Perspectives on Death and Dying

Books of Related Interest

The Cancer Book
Geoffrey M. Cooper

Carpe Diem: Enjoying Everyday Life with a Terminal Illness
Ed Maddan

A Challenge for Living: Dying, Death, and Bereavement
Inge B. Corless/Barbara B. Germino/Mary Pittman

*Dying, Death, and Bereavement: Theoretical Perspectives
and Other Ways of Knowing*
Inge B. Corless/Barbara B. Germino/Mary Pittman

Human Aging and Chronic Disease
Cary S. Kart/Eileen K. Metress/Seamus P. Metress

Life and Death: A Reader in Moral Problems
Louis P. Pojman

Life and Death: Grappling with the Moral Dilemmas of Our Time
Louis P. Pojman

Perspectives on Death and Dying

Gere B. Fulton, Ph.D., J.D.

Eileen K. Metress, Ph.D.

Department of Health Promotion and Human Performance
University of Toledo
Toledo, Ohio

Jones and Bartlett Publishers

Boston   *London*

Editorial, Sales, and Customer Service Offices
Jones and Bartlett Publishers
One Exeter Plaza
Boston, MA 02116
1-800-832-0034
617-859-3900

Jones and Bartlett Publishers
International
7 Melrose Terrace
London W67RL
England

Library of Congress Cataloging-in-Publication Data
Fulton, Gere B.
    Perspectives on death and dying / Gere B. Fulton, Eileen K.
Metress.
      p.   cm.
    Includes bibliographical references.
    ISBN 0-86720-926-7
    1. Death.   I. Metress, Eileen K.   II. Title.
    BD444.F86   1995
    306.9—dc20   94-333903
                                        CIP

Acquisitions Editor: Joseph E. Burns
Production Editor: Mary Cervantes Sanger
Design: Patricia Torelli
Manufacturing Buyer: Dana L. Cerrito
Editorial Production Service: WordCrafters Editorial Services, Inc.
Cover Design: Marshall Henrichs

Printed in the United States of America

98 97 96 95 94   10 9 8 7 6 5 4 3 2 1

Dedication

To the memory of those who have died and those who have survived,
whose stories are told in these pages,
who have taught us all so much about death and dying.

GBF

To the memory of my mother who taught me much
about love and life and living even in her dying.

EKM

Contents

CHAPTER 3   *Refusing Life-Sustaining Medical Treatment: Deciding for Others*   71

CHAPTER 4   *Controlling Your Medical Destiny Through Advance Directives*   117

CHAPTER 7   *Abortion*   259

CHAPTER 10   *Children and Death*   379

CHAPTER 11   *Suicide*   407

CHAPTER 12   *Medical Science and Post-Death Activities*   435

CHAPTER 13   *The Ritualization of Death: Funerals and Disposition of the Body*   461

Preface

SINCE THE EARLY 1970s, largely because of the unexpected and overwhelming success of Elisabeth Kubler-Ross's first book on the topic, *On Death and Dying,* U.S. society has demonstrated a growing fascination with the subject of death and dying. Prior to that time, there were few books on the topic, an almost nonexistent periodical literature, and aside from the occasional exploitative and sensationalist accounts in the tabloids, little in the way of real public interest in the subject. Although none could escape the reality that death was, and is, the destiny of all living things, there seemed to be an attitude of "the less said about it the better." Arguably we were, and the case can be made that we still are, a death-denying society; talking about death makes us (at least many of us) uncomfortable and, therefore, we do our best to avoid it.

We also can trace the beginnings of courses on death and dying to the early 1970s, the earliest ones perhaps owing their existence to the interest spawned by Kubler-Ross. Today these courses are offered in colleges and universities throughout the United States. They have even made their way into the high school curriculum and they are found more and more frequently in professional schools as well. We have been teaching an undergraduate class on Death and Dying at The University of Toledo since 1973. We, like many of our colleagues, first offered such a course because of interest expressed by students. Both of us have been trained in rather traditional programs for preparing health educators. Neither of us viewed ourselves then, nor do we now, as "death educators" or thanatologists. We were, and are, health educators and our interest in the topic arose from the linkage between our discipline, the health sciences, and death. Our subspecializations in the areas of aging, law, and medicine were, and are, an important part of our interest in death and dying and, in turn, provided us with a somewhat unique, at least different, avenue of approach. Now, after more than twenty years of experience of reading and studying, attending scores of conferences, and engaging in endless discussions with our colleagues and students, we find ourselves in a far different place than we were at the outset. Not only is it true that we have changed, but so has society. Most of the questions that motivate us, and many of the answers, are very different today than they were when we started. And they will continue to change.

We are convinced that learning about death and dying is best approached from a multidisciplinary perspective. Death and dying cannot be divorced from important underpinnings in philosophy, psychology, sociology, anthropology, law, and medicine. With the rapid changes that are taking place in the way health care is provided, or not provided, even such disciplines as economics, marketing, and management are becoming increasingly important. While none of us can be expected to demonstrate a mastery of all of these disciplines—there are few Renaissance scholars among us—we are firmly convinced that all of these play major roles in fully understanding the changing nature of the way we die.

Today, unlike the early 1970s, there is no shortage of books on the topic. Many of them are very good; some are outstanding. Each, however, fills a very special niche. Some are written from a psychological perspective, some sociological, some clinical, some cultural, and so on. We have read many of them; some have been tried as texts. Although we were literally awash in a sea of words, we could find nothing that seemed to meet our needs. What we wanted was an integrated approach that would address both the medical-legal and psychosocial aspects of death and dying. We felt, and continue to feel, that this type of approach to the topic would best prepare our students to understand and participate in the important personal and public policy decisions soon to confront them. What we were looking for was a book on medicine for nonphysicians, law for nonlawyers, and public policy for nonpoliticians. Like Goldilocks and the Three Bears, we wanted something that was not too hard, not too soft, but just right. That is what we have set out to create. We believe that our perspective, while it is but one of many that could be chosen, is a good place to begin an examination of the many important questions about death and dying.

In the following pages we will take you on a journey that touches many and varied dimensions of the topic at hand. We begin in Chapter 1 with a historical approach to death and many of the fears that have often accompanied the unpleasant thought of premature burial. Those fears, however, that the living might be regarded erroneously as dead, have been replaced by a new kind of fear, that the dead may be regarded erroneously as living. Newer methods of pronouncing death based on brain-referenced criteria have seemed to solve some problems, but they may have created new ethical challenges as well. This chapter is an attempt to bring some understanding to a topic that sometimes seems hopelessly muddled. It is also an important foundation for the discussion presented in the following two chapters, the so-called "right to die."

We can think of no topic more timely and few more important than that of Chapters 2 and 3. Medical technology has become increasingly adept at sustaining life where previously death would have been inevitable. The question that must be addressed is whether this kind of treatment is prolonging life or, rather, prolonging dying. In addition to the plight of the terminally ill, there is the growing problem posed by the permanently unconscious. We live in a society in which more than 30 million Americans have no health insurance and, consequently, little access to health care. At the same time, we are forcing some patients, or their families, to go to court to escape from medical treatment they do not want. How we got into this medical-ethical-legal thicket, and how we might find our way out, is the subject here. For ease in understanding what may seem like, to some, a terribly complex issue, we have divided our discussion of this topic into two parts. In the first of these, Chapter 2, we discuss the topic of making our own decisions about accepting or rejecting the use of life-sustaining medical treatment. In the second, Chapter 3, we ask, and answer, the question of who gets to make those decisions, and how, when we are no longer able to do so for ourselves.

Ours is a society that prizes the sovereignty of the individual. Respect for the autonomy of the patient is an important precept of medicine. While it is clear that competent patients have a right to direct the kind and amount of medical treatment that they will receive, many of us are concerned about what might happen to us when we no longer have the ability to decide for ourselves. Chapter 4 is about just that. Advance directives have been promoted as the only real way of guaranteeing that one's wishes concerning life-sustaining medical treatment will be respected when competence is lost. In this chapter, we describe the evolution of living wills and durable powers of attorney for health care as instruments of self-determination. We also discuss how the federal government, through the Department of Health and Human Services, has tried to ensure that patients in hospitals and skilled nursing homes are made aware of their rights to medical self-determination as consistent with state law. We also inject a cautionary note about advance directives, a sort of *caveat emptor,* and offer advice about ways in which you might pick your way around and through the legal maze that might otherwise prevent you from having your idiosyncrasies about medical treatment respected. Our purpose is to inform you about how advance directives can protect your loved ones and to motivate you to act on this knowledge.

Chapter 5 takes us into the debate about "euthanasia." In this chapter we begin with a historical look at the debate and proceed by examining the more recent events that have pushed the topic onto the front pages of our newspapers and to the forefront of controversy. Our discussion takes us from the pages of the medical and legal journals, to lonely cabins where hopeless people end their lives with medical assistance, to the voting booths of Washington and California, and to foreign countries where we look to find some channel markers to help us chart our way through these new, and potentially treacherous, waters.

Chapter 6 is likely to prove as frustrating for you to read as it was for us to write. Neonatology, the medical specialty that deals with treatment of premature or otherwise imperiled newborns, has given us awesome power to rescue babies who would have had no way of surviving were they born even a decade ago. We are now able to sustain younger and tinier, sicker and more debilitated infants than ever before. These "triumphs" are often achieved at great costs, both financial and in terms of the quality of the lives saved as well. The questions that need to be answered are: How much is too much? When does treatment become torture? Does having the *ability* to rescue mean we have the *obligation* to do so? Who gets to make these decisions? Parents? Physicians? Committees? Judges? Or, are there no decisions to be made? Should all anomalous newborns be treated as a matter of policy or law? These are heart-tugging issues and the decisions are sure to satisfy some while disappointing others, but decide we must. *Not* to decide is to decide in favor of the *status quo,* a decision by default. Like Prometheus, we have brought down fire from the gods. Our task now is to learn to use our power over life and death wisely.

Abortion has become one of the most divisive issues on the American political scene. Readers may be surprised to find that we have included a chapter on abortion in a volume of this type. We have done so for two major reasons. First, we include it because we believe, regardless of one's position on the issue of abortion, that it is scientifically and ethically correct to accept the premise that the embryo or fetus is alive throughout pregnancy and, therefore, that abortion results in its death. Whether or not the embryo or fetus is to be regarded as a person, or the equivalent of a person, is a philosophical and/or ethical question rather than a scientific one. The way in which one answers that question, however, is likely to have an influence on one's attitude toward abortion and one's reaction to a pregnancy ended in this way. Our second reason for including this topic is because of the way in which the abortion controversy has shaped the nature of the debate about life-sustaining medical treatment. The same arguments that undergird the abortion controversy—arguments about the sanctity of life versus the quality of life—are found in the debate about withholding or withdrawing life-sustaining medical treatment. This is seen in its clearest form in the neonatal care decisions, where the so-called pro-life movement has formed a partnership with the disability rights coalition, which has, in turn, produced a seemingly powerful political force. These same advocacies also may be seen in the cases that formed some of the content of Chapters 2 and 3, especially those regarding disabled and/or incompetent patients.

While we are realistic enough to realize that we do not have the answers that will resolve the controversy, we feel that those answers, if they are to be found, are most likely to emerge from a clear understanding of what the controversy is all about. In addition to tracing the history of abortion in this country and describing its present status, we also raise some questions about what lies on the horizon. While we doubt that it is possible to write a truly unbiased account of the controversy, and our own biases are likely to emerge from time to time, we have tried to be as objective as possible in our approach. We hope that we have succeeded in being both fair and informative.

In Chapter 8, we address the psychological issues surrounding the care of the terminally ill. Our goal here is to help the reader better understand the experience of dying so that he or she might better support those who are in the process of losing their lives. We pay homage to the important contributions of Elisabeth Kubler-Ross and describe the increasing popularity of hospice care as an important outgrowth of her pioneering work with the dying. The chapter ends with a discussion of the near-death experience.

Each of our lives will be touched by many losses. Some of these are, although important to us at the time, relatively insignificant: the loss of a valued object, a friendship, or failure to achieve a goal. Other losses may seem devastating: the loss of our independence, the failure of a marriage, or, probably of greatest impact, the death of a loved one. How we cope with these losses, our bereavement, and the resulting grief and mourning will have a major effect on the course of our lives. Chapter 9 addresses these issues and offers ways in which we might better understand these "necessary losses" and perhaps even use them as opportunities to further our growth.

Since parents are often greatly concerned about the effect of death on children, whether that of a sibling, parent, grandparent, or playmate, or the child's own impending death, the topic of children and death is presented next. Among the topics discussed in Chapter 10 is that of Sudden Infant Death Syndrome or SIDS. We have chosen to include this here, rather than in Chapter 9, because it is unlike, in many ways, the kind of deaths described there. We also offer suggestions here about helping children to understand and cope with death.

Chapter 11 deals with a major public health problem, that of suicide. After reviewing the statistical profile of those who take their own lives, we examine two populations that are especially at risk—the young and the old. Risk factors and some possible warning signs of suicide are also presented. Through the years, explanations for this curious, self-destructive act have been sought and we outline some of the major ones here. Statistics and theories, however, may do little to help us should we encounter a loved one or friend whom we suspect is contemplating suicide. Thus, we have included information on crisis intervention centers and individual intervention strategies that may be useful.

In modern society, various after-death activities involving the medical sciences have evolved. All deaths are officially registered via a death certificate signed by a physician. Collectively, death certificates serve as a public health record of the diseases or events (accidents, suicides, homicides) that cause

Americans to die. Additionally, certain deaths may be followed by a medical examiner's/coroner's investigation, an autopsy, tissue or organ donation, or donation of the body for anatomical study. These medically oriented procedures are examined in Chapter 12.

Our last chapter should be of great interest to anyone who has ever attended a funeral or other service for the memorialization of the dead. It is likely that each of us will, at sometime during our life, be responsible for making arrangements for a funeral or burial, or some alternative form of disposal of dead bodies. The costs of doing so are often quite high, depending on the alternatives chosen, and the decisions are often made at a time when intellect is likely to be clouded by emotion. Moreover, many of us are unaware of the options we have to choose from, having had little experience in making such arrangements. In Chapter 13 we describe those alternatives. As we have done throughout the book, we emphasize the importance of communication within families before a death occurs and advance planning as a means of sparing one's survivors unnecessary pain and sorrow. We feel that it is entirely possible for consumers of funeral goods and services to get exactly what they want but, in order to do so, they need to understand their alternatives.

There are several important themes that run like threads throughout the tapestry of this book. One of these is our belief in the importance of understanding how change—change in how we live and change in how we die—has influenced our attitudes about death and dying. Another is our belief that knowledge can be an important factor—perhaps the most important—in helping us understand and cope with the many crises and controversies surrounding the topic of death and dying. Our goal throughout the book has been to make death less a stranger and thereby help dispel some of the irrational fears that seem to haunt so many of us. We also hope to foster a willingness to talk about death and dying and to encourage the reader to communicate more effectively concerning death, whether one's own or that of others. We would like to eradicate the practice of isolating the dying in "emotional solitary confinement" where they are forced to die alone, surrounded by a "conspiracy of silence."

While this is clearly a book about death and dying, we hope that the reader will share our feelings that between these covers there is much to be learned about life and living. Although death is an inevitable and necessary part of life, there is much that we can do while alive to make our ultimate death much easier, both for ourselves and our families and friends. If this book provides some measure of help in achieving that goal, then we will have been richly rewarded for our effort.

Acknowledgments

As all authors realize, books like this are the product of many people. We would like to take this opportunity to thank some of them here. First there is Joe Burns, Vice President of Jones and Bartlett, who believed in this project enough to offer us a contract and then helped shape the book with his suggestions. Amina Sharma was there for us when we needed answers and it was she who guided us through the publishing maze and served as our link to the many bright and creative people at Jones and Bartlett. Our production editor, Mary Cervantes Sanger, helped bring our manuscript to life through her helpful suggestions. And finally, we offer our deepest gratitude to our copy editor, Laura Cleveland of WordCrafters Editorial Services, who helped turn our manuscript into the book you see before you. Laura is a fine wordsmith, but it was her sense of humor that often proved as valuable as her editorial pencil. Tim Jordan and Tim Mead spent hours pouring over our prose as they compiled the index for the book. Cynthia Sepic and Sue Fandry helped out with secretarial services, as did Jennifer Accetolla and Ruthe Jones.

We are also deeply indebted to our professional colleagues who reviewed drafts of the manuscript and offered valuable comment. Darrell Crase of Memphis State University, Dan Leviton of The University of Maryland at College Park, Robert Russell of Southern Illinois University at Carbondale, Elaine Vail of Western Illinois University, and William Yarber of Indiana University at Bloomington saved us from ourselves at more than one point and for that we are grateful. Although we benefited greatly from their good counsel, any errors that might remain are ours alone.

And, finally, we would like to thank the hundreds of students who studied from one of the several early editions of this manuscript. It was they who told us what "worked" and what didn't and who helped rekindle our enthusiasm with their own as we went back to the drawing board.

CHAPTER 1

Death

A Search for Definition

One question which would have never concerned our ancestors, except perhaps in a very specific religious sense, would be the question of a definition of death. The whole idea would have seemed ludicrous to them. They knew when a person was dead; he stopped breathing and his heart stopped beating. If a physician happened to be in attendance, and that was often not the case, he would sign a death certificate, thereby converting a biological fact into a legal one. But it's not so simple today. Nothing in life is simple anymore. Not even the leaving of it.

Willard Gaylin (1980), *Hard Choices: Death & Dying*

The only satisfactory proof of death is putrefaction.

J. B. Winslow (1742)

Lᴇᴛ's ʙᴇɢɪɴ with a working definition. Perhaps to you, the reader, this seems as "ludicrous" as Gaylin suggests that it would have seemed to your ancestors. Perhaps because we commonly assume that we understand what is meant when we hear that someone or something is dead, the very idea of asking, "What exactly do you mean by that?" would never even cross our minds. Death is the opposite of life. People or things are dead when they are no longer alive. While this is arguably correct, it is also more of a tautology than a definition. It describes death by contrasting it to life, but to rely on a description of what something is *not* to help us understand what it *is* seems less than satisfactory.

1

Black's Law Dictionary, a time-honored and respected source, defines death in the following way:

> DEATH. The cessation of life; the ceasing to exist; defined by physicians as a total stoppage of the circulation of the blood, and a cessation of the animal and vital functions consequent thereon, such as respiration, pulsation, etc. (Black, 1968)

Black seems to be telling us that death is to be defined by physicians and that it is based on such phenomena as the beating of the heart (as seen by "the circulation of the blood" and "pulsation," neither of which would be possible without the pumping action of the heart) and breathing (respiration). In fact, those are now and have been the traditional criteria for pronouncing death. We will refer to them as cardiopulmonary (heart/lung) criteria. The events are well known by every aficionado of the film genre known as "the western."

Most of the plots had a scene where the hero, the sheriff or "good guy" (as they used to be known in simpler times), confronted the villain ("bad guy") in a shoot-out. At the risk of dating ourselves, and realizing today that the opposition would more likely be a squadron of terrorists armed with nuclear weapons, let us continue our story. As the tension peaked, the hero would step out into an empty street, often in response to the taunts of his adversary, where the confrontation could be seen by the fear-ridden townspeople who had huddled behind shuttered windows. They walked slowly and ominously toward each other, with pistol hands poised, and when they got within bullet range, both parties went for their guns. Shots rang out in the deserted street and, after what seemed an interminable period, the bad guy fell to the ground. As the onlookers made their way into the street to cheer their champion, someone would inevitably approach the fallen body and feel for a pulse, or perhaps place a mirror up to the nostrils. If there were no pulse, or no breath to fog the mirror, the next line was usually, "You got him, sheriff, he ain't breathing. He's dead!"

While cardiopulmonary criteria were used to pronounce death throughout most of our history, and are still relied upon in most instances today, there are circumstances under which the use of these criteria would be inappropriate. Black tells us that there must be not only a stoppage of circulation and respiration, but that the stoppage must be total. To this we would add that the stoppage must be permanent or irreversible. Surely we don't regard the mere stoppage of circulation as indicative of death. When someone's heart stops beating we say that he or she had a cardiac arrest. We would pronounce the person dead only after we've been convinced that the arrest is permanent. As for breathing, any cessation here first signals the need for one of the various forms of artificial respiration, perhaps even the use of a machine, called a *respirator* (or more correctly, a *ventilator*), to breathe for the person. While either cardiac or pulmonary arrest may *lead* to death, the fact that there has been a cessation of function, if temporary, certainly does not support a conclusion that the person has died.

Medicine has produced an impressive array of technology which now enables the restoration and maintenance of both circulation and breathing under circumstances that previously would have resulted in inevitable death. This ability to apply medical technology to rescue the medically imperiled is, for many, a mixed blessing. While the technology is often capable of delaying death, it frequently is incapable of restoring health or function. Technology is certainly a major cause of the shift in the manner of how we die. While our ancestors tended to die at home, in the company of family and friends, death today occurs most frequently in institutions (hospitals and nursing homes) and often with tubes everywhere. It is not uncommon today to hear people say that while they don't fear dying (regardless of whether or not this is true), they don't want to die in the hospital with tubes in every orifice. While our ancestors' response to the approach of death might have been "Save me, Doctor," more and more today we hear the dying call out "Save me *from* the doctor."

Also, as we will discuss later in this chapter, our technology has tended to obscure, or at least blur, the once bright line that existed between the living and the dead. The same machines that, when used as a temporary substitute for spontaneous circulation and respiration, can save lives can also make it extremely difficult to tell when crucial organs, the heart and lungs, have permanently lost their ability to function. Thus, we have a new kind of problem. With the use of machines to assume and maintain vital functions of the body and, thereby, mask the usefulness of the traditional criteria to pronounce death or recognize inevitable death, there is a concern that we might treat the dead or dying as though they were neither. This is quite different from the death-related fears of our ancestors.

Fears of Premature Burial

While it is not uncommon today to hear concerns about medical technology being used to "maintain" the dying or even the dead, or that unbridled technology might create a situation whereby the dead are treated as though they were alive, our ancestors were often concerned about quite the opposite. For much of our history, including well into the late nineteenth and early twentieth centuries, there was a sense of great mystery and superstition surrounding death and that, coupled with a general distrust of physicians, manifested itself in concerns about being pronounced prematurely, and thereby erroneously, dead. Figure 1–1 shows a graphic depiction of this fear.

Mant (1976) collected a number of cases from the sixteenth through the

FIGURE 1–1   Fears of premature burial were common during the eighteenth and nineteenth centuries. Such fear is depicted in this painting by A. J. Wiertz (1796–1865). The stamp on the coffin reads: "MORT. CERTIFIE PAR NOS DOC-TEURS" (Dead, Certified by Our Doctors). (Reprinted by permission of the Musées Royaux des Beaux Arts, Brussels, Belgium)

eighteenth centuries that were indicative of premature burial. Although perhaps apocryphal, these tales are surely indicative of a widespread fear on the part of the general public. According to Mant, the fact that such cases, which were reliably authenticated, are quoted by many different authors suggests that errors, although admittedly occurring from time to time, were certainly not as common as was made out by the more sensationalist writers. Due to the plagues and epidemics that swept Europe in the seventeenth and eighteenth centuries, coupled with the primitive state of medicine, it is not surprising to learn of premature burial in the haste of disposing of infected bodies.

In writing about those allegedly buried alive, Mant states that:

> it would appear that some might have been saved were it not for superstition, disbelief and formality. One reads of persons hearing sounds from a fresh grave, disbelief and then many hours' delay before the formalities are completed for the exhumation. When the coffin is eventually opened we are told of the twisted shrouds, the doubled-up body, often with fresh injuries which have been bleeding, and all the signs of suffocation.

He warns the reader, however, that these accounts could well be erroneous. There could have been natural explanations, for example, the action of putrefaction or rodents or the plundering of vaults.

Arnold, Zimmerman, and Martin (1968), while focusing primarily on the public fears of premature burial during the nineteenth century, refer to "several hundred pamphlets and tracts written between 1700 and 1900" on the unreliability of diagnoses of death. It is difficult to tell the difference between some of these accounts and Poe's writings; the latter may well have been a case of fiction inspired by fact, or at least what was believed to be factual. In order to prevent burial in advance of death, various precautionary measures or safeguards were proposed. They included such things as application of boiling liquids or red-hot irons to the skin. Some of those most greatly troubled by this fear even specified such extreme measures as decapitation before burial (Mant, 1976, p. 225). Even such seemingly innocuous practices as washing the body and wailing during burial ceremonies have their origins, at least partially, in concerns about last-chance awakening of the apparently dead.

Although only one of the possible explanations underlying the introduction and popularization of embalming (c.f. Chapter 13), fear of premature burial was certainly a concern (Arnold et al., 1968, p. 1951). Embalming and burning of the corpse (cremation) were absolute guarantees against an untimely burial. The earliest mortuaries were created specifically as safeguards. There the corpse would be left to putrefy in hygienic isolation, for given the widespread belief that determining death was pretty chancy business, only the evidence of putrefaction could be relied upon. The morticians of the eighteenth century sometimes placed gloves on the corpses. The gloves were attached to an alarm by strings and the slightest movement of a finger caused a hammer to sound an alarm. The mortuary also contained a revival room and a pharmacy. Guards were on constant duty and punched time clocks on a regular basis. A physician directed the mortuary and made constant rounds. It wasn't until the nineteenth century that physicians widely criticized the use of the mortuary and the reliance on putrefaction as a sign of death. For even though mortuaries had existed for more than a hundred years, no corpse had ever sounded an alarm (Alexander, 1980, pp. 29–30).

Laennec's invention of the stethoscope, which he reported in 1819, ushered in a new era in the diagnosis of death. Auscultation, listening for the sounds of the beating heart, created renewed hope for diagnostic reliability. Even this, however, did not dispel the deep-seated fears that had permeated popular belief for centuries. It should be kept in mind, of course, that physicians were not always in attendance to pronounce death and, even if they had been, the state of the art (and the artist) was usually less than confidence inspiring.

Yet another attempt to avoid premature burial can be seen in the elaborate escape mechanisms and speaking tubes that were designed into coffins (see Figure 1–2). Arnold et al. (1968) describe one of these devices as follows:

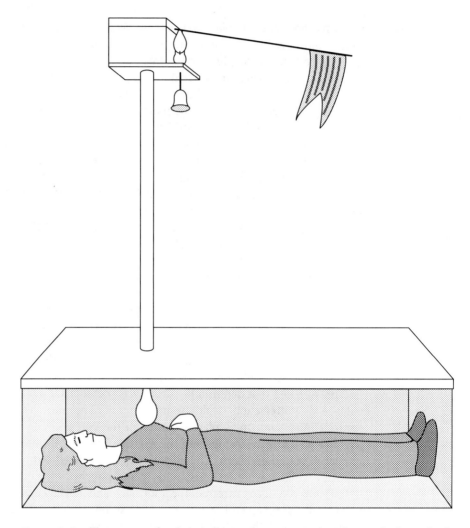

FIGURE **1–2**   Illustration of a device designed to protect the "deceased" from death from premature burial. (Adapted and reprinted with permission from John D. Arnold, Thomas F. Zimmerman, and Daniel L. Martin, "Public Attitudes and the Diagnosis of Death." *Journal of the American Medical Association*, 206(9): 1953. Copyright 1968, American Medical Association)

The apparatus [Figure 1–2] is described as a " . . . long tube three and one-half inches in diameter, and a hermetically sealed box. The box is fixed in an aperture in the coffin as soon as the latter is lowered in the grave. No gasses can escape from the tomb into the outside air, as the metallic box into which the upper end of the tube enters cannot be opened from the outside.

On the chest of the supposed dead body is placed a glass ball which communicates through the tube with an iron box above the ground. At the slightest movement of the chest wall, such as breathing or body movement, the glass ball releases a spring which opens the box immediately, thus admitting light and air to the coffin. At the same time a flag raises perpendicularly about four feet above the ground and a bell is set ringing which continues for about half an hour. In front of the box is a lamp which gives light after sunset to the coffin below. The tube also acts as a speaking tube which amplifies the voice of the inmate of the coffin, however feeble." (pp. 1952–1953)

While the effect that hearing a voice calling from the grave might have had on mourners at the gravesite or passers-by provides for some interesting speculation, there appear to be no reliable records of these elaborate devices ever resulting in the rescue of even one near victim of premature burial. (Figure 1–3 shows another casket design.) With increasing public trust in physicians, and the ever improving technology upon which they rely so heavily, public fears of premature burial began to fade.

Somewhere between the end of the nineteenth and the middle of the twentieth centuries, these public fears about being pronounced dead too soon were replaced with a concern, recognized first by the medical community, about not being pronounced dead soon enough. Irreversible cessation of cardiopulmonary function, the traditional standard used to declare death, had gradually given way to machines that could restart a stopped heart (defibrillators) and even regulate its beating if necessary (pacemakers). Respiratory function could be maintained indefinitely through the use of mechanical pumps called *ventilators*. The problem had become one of knowing when the person, whose vital functions were being maintained by this technology, had passed the point where, except for the technology, he or she would have been pronounced dead. Technology had obscured the once bright line, irreversible cessation of heartbeat and respiration, that had separated life and death. Once a person was put on these "life-support" systems, which could independently maintain respiration, and with it the circulation with which it was linked, how might we then know when death had occurred? Just as it was abhorrent to consider the likelihood that a person alive would be treated as though he or she were dead, it was also abhorrent, it was argued, to continue to treat a corpse as though it were alive.

A host of reasons were given in support of that conclusion. First, there was the emotional hardship for the family. If the person who had been placed on the "life-support" system had passed the point at which he or she was no longer capable of living, it would seem inhumane to subject the family to the ritual of visiting a breathing corpse and clinging to a baseless hope that life and recovery were still possible. If indeed this body were a corpse, and not a living person, it would seem far better to acknowledge such and allow for the grieving and mourning that typically follow death.

Second, there was the consideration of using scarce medical resources.

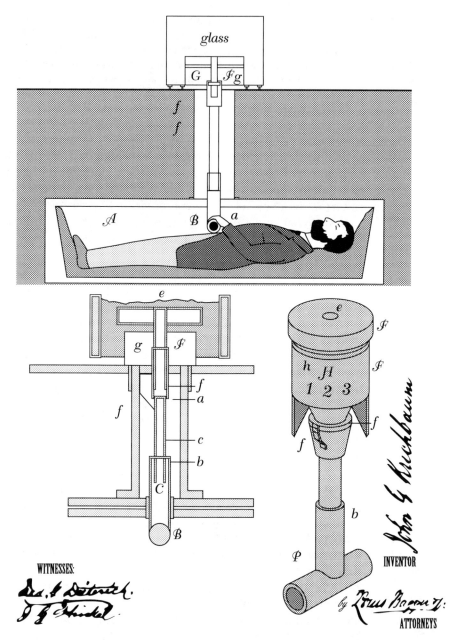

FIGURE 1–3   Another of the elaborately designed caskets resulting from fears and superstitions about premature burial.

Saving lives, regardless of the expense, had become commonplace in modern medicine, but maintaining a corpse in an intensive care unit would seem to be something else to consider. Not only would this mean that others who might be critically ill and in need of such treatment would be competing for, and sometimes denied, such care, which *for them* might be life saving, but it would also mean that this care, which today can easily exceed a thousand dollars a day, would have to be paid for. Individuals are seldom able to pay bills of this magnitude and, unless they are among the many millions of Americans who have no health insurance, the cost is usually borne by insurance companies, known as third-party payers. Even then, however, the cost of such care is distributed among many and is reflected in higher premiums. The same is true when government steps into the picture through Medicare or Medicaid coverage; when we say that government pays what we really mean is that we all pay. We, all of us, are the government. While money spent for health care is usually of high priority, we are entitled to ask if this is the kind of health care we want to spend our money on and, in addition, how much of our money we want to spend on health care as opposed to other services such as education, transportation, public housing, public utilities, or defense.

There is also the matter of our duty to treat the dead with respect. We have such a duty, it might be argued, in part from our obligations to the sensitivity of the family and loved ones. Although societies differ in their ideas about how this respect is properly manifested (discussed in Chapter 13), death rituals are one way in which this is carried out. By treating the dead with respect we also help insure that we, too, will be treated similarly at the time of our death. To continue to treat the dead as though they were alive would be, for many, a violation of our duties to treat the dead respectfully.

And, finally, there was the matter of procuring organs for transplantation. Organ transplantation is a phenomenon of the second half of the twentieth century. Although early attempts date back to 1906, the first successful kidney transplant was performed in Boston on monozygotic twins in 1954 (Flye, 1989, p. 10). Since kidneys are paired organs and life continues quite normally in the absence of one, early transplants relied upon donations from living, related donors. Family members were most likely to provide a good genetic match—an even more important consideration then than it is today with highly effective immunosuppressant drugs to combat rejection.

It was not until December 3, 1967, however, that the public was squarely confronted with a conceptual dilemma that had been taking place in the medical community concerning the traditional (cardiopulmonary) definition of death. It was on that day that Dr. Christiaan Barnard performed the world's first transplantation of a human heart. The event took place at Groote Shuur Hospital in Cape Town, South Africa. The recipient, Louis Washkansky, died of pneumonia eighteen days after the operation. A heart, which had long been symbolic of life itself, had been removed from one body and placed into another. If the person from whom it was taken was dead, as he or she surely must have been, how could the heart still be alive? And if the donor were alive at the time, surely the removal of his or her heart was the cause of death. The procedure was possible only because the technology existed to maintain a dead body long enough so that the still beating heart could be removed, quickly transferred to the body of a recipient whose own failing heart had been removed, and then stimulated to resume its pumping. The donor had been pronounced dead based on brain-referenced, rather than cardiopulmonary, criteria.

"Brain Death"

Although it had become increasingly obvious to physicians around the world that the new technology of intensive-care medicine could maintain respiration and circulation in a body where the brain had permanently stopped functioning, the leading American work on this condition was not published until 1968, the year after Barnard's triumph. A group of twelve scholars, all but three of whom were physicians, proposed the widespread adoption of a protocol for pronouncing death based on the permanent loss of brain function. Their paper, entitled "A Definition of Irreversible Coma," was subtitled as the "Report of the Ad Hoc Committee of the Harvard Medical School to Examine the Definition of Brain Death." It is unfortunate, in retrospect, that they chose the terminology "irreversible coma," and it is equally unfortunate that they introduced the terminology of "brain death." The meaning of the former—irreversible coma—seems to be hopelessly muddled in the literature (a point that will be discussed at some length later in this chapter) and the second—brain death—by placing the modifier (brain) before the noun death, seems to suggest that there are different ways of being dead: brain death, heart death, lung death and so on. That was not the goal of the committee, nor is it the desire of those who continue to use the terminology. What is being described here is a new way of diagnosing death (by looking at indicators of brain function) when life-support technology has obscured the traditional signs (cardiopulmonary function). Their introductory paragraph set the stage for their recommendations:

> Our primary purpose is to define irreversible coma as a new criterion for death. There are two reasons why there is need for a definition: (1) Improvements in resuscitative and support measures have led to increased efforts to save those who are desperately injured. Sometimes these efforts have only partial success so that the result is an individual whose heart continues to beat but whose brain is irreversibly damaged. The burden is great on patients who suffer permanent loss of intellect, on their families, on the hospitals, and on those in need of hospital beds already occupied by these comatose patients. (2) Obsolete criteria for the definition of death can lead to controversy in obtaining organs for transplantation.   (Ad Hoc Committee, 1968, p. 85)

This concept, that of a permanently nonfunctioning brain, originated in France in 1959. French neurologists called it *coma depasse* (literally "beyond coma") to describe a condition of irreversible unconsciousness associated with the permanent loss of the ability to breathe (Lamb, 1985, p. 4). Such patients lost all ability to respond to external stimuli and, even with the available life-support technology, had difficulty with the maintenance of homeostasis, especially the maintenance of blood pressure, which soon thereafter resulted in heart failure. The prognosis was then thought to be at most a few days, but sometimes as little as a few hours (Pallis, 1983, p. 34). The concept was slow in gaining popularity outside of France but, following the publication of the "Harvard Committee Report" it achieved worldwide recognition.

The committee stated that a permanently nonfunctioning brain could be diagnosed by the following criteria:

1. *Unreceptivity and unresponsitivity.* There is a total unawareness to externally applied stimuli and inner need and complete unresponsiveness—our definition of irreversible coma. Even the most intensely painful stimuli evoke no vocal or other response, not even a groan, withdrawal of a limb, or quickening of respiration.

2. *No movements or breathing.* Observations covering a period of at least one hour by physicians is [sic] adequate to satisfy the criteria of no spontaneous respiration or response to stimuli such as pain, touch, sound, or light. After the patient is on a mechanical respirator, the total absence of spontaneous breathing may be established by turning off the respirator for three minutes and observing whether there is any effort on the part of the subject to breathe spontaneously.

   The respirator may be turned off for this time provided that at the start of the trial period the patient's carbon dioxide tension is within the normal range, and provided also that the patient had been breathing room air for at least 10 minutes prior to the trial. [It is the carbon dioxide to oxygen ratio in the blood that triggers respiration, the so-called Herring-Brewer reflex.]

3. *No reflexes.* Irreversible coma with abolition of central nervous system activity is evidenced in part by the absence of elicitable reflexes. The pupil will be fixed and dilated and will not respond to a direct source of light. Since the establishment of a fixed, dilated pupil is clear-cut in clinical practice, there should be no uncertainty as to its presence. Ocular movement (to head turning and to irrigation of the ears with ice water) and blinking are absent. There is no evidence of postural activity (decerebrate or other). Swallowing, yawning, vocalization are in abeyance. Corneal and pharyngeal reflexes are absent.

   As a rule the stretch of tendon reflexes cannot be elicited; i.e., tapping the tendons of the biceps, triceps, and pronator muscles, quadriceps and gastrocnemius muscles with the reflex hammer elicits no contraction of the respective muscles. Plantar or noxious stimulation gives no response. (Ad Hoc Committee, 1968, pp. 85–86)

These three criteria are based on clinical observations and are sufficient for the diagnosis of a permanently nonfunctioning brain. If an electroencephalogram is available it will provide *confirmatory* data. An electroencephalogram is neither necessary nor, independent of the clinical observations, sufficient for the diagnosis.

4. *Flat electroencephalogram.* Of great confirmatory value is the flat or iso-electric EEG. We must assume that the electrodes have been properly applied, that the apparatus is functioning, and that the personnel in charge is competent. . . . There shall be no electroencephalographic response to noise or pinch.   (Ibid., p. 86)

The committee recommended that all the tests "be repeated at least 24 hours later with no change." Also, they caution, the validity of these indications depends on the exclusion of both hypothermia and central nervous system depressants, such as barbiturates. Hypothermia is defined as temperature below 90°F or 32.2°C (Ibid., pp. 85–86).

The patient's condition is to be determined only by a physician. Although the committee does not specify that the physician be either a neurologist or a neurosurgeon, since these determinations are typically made in the neurological intensive care unit (NICU or ICU), this is most likely to be the case. The committee also indicates that "when the patient is *hopelessly damaged as defined above* [emphasis added], the family and all colleagues who have participated in major decisions concerning the patient, and all nurses involved, should be so informed. Death is to be declared and *then* the respirator turned off (Ibid., p. 86).

In 1981 another prominent group of physicians, the Medical Consultants to the President's Commission for the Study of Ethical Problems in Medicine and Biomedical and Behavioral Research, published its recommendations for updating the Harvard Criteria (Medical Consultants 1981). While describing their recommendations as "one statement of currently accepted standards," acknowledging that other criteria might also be valid, they emphasized that the criteria used should "(1) eliminate errors in classifying a living individual as dead; (2) allow as few errors as possible in classifying a dead body as alive; (3) allow a determination to be made without unreasonable delay; (4) be adaptable to a variety of clinical situations; and (5) be explicit and accessible to verification" (Ibid., p. 2185).

While essentially reaffirming the Harvard criteria, the recommendations did indicate several areas where, in the light of knowledge gained in the intervening thirteen years, refinements might be appropriate. The most obvious of these had to do with the interval necessary between tests. Where the Harvard Committee had recommended an interval of twenty-four hours, the Medical Consultants indicated that, depending on the cause of the unconsciousness, an appropriate interval might be as short as six hours if there were EEG confirmation. In cases where the cause was unknown, especially if it arose from anoxia rather than trauma, observation for a period of twenty-four hours was preferred. And, in addition to the cautions about hypothermic and intoxicated patients that were part of the Harvard Committee recommendations, similar cautions were issued in regard to children under the age of five and in cases resulting from shock (Ibid., p. 2186). It is likely that there will be further refinements in the criteria for pronouncing death as new technology is developed.

THE FAR SIDE   By GARY LARSON

**"For crying out loud, I was *hibernating*! . . .
Don't you guys ever take a pulse?"**

FIGURE 1–4   (FAR SIDE copyright 1992 FARWORKS, INC./Dist. by UNIVERSAL PRESS SYNDICATE. Reprinted with permission. All rights reserved.)

Choosing a Definition of Death

Veatch is one of many writers who has attempted to distinguish between the "fact" of death and the concept, locus, and criteria of death (Veatch, 1976, 1989; see Table 1–1). Veatch would define death as "a complete change in the status of an [sic] living entity characterized by the irreversible loss of those characteristics that are essential to it" (1976, p. 25). Such a definition, he argues, would apply not only to humans, but to nonhuman animals, plants, organs, cells or "even metaphorically to a social phenomenon like a society or to any temporally limited entity like a research project, a sports event, or a language" (Ibid., p. 26).

A Concept of Death

In order to decide whether the entity had died it would first be necessary to agree on "those characteristics that are essential to it" and whether they had been irreversibly lost. To do so is to formulate a *concept* of death, a task that calls for philosophical rather than scientific inquiry. Because the nature of this inquiry is one to which scientists *qua* scientists, including physicians, bring no special skills, the concept of death should be based on a societal consensus. What is it about being alive, the loss of which should constitute death? Veatch offers several suggestions.

First, there is the consideration of the irreversible loss of flow of vital fluids. Death might be characterized by the cessation of movement of such vital fluids—breath and blood. This would seem to be the basis of the traditional or cardiopulmonary-referenced concept of death.

Alternatively, we might consider a more theological suggestion: the departure of the soul from the body. This is certainly an important part of the teachings of Christianity and, consequently, a conceptualization that might appeal to many of the faithful. The difficulty, however, comes when attempting to translate this occurrence into some measurable phenomenon. There have been attempts to demonstrate the passage of the soul by carefully weighing the dying person and comparing the weight before death to that after. Critics of this endeavor have suggested that any differences would most likely be due to the loss of tidal air in the lungs that would occur with total respiratory collapse.

Veatch's third suggestion involves the loss of the capacity for bodily integration. This is the condition described by the Harvard Committee as "brain death." Because it is the brain that controls the integrated function of the body, death of the brain, in this case the whole brain, would signal the death of the person. This would not require that all organs or cells be dead—the death of the *whole organism*—but rather that the organism no longer be capable of integrated function—the death of the organism *as a whole*. As we have seen from

TABLE 1–1 *Levels of the Definition of Death.* The various ways in which death might be conceptualized effect where we look and what we look for to determine whether death has occurred.

Formal Definition: Death means a complete change in the status of a living entity characterized by the irreversible loss of those characteristics that are essentially significant to it.

Concept of Death	*Locus of Death*	*Criteria of Death*
Philosophical or theological judgment of the essentially significant change at death	Place to look to determine if a person has died	Measurements physicians or other officials use to determine whether a person is dead—to be determined by scientific empirical study
1. The irreversible stopping of the flow of "vital" body fluids, i.e., the blood and breath	Heart and lungs	1. Visual observation of respiration, perhaps with the use of a mirror 2. Feeling of the pulse, possibly supported by electrocardiogram
2. The irreversible loss of the soul from the body	The pineal body? (according to Descartes) The respiratory track?	Observation of breath?
3. The irreversible loss of the capacity for bodily integration and social interaction	The brain	1. Unreceptivity and unresponsivity 2. No movements or breathing 3. No reflexes (except spinal reflexes) 4. Flat electroencephalogram (to be used as confirmatory evidence) —All tests to be repeated 24 hours later (excluded conditions: hypothermia and central nervous system drug depression)
4. Irreversible loss of consciousness or the capacity for social interaction	Probably the neocortex	Electroencephalogram

Source: Robert M. Veatch, *Death, Dying, and the Biological Revolution* (New Haven: Yale University Press, 1976), p. 53. Copyright © 1976 by Yale University Press. Reprinted by permission.
Note: The possible concepts, loci, and criteria of death are much more complex than the ones given here. These are meant to be simplified models of types of positions being taken in the current debate. It is obvious that those who believe that death means the irreversible loss of the capacity for bodily integration (3) or the irreversible loss of consciousness (4) have no reservations about pronouncing death when the heart and lungs have ceased to function. This is because they are willing to use loss of heart and lung activity as shortcut criteria for death, believing that once heart and lungs have stopped, the brain or neocortex will necessarily stop as well.

the previous discussion, it is precisely because most of the body's organs are capable of functioning beyond the point at which the brain has died that irreversible cessation of brain function has been embraced as an alternative criterion of death. Cell lines, if appropriately cultured, can live for years, even generations, after the persons from whom the cells were obtained have long since died.

Veatch's fourth suggestion is also brain oriented but, unlike the concept of

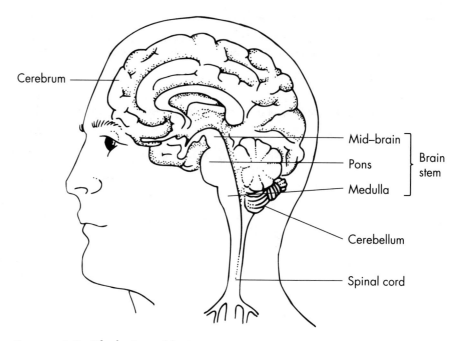

FIGURE 1–5   The brain and brain stem.

death proposed by the Harvard Committee, the focus here is not on the whole brain but, rather, the cerebrum or neocortex (see Figure 1–5). This concept would be based on the irreversible loss of the capacity for consciousness or social integration. After all, he writes, Homo sapiens is a rational animal, not merely a vegetative one. And, in addition to rationality, life is characterized by consciousness and the ability to interact socially with the environment. It is these minimal abilities, located primarily in the higher brain centers, that are "so essential that their loss ought to be taken as the death of the person" (1976, p. 42). While there is an interesting body of support for this position, especially within the philosophical literature, there is little reason to believe that it is likely to gain widespread public support. These arguments, both pro and con, will be examined more fully in Chapter 3.

The Locus of Death

Once a concept of death has been agreed upon, the next step is to identify "where to look" to see if death has occurred. Unlike the task of selecting a concept, which we identified as inherently philosophical, this aspect is anatomically based and, along with the identifying criteria, is best addressed by scientists. The traditional concept of death, characterized by the stoppage of breathing and circulation is, of course, linked to the function of the heart and lungs. The loss of the soul, being itself a philosophical or theological concept, poses a major problem for a scientist in search of a locus. This, says Veatch (1976, p. 44), "has not been dealt with definitively since the day of Descartes," who concluded it was most likely found in a "very small gland" situated in the middle of the brain. The concept of the soul residing in the pineal gland is likely to be viewed as strange today and perhaps it is best thought of as a construct, like the mind, which escapes dissection from the convolutions of the brain.

The locus for determining death conceptualized as loss of the capacity for bodily integration and social interaction is the brain. What is envisioned here is not the death of the whole person, but rather the death of the person as a whole. Sometimes this is described as the death of the *human* organism, with the emphasis on the word *human,* as opposed to the death of the human *organism*, with the emphasis on the word *organism* (Task Force, 1972, p. 49). This means, therefore, that the locus would have to include the whole brain, often described as "including the brain stem."

The locus for consciousness and capacity for social interaction, Veatch's fourth and, for him, preferred conceptualization of death, is "probably" the neocortex (Veatch, 1976). It certainly would not require death of the brain stem. This, of course, would mean that under such a concept it would be possible to pronounce as dead a breathing, though permanently unconscious, patient. Aside from the fact that this is viewed by some, including the members of the President's Commission, as a radical and inappropriate departure from the presently accepted concept of death, there is also a technical difficulty in diagnosing death of the neocortex as opposed to death of the whole brain. This problem will be addressed in Chapter 3.

The Criteria of Death

Having decided upon the locus (where to look) for finding out whether "those characteristics that are essential to life" have been lost, we turn to the question of measurement. What criteria can be used to provide the necessary evidence that death, as we have agreed to define it, exists? The criteria for the traditional definition based on cardiopulmonary function would be obvious. There is no heartbeat and no breathing. Other than insuring that these are permanent, there is nothing else to be done. The problem, as was discussed previously, arises when we are confronted by a case in which the "flow of vital fluids" is artificially sustained. This, of course, is the shortcoming of the "vital fluid" or cardiopulmonary concept of death and the very reason why an alternative way of diagnosing death has evolved.

Criteria for measuring the departure of the soul, like the task of knowing where to look, are far less reassuring. Since, says Veatch, the Greek term *pneuma* has the dual meaning of both "breath" and "soul or spirit," perhaps those who attempted to measure it by the final expiration of the dying were not far off the mark. The practical significance of this, however, seems nil. We encounter, at the very least, the same problem we confronted with the traditional cardiopulmonary concept when breathing is controlled by a ventilator.

The criteria for measuring the permanent loss of function in the brain, including the brain stem, are those of the Harvard Committee. Whether it is because the criteria are most clearly developed that the whole brain concept of death is so widely accepted or, conversely, because the whole brain concept is so widely accepted that the criteria are most clearly developed is debatable. The tests for "brain death," and with it the loss of the capacity for bodily integration, are well accepted within the scientific community and provide an alternative basis for pronouncing death throughout the United States and most of the western world.

Criteria that would differentiate the loss of the capacity for bodily integration (death of the whole brain) from the loss of capacity for consciousness or social integration (death of the neocortex or cerebrum) are much more controversial. The latter, which we discuss in the following chapters as permanent unconsciousness or persistent vegetative state, is diagnosed much more tentatively and only by gradually excluding other possible kinds of unconsciousness. Moreover, death of the neocortex can and does occur in association with a functioning brain stem. To declare such a person dead would force us to disregard the continuation of autonomic or vegetative functions such as spontaneous breathing and movement, something most people seem unwilling to do, at least at this time. Veatch (1989) and Gervais (1986) are among those who have urged adoption of neocortical death as death of the person. Recognizing significant societal reluctance to accept this notion, they have proposed that its adoption be optional. However, they treat the choice in alternative ways. Gervais proposes that the neocortical concept be adopted for routine use, but that there be a "conscience clause" reserved for those with a preference for the use of whole-brain criteria. A declaration of death based on the absence of *entire* brain function would, therefore, only be used in those instances where one's wishes were made known clearly beforehand. Veatch would maintain the current concept of death as general policy but would allow the application of the neocortical concept for those expressing such a preference.

Understanding "Brain Death"

Gaylin was right, nothing is simple anymore. "Brain death" is one of those terms that many of us have grown up with. It's part of our vocabulary. "What are you, brain dead? How many times do I have to explain it to you?" What we are going to suggest to you now is that (1) many, perhaps most, people don't understand the term; (2) the term is frequently used in incorrect and/or misleading ways; and (3) we would be better served by dropping it from our vocabulary.

The term "brain death," writes Molinari, "should now be abandoned, because it perpetuates professional and public confusion. It implies a degree or kind of deadness!" (1982, p. 401). By using the noun *brain* as a modifier of another noun, *death*, there seems to be a suggestion that there is more than one way of being dead. For example, when someone dies because he or she had a heart attack, we don't refer to it as heart death. When the cause of death is asphyxiation, we don't call it lung death. And when someone dies because of renal failure, we don't call it kidney death. We simply say that a person is dead. Whereas before we could make that diagnosis on the basis that the heart had permanently stopped beating and the person was no longer breathing, this was significant only because it inevitably lead to the death of the brain. Veith et al. state it in the following way:

> In practice death is only pronounced when the functions of circulation and respiration have ceased long enough to cause destruction of the brain and produce other signs of lifelessness. In these instances, cessation of circulation and respiration represent the specific criteria by which irreversible cessation of brain function is determined. (1977b, p. 1748)

The area seems to have become a semantic minefield. Plum and Posner (1980), who have written one of the definitive works on the topic, describe coma as one of a number of states of altered consciousness. Between consciousness and coma, which they regard at the extremes of a continuum, they list such states as *delirium* (disorientation), *obtundation* (mild to moderate reduction in alertness), *stupor* (deep sleep from which the person can be aroused by vigorous and repeated stimuli), and *coma* (a state of unarousable, eyes-closed unconsciousness). All of these are described as acute conditions.

Chronic alterations in consciousness include conditions such as *dementia* (decline in mental process accompanied by reduction in arousal), *hypersomnia* (excessive drowsiness), and the *persistent vegetative state* (awake but unaware). Also included here are *akinetic mutism* (silent, alert-appearing immobility), *appalic syndrome* (indicated to be a little-used term in English-speaking countries), and *locked-in syndrome* (total paralysis of the voluntary muscles or deefferentation). Only "brain death" and the persistent vegetative state will be addressed in this book.

Unlike the Harvard Committee, Plum and Posner make a distinction between "brain death" and irreversible coma. They use *irreversible coma* interchangeably with *cerebral death* (death of the cerebral hemispheres) and cite Korein, another highly respected neuroscientist, for the recommendation that the terms *irreversible coma* and *persistent vegetative state* do not allow for confusion and should be used in preference to the term *cerebral death* (1983, pp. 313–314).

This confusion is compounded by Walker (1985), another respected authority, whose book *Cerebral Death* is devoted to the description and diagnosis of neither irreversible coma nor persistent vegetative state, but of "brain death." Walker explains the dilemma in the following manner:

> Whether the dead-brain syndrome should be described as cerebral or brain death has occasioned differences of opinion. Some years ago cerebral death was the preferred term. Later, this phrase was used to denote a state of persistent brainstem function, especially respiration. Although there is disagreement as to whether these vegetating individuals with only a functioning brainstem and spinal cord should be considered alive, few physicians, theologians, or jurists would pronounce them dead. Brain death was reserved for the state of total absence of function of the brain.
>
> Because of this changing connotation of the term "cerebral death," although the former title has been retained in this edition, "brain death" will be used to refer to the permanent loss of all functions mediated by the brain. "Cerebral death" will be replaced by terms indicating the anatomical or physiological substrate. It is hoped that by means of this, some of the previous confusion will be avoided.   (pp. xiii–xiv)

Concerning the oft-abused term *coma*, Walker has this to say: "A number of modifiers, such as unresponsive and *irreversible* have been used to indicate presumed degrees of coma. These terms, often ill-defined, mean different states to different clinicians. A descriptive definition in clinical terms of responsivity which can be understood by all physicians is preferable" (p. 13, emphasis added).

As our final plea for semantic precision and clarity of meaning, we offer the cautionary recommendations of the Task Force on Death and Dying of the Institute of Society, Ethics, and the Life Sciences, now known as The Hastings Center:

> The proliferation and indiscriminate use of terms such as clinical death, physiological death, biological death, spiritual death, mind death, brain death, cerebral death, neocortical death, body death, heart death, irreversible coma, irreversible loss of consciousness, and virtual death only add to the confusion. The multiplicity of these terms and the difficulties encountered in defining them and in relating them to one another and to the idea of death of a person testify to the need for greater clarity in our understanding of the concept of death. Pending the advent of such clarity, it should be remembered that what is needed are criteria and procedures for determining that a man has died. The various abstract terms listed above do not contribute to the devision of such criteria. They are, perhaps, best avoided.   (1972, p. 51)

Since the term seems imbedded in our lexicon, to the extent that we find it necessary to use, we have found it helpful to refer to the condition as *brain-referenced death* or to place the term in quotation marks as so-called "brain death." The former properly recognizes that death, a unitary phenomenon, is being pronounced by reference to the death of the brain; the latter recognizes the term as a kind of shorthand or abbreviation for the same. The media, especially the print media, are the source of much of the confusion. Consider, for example, the following story which recently appeared in a newspaper serving a Midwestern city.

The headline read "Teenager Struck by Car Is Declared Brain-Dead." The story went on to recount how an anxious mother had spent hour after hour by the bedside of her fourteen-year-old son while doctors performed tests to see if he had any brain function. After nearly two days she was told the news she had been dreading—her son had no brain function. According to the newspaper, "the life-support system was disconnected at approximately 10:00 P.M. yesterday. The patient," the story continued, "was listed in critical condition this morning."

The confusion here is generated by the headline, which proclaimed that the child had been killed ("brain death" = death), and the text of the story, which states that the doctors disconnected the life-support system "yesterday" and that he was listed in *critical condition* "this morning."

This kind of misleading reporting is not limited to small town journalists. Witness, for example, the following account of a tragedy reported in *The New York Times*. The headline in this instance read, "Brain-Dead Baby Allowed to Die." The story explained that "Baby John" was born on Tuesday, declared "brain-dead" on Thursday but "kept alive" for possible organ donation, then allowed to die on Saturday when life support was removed (DeVettere, 1990, p. 102). Since the infant was medically and legally dead when declared "brain-dead," the newspaper was reporting that the baby was born on Tuesday, dead on Thursday, alive on Friday and then died (presumably a second time?) on Saturday.

One last illustration of confusion in the media should serve to make the point. Veatch offers the following:

> At 5:41 on the morning of Sunday, November 10, 1985, Philadelphia Flyers' star goaltender Pelle Lindbergh drove his $117,000 red Porsche into a concrete wall in front of a Somerdale, New Jersey, school. He and two companions were trapped in the car. Lindbergh suffered massive injuries to the brain and spinal cord, a broken hip, jaw, and two bones in his left leg. *The Washington Post* ran a story the next day with the headline "Flyers Goalie Lindbergh Is Declared Brain Dead." The same day *The New York Times* reported that Lindbergh "was brain dead and had no hope for recovery." The coverage of the story for the next two days continued to refer to him as "brain dead," yet spoke of him as "being kept alive on life-support systems," as "hovering near death," and as having "no chance to survive." One account reported that he was declared "clinically dead" on Monday. Finally, in stories dated Tuesday, two days after the accident and the apparent declaration of "brain death," it was reported that surgeons removed his organs for transplant

"at his family's request." The *Times* reported on Wednesday that he "died yesterday afternoon at the conclusion of a five hour operation to remove his organs for transplant."   (Veatch, 1989, p. 15)

Commenting on the foregoing, Veatch posits the following questions: "Were the writers of these stories aware of the fact that the state of New Jersey had not passed legislation authorizing the pronouncement of death based on brain [referenced] criteria? Did they contemplate the possibility that he could have been taken from the hospital in New Jersey across the nearby state line to a hospital in Pennsylvania where there is statutory authorization for pronouncing death based on the lack of brain function? If he had been moved, would Lindbergh then have died the moment he crossed the state line? And, what would have happened if he had been returned to New Jersey after being pronounced dead?" (Ibid., pp. 14–15). And, to these, we would add a final question: How can we ever expect ordinary people to understand brain-referenced death with this kind of reporting? It's no wonder that many people are confused.

Although "brain death" is widely accepted among the western nations, with the notable exception of Denmark, as illustrated by the material in Box 1–1, the Japanese have been reluctant to do so.

"Brain Death" and Public Policy

Pronouncing death has traditionally been the responsibility of the physician. The drafters of the Harvard Committee Report saw no reason why the use of the new criteria they were promoting should change anything. They suggested that:

> responsible medical opinion is ready to adopt new criteria for pronouncing death to have occurred in an individual sustaining irreversible coma as a result of permanent brain damage. If this position is adopted by the medical community, it can form the basis for change in the current *legal* concept of death. No statutory change in the law should be necessary since the law treats this question essentially as one of fact to be determined by physicians. The only circumstances in which it would be necessary that legislation be offered in the various states to define "death" by law would be in the event that great controversy were engendered surrounding the subject and physicians were unable to agree on the new medical criteria.   (1968, p. 87; emphasis added)

The American Medical Association agreed with this assessment and originally opposed any attempt to change the law on the statute books to accommodate pronouncements of death based on brain-referenced criteria (*AMA*,

B o x 1–1   *Death in Japan: Straight from the Gut*

The determination of death by brain-referenced criteria is not officially accepted in Japan, although it is favored by physicians. Public opinion is divided. There seem to be various reasons for this, including a distrust of physicians involved with transplantation, little concern about the misallocation of medical resources, and strong cultural feelings about "unnaturalness" arising from Buddhist beliefs.

While it may seem strange to westerners, many Japanese regarded the belly or gut, not the brain, as the master organ. For example, the Samurai warrior, when committing suicide (harikiri), plunged the sword into his belly, not into his heart or brain. This emphasis on the gut can also be observed linguistically. "At heart" in English is "at the bottom of the gut" in Japanese. To "have a heart-to-heart talk" in Japanese is to "open up one's gut."

This is not to suggest that the Japanese believe the gut to be biologically the master organ; many Japanese have no trouble identifying the brain as such. It just seems to be that the popular acceptance of "brain death" as the death of the person has not progressed nearly as far in Japan as it has in other modern societies with different cultural bases.

(Akatsu, 1990, p. 2)

1974). However, this attitude was soon to change. The "great controversy," which was dismissed as unlikely by Beecher and his colleagues (Harvard Committee), occurred, not because physicians were unable to agree on the criteria, but because challenges cropped up in the courts. The new criteria for pronouncing death gave rise to both criminal and civil litigation.

One of the first criminal cases, and the only one to make its way to a state's highest court (although in this case a Commonwealth rather than a state) was *Commonwealth* v. *Golston*, decided in 1977 (373 Mass. 249, 366, N. E. 2d 744). Golston, the defendant, had been charged with homicide by the Commonwealth of Massachusetts. There was no dispute about the facts. The defendant had struck his victim on the head with a baseball bat. The victim was hospitalized and a large portion of the skull removed to relieve pressure on the brain. Within the next forty-eight hours, his blood pressure and heartbeat were unobservable, he failed to breathe when removed from the ventilator, and the EEG was isoelectric (flat). These conditions persisted for the next two days and, in addition, there were no elicitable reflexes or responses to painful stimulation. After consultation with the family, the decision to remove the ventilator was made two days later, whereupon the victim's heart stopped. The defendant was convicted of criminal homicide.

The conviction was appealed on the basis that, according to the traditional (cardiopulmonary) definition of death, the victim was still alive at the time of the decision to remove him from the ventilator. Despite the fact that the Massachusetts legislature had not passed a law recognizing the legality of death based on brain-referenced criteria, the court ruled that "brain death" was appropriate to support a criminal conviction. While *Golston* was not the first criminal case to involve the question of recognizing death based on brain-referenced criteria, it was the first one to be decided by the highest court in a state system.

The following year, the Colorado Supreme Court addressed the issue of judicial recognition of brain-referenced death in a case where the trial court had adopted the provisions of the proposed, but not yet legislatively approved, Uniform [Brain Death] Act. The lower court had stated, "Our recognition of this concept of brain death does not preclude continuing recognition of the standard of death as determined by traditional criteria of cessation of respiration and circulation (*Lovato* v. *District Court*, 1979, p. 1081). The effect of the decision was to provide alternative determinations of death.

In upholding the decision, the court explicitly addressed two important issues: the relationship between judicial and legislative revision of the common law, and the grounds on which established precedent may sometimes be abandoned.

> We recognize the authority of, and indeed encourage, the General Assembly to pronounce statutorily the standards by which death is to be determined in Colorado. We do not, however, believe that in the absence of legislative action we are precluded from facing and resolving the legal issue of whether irretrievable loss of brain function can be used as a means of detecting the condition of death. Under the circumstances of his case we are not only entitled to resolve the question, but have a duty to do so. To act otherwise would be to close our eyes to the scientific and medical advances made worldwide in the past two or three decades.   (President's Commission, 1981, pp. 138–139)

As we shall see throughout this book, this is but one of many instances where the courts have felt compelled to enter the void resulting from legislative inactivity or unwillingness to deal with the issues of death and dying.

While state supreme court decisions tend to assure some consistency in the interpretation of law within the jurisdiction, lower court rulings sometimes produce conflicting results. Three years prior to the *Golston* decision, a California court adopted a brain-referenced pronouncement of death in the victim of a gunshot wound to the head. The victim had been pronounced "brain dead" just before his heart had been removed for transplantation. The jury was instructed as a matter of law that "the victim was legally dead before removal of organs from his body" (*People* v. *Lyons*, 1974).

Another California court, however, exhibited reluctance to impose a brain-referenced definition of death in the absence of legislative authority. The defendant in this case, who had been driving on the wrong side of a freeway while intoxicated, struck a young girl with his vehicle. At the hospital, she was pronounced dead on the basis of brain-referenced criteria and her heart was transplanted. The attorney for the defendant argued that since the legislature had not enacted a statute recognizing "brain death," only the traditional definition of death would support a conviction for manslaughter. The court agreed, holding that the evidence of the cause of death was not certain enough to support the charge. The dilemma, of course, was that a young girl was dead, and if the driver of the car that struck her didn't kill her, then what did? If she wasn't dead when the surgeons removed her heart, then they must have been responsible for her death. But no charges were ever brought against them. Surely someone must be responsible for her death.

As you might suspect, the case (*People* v. *Flores*, 1974) was appealed by the district attorney and the Superior Court authorized a manslaughter charge holding, as did the *Lyons* court, that as a matter of law, the victim was dead before her heart was removed. Curiously, however, although the defendant was subsequently convicted of both manslaughter and felony drunk driving, he received a sentence of less than five months. The deputy district attorney "explained" this lenient sentence as follows: "I cannot escape from the firm belief that the uncertain state of the case and statutory law on the subject of brain death was a sustained factor in the imposition of such a light sentence" (Veith et al., 1977b, p. 1746).

Civil courts were also confronted with the problem. One of the earliest such instances involved a claim for damages brought by the brother of the victim against the hospital where death had been pronounced prior to the removal of organs for transplantation (*Tucker* v. *Lower*, 1972). Claiming that his brother's heart was still beating just before the organs were removed, the plaintiff sought recovery of damages under the Wrongful Death Act. Only a prosecutor can institute criminal charges and there had been no attempt to do so. The attorney for the plaintiff, Douglas Wilder, has since become the first black governor in the history of the Commonwealth of Virginia.

The trial judge refused the defendants' motion to dismiss the case or to grant summary judgment in their favor, holding instead that the definition of death was the "all vital bodily functions" test established by the common law. Yet, at the last minute, the judge apparently reconsidered his decision and instructed the jury that:

> You shall determine the time of death in this case by using the following definition of the nature of death. Death is a cessation of life. It is the ceasing to exist. Under the law, death is not continuing, but occurs at a precise time,

---

Box 1–2 *Confusion About "Brain Death"?*

Youngner and his colleagues conducted a survey of a sample of 195 physicians and nurses "likely to be involved" in efforts at organ procurement for transplantation. Among other things, they were asked questions about "brain death." In response to a factual question about the use of the whole-brain criterion for pronouncing death, 123 (63 percent) answered correctly that the irreversible loss of all brain function was required for declaring a patient "brain dead." Most of the remaining one-third thought that irreversible loss of all cortical function alone was required for a patient to be declared "brain dead." The authors of the study concluded that "while there is widespread acceptance of the whole-brain criterion, there also is confusion about its legal and clinical applications."

(Youngner et al., 1989)

---

and that time must be established according to the facts of each specific case. In determining the time of death, as aforesaid, under the facts and circumstances of this case, you may consider the following elements, none of which should necessarily be considered controlling, although you may feel under the evidence, that one or more of these conditions are controlling: the time of the total stoppage of the circulation of the blood; the time of the total cessation of the other vital functions consequent thereto, such as respiration and pulsation; the time of complete and irreversible loss of all function of the brain; and, whether or not the aforesaid functions were spontaneously or were being maintained artificially or mechanically.   (President's Commission, 1981, pp. 140–141)

The jury acquitted the defendants. Because there was no appeal, higher courts did not have occasion to rule on the soundness of the trial judge's revision of the standards for determining death. Thus, the case did not establish a new rule on the legal standards to be used in Virginia for determining when death occurs. It did, however, prompt the Virginia medical society to support a statute that was adopted by the legislature the following year. In spite of the AMA's reluctance to endorse statutory support for the changed criteria for pronouncing death, legal actions against physicians and hospitals began to make it clear that such support was inevitable. Indeed, in most of the states where such cases were heard, the legislature responded by enacting a statute shortly thereafter (President's Commission, 1981, p. 140).

The Legislative Response

The Kansas legislature, in 1970, was first to enact a statutory definition of death. The statute provided for alternative definitions, one based on traditional cardiopulmonary criteria and the other on brain functions.

> A person will be considered medically and legally dead if, in the opinion of a physician, based on ordinary standards of medical practice, there is the absence of spontaneous respiratory and cardiac function and, because of the disease or condition which caused, directly or indirectly, these functions to cease, or because of the passage of time since these functions ceased, attempts at resuscitation are considered hopeless; and, in this event, death will have occurred at the time these functions ceased; or
>   A person will be considered medically and legally dead if, in the opinion of a physician, based on ordinary standards of medical practice, there is the absence of spontaneous brain functions; and if based on ordinary standards of medical practice, during reasonable attempts to either maintain or restore spontaneous circulatory or respiratory function in the absence of aforesaid brain function, it appears that further attempts at resuscitation or supportive maintenance will not succeed, death will have occurred at the time when these conditions first coincide. Death is to be pronounced before artificial means of supporting respiratory and circulatory function are terminated and before any vital organ is removed for purposes of transplantation. (President's Commission, *Defining Death,* 1981, p. 62)

Although there is no evidence that this statute or others that were patterned on it—such as Maryland (1972), or New Mexico, or Virginia (both enacted in 1973)—have been the cause of any mischief, by creating the appearance that different standards for pronouncing death will be applied on the basis of whether or not the person was a potential organ donor, a conceptual problem with "brain death" is perpetuated. As the President's Commission pointed out, organs are procured in only a small percentage of cases in which brain-referenced criteria are applied. "Medical concern," it concluded, "rests much less with any wish to facilitate organ transplantation than with the need both to render appropriate care to patients and to replace artificial support with more fitting and respectful behavior when a patient has become a dead body" (Ibid., p. 24).

The Capron-Kass Model

Alexander Capron and Leon Kass, a lawyer and physician respectively, drafted a proposed model statute designed to eliminate the confusion over the alternative definitions found in the earliest laws. It not only indicated how the two standards for pronouncing death were related, but it also eliminated the language in the Kansas statute concerning "hopeless" treatment, which might have suggested that the latter had to do with stopping treatment for the dying rather than defining when death had occurred (Capron and Kass, 1972).

The proposal was subsequently revised by Capron:

> A person will be considered dead if in the announced opinion of a physician, based on ordinary standards of medical practice, he has experienced an irreversible cessation of respiratory and circulatory functions, or in the event that artificial means of support preclude a determination that these functions have ceased, he has experienced an irreversible cessation of total brain functions. Death will have occurred at the time when the relevant functions ceased. (1978, p. 356)

Alaska, Iowa, and Michigan were the first states to enact laws based on the Capron-Kass model (President's Commission, 1981, p. 63).

The American Bar Association Model

Although uncharacteristically brief for anything inspired by a group of lawyers, the American Bar Association was next to step forward with a proposed statute: "For all legal purposes, a human body, with irreversible cessation of total brain function, according to usual and customary standards of medical practice, shall be considered dead" (Ibid., p. 64).

Tennessee was the first state to adopt this proposal as a statute. Although Illinois used the same language, it unfortunately inserted it as an amendment to its Uniform Anatomical Gift Act (which will be discussed in Chapter 12), creating the impression that it applied only to potential organ donors. This is precisely the kind of problem that did arise in Connecticut, a state which, like Illinois, made its statute on declaring death part of its organ transplantation law.

On January 30, 1981, Melanie Bacchiochi suffered a cardiac arrest while having her wisdom teeth removed under general anesthesia. She was resuscitated and admitted to the hospital. Nearly two weeks later, never having regained consciousness, she was diagnosed as being "brain dead," although her physician refused to remove her from the ventilator unless he were first granted immunity from prosecution by the Chief State's Attorney's Office. Ms. Bacchiochi's family went to court and, although the judge refused to reconcile the common law on death with the statute on organ donors, the state assured the physician and the hospital (which supported his position) that they would not prosecute if the ventilator were removed. On March 13, Melanie Bacchiochi was removed from the ventilator that had sustained her for nearly forty days. The irony was that had she been an organ donor, she could have been declared dead under Connecticut law and removed from the ventilator on

February 11. And, because this "solution" was based on agreement from the prosecutor, rather than a judicial decision, there was no precedence established to reassure other perhaps unduly cautious providers of care (Ibid., pp. 145–146).

The fact that such a definition mentions only loss of brain function as a basis for pronouncing death would seem to make it inapplicable to most deaths. This, however, is clearly not the case. As was mentioned earlier, the traditional or cardiopulmonary definition of death was also based on cessation of total brain function in recognizing that the cessation of cardiopulmonary function meant that the brain had or would inevitably stop functioning too.

The Uniform Brain Death Act

The next proposal to surface was that of the National Conference of Commissioners on Uniform State Laws, a group concerned with promoting uniformity of law among the states. This is the same group that has been so successful in establishing legal consistency from state to state concerning organ donation laws through the Uniform Anatomical Gift Act. Nevada (1979) was first to respond to its model: "For legal and medical purposes, an individual who has sustained irreversible cessation of all functioning of the brain, including the brain stem, is dead. A determination under this section must be made in accordance with reasonable medical standards" (Uniform Laws Annotated, Supp., 1981).

The American Medical Association Proposal

Undaunted by the proliferation of proposed statutes, perhaps realizing by now that their initial "just leave it up to us to decide" posture was failing to carry the day, the AMA stepped forward with its own version of a model law. While incorporating cardiopulmonary and brain-referenced alternatives for declaring death, unlike most of the other proposals it contained explicit provisions for limiting liability for physicians.

> *Section 1.* An individual who has sustained either (1) irreversible cessation of circulatory and respiratory functions, or (2) irreversible cessation of all functions of the entire brain, shall be considered dead. A determination of death shall be made in accordance with accepted medical standards.
>
> *Section 2.* A physician or any other person authorized by law to determine death who makes such determination in accordance with Section 1 is not liable for damages in any civil action or subject to prosecution in any criminal proceeding for his acts or the acts of others based on that determination.
>
> *Section 3.* Any person who acts in good faith in reliance on a determination of death is not liable for damages in any civil action or subject to prosecution

in any criminal proceeding for his act.   (President's Commission, 1980, pp. 117–118)

This proposal has failed to gain acceptance in any of the states.

Other Statutes

Although some of the states adopted the previously discussed proposals verbatim, others, while basing their law upon them, made minor modifications as the proposals made their way through the legislatures. Still others decided to come up with their own statutes "from scratch," so to speak. Legislatures are largely populated by lawyers, and it's not uncommon to find an attitude of "we can do it better," although the end result often raises doubts about such a claim. Figure 1–6 shows how the states responded to the need for a law to define death.

The Uniform Determination of Death Act

It was against this backdrop, the "Balkanization" of law that had arisen from the task of defining death, that the work of the President's Commission was initiated. The President's Commission, officially the President's Commission for the Study of Ethical Problems in Medicine and Biomedical and Behavioral Research, an unbelievably unwieldy name even by Washington standards, was created by Congress to study "the ethical and legal implications of the matter of defining death, including the advisability of developing a uniform definition of death" (42 U.S.C. § 1802, 1978).

The Commission, comprised of a distinguished group of scientists, held its first meeting in January 1980 and presented its final report to the president and the Congress on July 9, 1981. It made the following recommendations:

1. That recent developments in medical treatment necessitate a restatement of the standards traditionally recognized for determining that death has occurred.
2. That such a restatement ought preferably to be a matter of statutory law.
3. That such a statute ought to remain a matter of state law, with federal action at this time being limited to areas under current federal jurisdiction.
4. That the statutory law ought to be uniform among the several states.
5. That the "definition" contained in the statute ought to address general physiological standards rather than medical criteria and tests, which will change with advances in biomedical knowledge and refinements in technique.
6. That death is a unitary phenomenon which can be accurately demonstrated either on the traditional grounds of irreversible cessation of heart

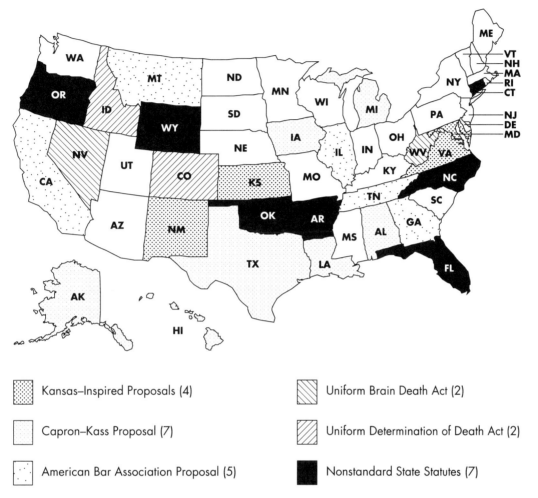

Kansas–Inspired Proposals (4)

Capron–Kass Proposal (7)

American Bar Association Proposal (5)

Uniform Brain Death Act (2)

Uniform Determination of Death Act (2)

Nonstandard State Statutes (7)

FIGURE 1–6 U.S. map showing the way in which the various states responded to the perceived need for a law defining death. Most of the statutes passed since 1981 seem to have been greatly influenced by the Uniform Determination of Death Act.

and lung functions or on the basis of irreversible loss of all functions of the entire brain.

7. That any statutory "definition" should be kept separate and distinct from provisions governing the donation of cadaver organs and from any legal rules on decisions to terminate life-sustaining treatment. (President's Commission, 1980, pp. 1–2)

To accomplish all this, the Commission recommended a new model identified as the Uniform Determination of Death Act (UDDA). Three organizations that had previously proposed model legislation of this subject—the American Bar Association, the American Medical Association, and the National Conference of Commissioners on Uniform State Laws—worked with the Commission and agreed to endorse this new model in place of their previous proposals.

Uniform Determination of Death Act (UDDA)

An individual who has sustained either (1) irreversible cessation of circulatory and respiratory functions, or (2) irreversible cessation of all functions of the entire brain, including the brain stem, is dead. A determination of death must be made in accordance with accepted medical standards.

While most states have exhibited reluctance to abandon their existing statutes to achieve the uniformity sought by the Commission, Colorado and Idaho adopted the Uniform Determination of Death Act even before the President's Commission report had been released. Only time will tell whether or not other states will follow suit. As illustrated by Box 1–3, sometimes even the existence of a rather well-defined statute doesn't eliminate the confusion about "brain death."

To the initial group of twenty-seven states that had adopted a statutory definition of death by 1981, within the next five years eight more had been added to the list: Mississippi (1981), Missouri (1983), Maine (1984–85), Ohio (1984), Rhode Island (1984), Pennsylvania, Vermont, and the District of Columbia (1985). In addition, three states have judicially recognized "brain death": Arizona (1979), Washington (1980), and New York (1984). Three other states have seemingly limited their recognition of "brain death" to homicide cases: Massachusetts (1977), Indiana (1981), and Nebraska (1982) (Martyn, 1986, p. 14).

The UDDA avoids the pitfalls found in some of the early attempts at legislation. It makes it clear that death is a unitary phenomenon that can be diagnosed either according to cardiopulmonary (traditional) or brain-referenced standards. Some critics have suggested that it introduces a redundancy by adding the brain stem, which is a part of the brain, to the diagnosis of cessation of all functions of the *entire* brain. Whether or not this is a valid criticism, given the current controversy about "*cerebral* death," remains to be seen. And, by leaving the *determination* of death as a matter for "accepted medical standards," the Commission has eliminated a concern that a statute might serve to "lock in" diagnostic criteria that are useful now but might quickly become outmoded as technology progresses.

For example, the original Harvard Committee recommendations for confirmation by EEG called for isoelectric readings before and after a twenty-four hour interval. While this was seen as necessary in 1968, it has subsequently

---

Box 1–3 *She's Dead, Isn't She?*

Sharon Ramirez, a resident of Ohio, had been beaten by her husband. When the EMT squad arrived at their home they found her unconscious and with highly irregular breathing. She was rushed to a nearby hospital and immediately placed on a ventilator in an attempt to stabilize her. Within a matter of days it became apparent that she had deteriorated further and had met the criteria for "brain death." The hospital, however, refused to authorize removing her from the life-support system without the consent of her next of kin. Mr. Ramirez, contacted at the county jail where he was being held awaiting trial, refused to give his permission.

At this point, the coroner petitioned the court to rule that she was dead and should be removed from the ventilator so that an autopsy could be performed. The hospital staff supported the request but stated that they "believe[d] they lack[ed] the authority to disconnect the respirator without the next of kin's consent." News reports stated that "the parties are uncertain of their legal obligations and want clarification from a judge." A hospital spokesperson was quoted as saying that the question "involves ethical questions that have been debated for centuries." Five days after she had been pronounced dead by her physicians, Mrs. Ramirez was taken off the respirator after her body "failed to respond." She was pronounced dead . . . again?

Ohio had passed a "death" law based on cardiopulmonary or brain-referenced criteria several years previously.

---

come to be regarded as greatly conservative and the current recommendations call for shortening the interval over which the patient must be observed. The proposed law does not lock in such diagnostic confirmatory measures as the EEG; other tests for brain activity can be accommodated, such as radioisotope cerebral angiography imaging or whatever newer and more efficient tests might become available as accepted medical standards. Once we have agreed societally, as seems to have been done, on a concept of death, the question of criteria to be employed can best be answered by those trained in medicine.

New Jersey is unique among the states in that it recognizes "brain death" but allows for exceptions based on religious objections (see Box 1–4).

"Live" Bodies and Dead Brains

Let us return again to the proposal of the Harvard Committee. After the medical personnel are satisfied that the appropriate tests have been conducted and the results demonstrate a permanently nonfunctioning brain, after everyone who has "participated in major decisions concerning the patient" has been in-

BOX 1–4   *"Brain Death" in New Jersey: Choosing Your Own Concept*

In 1991, New Jersey became the forty-ninth state to acknowledge, by statute, the cessation of brain function as a legal definition of death. Unlike any of the other states, however, New Jersey required physicians to consider religious beliefs before declaring the patient dead based on brain-referenced criteria. The religious exception was included largely to accommodate the orthodox Jewish population of the state and in spite of heavy lobbying from the state's medical and legal societies. Rather than requiring physicians to search for evidence of a patient's wishes, the law states that a physician is responsible for considering religious beliefs only if the beliefs are stated in the patient's medical record or if a relative or close friend provides the information. The new law provides that, when the religious exemption applies, death is to be declared, and the time of death fixed, only upon irreversible cessation of heartbeat and respiration, the traditional cardiopulmonary criteria.

(Olick, 1991; Phillips, 1991, p. 14)

formed, including the family, "death is to be declared and *then* the respirator turned off" (Ad Hoc Committee, 1968, p. 86, emphasis in original).

This is, we are told, a medical decision; "it is unsound and undesirable to force the family to make the decision" (Ibid., p. 86). We are also told that this decision must be made only by physicians who are not involved in any later effort to transplant organs or tissue from the deceased but, since this same provision is part of the Uniform Anatomical Gift Act, enacted into law in every state, the provision might be seen as unnecessary to the task at hand (Ibid., p. 87). Still again, for emphasis, the Committee states that

> the patient be declared dead before any effort is made to take him off a respirator, if he is then on a respirator. This declaration should not be delayed until he is taken off the respirator and all artificially stimulated signs have ceased. The reason for this recommendation is that in our judgment *it will provide a greater degree of legal protection to those involved.* Otherwise, the physicians would be turning off the respirator on a person who is, under the present strict, technical application of law, still alive.   (Ibid., emphasis added)

While the recommended procedures are designed to provide a safeguard against liability for the physician who disconnects the patient from the ventilator, surely the patient was just as dead before the machine was disconnected as after. If not, how could the patient be pronounced dead? And, if the patient was dead, which would seem to be clearly so, then why is it necessary to pull the plug? For, just as the pronouncement of death gives the physician the right to "pull the plug," it also conveys (surely in the case where the patient or the next of kin have given consent for organs to be used for transplantation) the right *not* to do so. Presumably, if one is dealing with a corpse, the moral imperative would be to preserve the organs for the benefit of the living in the best possible condition—by continuing the respiration process until they can be removed. Not only would there be no moral problems with such behavior, but, in fact, one might say that it would be morally irresponsible to run the risk of damaging valuable organs. In practice, this is just what is done. Typically, these newly dead though "functioning" cadavers are maintained only for relatively short periods of time—the time necessary to locate a recipient and harvest the organs. It would be possible, however, to extend this interval if so desired.

Psychiatrist Willard Gaylin, President of the Institute of Society, Ethics and the Life Sciences, now known as The Hastings Center, described this possibility in somewhat prophetic terms in a 1974 essay in *Harper's* magazine. Gaylin described these newly dead cadavers, which he called *neomorts* (neo = "new"; mort = "dead"; the newly dead), in the following manner:

> [They] would have the legal status of the dead with none of the qualities one now associates with death. They would be warm, respirating, pulsating, evacuating, and excreting bodies requiring nursing, dietary, and general attention—*and could probably be maintained so for a period of years.* If we chose to, we could, with the technology already at hand, legally avail ourselves of these new cadavers to serve science and mankind in dramatically useful ways. The autopsy, that most respectable of medical tradition, that last gift of the dying person to the living future, could be extended in principle beyond our current recognition. To save lives and relieve suffering—traditional motives for violating tradition—we could develop hospitals (an inappropriate word because it suggests the presence of living human beings), banks, or farms of cadavers which require feeding and maintenance, in order to be harvested. To the uninitiated, the "new cadavers" in their rows of respirators would seem indistinguishable from comatose patients now residing in wards of chronic neurological hospitals.   (Gaylin, 1974, p. 226)

According to Gaylin, some of the major uses to which the "neomort" might be put include:

1. *Training.* Uneasy medical students could practice routine physical examinations: auscultation, percussion of the chest, examination of the retina, rectal and vaginal examinations, and so on. All manner of tests could be practiced except neurological examinations, since the neomort by definition has no functioning central nervous system. Both student and patient could be spared the pain, fumbling, and embarrassment of the "first time."

Interns could practice standard and more difficult diagnostic procedures, from spinal taps to pneumoencephalography and the making of arteriograms, and residents could practice almost all of their surgical skills—in other words, most of the procedures that are now normally taught with the indigent in wards of major city hospitals could be taught with neomorts. Further, students could practice more exotic procedures often not available in a typical residency: eye operations, skin grafts, plastic facial surgery, amputation of useless limbs, and various forms of coronary surgery. They could also practice the actual removal of organs, whether they be kidneys, livers, or what have you, for delivery to the transplant team.

2. *Testing.* The neomort could be used for much of the testing of drugs and surgical procedures that are often performed on prisoners and volunteers. Diagnostic instruments, such as sophisticated electrocardiography, could be tested by selectively damaging various parts of the heart to see whether or how well the instrument could detect the damage.

3. *Experimentation.* An obvious form of experimentation would be testing cures for illnesses which would first be induced in the neomort. New antidotes could be tested for poisons administered to the neomort; validation and comparison of new therapies would be possible with cancers that had been intentionally induced. Again, because the neomort would have no brain function, there would be no psychological or placebo effect to cloud the interpretation of these trial therapies.

Gaylin's proposal was made in the early 1970s, at a time when he had no way of foreseeing the development of the AIDS epidemic now in our midst. AIDS, however, and the search for new therapies that are so urgently needed, presents us with a seductive case for the use of the neomort. New drugs could be tested in neomorts that had been injected with the AIDS virus. While this could also be done on living subjects, as is typically the case, the development of an AIDS vaccine might be speeded significantly by the kind of experimentation that is difficult to do with the living. First, there is always the problem of getting a significant number of volunteers for testing the safety and effectiveness of the vaccine. Depending on the form this vaccine might take, there would be a possibility, however slight, that the subjects might become infected. While this might be regarded as slight, many people still remember the problems with the swine flu vaccine of the 1970s. The complications from accidental infection with the acquired immunodeficiency virus are likely to be much greater than those associated with the swine flu vaccine. A vaccine presents yet another problem. Once the vaccine has been administered to a group of volunteers, given the pattern of transmission of the virus, how might one go about deciding whether or not the vaccine is effective? It would be necessary to differentiate between the effect of the vaccine and the fact that subjects might be reducing or eliminating high-risk behaviors. While, again, it would be unethical to intentionally expose a live volunteer, who had been (hopefully) immunized, directly to the virus, this could certainly be done with a population of neomorts.

4. *Banking*. Just as we now have blood banks, neomorts would make it possible to have banks for all transplantable organs or tissues.

5. *Harvesting*. A sizable population of neomorts could provide a steady supply of blood, since they would be capable of replenishing their own blood and could be used periodically as donors. Gaylin acknowledged at the time that were it not for the other valuable uses of the neomort, maintenance *only* for harvesting blood would probably not be cost effective. He suggested that the appropriate basis for evaluating cost would be similar to that used by the lumbering industry in the production of sawdust. Though it would be prohibitively expensive to set out to create sawdust by milling lumber, a product that is not commercially feasible has become a profitable dividend as waste from a more commercially useful harvest.

Here, again, Gaylin had no way of anticipating AIDS and the concerns it would create about the safety of blood banking. Although would-be donors who engage in high-risk behaviors are discouraged from giving blood, and all blood is screened for the presence of antibodies to the virus, it has not been commercially feasible to test the blood for the virus itself. What this means in practice is that it is possible for someone who has been infected with the virus but who has not yet become sero-positive (the body has not begun to produce antibodies to the virus) to unknowingly donate infected blood. If such blood is transfused, it is possible, but not certain, that the recipient will become infected. The risk of getting HIV-contaminated blood from a blood bank is very slight, much less than the risk of being exposed to the hepatitis virus. Awareness of this possibility, however, has created a trend toward autologous transfusion wherever possible. In this procedure, a person's own blood is drawn and stored prior to surgery for later use if needed.

Yet another use of the neomort, which Gaylin had no way of foreseeing, would be that of a gestational surrogate. Surrogate motherhood is a controversial topic. Much of the controversy has been generated by situations in which the woman, after carrying the pregnancy to term, experiences a change of heart and refuses to relinquish the baby to the contracting couple, who might even be the full genetic parents. While the legal status of such arrangements is unsettled, a fetus carried in the womb of a neomort would be less likely to lead to this particular problem. Whether fertilized naturally and then removed prior to implantation, or fertilized in a Petri dish (in vitro), the preembryo could then be implanted into the neomort's uterus for the duration of gestation. Birth would be by cesarean section. Not only would there be no concern about the relinquishment of the child after birth, but there would also be no need for concern about the surrogate engaging in activities that might be harmful to the fetus, such as smoking, drinking or using other drugs, not eating appropriately, not getting enough sleep, or contracting an infectious disease.

It is typical for many people, learning of Gaylin's proposal for the first time, to be somewhat repulsed by the idea. Using human bodies in such a way, even though dead, seems somehow disrespectful of the dead.

Jonas, a philosopher, published a paper on this subject in the same year that Gaylin's essay appeared in print (Jonas, 1974). Gaylin credits him with anticipating some of the ideas he proposes; their speculations on the uses to which these bodies might be put are remarkably similar. (Shane and Daly, 1986, have also written about living cadavers but without acknowledging either Gaylin or Jonas.) Their conclusions, however, are quite divergent.

Unlike Gaylin, Jonas seems willing to accept the report of the Harvard Committee as a means of diagnosing irreversible coma but *not* as a means of diagnosing death. "The Report," he claims, "has strictly speaking defined not death, the ultimate state, but a criterion for permitting it to take place unopposed—e.g., by turning off the respirator" (Ibid., pp. 132–133). Whether or not this position is valid is addressed later in this chapter; we conclude that it is not.

Because of his unwillingness to accept the conclusion that those who have been pronounced dead using brain-referenced criteria are *truly* dead, Jonas makes the following argument:

> We do not know with certainty the borderline between life and death, and a definition cannot substitute for knowledge. Moreover, we have sufficient grounds for suspecting that the artificially supported condition of the comatose patient may still be one of life, however reduced—i.e., for doubting that, even with the brain function gone, he is completely dead. In this state of marginal ignorance and doubt the only course to take is to lean over backward toward the side of possible life. It follows that interventions as I described [many of the same uses described for Gaylin's "neomorts"] should be regarded on a par with vivisection and on no account be performed on a human body in that equivocal or threshold condition. And the definition that allows them, by stamping as unequivocal what at best is equivocal, must be rejected. But mere rejection in discourse is not enough. Given the pressure of the—very real and very worthy—medical interests, it can be predicted that the permission it implies in theory will be irresistible in practice, once the definition is installed in official authority. Its becoming so installed must therefore be resisted at all costs. It is the only thing that still can be resisted; by the time the practical conclusions beckon, it will be too late. It is a clear case of *principiis obsta*.   (Ibid., p. 138)

Time has certainly proven Jonas right in one respect: the pressure of "medical interests" has proven to be irresistible. Neomorts, although seldom referred to as such, have quickly gone from theory to practice. Physicians have been seduced by seemingly irresistible temptations and, many would argue, by noble motives.

Although we first learned of this in 1978 (*Medical World News*, March 6, 1978), one of the most striking examples came in 1983. Again, we'll let the newspaper tell the story.

Woman on Respirator to Save Unborn Infant

New York (AP)—The life of an unborn child was at stake Wednesday as doctors fought to keep a pregnant mother of two alive with a respirator after she was declared medically "brain dead."

"She's alive, the baby's still alive," John Maniscalco said in explaining why the family is keeping his wife, Marie, 27, on a respirator at a Brooklyn hospital.

Mrs. Maniscalco collapsed a week ago at their Coney Island home, the husband said, after holding her head in pain and screaming, "I can't see you! Where are you?"

Mr. Maniscalco said doctors at Victory Memorial Hospital in Bay Ridge told him there was some kind of pressure on his wife's brain that could not be relieved and that she was "brain dead," meaning there is no sign of brain activity or brain waves.

The medical verdict was that it might be possible for the four-month-old fetus to develop normally despite the woman's condition.

"We all have a feeling there may be some hope," Mrs. Maniscalco's mother, Marie Catanzaor, who came from Virginia to be with her daughter, said. "If we can save one life that's something." (*The [Toledo] Blade*), December 1, 1983)

Was Mrs. Maniscalco dead? Yes. Was she being used as a neomort? Yes. Was it being done for a good cause? Again, many would argue that it was, especially where the next of kin were so supportive. What, however, might happen if there were disagreement among the next of kin? Or, perhaps even more dramatically, what might happen if the next of kin wanted to remove someone like Mrs. Maniscalco from the ventilator, so that they could bury their dead, and an outside party, or the state itself, opposed those wishes because it would result in the death of the embryo or fetus? Would it make any difference if the pregnancy had been planned or unplanned? What if the woman had been impregnated through rape or incest?

It has been demonstrated repeatedly that pregnant corpses can be maintained for increasingly longer periods before giving birth, by cesarean section, to seemingly healthy babies. Intervals of more than three months have been reported. (*Medical World News*, 1978, reported 21 days; Dillon et al., 1982, state that there are fewer than 200 successful instances of postmortem cesarean section in the literature; Field et al., 1988, cite 9 weeks at a cost of $217,784;

Bernstein et al., 1989, described as the "longest to date, 107 days at a cost of more than $100,000.)

The dilemma of "pregnant neomorts" took on an international flavor when, on October 4, 1992, eighteen-year-old Marion Ploch lost control of the car she was driving near the German city of Erlangen. The crash left the driver, an unmarried dental assistant, with severe head injuries and she was pronounced "brain dead" on October 8. Shortly after arriving at the hospital it was discovered that she was pregnant and, although the identity of the male who had impregnated her remained unknown, a specially recruited panel of medical, legal, and ethical specialists recommended that the young woman be maintained until the fetus could reach viability. Although her parents initially expressed a desire to bury their daughter as soon as possible, they eventually agreed to authorize the continuation of support and announced that they would raise the child as their own.

The case created a furor in Germany. Even Roman Catholic theologians were divided over the morality of the process. The pregnancy was ended on November 16 with the spontaneous delivery of a dead fetus. If the physicians had been successful in bringing the pregnancy to term, as they had intended, they would have set a record. None of the previously recorded cases involved a woman who died so early (thirteen weeks) in her pregnancy (Seibert, Waldrop, and Marshall, 1992; *The [Toledo] Blade,* 1992).

Although the current utilization of such bodies seems to have fallen far short of the multiplicity of uses envisioned by Gaylin and Jonas, the uses extend well beyond those just described. Even before Gaylin's essay appeared in print, and perhaps as part of the inspiration for it, there had been some successful experimentation in cleansing the blood of a living patient by temporarily shunting it through the liver of a "brain dead," but mechanically sustained, body (Summers et al., 1970). Among the other uses that have since been reported, in addition to the gestational experiments described previously, are testing of blood substitutes (Maugh, 1979), practicing intubation on both children (Carson, Rias, and Melker, 1981) and adults (Orlowski, Kanoti, and Mehlman, 1988), testing of the Jarvik-7, the artificial heart prototype that would be implanted in the chest of a Utah dentist, Dr. Barney Clark (Kolff et al., 1984; *Medical World News,* June 25, 1984, described the trials as being done on "cadavers"), and testing monoclonal antibodies as clotting inhibitors (Coller et al., 1988).

Gaylin was aware that his proposal, about which he expressed some ambivalence, would be condemned by some readers. New ideas are often slow in gaining acceptance. The very same feelings of revulsion that might be generated by the contemplation of neomorts were once attached to any experimental use of the human body. Dissection was widely opposed. Early anatomists, and the medical schools where they taught, often had to resort to nefarious schemes to obtain bodies for anatomical study. So clandestine had the task become that laws against grave robbing were passed to discourage what had become a growing problem. The situation now is quite different. For many people, donating one's body to a medical school is seen as an act of altruism. Consequently, rather than being threatened with a shortage of cadavers, most institutions today, particularly the "prestigious" ones, have a steady supply. Although not viewed as personally acceptable by some, anatomical gifts of this type are seldom criticized today.

Once death has occurred, the choices for disposal of the body are few. Either the body can be prepared for burial, entombment, or cremation or it can be donated to a medical school or other medical research institute. Since there is always a possibility that the body may not be suitable for such purposes, depending upon its condition at the time of death, or that the body may not be needed, it is always necessary to have alternative plans. Those who plan to donate their bodies for such uses, or who have had friends or relatives who have done so, usually view it as preferable to allowing the body to simply decompose. They would argue that it is better for some good to come out of their death, that the living might benefit in some way, rather than to merely dispose of the body. We will look closer at the procedures of donating one's body to science in Chapter 12.

Viewed in such a way, one might argue that the use of neomorts for studies of short duration would be the "ethical equivalent of organ donation" (Coller et al., 1988); studies that would require the maintenance of the neomort over longer periods of time would be more like the ethical equivalent of using cadavers for dissection. Even so, there are important legal and ethical issues that need to be addressed. Coller and his associates have proposed the following:

1. The research must address an important clinical problem.
2. Subjects should be excluded if they are candidates for organ donation. [This is based on their assertion that transplantation is a clinical procedure that has the *immediate* potential for saving lives and therefore it must take precedence over basic research done on neomorts.]
3. Subjects should be excluded if an autopsy to determine the cause of death is required.
4. The investigators should be prohibited from participating in deciding whether the patient meets the criteria for death and in determining the support systems. [This is the same principle that applies by law to organ transplantation.] Informed consent must be obtained from the next of kin; if the next of kin is not available, the research should not be conducted.
5. The death certificate must be signed before the experiment begins.
6. The materials to be injected must meet the same purity and production standards as would be required for an investigational new drug for

human use under the guidelines established by the Food and Drug Administration.

7. All procedures must be done in a manner identical to those that would be carried out on a living human.

8. Experiments should be designed to minimize the amount of time required for their completion.

9. Research on neomorts should be reviewed by an Institutional Review Board to insure independent assessment by a disinterested and expert group. (Coller et al., 1988, p. 638)

The guidelines are designed to insure that the body would be treated with respect. Like other anatomical gifts, including a gift of the whole body, the consent of the next of kin would be important. Unlike the provisions of the Uniform Anatomical Gift Act (UAGA), these recommendations do not seem to contemplate a donation made by a person while still alive. This is a rather insignificant point, however, for even though a donor's previously given consent is legally recognized under the provisions of the UAGA, in practice the decision is usually made by the family.

Orlowski and his colleagues (1988) wrote of the clinical need to use the newly dead for teaching and practicing intubation techniques. While recognizing the importance of this, they expressed their concern that the newly dead were being used in this way *without consent of the next of kin*. They acknowledge that ethically, morally, and legally it is always best to obtain consent from either the patient or the family, but they were concerned that a strict adherence to this would seriously reduce the opportunities for learning these techniques. The solution they propose is a novel one.

It is imperative that the skill of intubation be conveyed to trainees and that the principle of consent continue to be respected. Although no crisis in the education of trainees in intubation has occurred, it appears that such a crisis has been averted by the deceptive practice of using newly dead patients to teach intubation without consent. The practice is justified; the deception is not. We argue that the potential danger to those who need intubation mandates adoption of a program that *permits an exception to informed consent.* Through open disclosure that practice in intubation occurs and is both necessary and important, patients will have the opportunity to refuse the procedure specifically by advance directive. In the absence of expressed dissent, the practice should be permitted. (1988, p. 441, emphasis added)

This approach, sometimes described as an "opt out" system, operates from the assumption that either (1) no one would deny the use of his or her dead body for such important purposes or (2) if the practice is widely acknowledged and the person didn't expressly object while still alive, then we can presume that he or she would have consented. This approach, presumed consent, has also been suggested in the context of organ donation and will be discussed more fully when we come to that topic.

La Puma, writing in the same issue of *Annals of Internal Medicine* that contained the guidelines proposed by Coller and his associates, expressed his concern that although their recommendations provided a useful starting point, they failed to go far enough. To them he would add the following:

1. The dignity and humanity of the body should never be violated, even in the pursuit of the most valuable scientific knowledge.

2. The experiment should be precisely designed, and limited to a few minutes or hours, instead of days or weeks. [La Puma makes no attempt to reconcile this recommendation with the maintenance of the pregnant neomort for gestational purposes. Perhaps he would classify that as something other than "research."]

3. The diagnosis of brain death must be unequivocal, made in accordance with the standard of care and by the patient's clinicians. [This, of course, is currently required by law.]

4. The fully voluntary, knowledgeable consent of the next-of-kin is necessary; if possible, the next-of-kin must act as the patient would.

5. The experiment's medical importance must be clear and vital to clinicians; that is, the results should be likely to yield valuable information, such as safe, efficacious, innovative treatment for a lethal or severely disabling disease.

6. Prospective review and approval of the research protocol by an IRB [Institutional Review Board], with its community and ministry members in attendance is necessary.

7. Any charges for the time or resources spent on "life-support" systems after the declaration of death should be paid for by the investigators, not by the patient or the patient's family or their insurance carrier. [This, too, would resemble standard transplant practices where the donor family is relieved of all costs associated with recovery of tissues or organs.] (1988, p. 607)

It should be apparent from the foregoing that the practice of pronouncing death on the basis of brain-referenced criteria has helped resolve one difficult problem, or set of problems, but only at the expense of creating some completely new medical, moral, ethical, and legal dilemmas to challenge us. Who knows what lies in store for us as we march forward into the twenty-first century? One thing is certain: the problems will become even more challenging, not less. All of us have an obligation to participate in the public dialogue that will point the direction in which the technological revolution will invite us to go.

Summary

Our concepts and understanding of life and death have changed rather dramatically from the time of our early ancestors. Changes during the second half of this century, brought on primarily by advances in medical technology, have been especially swift. The realization that it is possible to keep bodies "alive" long after the brain has irreversibly stopped functioning has resulted in the development of new ways of diagnosing death, so-called "brain death." While most Americans have become increasingly comfortable with this transition, it appears that the concept of "brain death" is often misused and/or misunderstood. Regardless, the concept has been incorporated into the laws of all states, although some (New Jersey, for example) have made provisions for those who disagree with the concept on religious grounds.

Since death is a legal matter, as well as a medical and social one, we have traced the development of case and statutory law as the concept of "brain death" has evolved. In spite of convincing arguments in support of a standardized law (Uniform Determination of Death Act), few states have demonstrated a willingness to alter their existing statutes.

Finally, we discussed the implications of using brain function—whole-brain function—as a basis for stopping the use of mechanical life support. With the option to "pull the plug" there would also seem to be the option *not* to "pull the plug." The consequent use of lifelike cadavers in the service of mankind raises a host of new ethical issues.

Study Questions

1. What is the traditional legal definition of death?
2. What developments in medicine that took place somewhere between the end of the nineteenth century and the middle of the twentieth century produced a change in the public's fear of being pronounced dead prematurely?
3. What is meant by the term *brain death*?
4. Discuss the contribution of the Ad Hoc Committee of the Harvard Medical School to Examine the Definition of Brain Death to the expansion of the traditional cardiopulmonary definition of death.
5. What did the Harvard Ad Hoc Committee recommend as criteria of a permanently nonfunctioning brain?
6. What were the two reasons given by the Harvard Ad Hoc Committee for the need to recognize "brain-referenced" criteria as a measure of death?
7. How does the ethicist Robert Veatch differentiate among definitions, concepts, loci, and criteria of death?
8. What are some ways in which the term *brain death* has been misused?

9. What is the Uniform Determination of Death Act and why has it been proposed by the President's Commission?

10. What is a *neomort* and how, according to Gaylin, might neomorts be used for the benefit of mankind?

11. In what ways have *neomorts* actually been used?

References

Akatsu, H. (1990). The heart, the gut, and brain death in Japan. *Hastings Center Report* (March-April):2.

Ad Hoc Committee of Harvard Medical School to Examine the Definition of Brain Death. (1968). A definition of irreversible coma. *JAMA,* 205 (6):85–88.

Alexander, M. (1980). "The rigid embrace of the narrow house": Premature burial and the signs of death. *Hastings Center Report* (June): 25–21.

American Medical Association. (1974). Definition of death. *JAMA,* 227:728.

Arnold, J. D., T. F. Zimmerman, and D. L. Martin. (1968). Public attitudes and the diagnosis of death. *JAMA,* 206(9):1949–1954.

Bernstein, I. M. et al. (1989). Maternal brain death and prolonged fetal survival. *Obstetrics & Gynecology,* 74(3):2;434–437.

Black, H. C. (1968). *Black's law dictionary.* St. Paul: West Publishing Co.

Brain-dead patient, kept on life-support, miscarries. (1992) *The [Toledo] Blade.* November 17.

Capron, A. J. (1978). Legal definition of death. *Ann. N.Y. Acad. Sci.,* 315:349, 356.

Capron, A. M., and L. R. Kass. (1972). A statutory definition of the standards for determining human death: An appraisal and a proposal. *University of Pennsylvania Law Review,* 121:87–118.

Carson, R. A., J. L. Rias, and R. J. Melker. (1981). Research with brain-dead children. *IRB: Review of Human Subjects Research,* January:5–6.

Coller, B. S. et al. (1988). Inhibition of human platelet function *in vivo* with a monoclonal antibody (with observations on the newly dead as experimental subjects). *Annals of Internal Medicine,* 109:635–638.

Commonwealth v. *Golston,* 373 Mass. 249, 366 N. E. 2d 744 (1977), cert. denied, 434 U. S. 1039 (1978).

DeVettere, R. J. (1990). Neocortical death and human death. *Law, Medicine & Health Care,* 18(1–2):96–104.

Dillon, W. P. et al. (1982). Life support and maternal brain death during pregnancy. *JAMA,* 248(9):1089–1091.

Field, D. R. et al. (1988). Maternal brain death during pregnancy; medical and ethical issues. *JAMA,* 260(6):816–822.

Flye, M. W. (1989). *Principles of Organ Transplantation.* Philadelphia: W. B. Saunders.

Gaylin, W. (1974). Harvesting the dead. *Harper's* (September):223–230.

Gaylin, W. (1980). Hard choices: death and dying. Corporation for Public Broadcasting (videotape).

Gervais, K. G. (1986). *Redefining Death.* New Haven: Yale University Press.

Hirsh, H. L. (1975). Brain death. *Medical Trial Technique Quarterly* (Annual), 377–405.

Jonas, H. (1974). Against the stream: Comments on the definition and redefinition of death. In *Philosophical Essays.* Englewood Cliffs, NJ: Prentice Hall, 132–140.

Kolff, J. et al. (1984). The artificial heart in human subjects. *Journal of Thoracic & Cardiovascular Surgery*, 87:825–831.

Lamb, D. (1985). *Death, Brain Death and Ethics.* London: Croom Helm.

LaPuma, J. (1988). Discovery and disquiet: Research on the brain-dead. *Annals of Internal Medicine*, 109:606–608.

Lewis, H. (1990). Teenager struck by car is declared brain-dead. *The [Toledo] Blade*, September 9.

Lovato v. *District Court*, 601 P. 2d 1072 (Col. 1979) (en banc).

Mant, A. K. (1976). The medical definition of death. In Edwin S. Schneidman, ed., *Death: Current Perspectives.* Palo Alto: Mayfield, 218–231.

Martyn, S. R. (1986). Using the brain dead for medical research. *Utah Law Review*, 1(1):1–28.

May, W. (1973). Attitudes toward the newly dead. *Hastings Center Studies*, 1(1):3–13.

Medical Consultants on the Diagnosis of Death to the President's Commission for the Study of Ethical Problems in Medicine and Biomedical and Behavioral Research. 1981. Guidelines for the determination of death. *JAMA*, 246(19):2184–2186.

Molinari, G. F. (1982). Brain death, irreversible coma, and words doctors use. *Neurology*, 32:400–402.

New record birth of baby after mother's brain death. (1983). *Medical World News,* (August 8):28.

Olick, R. S. (1991). Brain death, religious freedom, and public policy: New Jersey: Landmark Legislative Initiative. *Kennedy Institute Ethics J.*, 1:275.

Orlowski, J. P., G. A. Kanoti, and M. J. Mehlman. (1988). The ethics of using newly dead patients for teaching and practicing intubation techniques. *NEJM*, 319(7):439–441.

Osborne, L. W. (1982). When RIP means research in progress—the use of brain dead subjects in medical research. *Australian Journal of Social Issues*, 17(2):171–180.

Pallis, C. (1983). *ABC of Brain Stem Death.* London: BMA House.

Parisi, J. E. et al. (1982). Brain death with prolonged somatic survival. *NEJM*, 306(1):14–16.

People v. *Flores,* Cal. Super. G. County, 7246-C, 1974.

People v. *Lyons*, 15 Criminal Law Reporter 2240 (Cal. Super. Alemeda Co., 1974).

Phillips, D. (ed.). (1991). New Jersey passes brain death law. *Hospital Ethics* (May-June): 14.

Plum, F. and J. B. Posner. (1980). *The Diagnosis of Stupor and Coma.* Philadelphia: F. A. Davis.

President's Commission for the Study of Ethical Problems in Medicine and Biomedical and Behavioral Research. (1981). *Defining Death.* Washington: U.S. Government Printing Office.

Searching for a common ground. (1984). *Medical World News* (June 25):43.

Seibert, S., T. Waldrop, and R. Marshall. (1992). A matter of death and life. *Newsweek* (November 16):55.

Shane, H. G., and W. J. Daly. (1986). How the dead can help the living. *Futurist* (Jan.-Feb.):24–26.

Summers, R. W., S. J. Curtis, C. E. Hartford, and J. L. Rubush (1970). Acute hepatic coma treated by cross circulation with irreversibly comatose donor. *JAMA*, 214 (13): 2297–2301.

Task Force on Death and Dying of the Institute of Society, Ethics, and the Life Sciences.

(1972). Refinements in criteria for the determination of death: An appraisal. *JAMA*, 221(1):48–53.

Tucker v. *Lower,* No. 2831, Richmond Va., Law and Equity Ct., May 23, 1972.

Veatch, R. M. (1976). *Death, Dying and the Biological Revolution*. New Haven: Yale University Press.

Veatch, R. M. (1989). *Death, Dying and the Biological Revolution* (rev. ed.). New Haven: Yale University Press.

Veith, F. J. et al. (1977a). Brain death I. A status report of medical and ethical considerations. *JAMA*, 238(15):1651–1655.

Veith, F. J. et al. (1977b). Brain death II. A status report of legal considerations. *JAMA*, 238(16):1744–1748.

Walker, A. E. (1985). *Cerebral Death*. Baltimore: Urban and Schwarzenberg.

Winslow, J. B. (1742). Dissertation sur l'incertitude des signes de la morte et l'abus des enternemens et embaumens precipites. Paris. [Cited in Walker (1985).]

Woman on respirator to save unborn infant. (1977). *The [Toledo] Blade*. December 1.

Youngner, S. J. et al. (1989). "Brain death" and organ retrieval. *JAMA*, 261(15):2205–2210.

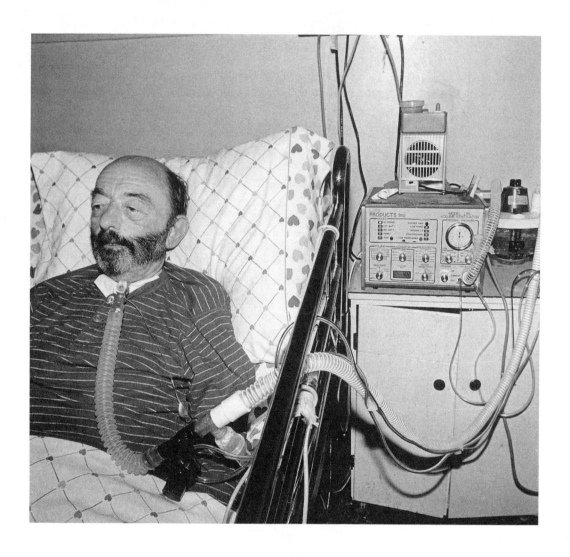

CHAPTER 2

Refusing Life-Sustaining Medical Treatment

Deciding for Yourself

I know not what course others may take, but as for me, give me liberty or give me death.

Patrick Henry, American Statesman, 1736–1779

It's not that I'm afraid to die. I just don't want to be there when it happens.

Woody Allen

IN THE PREVIOUS CHAPTER, we discussed the question, "When should a person be considered as dead?" In this and the following chapter, we shall examine the related, yet quite different, question: "When, and under what circumstances, may a person refuse to accept life-sustaining medical treatment (LSMT)?" We will limit our discussion in this chapter to those situations involving patients with decision-making capacity and reserve the arguably more difficult issue of making treatment decisions for those who lack decision-making capacity for Chapter 3.

This seemingly simple question has been the subject of great debate and litigation over the past twenty years or so. The answer, in some ways, is surprisingly straightforward. Assuming that persons are competent to make their own decisions about such things, they have the right to do so regardless of the consequences. According to the members of a presidential commission appointed to study such questions,

> the voluntary choice of a competent and informed patient should determine whether or not life-sustaining therapy will be undertaken, just as such choices provide the basis for other decisions about medical treatment. Health care institutions and professionals should try to enhance patients' abilities to make decisions on their own behalf and to promote understanding of the available treatment options. . . . Health care professionals serve patients best by maintaining a presumption in favor of sustaining life, while recognizing that competent patients are entitled to choose to forego any treatments, including those that sustain life.   (President's Commission, 1983, pp. 3–5)

Patients with Religiously Motivated Refusals: The Jehovah's Witnesses Cases

The operative words in the preceding quotation are *competent* and *informed.* The first of these, *competent,* would seem to imply that the person who is to make the decision is capable of doing so. In the view of the Commission,

> any determination of the capacity to decide on a course of treatment must relate to the individual abilities of a patient, the requirements of the task at hand, and the consequences likely to flow from the decision. Decision making capacity requires, to a greater or lesser degree: 1) possession of a set of values and goals; 2) the ability to communicate and to understand information, and 3) the ability to reason and to deliberate about one's choices.   (Ibid., pp. 57–60)

The requirement of capacity or competence is grounded in a respect for autonomy (literally "self-normative") or self-determination in decision making. There seems to be a long-standing and widely accepted commitment to the principle that each of us should be responsible for our own decisions, including decisions about whether or not to accept various forms of medical treatment. This concept often finds judicial expression in such language as, "Every human being of adult years and sound mind has a right to determine what shall be done with his own body" (*Schloendorff* v. *Society of New York Hosp.,* 1914, p. 93), and "[n]o right is held more sacred, or is more carefully guarded, by the common law, than the right of every individual to the possession and control of his own person, free from all restraint or interference of others, unless by clear and unquestionable authority of law" (*Union Pacific R. Co.* v. *Botsford,* 1891, p. 251).

Current law tends to link the provision of medical treatment to an even more stringent standard, requiring not only that there be consent, but that the consent be *informed*. This means, among other things, that the person giving, or withholding, the consent understands something about the risks versus the benefits of the proposed treatment, the nature of the treatment itself, and any alternatives to the treatment that might exist.

All too often, however, decisions about competence have been based on whether or not a physician agrees with a patient's decision. An unwillingness to accept another's decision, especially when it involves foregoing life-sustaining medical treatment, is sometimes rationalized by insisting that the patient is not competent. Some would go even further and insist that a decision to refuse life-sustaining medical treatment is, a priori, unreasonable and, therefore, could not have been made by a competent person. This kind of reasoning, this "I know better than you what is the right decision for you to make," is an example of paternalism and the antithesis of autonomy. Although the term *paternalism* is deeply ingrained in the bioethical literature, it would probably be better labeled and less sexist to refer to it as *parentalism*, since it is characteristic of both mothers (maternalism) and fathers (paternalism). Regardless, while it is often appropriate within the confines of the parent-child relationship, it has no place in the context of the health care system.

In spite of a long-standing respect for autonomy, at least in word if not in deed, the legal literature is filled with examples where seemingly competent patients have had treatment forced upon them. Many of the earliest cases involved members of Jehovah's Witnesses who would have probably died had it not been for court-ordered intervention. One of the best known examples of such intervention took place in the District of Columbia in 1964 (*Application of the President and Directors of Georgetown College, Inc.*).

The Georgetown College Case

The patient, a twenty-five-year-old mother of a seven-month-old child, had been brought to Georgetown University Hospital by her husband, having lost a large volume of blood from a ruptured ulcer. Mrs. Jones and her husband were both Jehovah's Witnesses and, according to their religious beliefs, they were prohibited from receiving blood transfusions. When it appeared to the members of the hospital staff that she would die without a transfusion, the hospital attorney sought court permission to administer blood over her objections and those of her husband. The petition was denied by the District Court.

However, permission was granted by a single judge, Judge Skelly Wright of the Appellate Court, who visited the patient and her husband at the hospital and conferred with members of the hospital staff. Although the husband continued to resist the transfusion of his by-then weakened wife, whose only audible words were "Against my will," the judge proceeded to authorize the procedure. In an opinion that seems, to many, a masterpiece of rationalization and obfuscation, the judge offered the following justifications for overriding the religiously motivated wishes of the patient and her husband.

First, Judge Wright indicated that while the patient repeatedly refused permission for the transfusion, there was some ambivalence as to whether or not she would oppose it if it were ordered by the court. After reporting that the "only audible reply" which could be heard was "Against my will," the judge stated that when he asked about opposition to a court order, Mrs. Jones murmured "as best I could make out, that it would not then be her responsibility." The judge also stated that the order was necessary to "maintain the status quo" and prevent the issue regarding the rights of the parties from becoming moot before "full consideration" was possible (Ibid., p. 1007).

The decision was also based, at least in part, on the fact that the patient was the mother of an infant child whom, through her otherwise avoidable death, she would be abandoning. Judge Wright argued that the patient had "a responsibility to the community to care for her infant [and] thus the people had an interest in preserving the life of the mother" (Ibid., p. 1008).

Concerns about civil and criminal liability were also underlying factors in his decision. The judge suggested that Mrs. Jones had put the physicians and hospital in a precarious position. "Death resulting from failure to extend *proper medical care*, where there is a duty of care, is manslaughter in the District of Columbia," he stated. Mrs. Jones' religious beliefs about transfusions were dismissed by stating that she

> had no wish to be a martyr and her religion merely prevented her consent to a transfusion. If the law undertook the responsibility of authorizing the transfusion without her consent, no problem would be raised with respect to her religious practice. Thus, the effect of the order was to preserve for Mrs. Jones the life she wanted without the sacrifice of her religious beliefs. (Ibid., p. 1009)

The judge concluded his justification with the statement that since "a life hung in the balance" and "there was no time for research and reflection," he was "determined to act on the side of life" (Ibid., p. 1001).

Less than a month after the court-ordered transfusion, Mrs. Jones' attorneys filed a petition for a rehearing of the case by the entire Court of Appeals. The petition was denied, but three of the nine judges, including Warren Burger, who would later be appointed by President Richard Nixon as Chief Justice of the United States Supreme Court, would have granted the petitioner's request. Among other things, the dissenters argued that rather than preserving the status quo, as Judge Skelly Wright claimed, his order completely changed it by granting fully and finally all of the relief sought, thus disposing of the matter on its merits. Judge Burger cited with approval the words of a former Supreme Court Justice, Louis D. Brandeis, that

> the makers of our Constitution . . . sought to protect Americans in their beliefs, their thoughts, their emotions and their sensations. They conferred, as against the Government, the right to be let alone—the most comprehensive of rights and the right most valued by civilized man. (Ibid., pp. 1016–1017)

He went on to say that

> nothing in this utterance suggests that Justice Brandeis thought an individual possessed these rights only as to *sensible* beliefs, *valid* thoughts, *reasonable* emotions, or *well-founded* sensations. I suggest he intended to include a great many foolish, unreasonable and even absurd ideas which do not conform, such as refusing medical treatment even at great risk.   (Ibid, p. 1017)

It was not uncommon for courts, including appellate courts, to disregard the wishes of patients to refuse blood transfusions, at least where the wishes were based on religious convictions and the prognosis was otherwise favorable. In one of the few such cases to reach a state supreme court (*John F. Kennedy Memorial Hospital* v. *Heston,* 1971) in a state which incidentally has since come to occupy a leading position in the adjudication of such cases, the New Jersey Supreme Court stated, in *dicta*, that "it seems safe to say there is no constitutional right to choose to die" (p. 672).

Box 2–1 explains the U.S. judicial system.

John F. Kennedy Memorial Hospital v. *Heston*

Delores Heston was a twenty-two-year-old single woman who had been severely injured in an automobile accident. She had a ruptured spleen that was expected to cause her death unless surgery was performed with a requisite transfusion. She and her parents were Jehovah's Witnesses. A judge appointed a guardian for Ms. Heston with directions to consent to transfusion if needed. The transfusion was administered. Although recognizing that the controversy was by then moot, the New Jersey Supreme Court agreed to hear arguments because resolution of the issue was in the public interest. Citing with approval earlier decisions ordering transfusions for the infant child of Jehovah's Witnesses parents (*State* v. *Perricone,* 1962) and for a pregnant woman, also a member of Jehovah's Witnesses, where it was argued that the transfusion was necessary to preserve her life and thereby the life of the fetus she was carrying (*Raleigh Fitkin-Paul Morgan Memorial Hospital* v. *Anderson,* 1964), the court proceeded to affirm the decision of the lower court.

The court indicated that it might have held differently if the treatment were likely to cause either death or serious infirmity, neither of which would likely result from transfusion. Moreover, like Judge Skelly Wright, the court raised concerns about whether the hospital or physicians might not incur liability for failure to provide something as simple and well-established as a transfusion, regardless of the patient's convictions. While it is difficult to attempt to pinpoint just when this attitude began to change, that it has changed, and dramatically so, can best be illustrated by a more recent case from Florida (*Wons* v. *Public Health Trust,* 1989).

B o x 2–1   *The Structure of the Judicial System*

Although there are slight variations from state to state, the judicial system within each is typically comprised of a variety of lower courts (trial courts) and two levels of appellate courts: intermediate courts and high courts. The intermediate courts are generally referred to as Courts of Appeal and the high courts are known as Supreme Courts, although in New York the designations are reversed, with the Court of Appeals being the highest court in the state and the Supreme Court functioning as an intermediate court. There are various kinds of trial courts, each of which has jurisdiction over only certain kinds of disputes. Probate courts typically deal with questions concerning guardianship and death, including the distribution of certain assets of the deceased. There are also courts specially designated to hear criminal cases (Common Pleas); family matters such as divorce, child custody, and support (Domestic Relations); and so on. Since requests to withhold or withdraw treatment from an uncommunicative patient often involve competency adjudication and the appointment of a guardian, they are within the jurisdiction of the Probate Court.

Only trial courts assemble evidence by calling witnesses to testify and introduce exhibits or documents (physical evidence). Juries, where appropriate, are only found at this first level of the judicial system. Appellate courts review disputes based on the record (transcript) of the trial court and they must accept the facts as found by either the jury (if there was one) or judge (if there was not). The role of the appellate court is to determine whether the law was appropriately applied, not whether the "facts" were or were not true. Decisions of trial courts may have precedential value, but they are not binding on other courts. Decisions of intermediate courts are binding on all trial courts within their jurisdiction. Decisions of the highest court in the state are binding on all of the lower courts in that state but have no legal effect on the courts of other states. Most, but not all, of the cases involving LSMT disputes are under the jurisdiction of state courts; some cases (for example, where the patient is being treated in a federally funded institution such as Veteran's Administration Hospital) are handled by the federal judicial system.

The federal system parallels the state system but jurisdiction is limited to questions involving federal law, disputes involving parties of different states (called *diversity of citizenship*), and cases involving interpretations of constitutional rights. Cases originating in the state judicial system that have resulted, through appeal, in a decision by the state supreme court may sometimes be appealed to the United States Supreme Court. This is done by filing a request, called a petition for *certiorari*, which the Court may, but is not obligated to, grant. The trial courts of the federal system are called District Courts. The intermediate courts—courts of appeal—are known as Circuit Courts. As with the state judicial system, decisions of District Courts are binding only on parties residing within their jurisdiction. Circuit Court decisions are precedential for all the District Courts within that particular circuit. Decisions of the United States Supreme Court are "the law of the land." Following is a simple chart of the two judicial systems, state and federal:

Box 2-1 (*Continued*)

The State and Federal Judicial System

State	Federal
Trial Courts	District Courts
Probate Courts	
Common Pleas	
Domestic Relations	
Courts of Appeal	Circuit Courts
Supreme Court	United States Supreme Court

A map of the federal judicial system, indicating the number and location of each of the circuit courts, may help in simplifying the pattern of organization of the system (see Figure 2–1).

Wons v. Public Health Trust

Norma Wons, a practicing Jehovah's Witness and mother of two minor children, entered a medical facility operated by the Public Health Trust of Dade County (Florida) with a condition known as dysfunctional uterine bleeding. When informed by physicians that she would require a blood transfusion, Mrs. Wons, who was conscious and competent, refused to give consent. The hospital petitioned the court for permission to administer blood. The judge reasoned that minor children have a right to be reared by two loving parents, a right which trumped the mother's rights of privacy and free exercise of religion. The blood was transfused while Mrs. Wons was unconscious.

Upon regaining consciousness, Mrs. Wons appealed the decision. The Court of Appeals held that the case was not moot due to the recurring nature of Mrs. Wons's condition and it held that her constitutional rights of religion and privacy could not be overridden by the state's purported interests.

In reversing the decision of the trial court, the appellate court stated:

> Surely nothing, in the last analysis, is more private or more sacred than one's religion or view of life, and here the courts, quite properly, have given great deference to the individual's right to make decisions vitally affecting his private life according to his own conscience. It is difficult to overstate this right because it is, without exaggeration, the very bedrock upon which this country was founded. (Ibid., p. 98)

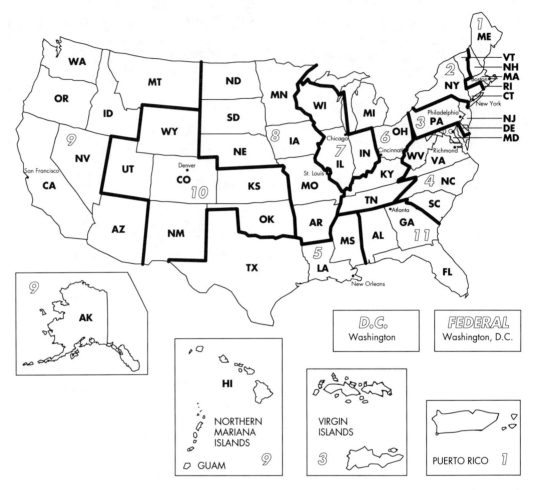

FIGURE 2–1   The Federal Appellate Courts. (Reprinted from *West's Law Finder: A Legal Research Manual.* Copyright 1993 by West Publishing Corporation. Reprinted with permission)

In a concurring opinion, concerning the question of Mrs. Wons's responsibility to her children, the Chief Justice pointed out that:

> The medical profession may consider a blood transfusion a rather ordinary and routine procedure, but, given Mrs. Wons' religious beliefs, that procedure for her is extra-ordinary. . . . [W]e must not assume from her choice that Mrs. Wons was not considering the best interests of her children. She knows they will be well cared for by her family. As a parent, however, she must consider the example she sets for her children, how to teach them to follow what she believes is God's law if she herself does not. The choice for her cannot be an easy one, but it is hers to make. It is not for this court to judge the reasonable-

ness or validity of her beliefs. Absent a truly compelling state interest to the contrary, the law must protect her right to make that choice. (Ibid., p. 102)

Fosmire v. *Nicoleau*

Yet a more recent decision, this one from the highest court in New York, further affirms the right of a competent person to make his or her own medical decisions, even if that decision were to result in an otherwise preventable death.

Denise Nicoleau was a practical nurse and her husband was a radiologist. Both were Jehovah's Witnesses. When Mrs. Nicoleau became pregnant, she informed her physician that her religious convictions prevented her from receiving "the administration of blood, pooled plasma or other derivatives" (*Fosmire* v. *Nicoleau*, 1990, p. 78), and she noted this on the medical consent form that she signed upon admission to the hospital. On December 29, 1988 she went into labor prematurely, a Cesarean section was performed, and a healthy baby boy was delivered. Following the delivery, she began to hemorrhage and additional surgery was required. Because she had lost a substantial amount of blood, she was informed that it was her physician's opinion that she would die without a transfusion. Both she and her husband, basing their decision on their religious beliefs, refused to consent. She was thirty-six years old and, except for the loss of blood, apparently in good health.

The hospital decided to seek a court order authorizing the transfusion. The court, without even giving notice to Mrs. Nicoleau or her husband, ordered the first of two transfusions she received over a three-day period. Shortly thereafter, she and her husband filed an appeal arguing that the refusal was based not only on her religious beliefs but also on her "concern for the dangers associated with transfusions, particularly the risk of contracting a communicable disease such as AIDS" (Ibid., p. 79).

The appeals court, by a divided vote, vacated the order on the grounds that Mrs. Nicoleau had been denied notice and an opportunity to be heard. The Court of Appeals, which is New York's supreme court, held that Mrs. Nicoleau, as a competent adult, had both a common-law and statutory right to determine the course of her own medical treatment, which includes the right to decline blood transfusions, and the state had failed to show it had superior interests in preventing her from exercising that right.

The court was unresponsive to arguments that Mrs. Nicoleau's rights should be subordinate to the state's interest in maintaining the unity of the family and parental ties between parents and their children.

The State's interest in promoting the freedom of its citizens generally applies to parents. The State does not prohibit parents from engaging in dangerous activities because there is a risk that their children will be left orphans. There are instances, as the hospital notes, where the State has prohibited the public from engaging in an especially hazardous activity or required that special safety precautions be taken by participants. But we know of no law in this State prohibiting individuals from participating in inherently dangerous activities or requiring them to take special safety precautions simply because they have minor children. There is no indication that the State would take a more intrusive role when the risk the parent has assumed involves a very personal choice regarding medical care. On the contrary, the policy of New York, as reflected in the existing law, is to permit all competent adults to make their own personal health care decisions without interference from the State.   (Ibid., p. 84)

While the Jehovah's Witnesses cases present an interesting perspective on the interests of the state in preserving life and/or protecting minor children from abandonment, the development of the right of a competent adult to refuse life-sustaining medical treatment simply because life itself has become too burdensome is best illustrated by a pair of California cases.

Bartling v. Superior Court

William Bartling was a seventy-year-old man with a history of chronic anxiety/depression and alcoholism (*Bartling* v. *Superior Court,* 1984). He entered Glendale Adventist Medical Center on April 8, 1984, for treatment for depression. A routine physical examination, including a chest X-ray, was performed, and a tumor was discovered on Mr. Bartling's lung. A biopsy was performed by inserting a needle into the tumor, which caused the lung to collapse. Tubes were inserted in his chest and through his nasal passage and throat in order to reinflate the lung. Since Mr. Bartling also suffered from emphysema, a form of chronic lung disease, the hole made by the biopsy needle did not heal properly and attempts to expand (reinflate) the lung were unsuccessful. A tracheotomy was performed and he was placed on a ventilator.

When it became clear that he had become respirator dependent and that there was no likelihood that he would regain the ability to breathe on his own, he became increasingly despondent. Several times Mr. Bartling tried to remove the ventilator tube from the opening in his neck. To prevent him from doing so, his wrists were tied to the bed (soft restraints). Despite repeated requests from both Mr. Bartling and his wife, Glendale Adventist and his physicians refused to remove either the ventilator or the restraints. In addition to his tumor, which turned out to be malignant (cancerous), examinations revealed that Mr. Bartling also had arteriosclerosis (hardening of the arteries) and an abdominal aneurysm (a "ballooning" of the abdominal aorta, the large vessel carrying blood from the heart to the lower extremities).

To further convince the hospital administration and his physicians of his sincerity and to expedite their compliance with his wish to be set free of the ventilator, Mr. Bartling filed a complaint in Superior Court. Attached to the complaint were a Living Will and a Durable Power of Attorney for Health Care (both living wills and durable powers of attorney for health care will be discussed in Chapter 4) appointing his wife to act as his surrogate (attorney-in-fact), and a declaration attesting to his understanding of his situation and his desire to discontinue the ventilator.

> While I have no wish to die, I find intolerable the living conditions forced upon me by my deteriorating lungs, heart and blood vessel systems, and find intolerable my being continuously connected to this ventilator, which sustains my every breath and my life for the past six and one-half (6 1/2) weeks. Therefore, I wish this Court to order that the sustaining of my respiration by this mechanical device violates my constitutional right, is contrary to my every wish, and constitutes a battery upon my person. I fully understand that my request to have the ventilator removed and discontinued, which I have frequently made to my wife and to my doctors, will very likely cause respiratory failure and ultimately lead to my death. I am willing to accept that risk rather than to continue the burden of this artificial existence which I find unbearable, degrading, and dehumanizing. I also suffer a great deal of pain and discomfort because of being confined to bed, being on this ventilator, and from the other problems which are occurring.   (Ibid., p. 222)

Additionally, Mr. and Mrs. Bartling and Mr. Bartling's daughter all executed documents releasing Glendale Adventist and its doctors from any claim of civil liability should Mr. Bartling's wishes be honored.

Since Mr. Bartling could not be present in court, a videotape deposition was taken on the day before the Superior Court hearing. Mr. Bartling could not speak but he could nod or shake his head to indicate yes or no answers. Mr. Bartling indicated that he wanted to live, that he did not want to live on the ventilator, and that he understood that if the ventilator were removed he might die.

It was the opinion of his physicians that Mr. Bartling's illness was not terminal and that he could live for at least a year if he were "weaned" from the ventilator. However, "weaning was unlikely because of his medical and psychological problems that were not under control" (Ibid., p. 223).

The trial court made several "findings of fact" which included that (1) Mr. Bartling's illnesses were serious but not terminal, (2) although Mr. Bartling was attached to a ventilator to facilitate breathing, he was not in a vegetative state and was not comatose, and (3) Mr. Bartling was competent. Relying substantially on the New Jersey Supreme Court's *Quinlan* decision, which will be discussed in detail in the following chapter, the court concluded that as long as there was some potential to restore Mr. Bartling to a "cognitive, sapient life," it would be inappropriate to order removal of the ventilator. Glendale Adventist had argued that it was a Christian hospital devoted to the preservation of life and that it would be unethical for their physicians to disconnect life-support systems from patients whom they viewed as having the potential for cognitive, sapient life.

Mr. Bartling died, still connected to the ventilator, the day before his appeal was heard. In reversing the Superior Court, the Court of Appeals held that limiting the right to termination of life-support equipment to comatose, terminally ill patients or their representatives was in error. The court held that once the threshold issue of whether or not Mr. Bartling was legally competent had been resolved in his favor, his right to refuse unwanted medical treatment outweighed any interest that the State of California might have had in either (1) preservation of life, (2) prevention of suicide, or (3) maintaining the ethical integrity of the medical profession. According to the court, "if the right of the patient to self-determination as to his own medical treatment is to have any meaning at all, it must be paramount to the interests of the patient's hospitals and doctors. The right of a competent adult patient to refuse medical treatment is a constitutionally guaranteed right which must not be abridged" (Ibid., p. 225). The court dismissed any concerns about suicide by stating that rather than causing Mr. Bartling's death by unnatural means, the action requested here "would merely have hastened his inevitable death by natural causes" (Ibid.).

Subsequent to the Court of Appeals decision, Mrs. Bartling filed a claim with the Superior Court to recover attorneys fees on a private-attorney-general theory. The theory rests on the "policy of encouraging private actions to vindicate important rights affecting the public interest, without regard to material gain" (*Bartling* v. *Glendale Adventist Medical Center,* 1986, p. 850). Although, as with the initial complaint brought to force discontinuation of the ventilator, the motion was denied at trial, the Court of Appeals ruled that the denial was based on inappropriate grounds and remanded the decision for a ruling on the merits. Mrs. Bartling eventually prevailed and was awarded attorneys fees in the amount of $160,000.

While *Bartling* makes it clear that a competent patient has the right to refuse invasive forms of life-sustaining medical treatment where there is no likelihood of restoration of health, in the *Bouvia* case (*Bouvia* v. *Superior Court,* 1986), decided by the same California Appellate Court as *Bartling* some two years later, the case is made even more strongly.

Bouvia v. Superior Court

Elizabeth Bouvia was a twenty-eight-year-old woman who had been afflicted since birth with cerebral palsy. She was also quadriplegic. Her physical handicaps had progressed to the point where she was completely bedridden. Except for a few fingers of one hand and some slight head and facial movements, she had become immobile. She was physically helpless and unable to care for herself. (See Figure 2–2.)

Ms. Bouvia was described as intelligent and mentally competent. She had earned a college degree. She was married but her husband had left her. She had been pregnant but had experienced a miscarriage. She lived with her parents until her father told her that they could no longer care for her. After that she lived intermittently with friends and at public facilities. A search for a permanent place to live, where she might receive the constant care she needed, had been unsuccessful. She was without financial means to support herself and, therefore, had to rely on public assistance for medical and other care.

On several occasions she expressed a desire to die. In 1983 she sought the right to be cared for in a public hospital in Riverside County (California) while she intentionally "starved herself to death." A court denied her judicial assistance to accomplish that goal. She later abandoned an appeal from that ruling. Thereafter, friends took her to several different facilities, both public and private. Efforts to find an apartment of her own with publicly paid live-in help or regular visiting nurses to care for her, or some other suitable facility, proved fruitless.

In the winter of 1986, Ms. Bouvia was admitted to High Desert Hospital in Lancaster. Ms. Bouvia had to be spoon fed. Because she was unable to retain solids, she was fed soft, liquidlike food. She stopped eating when she could no longer swallow without nausea and vomiting. Because of her previously announced resolve to starve herself, the medical staff feared that her weight loss might reach a life-threatening level. Since her weight seemed to hover between sixty-five and seventy pounds, her physicians inserted a nasogastric tube against her will and contrary to express written instructions.

Whether or not the nasogastric tube was necessary to prevent life-threatening weight loss, said the Court of Appeals, was immaterial. A patient has the right to refuse any medical treatment or medical service, even when such treatment is labeled "furnishing nourishment and hydration." This right exists even if its exercise creates a "life threatening condition" (*Bouvia* v. *Superior Court*, 1986, p. 1137).

The court went on to state that "the right to refuse medical treatment is basic and fundamental. It is recognized as a part of the right of privacy protected by both state and federal constitutions" (Ibid.). Its exercise requires no one's approval. It is not merely one vote subject to being overridden by medical opinion. The court also cited with approval a statement by the President's Commission:

> The voluntary choice of a competent and informed patient should determine whether or not life-sustaining therapy will be undertaken, just as such choices provide the basis for other decisions about medical treatment. Health care institutions and professionals should try to enhance patients' abilities to make

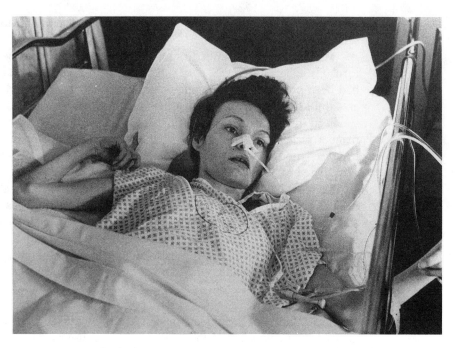

FIGURE 2–2   Elizabeth Bouvia. (Reprinted with permission of AP/Wide World Photos)

decisions on their own behalf and to promote understanding of the available treatment options. . . . Health care professionals serve patients best by maintaining a presumption in favor of sustaining life, while recognizing that competent patients are entitled to choose to forego any treatments, including those that sustain life.   (President's Commission, 1983, p. 3)

The court also cited the Policy and Statement of Patients' Choices of Treatment Options, as approved by the American Hospital Association, stating in pertinent part: "Whenever possible, however, the authority to determine the course of treatment, if any, should rest with the patient" and "the right to choose treatment includes the right to refuse a specific treatment *or all treatments*" (*Bouvia* v. *Superior Court,* 1986, p. 1141).

The court further buttressed its holding with a March 15, 1986, statement adopted by the Council on Ethical and Judicial Affairs of the American Medical Association. The statement, entitled Withholding or Withdrawing Life Prolonging Medical Treatment, declares:

The social commitment of the physician is to sustain life and relieve suffering. Where the performance of one duty conflicts with the other, the choice of the patient, or his family or legal representative if the patient is incompetent to act in his own behalf, should prevail.

Life prolonging medical treatment includes medication and artificially or technologically supplied respiration, nutrition or hydration. In treating a terminally ill or irreversibly comatose patient, the physician should determine the benefits of treatment outweigh its burdens. At all times, the dignity of the patient should be maintained.   (Ibid.)

In a strongly worded passage, the court seemed to identify with Elizabeth Bouvia's predicament:

Here, if force fed, [she] faces 15 to 20 years of painful existence, endurable only by the constant administrations of morphine. Her condition is irreversible. There is no cure for her palsy and arthritis. [She] would have to be fed, cleaned, turned, bedded, and toileted by others for 15 to 20 years! Although alert, bright, sensitive, perhaps even brave and feisty, she must lie immobile, unable to exist except through physical acts of others. Her mind and spirit may be free to take great flights but she herself is imprisoned and must lie physically helpless subject to the ignominy, embarrassment, humiliation and dehumanizing aspects created by her helplessness. We do not believe it is the policy of this state that all and every life must be preserved against the will of the sufferer. It is incongruous, if not monstrous, for medical practitioners to assert their right to preserve a life that someone else must live, or, more accurately, endure, for "15 to 20 years." We cannot conceive it to be the policy of this state to inflict such an ordeal upon anyone.   (Ibid., pp. 1143–1144)

The court also stated that the motive underlying the refusal of treatment was irrelevant.

If a right exists, it matters not what "motivates" its exercise. We find nothing in the law to suggest the right to refuse medical treatment may be exercised only if the patient's *motives* meet some else's approval. It certainly is not illegal or immoral to prefer a natural, albeit sooner, death than a drugged life attached to a mechanical device.   (Ibid., p. 1145)

The court recognized that Ms. Bouvia was financially unable to go to a private hospital and that, apparently, the public hospital where she was a patient was required to accept her. But, cautioned the court, "having done so it may not deny her relief from pain and suffering merely because she [had] chosen to exercise her fundamental right to protect what little privacy [remained] to her" (Ibid., p. 1145).

Judge Compton, writing in concurrence with a unanimous court, would have gone even further. Agreeing with his judicial colleagues that Ms. Bouvia had an absolute right to effectuate her decision to end her existence, he suggested that "this state and the medical profession, instead of frustrating her desire, should be attempting to relieve her suffering by permitting and in fact assisting her to die with ease and dignity. The fact that she is forced to suffer from the ordeal of self-starvation to achieve her objective is in itself inhumane" (Ibid., p. 1147).

As seen by Judge Compton, "the right to die is an integral part of our right to control our own destinies so long as the rights of others are not affected. That right should," he suggested, "include the ability to enlist assistance from others, including the medical profession, in making death as painless and quick as possible" (Ibid., p. 1147). We will return to a discussion of this proposal—physician-assisted suicide—in Chapter 5.

Even after Ms. Bouvia had won the right to have her feeding tube removed, the hospital refused to comply with the totality of the decision. Two days after the ruling, her physicians decided to withdraw her morphine. Her lawyer succeeded in getting a court order transferring her to another hospital which would agree to control her pain without conditioning it upon the acceptance of tube feeding. As this book went to print, this tragic story was still being played out somewhere in California.

Elizabeth Bouvia is not the only severely handicapped person who had to fight for the right to refuse unwanted medical treatment. In 1989 there were two such incidents, both of which resulted in similar rulings, but with quite dissimilar outcomes.

Petition of Rivlin

David Rivlin was a Michigan man who sustained a 1971 bodysurfing accident in California which left him quadriplegic, though with some use of his arms. His condition was complicated further by a 1986 operation to remove an aneurysm of the second cervical vertebrae which left him unable to use his arms or to breathe on his own. For the next three years, he was confined to a nursing home near Detroit.

In May 1989, he petitioned a circuit court for permission to have a physician sedate him and then disconnect his ventilator. "Life," said Mr. Rivlin, "is more than surviving. It's interacting with other people, it's having a family, it's having a career, it's having a wife. It's all of those things and I can't have them. It might sound selfish that I can't have these and I want to terminate my life. I want to lead a full life, not just a shell of a life" (*Coldwater [MI] Daily Reporter*, May 20, 1989). In June 1989, the Circuit Court for Oakland County granted his petition. He died shortly thereafter.

Georgia v. McAfee

Larry McAfee also went to court to get permission to stop treatment. The trial judge decided in his favor but ordered the ruling appealed to the Georgia Supreme Court to obtain a legal precedent. The state's highest court affirmed the judge's decision (*Georgia v. McAfee*, 1989). But then McAfee changed his mind.

McAfee, who had been an avid outdoorsman prior to a motorcycle accident that left him quadriplegic, argued that he had no desire to go on living under his present circumstances. After his private insurance, which had paid for his hospitalization and care in an apartment after his discharge, expired, his care was paid for by Medicare. When those benefits ran out, the cost of his care was picked up by Medicaid which, in Georgia, provided $100 a day, considerably less than he had been receiving under Medicare. Medicare is a federally administered program whereas Medicaid is administered by the states and relies upon both federal and state contributions. Medicaid payments to the disabled vary from state to state. It had been estimated that it would cost approximately $265 a day ($96,725 yearly) to provide a live-in attendant and other support for him to live in his own apartment, but neither Medicare nor Medicaid would pay for that in-home support.

In many ways, his plight is representative of the barriers that many handicapped people encounter in a society that is all too often insensitive to their needs. After Mr. McAfee's private insurance ran out, he was transferred from one facility to another. Since Georgia had no nursing homes equipped for ventilator patients, he was first sent to an Ohio nursing home and from there to a hospital in Atlanta. His daily routine consisted of being cleaned and having his lungs suctioned. Then he was dressed in a jogging suit and athletic shoes and left in his wheelchair, which he moved with a breath-activated device, with little more to do than watch television. His parents testified at his trial that they had tried to help him find adequate care, but they agreed that the decision to shut off the ventilator should be his.

Like Elizabeth Bouvia, having gained some control over his life by having his wishes granted, McAfee's interest in living seemed to be revived. The problem was seen, by the disability rights movement, as one of confinement in a restrictive environment, not the severity of his condition. Shortly after his victory in court, McAfee left Atlanta's Grady Memorial Hospital, where he had been confined to the intensive care unit, to live in a nursing home in Alabama. In January 1990, he testified before the Georgia legislature in behalf of state funding for independent living for persons like himself (Longmore, 1992). McAfee was quoted as saying that "turning off the ventilator still remains a very viable option to me, but I want to look into the possibilities to see what's available first. I want to give it a try" (Applebome, 1990).

The McAfee case has become a rallying point for a coalition of disability-rights groups and antiabortion activists. The former regard this case as yet another example of discrimination against the handicapped, and the latter seem to regard it as a violation of the sanctity of life ethic which lies at the core of their movement. It has also seemed to pit civil libertarians, who argue that the disabled should have the same right to make medical treatment decisions as the able-bodied, against those who would argue that this is a form of discrimination against the handicapped. Ordinarily, these groups would be found on the same side of most issues.

McKay v. Bergstedt

As a final example of the way in which these difficult issues are played out, we turn now to the case of Kenneth Bergstedt as decided by the Supreme Court of Nevada. Mr. Bergstedt, like Messrs. Rivlin and McAfee, was a young man (age thirty-one) who in 1969 had become quadriplegic and ventilator-dependent from an injury he sustained in a swimming pool. For twenty-one years, he relied upon a ventilator to sustain his breathing. Since the death of his mother in 1978, he had depended entirely on the care and companionship of his father. Becoming increasingly fearful concerning his father's failing health and realizing that his death would likely result in a dramatic change in his already greatly compromised "life style," he petitioned the court for permission to have his ventilator disconnected in order that he might die. The request was granted but the decision was appealed to the Nevada Supreme Court. Although the cause is not stated in the Court's opinion, Kenneth Bergstedt died before the appeal could be heard. Perhaps confirming his apprehension, his father also died within a matter of days thereafter.

In affirming the trial court's decision to grant his request, accompanied by a desire that he also be sedated prior to the removal of the ventilator, the Supreme Court emphasized that he had been examined by a psychiatrist and found to be competent and that the decision had been made after "substantial deliberation." The court also noted that his father understood the basis for his son's decision and, reluctantly, approved.

The court stated that Mr. Bergstedt's right to discontinue his life-sustaining treatment had to be balanced against a number of legitimate state interests. These interests were first enunciated in *Saikewicz,* a Massachusetts case that will be discussed in the next chapter, and they have become common in the deliberations of most of the courts that have considered these issues. As articulated by the Nevada Supreme Court, they are:

1. The interest of the state in preserving the sanctity of all life, including that of the particular patient involved in a given action.
2. The interest of the state in preventing suicide.
3. The interest of the state in protecting innocent third parties who may be adversely affected by the death of the party seeking relief.
4. The state's interest in preserving the [ethical] integrity of the medical profession.

To these, the court added a fifth concern, "the interest of the state in encouraging the charitable and humane care of those whose lives may be artificially extended under conditions which have the prospect of providing at least a modicum of quality living" (*McKay* v. *Bergstedt,* 1990, p. 621). The court made it quite clear that it was concerned that people like Mr. Bergstedt were, indeed, in a vulnerable position and needed assurance "that society would not cast him adrift in a sea of indifference after his father's passing" (Ibid., p. 628). While acknowledging that the available support systems—whether governmental, private, or charitable—might not have been adequate to alleviate his fears, they stated that had he not died before the appeal was heard, they would have required that he be fully informed of the alternatives available to him after his father's death or incapacity before exercising his right to discontinue treatment.

So that decisions of this type might be facilitated without always resorting to the courts, at least in Nevada, the court established the following procedure. In the case of a competent adult patient desiring to refuse or discontinue treatment, two nonattending physicians must examine the patient and certify in writing that (a) the patient is mentally competent and has been apprised of all treatment alternatives, (b) the patient's condition is irreversible, (c) there has been no coercion, and (d) if the patient was not terminally ill that he or she was informed of all available care options.

If such a patient has a life expectancy of six months or less, the patient's constitutional and common law rights of self-determination will prevail over any of the aforementioned state interests. Moreover, any physician or health care provider assisting the patient, including the administration of any sedative or pain medication to ease the patient's predeath anxieties or pain, will be free of any liability, either civil or criminal. If, however, the patient is nonterminal, that is, has a life expectancy of greater than six months, then the patient's rights must be weighed against the interests of the state in a court of law. A decision in favor of the patient shall be final; the decision of the court shall not be subject to appeal unless the court finds in favor of the state. In such instances, the patient shall be entitled to an expedited appeal in the event that such is desired (Ibid.).

As should be obvious to the reader, there has been a considerable evolution in the law regarding the right of a competent person to refuse life-sustaining medical treatment. Whereas the cases decided prior to the 1970s were likely to defer to the judgment of physicians and override the wishes of the patient, more recent cases clearly illustrate a growing respect for autonomy and self-determination exercised by a competent patient.

While these cases clearly illustrate that a competent person has the right to refuse unwanted medical treatment including, in most instances, treatment necessary to sustain life, the issue becomes somewhat more complicated when there is a loss of decision-making capacity. What would happen, for example, should the patient be in a state of unconsciousness or otherwise be unable to express a desire about the acceptance or refusal of life-sustaining medical treatment? This question will be addressed in the following pages.

Summary

The cases in this chapter were selected to illustrate the changes that have been taking place in the past several decades regarding the right of competent adults to refuse all forms of medical treatment, including treatment thought necessary to sustain life. While the early cases dealing with religiously motivated refusals (the *Georgetown College* and *Heston* cases) demonstrate a paternalistic or parental attitude on the part of both physicians and judges to either disregard the right of the patient or to find some way to circumvent it, the recent decisions (the *Wons* and *Nicoleau* cases) reflect the influence of the "patient's rights" movement and the growing respect for autonomy it has championed. The cases dealing with treatment refusal decisions by the disabled, while also indicative of respect for autonomy, raise important questions about the way in which discrimination against the disabled might unduly influence the kind of LSMT decisions they make. Although it would seem discriminatory in itself to argue that Kenneth Bergstedt ought not to have the same right to refuse treatment that William Bartling or Denise Nicoleau do, the actions of Elizabeth Bouvia and Larry McAfee should be powerful reminders of the forces that often influence our decisions. Although we clearly need to continue the work that has been done to empower the disabled and eliminate the various barriers that prevent their full participation in society, denying them the right to make their own choices about medical treatment would be a questionable way to achieve this goal.

Study Questions

1. According to the President's Commission, what should be the basis for deciding whether a person should be permitted to refuse medical treatment, including life-sustaining medical treatment?

2. How have many of the "early" (prior to the 1970s) courts balanced the right of a pregnant woman to follow her own religious beliefs about refusing blood transfusions against the public interest in saving her life and that of the fetus she was carrying? How have the modern courts tended to address this same dilemma?

3. How have the modern courts addressed the question of withholding or withdrawing life-sustaining medical treatment from competent patients requesting such when they are not terminally ill?

4. In what ways are these decisions influenced when the request to stop life-sustaining medical treatment is based upon disability or handicap experienced by a young and otherwise healthy person as opposed to an older person with failure in one or more major organs?

5. Are there circumstances which, according to the decision in the *Bergstedt* case, might result in the refusal of the request by a disabled person to discontinue life-sustaining medical treatment?

References

Applebome, P. (1990). An angry man fights to die, then tests life. *The New York Times,* February 7.

Application of the President and Directors of Georgetown College, Inc., 331 F. 2d 1000 (D.C. Cir.), *aff'd*, 331 F. 2d 1010 (D. C. Cir.), *cert. denied*, 337 U.S. 978 (1964).

Bartling v. *Glendale Adventist Medical Center*, 184 Cal. App. 3d 961, 229 Cal. Rptr. 360 (1986).

Bartling v. *Superior Court*, 163 Cal. App. 3d 186, 209 Cal. Rptr. 220 (1984).

Bouvia v. *Superior Court* (Glenchur), 179 Cal. App. 3d 1127, 225 Cal. Rptr. 297 (1986).

Cruzan v. *Director, Missouri Department of Health,* 110 S. Ct. 2841 (1990).

Fosmire v. *Nicoleau,* 551 N. E. 2d 77 (N.Y. 1990)

Georgia, State of v. *McAfee*, 385 S.E. 2d 651 (1989).

John F. Kennedy Memorial Hospital v. *Heston*, 58 N.J. 576, 279 A. 2d 670 (1971).

Longmore, P. K. (1992). Assisted suicide—What euthanasia activists say, what people with disabilities say. *Western Journal of Medicine,* 157(2): 190–191.

McKay v. *Bergstedt*, 801 P. 2d 617 (Nev. 1990).

President's Commission for the Study of Ethical Problems in Medicine and Biomedical and Behavioral Research. (1983). *Deciding to Forego Life-Sustaining Medical Treatment.* Washington, D.C.: U.S. Government Printing Office.

Raleigh Fitkin-Paul Morgan Memorial Hosp. v. *Anderson*, 42 N.J. 421, 201 S. 2d 537, *cert. denied*, 377 U.S. 985 (1964).

Rivlin, Petition of, Case No. 89-369904, Oakland 6 Circuit Ct. (Mi., 1989)

Schloendorff v. *Society of New York Hosp.*, 211 N.Y. 125, 105 N.E. 92 (1914).

State v. *Perricone*, 37 N.J. 462, 181 A. 2d 751 (1962).

Union Pac. R. Co. v. *Botsford,* 141 U.S. 250 (1891).

Wons v. *Public Health Trust*, 500 So. 2d 679 (Fla. Dist. Ct. App., 1987), *aff'd,* 541 So. 2d 96 (Fla. 1989).

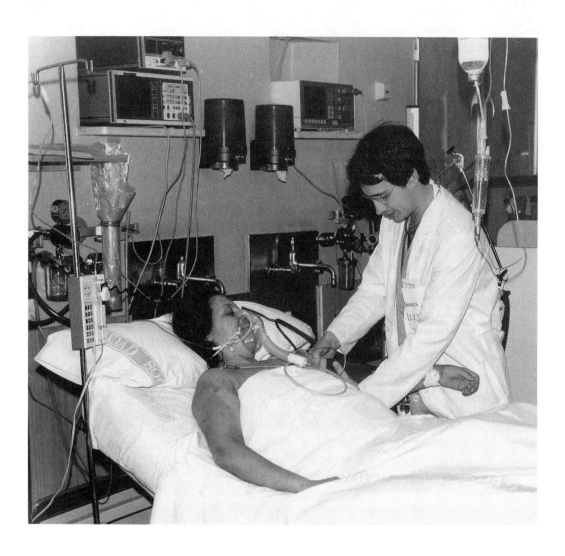

CHAPTER 3

Refusing Life-Sustaining Medical Treatment

Deciding for Others

Vex not his ghost: O! let him pass; he hates him
That would upon the rack of this tough world
Stretch him out longer.

William Shakespeare, *King Lear,* Act V, Scene III

Medical technology has effectively created a twilight zone of
suspended animation where death commences while life, in some
form, continues. Some patients, however, want no part of a life
sustained only by medical technology. Instead, they prefer a plan of
medical treatment that allows nature to take its course and permits
them to die with dignity.

Chief Justice Frank X. Gordon, Jr., Supreme Court of Arizona,
Rasmussen v. *Fleming* (1987)

THE PRINCIPLE OF AUTONOMY—the right of competent persons to
make their own decisions about the kind of medical care they will receive—has
become increasingly well accepted in our society. Unfortunately, there are
often tragic circumstances where patients have lost, or perhaps have never
even possessed, the capacity for making their own decisions about life-sustaining medical treatment. This means that members of their families or other
loved ones are faced with making these difficult choices. While there is, understandably and quite appropriately, a reluctance to grant others the same range
of decision-making authority as might be exercised by oneself, there are situations where the delegation of such authority is unavoidable. Where there is a
decision that has to be made, *someone* has to make it. The question then becomes that of identifying the appropriate decision maker. Should it be the

physicians? The hospital administration? The family? The courts? The state? We will explore these issues in this chapter.

While a number of factors could result in the absence of decision-making capacity, we will first turn to those cases where the patient has experienced a permanent loss of consciousness, the so-called persistent vegetative state (PVS).

The Previously Competent Patient in a PVS

In re Quinlan

Her name was Karen Ann Quinlan. She was twenty-one years old and were it not for a tragic accident on an April night in 1975, she might never have been known beyond the small New Jersey town of Landing. Ms. Quinlan, however, was destined to become famous as the central character in a conflict between the ability of modern medical technology to sustain life and the wishes of parents to allow a stricken daughter to die with peace and dignity (see Figure 3–1).

Ms. Quinlan had been partying with a small group of friends when it was noticed that she had stopped breathing. Her friends tried mouth-to-mouth resuscitation unsuccessfully and, in a state of panic, they called the rescue squad. Within what seemed a few minutes, a policeman arrived at the house and was able to restore labored breathing. Ms. Quinlan was rushed to Newton Memorial Hospital and placed on a ventilator to stabilize her.

The cause of her respiratory arrest was never clearly determined. She had been drinking gin and tonic but not nearly enough, according to her friends, to account for her loss of consciousness. Although both her friends and parents agreed that she wasn't into drugs, there was a nearly full bottle of Valium in her purse. The physicians tentatively diagnosed the cause of her asphyxia as the result of an interaction between two drugs, alcohol and Valium. Ms. Quinlan, like many young women, had been dieting and perhaps the reaction had in some way been related to her self-deprivation of food. Whatever the reason, she lay unconscious, her breathing sustained by the ventilator.

Within several days she opened her eyes. Her parents were hopeful that this was to be the start of her recovery, but it wasn't to be. As her physicians came to diagnose over time, she was in a state of permanent unconsciousness called a *persistent vegetative state* (PVS). The term had been coined in 1972 by Jennett and Plum to describe those patients who exhibited brain stem functions but a total absence of activity in the cerebral cortex. Unlike the eyes-closed, sleeplike unconsciousness typically seen with comatose patients, those in a PVS experience alternate cycles of eyes-open and eyes-closed unconsciousness. "Awake, but unaware" is how it is often described.

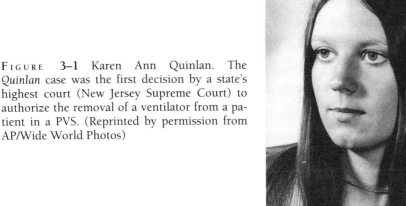

F I G U R E   3–1   Karen Ann Quinlan. The *Quinlan* case was the first decision by a state's highest court (New Jersey Supreme Court) to authorize the removal of a ventilator from a patient in a PVS. (Reprinted by permission from AP/Wide World Photos)

The human brain may be divided into two parts: the upper or higher brain centers comprised of the cerebral hemispheres and the lower brain known as the brain stem. The upper brain, also known as the cerebrum or neocortex, is the most highly evolved portion of the brain and is responsible for the processes of thinking and reasoning that are associated with being human. The brain stem contains the centers that control the "vegetative" functions of the body such as breathing or swallowing. The brain cells (neurons) that make up the cerebrum, and especially its outer covering, the cerebral cortex, are especially sensitive to oxygen deprivation. Permanent damage to the cerebrum typically occurs with levels of asphyxia far less than necessary for comparable damage to the brain stem. Since the death of the brain proceeds from the top down, in a so-called rostral-caudal direction, patients with death of the brain stem will also have lost all function at the level of the cerebrum. And, as was explained in Chapter 1, it is death of the brain stem that is critical to the pronouncement of death based on brain-referenced criteria, so-called "brain death."

To the uninitiated, seeing someone in a persistent vegetative state can be a disturbing experience. Their eyes are open but they don't focus on anything; they seem to be staring aimlessly into space. They sometimes yawn or grimace as though in pain but, neurologists tell us, they are incapable of experiencing pain.

In the opinion of her physicians, Ms. Quinlan had a "negligible chance of recovering to a cognitive, sapient state"; her prognosis was bleak. If she were to continue on the ventilator, along with the tubes that provided her with food and fluids and the catheter that had been placed to empty her bladder, she was capable of living indefinitely in her severely impaired condition. The record for survival in a PVS belonged, at that time, to a woman from Tarpon Springs, Florida.* Elaine Esposito experienced an anesthesia accident on August 6, 1941, and lived for 37 years, 111 days until her death in 1978, without regaining consciousness (see Figure 3–2). The thought of that happening to their daughter was more than the Quinlans could bear. So, secure in their belief that they were doing what Karen would have wanted, the Quinlans told her caregivers that they wanted her removed from the ventilator. She had been unconscious for slightly more than three months at the time of their request.

Joe and Julia Quinlan, Karen's parents, were devout Catholics and they had sought counsel with their parish priest before making their decision. They were comforted to learn that church teaching supported their decision. Neither parent wanted Karen to die. They simply wanted, in Joe Quinlan's terminology, "to return Karen to God's hands; to remove her from the machine that was frustrating God's will." The use of a ventilator to maintain life under such tragic circumstances was, they believed, extraordinary and not obligatory. Their position was based on a statement by Pope Pius XII, in a 1957 address to a conference of anesthesiologists, that Catholics were obliged to use only ordi-

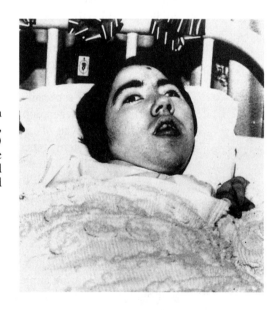

FIGURE 3–2 Although little was known about permanent unconsciousness at the time, and the term persistent vegetative state (PVS) wasn't even in use until the early 1970s, Elaine Esposito demonstrated that people so afflicted can survive for long periods of time. (Reprinted by permission of AP/Wide World Photos)

*As of January 1991, Rita Greene had been maintained in a PVS, with the support of a feeding tube, at Washington (D.C.) General Hospital for more than 40 years. She lost consciousness on October 25, 1951, following a cardiac arrest (McCormick, 1991).

nary means to sustain life and that there was no need to strive to maintain life when there is no hope for recovery.

This distinction between ordinary and extraordinary means was further developed in a 1974 document prepared by the Family Life Division of the United States Catholic Conference and issued in the name of the National Conference of Catholic Bishops. According to this report, ordinary means are described as "all medicines, treatments, and operations which offer a reasonable hope of benefit and can be obtained and used without excessive pain, expense, or other inconvenience." By extraordinary means are meant "all medicines, treatment, and operations which cannot be obtained or used without excessive pain, expense, or other inconveniences, or which, if used, would not offer a reasonable hope of benefit" (Respect Life, 1974, p. 33).

The physicians and hospital administration refused to honor the Quinlans' request. Although Ms. Quinlan was terribly impaired—she had experienced an irreversible loss of function of her cerebral cortex—she was not dead. Moreover, since she was alive and dependent on the ventilator to maintain her breathing, to remove her from it would cause her death and would, arguably, be an act of homicide.

Since this seemed to be a case of first impression—without precedence in the medical or legal literature—the Quinlans decided, because their daughter was twenty-one at the time of the accident, to ask the court for guardianship in order to remove her from the ventilator. They hired a young lawyer, Paul Armstrong, to represent them.

The Quinlans argued their case before Judge Robert Muir of the New Jersey Superior Court in late October of 1975. They were opposed by the State of New Jersey, represented by the Attorney General. There was no dispute about the medical facts. The only issue at stake was whether they should be given permission to discontinue the ventilator that was keeping their daughter alive.

On October 10, Judge Muir delivered his decision. He ruled against the Quinlans. Each of their arguments had been rejected.

1. Continued treatment of Karen Ann did not constitute "cruel and unusual punishment" under the Eighth Amendment to the Constitution.
2. The ventilator was not an example of "extraordinary means" and discontinuation would constitute homicide and an act of euthanasia.
3. Karen Ann's previous statements that she would not want her life artificially prolonged were dismissed as "theoretical."
4. There is no constitutional right to die that can be asserted by a parent for an incompetent child.

The Quinlans appealed the decision and the case was argued before the seven justices of the New Jersey Supreme Court on January 17, 1976. It was slightly more than two months until the court reached a decision. In a unanimous opinion, it reversed the decision of the lower court and granted immunity for the withdrawal of the ventilator. Bootstrapping a 1973 decision of the U.S. Supreme Court which struck down a Texas abortion law (*Roe* v. *Wade*), the court held that the constitutionally protected right of privacy that had been enunciated in *Roe* was broad enough to encompass a decision to refuse life-sustaining medical treatment. This was to be the first of many courts to use the right of privacy to justify decisions of this sort. The court also stated that such constitutional rights are not lost when one becomes incompetent and that, in this case, Karen's father could appropriately exercise it on her behalf.

The decision was also an important stimulus to the growth and development of ethics committees in hospitals. The court ruled that the ventilator could be removed only if Karen's physicians agreed that there was no likelihood of her recovery and that judgment was affirmed by an ethics committee. In retrospect, there seem to be two basic problems with the procedural end of the court's decision. First, at the time of the decision, there were no ethics committees in hospitals. The recommendation was based on a short paper written by pediatrician Karen Teel, which had appeared in the *Baylor Law Review* (1975). In her paper, Teel suggested that ethics committees might be an appropriate way of dealing with biomedical controversies in the same way that institutional review boards (IRBs) functioned in protecting human subjects in government-sponsored research. The second problem with the court's prescription had to do with the composition and function of ethics committees. Here the court seemed to get *ethics* confused with *prognosis*. Ethics committees, which will be discussed later in this volume, are typically comprised of physicians, lawyers, hospital administrators, nurses, social workers, clergy, and others. Whatever else they might be, they are not designed to be physician controlled or dominated. Such being the case, it would seem highly inappropriate for such an assortment of people to dabble in prognosis. Agreeing or disagreeing with the prognosis of the attending physicians is a task for, and only for, other similarly qualified physicians. Indeed, the court seems to have confused an ethical question with a medical one. An example of the latter would be, "Given the results of appropriate tests conducted on the patient, do you agree with the assessment that there is no likelihood of recovery of consciousness?" This is a question that might be presented to a prognosis committee comprised of, in this case, neurologists. An example of an ethical question would be, "Given a situation in which there is agreement that the patient is unlikely to regain consciousness, is it ethically permissible to discontinue the mechanical ventilation that is sustaining life?" Answers to questions of this type, unlike those about prognosis, are best provided by a multidisciplinary committee. Which of these two tasks was envisioned by the *Quinlan* court is not clear from the opinion.

Buoyed by the ruling of the court, the Quinlans again approached Karen's physicians with their request to have her removed from the ventilator. They refused to do so. It was not until six weeks after the ruling that one of her physicians proposed a way out by attempting to wean her from the ventilator. Although this had been unsuccessfully attempted several times throughout her hospitalization, all parties desperately agreed to try it one more time. To their astonishment, Karen began to breath on her own and, by the end of the week, she was free of the ventilator for good.

Since there was an expectation that Karen would die without the ventilator, this new development was met with a mixture of surprise and relief. Now that she was free of the ventilator, there was no longer any reason for Karen to be hospitalized. Plans were made to transfer her to a nursing home on June 9, 1976, and she remained there, and unconscious, until her death on June 11, 1985. She had been unconscious for ten years and nearly two months. During her stay, she was fed through a gastrostomy tube and her urine was drained through an indwelling Foley catheter. She was given regular nursing care to prevent infection and the development of decubitus ulcers (bed sores) and she received anticonvulsant medication through her feeding tube.

The cost of Karen's care during her first year of hospitalization came to $188,000. An additional $50,000 was spent on round-the-clock police protection. The hospital was fearful that someone might try to take matters into his or her own hands by "pulling the plug;" her parents were concerned that someone might take Karen's picture. They had denied permission for this repeatedly. The cost of her care in the nursing home was estimated at approximately $100 a day. Most of these costs were paid by Medicaid.

That Karen Ann Quinlan would be able to breathe on her own was clearly unexpected. It was precisely because of a belief that she wouldn't be able to, that she would die if the ventilator were removed, that her parents' request was opposed by her physicians, the hospital, and the State of New Jersey. It is now widely understood medically that most, if not all, patients in a PVS are capable of breathing unassisted. We might ask, however, if it is legally and ethically appropriate to remove a permanently unconscious patient from a ventilator with the expectation that doing so will result in death, why would it not be equally appropriate to remove other forms of life-sustaining medical treatment? Why not, for example, feeding tubes?

It took nearly seven years for the question to arise and when it did it was in the context of a charge of homicide that had been brought against two physicians.

Barber v. Superior Court

Clarence Herbert was a fifty-six-year-old man who, in 1981, had entered Kaiser-Permanente Hospital in Harbor Springs, California, for closure of an ileostomy that had been created several months earlier to relieve a bowel obstruction. The operation, performed by Dr. Robert Nejdl, was uneventful. However, during Mr. Herbert's first hour in the recovery room, he suddenly stopped breathing. He lost consciousness and was placed on a ventilator. A hospital neurologist diagnosed severe brain damage due to anoxia. The next morning, Mrs. Herbert was approached by Dr. Neil Barber, the attending internist, who, according to her, said that Mr. Herbert was "brain dead." The next day Dr. Barber removed Mr. Herbert from the ventilator. While removing a "brain dead" patient from a ventilator is clearly appropriate, with or without consent of the next of kin, Mr. Herbert was obviously not such. When removed from the ventilator he began to breathe on his own!

The next day, Mrs. Herbert and the other members of her family signed a consent form indicating that the family wanted "all machines taken off that are sustaining life." Shortly thereafter, Dr. Barber ordered all IV feeding stopped; Dr. Nejdl next ordered the nasogastric tube removed. Mr. Herbert was transferred from intensive care to a private room and six days later he died from pneumonia and dehydration.

The Los Angeles County Prosecutor's office was notified of the situation by a nursing supervisor who was distraught over what had taken place. The prosecutor charged the physicians with murder, but the charges were dismissed by the Municipal Court at a preliminary hearing. The dismissal was appealed by the prosecution and the case was subsequently reinstated by the Superior Court. The Court of Appeals heard an appeal and ruled that there was no basis for proceeding to trial. Decisions to discontinue treatment, they said, including artificially administered feeding and hydration, belonged appropriately to the physicians who were caring for the patient.

According to the court, decisions to discontinue tube feeding should be made on the same basis as other medical treatment decisions—whether or not it is proportionate or disproportionate in terms of the benefits to be gained versus the burdens caused. Noting that physicians are authorized under the standards of medical practice to discontinue forms of therapy which in their medical judgment are useless—that is, continuation cannot and does not improve the prognosis for recovery—the court stated that this essentially medical determination should be made on the basis of facts that are unique to each case (*Barber v. Superior Court*, 1983, p. 491).

The importance of the case lies in the fact that it was the first time that the question of the withdrawal of tube feeding was addressed by a court. While it resulted in a dismissal of the charges against Drs. Barber and Nejdl, there were a number of questions left unanswered. For example, was the diagnosis of Mr. Herbert's condition made too quickly? Keep in mind that he had been diagnosed as being in a persistent vegetative state within three days after he had stopped breathing in the recovery room. The physicians should not be criticized for failing to adhere to standards that were not even in existence until six years later. In 1989 the American Academy of Neurology published the following recommendations concerning the diagnosis of PVS:

> The primary basis for the diagnosis of PVS is the careful and extended clinical observation of the patient, supported by laboratory studies. PVS patients will show no behavioral response whatsoever over an extended period of time. The diagnosis of permanent unconsciousness can usually be made with a high degree of medical certainty in cases of hypoxic-ischemia after a period of one to three months. (p.125)

There might also have been some reason for concern about the rather hasty decision to pull Mr. Herbert's feeding tube in that Kaiser-Permanente was operating as a Health Maintenance Organization (HMO). HMOs are designed on the premise that it is better for the patient and more cost efficient to prevent illnesses and hospitalizations rather than to provide extended in-patient care. The hospitals and physicians profit by keeping members of the HMO healthy. They lose money when members become sick and require prolonged hospital care. Under such circumstances, there is a significant loss entailed by providing extended care for someone in a PVS.

Regardless of the reason, the *Barber* case is not an ideal case on which to base a discussion of the merits of withholding or withdrawing feeding tubes. However, it was the first such case to be decided by a court.

Brophy v. *New England Sinai Hospital, Inc.*

The first tube-feeding case to reach the highest court in any jurisdiction was decided by the Supreme Judicial Court of Massachusetts in 1986 (*Brophy* v. *New England Sinai Hospital, Inc.*). Paul Brophy was forty-five years old and had been admitted to the hospital after complaining of a severe headache and suffering a subsequent loss of consciousness. The symptoms had resulted from an aneurysm—a weak spot in a blood vessel—in his brain. An attempt to surgically repair the problem was unsuccessful. Mr. Brophy never regained consciousness. With the passage of time, he was diagnosed as being in a PVS. A gastrostomy tube was inserted through his abdomen and into his stomach so that he could be adequately nourished.

Paul Brophy had been a firefighter and Emergency Medical Technician (see Figure 3–3). According to his wife, Mr. Brophy had strong feelings about not wanting to have his life sustained under such circumstances as he now found himself. Ten years previously, at a time when the *Quinlan* case was very much in the news, he stated to his wife, "I don't ever want to be on a life-support system. No way do I want to live like that; that is not living" (Ibid., p. 632). Some time thereafter he helped to rescue a man from a burning truck. The man was extensively burned and died a few months later. Mr. Brophy received a commendation for bravery but tossed the medal in the trash saying, "I should have been five minutes later. It would have been all over for him." Regarding the incident, he said to his brother, "If I'm ever like that, just shoot me, pull the plug" (Ibid.).

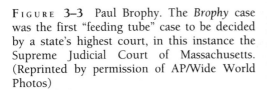

FIGURE 3–3 Paul Brophy. The *Brophy* case was the first "feeding tube" case to be decided by a state's highest court, in this instance the Supreme Judicial Court of Massachusetts. (Reprinted by permission of AP/Wide World Photos)

About a week prior to his illness, in discussing a local teenager who had been put on a life-support system he said, "No way, don't ever let that happen to me, no way." And, while in the hospital prior to his unsuccessful surgery, when he tried to sit up to hug one of his daughters and was told that it was inadvisable for him to do so, he responded, "If I can't sit up to kiss one of my beautiful daughters, I may as well be six feet under" (Ibid.).

After Mr. Brophy had been sustained by his feeding tube for nearly twenty-two months, his wife asked to have the tube feeding stopped. She did so in the belief that that is what her husband would clearly have wanted. She also had the support of her family and relatives. The Brophys had been married for twenty-seven years and had five adult children. His mother, age ninety-one, was alive, as were his four brothers and three sisters. When the physicians and hospital refused to comply with the request, Mrs. Brophy sought a court order granting her authority to direct "the withholding or discontinuation of all medical treatment, including the artificial provision of nutrition and hydration" (Ibid., p. 331).

The petition was denied by the Probate Court. Although the court found that there was no evidence that Mrs. Brophy had been motivated by concerns other than the best interests of her husband and that financial considerations played no part in her decision, it held that "it is ethically inappropriate to cause the preventable death of Brophy by the deliberate denial of food and water, which can be provided to him in a noninvasive, nonintrusive manner which causes no pain and suffering, irrespective of the substituted judgment of the patient. The proper focus should be the *quality of treatment* furnished to Brophy, and not on the quality of Brophy's life" (Ibid., p. 341, emphasis added). Although Mrs. Brophy had requested, and the hospital had agreed to, placement of a Do-Not-Resuscitate (DNR) order in the chart, to effectuate a desire that Mr. Brophy not be "rescued" if he were to experience a cardiac arrest or other life-threatening crisis, there was no expectation that such a "fortuitous accident" was likely to occur. Mr. Brophy, if he were to continue receiving food and water by tube, could be expected to go on living for years.

The Probate Court seemed to be particularly influenced by the symptoms it hypothesized that Mr. Brophy would experience if the petition were granted:

- His mouth would dry out and become caked or coated with thick material.
- His lips would become parched and cracked or fissured.
- His tongue would become swollen and might crack.
- His eyes would sink back into their orbits.
- His cheeks would become hollow.
- The mucosa (lining) of his nose might crack and cause his nose to bleed.
- His skin would hang loose on his body and become dry and scaly.
- His urine would become highly concentrated, causing burning of the bladder.
- The lining of his stomach would dry out causing dry heaves and vomiting.
- He would develop hyperthermia, a very high body temperature.
- His brain cells would begin drying out, causing convulsions.
- His respiratory tract would dry out, giving rise to very thick secretions, which could plug his lungs and cause death.
- Eventually his major organs would fail, including his lungs, heart and brain. (Ibid., pp. 338–339)

The court concluded that these symptoms would be extremely painful and that, in fact, Mr. "Brophy's attending physician was unable to imagine a more cruel and violent death than thirsting to death" (Ibid., p. 339). (See Box 3–1.)

Mrs. Brophy took her appeal to the Supreme Judicial Court of Massachusetts which, on September 11, 1986, some nineteen months after the

---

Box 3–1   Pain and PVS

One aspect of the debate about stopping treatment in PVS focuses on a concern that the afflicted person will experience suffering after treatment is stopped (e.g., will experience dyspnea after removal of a respirator or face discomfort associated with starvation and dehydration after removal of a feeding tube). The most obvious contradiction to this projection is that, by definition, in PVS both the person's capacity to perceive a wide range of stimuli and the neocortical or higher brain functions that are needed to generate a self-perceived affective response to any such stimuli are destroyed. Pain cannot be experienced by brains that no longer retain the neural apparatus for suffering.

(Council on Scientific Affairs and Council on Ethical and Judicial Affairs, 1990, p. 428)

Probate Court had ruled against her and nearly three and one-half years after her husband had lost consciousness, granted her petition—by a four to three vote. Obviously concerned about the effect of ordering unwilling physicians to participate in the clamping of Mr. Brophy's feeding tube, the court tried to resolve the problem by authorizing Mrs. Brophy to transfer care of her husband to other physicians who would honor her request. Referring to the position taken by the American Academy of Neurology, which had filed a brief in support of removal of the tube, the majority found that the Probate Court's comments about the painfulness of death by dehydration to be inconsistent with medical authority. According to the Academy, patients in a PVS, like Mr. Brophy, are unable to experience pain and suffering. The court also cited the Report of the President's Commission that "pain and suffering are absent, as are joy, satisfaction, and pleasure" (President's Commission, pp. 181–182).

The majority addressed the Probate Court's concern about the "ethical inappropriateness" of discontinuing tube feeding by calling attention to a 1986 Statement of the AMA Council on Ethical and Judicial Affairs:

> Even if death is not imminent but a patient's coma is beyond doubt irreversible and there are adequate safe-guards to confirm the accuracy of the diagnosis and with the concurrence of those who have responsibility for the care of the patient, it is not unethical to discontinue all means of life-prolonging medical treatment.
>
> Life-prolonging medical treatment includes medication and artificially or technologically supplied respiration, nutrition or hydration. In treating a terminally ill or irreversibly comatose patient, the physician should determine whether the benefits of treatment outweigh its burdens. At all times the dignity of the patient should be maintained.   (Ibid., pp. 638–639)

Although each of the dissenting justices wrote separate opinions as to why they thought the decision was wrong, at least one of them, Justice Nolan, was as critical of what the holding seemed to *represent* as he was of the immediate outcome. "The court today," he wrote, "has rendered an opinion which affronts logic, ethics, and the dignity of the human person." He found it "outrageously erroneous" to regard tube feeding as medical treatment, seeing it instead as "basic human needs." He went on to accuse the majority of endorsing "euthanasia and suicide." His short, but obviously angry, dissent ended with the following:

> Finally, I can think of nothing more degrading to the human person than the balance which the court struck today in favor of death and against life. It is but another triumph for the forces of secular humanism (modern paganism) which have now succeeded in imposing their anti-life principles at both ends of life's spectrum.   (Ibid., p. 640)

While arguably intemperate from the perspective of judicial tone, Justice Nolan's dissent capsulizes much of the debate concerning the extent to which life must always be preserved. In his reference to "both ends of life's spectrum," Justice Nolan was clearly expressing his dissatisfaction not only with withdrawal of treatment, in this case tube feeding, from the permanently unconscious, but with abortion as well. Indeed, these two issues, along with the equally controversial issue of treatment decisions concerning imperiled newborns—which will be discussed in Chapter 6—are illustrative of an underlying disagreement about the inviolate nature of human life itself.

To some, life is the most fundamental value—often described as the paramount human right—and it must always be protected and preserved, regardless of any concern for its quality. This position is typically described as *vitalism* or representative of a sanctity of life ethic. In its purest form it would oppose any decision that would shorten life, either by allowing death to occur by withholding or withdrawing treatment or by an act that would intentionally cause death. To the vitalist, asking questions about the quality of life being sustained—a balancing of benefits and burdens—is likely to take one onto slippery slopes where seemingly reasonable choices will result inevitably in both unreasonable and unethical ones. The same arguments used to support a decision to remove a feeding tube from someone like Paul Brophy, argues the vitalist, will next be used to justify stopping treatment on mentally retarded children or the senile elderly. By disregarding the sanctity of life of the "unborn," so the argument goes, the stage has been set for the death of people like Paul Brophy who might otherwise have been kept alive merely by feeding them. This "right to life" is seen as the basic human right upon which all other rights clearly depend.

For others, however, the issue is not simply one of life. While important in and of itself, the value of life must always be placed in the context of other important considerations such as the individual's level of functioning, loss of dignity, life expectancy, and medical prognosis, as well as the risks and benefits and the treatment options open to the patient. Failure to recognize the right of the individual to make these decisions for him- or herself based on individual and idiosyncratic values about quality of life deprives him or her of the autonomy and respect that lie at the core of democratic societies. This quality of life ethic, or *relativism* as it is sometimes called, would argue that it is only by allowing each of us to make such decisions for ourselves or, if we are unable to do so, by those closest to us acting on our behalf, that we honor life by preserving its dignity. Relativists would place autonomy at the top of their value system.

In practice, as opposed to theory, one seldom sees—outside the context of the most rigid opposition to abortion under *any* circumstances—advocacy of vitalism in its purest form. Although the New Jersey Supreme Court specifically noted that its decision in the *Quinlan* case was *not* based on the quality of Ms. Quinlan's life, it is difficult to understand the decision on any other basis. Regardless, there has been little controversy in the wake of *Quinlan* about removing permanently unconscious patients from ventilators; the controversy has focused on feeding tubes which, to opponents, are different from other forms of *medical* care. Whereas ventilators are seen as invasive medical treatment, the process of feeding, in the words of Justice Nolan, "is simply not medical treatment and is not invasive. . . . Food and water are basic human needs. They are not medicines and feeding them to a patient is just not medical treatment" (Ibid.).

Cruzan v. *Director, Missouri Department of Health*

It is against this backdrop of controversy over tube feeding of the permanently unconscious that the *Cruzan* case took on such importance. In the early morning hours of January 11, 1983, Nancy Cruzan's car skidded on a rural Missouri road (see Figure 3–4). It struck some small trees and a mailbox before swerving back across the road. It then crashed through a fence and rolled several times before coming to rest on its top. Ms. Cruzan was thrown from the car and landed face down in a ditch. When the Carthage Fire Department arrived at the scene, nineteen minutes after the accident, they found Ms. Cruzan lifeless, in total cardiac and respiratory arrest. She seemed to have experienced only minor cuts and bruises, although she did have a "massive swelling" of the face.

Life-support procedures were instituted within two minutes of arrival. Within one or two minutes there was evidence of a pulse and respiration and she was transported to the hospital emergency room with vital signs of BP 110/80, pulse 92, and respiration 14 and spontaneous. An exploratory laparotomy disclosed a laceration to her liver which was repaired. Multiple facial fractures were repaired by an oral surgeon. Estimates of the duration of her anoxia ranged from six to twenty minutes with the most probable duration twelve to fourteen minutes.

Her recovery from surgery was uneventful. She remained in a "coma" for approximately three weeks when she appeared to have progressed to a PVS. Several weeks after her accident, on February 1, 1983, with the consent of her then-husband, a gastrostomy tube was inserted. She was discharged from the hospital on February 21 and admitted to a rehabilitation facility where she was treated for six weeks. From there she was discharged as unimproved and unresponsive to rehabilitation. Her husband took her to his grandmother's home where she was attended constantly by professional nurses. Within two or three weeks she developed pneumonia, probably from food aspiration as a result of oral feeding efforts, and she was rehospitalized for a short time before returning to the grandmother's home.

Shortly thereafter, she was admitted to a nursing home where, after several days, she was rehospitalized with a fever of 107 degrees from some kind of infection. She was discharged and then admitted to Mount Vernon State Hospital on October 19, 1983.

By 1987, after nearly four and one-half years had passed without any sign of recovery, her parents asked the hospital physicians to remove her feeding tube. The physicians and the hospital administrator refused to honor the request unless it was approved by the Probate Court. Their petition to the court was granted by Judge Charles E. Teel, Jr., who found that there was "clear and convincing evidence" that "the intent of [Nancy Cruzan], if mentally able, would be to terminate her nutrition and hydration" (*Cruzan* v. *Harmon,* 1988, p. 444). The Probate Court, as is typical in proceedings of this type, appointed a guardian *ad litem* to represent Ms. Cruzan's interests during the hearing. The decision of the court was appealed by both the State of Missouri and the guardian *ad litem* who, while he agreed with the decision of the Probate Court, felt that a decision of such importance should be reviewed by the Missouri Supreme Court.

The Missouri Supreme Court heard arguments in the case and, in November 1988, by a four to three decision, reversed the decision of the Probate Court. At the time of the oral arguments, Ms. Cruzan had been unconscious for nearly six years. The majority wrote that it is "definitionally impossible for a person to make an informed decision—either to consent or refuse—under hypothetical circumstances" (Ibid., p. 417). This would seem to run counter to the terms of Missouri law under which a 1986 Act would allow a competent person to execute a Living Will. Under the law, however, one of the things that a person could not refuse through a Living Will was food and water (Sections 459.010 et seq., RSMo, 1986). Also, contrary to the findings of the Probate Court, the Supreme Court asserted that there was no reliable evidence that Ms. Cruzan would have refused artificial feedings. What was the evidence that the Court regarded as unreliable?

> The trial [Probate] court had relied on the testimony of Athena Comer, a long-time friend, co-worker and a housemate for several months, as sufficient

to show that [Ms. Cruzan] would wish to be free of medical treatment under her present circumstances. Ms. Comer described a conversation she and Nancy had while living together, concerning Ms. Comer's sister who had become ill suddenly and died during the night. The Comer family had been told that if she had lived through the night, she would have been in a vegetative state. [Ms. Cruzan] had lost a grandmother a few months before. Ms. Comer testified that: "Nancy said she would never want to live [as a vegetative state] because if she couldn't be normal or even, you know, like half way, and do things for yourself, because Nancy always did, that she didn't want to live . . . and we talked about it a lot." She said "several times" that "she wouldn't want to live that way because if she was going to live, she wanted to be able to live and not to just lay in a bed and not be able to move because you can't do anything for yourself." [S]he said that she hoped that [all the] people in her family knew that she wouldn't want to live [as a vegetable] because she knew it was usually up to the family whether you lived that way or not.

The conversation took place approximately a year before [Ms. Cruzan's] accident and was described by Ms. Comer as a "very serious" conversation that continued for approximately half an hour without interruption. The Missouri Supreme Court dismissed Nancy's statement as "unreliable" on the ground that it was an informally expressed reaction to other people's medical conditions.

The Missouri Supreme Court did not refer to other evidence of [Ms. Cruzan's] wishes or explain why it was rejected. [Ms. Cruzan's] sister, Christy, to whom she was very close, testified that she and Nancy had two very serious conversations about a year and a half before the accident. A day or two after a niece was stillborn (but would have been badly damaged if she had lived), Nancy had said that maybe it was part of a "greater plan" that the baby had been stillborn and did not have to face "the possible life of mere existence." A month later, after their grandmother had died after a long battle with heart problems, Nancy said that "it was better for my grandmother not to be brought back and forth [by] medical [treatment], brought back from a critical near point of death. . . . "

[Ms. Cruzan's] sister, Christy, [her] mother, and another of her friends, testified that [Ms. Cruzan] would want to discontinue the hydration and nutrition. Christy said that "Nancy would be horrified at the state she is in." Based on "a lifetime of experience [I know Nancy's wishes] are to discontinue the hydration and nutrition." [Ms. Cruzan's] mother testified: "Nancy would not want to be like she is now. [I]f it were me up there or Christy or any of us, she would be doing for us what we are trying to do for her. I know she would . . . as her mother."   (*Cruzan* v. *Director*, 1990, pp. 4931–4932)

Judge Welliver, dissenting from the decision of the majority in regard to their reliance on the public policy represented by the Missouri Living Will law, characterized the law as "a fraud on the people of Missouri from the beginning and which . . . , if directly attacked, must, . . . be held to be unconstitutional" (*Cruzan* v. *Harmon*, 1988, p. 441).

The *Cruzan* decision was appealed to the U.S. Supreme Court. By the time the Missouri Supreme Court had decided the case, many state courts had heard and decided similar cases concerning treatment of PVS patients, some

FIGURE 3–4   Nancy Cruzan. The *Cruzan* case was the first so-called "right to die" case to be decided by the U.S. Supreme Court. At the time of her death, Ms. Cruzan had been unconscious for nearly eight years. (Reprinted by permission of AP/Wide World Photos)

involving feeding tubes. One of the dissenters in *Cruzan* made reference to the fact that "the majority cites more than 50 appellate decisions from 16 jurisdictions that support and validate the trial [Probate] court's findings of fact, conclusions of law and the judgment in this case; yet, ironically, it reverses the judgment in favor of Ms. Cruzan by finding "that the trial court erroneously declared the law" (Ibid., p. 430). Some of these cases had even been unsuccessfully appealed to the U.S. Supreme Court. *Quinlan* was appealed, but the Court refused to hear the appeal, thereby allowing the decision of the New Jersey Supreme Court to stand. Since the Supreme Court had yet to rule on a so-called "right to die" case and the vast majority of state courts to hear such cases had sided with the family in support of their request to discontinue life-sustaining treatment, there was some reason to believe that the Court would accept the *Cruzan* appeal. But, when the Court agreed to do so, early in 1988, public expectations were mixed. Some, reasoning the Court had refused to hear other cases that had been appealed because the Court agreed with the decision to allow discontinuation of treatment, viewed the acceptance of the *Cruzan* appeal as an indication that the Court was prepared to overturn the decision of the Missouri Supreme Court. Others, mindful that the Supreme Court had become increasingly conservative in the intervening years since *Quinlan* was denied a hearing, were fearful that a more conservative Court might affirm the decision of the Missouri Supreme Court and, in so doing, indirectly overturn all of the cases previously decided by state courts in favor of discontinuation of treatment.

Arguments were heard on December 6, 1989, and a decision was handed down on June 25 of the following year. It was a five to four decision with the justices voting along fairly predictable lines. Chief Justice Rehnquist, writing the opinion for the majority, avoided any reference to the Missouri Living Will law, which Justice Welliver had criticized as "a fraud on the people of Missouri," in his dissent. Instead, he simply upheld the right of the State of Missouri to demand that Ms. Cruzan's wishes be established by "clear and convincing evidence" which, according to the Missouri Supreme Court, her family had failed to do. Unless and until they were able to meet such a burden of proof, Nancy Cruzan must continue to receive artificial feeding and hydration. Although this was certainly bad news to the Cruzan family and those who sympathized with their plight, there was also some good news to be found in the Court's decision. First, eight of the justices—all but Justice Scalia—agreed that there was a constitutionally protected right for competent persons to refuse medical treatment, even life-sustaining medical treatment. The Court also held that there was no difference between artificially provided nutrition and hydration and other forms of medical treatment that might be refused. Furthermore, the Court held that these rights are not lost when a person becomes incompetent like Nancy Cruzan.

Justice O'Connor, and presumably the members of the minority (Justices Brennan, Marshall, Blackmun, and Stevens) would extend the right to refuse treatment even further. "[T]he Court does not today decide the issue whether a State must also give effect to the decisions of a surrogate decision maker. In my view, such a duty may well be constitutionally required to protect the patient's liberty interest in refusing medical treatment" (Ibid., p. 4923).

Justice Scalia joined in the opinion of the majority but wrote a separate concurring opinion to express his view that "the federal courts have no business in this field" (Ibid., p. 4924). Characterizing Ms. Cruzan's "right" as analogous to the claim of a right to commit suicide, he argued that whether or not the residents of a state wished to tolerate such behavior was a matter for them to decide through their elected representatives. Justice Scalia was the only member of the Court who supported either the conclusion that refusal of artificially administered food and/or water should be regarded as suicide or that such cases should not be heard by the federal courts.

Justice Brennan wrote a dissenting opinion that was joined by Justices Marshall and Blackmun. He began by quoting from a decision of the Arizona Supreme Court in *Rasmussen* v. *Fleming* (1987):

> Medical technology has effectively created a twilight zone of suspended animation where death commences while life, in some form, continues. Some patients, however, want no part of a life sustained only by medical technology. Instead, they prefer a plan of medical treatment that allows nature to take its course and permits them to die with dignity.   (211, 678)

Of the approximately 1.6 million people who die in hospitals in the United States every year, he wrote, perhaps 70 percent do so after a decision to forgo life-sustaining treatment has been made, and nearly every death involves a decision whether to undertake some medical procedure that could prolong the process of dying. To the dissenters, the right to be free of unwanted medical treatment was not merely a *liberty interest,* as it was cast by the majority, but a *fundamental right.* Unlike liberty interests, which can be overcome by state laws that bear a rational relationship to the attainment of a legitimate state interest, fundamental rights can be overcome only by a compelling state interest that is reflected in a narrowly drawn law designed to accomplish a legitimate state purpose. Fundamental rights place a much higher burden on the state and federal government in any attempt to restrict activities embodying such rights.

To the dissenters, the delivery of food and water through a tube was clearly one such form of medical treatment that could be refused. In support of this, they cited to such conclusions by the American Academy of Neurology, the American Medical Association, and the President's Commission. They also indicated that the federal government permits the cost of medical devices and formulas used in tube feeding to be reimbursed under Medicare and that the formulas are regulated by the Food and Drug Administration as "medical foods," while the tubes are regulated as medical devices.

In response to the claim advanced by the State of Missouri that Ms. Cruzan's desire to refuse medical treatment should be subordinated to the state's interest in preserving her life, as long as she is free of pain and physical discomfort, Justice Blackmun offered the following rebuttal:

> If Missouri were correct . . . it is not apparent why a State could not choose to remove one of her kidneys without consent on the ground that society would be better off if the recipient of that kidney were saved from renal poisoning. Nancy cannot feel surgical pain. Nor would removal of one kidney be expected to shorten her life expectancy. Patches of her skin could also be removed to provide grafts for burn victims, and scrapings of bone marrow to provide grafts for someone with leukemia. Perhaps the State could lawfully remove more vital organs for transplanting into others who would then be cured of their ailments, provided the State placed Nancy on some other life-support equipment to replace the lost function. Indeed, why could the State not perform medical experiments on her body, experiments that might save countless lives, and would cause her no greater burden than she already bears by being fed through the gastrostomy tube? This would be too brave a new world for me and, I submit, for our Constitution.   (Ibid., p. 4929)

Referring to public opinion polls which demonstrated that the vast majority of Americans would not choose to have their lives maintained under circumstances such as Ms. Cruzan was in, the dissenters argued that the only legitimate interest of the State of Missouri was in safeguarding the accuracy of determining her wishes. Here, however, the state had failed to do so. The state, contrary to public opinion, had established a presumption in favor of continuing treatment and had required a high standard of proof (clear and convincing evidence) to rebut that assumption, but no proof was required to support a finding that the incompetent person would wish to continue treatment.

Rather than continuing to treat Ms. Cruzan, contrary to the wishes of parents who believed that they were doing what she would want done, where firm evidence of the patient's wishes is absent, the dissenters would establish a presumption in favor of the family. The majority acknowledged that while close family members might well have strong feelings about the decision, "there is no automatic assurance that [their] view will necessarily be the same as the patient's would have been had she been confronted with the prospect of her situation while competent" (Ibid., p. 4933).

To this, Justice Blackmun commented:

> I cannot quarrel with this observation. But it leads only to another question: Is there any reason to suppose that a State is *more* likely to make the choice that the patient would have made than someone who knew the patient intimately? To ask this is to answer it. As the New Jersey Supreme Court observed: "Family members are best qualified to make substituted judgments for incompetent patients not only because of their peculiar grasp of the patient's approach to life, but also because of their special bonds with him or her. . . . It is . . . they who treat the patient as a person, rather than a symbol of a cause." (Ibid., p. 4933)

On November 1, 1990, Mr. and Mrs. Cruzan again appeared before Judge Charles E. Teel, Jr., the same Probate Court judge who had granted their petition some three years earlier. Having successfully defended the position of the State of Missouri, Attorney General William L. Webster announced that the state would not be a party to any further court actions brought by the Cruzan family. The family presented additional witnesses who testified to the fact that they, too, had had conversations with Ms. Cruzan, whom they knew as Nancy Davis (Davis was her married name), in which she shared with them her wishes not to be maintained under such circumstances. Although there were no opposing parties before the court, there were opposing briefs filed by several right-to-life groups, including the International Anti-Euthanasia Task Force, the National Legal Center for the Medically Dependent and Disabled, and Missouri Citizens for Life. As he had done before, Judge Teel noted that there was clear and convincing evidence that Ms. Cruzan would not choose to continue tube feeding and hydration under her present circumstances and that her parents were authorized to direct the removal of the gastrostomy tube.

The decision was entered in the record on December 14, 1990. Although there were last-minute legal maneuvers by opponents and protesters holding candlelight vigils on the front steps of the hospital, for the Cruzan family the tragedy was finally over. Nancy Cruzan died on December 26, 1990, twelve days after the tube feeding was stopped and nearly nine years after she became unconscious.

The major lesson to be learned from the Cruzan case is quite simple: *WRITE IT DOWN!* While states are not compelled to demand high levels of proof of the wishes of incompetents before stopping treatment and, aside from Missouri, few other states have asserted such high levels of proof, the majority opinion clearly supports those states that might wish to follow Missouri's lead. Indeed, one of the major developments in the wake of the Cruzan case was the passage of new federal legislation, the Patient Self-Determination Act, which would encourage patients in federally funded institutions, those that receive Medicare and/or Medicaid funds, to set forth their wishes about life-sustaining medical treatment in the form of an advance directive. This will be discussed in detail in Chapter 4.

The Case of Helga Wanglie

To this point in the book, we have been discussing the difficulties often experienced by family members in their attempts to have all forms of LSMT withdrawn from a loved one now in a persistent vegetative state (PVS). We have also seen how the courts and commentators have responded to these desires by acknowledging that treatment can be stopped when there is some reliable evidence that this is what the patient would have chosen if able to do so. The lesson to be learned from *Cruzan* is that states may require, if they wish, high levels of proof ("clear and convincing" evidence) but that other states are free to set lower standards if they so desire. Some commentators, including the members of the President's Commission, would, in the absence of any evidence about what the patient would choose, defer the decision to the family under a best interest standard.

The case of Helga Wanglie (*In re: The Conservatorship of Helga Wanglie,* 1991) forces us to look at the question from a different perspective. It is, in a sense, the flip side of the *Quinlan-Cruzan* line of cases in which families wanted to stop treatment and they were opposed by the medical establishment.

Helga Wanglie was eighty-five years old when she was moved from a nursing home to Hennepin County Medical Center (Minneapolis) because of difficulty in breathing. She required emergency intubation and was placed on a ventilator. Although she was conscious, she was unable to communicate clearly. She recognized her family and occasionally expressed discomfort.

Some four months later, after attempts to wean her from the ventilator were unsuccessful, she was discharged to a chronic care hospital. A week later, during another weaning attempt, her heart stopped; she was resuscitated and taken to another hospital for intensive care. When she failed to regain consciousness it was suggested that it would be appropriate to withdraw life support. The family rejected the advice and, instead, transferred her back to Hennepin County Medical Center. Two weeks after she had been readmitted her physicians diagnosed her as being in a PVS. She was maintained by a ventilator, antibiotics, frequent airway suctioning, air flotation bed, feeding tube, and biochemical monitoring (Miles, 1991). The family had agreed, reluctantly, to a do-not-resuscitate order, based on the improbability of Mrs. Wanglie's surviving a cardiac arrest.

Throughout June and July, the physicians continued to suggest that treatment be withdrawn since it was *of no benefit* to her. Her family, however, unlike those situations we have been discussing until now, insisted on continued treatment. Her husband and two adult children, a daughter and son, stated that "physicians should not play God, that the patient would not be better off dead, that removing life support showed moral decay in our civilization, and that a miracle could occur" (Ibid., p. 513). Although initially her husband said that she had never stated her preferences regarding LSMT, several months later he claimed that his wife had consistently told him that she wanted "respirator support" under such circumstances. Treatment was continued and by August there was a consensus among the nurses that it seemed inappropriate.

By October, a new attending physician had consulted with specialists and confirmed the diagnosis of PVS which had been made in mid-June. He concluded that Mrs. Wanglie was "at the end of her life and that the respirator was 'non-beneficial,' in that it could not heal her lungs, palliate her suffering, or enable this unconscious and permanently respirator-dependent woman to experience the benefits of the life afforded by respirator support" (Ibid.). Because the respirator could prolong life, it was not characterized as futile.

Approximately a month later, Mrs. Wanglie's physician, with the concurrence of the hospital ethicist, informed the family that he was unwilling to continue to prescribe the ventilator. The husband, a retired attorney, refused to approve the hospital's proposal to either transfer his wife to another facility or to seek a court order mandating treatment. In January, the hospital's board of directors, by a four-to-three vote, decided to pursue a resolution of the conflict in court. The hospital had no financial interest in stopping treatment; Mrs. Wanglie's care was being paid through a combination of Medicare and private insurance. From February through May, the family and the hospital searched for another facility that would accept Mrs. Wanglie. They were unsuccessful.

The case was heard in late May and the court issued a decision on July 1, 1991. It had been slightly more than a year since Mrs. Wanglie had been first diagnosed as being in a PVS. The court found that Mr. Wanglie was the person best able to represent his wife's interests. It further stated that since no specific request to stop treatment had been made it would not speculate on the legality of such an order. In view of "uncertainty" about its legal obligation to continue treatment, the hospital agreed that it would continue to do so. Three days later, Mrs. Wanglie, still attached to the ventilator, died. The family declined an autopsy and they stated that Mrs. Wanglie had received excellent care.

While the court's decision to vest authority in the family, rather than with the physicians, seems to be consistent with the other cases we have been looking at, the situation raises some interesting questions about the kinds of treatment that providers are required to furnish. For example,

> a patient's request for a treatment does not necessarily oblige a provider or the health care system. Patients may not demand that physicians injure them (for example, by mutilation), or provide plausible but inappropriate therapies (for example, amphetamines for weight reduction), or therapies that have no value (such as laetrile for cancer). Physicians are not obliged to violate their personal moral views on medical care so long as patients' rights are served. (Ibid., pp. 513–514)

An editorial in *The New England Journal of Medicine,* which ran in the same issue as Steven Miles', a clinical ethicist at Hennepin County Medical Center, essay describing the case from the hospital's perspective, supported the decision of the court to vest decision-making authority with Mr. Wanglie. Dr. Marcia Angell, the editor of *The Journal*, depicted the case as one of conflicting views about goals. The hospital saw the ventilator as "nonbeneficial" because it would not restore Helga Wanglie to consciousness; the family viewed maintaining her life, however diminished, as its goal. While it would appear that most people would not wish to have their lives maintained under such circumstances, Angell argued that the decision is best left in the hands of the patient's family especially, as in this case, where there was no evidence that the patient would have chosen otherwise (Angell, 1991).

A director of an intensive care unit, writing in the *Hastings Center Report*, disagreed. In support of the view that the hospital had no obligation to provide treatment, he cited a consensus report on the ethics of forgoing life-sustaining treatment in the critically ill which had been prepared by the Society of Critical Care Medicine:

> Treatments that offer no benefit and serve to prolong the dying process should not be employed. In light of a hopeless prognosis, the indefinite maintenance of patients reliably diagnosed as being in a persistent vegetative state (PVS) raises serious ethical concerns both for the dignity of the patient and for the diversion of limited medical and nursing resources from alternative applications that could offer medical and nursing benefit to others. The PVS patient should be removed from the ICU unless it is not possible otherwise to meet the patient's nursing care needs. A PVS patient should not be main-

tained in the ICU to the exclusion of a patient who can derive benefit from ICU care.   (Rie, 1991, p. 25)

A different conclusion was reached by another commentator, perhaps even more stridently, who viewed the conflict as a clash of values rather than a difference about medical appropriateness.

> A clear case of medical inappropriateness would be an attempt to cure cancer with laetrile, since medicine has presumably shown that laetrile cannot cure cancer. Moreover, since laetrile's clinical ineffectiveness is a technical medical fact about which doctors are supposed to have professional expertise, it is professionally appropriate for doctors to refuse to grant a patient's request to have laetrile prescribed for cancer. But HCMC's [the hospital's] disagreement with Mrs. Wanglie's family is not a technical dispute about a matter where doctors can be presumed to have greater expertise than laymen. The parties to the dispute do not disagree about whether maintaining Mrs. Wanglie on a respirator is likely to prolong her life; they disagree about whether her life is worth prolonging. This is not a medical question, but a question of values. Hence their term "medically inappropriate," with its implication of the relevance of technical medical expertise, is itself inappropriate in this context. It is as presumptious and *ethically* inappropriate for doctors to suppose that their professional expertise qualifies them to know what kind of life is worth prolonging as it would be for meteorologists to suppose their professional expertise qualifies them to know what kind of destination is worth a long drive in the rain.   (Ackerman, 1991, p. 28)

This view, however, fails to adequately address the problem of allocating scarce resources, both medical and financial, in providing continuing treatment under such circumstances. Although the approximately $800,000 in care which Mrs. Wanglie had received from the hospital was being paid for by private insurance, and the insurance company had expressed no reluctance to continue payment, its costs would eventually be passed along to other policyholders in the form of higher premiums.

Since few of us, or our families, would likely choose to continue treatment under circumstances such as this, the impact of the court's decision in the *Wanglie* case is hard to predict. It would seem clear, however, that the debate about the proper treatment of the nonautonomous patient in a PVS without an advance directive will continue to be a vigorous one.

The Persistent Vegetative State: An Evolving Understanding

As we stated earlier in this chapter, our understanding of the persistent vegetative state is, historically speaking, relatively new. Jennet and Plum (1972) were the first to use the term. At the time that *Quinlan* was decided, there was confusion as to whether patients in a PVS were able to breathe without a ventilator. Karen Ann Quinlan's physicians refused to remove her from the ventilator because they thought it would cause her death. When her parents were finally able to have it removed, Karen unexpectedly continued breathing unassisted and managed to continue doing so for nearly nine years before she died. It is now widely understood that most patients in a PVS are able to breathe without support.

Because of the confusion surrounding the diagnosis, prognosis, and proper care of the patient in a PVS, the American Academy of Neurology (ANA) published a position paper on the condition in 1989. In addition to describing the characteristics of the PVS as it was understood then, the Academy took the position that "artificial provision of nutrition and hydration is a form of medical treatment and may be discontinued in accordance with the principles and practices governing the withholding and withdrawal of other forms of medical treatment" (American Academy of Neurology, 1989, p. 125). This position was affirmed by a majority of the U.S. Supreme Court in the *Cruzan* decision.

Regardless, the controversy about the diagnosis, prognosis, and appropriateness of care for the patient in a PVS continued. In 1993, the American Neurological Association (ANA) Committee on Ethical Affairs published a paper asserting that "the public must be assured that the PVS can be diagnosed with a high degree of certainty by well-defined clinical criteria" (1993, p. 386). They commented that, "*Persistent vegetative state* is . . . a vegetative state that has continued or endured for at least 1 month. This operational definition does *not* imply either *permanency* or *irreversibility*. Patients in PVS occasionally improve to a state of partial recovery or rarely to total recovery; most often, they progress to a PVS [*permanent* vegetative state] or death" (Ibid., p. 387).

In an editorial accompanying the report, the chair of the committee announced that the ANA had supported the formation of a Multi-Society Task Force on PVS because of a "need for the neurosciences to speak with a single voice" on this issue (Celesia, 1991, p. 391). The task force, comprised of representatives of the American Neurological Society, the American Academy of Neurology, the Child Neurology Society, the American Association of Neurological Surgeons, and the American Academy of Pediatrics was formed in 1992 and was to prepare a position paper on the medical aspects of PVS.

The long-awaited Multi-Society report appeared in *The New England Journal of Medicine* in late May and early June of 1994. In the first of this two-part report, the Task Force "define[d] the persistent vegetative state and related terms and conditions and discusse[d] the epidemiology, causes, and pathological features, as well as ancillary diagnostic studies. The second part adresse[d] the prognosis for recovery and long-term survival of patients in a persistent vegetative state and discusse[d] issues related to pain and suffering and treatment (Multi-Society Task Force on PVS, 1994a, p. 1500).

The vegetative state is to be diagnosed according to the following criteria:

- No evidence of awareness of self or environment and an inability to interact with others.

- No evidence of sustained, reproducible, purposeful, or voluntary behavioral responses to visual, auditory, tactile, or noxious stimuli.

- No evidence of language comprehension or expression.

- Intermittent wakefulness manifested by the presence of sleep-wake cycles.

- Sufficiently preserved hypothalamic and brain-stem autonomic functions to permit survival with medical and nursing care.

- Bowel and bladder incontinence.

- Variably preserved cranial-nerve reflexes (pupillary, oculocephalic, corneal, vestibulo-ocular, and gag) and spinal reflexes.   (Ibid.)

The Task Force differentiated between "persistent" vegetative state and "permanent" vegetative state, describing the former as referring "only to a condition of past and continuing disability with an uncertain future" and the latter as implying "permanent" irreversibility. "Persistent vegetative state is a diagnosis; permanent vegetative state is a prognosis" (Ibid.). The permanence of the condition, "like all clinical diagnoses in medicine, is based on probabilities, not absolutes" (Ibid.). The Task Force added that "a patient in a persistent vegetative state becomes permanently vegetative when the diagnosis of irreversibility can be established with a high degree of clinical certainty—that is, when the chance that the patient will regain consciousness is exceedingly small" (Ibid.).

The Task Force estimated that in the United States there are 10,000 to 25,000 adults and 4,000 to 10,000 children in a persistent vegetative state. The prognosis depends upon the underlying disease process. Underlying causes were categorized as (1) acute traumatic and nontraumatic injuries, (2) degenerative and metabolic disorders, and (3) developmental malformations. The first category was further divided into those cases arising from head trauma and those arising from hypoxic-ischemic encephalopathy, that is, deprivation of oxygen to the brain not related to a blow to the head (Ibid., pp. 1503–1504).

In the second part of the report, the Task Force stressed that "there are two dimensions of recovery from a persistent vegetative state: recovery of consciousness and recovery of function" and that the former may occur without the latter. Concerning recovery of consciousness, they stated that it is unlikely after twelve months when the cause of unconsciousness has been trauma. When the cause of unconsciousness has been nontraumatic, recovery of consciousness is "rare" after three months. Recall, as discussed earlier in this chapter, that in the 1988/89 position paper of the American Academy of Neurology, it was stated that "the diagnosis of permanent unconsciousness can usually be made with a high degree of medical certainty in cases of hypoxic-ischemic encephalopathy [nontrauma] after a period of 1 to 3 months" (1989, p. 125).

The Task Force reported that "few patients in a persistent vegetative state have undergone a verified recovery of consciousness more than 12 months after a traumatic injury or more than 3 months after a nontraumatic injury" (Multi-Society Task Force on PVS, 1994b, p. 1575). Acknowledging that stories of unexpected recovery are sometimes reported in the popular media, the Task Force stressed that such reports are "poorly documented, the nature of the patient's neurological condition is unclear, or the timing of the entry into the vegetative state is extremely atypical" (Ibid., citations omitted). Although they combed the medical literature, the Task Force was able to verify reports of only a few patients who had regained consciousness after being properly diagnosed as PVS and all were left with moderate to severe disability.

At a time when the national focus is on health care reform, especially in regard to universal access and cost containment, the expense of providing long-term care for the permanently unconscious is a legitimate concern. Although difficult to estimate:

> The cost of hospital care for the first three months is estimated to be $149,200. The estimated cost of long-term care in a skilled nursing facility ranges from approximately $350 per day ($126,000 per year) to approximately $500 per day ($180,000 per year). For children in a persistent vegetative state, the estimated annual cost of care at home is $129,000 (±$51,000) for the first year and $97,000 for subsequent years. A rough approximation of the total annual cost in the United States for the care of adults and children in a persistent vegetative state is $1 billion to $7 billion.　(Ibid., p. 1576, citations omitted)

The report concludes by joining the earlier recommendations of the President's Commission for the Study of Ethical Problems in Medicine and Biomedical and Behavioral Research, the Hastings Center, the American Academy of Neurology, the American Medical Association, and the United Kingdom Institute of Medical Ethics Working Party on the Ethics of Prolonging Life and Assisting Death that "surrogate decision makers and patients acting through advance directives have the right to terminate all forms of life-sustaining medical treatment, including hydration and nutrition" (Ibid., p. 1577, citations omitted).

Only time will tell whether this latest report will still or stir the public debate over the appropriate treatment of the PVS.

The Previously Competent Patient in Dementia

If we are to consider that a previously competent person who is now permanently unconscious has a right to refuse life-sustaining medical treatment, preferably based on clear expression of those wishes prior to incapacitation, should those same wishes also be respected if the person is somewhat less than permanently unconscious, in dementia? This is a state of awareness somewhere between competence and unconsciousness. Let's begin with a case.

In re Conroy

Claire Conroy was eighty-four years old and bedridden, unable to move from a semifetal position. She suffered from arteriosclerotic heart disease, hypertension, and diabetes mellitus. Her left leg was gangrenous to her knee and she had several decutitus ulcers (bed sores) on her left foot, leg, and hip. She had an eye problem that required irrigation. Her bladder was being drained through a catheter and she had no control over her bowels. She was unable to speak and her ability to swallow was limited.

Ms. Conroy had been hospitalized twice for dehydration. During the second of these hospitalizations it was noticed that she had gangrenous ulcers on her left foot. Two orthopedic surgeons recommended that her leg be amputated to save her life. Since Ms. Conroy was confused, disoriented, and physically dependent, her nephew, Thomas Whittemore, who had been appointed as her guardian, was asked to consent to the surgery. He refused, indicating that he was confident that she would not have wanted it. Contrary to the surgeon's prognosis, Ms. Conroy did not die from the gangrene.

Since Ms. Conroy was not eating adequately, the physician who cared for her in the nursing home where she had been admitted inserted a nasogastric tube. Several months later the tube was removed and Ms. Conroy was fed by hand through her mouth for two weeks. However, she was unable to eat a sufficient amount in this manner and the tube was reinserted.

Ms. Conroy was able to interact with her environment in some limited ways. She could move her head, neck, hands, and arms slightly. She was able to scratch herself and she had pulled at her bandages, feeding tube, and catheter. She moaned occasionally when moved or fed through the tube or when her bandages were changed. Her eyes sometimes followed individuals in the room. Her facial expressions were different when she was awake from when she was asleep. She smiled sometimes when her hair was combed or when she received a comforting rub.

Her physicians agreed that she was not brain dead, comatose, or in a persistent vegetative state. They agreed that her intellectual capacity was "very limited" and that her mental condition would probably never improve. She was described as "severely demented" and, as far as could be determined, she was unable to respond to verbal stimuli, and seemed to have no higher functioning or consciousness.

It was at this point that her nephew asked her physician to remove the nasogastric tube through which Ms. Conroy was receiving nourishment. Her physician refused to do so without a court order. The trial court granted Mr.

Whittemore permission to authorize removal of the tube but the decision was reversed on appeal. The case was subsequently heard by the New Jersey Supreme Court.

The testimony at trial had been inconclusive as to whether, or to what extent, Ms. Conroy was capable of experiencing pain. One of her physicians suggested that it was possible that she might be experiencing pain from her severely contracted limbs, or that the contractures were a reaction to pain, but that she did not necessarily suffer pain from the sores on her legs. Another of the physicians testified that it was "unclear" whether the feeding tube caused her pain or whether it was even possible that she was capable of experiencing pain. Both physicians testified that if the nasogastric tube were removed, Ms. Conroy would die of dehydration in about a week. Both agreed that the resulting thirst could be painful, but one of them testified that she would be unconscious long before she died. The two physicians disagreed as to whether removing the tube would be accepted medical practice.

Ms. Conroy had been described as leading a rather cloistered life. She had worked all her life for a cosmetics company and had never moved from her childhood home. She never married and had very few friends. She had been very close to her three sisters, all of whom had died. She had been retired for approximately fifteen years at the time of her hospitalization.

Thomas Whittemore was her only surviving relative. He had known her for over fifty years and had visited her weekly for four or five years prior to her hospitalization and had continued to visit her regularly since. The trial court concluded that there was no question that Mr. Whittemore had good intentions and that there was no conflict of interest due to any possible inheritance he might receive from his aunt's death.

Like the Quinlans, Ms. Conroy was a member of the Catholic Church and, as had been their situation, the request to remove the nasogastric tube was supported by a priest testifying that tube feeding of someone in such a condition was an example of extraordinary procedures. Ms. Conroy, like Mr. Bartling, died with the tube in place before the trial court decision could be heard by the appeals court. In reversing the decision of the trial court, the Appellate Division held that the right to terminate life-sustaining medical treatment based on a guardian's judgment was "limited to incurable and terminally ill patients who are brain dead, irreversibly comatose, or vegetative, and who would gain no medical benefit from continued treatment" (*In re* Conroy, p. 1219). It also ruled that a guardian's decision may "never be used to withhold nourishment, as opposed to the treatment or attempted curing of a disease, from an incompetent patient who is not comatose, brain dead, or vegetative, and whose death is not irreversibly imminent" (Ibid.). Both holdings were seen as being consistent with the decision of the New Jersey Supreme Court in *Quinlan*. Since the court of appeals decision in this case was reached at about the same time as that of the California Superior Court in the *Barber* case, one commentator suggested that removing feeding tubes was "Lawful Killing in CA, Homicide in NJ" (Annas, 1983).

The New Jersey Supreme Court reversed. Six of the seven justices joined in the opinion of the court. The sole dissenter concurred in the judgment but argued that the procedures the majority had endorsed were far too restrictive. The court was also eager to point out that its holding was restricted to nursing home residents (with a life expectancy of approximately one year or less) because they are governed by a number of state statutes that do not apply to elderly persons in other settings, such as those in hospitals or who are receiving care in their own homes.

The court began its analysis by restating its belief that the right to make medical care decisions is grounded in the common law doctrine of informed consent and the federal constitutional right of privacy (*In re* Conroy, p. 1222). Rejecting the argument that a death resulting from the refusal of medical treatment would be suicide, the court described the difference as being between self-determination (in the former case) and self-infliction or self-destruction (in the latter). Moreover, the court stated, "to the extent that our decision in *John F. Kennedy Memorial Hospital* v. *Heston* [one of the Jehovah's Witnesses cases discussed in the previous chapter] implies the contrary, we now overrule it" (Ibid., p. 1124, citation omitted).

There were several procedural mechanisms by which a decision to refuse or discontinue life-sustaining treatment, including feeding tubes, for persons like Ms. Conroy could be made. The first of these was described as a *subjective standard.*

The subjective standard would be satisfied when it could be clearly demonstrated that the decision is one that the incompetent person would make if able to do so. Such might be shown by a written document, such as a Living Will, or even an oral directive given to a family member, friend, or health care provider. It might also consist of a durable power of attorney or "it might take the form of reactions that the patient voiced regarding medical treatment administered to others" (Ibid., p. 1230).

This standard was *subjective.* The question is not what a *reasonable* or *average* person would have chosen to do under the circumstances, but what the particular patient would have done if able to choose for him or herself (Ibid., p. 1229).

There are often situations, suggested the court, where evidence that would satisfy such a standard doesn't exist. This, however, should not in and of itself preclude refusal or withdrawal of treatment when the patient is incompetent. In such situations, one might resort to either of two best interests tests: a limited-objective or a pure-objective test.

Under a *limited-objective* test, treatment could be withheld or withdrawn when there is *some* trustworthy evidence that the patient would have refused the treatment and the decision maker is satisfied that it is clear that the burdens to the patient's continued life with treatment outweigh the benefits of that life for him or her.

The *pure-objective* test was described as applying in the absence of trustworthy evidence, or any evidence at all, that the patient would have declined treatment. Even here, treatment might be refused if the burdens of the patient's life with treatment clearly and markedly outweigh the benefits that the patient derives from life. The court stressed that the "recurring, unavoidable and severe pain of the patient's life with the treatment should be such that the effect of administering life-sustaining treatment would be inhumane" (Ibid., p. 1232).

Recognizing that patients in nursing homes are usually "vulnerable" to abuse, the court established procedural requirements that would have to be met before any refusal of treatment could be honored. Because these mechanisms are largely unique to New Jersey, the interested reader is directed to the opinion itself for this information.

Since Ms. Conroy had died before either of the appeals had been decided, we have no way of knowing whether or not there would have been sufficient evidence for her to meet any of the standards described by the Supreme Court. The sole dissenter, Justice Handler, sensing that she would most likely have fallen into the pure-objective category, criticized the majority for the "overly restrictive" way in which they had described the requirements for meeting that standard. By focusing as they did on pain, he argued, the court had obviated other extremely important considerations.

> [S]ome people abhor dependence on others as much, or more, than they fear pain. Other individuals value personal privacy and dignity, and prize independence from others when their personal needs and bodily functions are involved. Finally, the ideal of bodily integrity may become more important than simply prolonging life at its most rudimentary level. Persons, like Miss Conroy, "may well have wished to avoid . . . [t]he ultimate horror [not of] death but the possibility of being maintained in limbo, in a sterile room, by machines controlled by strangers."   (Ibid., p. 1248, quoting Steel, 1976, p. 93)

Justice Handler also cited the President's Commission in support of his proposal that one must consider the *quality* of the life being sustained rather than merely life itself (President's Commission, 1983, p. 135). The total situation of the person *in extremis*, regardless of the presence or amount of physical pain, should be taken into consideration. This would include such things as the "presence of progressive, irreversible, and extreme physical deterioration, such as ulcers, lesions, gangrene, infection, incontinence and the like, which frequently afflict" such patients (Ibid., p. 1249). Caring for patients like this entails constant and extensive handling and manipulation of the body.

> At some point, such a course of treatment upon the insensate patient is bound to touch the sensibilities of even the most detached observer. Eventually pervasive bodily intrusions, even for the best motives, will arouse feelings akin to humiliation and mortification for the helpless patient. When cherished values of human dignity and personal privacy, which belong to every person living or dying, are sufficiently transgressed by what is being done to the individual, we should be ready to say, enough.   (Ibid., p. 1250)

In rather stark contrast to the way in which the New Jersey Supreme Court approached the *Conroy* case, New York's highest court, the Court of Appeals, ruled that a patient like Claire Conroy must continue to receive tube feedings unless there was clear and convincing evidence that she would have refused it if able to do so. Aside from Missouri, New York (and possibly Maine) is the only state to require such a high standard of proof as a precondition to stopping or, presumably, refusing treatment.

In re O'Connor

Mary O'Connor was a seventy-seven-year-old widow with two daughters, both of whom were practical nurses. Since the death of her husband she had been living alone for nearly twenty years. Until the time of her retirement in her early seventies, she had been employed in hospital administration for twenty years.

Mrs. O'Connor was not unfamiliar with death and dying. She had seen a number of her close relatives die from cancer, including her husband, who died from a brain tumor, and two of her brothers. Her stepmother had also died of cancer.

In 1985, Mrs. O'Connor suffered the first in a series of strokes causing brain damage and related disabilities, leaving her unable to care for herself. After discharge from the hospital, she lived with one of her daughters and was cared for by both. Less than two years later, she suffered another major stroke which further impaired her already severely limited ability to function. Since her daughters were unable to care for her at home, she was transferred from the hospital to a long-term geriatric care facility associated with it.

In conjunction with this transfer, her daughters submitted a document signed by both of them, indicating that their mother had expressed the wish in many conversations that "no artificial life support be started or maintained in order to continue or sustain her life" and that they wanted the request to be honored. The document was placed in Mrs. O'Connor's file.

When her condition worsened she was transferred back to the hospital. She was suffering from dehydration, sepsis (infection), and probably pneumonia. She had lost her gag reflex and it was impossible for her to swallow foods or liquid. Although still incompetent, she seemed to improve after receiving fluids, limited nourishment, and antibiotics intravenously; however, her inability to swallow persisted and her physician planned to insert a nasogastric tube. Her daughters objected and the matter was presented to the hospital ethics committee which concluded that it would be inappropriate to withhold the intubation.

The hospital sought a court order authorizing the insertion of the nasogastric tube. The court heard testimony stating that Mrs. O'Connor was suffering from "multiinfarct dementia as a result of the strokes" (*In re O'Connor,* 1988, p. 609). She was conscious and capable of responding to simple questions or requests, sometimes by squeezing the questioner's hand and sometimes verbally. It was stated that it was doubtful that she would ever regain significant mental capacity. Her physician stated that "death by starvation and especially thirst was a painful way to die and that Mrs. O'Connor would, therefore, experience extreme, intense discomfort since she is conscious, alert, capable of feeling pain, and sensitive even to mild discomfort" (Ibid., p. 610). This opinion was contested by another neurologist testifying on behalf of Mrs. O'Connor and her daughters. He felt that her extensive brain damage would prevent her from feeling pain and that she would simply become more lethargic and unresponsive and would ultimately die. Any pain that she might experience, he felt, could be controlled with drugs to keep her comfortable.

Neither of these two physicians had known Mrs. O'Connor prior to her hospitalization and, therefore, knew nothing of her attitudes toward the use of life-sustaining measures. However, there was testimony from a longtime friend and co-worker, as well as from her daughters, that Mrs. O'Connor had strong feelings about the use of life-sustaining medical treatment, having previously said such things as, "I would never want to be a burden on anyone and I would never want to lose my dignity before I passed away" and expressing the opinion that it is "monstrous to keep someone alive by using machinery, things like that, when they are not going to get better" (Ibid., p. 611). Mrs. O'Connor was described as a "very religious woman" who "felt that nature should take its course and artificial means" should not be used to prolong life (Ibid.). The trial court granted the hospital's application because all three witnesses agreed that Mrs. O'Connor had never specifically discussed providing food or water with medical assistance nor had she ever said that she would refuse treatment even if it would produce a painful death. The decision was affirmed by both the appellate court and the high court by a five-to-two decision.

In reviewing the decisions of two lower courts, the Court of Appeals minimized the significance of Mrs. O'Connor's previous expressions about life-sustaining treatment:

> Although Mrs. O'Connor's statements about her desire to decline life-sustaining treatments were repeated over a number of years, there is nothing, other than speculation, to persuade the fact finder that her expectations were more than immediate reactions to the unsettling experience of seeing or hearing of

another's unnecessarily prolonged death. Her comments—that she would never want to lose her dignity before she passed away, that nature should be permitted to take its course, that it is "monstrous" to use life-support machinery—are, in fact, no different than those that many of us might make after witnessing an agonizing death. Similarly, her statements to the effect that she would not want to be a burden to anyone are the type of statements that older people frequently, almost invariably make. If such statements were routinely held to be clear and convincing proof of a general intent to decline all medical treatment once incompetency sets in, few nursing home patients would ever receive life-sustaining medical treatment in the future. The aged and infirm would be placed at grave risk if the law uniformly but unrealistically treated the expression of such sentiments as a calm and deliberate resolve to decline all life-sustaining medical assistance once the speaker is silenced by mental disability. That Mrs. O'Connor made similar statements over a long period of time does not, by itself, transform them from the type of comments that are often made casually into the type of statements that demonstrate a seriousness of purpose necessary to satisfy the "clear and convincing evidence" standard. (Ibid., p. 614)

Two factors seemed to influence the court's decision in the *O'Connor* case, the first more so than the second. The first factor was that Mrs. O'Connor had failed to express her wishes about the kind of life-sustaining treatment she would wish to refuse and the circumstances under which she would refuse it. It might be argued that few people would have the foresight to do this and that failure to predict their fate should not be used to frustrate their will. The second factor was the concern about the kind of death that would likely result from dehydration and/or starvation. While there is a differing of opinion in the literature about the "painfulness" of such a death, there seems to be an emerging consensus that such deaths are not always painful and that they need not be experienced as such.

Dame Cicely Saunders, founder of the modern hospice movement and chairperson of St. Christopher's Hospice in England, is but one of many to suggest that nutrition and/or hydration provided by tube may do little to benefit the dying patient. Rather than dying of starvation, or even of acute dehydration, the withholding of food and/or water by tube often allows death to occur from a debilitation of all systems; the provision of food and water by tube may only serve to increase discomfort. Any feelings of thirst are better addressed by offering fluids gently by mouth, by providing ice to suck, and by good mouth care (*Concern for Dying Newsletter*, Fall 1986). For the terminally ill patient, tube feeding might even exacerbate painful symptoms such as nausea, diarrhea, bloating, and other forms of gastrointestinal distress.

For those who wish to avoid having their dying technologically prolonged, and long for the "good old days" where people died quietly in their beds, it would be useful to realize that such deaths were often accompanied by and frequently the result of dehydration and starvation. As people approached the time of death, they often drastically limited their consumption of food and liquids. Rather than regarding themselves as "deprived" of such, they seemed to lose their appetites and would often stop eating altogether. They became progressively weaker and death would be the inevitable outcome. Their deaths were seldom attributable to "starvation" or "dehydration" but were, instead, regarded as "natural causes."

Even among those who have died as a result of hunger strikes or prolonged fasting, there are seldom complaints about pain or discomfort. Now, however, when an ill and/or elderly person stops eating, it is seen as a problem that needs to be remedied and the cure is typically the insertion of a feeding tube. The question to be asked is whether this always provides a net benefit for the patient.

The Never Competent Patient

Our final consideration in an attempt to understand the various dimensions of the right to refuse life-sustaining medical treatment will raise the question of decision making when the person on behalf of whom treatment is to be refused or withdrawn has never been competent to express his or her wishes on the subject. Does this mean, as would seem to be suggested from the previous cases of now incompetent, but previously competent, adults, that treatment can never be refused by their next of kin or other appropriate surrogates, or are there circumstances under which such decisions would be respected? While the law here is less settled than with the previously discussed circumstances, there are some cases that might help light the way.

Superintendent of Belchertown State School v. Saikewicz

The first case to address this issue involved Joseph Saikewicz, a sixty-seven-year-old man who was a resident of Belchertown State School in Massachusetts. Mr. Saikewicz was described as "profoundly retarded," with an IQ estimated at ten and a mental age of two years and eight months. He had been institutionalized all his life and was unable to communicate verbally. When Mr. Saikewicz was diagnosed as having acute myeloblastic leukemia, an attorney at the institution petitioned the Probate Court for the appointment of a guardian with the authority to make decisions concerning his medical care. Although he had two elderly sisters, they had not been involved in his life and they choose not to participate in any treatment decisions. A guardian *ad litem* was appointed to represent Mr. Saikewicz's interests. The guardian *ad litem* reported that the illness was incurable and that, although chemotherapy was the medically indicated course of treatment, it would cause Mr. Saikewicz significant adverse side effects and discomfort. These, he stated, as well as the inability of Mr. Saikewicz to understand the treatment and the fear and pain he would suffer as a result, outweighed the limited prospect of any benefit from treatment, namely, the possibility of some uncertain, but limited, extension of life. He recommended that "not treating Mr. Saikewicz would be in his best interests" (*Superintendent of Belchertown State School* v. *Saikewicz*, 1977, p. 419).

The Probate Court held that the chemotherapy need not be provided. The judge seemed to rely primarily upon testimony, including that of two physicians, that indicated (1) that persons over age sixty have more difficulty tolerating chemotherapy and the treatment is likely to be less successful than in younger patients; (2) the treatments cause severe anemia and this, along with the possibility of bleeding and infections, will require a number of transfusions; (3) remission of the leukemia is achieved in only 30 to 50 percent of the cases; and (4) if remission does occur it typically lasts for between two and thirteen months, although longer periods are possible (Ibid., p. 420).

Clearly, the decision was influenced by Mr. Saikewicz's mental status:

> There was testimony as to the importance of having the full cooperation of the patient during the initial weeks of the chemotherapy procedure as well as during follow-up visits. For example, the evidence was that it would be necessary to administer drugs intravenously for extended periods of time—twelve or twenty-four hours a day for up to five days. The inability of Saikewicz to comprehend the purpose of the treatment, combined with his physical strength [he had been described as "physically strong and well built"], led the doctors to testify that Saikewicz would probably have to be restrained to prevent him from tampering with the intravenous devices. Such forcible restraint could, in addition to increasing the patient's discomfort, lead to complications such as pneumonia.   (Ibid., p. 421)

The decision of the Probate Court was appealed directly to the Supreme Judicial Court, the state's highest court, which unanimously affirmed on July 9, 1976. Mr. Saikewicz died slightly less than two months later. Death was due to bronchial pneumonia, a complication of the leukemia. His death was described as being without pain or discomfort (Ibid., p. 422).

The Saikewicz court was the first in a long succession to identify the "interests of the State," against which the right of a patient to refuse treatment must be balanced. These interests were distilled from a review of the legal literature and were identified as (1) the preservation of life, (2) the protection of the interest of innocent third parties, (3) the prevention of suicide, and (4) maintaining the ethical integrity of the medical profession (Ibid.). Against these were balanced the factors which the Probate Court had identified as weighing against the administration of chemotherapy. They were (1) Mr. Saikewicz's age, (2) the probable side effects of treatment, (3) the low chances of producing a remission, (4) the certainty that treatment would cause suffering, (5) his inability to cooperate, and (6) the quality of life possible for him even if the treatment would produce a remission. It was in regard to this final factor, his quality of life, that the Supreme Court seemed to feel that an interpretive comment was necessary.

The court stated that "to the extent that this . . . equates the value of life with any measure of their quality of life, we firmly reject it" (Ibid., p. 432). Commenting that this did not seem to be the intent of the Probate Court and that there was every indication that the judge and all the parties had demonstrated great respect for the dignity and worth of Mr. Saikewicz's life, the Court offered the following "clarification." It suggested that, "rather than reading the judge's formulation in a manner that demeans the value of the life of one who is mentally retarded, the vague, and perhaps ill-chosen, term 'quality of life' should be understood as a reference to the continuing state of pain and disorientation precipitated by the chemotherapy treatment" (Ibid., p. 432).

The court endorsed a substituted-judgment standard for making decisions in cases such as this. In essence, this requires the decision maker to "stand in the shoes of the incompetent" and make the decision that he or she would make if he or she were able to do so. While such might be reasonable in situations where the surrogate had some knowledge of the values of the incompetent, as was the case with the parents of Karen Ann Quinlan and Nancy Cruzan, for some like Mr. Saikewicz, who had never been competent, the task becomes much more elusive. The task was complicated even further by the court's instructions that the decision "should be that which would be made by the incompetent person, if that person were competent, but taking into account the present and future incompetency of the individual as one of the factors which would necessarily enter into the decision-making process of the competent person" (Ibid., p. 431). What the court seems to be saying here is that if Mr. Saikewicz, who had been incompetent all his life, were suddenly lucid at the age of sixty-seven and realized he had leukemia, realized the benefits and risks of the proposed treatments and further realized that immediately after making his decision he would return to his previously incompetent state, the decision to be honored is that which he would have made. In their scramble to avoid endorsing a decision to allow someone else to simply say that, given the facts of the case, it would be in Mr. Saikewicz's best interests to refuse treatment, the Supreme Judicial Court produced an explanation worthy of Lewis Carroll's Mad Hatter.

Yes, the term *quality of life* can be vague and ill chosen. And yes, it is neither wise nor desirable, under most circumstances, to allow others to refuse or discontinue treatment for incompetents based on the decision maker's view of the quality of an incompetent's life. And it should especially concern us if that power were to be put into the hands of parties unrelated to and/or emotionally uninvolved with the incompetent, even more so if that power were to reside with "government" or "the state." But, that is not to suggest that there may not be situations where the quality of life, as seen through the eyes of the incompetent, is not the appropriate basis for refusal or discontinuation of life-sustaining medical treatment. And, in spite of the fact that the *Quinlan* court specifically disavowed that the decision to allow removal of the ventilator was based on the quality of Ms. Quinlan's life, it is easily argued that it was. And that doing so was, and is, appropriate both ethically and legally.

In re Storar

A similar case arose in New York State several years later, concerning a profoundly retarded man by the name of John Storar. Mr. Storar, who was reported to have a mental age of "about eighteen months" was fifty-two years old and had been a resident of a state facility for the mentally retarded since age five. His closest relative was his seventy-seven-year-old mother, a widow, who visited him almost daily. He was her only child.

The problem began with blood in his urine. When physicians first noticed it they asked his mother for permission to conduct the necessary diagnostic tests. She initially refused, but after further discussions, she gave consent. The tests showed cancer of the bladder. The recommended treatment was radiation therapy. Mrs. Storar was appointed as guardian and, with her consent, Mr. Storar received therapy for six weeks, after which the disease was reported to be in remission.

Approximately six months later, there was, again, blood in his urine. Cauterization was tried unsuccessfully. At that point, the physicians concluded that the cancer was terminal. Since Mr. Storar was being weakened by the blood loss, the physicians asked his mother for permission to administer transfusions. Although initially she refused to authorize the transfusions, she shortly thereafter withdrew her objection. Mr. Storar had been receiving approximately two units of blood every two weeks or so when, after several such treatments, his mother asked that the transfusions be stopped. At this point, the director of the institution where Mr. Storar resided petitioned the Probate Court for permission to continue with the transfusions.

All of the testimony at trial was consistent. John Storar had metastatic bladder cancer. His life expectancy was estimated at three to six months. It was also conceded that Mr. Storar found the transfusions disagreeable. He was often sedated before his transfusions to calm him. There was some testimony to the fact, that, given the status of his cancer, the transfusions may only prolong suffering and that treatment could properly be limited to administering pain killers. Mrs. Storar stated that she only wanted her son to be "comfortable" (*In re* Storar, p. 368). The Probate Court found that his mother was the person in the best position to determine what he would want and that she "wants his suffering to stop and believes that he would want this also" (Ibid.). The case was appealed and the decision was affirmed. A divided Court of Appeals—which, as was mentioned earlier, is the highest court in the State of

New York—reversed the decision. In spite of the transfusions, which continued regularly while the case was on appeal, Mr. Storar died after arguments were held but before the Court of Appeals had issued an opinion. The majority stated that a parent may not deprive a child of life-saving treatment, however well intentioned.

The matter of making decisions about the use of life-sustaining medical treatment is, indeed, a difficult one, especially if the incompetency has been lifelong. On the same day that the New York Court of Appeals handed down its decision in the *Storar* case, they also decided an appeal brought on behalf of an elderly man in a PVS (*Eichner* v. *Dillon*, 1981). The major difference between the two cases, both of which involved "incompetents," was that the PVS patient had been competent for all of his life before the tragic accident that had permanently incapacitated him.

Eichner v. *Dillon*

Brother Fox was an eighty-three-year-old member of the Society of Mary, a Catholic religious order, for over sixty-six years. He sustained a hernia while working in the garden one day. He was, at the time, in good health, except for the hernia. While undergoing surgery for repair of the hernia, Brother Fox went into cardiac arrest and his subsequent brain damage left him in a state of permanent unconsciousness. Like Karen Ann Quinlan, he was maintained on a ventilator.

Father Eichner, who was described as Brother Fox's closest friend and the Director of the Society, asked that the ventilator be removed. The request was supported by Brother Fox's ten nieces and nephews, his only surviving relatives. In affirming the decisions of the two lower courts that had agreed that Father Eichner's petition should be granted, the high court found it persuasive that Brother Fox had clearly and repeatedly expressed his unwillingness to be maintained under such circumstances, beginning with discussions about the *Quinlan* case which had arisen some years previously. As so often happens when cases like this get into the legal system, Brother Fox died, still attached to the ventilator, during the appeals.

Conclusions

Although there are some scattered cases, primarily those decided by lower courts many years ago, that would suggest differently, there seems to be a strong consensus that competent patients have an unrestricted right to refuse all forms of life-sustaining medical treatment. The common law doctrine of informed consent forbids physicians from forcing treatment on unwilling or inadequately informed patients. There are also constitutional underpinnings of a

Box 3–2 *Withholding or Withdrawing Life-Prolonging Medical Treatment*

The social commitment of the physician is to sustain life and relieve suffering. Where the performance of one duty conflicts with the other, the preferences of the patients should prevail. If the patient is incompetent to act in his own behalf and did not previously indicate his preferences, *the family or other surrogate decision maker*, in concert with the physician, must act in the *best interest* of the patient.

(*Current Opinions of the Council of Ethical and Judicial Affairs of the American Medical Association—1989.* Chicago, IL: American Medical Association, 1989, Section 2.20, emphasis added)

right of self-determination in choosing the kind and amount of medical treatment that is to be provided. Although some courts, starting with the New Jersey Supreme Court in *Quinlan,* have identified this as a fundamental right of privacy, the majority of the U.S. Supreme Court in *Cruzan* refused to do so; they regarded it, instead, as a liberty interest. The difference would seem to be that, in previous Supreme Court cases, privacy has been treated as a right of such importance that it virtually trumps any state interests that would restrict it unless those interests were compelling and the restrictions were very narrowly drawn. A liberty interest, by comparison, will ensure some rights, but the burden the state must bear to demonstrate an interest sufficient to overcome the right in question is much less. The difference between fundamental and less important rights will be discussed quite fully in Chapter 7.

In those situations where the question is whether or not treatment can be refused by someone acting on behalf of an incompetent patient, the controversy is mainly about the wishes of the incompetent. In cases that have involved previously competent patients, the decisions have hinged on whether or not the patient, now incompetent, had previously expressed an intention. Courts in some states have required that their evidence of such be "clear and convincing;" most states have demonstrated a willingness to accept less stringent levels of proof.

Where the patient is incompetent, and has been so throughout life, or where the patient is now incompetent and although previously competent has never expressed an opinion about the use of life-sustaining medical treatment, the decision-making process becomes somewhat more difficult. Massachusetts, in *Saikewicz,* and New York, in *Storar,* are examples of states that arrived at quite different decisions with rather similar circumstances.

Many states, and most commentators, seem to agree that the absence of information about the desires of the incompetent should not foreclose any decision to withhold or withdraw treatment. While it is preferable to make decisions based on principles such as autonomy and substituted judgment, decisions based on the best interests of the patient should be honored in the absence of such information. Whereas the former are subjective standards based on idiosyncratic or highly personal values, the latter is an objective standard based on what an "average, reasonable person in the patient's position" would do (President's Commission, 1983, pp. 134–136; Weir and Gostin, 1990; National Center for State Courts, 1991; The Hastings Center, 1987). Since polls have repeatedly shown the vast majority of Americans would choose not to have their lives sustained under circumstances of permanent unconsciousness, a best interests standard would support decisions such as those of the Quinlan, Brophy, and Cruzan families.

There also seems to be consensus that these problems should, to the extent possible, be kept out of the courts. Writing in *The New England Journal of Medicine,* Lo, Rouse, and Dornbrand expressed this as follows:

> We suggest that families generally be allowed to make decisions based on the previously expressed wishes and best interests of incompetent patients. In the cases presented here [writing about *Cruzan* and *O'Connor*], there was considerable evidence that the patients would not have wanted treatment and that their families were motivated by love. Nor was there any disagreement among the family members. We believe that the courts should be involved only when the surrogates are not acting in good faith or when the decisions of surrogates cannot be considered by a reasonable person to be consistent with the patient's wishes or best interests. Physicians or hospitals that challenge the family's decisions ought to have the burden of proof in court. (1990, p. 1231)

Although the cases discussed in this chapter, and many others like them, have attracted a great deal of attention, it should be noted that most decisions to withhold or withdraw life-sustaining medical treatment are not made by courts. They are made quietly at the bedside of the patient. Often they wind up in court because physicians and/or hospitals, often driven by overly cautious hospital attorneys, have refused to stop aggressive and unwanted treatment, not because they feel that it will provide a net benefit to the patient, but because they fear incurring some liability if they don't treat. Such a fear is entirely ungrounded. There are no cases in which a physician or hospital has been successfully sued for withholding or withdrawing life-sustaining medical treatment for an incompetent patient at the request of the family (Meisel, 1989, p. 160).

Even the courts that have handed down these widely publicized cases have cautioned that the decisions are best made outside the legal system. Some, like the New Jersey Supreme Court, have suggested that the matter is best suited to resolution by the legislature. They have recommended that state legislatures pass laws to clarify the process by which decisions about LSMT are to be made. These laws are the subject of the next chapter.

Summary

Although it is well recognized in both law and medicine that a competent person has the right to make his or her own decisions about all forms of medical treatment, including the refusal of life-sustaining medical treatment, deciding about the appropriate course of treatment when the person is no longer competent is much more problematic. The many difficulties presented in these situations are illustrated by the cases described in this chapter. The *Quinlan* case was the first to address the respective rights of the patient, the patient's family, and the state where the question was whether or not a ventilator could be removed from a patient diagnosed as being in a persistent vegetative state. The controversy broadened when, in the line of cases beginning with Clarence Herbert (*Barber* v. *Superior Court*), the treatment in question shifted from a ventilator to a feeding tube. For some, the distinction was based on the *kind* of treatment in question: ventilators were an example of extraordinary medical care that could be refused; feeding tubes were part of basic care, simple treatment that must always be provided to all patients regardless of the circumstances. The Massachusetts Supreme Judicial Court was the first State Supreme Court to rule, in the *Brophy* case, that the use of feeding tubes should be evaluated in the same way as other forms of life-sustaining medical treatment. The question would ultimately be addressed by the U.S. Supreme Court in the case of Nancy Cruzan. In its *Cruzan* decision, the court affirmed this position, that competent adults had the right to refuse all forms of life-sustaining medical treatment, including feeding tubes, but that the State of Missouri—where Nancy Cruzan resided—had the right, if it so chose, to require that there be clear and convincing evidence that this would be the choice Nancy would make if she were able to do so.

The *Wanglie* case in Minnesota provides an opportunity to examine the flip side of the line of cases culminating with *Cruzan*. What should the outcome be when it is the physicians who are seeking to stop life-sustaining medical treatment for a person in a persistent vegetative state and they are opposed by the patient's family? Like *Cruzan*, the decision is to be based upon the choice that the patient would have made if able to do so.

The persistent vegetative state would seem to many to be a fate worse than death. It is a condition where life can be sustained indefinitely although the patient is completely devoid of the experience of living. For those who hold such a view, the decision to stop treatment is an easy one. But what about those cases where the degree of participation in the experience of living is somewhat less drastically impaired? What of those who are merely (?) demented? Here, as in the *Conroy* and *O'Connor* cases, the courts have been more reluctant to authorize abatement of treatment decisions made by family members. So, too, with some of the cases involving never competent patients such as John Storar.

These cases, true life stories all, should serve to convince all of the need to put their wishes in writing about the kind of medical treatment they would consider appropriate should the time come when they are no longer able to make their own decisions. Whether motivated by a concern about preserving one's own sense of personal dignity or by concerns about the well-being—either emotional or financial or both—of their family, this is a step that each of us needs to take . . . now.

Study Questions

1. What is the significance of the Quinlan case in regard to the right to refuse life-sustaining medical treatment on behalf of a person in a persistent vegetative state?

2. How does the persistent vegetative state (PVS) differ from "brain death"?

3. Although the early cases, including *Quinlan,* often used the terms *ordinary* and *extraordinary* to describe the kind of treatment which could not and could be required, this distinction is no longer in vogue. What terminology is now being used to differentiate between treatment that is likely to be required and that which might be declined?

4. In the text there is a suggestion that the *Quinlan* court may have confused the role of an ethics committee with that of a prognosis committee. In what way might this be so?

5. Since *Quinlan* was the first case involving a patient diagnosed as being in a PVS where the court approved the abatement of LSMT, of what significance is the case involving Clarence Herbert (*Barber* v. *Superior Court*)?

6. What did Justice Nolan mean when he wrote in his dissent in the *Brophy* case that the decision was "but another triumph for the forces of secular humanism (modern paganism) which have now succeeded in imposing their anti-life principles at both ends of life's spectrum"?

7. What were the similarities between the *Quinlan* and the *Cruzan* cases? What were the differences?

8. The authors refer to the *Cruzan* decision by the United States Supreme Court as a "good news/bad news" decision. What was the "good" news? The "bad"?

9. What is the difference between the following standards of proof (a) beyond a reasonable doubt, (b) the preponderance of the evidence, and (c) clear and convincing evidence. Which of these is typically used in deciding civil disputes?

10. The U.S. Supreme Court, in *Cruzan,* did *not* describe the right to refuse unwanted medical treatment as a *fundamental right* but, rather, as a *liberty interest.* What is the significance of this distinction?

11. Why do the authors describe the *Wanglie* case as the flip side of the *Quinlan-Cruzan* line of cases?

12. The *Quinlan* and *Conroy* cases were both decided by the same court, yet the decisions differed. In what ways were the facts in these two cases different and how did the decisions differ?

13. How did the decision of New Jersey's highest court, in *Conroy,* differ from that of New York's highest court, in *O'Connor* ? Are the facts in *O'Connor* more like those in *Conroy* or *Quinlan*?

14. *Saikewicz* and *Storer* are both about never competent patients. In what ways do

cases such as these raise issues that are not found in the cases that precede them in the text?

15. Aside from the fact that they were decided by different courts, what was the basis for the difference in the decisions in the *Saikewicz* and *Storar* cases?

References

Ackerman, F. (1991). The Significance of a Wish. *Hastings Center Report* (July-August): 27–29.

American Academy of Neurology. (1989). Position of the American Academy of Neurology on certain aspects of the care and management of the persistent vegetative state patient. *Neurology,* 39:125–126.

American Medical Association, Statement of the Council on Ethical and Judicial Affairs. (1986). *Withholding or Withdrawing Life Prolonging Medical Treatment.* Chicago: Author.

American Neurological Association (ANA) Committee on Ethical Affairs. (1993). Persistent vegetative state: Report of the American Neurological Association Committee on Ethical Affairs. *Annals of Neurology,* 33:386–390.

Angell, M. (1984). Respecting the autonomy of competent patients. *NEJM,* 310:1115–1116.

___. (1991). The case of Helga Wanglie: A new kind of "right to die" case. *NEJM,* 325(7): 511–512.

Annas, G. J. (1983). Nonfeeding: Lawful killing in CA, homicide in NJ. *Hastings Center Report* (December): 19–20.

___. (1985). Fashion and freedom: When artificial feeding should be withdrawn. *AJPH,* 75:685–688.

Barber v. *Superior Court,* 147 Cal. App. 3d 1006, 195 Cal. Rptr. 484 (1983) aff'g *People* v. *Barber,* No. A025586 (Los Angeles Mun. Ct., Mar. 9, 1983).

Brophy v. *New England Sinai Hosp., Inc.,* 398 Mass. 417, 497 N.E. 2d 626 (1986).

Celesia, G. G. (1993). Persistent vegetative state. *Annals of Neurology,* 33:391.

Conroy, In re, 188 N.J. Super. 523, 457 A. 2d 1232 (Ch. Div.), rev'd 190 N. J. Super. 453.

Council on Scientific Affairs and Council on Ethical and Judicial Affairs (American Medical Association). (1990). Persistent vegetative state and the decision to withdraw or withhold life support. *JAMA,* 263:426–430.

Cruzan v. *Director, Missouri Department of Health,* 497 U.S. 261, 110 S. Ct. 2841 (1990).

Cruzan v. *Harmon,* 760 S. W. 2d 408 (1988).

Denial of tube feeding not typically painful, Dame Cicely writes. (1986, fall). *Concern for Dying Newsletter,* 12:3, p. 2.

Eichner v. *Dillon* (In re *Eichner*), 102 Misc. 2d 184, 423 N.Y.S. 2d 517 (1980), *modified,* 52 N.Y. 2d 363, 420 N.E. 2d 64, 438 N.Y.S. 266, *cert. denied,* 454 U.S. 858 (1981).

Family Life Division, U.S. Catholic Conference. (1974). *Respect Life.* Washington, D.C.: Author.

Hastings Center, The. (1987). *Guidelines on the Termination of Life-Sustaining Treatment and the Care of the Dying.* Briarcliff Manor, NY: Author.

In re: The Conservatorship of Helga M. Wanglie (1991), reprinted in *Issues in Law & Medicine,* 7(3): 369–377.

Jennett, B., and F. Plum. (1972). Persistent vegetative state after brain damage: A syndrome in search of a name. *Lancet,* 1:734–737.

Lo, B., F. Rouse, and L. Dornbrand. (1990). Family decision making on trial: Who decides for incompetent patients? *NEJM,* 332:1228–1232.

McCormick, B. (1991). Not enough data on lives, costs. *American Medical News* (January 7): 23.

Meisel, A. (1989). *The Right to Die.* New York: John Wiley & Sons.

Miles, S. H. (1991). Informed demand for "non-beneficial" medical treatment. *NEJM,* 325(7): 512–515.

Multi-Society Task Force on PVS. (1994a). Medical aspects of the persistent vegetative state: (First of two parts). *NEJM,* 330: 1499–1508. (1994b). Medical aspects of the persistent vegetative state: (Second of two parts). *NEJM,* 330: 1572–1579.

National Center for State Courts. (1991). *Guidelines for State Court Decision Making in Authorizing or Withholding Life-Sustaining Medical Treatment.* Williamsburg, VA: Author.

O'Connor, In re, 72 N.Y. 2d 517, 531 N.E. 2d 607, 534 N.Y.S. 2d 886 (1988).

President's Commission for the Study of Ethical Problems in Medicine and Biomedical and Behavioral Research. (1983). *Deciding to Forego Life-Sustaining Treatment.* Washington, D.C.: U.S. Government Printing Office.

Quinlan, In re, 137 N.J. Super. 227, 348 A. 2d 801 (Ch. Div., 1975), rev'd, 70 N.J. 10, 355 A. 2d 647, *cert. denied sub nom. Garger v. New Jersey,* 429 U.S. 922, 50 L. Ed. 2d 289, 97 S. Ct. 319 (1976) overruled in part, *In re Conroy,* 98 N. J. 321, 486 A. 2d 1209 (1985).

Rasmussen v. Fleming, 154 Ariz. 207, 741 P. 2d 674 (1987).

Rie, M. A. (1991). The limits of a wish. *Hastings Center Report,* July/August, pp. 24–27.

Roe v. Wade, 410 U.S. 113 (1973).

Storar, In re, 106 Misc. 2d 880, 433 N.Y.S. 2d 388 (Sup. Ct.) aff'd, 78 A. 2d, 1013, 434 N.Y.S. 2d 46 (1980), rev'd 52 N.Y. 2d 363, 420 N.E. 2d 64, 438 N.Y.S. 2d 266, *cert. denied,* 454 U.S. 858 (1981).

Superintendent of Belchertown State School v. Saikewicz, 373 Mass. 728, 370 N.E. 2d 417 (1977).

Teel, K. (1975). The physician's dilemma: A doctor's view: What the law should be. *Baylor L. Rev* 27(1):6–9.

Weir, R. F. (1989). *Abating Treatment with Critically Ill Patients: Ethical and Legal Limits to the Medical Prolongation of Life.* New York: Oxford University Press.

Weir, R. F., and L. Gostin. (1990). Decision to abate life-sustaining treatment for nonautonomous patients: Ethical standards and legal liability for physicians after *Cruzan. JAMA,* 264:1846–1853.

CHAPTER 4

Controlling Your Medical Destiny Through Advance Directives

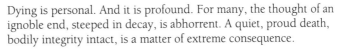

Dying is personal. And it is profound. For many, the thought of an ignoble end, steeped in decay, is abhorrent. A quiet, proud death, bodily integrity intact, is a matter of extreme consequence.

Justice Harry A. Blackmun, Dissent in *Cruzan* v. *Director* (1990)

Every human being of sound mind and adult years has a right to determine what shall be done to his own body.

Justice Benjamin H. Cardozo, *Schloendorff* v. *Society of New York Hospital* (1914)

As should be obvious from the preceding two chapters, competent patients have the right to refuse medical treatment, all forms of medical treatment, regardless of the consequences. The foundations of this right are found in the common law (judicial decisions that have become part of the Anglo-American heritage), in Constitutions (both state and federal), and in statutes (the laws passed by legislative bodies at the state and national level). The common law moorings of this right were recognized more than a hundred years ago by the United States Supreme Court: "[N]o right is held more sacred, or is more carefully guarded by the common law, than the right of every individual to the possession and control of his person, free from all restraint or interference of others, unless by clear and unquestionable authority of law" (*Union Pacific R. Co.* v. *Botsford,* 1891, p. 251).

Cruzan was but one of the most recent in a long line of cases heard in both state and federal courts to recognize this freedom to decide for oneself whether to accept or refuse even life-sustaining medical treatment. The majority of the *Cruzan* court viewed this right as part of a Fourteenth Amendment liberty interest; at least some members of the minority saw it as falling within the fundamental right of privacy guaranteed by the Constitution. Consequently, it would be unusual to find a situation today where medical care was being forced upon an unwilling recipient capable of making a decision to refuse it. The difficulty, as was shown in the line of cases beginning with *Quinlan,* typically arises only when the person who is the recipient of the care is not competent to make decisions, either because he or she has never been competent or has become incompetent through accident or illness.

People in the former category, the never competent, present a particularly perplexing problem. Because they have never possessed the qualities of intellect or reason to enable them to make such decisions, some courts have refused to allow medical treatment to be withheld or withdrawn under any circumstances. This was the outcome of the *Storar* case discussed in the previous chapter. Still other courts, as was true with the *Saikewicz* case, have allowed the withholding or withdrawal of LSMT if it could be demonstrated to be what the person would have chosen had he or she been able to do so. Although the *Saikewicz* court called this a *substituted-judgment* test, and it has been criticized for it, it seems that what the court was really talking about was whether or not the proposed course of action was in the *best interest* of the patient. That is, would a reasonable person in such a situation make the decision that the court is being asked to approve.

The use of the phrase "substituted judgment" should more correctly be reserved for those situations wherein a decision is to be made for a previously competent person on the basis of attitudes and/or values that were either directly expressed or might be inferred from behavior or life style before losing competence. Even then, some courts, as was true with the Supreme Court decision in *Cruzan,* may require that such evidence be of the highest and most reliable caliber, that is, clear and convincing. The majority of courts that have been asked to rule on cases of this type, however, have required a lesser standard of proof, insisting only that the choice be supported by a preponderance of the evidence, that is, that it is more likely than not that such is the choice that the previously competent patient would make if he or she were now able to do so. Although the problem of decision making has increased with the growing ability of medicine to sustain life for ever-lengthening periods of time under increasingly fragile circumstances, the problem is not a new one.

Living Wills

The idea of putting your wishes about LSMT in writing as a means of protecting your right to exercise control over such decisions when incompetent was first proposed by Luis Kutner in 1930. Kutner (1987) coined the term *living will* to describe such a directive. Although it was not widely accepted at first, its popularity was boosted by a number of occurrences.

The concept was endorsed by right-to-die groups which were founded in the middle to late 1930s. It was not until 1967, when the newly formed Euthanasia Educational Council decided to promote the use of the living will, that the document became widely recognized. The Euthanasia Educational Council, which will be discussed more fully later in the book, was started as a sister organization of the Society for the Right to Die, which was formed in 1938. The living will was also popularized through the media, especially by the widely read syndicated advice columnists Abigail Van Buren ("Dear Abby") and her twin sister Ann Landers ("Dear Ann Landers"). Living wills were further popularized from publicity about the *Quinlan* (1976) case in New Jersey, the passage of state laws granting them statutory recognition, and, most recently, the *Cruzan* (1990) decision by the United States Supreme Court.

A living will is a document you execute while competent to describe the kind of medical care you would want to receive or refuse if a time comes when you are unable to make decisions for yourself. It, along with durable powers of attorney for health care (to be discussed below), is referred to as an *advance directive*. Because living wills typically specify the conditions or circumstances under which you would choose to refuse (or accept) treatment, they are known as *instructional* advance directives. (See Box 4–1.)

Another type of advance directive that can be used for the same purpose involves the appointment of a representative to make the kind of decisions for you that you would make for yourself if you were able to do so. Sometimes described as a *proxy* advance directive, this, too, has gained wide acceptance since the first law (statute) recognizing it as a legal form of delegated decision-making authority was passed by the State of Delaware in 1982. Since it is difficult to predict the various circumstances you might encounter in the future, many people feel that it makes better sense to entrust decision-making to a carefully chosen surrogate rather than to speculate about unforeseen circumstances. This type of advance directive is known as a *durable power of attorney for health care* (DPAHC).

There has traditionally been a belief that living wills are legal documents only when they have been authorized by statute. While that may or may not have been an accurate statement of the law of advance directives in at least some states *prior* to the *Cruzan* decision, it is arguably no longer so. *Cruzan*

B o x 4–1   *Even Judges Need Living Wills*

Charles E. Teel, Jr., was the Probate Judge who heard the initial arguments in the Nancy Cruzan case. His decision, to grant the Cruzans permission to discontinue their daughter's tube feeding which had been maintaining her for more than four years, was overturned by the Missouri Supreme Court. That decision, that the feeding tube could not be discontinued unless there were "clear and convincing evidence" of Nancy's desire to do so, was ultimately upheld by the United States Supreme Court.

Nearly three years after he had first ruled in their favor, the Cruzans again stood before Judge Teel with additional witnesses to testify that Nancy would have wanted to stop treatment. In the interval between these two trials, Judge Teel had experienced a serious heart attack. Although he was in a position to appreciate, far better than most, the importance of having a living will, he told *The New York Times* that he had none.

(Gibbons, 1991, p. 2)

---

seems to have provided legal recognition, constitutional if not statutory, for both forms of advance directives by focusing the legal inquiry on the wishes of the formerly competent patient. Perhaps a more important aspect of advance-directive statutes is the immunity from civil and criminal liability they confer on health care workers (especially physicians) and institutions that act on them in good faith.

The first bill that proposed to make the living will a legally binding document was introduced in 1968 by Dr. Walter Sackett, a Florida legislator. It failed to gain approval. Not until sixteen years later would Florida join the states (then numbering twenty-three) that had passed such laws.

In 1976, the California legislature, perhaps responding to some of the issues raised by the *Quinlan* case, passed the nation's first living will law—the California Natural Death Act. The law, as seen from our current perspective, was a modest (and rather ineffective) foray into a then-controversial area. First, the statute applied only to the terminally ill. A "qualified patient," defined as one who was afflicted by a "terminal condition," could draft a directive no sooner than fourteen days after the diagnosis had been confirmed by two physicians. Moreover, *terminal condition* was defined as an "incurable condition caused by injury, disease, or illness, which, regardless of the application of life-sustaining procedures, would, within reasonable medical judgment, produce death, and where the application of life-sustaining procedures serve only to postpone the moment of death of the patient" (§§7187, Cal. Stat., Chapter

1439, Code § Health and Safety, Sept. 30, 1976). To the extent that the publicity concerning the *Quinlan* case was in any way responsible for the passage of this law, it should be noted that Karen Ann Quinlan would not have been a "qualified patient" for whom the law would be applicable. Also, because the law allows termination of LSMT only where the underlying condition would cause death *regardless of medical treatment*, it would seem to imply that only futile forms of treatment could be refused. But, it might be argued, what is the importance of refusing treatment in those situations where death is imminent regardless of the treatment? The reason that most people would choose to refuse treatment when they are terminally ill is because the treatment is keeping them from dying more quickly. Clearly the statute granted less freedom to citizens of California who had signed living wills than that possessed by other citizens who did not have to rely upon a written expression of their wishes about LSMT.

In addition to these restrictions, the California statute placed a five-year limitation on living wills and stated that they would not be respected if the person making the declaration (the declarant) was pregnant (Ibid., §7188). Although there is reason to believe that the latter restriction, which is found in living will laws from many other states as well, would not withstand constitutional challenge, the situation would seem to occur so infrequently that there has been no such test of the law in court to date (Benton, 1990; Macavoy-Snitzer, 1987). Figure 4–1 shows a breakdown by state of laws governing living wills and appointing health care agents.

Durable Powers of Attorney for Health Care

The use of proxy advance directives is a more recent phenomenon. Delaware was the first state to specifically provide for the appointment of a proxy to represent an incapacitated patient, an alternative contained in its Death with Dignity Act passed in 1982 (Del. Code Ann. Tit. 16, §§2502 (July 12, 1982). Today more than forty states have statutes authorizing the use of health care proxies and all states provide for the use of durable powers of attorney, without specifically indicating "for health care" (see Figure 4–2). The President's Commission, the American Bar Association Commission on Legal Problems of the Elderly, and many legal scholars have taken the position that, in the absence of statutory limitations on the use of these "general" powers of attorney, nothing should prevent their use for appointing a surrogate to make health care decisions (President's Commission, 1983, pp. 146–147; Mishkin, 1986, p. 28; Sabatino, 1990).

There are several important reasons for preparing an advance directive.

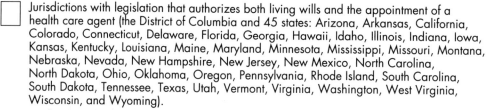

Jurisdictions with legislation that authorizes both living wills and the appointment of a health care agent (the District of Columbia and 45 states: Arizona, Arkansas, California, Colorado, Connecticut, Delaware, Florida, Georgia, Hawaii, Idaho, Illinois, Indiana, Iowa, Kansas, Kentucky, Louisiana, Maine, Maryland, Minnesota, Mississippi, Missouri, Montana, Nebraska, Nevada, New Hampshire, New Jersey, New Mexico, North Carolina, North Dakota, Ohio, Oklahoma, Oregon, Pennsylvania, Rhode Island, South Carolina, South Dakota, Tennessee, Texas, Utah, Vermont, Virginia, Washington, West Virginia, Wisconsin, and Wyoming).

States with legislation that authorizes only living wills (2 states: Alabama and Alaska).

States with legislation that authorizes only the appointment of a health care agent (3 states: Massachusetts, Michigan, and New York).

Note: The specifics of living will and health care agent legislation vary greatly from state to state. In addition, many states also have court-made law that affects residents' rights. For information about specific state laws, please contact Choice In Dying.

FIGURE 4–1 State statutes governing living wills and appointment of health care agents. [Reprinted by permission of Choice In Dying (formerly Concern for Dying/Society for the Right to Die), 200 Varick Street, New York, NY 10014–4810; (212)366–5540]

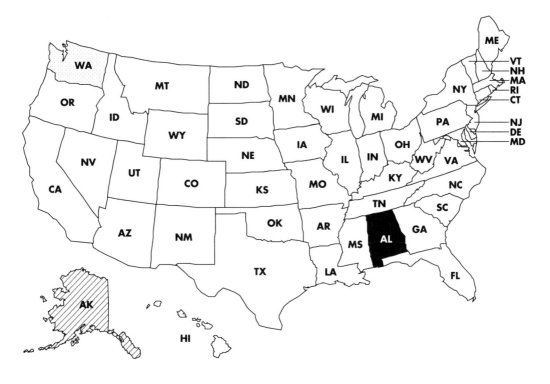

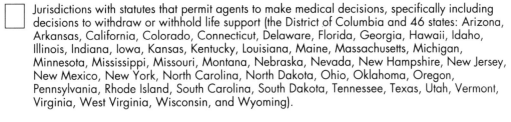

Jurisdictions with statutes that permit agents to make medical decisions, specifically including decisions to withdraw or withhold life support (the District of Columbia and 46 states: Arizona, Arkansas, California, Colorado, Connecticut, Delaware, Florida, Georgia, Hawaii, Idaho, Illinois, Indiana, Iowa, Kansas, Kentucky, Louisiana, Maine, Massachusetts, Michigan, Minnesota, Mississippi, Missouri, Montana, Nebraska, Nevada, New Hampshire, New Jersey, New Mexico, New York, North Carolina, North Dakota, Ohio, Oklahoma, Oregon, Pennsylvania, Rhode Island, South Carolina, South Dakota, Tennessee, Texas, Utah, Vermont, Virginia, West Virginia, Wisconsin, and Wyoming).

States with statutes interpreted by court decisions, Attorney General Opinions or other statutes to permit agents to make medical decisions, including decisions to withhold or withdraw life support (2 states: Maryland and Washington).

State with a statute that authorizes consent to medical treatment, but specifically bars agents from consenting to the withholding/withdrawal of life support (Alaska).

State with no statutory means of appointing an agent to make medical decisions (Alabama).

FIGURE 4–2 State law governing Durable Powers of Attorney, health care agents, and proxy appointments. [Reprinted by permission of Choice In Dying (formerly Concern for Dying/Society for the Right to Die), 200 Varick Street, New York, NY 10014–4810; (212)366–5540]

First, they help ensure that your wishes concerning treatment options will be respected. Second, they protect your family members, health care professionals, and others from the stress and potential conflict of making critical decisions without sufficient information concerning your wishes if you are incompetent. One has only to consider the families of Karen Quinlan, Paul Brophy, and Nancy Cruzan to realize the anguish that so often accompanies such tragedies. Even in those situations where the family does not get caught up in the legal system, it is often much easier for them to make decisions if they know that they are doing what you would have wanted them to do.

The earliest versions of living wills were rather broad and vague in terms of the guidance offered. An example of this is one of the early documents prepared and distributed by the Euthanasia Educational Council, the forerunner of Concern for Dying, which, in turn, recently merged with the Society for the Right to Die to form an entity known as Choice In Dying (see Figure 4–3).

While one of the purposes of the living will is to protect the patient from receiving unwanted treatment, an equally important purpose is to provide immunity from civil and/or criminal liability to physicians who rely upon such documents in withholding or withdrawing LSMT. By freeing them from concerns about liability, the assumption is that they will be more willing to respect the previously stated wishes of the now incompetent patient. Such being the case, it would seem preferable that the living will also be accorded legal recognition by statute, for only the state can grant freedom from criminal liability.

Many of the earliest statutes, while recognizing the right of a qualified patient to prepare a living will and granting immunity to health care providers who acted upon it in good faith, did little or nothing to "encourage" reluctant providers to comply with it. While some of the more recently enacted statutes address this by requiring that unwilling physicians transfer the care of the patient to a provider who is willing to abide by the provisions of the living will, the penalties for failure to do so are more likely to be in the form of professional sanctions rather than any legal remedies in the form of monetary damages. The exceptions to this have been few (*Bartling* v. *Superior Court,* 1984; Miller, 1988). With the passage of living will laws, states have often prescribed the form that the documents must take and placed limitations on the range of decisions that will be respected. See Figures 4–4(a) and 4–4(b).

Although there are few remaining states without living will laws (refer to Figure 4–1), even before the *Cruzan* decision there was reason to suspect that courts would grant legal recognition to living wills in the absence of statutory recognition. For example, in 1984 the Florida Supreme Court held that a living will executed by Francis B. Landy some nine years prior to the enactment of a living will statute by the Florida legislature must be respected. This decision also applied where the patient, as was the case with Mr. Landy, did not fall within the terms of the Life-Prolonging Procedure Act, which applied only to

TO MY FAMILY, MY PHYSICIAN, MY LAWYER, MY CLERGYMAN

TO ANY MEDICAL FACILITY IN WHOSE CARE I HAPPEN TO BE

TO ANY INDIVIDUAL WHO MAY BECOME RESPONSIBLE FOR MY HEALTH, WELFARE OR AFFAIRS

Death is as much a reality as birth, growth, maturity and old age—it is the one certainty of life. If the time comes when I, _____ can no longer take part in decisions for my own future, let this statement stand as an expression of my wishes, while I am still of sound mind.

If the situation should arise in which there is no reasonable expectation of my recovery from physical or mental disability, I request that I be allowed to die and not be kept alive by artificial means or "heroic measures". I do not fear death itself as much as the indignities of deterioration, dependence and hopeless pain. I, therefore, ask that medication be mercifully administered to me to alleviate suffering even though this may hasten the moment of death.

This request is made after careful consideration. I hope you who care for me will feel morally bound to follow its mandate. I recognize that this appears to place a heavy responsibility upon you, but it is with the intention of relieving you of such responsibility and of placing it upon myself in accordance with my strong convictions, that this statement is made.

Signed _____

Date _____

Witness _____

Witness _____

Copies of this request have been given to _____

_____

_____

_____

FIGURE 4–3 An example of one of the early versions of a Living Will distributed by the Euthanasia Educational Council. Notice the use of terminology like "heroic measures" rather than, as is the case with more modern documents, a description of the kind of treatment to be refused, such as feeding tube or ventilators. [Reprinted by permission of Choice In Dying (formerly Concern for Dying/Society for the Right to Die), 200 Varick Street, New York, NY 10014–4810; (212)366–5540]

the terminally ill. Mr. Landy had been diagnosed as being in a persistent vegetative state. This was the first time that the highest court in any state had addressed the subject of a living will and recognized its validity in decision making for incompetent patients (*John F. Kennedy Memorial Hospital, Inc.* v. *Bludworth*, 1984).

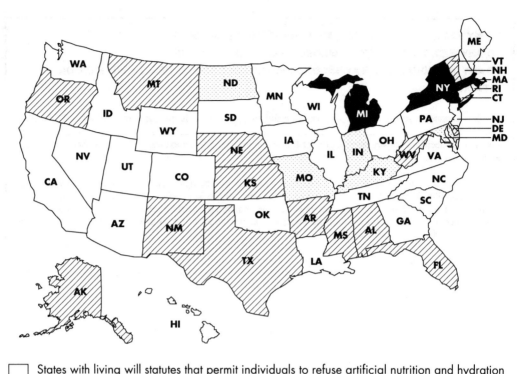

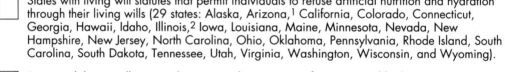

States with living will statutes that permit individuals to refuse artificial nutrition and hydration through their living wills (29 states: Alaska, Arizona,[1] California, Colorado, Connecticut, Georgia, Hawaii, Idaho, Illinois,[2] Iowa, Louisiana, Maine, Minnesota, Nevada, New Hampshire, New Jersey, North Carolina, Ohio, Oklahoma, Pennsylvania, Rhode Island, South Carolina, South Dakota, Tennessee, Utah, Virginia, Washington, Wisconsin, and Wyoming).

States with living will statutes that require the provision of nutrition and hydration except in very limited circumstances (5 states: Indiana,[3] Kentucky, Maryland,[4] Missouri,[3] and North Dakota).

Jurisdictions whose living will statutes do not explicitly permit the refusal of, or explicitly require the application of, artificial nutrition and hydration (the District of Columbia and 13 states: Alabama, Arkansas, Alaska, Delaware, Florida, Kansas, Mississippi, Montana, Nebraska, New Mexico, Oregon, Texas, Vermont, and West Virginia).

States without living will statutes (3 states: Massachusetts, Michigan, New York).

[1] The authority to withhold or withdraw artificial nutrition and hydration is only explicitly mentioned in the sample document
[2] Artificial nutrition and hydration cannot be withheld or withdrawn if the resulting death is due to starvation or dehydration
[3] The medical power of attorney statutes in Indiana and Missouri permit appointed agents to refuse artificial nutrition and hydration on behalf of the principal.
[4] Although the act requires the "administration of food and water," a Maryland Attorney General's Opinion has stated that artificial nutrition and hydration may be refused through a living will.

FIGURE 4–4(a)   Artificial nutrition and hydration in Living Will statutes. (Reprinted by permission of Choice In Dying (formerly Concern for Dying/Society for the Right to Die), 200 Varick Street, New York, NY 10014–4810; (212)366–5540]

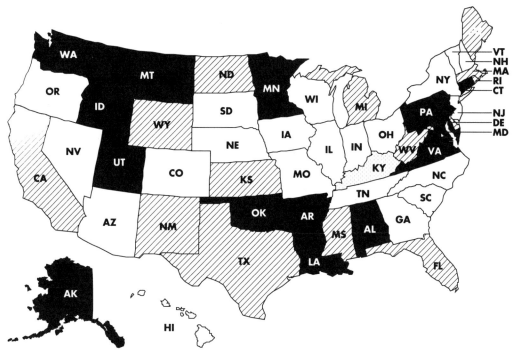

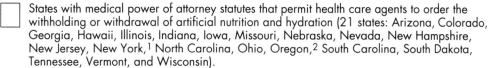
States with medical power of attorney statutes that permit health care agents to order the withholding or withdrawal of artificial nutrition and hydration (21 states: Arizona, Colorado, Georgia, Hawaii, Illinois, Indiana, Iowa, Missouri, Nebraska, Nevada, New Hampshire, New Jersey, New York,[1] North Carolina, Ohio, Oregon,[2] South Carolina, South Dakota, Tennessee, Vermont, and Wisconsin).

States with medical power of, attorney statutes that explicitly require the provision of nutrition and hydration except in very limited circumstances (1 state: Kentucky).

Jurisdictions whose medical power of attorney statutes do not explicitly permit the refusal of, or explicitly require the application of, artificial nutrition and hydration (the District of Columbia and 13 states: California, Florida, Kansas, Maine, Massachusetts, Michigan, Mississippi, New Mexico, North Dakota, Rhode Island, Texas, West Virginia and Wyoming).

States without medical power of attorney statutes (15 states: Alabama, Alaska, Arkansas, Connecticut, Delaware, Idaho, Louisiana, Maryland, Minnesota, Montana, Oklahoma, Pennsylvania, Utah, Virginia, and Washington).

[1] Agents are permitted to order the withholding or withdrawal of artificial nutrition and hydration only if they know the wishes of the principal concerning such action.

[2] Agents are permitted to order the withholding or withdrawal of artificial nutrition and hydration only if the principal had expressly rejected artificial nutrition and hydration before incompetence.

FIGURE 4–4(b) Artificial nutrition and hydration in Medical Durable Power of Attorney statutes. [Reprinted by permission of Choice In Dying (formerly Concern for Dying/Society for the Right to Die), 200 Varick Street, New York, NY 10014–4810; (212)366–5540]

The Problem of Artificial Feeding and Hydration

One of the most common restrictions is the limitation placed upon decisions to refuse artificially provided nutrition and/or hydration. While it is unlikely that any such restrictions will withstand judicial scrutiny in the wake of the *Cruzan* case, even before *Cruzan* there was evidence that courts would be unwilling to uphold such limitations. The first such appellate court to overturn a restriction of this type was in Florida. The Florida Life Prolonging Procedure Act stated that artificial feeding could not be withheld or withdrawn under the Act. Mrs. Helen Corbett, age seventy-three, was in a PVS and being fed through a naso-gastric tube. After three years, her husband of forty-eight years, with the support of Mrs. Corbett's physicians, decided that continued use of the feeding tube was serving no valid purpose. Although she had not prepared a living will, Mr. Corbett claimed to be acting on what he knew to be his wife's wishes. The treating physicians were in agreement with his decision, but they felt constrained by the provisions of the Act. The court ruled that they were unable to make a legal, scientific, or moral distinction between forced sustenance or the forcing of other vital functions and that the right to have a nasogastric tube removed is a constitutionally protected right that could not be limited by legislation. The Florida Supreme Court declined a request to review the decision of the appeals court (*Corbett* v. *D'Alessandro*, 1986).

As was discussed in the previous chapter, the living will law that had been passed by the Missouri legislature also included a restriction on the refusal of artificially provided nutrition and/or hydration (Section 459.010 et seq. R.S. Mo., 1986). While Nancy Cruzan had not executed a living will and the legality of such restrictions, either constitutionally or otherwise, was not before any of the courts to hear arguments in *Cruzan*, there was support in the decision of the U.S. Supreme Court for the position that there is no significant distinction to be made between artificially provided nutrition and/or hydration and other forms of medical treatment that might be refused. Moreover, since Nancy Cruzan's parents were subsequently successful in obtaining judicial approval to discontinue the use of the feeding tube, there are only two conclusions that could be drawn about the legal status of the feeding tube restrictions in the Missouri Living Will Law.

The first of these, and the most logical, is that those restrictions are no longer valid after *Cruzan*. If that is not the case, why else would the Missouri Supreme Court permit the Probate Court to allow the Cruzans to authorize removal of their daughter's feeding tube? The other conclusion, a rather bizarre one, would be that patients like Nancy Cruzan, who do not have living wills, enjoy a broader array of rights to refuse treatment than do those patients who have executed a living will according to the directives of the legislature.

The Medical Directive

A more recent variation of the living will is the Medical Directive, described as a "new comprehensive advance care document," by its developers, Linda L. and Ezekiel J. Emanuel. The Medical Directive was designed to provide for greater specificity in both planning for and executing an advance directive. The original form was published in the *Journal of the American Medical Association* (Emanuel and Emanuel, 1989) and, subsequently, as a supplement to the *Harvard Medical School Health Letter* (1990). The directive posits "four paradigmatic scenarios"—four different circumstances—and asks readers to choose among twelve different treatment options. The readers are asked to rate each of the options according to whether they would (1) want it to be used, (2) not want it to be used, (3) be undecided about having it used, or, in certain cases, (4) whether they would want it used on a trial basis with discontinuation if there were no clearly beneficial effect. The circumstances are described as:

A. "Coma" or persistent vegetative state.
B. "Coma" with "small likelihood of recovering fully, a slightly larger likelihood of surviving with permanent brain damage, and a much larger likelihood of dying."
C. Brain damage or brain disease which is irreversible and which results in an inability to recognize people or speak understandably, along with a terminal illness.
D. Brain damage or brain disease as in C but without a terminal illness.

The various treatments to be considered are:

1. Cardiopulmonary resuscitation
2. Mechanical breathing
3. Artificial nutrition and hydration
4. Major surgery
5. Kidney dialysis
6. Chemotherapy
7. Minor surgery
8. Invasive diagnostic tests
9. Blood or blood products
10. Antibiotics
11. Simple diagnostic tests

12. Pain medications, even if they dull consciousness and indirectly threaten life.

Figure 4–5 shows how this might be presented using the example of permanent unconsciousness.

The Emanuels recommend that the checklist be attached to or incorporated into a durable power of attorney document so that the choices selected can be used to guide the attorney-in-fact in making decisions about the appropriateness of various treatment proposals. They also suggest incorporation of a statement about organ donation if desired (1989, p. 3290).

Convinced by experience in using the directive in clinical trials that there were some interpretation problems, Linda Emanuel proposed a "remodeling" of the document (Emanuel, 1991). The revised directive contained two additional scenarios, condensed the treatment options from twelve to six, and added a series of choices about the "goal" of medical care. The two new scenarios were:

Situation D. Incurable chronic illness which involves mental disability or physical suffering and ultimately causes death, and in addition an illness that is immediately life threatening but reversible.

Situation E. Current state of health (to be described) and have a life-threatening but reversible illness.

Under each of the situations, the document would only be used to guide decisions if the person executing it were unable to do so because of permanent loss of decision-making capacity. The remodeled directive, using the same situation presented before, is shown in Figure 4–6. Whether or not greater specificity is a desirable goal, especially at the risk of the potential for greater confusion resulting from increased complexity, has yet to be demonstrated.

An alternative to the use of a living will, and the possible vagueness and difficulty in predicting unforeseen circumstances that might accompany it, is the appointment of a surrogate or proxy decision maker through a durable power of attorney for health care (DPAHC). A power of attorney is a document whereby you, the principal, authorize someone else, who now becomes your agent or attorney-in-fact, to act on your behalf. One of the most common uses of power of attorney is in property transactions. In granting another power to act legally on your behalf it becomes possible to buy and sell real property without being personally in attendance. Your attorney-in-fact, who need not be, in fact, an attorney (attorney-at-law), has a duty to act in your best interest. This duty is often described as a fiduciary duty. It means, at its simplest, that he or she may not knowingly act contrary to your wishes or benefit at your ex-

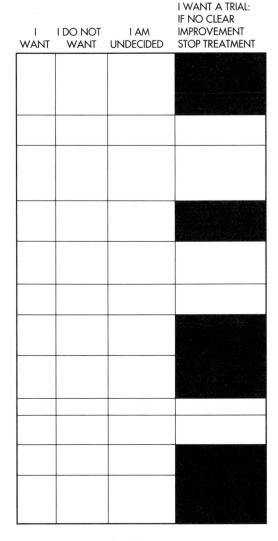

SITUATION (A)

If I am in a coma or in a persistent vegetative state, and in the opinion of my physician and several consultants have no known hope of regaining awareness and higher mental functions no matter what is done, then my wishes regarding use of the following, if considered medically reasonable, would be:

	I WANT	I DO NOT WANT	I AM UNDECIDED	I WANT A TRIAL: IF NO CLEAR IMPROVEMENT STOP TREATMENT
1. CARDIOPULMONARY RESUSCITATION— if on the point of dying the use of drugs and electric shock to start the heart beating and artificial breathing.				■
2. MECHANICAL BREATHING— breathing by a machine.				
3. ARTIFICIAL NUTRITION AND HYDRATION— nutrition and fluid given through a tube in the veins, nose, or stomach.				
4. MAJOR SURGERY— such as removing the gall bladder or part of the intestines.				■
5. KIDNEY DIALYSIS— cleaning the blood by machine or by fluid passed through the belly.				
6. CHEMOTHERAPY— drugs to fight cancer.				
7. MINOR SURGERY— such as removing some tissue from an infected toe.				■
8. INVASIVE DIAGNOSTIC TESTS— such as using a flexible tube to look into the stomach.				
9. BLOOD OR BLOOD PRODUCTS				
10. ANTIBIOTICS— drugs to fight infection.				
11. SIMPLE DIAGNOSTIC TESTS— such as blood tests or x-rays.				■
12. PAIN MEDICATIONS. EVEN IF THEY DULL CONSCIOUSNESS AND INDIRECTLY SHORTEN MY LIFE—				

FIGURE 4–5 The Medical Directive. Using the example of permanent unconsciousness, one of four "paradigmatic scenarios," the reader is asked to choose which of twelve treatments he or she would want to have provided. (Emanuel and Emanuel, 1989)

SITUATION (A)

If, in the opinion of my physician and two consultants, I am in a coma or in a persistent vegetative state, and have no known hope of regaining awareness and higher mental functions no matter what is done, then my wishes, if medically reasonable, for this and any additional illness would be:

	want	don't want	unsure	treatment trial; stop for no improvement
Resuscitation:				
Mechanical breathing, surgery, chemotherapy, dialysis:				
Blood transfusion:				
Artificial nutrition & fluid:				
Simple diagnostic tests, antibiotics:				
Pain medication even if indirectly shortening life:				

The goal of medical care should be:
—prolong life, treat everything
—comfort care only
—other (specify)
(check one)

FIGURE 4-6   The "Revised" Medical Directive. In this 1991 "remodeling" of the Medical Directive, the number of treatments has been reduced from twelve to six and, in addition, the reader is asked to indicate a choice about the "goal" of medical care. (Emanuel, 1991)

pense. A power of attorney typically expires with the death or incompetence of the principal.

To overcome this limitation—expiration upon death or mental disability—a power of attorney can be designated as durable. This allows your attorney-in-fact to continue to represent you and manage your affairs. To create a durable power of attorney, the document must state that it is intended to be durable, or that the power created will not be affected by the incapacity of the principal.

Although the word *attorney* is used in the phrase "power of attorney," powers of attorney may be given to almost anyone. There may be some limitations under state laws, primarily to prevent health care providers or nursing home administrators from being placed in a potential conflict of interest, but the power certainly can be given to family members, friends, or clergy.

Theoretically, your representative, called an attorney-in-fact, a surrogate, or a proxy, should be able to make all those decisions that you, the now incompetent patient, would otherwise have been able to make for yourself. In practice, however, the statutes that authorize the creation of the power often put limitations on the extent of the power granted. This will be discussed in greater detail later in the chapter.

Like living wills, durable powers of attorney for health care must be authenticated in the manner prescribed by statute, either by witnessing or by notarization. The statutes often call for two witnesses, both of whom must witness your signature and typically certify that you seem to be of sound mind, that you are not signing under duress, and that there has been no coercion to get you to sign. Unlike the designation of the person holding the power, it is usually advised that you choose witnesses who are "disinterested," meaning that they do not stand to inherit property under the terms of your will or by operation of state law should you die intestate.

It is usually a good idea to designate one or more successor agents to represent you in the event that your original designee is unable or unwilling to do so. Of course, to avoid the latter, it is recommended that you discuss your plan to create a DPAHC with your intended agent before designating him or her as such, as is also true for the successor agents. Each of the potential agents should be given a copy of the document after it has been authenticated.

Although statutes authorizing the creation of living wills and/or DPAHC have been in existence in many states for a decade or more, comparatively few people have taken advantage of them. It is estimated that fewer than 15 percent of Americans and an even lower percentage of Canadians have prepared such documents (Singer and Siegler, 1992). Although public awareness of the plight of the Cruzan family and the widespread publicity of the decision of the U.S. Supreme Court seemed to provide a brief surge of interest, there is still a tremendous need to get this message to the public at large.

The Patient Self-Determination Act of 1990

Federal legislation, passed in the wake of *Cruzan*, is likely to provide a boost to the use of advance directives. On December 1, 1991, the Patient Self-Determination Act (PSDA) became law (see Box 4–2). The legislation was introduced in the Senate by Daniel P. Moynihan of New York and John Danforth of Missouri. Interestingly, the sponsors represent the two states that have placed the most stringent requirements on families wishing to discontinue LSMT for their loved ones (i.e., *Storar*, 1981, and *O'Connor*, 1988, both in New York, and *Cruzan*, 1990, in Missouri). The corresponding legislation in the

---

Box 4–2   *The PSDA: A Double-Edged Sword?*

Besides the possibility that it [the PSDA] will have little impact, the Act may be counterproductive; patients could be incorrectly informed about their rights. The Act requires informing patients of their rights under *state* law. Patients' rights under the laws of their state may be less than their rights under the U.S. Constitution; many existing statutes limit the kinds of directives that patients can give and the conditions under which patients can give directions. For example, a state's living will statute may apply only to terminally ill patients or may exclude feeding tubes. Also, only 43 states have living will statutes; only 24 states have health care proxy statutes. The *Cruzan* decision's discussion of federal constitutional law suggests that people are free to write advance directives regardless of whether their instructions exceed what their state's statute allows, and regardless of whether their state has a statute.

(La Puma, Orentilicher, and Moss, 1991, p. 404, citations omitted)

House of Representatives was introduced by Congressman Sander Levin of Michigan. The law was passed as part of a comprehensive budget reconciliation package and was signed by President George Bush on November 5, 1990. It is codified as Public Law No. 101–508.

The law requires that any hospitals, skilled nursing facilities, home health agencies, hospices, and health maintenance organizations (HMOs) serving Medicare and/or Medicaid patients develop written policies and procedures to provide written information to adults to whom they provide care. The written material must describe:

- An individual's rights under state law (including both statutory and case law) to make decisions about medical care, including the right to accept or refuse medical and surgical treatment.
- An individual's rights under state law to formulate advance directives such as a living will or durable power of attorney for health care.
- The policies and procedures that the institution has developed to honor these rights.

Under this federal law, there must be a protocol for documenting in the medical record whether or not the individual has either a living will or a durable power of attorney for health care. It also requires institutions to have a policy ensuring compliance with state law governing advance directives. The written information is to be provided when the patient is first admitted. In the case of a hospital or skilled nursing home, the advance directive, if the patient has one, is to be made a part of the medical record.

The law requires recipients of federal Medicare and/or Medicaid funding to provide (individually or with others) education for staff and community on issues concerning advance directives. All providers are cautioned that they may not condition the provision of care or otherwise discriminate against an individual based on whether or not he or she has executed an advance directive.

The Secretary of Health and Human Services is charged with responsibility for developing a national campaign to educate the public about advance directives, including the mailing of information to Social Security recipients and adding a page to the Medicare handbook, and to provide assistance to the states in implementing the new law. Unfortunately, Congress failed to appropriate any funds for implementation of the new law and the educational campaign envisioned has been virtually nonexistent.

While the PSDA should be useful in informing patients of their rights to make decisions about all forms of medical and/or surgical treatment, including LSMT, even after they may experience a loss of decision-making capacity, there are concerns that such decisions are not best made at the time of hospital admission. Ideally, the discussions with physicians, family, and close friends that should precede those decisions would take place well in advance of hospitalization. While it is still too soon to comment on how hospitals and other health care providers have handled these new requirements, it will be important to monitor this on an on-going basis to make sure that the PSDA is performing as desired by Congress.

While the use of advance directives, either living wills or durable powers of attorney for health care, is highly recommended, one should proceed with caution. Although one would expect that legislation, both state and federal, would clarify the right to refuse unwanted medical treatment, that has not always been the case. Laws are the product of the political process and they often reflect compromises that fall short of their sponsor's anticipations. Ohio provides the material for an illustration of what can happen when the politicians step into the arena.

The Ohio Advance Directive Law: A Case Study

As of November 5, 1990, the date President Bush signed the PSDA into law, Ohio was among that minority of states, then numbering fewer than eight, that had not provided statutory recognition of living wills. That the legislature had failed to do so, however, was not for a lack of interest in the topic. A living will bill was first introduced in 1977. From then until 1989, the legislature refused to pass living will legislation, although bills were introduced each year.

Proponents of living will legislation encountered formidable opposition from the Catholic Conference of Ohio and the Ohio Society for the Right to Life, both of which seemed to view such legislation as part of a trend toward what they saw as a diminishing respect for human life. Their passion was fueled by hostility toward the U.S. Supreme Court's decision in *Roe* v. *Wade* (1973), which legalized abortion throughout the country, and their linkage of abortion and "euthanasia," which they viewed as part of the living will movement, as equally objectionable.

It took twelve years to get a bill through the legislature (Fulton, 1991). In 1989, the General Assembly passed legislation creating a Durable Power of Attorney for Health Care. Much like the earlier efforts in California, the 1989 bill included restrictions that greatly limited its usefulness in protecting personal autonomy in controlling one's medical destiny. First, it was limited to those who were "terminally ill," which was defined in such a way as to clearly exclude those who might be permanently unconscious. Second, an attorney-in-fact could only be authorized to refuse or discontinue treatment if death were *imminent* regardless of the treatment employed. This would mean that only futile treatment could be rejected and, moreover, if death would occur soon (imminent) *regardless* of the treatment, then there was little reason to be concerned about stopping treatment. It is only in cases in which death could be postponed indefinitely by the use of medical technology where patients, or those acting on their behalf, have typically expressed a desire to discontinue treatment. The Ohio law seemed to be saying that you could only refuse life-sustaining medical treatment where it didn't make any difference if you refused it or not! In addition to this, the law also specified that food and water, administered by tube, were forms of treatment that could never be refused.

A month before the law was scheduled to become effective, it was cited by a County Appeals Court Judge as indicative of a "public policy against the withdrawal of artificially administered nutrition and/or hydration" (*Couture* v. *Couture,* 1989). Daniel Couture, age twenty-nine, had been in a PVS for nearly four months. His mother, who had been appointed as his guardian, had been granted permission by the probate court to have tube feeding and hydration discontinued, but the decision was appealed by Daniel's father (the parents were separated) and the Court of Appeals reversed. Almost immediately, the Ohio legislature responded to what was called a "misinterpretation" of the new law by attaching statements to several versions of living will bills then introduced, explaining that it was never the intent of the legislature to establish such a public policy. The legislature claimed that it merely wanted to limit the decision-making power of agents appointed by the patient under the durable power of attorney for health care law, which it seemed to regard as potentially subject to greater abuse than similar decisions made by guardians appointed and supervised by the court.

The decision of the U.S. Supreme Court in *Cruzan* and the passage of the

Patient Self-Determination Act by Congress provided a strong incentive for the Ohio General Assembly to revise this earlier attempt to authorize the appointment of decision-making surrogates and to enact a living will law. *Cruzan* clearly indicated that competent adults had a right to refuse all forms of unwanted medical treatment, including hydration and/or nourishment supplied by tube, and, in *dicta*, that those same decisions could be made by a properly delegated proxy. The PSDA required that patients be informed of their rights "under state law" to make decisions about medical care, including their right to formulate advance directives such as living wills or durable powers of attorney for health care. Although the state medical and legal societies had never taken a position of either leadership or support with any of the advance directive bills that had been introduced into the General Assembly, both seemed to sense that the time was at hand to bring the state into compliance with these new legal requirements.

During the summer and early fall of 1990—Cruzan had been decided in June—a joint committee of the Ohio State Medical Association (OSMA) and the Ohio State Bar Association (OSBA) worked to draft a model living will/durable power of attorney for health care bill. The leadership of the Ohio Senate agreed to give the bill priority consideration. Significantly, the Ohio Catholic Conference announced that it would not oppose the bill. The only announced opposition came from the Ohio Right-to-Life Society.

The bill was introduced on January 22, 1991. Originally some forty pages long, by the time it was signed by Governor George Voinovich on July 11 of that same year, it had accrued thirty-seven pages of amendments! Although the original bill was less than a model of clarity and/or brevity, the new law gave Ohio the distinction of having the nation's most wordy and arguably most complicated advance directive legislation. The law was described by its sponsors as a "political compromise," a term that should serve as a caution for all, regardless of their attitude about advance directives in general. Since the law is written in unusually repetitious and ponderous language, and has yet to be interpreted or otherwise ruled on by any of the higher courts in the state, there is likely to be debate and disagreement about its many nuances. The story of what happened in Ohio, however, provides an excellent illustration of what can happen when difficult medical-legal-ethical issues of this type are cast into the political forum. The law is fully described elsewhere (Fulton, 1991); only selected aspects will be presented here for their illustrative value.

The Ohio law provides for the following: (1) the creation of a durable power of attorney for health care, thereby supplanting the earlier law which had been in existence for approximately two years and which had been the source of controversy in the *Couture* case; (2) the creation of a living will; and (3) a process for making decisions about LSMT when there is no advance directive.

Both the DPAHC and the living will provisions allow the refusal or withdrawal of LSMT only in cases of terminal illness or permanent unconsciousness. They also establish unusually precise wording that must be in the document if the maker (known as a "declarant") wishes to refuse hydration or nourishment by tube. Both require notification to next of kin or others who might be designated by the declarant and allow for those so notified to contest the legitimacy of the documents or the accuracy of the diagnosis.

Both documents are restricted to use by adults (eighteen years of age or older) and have clauses indicating that they will not be recognized to abate treatment on a pregnant woman if doing so would terminate the pregnancy, unless the pregnancy or health care would pose a substantial risk to the woman's life or there was medical agreement that the fetus would not be born alive.

The most controversial provision of the Ohio law has to do with the permanently unconscious, but not terminally ill, patient who has failed to execute an advance directive. Although there is considerable legal authority for granting decision-making responsibility to the next of kin under such circumstances (Areen, 1987; Weir, 1989; Weir and Gostin, 1990) without resorting to guardianship or other judicial proceedings, such responsibility is greatly circumscribed in Ohio where the treatment is feeding and/or hydration by tube (see Box 4–3).

If the patient, a nondeclarant, has been diagnosed as being permanently unconscious, a diagnosis which the American Academy of Neurology indicates can be reliably made in "no less than one and no more than three months" (1989), and the next of kin wish to have the feeding/hydration tubing removed, they are required to do so through the probate court. They must first, however, wait at least twelve months after the diagnosis has been confirmed before they can present a petition to the court for authority to stop treatment. The court then has up to two months to act on the petition. This could easily mean that the patient would have been receiving LSMT by feeding tube for nearly a year and a half before it could be stopped. Moreover, in spite of the fact that there is no advance directive (or, perhaps, because of such), the probate court is instructed to grant the petition only if there is "clear and convincing" evidence that this is the decision that the patient would make if he or she were able to do so. This, of course, presents a seemingly insurmountable barrier to stopping treatment where the patient is a child or an adult with lifelong incompetency and, arguably, for most previously competent adults as well. While there is clearly an interest on the part of the state in ensuring an accurate diagnosis before treatment can be stopped, the establishment of a twelve-month waiting period *after* confirmation of the diagnosis is, it could be argued, arbitrary and capricious. Not only does it force futile treatment upon the patient, but it also requires the family to incur the considerable costs and emotional stress that accompany the legal process. Although the constitutionality of this part of the law has yet to be ruled upon by an appellate court, the several

---

B O X 4–3   *On Restrictions in Advance Directive Statutes*

All of these restrictions have led many health care professionals, administrators, and even lawyers wrongly to maintain that a directive broader than the statute is without legal effect. They make the common mistake of believing that once the legislature has recognized one means of protecting individual rights, there are no other means. They misconstrue every other effort to express treatment preferences as if it were a ball hit out of bounds.

In fact, any expression of treatment preferences has legal effect. A directive broader than the state statute is not out of bounds. Health care professionals are obligated to pay careful attention to such directives. But to see why, you have to understand something about the relationship of the statutory rights provided by state legislatures, the additional common law rights recognized by judges, and the rights provided by the state and federal constitutions. Patients have all three.

So what are these other nonstatutory rights? Judges have long since recognized that patients have a common law right to be free of unwanted bodily invasion. This is the basis of the legal obligation to obtain a patient's informed consent before performing invasive procedures. In case after case, judges have declared that patients have a common law right to refuse unwanted life-sustaining treatment. That right is not confined to the terminally ill, and applies to the refusal of all life-sustaining treatment modalities including artificial nutrition and hydration.

(Wolf, 1991)

---

lower court decisions that have involved permanently unconscious non-declarants have authorized the discontinuation of treatment as though this section of the law had never existed (*In re Crum*, 1991; *In re McInnis*, 1991; *In re Myers*, 1993).

Although the Ohio law grants immunity to physicians and other health care providers who act in good faith in relying upon the provisions of an advance directive, advance directives, although *sufficient* to support such decisions, are not *necessary* to stop treatment. There is, as was previously stated, considerable authority for stopping LSMT when it is in the *best interest* of the patient to do so. While a decision to abate treatment on a best-interest basis does not carry with it a blanket grant of immunity, there are no instances in the legal literature where a physician or other health care provider has been successfully sued for so acting. Physicians routinely stop treatment now, just as they have traditionally, when it no longer provides a net benefit to the patient. Physicians have no obligation to provide futile treatment and this should be especially so where the decision to stop is unanimously supported by the next of

---

BOX **4–4**   *Beware of Restrictive Advance Directive Legislation*

Most of the courts that have addressed the issue of the withdrawal of artificial life supports have recognized that individuals have a common law or constitutional right to refuse treatments in settings other than those covered by a living will statute [citing to *In re Jobes*, 108 NJ 394, 529 A2d 434 (NJ 1987)]. Consequently, if a patient expressed treatment preferences in a living will for circumstances that went beyond the scope of the living will statute, the preferences would likely be upheld under common or constitutional law. However, the limitations in a state's living will statute may influence patients when they compose their wills. Many patients are likely to use the model living will form that is published as part of the state's living will statute. In addition, courts may be influenced by the scope of the living will statute in deciding the scope of a patient's common law or constitutional right to refuse artificial life supports [citing to *Couture* v. *Couture*, 48 Ohio App. 3d 208 (Ohio Ct. App. 1989)].

(Orentlicher, 1990, p. 2365)

---

kin (Veatch and Spicer, 1992; Areen, 1987; Weir and Gostin, 1990). See Box 4–4.

Beyond the Statutory Limits

There is yet another problem with the Ohio law and others like it. While the law authorizes discontinuation of LSMT pursuant to the terms of a living will or DPAHC when the patient is either terminally ill or permanently unconscious, these are not the only circumstances under which persons might wish to refuse LSMT. Although PVS represents a dramatic illustration of incapacity, and the tragedies of the Quinlan and Cruzan families have created broad public awareness of this particular problem, the likelihood of permanent unconsciousness happening to many people is quite low. Of much greater probability is the development of Alzheimer's disease or other forms of severe dementia. Many of us fear what might happen if we were to develop such a form of debilitation and, along with this, require some form of LSMT. Think about this if you will. Suppose that you were to develop Alzheimer's disease and you were subsequently diagnosed with kidney failure. Would you choose to have treatment? Would you, if you had the ability to do so, consent to either hemodialysis or a kidney transplant? Would you sooner die from the complications of end-stage renal disease or receive treatment and perhaps go on living in your mentally impaired state for years? Keep in mind, of course, that you could refuse any form of treatment if you were competent to do so. Also keep in mind that we are talking only about your making decisions for *yourself*. To decide that you would not wish to have *your* life prolonged under circumstances such as this is not to suggest that others who might feel differently should be bound by *your* choice. Further keep in mind that since your condition is neither a terminal illness nor a form of permanent unconsciousness, your treatment decision does not fall within the framework of many advance directive laws. This, however, should not prevent you from executing a valid advance directive that would protect your right to make even this decision if you follow the approach recommended below.

Let's look at another example. Just as some people are concerned about what might happen to them if they were to develop Alzheimer's disease or other forms of severe dementia, others fear the loss of mobility and total dependence upon the care of others. Such might occur in the case of a massive insult to the brain resulting from a stroke or accidental injury. Suppose, for example, that you were totally and irreversibly paralyzed and unable to communicate in any way. Further suppose that in this severely impaired condition you were to develop pneumonia. The pneumonia could be treated with antibiotics and your life could be saved. Would you want to be treated? Would you sooner die from the complications of pneumonia or continue to live as you are? Again, you fail to fit the common definition of either terminally ill or permanently unconscious and the provisions of your statutorily based advance directive may not apply. Again, let us emphasize that there are likely to be people who would choose treatment under either of these situations and we fully support their right to make such decisions. However, for those who would choose differently, they need not have the scope of their decision-making authority restricted to those conditions recognized by statute.

Rather than allowing their choices to be limited to those approved by the legislature, they might instead state the circumstances under which *they* would wish to have LSMT withheld or withdrawn. While such choices might well exceed those authorized by statute, their right to refuse treatment is secured by other parts of "the law"—the common law and the constitutions of the United States and, perhaps, the state in which they reside. As illustrated in Figure 4–7, what we commonly refer to as "the law" is really a somewhat amorphous assembly of rules and regulations, rights and responsibilities, and liberties and restrictions that can be found in a wide variety of documents. First, there is the law as enunciated by judges which has been compiled in record books over many centuries. Together these form the body of what is known as common law and it is upon such law that many of our most cherished freedoms rest. For example, the law of informed consent, and its corollary, informed refusal, is largely a result of judicial interpretations of the law of battery or uncon-

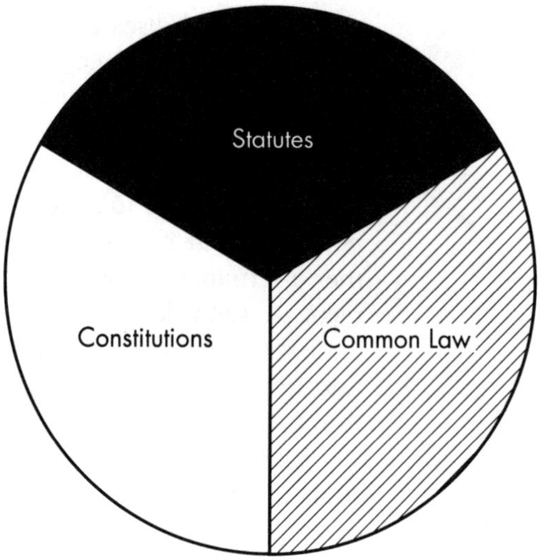

FIGURE 4-7 Sources of Law. "Rights," as defined by law, are the result of judicial decisions (common law) and interpretations of the constitution (both state and federal) as well as laws passed by the legislature (statutes).

sented touching. The law of informed consent is deeply imbedded in our legal tradition and it has been cited in many of the cases discussed earlier in this volume.

Second, there is the law as found in constitutions and their interpretations by judges. While most people are well aware of the privileges and immunities conferred by the United States Constitution, and the restrictions it places on government intervention into the lives of citizens, they are often far less aware of similar, and sometimes even more extensive, freedoms guaranteed by state constitutions. It is these documents to which we turn to find the meanings of terms like *privacy* and *liberty,* both of which have been cited as providing a foundation for the freedom to refuse unwanted medical treatment. Many courts, including the U.S. Supreme Court, have described the right to privacy as a fundamental right, meaning that it may not be restricted by the government, either state or federal, without demonstration of a compelling reason for so doing.

As a practical matter, fundamental rights are nearly always upheld by the courts against government attempts to prescribe limits on them. The privacy right was first successfully asserted in the *Quinlan* case and was relied upon by a number of other state courts deciding similar controversies. But in the *Cruzan* case, the U.S. Supreme Court retreated from this, characterizing the right to refuse unwanted treatment as a "liberty interest," a somewhat "weaker" right which allowed the State of Missouri to intervene in the decision making in a way that a fundamental right would likely have precluded. Since the freedoms granted under state constitutions are not constrained by interpretations of the U.S. Constitution, it is possible that even greater protections for individual rights may be found there.

The third component of "the law" is the collection of rules and regulations, called *statutes,* passed by the legislative branch of government, both state and federal. The scope of such laws is limited by interpretations of the Constitution as found in the decisions of our highest courts. A given state legislature may pass an advance directive law granting immunity to health care providers acting pursuant to it contingent upon terminal illness or permanent unconsciousness. However, it clearly does not have the authority to deprive citizens of the constitutional and/or common law right to execute more expansive advance directives. A health care provider acting pursuant to a condition in an advance directive outside the letter of the statute, such as withholding antibiotics from an Alzheimer's disease patient who develops pneumonia, will not have a blanket grant of immunity from the legislature, but the right of the patient to express such a wish and the expectation that it will be respected is no less secure. See Box 4–5.

While it is important for everyone preparing an advance directive to become fully aware of the statutory requirements and restrictions in their particular state, it is important for them to understand that the statute represents the *minimal* level of protection that their decision will be accorded.

Let us return to the case of Ohio to illustrate the importance of this final point. Shortly after the governor signed the advance directive bill into law, the Ohio State Bar Association formed a committee to draft model forms to be used to comply with the requirements of the new law for either a living will or a DPAHC. These forms were subsequently approved by the Ohio State Medical Association and prepared for distribution bearing the seals of both organizations. The organizations also initiated an educational campaign to inform the public about the new law and to encourage them to sign one of these standardized or "generic" forms. While stressing that the documents would serve to protect their rights to determine their own medical treatment under the statute, there was no indication that their choices could legally exceed those bounds if desired. Instead, it is reasonable to believe that most Ohioans, upon securing a copy of a form endorsed by two such prestigious organizations, signed the documents thinking that they had done all that they could do to protect themselves and their families. It was with such a problem in mind that LaPuma and others (1991, p. 404), writing in the *Journal of the American Medical Association* about the implications of the PSDA, expressed a concern that the Act might be, in some ways, counterproductive; that patients might be *incorrectly* informed about their rights. They noted that while the Act requires informing patients about their rights under *state* law, they may never be told that their rights under the U.S. Constitution may be much broader.

Box 4–5 *Advance Directive Statutes: Death Warrants or Life Sentences?*

Most thoughtful analyses [citations omitted] of the Supreme Court justices' different *Cruzan* opinions argue persuasively that, taken together, these opinions stand for the propositions that: (1) the Fourteenth Amendment Due Process liberty interest includes the right of a decisionally capable person to make LSMT decisions, presently or prospectively through an instruction or proxy advance directive, and that a state statute is not necessary to effectuate this right and it certainly may not intrude upon this right; (2) the constitutional right to make and have carried out LSMT decisions is not limited (and could not be limited under the Fourteenth Amendment's Equal Protection clause) to terminally ill or PVS patients; (3) there is no meaningful distinction between withdrawing treatment and withholding its initiation in the first place; and (4) there is no meaningful legal distinction between decisions concerning artificial feeding tubes and other forms of LSMT. Thus, state statutes that limit patient autonomy concerning LSMT decisions are subject to constitutional challenge and judicial invalidation, as has occurred in the several cases to date in which the issue has been raised [citing to *McConnell* (Conn. 1989); *Browning* (Fla. 1990); and *Corbett* (Fla. 1986)].

   The big problem, however, is that physicians and other health care professionals quite understandably do not usually compehend and act upon the law in the same way that sophisticated appellate judges and law professors do. Instead, misperceptions of legal requirements that feed into their natural risk-adverse predilections (at least when it comes to their own legal exposure), often fueled by the overly conservative advice supplied by in-house counsel and risk managers, frequently cause physicians to follow the path of apparent least resistence even at the expense of patient and family autonomy and their own ethical and clinical preferences. To many physicians, the advance-directive and/or family-consent statutes on the books in their particular jurisdiction, however restrictive and counterproductive, represent *the* applicable law on LSMT decision making, and astute lectures explaining how these statutes fit with and supplement rather than supplant constitutional and common law rights may have little impact on medical behavior [citation omitted].

Reprinted with permission from Marshall B. Kapp, "State Statutes Limiting Advance-Directives: Death Warrants or Life Sentences?", *Journal of the American Geriatric Society*, 40: 772–776.

Unfortunately, health care providers may be similarly misinformed (Fulton, 1992).

   Although living wills are typically created to express limitations on the use of LSMT, they also can be used to express a desire to receive a particular kind of treatment or even a wish for all available treatment for as long as possible.

While it seems that this is not what most people would wish (Greco et al., 1991), there is evidence that some people would. This, for example, was the situation in the *Wanglie* case that was discussed in Chapter 3. Although Mrs. Wanglie, who was diagnosed as being permanently unconscious, did not have an advance directive, her husband was convinced, from previous conversations with his wife, that she would want to have all possible treatment continued.

An Alternative to Traditional Forms of Advance Directives

Finally, we leave you with an example of a document that expresses a desire for the continuation, rather than refusal, of all forms of LSMT. The document, called a Will to Live, first appeared in the March 24, 1992, issue of the *National Right to Life News,* a publication of the National Right to Life Committee. Although the National Right to Life Committee is most often associated with opposition to abortion, as will be discussed in Chapter 7, it has also opposed various forms of living will legislation. The Will to Live is being promoted as an alternative form of advance directive that "starts from the principle that the presumption should be for life." The document, it is claimed, is designed to protect the individual against the "pro-euthanasia views widespread in society" and to prevent the starving to death of the "disabled." The directive, which has been reproduced as Figure 4–8, would *never* authorize the withholding or withdrawal of food and/or water and would authorize the elimination of other forms of LSMT only when death was imminent or during the final stages of a terminal condition. The former is defined as having an incurable terminal illness or injury that will cause death within a week or less regardless of the kind of treatment provided. This would be an example of the kind of futile treatment described earlier. The latter is defined as having an incurable terminal illness or injury from which death would be likely, not within a week, but within "three months or less."

Whether you wish to have all forms of LSMT, including tube feeding and/or hydration, withheld or withdrawn when you are terminally ill, permanently unconscious, or under any of a number of idiosyncratically intolerable conditions or if you wish to have all forms of LSMT provided for as long as possible regardless of the circumstances, or anything in between, the important thing is that you put your wishes in writing NOW. These are difficult and uncomfortable issues for many people to contemplate, but the time and effort that you spend now may well be of immeasurable comfort to your loved ones if they find themselves confronted by these tragic choices. When such decisions have to be made, someone has to make them. The questions to be faced are (1) who gets to make them and (2) what will those decisions be? The choices are quite clear.

WILL TO LIVE AND ACCOMPANYING SUGGESTIONS

WILL TO LIVE

GENERAL PRESUMPTION FOR LIFE

I direct my health care provider(s) and health care agent to make health care decisions consistent with my general desire for the use of medical treatment that would preserve my life, as well as for the use of medical treatment that can cure, improve, or reduce or prevent deterioration in, any physical or mental condition.

Food and water are not medical treatment, but basic necessities. I direct my health care provider(s) and health care agent to provide me with food and fluids orally, intravenously, by tube, or by other means to the full extent necessary both to preserve my life and to assure me the optimal health possible.

I direct that medication to alleviate my pain be provided, as long as the medication is not used in order to cause my death.

I direct that the following be provided:
- the administration of medication;
- cardiopulmonary resuscitation (CPR); and
- the performance of all other medical procedures, techniques, and technologies, including surgery,

all to the full extent necessary to correct, reverse, or alleviate life-threatening or health-impairing conditions, or complications arising from those conditions.

I also direct that I be provided basic nursing care and procedures to provide comfort care.

I reject, however, any treatments that use an unborn or newborn child, or any tissue or organ of an unborn or newborn child, who has been subject to an induced abortion. This rejection does not apply to the use of tissues or organs obtained in the course of the removal of an ectopic pregnancy.

I also reject any treatments that use an organ or tissue of another person obtained in a manner that causes, contributes to, or hastens that person's death.

The instructions in this document are intended to be followed even if suicide is alleged to be attempted at some point after it is signed.

I request and direct that medical treatment and care be provided to me to preserve my life without discrimination based on my age or physical or mental disability or the "quality" of my life. I reject any action or omission that is intended to cause or hasten my death.

I direct my health care provider(s) and health care agent to follow the above policy, even if I am judged to be incompetent.

During the time I am incompetent, my agent, as named below, is authorized to make medical decisions on my behalf, consistent with the above policy, after consultation with my health care provider(s), utilizing the most current diagnoses and/or prognosis of my medical condition, in the following situations with the written special conditions.

(OVER)

Notice: Although this is the content of the Will to Live, it is not itself a legal document. Different forms exist for each state. Do not attempt to sign this version. Instead, to obtain the Will to Live valid in your state, send a self-addressed, stamped business (9 1/2 " wide) envelope to Will to Live Project, Suite 500, 419 Seventh St., N.W., Washington, D.C. 20004.

FIGURE 4–8   The Will to Live is a document developed by the National Right to Life Committee in reaction to what it sees as a trend toward withholding and/or withdrawing LSMT from vulnerable patients without their consent. (Reprinted by permission of the National Right to Life Committee, Inc., Washington, D.C.)

WHEN MY DEATH IS IMMINENT

A. If I have an incurable terminal illness or injury, and I will die imminently — meaning that a reasonably prudent physician, knowledgeable about the case and the treatment possibilities with respect to the medical conditions involved, would judge that I will live only a week or less even if lifesaving treatment or care is provided to me — the following may be withheld or withdrawn:

(Be as specific as possible; SEE SUGGESTIONS.): _____

_____

_____

_____

(Cross off any remaining blank lines.)

WHEN I AM TERMINALLY ILL

B. Final Stage of Terminal Condition. If I have an incurable terminal illness or injury and even though death is not imminent I am in the final stage of that terminal condition — meaning that a reasonably prudent physician, knowledgeable about the case and the treatment possibilities with respect to the medical conditions involved, would judge that I will live only three months or less, even if lifesaving treatment or care is provided to me — the following may be withheld or withdrawn:

(Be as specific as possible; SEE SUGGESTIONS.): _____

_____

_____

_____

(Cross off any remaining blank lines.)

C. OTHER SPECIAL CONDITIONS: **(Be as specific as possible; SEE SUGGESTIONS.):** _____

_____

_____

_____

(Cross off any remaining blank lines.)

IF I AM PREGNANT

D. Special Instructions for Pregnancy. If I am pregnant, I direct my health care provider(s) and health care agent to use all lifesaving procedures for myself with none of the above special conditions applying if there is a chance that prolonging my life might allow my child to be born alive. I also direct that lifesaving procedures be used even if I am legally determined to be brain dead if there is a chance that doing so might allow my child to be born alive. Except as I specify by writing my signature in the box below, no one is authorized to consent to any procedure for me that would result in the death of my unborn child.

> If I am pregnant, and I am not in the final stage of a terminal condition as defined above, medical procedures required to prevent my death are authorized even if they may result in the death of my unborn child provided every possible effort is made to preserve both my life and the life of my unborn child.
>
> _____

FIGURE 4–8 *(Continued)*

SUGGESTIONS
FOR PREPARING WILL TO LIVE/DURABLE POWER OF ATTORNEY

(PLEASE READ THE DOCUMENT ITSELF BEFORE READING THIS. IT WILL HELP YOU BETTER UNDERSTAND THE SUGGESTIONS.)

YOU ARE NOT REQUIRED TO FILL OUT ANY PART OF THIS "WILL TO LIVE" OR ANY OTHER DOCUMENT SUCH AS A LIVING WILL OR DURABLE POWER OF ATTORNEY FOR HEALTH CARE. NO ONE MAY FORCE YOU TO SIGN THIS DOCUMENT OR ANY OTHER OF ITS KIND.

The Will to Live form starts from the principle that the presumption should be for life. If you sign it without writing any "SPECIAL CONDITIONS," you are giving directions to your health care provider(s) and health care agent(s) to do their best to preserve your life.

Some people may wish to continue certain types of medical treatment when they are terminally ill and in the final stages of life. Others may not.

If you wish to refuse some specific medical treatment, the Will to Live form provides space to do so ("SPECIAL CONDITIONS"). You may make special conditions for your treatment when your death is imminent, meaning you will live no more than a week even if given all available medical treatment; or when you are incurably terminally ill, meaning you will live no more than three months even if given all available medical treatment. There is also space for you to write down special conditions for circumstances you describe yourself.

The important thing for you to remember if you choose to fill out any part of the "SPECIAL CONDITIONS" sections of the Will to Live is that *you must be very specific in listing what treatments you do not want*. Some examples of how to be specific will be given shortly, or you may ask your physician what types of treatment might be expected in your specific case.

Why is it important to be specific? Because, given the pro-euthanasia views widespread in society and particularly among many (not all) health care providers, *there is great danger that a vague description of what you do not want will be misunderstood or distorted so as to deny you treatment that you do want.*

Many in the medical profession as well as in the courts are now so committed to the quality of life ethic that they take as a given that patients with severe disabilities are better off dead and would prefer not to receive either life-saving measures or nutrition and hydration. So pervasive is this "consensus" that it is accurate to say that in practice it is no longer true that the "presumption is for life" but rather for death. In other words, instead of assuming that a now incompetent patient would want to receive treatment and care in the absence of clear evidence to the contrary, the assumption has virtually become that since any "reasonable" person would want to exercise a "right to die," treatment and care should be withheld or withdrawn unless there is evidence to the contrary. The Will to Live is intended to maximize the chance of providing that evidence.

It is important to remember that you are writing a legal document, not holding a conversation, and not writing a moral textbook. The language you or a religious or moral leader might use in discussing what is and is not moral to refuse is, from a legal standpoint, often much too vague. Therefore, it is subject to misunderstanding or deliberate abuse.

The person you appoint as your health care agent may understand general terms in the same way you do. But remember that the person you appoint may die, or become incapacitated, or simply be unavailable when decisions must be made about your health care. If any of these happens, a court might appoint someone else you don't know in that person's place. Also remember that since the health care agent has to follow the instructions you write in this form, a health care provider could try to persuade a court that the agent isn't really following your wishes. A court could overrule your health care agent's

Figure 4–8   *(Continued)*

insistence on treatment in cases in which the court interprets any vague language you put in your "Will to Live" less protectively than you meant it.

So, for example, **do not** simply say you don't want "extraordinary treatment." Whatever the value of that language in moral discussions, there is so much debate over what it means legally that it could be interpreted very broadly by a doctor or a court. For instance, it might be interpreted to require starving you to death when you have a disability, even if you are in no danger of death if you are fed.

For the same reason, **do not use** language rejecting treatment which has a phrase like "excessive pain, expense or other excessive burden." Doctors and courts may have a very different definition of what is "excessive" or a "burden" than you do. **Do not use** language that rejects treatment that "does not offer a reasonable hope of benefit." "Benefit" is a legally vague term. If you had a significant disability, a health care provider or court might think you would want no medical treatment at all, since many doctors and judges unfortunately believe there is no "benefit" to life with a severe disability.

What sort of language is specific enough if you wish to write exclusions? Here are some examples of things you might--or might not--want to list under one or more of the "Special Conditions" described on the form. Remember that any of these will prevent treatment ONLY under the circumstances — such as when death is imminent — described in the "Special Condition" you list it under. (The examples are not meant to be all inclusive — just samples of the type of thing you might want to write.)

"Cardiopulmonary resuscitation (CPR)." (If you would like CPR in some but not all circumstances when you are terminally ill, you should try to be still more specific: for example, you might write "CPR if cardiopulmonary arrest has been caused by my terminal illness or a complication of it." This would mean that you would still get CPR if, for example, you were the victim of smoke inhalation in a fire.)

"Organ transplants." (Again, you could be still more specific, rejecting, for example, just a

"heart transplant.")

"Surgery that would not cure me, would not improve either my mental or my physical condition, would not make me more comfortable, and would not help me to have less pain, but would only keep me alive longer."

"A treatment that will itself cause me severe, intractable, and long-lasting pain but will not cure me."

Pain Relief. Under the "General Presumption for Life," of your Will to Live, you will be given medication necessary to control any pain you may have "as long as the medication is not used in order to cause my death." This means that you may be given pain medication that has the secondary, but unintended, effect of shortening your life. If this is not your wish, you may want to write something like one of the following under the third set of "Special Conditions" (the section for conditions you describe yourself):

"I would like medication to relieve my pain but only to the extent the medication would not seriously threaten to shorten my life." OR

"I would like medication to relieve my pain but only to the extent it is known, to a reasonable medical certainty, that it will not shorten my life."

Think carefully about any special conditions you decide to write in your "Will to Live." You may want to show them to your intended health care agent(s) and a couple of other people to see if they find them clear and if they mean the same thing to them as they mean to you. *Remember that how carefully you write may literally be a matter of life or death--your own.*

AFTER WRITING DOWN YOUR SPECIAL CONDITIONS, IF ANY, YOU SHOULD MARK OUT THE REST OF THE BLANK LINES left on the form for them (just as you do after writing out the amount on a check) to prevent any danger that somebody other than you could write in something else.

It is wise to review your Will to Live periodically to ensure that it still gives the directions you want followed.

March, 1992
Prepared by National Right to Life Committee, Will to Live Project
419 7th St. N.W. • Suite 500 • Washington, D.C. 20004 • (202) 626-8800

FIGURE 4–8 *(Continued)*

Summary

Because of changes in the way in which we die, both in terms of how and where, there has been a growing interest in the way in which decisions about life-sustaining medical treatment are made when the patient is no longer able to participate in that process. This interest has also been intensified by the highly publicized cases of Karen Ann Quinlan and Nancy Cruzan. The Quinlan case, in particular, was instrumental in the passage of the first state living will statute, The California Natural Death Act of 1976. Since then every state has passed laws authorizing either living wills or durable powers of attorney for health care or both.

Although patients have the right under the Constitution—the U.S. Constitution definitely and probably their state constitutions as well—to refuse all forms of unwanted medical treatment, advance directive statutes are often more restrictive in the kinds of decisions they seem to acknowledge. Many advance directive statutes apply only when the patient is either terminally ill or permanently unconscious. Those wishing to assure that treatment is withheld or withdrawn under other specified circumstances such as permanent mental impairment or severe loss of motor function may have to rely upon constitutional and common law rights rather than upon statutes. Some state advance directive laws also differentiate between artificially provided feeding and hydration and other forms of medical treatment, often putting special restrictions upon decisions to forgo the former. You would be well advised to carefully examine the advance directive law(s) in your state of residence to see whether their decisions about treatment are fully respected before signing any "standardized" forms; an individualized or idiosyncratic statement of their wishes meeting all of the required formalities may be advisable.

The Patient Self-Determination Act was passed by Congress and signed by President Bush in November 1990. It became effective on December 1, 1991. All hospitals and other health providers receiving funding under Medicare and/or Medicaid are now required to inquire about advance directives whenever patients are admitted to receive services. It is still too early to judge what effect this will have on the number of people preparing advance directives.

Advance directives can spare families and loved ones the tremendous stress of trying to make the "right" decision where the wishes of the patient are unknown. They can also help avoid the kind of legal entanglements that were experienced by the Quinlans and the Cruzans. Even if your decision would be to continue all forms of treatment for as long as possible, rather than to restrict treatment, advance directives—as illustrated by the Will to Live—can effectuate that choice. Most importantly, whatever your wishes, be sure to take action now. This is not something that should be considered only by "older" persons. Karen Ann Quinlan was twenty-one and Nancy Cruzan was twenty-five when they lost consciousness, and with it the ability to make their own decisions. Don't put this off until "later." This is an important gift that you can give to your loved ones. Do it now!

Study Questions

1. What is an *instructional* advance directive?

2. What is a *proxy* advance directive?

3. In what way might "the Medical Directive," as proposed by Emanuel and Emanuel, be useful in formulating one's wishes about the use of life-sustaining medical treatment?

4. What are the *procedural* requirements in executing a valid form of advance directive?

5. What is the Patient Self-Determination Act and how does it work?

6. In what ways might advance directives executed according to state law actually serve to restrict rather than fully implement patient autonomy?

7. The "Will to Live," prepared and distributed by the National Right to Life Committee, represents a departure from the typical form of advance directive. In what ways does it differ and what are the philosophical underpinnings of this approach to making medical treatment decisions?

References

Areen, J. (1987). The legal status of consent obtained from families of adult patients to withhold or withdraw treatment. *JAMA,* 258:229–235.

Bartling v. *Superior Court,* 163 Cal. App. 196, 2098 Cal. Rptr. 220 (1984).

Benton, E. C. (1990). The constitutionality of pregnancy clauses in living will statutes. *Vanderbilt Law Review,* 43:1821–1837.

California Natural Death Act, 1976 Cal. Stat., Chapter 1439, Code § Health and Safety, § 7185–7195 (Sept. 30, 1976).

Corbett v. *D'Alessandro,* 487 So.2d 368 (Fla. Dist. Ct. App.), *review denied,* 492 So.2d 1331 (Fla. 1986).

Couture v. *Couture,* 48 Ohio App. 3d 208, 549 N.E.2d 571 (1989).

Crum, In re, 61 Ohio Misc.2d 596, 580 N.E. 2d 876 (Probate Ct., Franklin County, 1991).

Cruzan v. *Director, Missouri Dept. of Health,* 497 U.S. 261, 110 S. Ct. 2841, 111 L. Ed.2d 224 (1990).

Del. Code Ann. Tit. 16, §2502 et. seq. (July 12, 1982).

Emanuel, L. L., and E. J. Emanuel. (1989). The medical directive: A new comprehensive advance care document. *JAMA,* 261:3288–3293.

___. (1990). The medical directive: A new comprehensive advance care document. *Harvard Medical School Health Letter,* (Supplement), June.

Emanuel, L. (1991). The health care directive: Learning how to draft advance care documents. *JAGS,* 39:1221–1228.

Fulton, G. B. (1991). *Your Guide to Living Wills and Durable Powers of Attorney for Health Care in Ohio* (Lawyer's Edition). Holland, OH: Health Law Press.

___. (1992). What the physician needs to know about advance directives. *Toledo Medicine* (January/February): 22–23.

Gibbons, D. L. (1991). Doctors need to be nudges on D-words. *Medical World News* (January).

Greco, P. J., K. A. Schulman, R. Lavizzo-Mourey, and J. Hansen-Flaschen. (1991). The Patient Self-Determination Act and the future of advance directives. *Annals of Internal Medicine,* 115:639–643.

Hastings Center, The. (1987). *Guidelines on the Termination of Life-Sustaining Treatment.* Briarcliff Manor, NY: Author.

John F. Kennedy Memorial Hospital, Inc. v. *Bludworth (Landy)* , 452 So. 2d 921 (Fla. 1984).

Kapp, M. B. (1992). State statutes limiting advance-directives: Death warrants or life sentences? *JAGS,* 40: 772–776.

Kutner, L. (1987). The living will: The epitome of human dignity in coping with the historical event of death. *University of Detroit Law Review,* 64:661–686.

LaPuma, J. D. Orentilicher, and R. J. Moss. (1991). Advance directives on admission: Clinical implications and analysis of the Patient Self-Determination Act of 1990. *JAMA,* 266:402–405.

MacAvoy-Snitzer, J. (1987). Pregnancy clauses in living will statutes. *Columbia Law Review,* 87:1280–1300.

McInnis, In re, 61 Ohio Misc.2d 790, 584 N.E.2d 1389 (Probate Ct., Stark County 1991).

Miller, D. H. (1988). Right to die damage actions: Developments in the law. *Denver University Law Review,* 65:181–212.

Mishkin, B. (1986). *A Matter of Choice: Planning Ahead for Health Care Decisions.* Washington, DC: AARP.

Myers, In re, 62 Ohio Misc. 2d 763, 610 N.E. 2d 663 (Probate Ct., Summit County, 1993).

Ohio Revised Code §§1337.11–1337.17; 2133.01–2133.15 (effective October 10, 1991).

Orentlicher, D. (1990). Advance medical directives. *JAMA,* 263:2365–2367.

Patient Self-Determination Act of 1990, The, Public Law No. 101–50–8, Section 4206 U.S. Code Cong. & Admin. News (104 Stat.) 291; Public Law No. 101–508, Section 4751, 1990 U.S. Code Cong. & Admin. News (104 Stat.) 519.

Position of the American Academy of Neurology on certain aspects of the care and management of the persistent vegetative state patient. (1989). *Neurology,* 39:125–126.

President's Commission for the Study of Ethical Problems in Medicine and Biomedical and Behavioral Research. (1983). *Deciding to Forego Life Sustaining Treatment.* Washington, DC: Author.

Quinlan, In re, 137 N.J. Sup. 227, 348 A. 2d 801, *modified and remanded,* 70 N.J. 10, 355 A. 2d 647, *cert. denied sub nom. Garger* v. *New Jersey,* 429 U.S. 922 (1976).

Roe v. *Wade,* 410 U.S. 113, 93 S. Ct. 705 (1973).

Sabatino, C. P. (1990). *Health Care Powers of Attorney.* Washington, DC: American Bar Association.

Schloendorff v. *Society of New York Hospital,* 22 N.Y. 125, 105 N.E. 92 (1914).

Section 459.010 et. seq. R.S. Mo., 1986.

Singer, P. A., and M. Siegler. (1992). Advancing the cause of advance directives. *Arch. Intern. Med.,* 152:22–24.

Union Pacific R. Co. v. *Botsford,* 141 U.S. 250 (1891).

Veatch, R. M., and C. M. Spicer. (1992). Medically futile care: The role of the physician in setting limits. *American Journal of Law & Medicine,* 28:15–36.

Weir, R. F., and L. Gostin. (1990). Decisions to abate life-sustaining treatment on non-autonomous patients: Ethical standards and legal liability for physicians after Cruzan. *JAMA,* 264:1846–1853.

Westchester County Med. Center, In re (O'Connor), 72 N.Y. 2d 517, 534 N.Y.S. S2d 886, 531 N.E. 2d 607 (1988), amended 1988.

Wolf, S. M. (1991). Honoring broader directives. *Hastings Center Report* (Special Supplement on Practicing the PSDA) (September/October): S8–9.

Appendix

Right-to-Die Case and Statutory Citations— State-by-State Listing

Note: Below is a list of statutes and cases concerning the right to die. The cases are arranged alphabetically (case names beginning with "In re" alphabetized according to the first party's name). The year(s) within brackets following the name of the act indicate the year of enactment and any subsequent amendments.

Alabama

Alabama Natural Death Act [1981], Ala. Code §§22-8A-1 to 22-8A-10 (1990).

Camp v. White, 510 So. 2d 166 (Ala. 1987).

Alaska

Alaska Rights of Terminally Ill Act [1986], Alaska Stat. §§18.12.010 to 18.12.100 (1991).

Alaska Statutory Form Power of Attorney Act [1988], Alaska Stat. §§13.26.332 to 13.26.356 (Supp. 1992).

Arizona

Arizona Living Wills and Health Care Directives Act [1985, 1991, 1992], Ariz. Rev. Stat. Ann. §§36–3201 to 36–3262 (Supp. 1992).

Lurie v. Samaritan Health Service, No. C510198 (Ariz. Super. Ct. Maricopa Co. March 24, 1984).

Rasmussen v. Fleming, 154 Ariz. 207, 741 P.2d 674 (1987).

Arkansas

Arkansas Rights of the Terminally Ill or Permanently Unconscious Act [1977, 1987], Ark. Code Ann. §§20-17-201 to 20-17-218 (Michie 1991).

California

California Natural Death Act [1976, 1991], Cal. Health & Safety Code §§7185 to 7194.5 (West Supp. 1993).

Reprinted by permission of Choice In Dying (formerly Concern for Dying/Society for the Right to Die), 200 Varick Street, New York, NY 10014–4810/(212) 366–5540.

California Durable Power of Attorney for Health Care Act [1984, 1985, 1988, 1990, 1991, 1992, 1993], Cal. Civil Code §§2430 to 2444 (West Supp. 1993 & A.B. 346, signed July 19, 1993).

California Statutory Form Durable Power of Attorney for Health Care Act [1984, 1985, 1988, 1990, 1991, 1992], Cal. Civil Code §§2500 to 2508 (West Supp. 1993).

Barber v. Superior Court, 147 Cal. App. 3d 1006, 195 Cal. Rptr. 484 (Ct. App. 1983).

Bartling v. Glendale Adventist Medical Center, 184 Cal. App. 3d 97, 228 Cal. Rptr, 847 (Ct. App. 1986), *on remand,* No. 500735 (Cal. Super. Ct. L.A. Co. Oct. 14, 1987) (attorney fees) (Riley, J.).

Bartling v. Glendale Adventist Medical Center, 184 Cal. App. 3d 961, 229 Cal. Rptr. 360 (Ct. App. 1986) (damages).

Bartling v. Superior Court, 163 Cal. App. 3d 186, 209 Cal. Rptr. 220 (Ct. App. 1984).

Bouvia v. Glenchur, 195 Cal. App. 3d 1075, 241 Cal. Rptr. 239 (Ct. App. 1987) (attorney fees).

Bouvia v. County of Riverside, No. 159780 (Cal. Super. Ct. Riverside Co. Dec. 16, 1983) (Hews, J.).

Bouvia v. Superior Court (Glenchur), 179 Cal. App. 3d 1127, 225 Cal. Rptr. 297 (Ct. App. 1986), *review denied* (June 5, 1986).

Cantor v. Weiss, No. 626163 (Cal. Super. Ct. L.A. Co. Dec. 30, 1986) (Newman, J.).

Childs v. Abramovice (Morrison), 206 Cal. App. 3d 304, 253 Cal. Rptr, 530, 88 Daily Journal D.A.R. 14963 (Cal. Ct. App. 1988) (King, J.).

In re Cruse, No. J914410 (Cal. Super. Ct. L.A. Co. Feb. 15, 1979) (Byrne, J.).

In re Conservatorship of Drabick, 200 Cal. App. 3d 185, 245 Cal. Rptr. 840 (Cal. Ct. App. 1988), *rehearing denied* (May 12, 1988), *review denied* (July 28, 1988), *cert. denied sub nom. Drabick v. Drabick,* 488 U.S. 958 (1988), *rehearing denied,* 488 U.S. 1024 (1989).

Foster v. Tourtellotte, No. CV 81–5046-RMT (C.D. Cal. Nov. 16, 17, 1981), *connected case,* 704 F.2d 1109 (9th Cir. 1983).

Gary v. California (Hirth), No. 576 123 (Cal. Super. Ct. San Diego Co. March 5, 23), *modified in part* (April 15, 1987) (Milkes, J.).

Gary v. Superior Court, No. D006166 (Cal. Ct. App. 4th Dist. Sept. 25, 1987) (Kremer, J.).

McMahon v. Lopez (Flott), 199 Cal. App. 3d 829, 245 Cal Rptr. 172 (Ct. App. 1988).

Thor v. Superior Court, 5 Cal. 4th 725, 21 Cal. Rptr. 2d 357, 855 P.2d 375 (1993).

Sanchez v. Fairview Developmental Center, No. CV 88-0129 FFF(Tx) (C.D. Cal. March 30, 1988) (Fernandez, J.), 4 Issues in L. & Med. 129; *connected case,* No. 563–313 (Cal. Super. Ct. Orange Co. Sept. 2, 1988) (McDonald, J.).

Westhart v. Mule, 213 Cal. App. 3d 542, 261 Cal. Rptr. 640, 89 Daily Journal D.A.R. 10903 (Ct. App. 1989) (Bauer, J.), *opinion withdrawn,* 1989 Cal. Lexis 4990 (Cal. 1989).

In re Young, No. A 100863 (Cal. Super. Ct. Orange Co. Sept. 11, 1979) (Summer, J.).

COLORADO

Colorado Medical Treatment Decision Act [1985, 1989], Colo. Rev. Stat. §§15-18-101 to 15-18-113 (1987 & Supp. 1992).

Colorado Patient Autonomy Act [1992], Colo. Rev. Stat. §§15-14-501 to 15-14-509 (Supp. 1992).

In re Carothers, No. 89PR66 (Colo. Dist. Ct. Mesa Co. Sept. 15, 1989) (Buss, J.)

In re Carothers, No. 89PR66 (Colo. Dist. Ct. Mesa Co. Feb. 12, 1990) (Buss, J.) (attorney fees).

In re Peterson, No. 90PR0827 (Colo. Dist. Ct. El Paso Co. July 6, 1991) (Bromley, J.).

In re Rodas, No. 86PR139 (Colo. Dist. Ct. Mesa Co. Jan. 22, 1987, *as modified,* April 3, 1987) (Buss, J.).

Ross v. Hilltop Rehabilitation Hospital, 676 F. Supp. 1528 (D. Colo. 1987) (Rodas damage claim).

CONNECTICUT

Connecticut Removal of Life Support Systems Act [1985, 1991, 1993], Conn. Gen. Stat. §§19a-570 to 19a-580c (1993 & Substitute Bill 7244, signed June 29, 1993).

Connecticut Statutory Short Form Durable Power of Attorney Act [1990, 1991], Conn. Gen. Stat. §§1-43 to 1-54a (Supp. 1992).

Foody v. Manchester Memorial Hospital, 40 Conn. Supp. 127, 482 A.2d 713 (Super. Ct. 1984).

McConnell v. Beverly Enterprises, 209 Conn. 692, 553 A.2d 596 (1989).

DELAWARE

Delaware Death with Dignity Act {1982, 1983], Del. Code Ann. tit. 16, §§2501 to 2509 (1983).

In re Severns, 425 A.2d 156 (Del. Ch. 1980).

Severns v. Wilmington Medical Center, Inc., 421 A.2d 1334 (Del. 1980).

In re Shumosic, No. 5515 (Del. Ch. Sept. 27, 1988) (Allen, C.).

DISTRICT OF COLUMBIA

District of Columbia Natural Death Act of 1981 {1982], D.C. Code Ann. §§6-2421 to 6-2430 (1989).

District of Columbia Health-Care Decisions Act of 1988 [1988, 1992], D.C. Code Ann. §§21-2201 to 21-2213 (1989 & Supp. 1992).

In re A.C., 573 A.2d 1235 (D.C. Ct. App. 1990).

Tune v. Walter Reed Army Medical Hospital, 602 F. Supp. 1452 (D.D.C. 1985).

FLORIDA

Florida Health Care Advance Directives Act [1984, 1985, 1990, 1992], Fla. Stat. Ann. §§765.101 to 765.401 (Supp. 1993).

Florida Durable Power of Attorney Act [1974, 1977, 1983, 1988, 1990, 1992], Fla. Stat. Ann. §709.08 (Supp. 1993).

In re Axelrod, No. 91-241-CG (Fla. Cir. Ct. Palm Beach Co. July 3, 1991) (Gersten, J.).

In re Guardianship of Barry, 445 So. 2d 365 (Fla. Dist. Ct. App. 1984) (Scheb, J.).

In re Guardianship of Browning, 568 So. 2d 4 (Fla. 1990).

Corbett v. D'Alessandro, 487 Sp. 2d 368 (Fla. Dist. Ct. App.), *review denied,* 492 So. 2d 1331 (Fla. 1986).

Gilbert v. State, 487 So. 2d 1185 (Fla. Dist. Ct. App.), *review denied,* 494 So. 2d 1150 (Fla. 1986).

Helstrom v. Florida Life Care, No. 88-1870-CA-01 (Fla. Cir. Ct. Sarasota Co. May 10, 1988) (Boylston, J.).

Hoffmeister v. Coler, 544 So. 2d 1067 (Fla. Dist. Ct. App. 4th Dist. 1989) (attorney fees).

Hoffmeister v. Satz, No. 87-28451 CR (Fla. Cir. Ct. 17th Dist. Broward Co. Feb. 22, 1988).

John F. Kennedy Memorial Hospital, Inc. v. Bludworth, 452 So. 2d 921 (Fla. 1984).

In re Baby Girl Muller, No. 88-1073 (Fla. Cir. Ct. Hillsborough Co. Feb. 9, 1988) (Evans, J.).

In re Ray, No. 91-2202 CAA (Fla. Cir. Ct. Okaloosa Co. July 29, 1991) (Barron, J.).

Rekstad v. Florida Life Care, Inc., No. 87-4285-CA-01 (Fla. Cir. Ct. Sarasota Co. Sept. 18, 1987) (Walker, J.).

In re Guardianship of Rothblatt, No. 87-256-41 (Fla. Cir. Ct. Penellas Co. Aug. 24, 1987) (Ward, J.).

In re Guardianship of Stone, No. 90-5867 (Fla. Cir. Ct. Broward Co. June 24, 1991).

Satz v. Perlmutter, 362 So. 2d 160 (Fla. Dist. Ct. App. 1978), *affirmed,* 379 So. 2d 359 (Fla. 1980).

In re Underwood, No. 85-8107-Ca-T (Fla. Cir. Ct. Brevard Co. Aug. 30, 1985).

In re Zahn, No. 85-3723 (Fla. Cir. Ct. Broward Co. Nov. 20, 1986) (Hare, J.).

GEORGIA

Georgia Living Wills Act [1984, 1986, 1987, 1989, 1992], Ga. Code Ann. §§31-32-1 to 31-32-12 (Michie Supp. 1992).

Georgia Durable Power of Attorney for Health Care Act [1990], Ga. Code §§31-36-1 to 31-36-13 (Michie 1991).

In re Jane Doe, No. D 56730 (Ga. Super. Ct. Fulton Co. July 13, 1988) (Williams, J.).

In re Jane Doe, No. D 62058 (Ga. Super. Ct. Fulton Co. Nov. 30, 1988) (Langham, J.).

In re Jane Doe, No. D 93064 (Ga. Super. Ct. Fulton Co. Oct. 17, 1991) (Sears-Collins, J.).

In re Jane Doe, 262 Ga. 389, 418 S.E.2d 3 (1992).

Kirby v. Spivey, 167 Ga. App. 751, 307 S.E.2d 538 (Ct. App. 1983).

In re L.H.R., 253 Ga. 439, 321 S.E.2d 716 (1984).

In re McAfee, 259 Ga. 579, 385 S.E.2d 651 (1989).

University Health Services, Inc. v. Piazzi, No. CV86-RCCV-464 (Super. Ct. Richmond Co. Aug. 4, 1986) (Fleming, J.).

Young v. Emory University, No. 83–6143–5 (Ga. Super. Ct. Dekalb Co. Aug. 10, 29, 1983) (Fuller, J.).

Zodin v. Manor Health Care, No. 9010821007 (Ga. Super. Ct. Cobb Co. Nov. 21, 1990) (White, J.).

HAWAII

Hawaii Medical Treatment Decisions Act [1986], Hawaii Rev. Stat. §§327D-1 to 327D-27 (Supp. 1992).

Hawaii Durable Power of Attorney for Health Care Decisions Act [1992], Hawaii Rev. Stat. §551D-1 to 551D-7 (Supp. 1992).

In re Guardianship of Crabtree, No. 86-0031 (Hawaii Fam. Ct. 1st Cir. April 26, 1990) (Heeley, J.).

Wilcox v. Hawaii, Civ. No. 860116 (Hawaii Cir. Ct. 5th Cir. June 16, 1986) (Hirano, J.).

IDAHO

Idaho Natural Death Act [1977, 1986, 1988], Idaho Code §§39-4501 to 39-4509 (1985 & Supp. 1992).

ILLINOIS

Illinois Living Will Act [1984, 1988], Ill. Ann. Stat. ch. 110 1/2, §§701 to 710 (Smith-Hurd Supp. 1992).

Illinois Powers of Attorney for Health Care Act [1987, 1988], Ill. Ann. Stat. ch. 110 1/2, §§804-1 to 804-12 (Smith-Hurd Supp. 1992).

In re Greenspan, 137 Ill. 2d 1, 558 N.E.2d 1194, *remanded,* No. 88P8726 (Cir. Ct. Cook Co. Oct. 3, 1990) (Dowdle, J.).

In re Estate of Longeway, 133 Ill. 2d 33, 549 N.E.2d 292 (1989).

In re Estate of Prange, 166 Ill. App. 3d 1091, 520 N.E. 2d 946 (Ct. App.), *vacated,* 527 N.E.2d 303, *cert. denied sub nom. Murphy v. Benson,* 102 L. Ed. 2d 219, 109 S. Ct. 229, 57 U.S.L.W. 3259 (1988).

INDIANA

Indiana Living Wills and Life-Prolonging Procedures Act [1985], Inc. Code Ann. §§16-8-11-1 to 16-8-11-22 (Burns 1990).

Indiana Powers of Attorney Act [1991], Ind. Code Ann. §§30-5-1-1 to 30-5-10-4 (Burns Supp. 1992).

In re Lawrance, 579 N.E.2d 32 (Ind. 1991).

IOWA

Iowa Life-sustaining Procedures Act [1985, 1987, 1992], Iowa Code Ann. §§144A.1 to 144A.12 (1989 & Supp. 1993).

Iowa Durable Power of Attorney for Health Care Act [1991], Iowa Code Ann. §§144B.1 to 144B.12 (Supp. 1993).

Morgan v. Olds, 417 N.W.2d 232 (Iowa Ct. App. 1987).

KANSAS

Kansas Natural Death Act [1979], Kan. Stat. Ann. §§65-28,101 to 65-28,109 (1992).

Kansas Durable Power of Attorney for Health Care Decisions Act [1989], Kan. Stat. Ann. §§58–625 to 58–632 (Supp. 1992).

KENTUCKY

Kentucky Living Will Act [1990], Ky. Rev. Stat. §§311.622 to 311.644 (Michie/Bobbs-Merrill Supp. 1992).

Kentucky Health Care Surrogate Act [1990], Ky. Rev. Stat. §§311.970 to 311.986 (Michie/Bobbs-Merrill Supp. 1992).

DeGrella v. Elston, 858 S.W.2d 698 (Ky. 1993).

LOUISIANA

Louisiana Life-Sustaining Procedures Act [1984, 1985, 1990, 1991], La. Rev. Stat. Ann. §§40:1299.58.1 to 40:1299.58.10 (West Supp. 1992).

Louisiana Power of Attorney Act [1981, 1990], La. Civ. Code Ann. art. 2997 (West Supp. 1993).

In re P.V.W., 424 So. 2d 1015 (La. 1982).

MAINE

Maine Uniform Rights of the Terminally Ill Act [1985, 1990, 1991], Me. Rev. Stat. Ann. tit. 18-A, §§5-701 to 5-714 (West Supp. 1992).

Maine Powers of Attorney Act [1986, 1991], Me. Rev. Stat. Ann. tit. 18-A, §§5-501 to 5-506 (West Supp. 1992).

In re Gardner, 534 A.2d 947 (Me. 1987).

In re Hallock, No. 88381 (Me, P. Ct. Kennebec Co. Sept. 26, 1988) (Mitchel, J.).

In re Swan, 569 A.2d 1202 (Me. 1990).

In re Weaver, No. 896177 (Me. P. Ct. Cumberland Co. Feb. 27, 1989) (Childs, J.), *motion to Intervene and for Reconsideration denied,* No. 89-177 (P. Ct. Cumberland Co. March 28, 1989) (Childs, J.).

MARYLAND

Maryland Health Care Decision Act [1985, 1986, 1987, 1993], Md. Health-Gen. Code Ann. §§5–601 to 5–618 (1990 & H.B. 1243, signed May 11, 1993).

Mack v. Mack, 329 Md. 188, 618 A.2d 744 (1993).

In re Riddlemoser, 317 Md. 496, 564 A.2d 812 (1989).

MASSACHUSETTS

Massachusetts Health Care Proxies by Individuals Act [1990], Mass. Gen. L. ch. 201D (Supp. 1992).

In re Care and Protection of Beth, 412 Mass. 188, 587 N.E.2d 1377 (1992).

Brophy v. New England Sinai Hospital, Inc., 398 Mass. 417, 497 N.E.2d 626 (1986).

In re Dinnerstein, 6 Mass. App. 466, 380 N.E.2d 134 (Ct. App. 1978).

In re Guardianship of Jane Doe, 411 Mass. 512, 583 N.E.2d 1263 (1992), *cert. denied sub nom. Doe v. Gross,* 112 S. Ct. 1512 (1992).

In re Hier, 18 Mass. App. 200, 464 N.E.2d 959 (Ct. App.), *review denied,* 392 Mass. 1102, 465 N.E.2d 261 (1984).

Lane v. Candura, 6 Mass. App. Ct. 377, 376 N.E.2d 1332 (1978).

In re Laws, Np. 226215 (Mass. P. & Fam. Ct. Essex Div. May 4, 1987) (Buczko, J.).

Custody of a Minor (1), 375 Mass. 733, 379 N.E.2d 1053, 97 A.L.R.3d 401 (1978) (leukemia & chemotherapy); *Custody of a Minor (2),* 378 Mass. 732, 393 N.E.2d 836 (1979) (related case involving leukemia, chemotherapy and laetrile).

Custody of a Minor, 385 Mass. 697, 434 N.E.2d 601 (1982) ("no code").

In re Spring, 380 Mass. 629, 405 N.E.2d 115 (1980).

Superintendent of Belchertown State School v. Saikewicz, 373 Mass. 728, 370 N.E.2d 417 (1977).

MICHIGAN

Michigan Power of Attorney for Health Care Act [1990], Mich. Comp. Laws, §§700.496 (West Supp. 1992).

In re Blodgett, No. 83-26514-AZ (Mich. Cir. Ct. Washtenaw Co. May 25, 1984) (Ager, J.).

In re Culham, No. 87-340537-AZ (Mich. Cir. Ct. Oakland Co. Dec. 15, 1987) (Breck, J.).

In re Hayes, No. 90-113,811-GD (Mich. P. Ct. Macomb Co. Aug. 30, 1990) (Nowicki, J.).

Hobbins, et al. v. Attorney General, No. 93-3060178 CZ (Mich. Cir. Ct. Wayne County May 24, 1993) (struck down Michigan anti-assisted suicide law as unconstitutional under state constitution).

In re Martin, No. 161431 (Mich. Ct. App. July 19, 1993).

In re Rivlin, No. 89-369904-AZ (Mich. Cir. Ct. Oakland Co. July 18, 1989) (Gage, J.).

In re Rosebush, 195 Mich. App. 675, 491 N.W.2d 633 (1992).

In re Rosebush, No. 88-349180-AZ (Mich. Cir. Ct. Oakland Co. Nov. 30, 1988) (Kuhn, J.) (attorney fees).

In re Yetzke, No. 93-155558-GD (Mich. P. Ct. Kent Co. June 14, 1993) (Haynes, J.).

MINNESOTA

Minnesota Adult Health Care Decisions Act [1989, 1992, 1993], Minn. Stat. §§145B.01 to 145B.17 (Supp. 1993 & S.F. 40, signed May 20, 1993).

Minnesota Durable Power of Attorney for Health Care Act [1993], Minn. Stat. §§145C.01 to 145C.15 (S.F. 40, signed May 20, 1993).

In re Welfare of Steinhaus, (Minn. Redwood Co. Ct., Juv. Div. Sept. 11), *reversed,* (Redwood Co. Ct., Fam. Div. Oct. 13, 1986).

In re Torres, 357 N.W.2d 332 (Minn. 1984).

In re Conservatorship of Wanglie, No. PX-91-283 (Minn. Dist. Ct. Hennepin Co. July, 1991) (Belois, J.).

MISSISSIPPI

Mississippi Withdrawal of Life-Saving Mechanisms Act [1984], Miss. Code Ann. §§41-41-101 to 41-41-121 (Supp. 1992).

Mississippi Durable Power of Attorney for Health Care Act [1990, 1993], Miss. Code Ann. §§41-41-151 to 41-41-183 (Supp. 1992 & S.B. 2830, signed March 16, 1993).

MISSOURI

Missouri Life Support Declarations Act [1985], Mo. Ann. Stat. §§459.010 to 459.055 (Vernon 1992).

Missouri Durable Power of Attorney for Health Care Act [1991], Mo. Ann. Stat. §§404.800 to 404.870 (Vernon Supp. 1992).

In re Busalacchi, No. 73677 (Mo. January 26, 1993).

Cruzan v. Harmon, 760 S.W.2d 408 (Mo. 1989).

Cruzan v. Mouton, No. CV384–9P (Mo. Cir. Ct. Jasper Co. Dec. 14, 1990) (Teel, J.).

In re Warren, No. WD 46420 (Mo. Ct. App. W. Dist. July 13, 1993).

Sullivan v. St. John's Mercy Medical Center (Stoppe), No. 561631 (Mo. Cir. Ct. St. Louis Co. June 8, 1987) (Weinstock, J.).

MONTANA

Montana Rights of the Terminally Ill Act [1985, 1989, 1991], Mont. Code Ann. §§50-9-101 to 50-9-111, 50-9-201 to 50-9-206 (1991).

Montana Durable Power of Attorney Act [1974, 1985], Mont. Code Ann. §§72-5-501 to 75–5-502 (1991), as interpreted by Rights of the Terminally Ill Act, §50-9-103(4).

NEBRASKA

Nebraska Rights of the Terminally Ill Act [1992], Neb. Rev. Stat. §§20-401 to 20-416 (Supp. 1992).

Nebraska Power of Attorney for Health Care Act [1992, 1993], Neb. Rev. Stat. §§30-3401 to 30-3432 (Supp. 1992 & L.B. 782, signed June 10, 1993).

NEVADA

Nevada Uniform Act on the Rights of the Terminally Ill [1977, 1985, 1987, 1991], Nev. Rev. Stat. §§449.535 to 449.690 (1991).

Nevada Durable Power of Attorney for Health Care Act [1987, 1991], Nev. Rev. Stat. Ann. §§449.800 to 449.860 (1991).

McKay v. Bergstedt, 106 Nev. 808, 801 P.2d 617 (1990).

NEW HAMPSHIRE

New Hampshire Living Wills Act [1985, 1991, 1992], N.H. Rev. Stat. Ann. §§137-H:1 to 137-H:16 (1990 & Supp. 1992).

New Hampshire Durable Power of Attorney for Health Care [1991], N.H. Rev. Stat. Ann. §§137-J:1 to 137-J:16 (Supp. 1992).

NEW JERSEY

New Jersey Advance Directives for Health Care Act [1991], N.J. Stat. Ann. §§26:2H-53 to 26:2H-78 (West Supp. 1992).

In re Clark, 210 N.J. Super. 548, 510 A.2d 136 (Super. Ct. Ch. Div. 1986); 212 N.J. Super. 408, 515 A.2d 276 (Super Ct. Ch. Div. 1986), *affirmed,* 216 N.J. Super. 497, 524 A.2d 448 (Super. Ct. App. Div. 1987) (attorney fees).

In re Conroy, 98 N.J. 321, 486 A.2d 1209 (1985).

In re Donlan, No. A-3103-89T5F (N.J. Super. Ct. App. Div. Oct. 24, 1990).

In re Farrell, 108 N.J. 335, 529 A.2d 404 (1987).

In re Fields, (N.J. Super. Ct. Ch. Div. Salem Co. Nov. 6, 1986) (Miller, J.).

Fuhrmann v. Kean, No. 86-1951 (D.N.J. July 13, 1987) (Cowen, J.).

Iafelice v. Luchs, 206 N.J. Super. 103 (1985).

In re Jobes, 210 N.J. Super. 543, 510 A.2d 133 (Super. Ct. Ch. Div.), *review denied* (N.J. March 10, 1986).

In re Jobes, 108 N.J. 394, 529 A.2d 434 (1987).

McVey v. Englewood Hospital Association, 216 N.J. Super. 502, 524 A.2d 540 (Super. Ct. App. Div. 1987) (per curiam), cert. denied, 108 N.J. 182, 528 A.2d 12 (1987).

In re Moorhouse, 250 N.J. Super. 307, 593 A.2d 1256 (Super. Ct. App. Div. 1991).

In re Peter, 108 N.J. 365, 529 A.2d 419 (1987).

In re Putzer, No. P21–87E (N.J. Super. Ct. Ch. Div. Essex Co. July 9, 1987) (Margolis, J.).

In re Quackenbush, 156 N.J. Super. 282, 383 A.2d 785 (1978).

In re Quinlan, 70 N.J. 10, 355 A.2d 647, *cert. denied sub nom. Garger v. New Jersey,* 429 U.S. 922, 50 L. Ed. 2d 289, 97 S. Ct. 319 (1976), *overruled in part, In re Conroy,* 98 N.J. 321, 486 A.2d 1209 (1985).

In re Requena, 213 N.J. Super. 475, 517 A.2d 886 (Super. Ct. Ch. Div.), *affirmed,* 213 N.J. Super. 443, 517 A.2d 869 (Super. Ct. App. Div. 1986) (per curiam).

In re Schiller, 148 N.J. Super. 168, 372 A. 2d 360 (1977).

In re Smerdon, No. A-6031-89T1 (N.J. Super. Ct. App. Div. April 8, 1991), *cert. denied,* 126 N.J. 336, 598 A.2d 893 (1991).

Strachan v. John F. Kennedy Memorial Hospital, 109 N.J. 523, 538 A.2d 346 (1988).

In re Visbeck, 210 N.J. Super. 527, 510 A.2d (Super. Ct. Ch. Div. 1986).

NEW MEXICO

New Mexico Right to Die Act [1977, 1984], N.M. Stat. Ann. §§24-7-1 to 24-7-11 (1991).

New Mexico Durable Power of Attorney Act [1989], N.M. Stat. Ann. §§45-5-501 to 45–5-502 (supp. 1991).

New Mexico ex rel. Smith v. Fort, No. 14,768 (N.M. 1983).

NEW YORK

New York Health Care Proxy Act [1990], N.Y. Pub. Health Law §§2980 to 2994 (McKinney Supp. 1993).

A.B. v. C., 477 N.Y.S.2d 281 (N.Y. Sup. Ct. Schenectady Co. 1984).

In re Application of Alderson (Kimbrough), No. 90193/86 (N.Y. Sup. Ct. N.Y. Co. Aug. 3, 1988) (Ciparick, J.); N.Y.L.J. Aug. 9, 1988, at 18, col. 2.

In re Beth Israel Medical Center (Weinstein), 136 Misc. 2d 931, 519 N.Y.S.2d 511 (Sup. Ct. N.Y. Co. 1987).

In re Application of Brooks (Leguerrier), (N.Y. Sup. Ct. Albany Co. June 10, 1987) (Conway, J.).

Delio v. Westchester Co. Medical Center, 129 A.D.2d 1, 516 N.Y.S.2d 677 (2d Dep't 1987).

In re Petition of the Department of Veterans Affairs Medical Center, 749 F. Supp. 495 (S.D.N.Y.), *aff'd without opinion,* 914 F.2d 239 (2d Cir. 1990).

In re Eichner, 52 N.Y.2d 363, 438 N.Y.S.2d 266, 420 N.E.2d 64, *cert. denied,* 454 U.S. 858 (1981).

Elbaum v. Grace Plaza of Great Neck, Inc., 148 A.D.2d 244, 544 N.Y.s.2d 840 (2d Dep't 1989).

Evans v. Bellevue Hospital (Wirth), No. 16536/87 (N.Y. Sup. Ct. N.Y. Co. July 27, 1987) (Sandifer, J.); N.Y.L.J. July 28, 1987, at 11, col. 1.

In re Finsterbach (N.Y. Sup. Ct. Oneida Co. June 12, 1990) (Tenney, J.).

Fosmire v. Nicoleau, 75 N.Y.2d 218, 551 N.Y.S. 2d 876, 551 NE 2d 77 (1990).

In re Application of Gannon (Coons), No. 0189–017460 (N.Y. Sup. Ct. Albany Co. April 3), *vacated,* No. 0189–017460 (sup. Ct. Albany Co. April 11, 1989); N.Y.L.J. April 7, 1989 at 29, col. 9.

Grace Plaza of Great Neck, Inc. v. Elbaum, No. 162 (N.Y. Oct. 14, 1993) (mandating payment of nursing home fees for unwanted services).

In re Hallahan, No. 16338/1989 (N.Y. Sup. Ct. Bronx Co. Aug. 28, 1989).

Halperin v. North Shore University Hospital Center, No. 93-020905 (N.Y. Sup. Ct. Nassau Co. August 13, 1993) (Alpert, J).

Hayner v. Child's Nursing Home, No. 0188 015609 (N.Y. Sup. Ct. Albany Co. Dec. 5, 1988) (McDermott, J.).

In re Hofbauer, 47 N.Y.2d 648, 419 N.Y.S.2d 936, 393 N.E.2d 1009 (1979).

In re Application of Kerr (O'Brien), 135 Misc. 2d 1076, 517 N.Y.S.2d 346 (Sup. Ct. N.Y. Co. 1986).

In re Application of Kerr (Essner), No. 21748/86 (N.Y. Sup. Ct. Bronx Co. Dec. 17, 1986) (Turret, J.).

Kurzweil v. Harrison, No. 14810/91 (N.Y. Sup. Ct. New York Co. July 30, 1991) (Miller, J.) (petition for revocation of health care proxy denied); N.Y.L.J. Aug. 16, 1991 at 22.

In re Application of Kruczlnicki (Keyes), No. 26796 (N.Y. Sup. Ct. Warren Co. Feb. 16, 1989) (Dier, J.).

In re Application of Licopoli (Akullian), No. 1172-88 (N.Y. Sup. Ct. Albany Co. March 10, 1988) (Prior, J.).

In re Lydia E. Hall Hospital, 116 Misc. 2d 477, 455 N.Y.S.2d 706 (Sup. Ct. Nassau Co. 1982); 117 Misc. 2d 1024, 459 N.Y.S.2d 682 (Sup. Ct. Nassau Co. 1982).

Marie v. Astoria General Hospital, No. 03607/88 (N.Y. Sup. Ct. Queens Co. March 23, 1988) (Zelman, J.).

In re Marrazzo, No. 90–14709 (N.Y. Sup. Ct. Suffolk Co. Jan. 2, 1991) (Gowan, J.); N.Y.L.J. Jan. 15, 1991 at 26, col. 6.

In re Moschella, No. 5806/84 (N.Y. Sup. Ct. Queens Co. May 10, 1984) (Kassoff, J.); N.Y.L.J. May 22, 1984, at 12, col. 2.

In re Application of Plaza Health and Rehabilitation Center, (N.Y. Sup. Ct. Onondaga Co. Feb. 2, 1984) (Miller, J.).

In re Ramos, No. 7715-90 (N.Y. Sup. Ct. Bronx Co. March 13, 1990) (Salmon, J.).

Saunders v. State, 129 Misc. 2d 45, 492 N.Y.S.2d 510 (Sup. Ct. Nassau Co. 1985).

In re Storar, 52 N.Y.2d 363, 438 N.Y.S.2d 266, 420 N.E.2d 64, *cert. denied,* 454 U.S. 858 (1981).

In re Strauss, No. 8378/87 (N.Y. Sup. Ct. Bronx Co. July 1, 1987) (Tompkins, J.).

In re Triarsi, No. 86-14241 (N.Y. Sup. Ct. Suffolk Co. Aug, 21, 1986) (Yachnin, J); N.Y.L.J. Sept. 18, 1986, at 12, col. 5.

U.S.A. v. University Hospital, 575 F. Supp. 607, (E.D.N.Y. 1983), *affirmed,* 729 F.2d 144 (2nd. Cir. 1984).

In re Vogel, 134 Misc. 2d 395, 512 N.Y.S.2d 622 (Sup. Ct. Nassau Co. 1986), *declined to follow in Delio v. Westchester Co. Medical Center,* 129 A.D.2d 1, 516 N.Y.S.2d 677 (2d Dep't 1987).

Weber v. Stony Brook Hospital, 95 App. Div. 2d 587, 467 N.Y.S.2d 685, *affirmed,* 60 N.Y.2d 208, 456 N.E.2d 1186, 469 N.Y.S.2d 63, *cert. denied,* 464 U.S. 1026 (1983).

In re Weiland (Juchnewicz), No. 89–033 (N.Y. Sup. Ct. Suffolk Co. January 19, 1989) (Colby, J.).

In re Westchester County Medical Center (O'Connor), 72 N.Y.2d 517, 534 N.Y.S.2d 886, 531 N.E.2d 607 (1988).

Wickel v. Spellman, 159 A.D.2d 576, 552 N.Y.S.2d 437 (2d Dep't 1990).

Workmen's Circle Home and Infirmary for the Aged v. Fink, 135 Misc. 2d 270, 514 N.Y.S.2d 893 (Sup. Ct. Bronx Co. 1987), *declined to follow in Delio v. Westchester County Medical Center,* 129 A.D.2d 1, 516 N.Y.S.2d 677 (2d Dep't 1987).

NORTH CAROLINA

North Carolina Right to Natural Death Act [1977, 1979, 1981, 1983, 1991], N.C. Gen. Stat. §§90-320 to 90-322 (1990 & Supp. 1992).

North Carolina Health Care Powers of Attorney Act [1991, 1993], N.C. Gen. Stat. §§32A-15 to 32A-26 (1991 & H.B. 1043, ratified July 24, 1993).

Rettinger v. Littlejohn, No. 91CVD4155 (N.C. Super. Ct. Forsyth Co. Sept. 12, 1991) (Reingold, J.).

NORTH DAKOTA

North Dakota Uniform Rights of the Terminally Ill Act [1989, 1991, 1993], N.D. Cent. Code §§23-06.4-01 to 23-06.4-14 (1991 & S.B. 2394, signed April 21, 1993).

North Dakota Durable Powers of Attorney for Health Care Act [1991, 1993], N.D. Cent. Code §§23-06.5-01 to 23-06.5-18 {1991 & S.B. 2417, signed March 26, 1993).

In re Bayer, No. 4131 (N.D. Burleigh Co. Ct. Feb. 5, 11 and Dec. 11, 1987) (Riskedahl, J.).

OHIO

Ohio Modified Uniform Rights of the Terminally Ill Act [1991], Ohio Rev. Code Ann. §§2133.01 to 2133.15 (Anderson Supp. 1992).

Ohio Power of Attorney for Health Care Act [1989, 1991], Ohio Rev. Code Ann. §§1337.11 to 1337.17 (Anderson Supp. 1992).

Anderson v. St. Francis-St. George Hospital (Winter), 83 Ohio App. 3d 221, 614 N.E.2d 841 (1992) (no damages award for battery claim).

Couture v. Couture, 48 Ohio App. 3d 208, 549 N.E.2d 571 (Ct. App. 1989), *superseded by statute as stated in In re Guardianship of Crum,* 61 Ohio Misc. 2d 596, 580 N.E.2d 876 (Ct. App. 1991).

In re Guardianship of Crum, 61 Ohio Misc. 2d 596, 580 N.E.2d 876 (Ct. App. 1991).

In re Guardianship of Dial, No. 333,119 (Ohio Ct. Com. Pl. Prob. Div. Franklin Co. Feb. 26, 1985) (Metcalf, J.); *Bloom v. Grant Hospital,* No. 85 CV-0201081 (Ohio Ct. Com. Pl. Franklin Co. Feb. 26), *writ of mandamus dismissed sub nom. State of Ohio ex rel. Bloom,* No. 85-332 (Dec. 4, 1985).

Leach v. Akron General Medical Center, 68 Ohio Misc. 1, 426 N.E.2d 809 (Com. Pl. 1980).

Leach v. Shapiro, 13 Ohio App. 3d 393, 469 N.E.2d 1047 (Ct. App. 1984).

In re Milton, 29 Ohio St. 3d 20, 505 N.E.2d 255, *cert. denied sub nom. Ohio Dep't Mental Health v. Milton,* 484 U.S. 820, 98 L. Ed. 2d 41, 108 S. Ct. 79 (1987).

In re Guardianship of Myers, No. G-92-12-049 (Ohio Ct. Com. Pl. P. Div. Summit Co. Jan. 29, 1993) (Spicer, J.).

In re Thompson, No. 60553 (Ohio Ct. Com. Pl. P. Div. Scioto Co. June 16, 1993) (Kirsch, J.).

OKLAHOMA

Oklahoma Rights of the Terminally Ill or Persistently Unconscious Act [1985, 1987, 1990, 1992], Okla. Stat. Ann. tit. 63, §§3101.1 to 3101.16 (West Supp. 1993).

Oklahoma Hydration & Nutrition for Incompetent Patients Act [1987, 1990, 1992], Okla. Stat. Ann. tit. 63, §§3080.1 to 3080.5 (West Supp. 1993).

OREGON

Oregon Rights with Respect to Terminal Illness Act [1977, 1983, 1987, 1993], Or. Rev. Stat. §§127.605 to 127.650 (1990 & S.B. 286, signed August 31, 1993).

Oregon Durable Power of Attorney for Health Care Act [1989], Or. Rev. Stat. §§127.505 to 127.585 (1990).

Evans v. District Attorney of Douglas County, No. E82-2173 (Or. Cir. Ct. Douglas Co. Dec. 13, 1982).

PENNSYLVANIA

Pennsylvania Advance Directive for Health Care Act [1992], P. Stat. Ann. tit. 20, §§5401 to 5416 (S.B. 3, signed April 16, 1992).

Pennsylvania Durable Powers of Attorney Act [1982], Pa. Stat. Ann. tit. 20, §§5601 to 5607 (Supp. 1992), *as interpreted by Pocono Medical Center v. Harley,* No. 3467 (Pa. Ct. Com. Pl. Monroe Co. Dec. 14, 1990).

In re E.L.K. Incompetent, No. 72065 (Pa. Ct. Com. Pl. Orphan's Ct. Div. Berks Co. Jan. 18, 1991).

In re Jane Doe, 16 Phila. 229 (Pa. Ct. Com. Pl. Philadelphia Co. 1987).

In re Fiori, No. 49355 (Pa. Ct. Com. Pl. Bucks Co. Feb. 3, 1993) (Sokolove, J.).

Neuman Medical Center v. Popowich, No. 5663 (Pa. Ct. Com. Pl. Philadelphia Co. April 26, 1990).

Pocono Medical Center v. Harley, No. 3467 (Pa. Ct. Com. Pl. Monroe Co. Dec. 14, 1990).

Ragona v. Preate, No. 90 Equity 118 (Pa. Ct. Com. Pl. Lackawanna Co. Nov. 30, 1990).

RHODE ISLAND

Rhode Island Rights of the Terminally Ill Act [1991, 1992], R.I.Gen. Laws §§23-4.11-1 to 23-4.11-14 (Supp. 1992).

Rhode Island Health Care Power of Attorney Act [1986, 1989, 1992, 1993], R.I. Gen. Laws §§23-4.10-1 to 23.4.10-12 (supp. 1992 & H.B. 6313, signed July 6, 1993).

Gray v. Romeo, 697 F. Supp. 580 (D.R.I. 1988).

Gray v. Romeo, 709 F. Supp. 325 (D.R.I. 1989) (attorney fees).

SOUTH CAROLINA

South Carolina Death with Dignity Act [1986, 1988, 1991], S.C. Code Ann. §§44-77-10 to 44-77-160 (Law Co-op Supp. 1992).

South Carolina Powers of Attorney Act [1986, 1990, 1992], S.C. Code Ann. §§62-5-501 to 62-5-505 (Law Co-op Supp. 1992).

SOUTH DAKOTA

South Dakota Living Will Act [1991], S.D. Codified Laws Ann. §§34-12D-1 to 34-12D-22 (Supp. 1992).

South Dakota Durable Powers of Attorney Act [1977, 1979, 1990, 1992], S.D. Codified Laws Ann. §§59-7-2.1 to 59-7-2.8, 59-7-8 (Supp. 1992).

TENNESSEE

Tennessee Right to Natural Death Act [1985, 1991, 1992], Tenn. Code Ann. §§32-11-101 to 32-11-112 (Supp. 1992).

Tennessee Durable Power of Attorney for Health Care Act [1990], Tenn. Code Ann. §§34-6-201 to 34-6-214 (1991).

Dockery v. Dockery, 559 S.W. 2d 952 (Tenn. Ct. App. 1977), *cert. denied* (Tenn. 1977).

Jan Doe v. Wilson, No. 90-364-II (Tenn. Ch. Ct. Davidson Co. February 16, 1990) (High, Ch.).

TEXAS

Texas Natural Death Act [1977, 1979, 1983, 1985, 1990], Tex. Health & Safety Code Ann. §§672.001 to 672.021 (1992).

Texas Durable Power of Attorney for Health Care Act [1989], Tex. Civil Practice & Remedies Code Ann. §§135.001 to 135.018 (Vernon Supp. 1993).

Newman v. William Beaumont Army Medical Center, No. EP-86-CA-276 (W.D. Tex. Oct. 30, 1986) (Hudspeth, J.).

In re Guardianship Estate of Petersen, No. E117,982 (Tex. Dist. Ct. Jefferson Co. Aug. 4, 1983) (Thomas, J.).

UTAH

Utah Personal Choice and Living Will Act [1985, 1988, 1993], Utah Code Ann. §§75-2-1101 to 75-2-1119 (Supp. 1992 & H.B. 299, signed March 10, 1993 & S.B. 133, signed March 15, 1993).

VERMONT

Vermont Terminal Care Document Act [1982], Vt. Stat. Ann. tit. 18, §§5251 to 5262 and tit. 13, §1801 (1987).

Vermont Durable Powers of Attorney for Health Care Act [1987], Vt. Stat. Ann. tit. 14, §§3451 to 3467 (1989 & Supp. 1992).

VIRGINIA

Virginia Health Care Decisions Act [1983, 1988, 1989, 1991, 1992], Va. Code §§54.1-2981 to 54.1-2993 (Supp. 1992).

Alexandria Hospital v. McLellan, No. CH 13009 (Va. Cir. Ct. Jan. 19, 1982) (Grenadier, J.).

In Re Baby "K", NO. 93–66-A (E.D. Va. July 1, 1993).

Hazelton [sic] v. Powhatan Nursing Home, Inc., No. CH 98287 (Va. Cir. Ct. Fairfax Co. Aug. 29), *order signed* (Sept. 2) (Fortkort, J.), *appeal denied,* Record No. 860814 (Va. Sept. 2, 1986), 6 Va. Cir. Ct. Op. 414 (Aspen 1987).

WASHINGTON

Washington Natural Death Act [1979, 1992], Wash. Rev. Code Ann. §§70.122.010 to 70.122.920 (Supp. 1993).

Washington Durable Power of Attorney—Health Care Decisions Act [1989], Wash. Rev. Code Ann. 11.94.010 (Supp. 1993).

In re Colyer, 99 Wash. 2d 114, 660 P.2d 738 (1983), *modified In re Guardianship of Hamlin,* 102 Wash. 2d 810, 689 P.2d 1372 (1984).

Dinino v. State ex rel Gorton, 102 Wash. 2d 327, 684 P.2d 1297 (1984).

In re Guardianship of Grant, 109 Wash. 2d 545, 747 P.2d 445 (1987), *modified,* 757 P.2d 534 (1988).

In re Guardianship of Hamlin, 102 Wash. 2d 810, 689 P.2d 1372 (1984).

In re Guardianship of Ingram, 102 Wash. 2d 827, 689 P.2d 1363 (1984).

Strickland v. Deaconess Hospital, 47 Wash. App. 262, 735 P.2d 74 (Ct. App.), *review denied* (Wash. July 1, 1987).

WEST VIRGINIA

West Virginia Natural Death Act [1984, 1991], W. Va. Code §§16-30-2 to 16-30-13 (1991 & Supp. 1992).

West Virginia Medical Power of Attorney Act [1990], W. Va. Code §§16-30a-1 to 16–30a-20 (1991).

Belcher v. Charleston Area Medical Center, 188 W. Va. 105, 422 S.E.2d 827 (1992).

WISCONSIN

Wisconsin Natural Death Act [1984, 1986, 1988, 1991, 1992], Wisc. Stat. Ann. §§154.01 to 154.15 (West 1989 & Supp. 1992).

Wisconsin Power of Attorney for Health Care Act [1990, 1992], Wisc. Stat. Ann. §§155.01 to 155.80 (Supp. 1992).

In re Guardianship of L.W., 167 Wisc. 2d 53, 482 N.W.2d 60 (1992).

WYOMING

Wyoming Living Will Act [1984, 1985, 1987, 1991, 1992], Wyo. Stat. §§35-22-101 to 35-22-108 (Supp. 1992).

Wyoming Durable Power of Attorney for Health Care Act [1991, 1992], Wyo. Stat. §§3-5-201 to 3-5-213 (Supp. 1992).

UNITED STATES

Patient Self-Determination Act [1990], Pub. L. 101-508 §§4206, 4751 (OBRA), 42 U.S.C. 1395 cc(a) et seq. (1990).

Bowen v. American Hospital Association, 476 U.S. 160 (1986).

Cruzan v. Director, Missouri Department of Health, 497 U.S. 261, 110 S. Ct. 2841 (1990).

SEE ALSO

Uniform Rights of the Terminally Ill Act [1985, 1987, 1989], §§1-18, 9B U.L.A. 96-115 (Supp. 1992).

CHAPTER 5

Euthanasia

It is rather the mark of a good and holy God that He permits so
many of his children to undergo that suffering here on earth.
Suffering is almost the greatest gift of God's love.

Joseph V. Sullivan, *Catholic Teaching on the Morality of Euthanasia*
(1949)

It's easy to bear adversity. Another man's I mean.

Mark Twain (Samuel Langhorne Clemens)

There is but one truly serious philosophical problem, and that is
suicide.

Albert Camus, *An Absurd Reasoning* (1955)

THE PUBLIC DEBATE ABOUT euthanasia rages. As we will demonstrate in this chapter, it has been discussed in the public policy arena since
early in this century, but the events of the past twenty years have greatly intensified the tone of the debate. Unfortunately, the debate often takes place in the
absence of any agreement as to exactly what it is that is being debated.

The *American Heritage Dictionary of the English Language* defines euthanasia
as (1) the action of inducing the painless death of a person for reasons assumed
to be merciful, or (2) an easy or painless death. It indicates that the word is derived from the Greek: *eu-*, meaning good and *thanatos*, meaning death. It is
sometimes referred to as "the good death" or "death with dignity." For many
people, the term is seen as being synonymous with "mercy killing." Often these

words or phrases are injected into the public debate in ways that seem to be intended to obscure rather than illuminate the differences between the various meanings, creating what the members of the President's Commission characterized as the disservice of "empty rhetoric" (President's Commission, 1983). According to them, phrases such as "death with dignity" and "euthanasia," along with "right to die," "right to life," and "quality of life" have often been used as "slogans" or "code words." Their meanings, if they were ever clear, have become hopelessly blurred. The issues are much more likely to be understood if the exact meanings of these "rhetorical devices" are spelled out (Ibid., p. 24).

It would seem to be desirable at this point to introduce some definitions. Although the term *euthanasia* is all too often used by itself, this often causes a great deal of confusion. We would suggest that the use of modifiers is necessary to achieve some clarity. First, we can define euthanasia as either *passive* or *active*. *Passive* euthanasia would refer to allowing the patient to die by withholding or withdrawing LSMT which was no longer desired by the patient or, in cases where the patient was unable to make such a decision, where there was agreement that the treatment was no longer serving the best interests of the patient. This would be described as *voluntary*, passive euthanasia in the former case and *nonvoluntary*, passive euthanasia in the latter. *Active* euthanasia would describe those actions taken to shorten the life of the patient, although such shortening might come about either *directly* or *indirectly*. *Indirect*, active euthanasia would describe a situation where death was hastened as a secondary and unintended, but foreseeable, consequence of a primary intent to relieve pain. For example, morphine is the drug of choice for pain relief but, as is true for all depressant drugs, there is a tendency for tolerance to develop rather rapidly. In order to get the therapeutic effect, it is necessary to escalate the dosage. With stronger doses there is a depression of respiration and one predictable consequence of diminished respiratory response is the development of pneumonia, which often causes death. Since the intent in prescribing the morphine is to relieve the patient's pain rather than to cause death, this is a common medical practice and, like the passive euthanasia described earlier, with the exception of withholding or withdrawing feeding and/or hydration tubes from the nonterminally ill, it is seldom criticized.

The final category, *direct*, active euthanasia is the most controversial. Here the intent is to cause death as quickly and humanely as possible in order to spare the patient a lingering and/or painful process of dying. This form of euthanasia is sometimes called "mercy killing" and it has, for reasons that will be described later, been receiving increasing attention. In addition to the modifiers described, it is also important to draw a distinction between *voluntary* and *involuntary* euthanasia. Euthanasia would be voluntary if it were performed by, or at the request of, a competent patient who had decided that there was nothing to be gained by continued living. It would be described as involuntary when it was a decision imposed on someone who desired to go on living. Unfortunately, this distinction is sometimes blurred, perhaps intentionally, by those who oppose voluntary euthanasia by simply describing (all) euthanasia as Hitlerian. It should be clear to all that the genocidal policies of the Third Reich were neither motivated by mercy nor based on consent. Davies (1988) has suggested that voluntary euthanasia, which she describes as "helping to die," is as different from involuntary euthanasia ("killing") as raping is from making love. While the act may be similar, the circumstances are quite distinguishable.

It appears that the term was originally used to refer to an action that would allow the hastening of death as a humane act to end suffering. This was the goal underlying the formation of the Euthanasia Society of America in 1938, a group that was modeled after the Voluntary Euthanasia Society in Great Britain. The development of the life-sustaining technology that would later necessitate a distinction between allowing to die (passive euthanasia) and hastening death (active euthanasia), primarily ventilators and feeding tubes, were not part of medical practice at the time. Unfortunately, the term *euthanasia* today is frequently used to describe both of these situations and often without attempting to differentiate between them.

Perhaps some of the subtleties concerning "euthanasia" may be illustrated by Table 5–1.

It would appear that many people have rather strong feelings about what, for them, might constitute a "bad" death. To die with a great deal of pain and suffering or to have their dying prolonged in such a way that it would seem dehumanizing—to strip one of one's dignity—is widely abhorred. In clinical practice, for example, there is typically an understanding that a person in the agonal stages of terminal cancer would not be "coded" if they were to experience heart failure. DNR (Do Not Resuscitate) orders are placed on the charts of such patients to comply with protocols established by hospitals in accordance with national accreditation standards. To "drag a patient back from death's

TABLE 5–1 *Semantics of Euthanasia*

Dysthanasia (Bad Death)	Euthanasia (Good Death)		
	Passive	*Active*	
Intentionally prolonging the dying process, e.g., resuscitating or defibrillating a patient with terminal cancer who has experienced a pulmonary or cardiac arrest; refusal to provide pain control if it would shorten life.	An act of omission. Either withholding LSMT or discontinuing treatment that no longer provides a benefit to the patient.	*Indirect:* Treatment that shortens life as an unintended but forseeable side effect of a desired goal, e.g. the use of morphine to control pain.	*Direct:* An act intended to cause the death of the patient and thereby reduce suffering. Sometimes called "mercy killing."

door" only so that he or she might experience additional days or weeks of suffering might well be viewed as a violation of one of the first rules of medicine—*primum non nocere* (first do no harm).

Consequently, when experiencing a loved one dying from the ravages of cancer, watching him or her suffer over a period of weeks or even months before dying of heart failure or perhaps pneumonia, feelings of relief sometimes outweigh feelings of sadness. The occurrence of such a "fortuitous accident" has freed the dying person from a life filled with suffering.

A Short History of Euthanasia Legalization

While the discussion of euthanasia, defined as killing motivated by mercy rather than malice, and rational suicide, defined as the taking of one's own life when confronted by intolerable alternatives, has been discussed since well before the turn of the twentieth century, events of the past ten to twenty years have greatly increased public interest. Support for the concept has grown appreciably since 1906 when a bill was introduced into the Ohio legislature—the first such bill introduced in any English-speaking country—which would have legalized euthanasia for certain "incurable sufferers" (Russell, 1975, p. 60). The bill was subsequently defeated by a vote of approximately three to one and both it and its sponsor were widely attacked in the press. An editorial concerning the bill stated that

> the way would be opened for guardians and relatives to rid themselves of their burdens, for quacks to conceal their failures, for heirs to resort to corrupt practices, for confidence in the medical profession to be eroded, and it would add to the terrors of the sick bed by stimulating fears . . . the patient would look forward to the visit of the physician with dread.   (Ibid., p. 61)

The Voluntary Euthanasia Legalization Society was organized in Great Britain in 1935 and was instrumental in getting a bill introduced into the House of Lords the following year. As it had been in Ohio, it was defeated by a convincing margin. An American counterpart, the Euthanasia Society of America, was organized in New York in 1938. The work of both of these organizations was strongly opposed by the mainstream of organized religion and medicine. Among members of the public, however, there was considerable support. Public opinion polls of the time showed only a slight majority opposing "mercy deaths under government supervision for hopeless invalids" (Ibid., p. 82) and, among some segments of the public, supporters slightly predominated. This, as we shall show, is true today when public support for the concept seems to be significantly greater than prevailing attitudes within either organized religion or medicine. This should not be interpreted to suggest that there are not individual bodies or members within either of these groups who might disagree, sometimes strongly, with these positions.

Although there were isolated cases of "mercy killings" that came to trial and attracted great publicity during the 1930s and 1940s, the move for decriminalization of medically supervised euthanasia was greatly slowed by news of the Nazi atrocities of World War II. The leadership of the Euthanasia Society of America were men and women who were widely respected in the professions, but their efforts were met with considerable hostility. They were labeled as anti-God, un-American, and as public menaces. In 1947 the Society was able to form a "Committee of 1776 Physicians for Legalizing Voluntary Euthanasia in New York State" and a bill was drafted under which an "incurable sufferer" could seek court approval of direct, active euthanasia. The petition to the court would require an affidavit from the diagnosing physician and review by a court-appointed, physician-dominated committee, but the bill died for lack of a legislative sponsor. Nevertheless, support for the idea continued to grow. Two years later, in 1949, 379 Protestant and Jewish clergy petitioned the New York legislature in support of voluntary euthanasia. The legislature failed to act on their request.

Euthanasia in the Courts

Although legislators have been unwilling to legalize direct, active, voluntary euthanasia, the courts have demonstrated exceptional leniency in dealing with those charged with mercy killing, often where the acts have taken place *without* the consent of the one killed. As compiled by Glantz (1987/88), some of the principal cases follow:

1. In 1939, Harry Johnson was arrested for asphyxiating his cancer-stricken wife. The grand jury refused to indict, finding instead that Johnson had been temporarily insane at the time of the act.

2. Also in 1939, Louis Greenfield chloroformed his "imbecile" teenage son to death. For seventeen years he had cared for the boy, who had "the mentality of a two-year-old and who spoke in a mumble understandable only by his mother" (Kamisar, 1958, p. 1021). He claimed that he did it because "I loved him, it was the will of God." He was acquitted of first-degree murder.

3. Louis Repouille, in that same year, after reading about the Greenfield case, chloroformed his thirteen-year-old "mongoloid," blind, bedridden, "imbecile" son. He was indicted for first-degree manslaughter,

convicted of a second-degree manslaughter, and freed on a suspended five- to ten-year sentence.

4. In 1943, John Noxon, a wealthy lawyer, electrocuted his six-month-old "mongoloid" son by draping a wire around him, dressing him in wet diapers, and placing him on a silver serving tray. Noxon claimed his son's death was an accident. He was convicted of first-degree murder. His death sentence was commuted to life imprisonment and later reduced to six years to life to make him eligible for parole, which was granted. He spent about four years in prison.

5. In 1950, Eugene Braunsdorf, a symphony musician, took his twenty-nine-year-old daughter, who was "spastic and incapable of speech," from the private sanitarium where she lived, shot her to death, and then attempted suicide by shooting himself in the chest twice and, upon reviving, twice more. He claimed he was worried about his health and about his daughter's future should he die. He was found not guilty by reason of temporary insanity.

6. In 1973, Lester Zygmanik shot to death his brother George, who had been paralyzed from the neck down in a motorcycle accident. It was claimed that George begged Lester to kill him. Lester was acquitted by reason of temporary insanity after the jury deliberated for two hours and forty minutes. The story was later published as a book, *Act of Love*, by Paige Mitchell (1976), and produced as a made-for-television docudrama.

These cases have been taken from a listing of nineteen such happenings described by Glantz, who also comments that of them, "only two defendants were sentenced to jail" and that one of them, John Noxon, "had tried to deny his actions by claiming that his son was accidentally electrocuted" (Glantz, 1987/88, p. 234).

Only three of the nineteen cases involved medical professionals, two of them physicians and the other a nurse. One of the physicians, Dr. Herman Sander, a Manchester, New Hampshire general practitioner, was accused of killing a cancer patient in 1950. He even recorded his attempt to kill his patient in the medical record: "Patient was given 10 cc of air intravenously repeated four times. Expired within ten minutes after this was started" (Ibid., p. 233). At trial, the defense claimed that the patient was dead when the air was injected and that Dr. Sander, therefore, did not cause the death. He was acquitted. Although his license to practice medicine in New Hampshire was at first revoked, it was later restored. He was also dismissed from his county medical society, but after a four-year struggle, he was admitted to another one. It is reported that 90 percent of the townspeople signed a petition supporting Dr. Sander (Ibid.).

If the claim of the defense—that the patient was already dead when the air embolus was injected—was true, surely Dr. Sander would have known that. And, if he had known that death had already occurred, why then would he have injected the air? If the patient was dead and Dr. Sander didn't know it, what difference should it have made? Surely he intended to kill his patient, didn't he? And, should his act be excused only because of his error in judging his patient to be alive?

The other case reported by Glantz that involved a physician took place in 1973. Dr. Vincent Montemarano was, while chief surgical resident at Nassau County Medical Center on Long Island, New York, accused of killing one of his patients who was suffering from pharyngeal cancer. The cause of death was claimed by the prosecution to be potassium chloride and, as in the *Sander* trial, the defense claimed that the patient was already dead or had died from other causes. Like Dr. Sander, Dr. Montemarano was acquitted.

In Glantz's only case involving a nurse, Ann Capute was charged with murdering a patient in 1981 by administering large doses of morphine. She, like Dr. Sander, documented the event in the medical record. The prosecution presented more than twenty witnesses, including four medical experts, who testified that the morphine had been the cause of death. The defense countered with three medical experts who testified that the patient, age fifty-one, had died from the disease. Like the physicians, the nurse was acquitted.

In addition to these, there are at least two other widely known examples of physicians who caused, or attempted to cause, the death of patients. In August 1985, Dr. John Kraai, an elderly physician from a small town in upstate New York, was arrested and charged with second-degree murder of his patient and old friend, Frederick Wagner. Mr. Wagner, who was eighty-one, had suffered from Alzheimer's disease for five years and had also developed gangrene in one foot as a result of ulcerous sores. He was said to be in pain and no longer able to recognize anyone. Dr. Kraai allegedly injected Mr. Wagner with several large doses of insulin. The Kraai case never went to trial. While released on bond, Dr. Kraai took his own life with a massive dose of Demerol. His widow stated that he probably took his life to spare his family from the stress of a trial. Like Dr. Sander, there was a strong showing of community support for Dr. Kraai (Humphry and Wickett, 1986, pp. 140–141).

And finally, the case of Dr. Joseph Hassman. Dr. Hassman, a New Jersey family practitioner, was sentenced to two years' probation and fined $10,000 for injecting Demerol into the feeding tube of his eighty-year-old mother-in-law. It was suggested that he may have "succumbed to family pressures" to end her suffering from Alzheimer's disease. It was claimed by the prosecutor that Dr. Hassman administered the drug in the presence of his wife and his father-in-law and that it was a family decision. He had entered a guilty plea (Mercy Killing Draws Probation, 1987).

These cases seem to illustrate an ambivalence on the part of the courts about using the criminal law to punish those who act "mercifully" to end life in spite of the fact that the law does not take the motive of the actor into consideration in assessing the criminality of the act. *Murder* is a homicide (killing of one person by another) committed with malice aforethought. Malice, however, does not mean ill will or hatred but, rather, an intention to kill and forseeability that the act performed is likely to result in death. It is also murder to act in "wanton and willful disregard of the obvious likelihood of causing death or great bodily injury" if the death of another results. *Manslaughter* is unlawful homicide committed without malice aforethought. Manslaughter can be voluntary, as when one person kills another in a rage of passion, or involuntary, as when death results from gross negligence. Glantz relates this to the foregoing discussion in the following manner:

> The common thread tying these various forms of unlawful homicide together is that the death of the other person must be caused by a wrongful or illegal act. Ordinarily, one must commit a positive act such as a poisoning, shooting, or stabbing to commit a crime. One cannot commit a crime by omitting to act, unless there is a *legal* (not moral) duty to act. Thus it is a crime to omit to file an income tax return, because there is a legal requirement to do so. Whether or not a physician is breaching a duty to act when he withdraws or withholds treatment is a key consideration in determining criminal liability. Furthermore, killing someone out of a good motive, such as to relieve pain, is not a defense to homicide. It is not the *motive* of the killer but, rather, the *intent* to kill that is the key element in unlawful homicide. Furthermore, the consent of the victim [a rather slanted way of describing the one who is killed and who may, in reality, view him- or herself as a "victim" of the disease or disability rather than the "killer"] is not a defense against a charge of murder. (1987/88, p. 232)

Not only have the courts shown a proclivity for accepting a rather tortured explanation of the facts, such as the patient already being dead when the lethal act was performed, and a willingness to impose exceptionally lenient "probationary" sentences on those who were convicted, but there also seems to be a disturbing avoidance of the issue by labeling those who admit to killing with merciful motive as suffering from temporary insanity. In acquitting Lester Zygmanik, for example, the court put its stamp of approval upon the following sequence of events. Lester Zygmanik was sane up until he pulled the trigger of the gun that killed his brother. He was insane when he committed the act. The insanity, however, was only temporary for he is now sane again. Perhaps a more tenable explanation would be that although the act of killing was illegal and committed by a clearly sane person, the motive—to do what his stricken brother and all members of his family agreed was the "right" thing to do—evoked the sympathy of the jurors. Realizing that the alternative would be to punish Lester for what he did, they chose to excuse him by the only route open to them—by finding him not guilty by reason of temporary insanity. What they might well have been saying is, "If I were ever to find myself in the predicament of George Zygmanik, I hope that I would have someone who loved me to do what Lester did for George!"

There are numerous factors underlying what seems to be a change in public attitude about the medical prolongation of life. Not only are there fears about lingering painfully or meaninglessly with diseases such as cancer, AIDS (acquired immunodeficiency syndrome), and Alzheimer's disease, but there is also the fear of dying while a prisoner of medical technology, in what has been described as a modern Procrustean bed (Singer and Siegler, 1990, p. 1882). In Greek mythology, Procrustes was a giant who was a thief and a murderer. He would capture travelers and tie them to an iron bed. If his victims were longer than the bed, he would hack off their limbs to fit it; if they were too short, he would stretch them to the right size. Much of the "patient's rights" and "right to die" movement has been fueled by concerns about overtreatment in the modern hospital and the "never say die" (literally) attitude of some physicians. Although the *Quinlan* case opened the door for a public dialogue about refusing certain forms of LSMT, the issue that has recently been the focus of heated debate is whether or not it might not be better, at least under certain circumstances, to take steps to hasten death rather than await the fortuitous accident (such as cardiac or respiratory arrest) or withholding or withdrawing treatment.

Although the issue has been debated in this country for the better part of a century, events of the last decade or so have greatly intensified the tone of the debate. It would be useful to review several of them here.

The National Hemlock Society

The Hemlock Society was formed in 1980 by Derek Humphry (see Figure 5–1) and his wife, Ann Wickett. While originally in Los Angeles, the Society today is headquartered in Eugene, Oregon. Humphry was motivated by the experience he had in helping his first wife, Jean, who was dying from ovarian cancer, end her own life by poisoning. They had come to an agreement that when her cancer became too distressing to her she would take her own life and he would help. After much difficulty in finding a physician who would provide a prescription for a lethal dose, they finally succeeded. Humphry told the story of their experience in a book, *Jean's Way*, which he wrote soon after her death. Humphry, who had been living in England at the time, later moved to California with his second wife, Ann Wickett. The Society's name is derived from the story of the death of Socrates wherein the Athenian philosopher chose to end his own life by drinking hemlock after he had been condemned to death by the Senate (see Figure 5–2). In addition to *Jean's Way*, the society

Figure 5–1 Derek Humphry, founder of the Hemlock Society and author of *Final Exit*. (Reprinted by permission of AP/Wide World Photos)

publishes a number of books including *Let Me Die Before I Wake*, described as a "Book of Self Deliverance for the Dying." It contains information on the legal aspects, psychology, and actual methods (drug doses) for a terminally ill person to take his or her own life. Hemlock claims that over 100,000 copies of the book have been sold.

As stated by the Society, there are four *General Principles* upon which it is based:

1. HEMLOCK will seek to provide a climate of public opinion which is tolerant of the rights of people who are terminally ill to end their own lives in a planned manner.

2. HEMLOCK does not encourage suicide for any primary emotional, traumatic, or financial reasons in the absence of terminal illness. It approves of the work of those involved in suicide prevention.

3. The final decision to terminate life is ultimately one's own. HEMLOCK believes this action, and most of all its timing, to be an extremely personal decision, wherever possible taken in concert with family, close friends, and personal physician.

4. HEMLOCK speaks only to those people who have mutual sympathy with its goals. Views contrary to its own which are held by other religions and philosophies are respected.

The National Hemlock Society describes itself as a "nonprofit organization of over 31,000 members" with chapters throughout the United States. It is sup-

FIGURE 5–2   The Death of Socrates by Jacques Louis David. (Reprinted by permission of The Metropolitan Museum of Art, Wolfe Fund, 1931. Catharine Lorillard Wolfe Collection. All rights reserved, The Metropolitan Museum of Art.)

ported by membership fees, donations, and the sales of books and other literature (*Newsletter,* July 1989). Hemlock's objectives are:

- Continuing a dialogue to raise public consciousness of active voluntary euthanasia through the news media, public meetings, and with the medical and legal professions, and others.
- Supporting the principle of legislation to permit a dying person to lawfully request a physician to help them die. [The Humane and Dignified Death Act]
- Publishing informational material to help members decide the manner and means of their death. *Let Me Die Before I Wake* is the only guide to self-deliverance for the dying in the USA. [Humphry's best-seller, *Final Exit,* had not yet been published.]
- Issuing a quarterly newsletter to members providing up-to-date information on issues of death and dying.
- Providing members upon joining a free Living Will and Durable Power of Attorney for Health Care, plus a medical treatment card for purse or wallet. (Ibid.)

Humphry and Wickett have also written a full-length book on euthanasia—*The Right to Die* (1986)—for a major publishing house.

In October 1991, Ann Wickett, at the age of forty-nine, took her own life. She had been diagnosed as having breast cancer and her marriage to Humphry had ended in a bitter divorce.

Last Wish

Betty Rollin, a journalist, TV correspondent, and author has worked for NBC News and ABC News and has written articles for national publications including *The New York Times* and *McCall's* (see Figure 5–3). She is also the author of a best-selling book, *First, You Cry* (1976), in which she describes her own experience in dealing with a life-threatening disease—breast cancer. Perhaps her most compelling work, however, is the story of how she helped her mother—seventy-six years old and dying from cancer—end her own life by suicide.

For two and a half years, Ida Rollin struggled with her disease. At first she was optimistic. After all, she had watched her daughter triumph over breast cancer. But after two bouts of chemotherapy, with a "relatively good" period of six months in between, she said, "Enough! I'm ready to die . . . now!" She saw her health and life slowly slipping away and she wanted no more of the sickness and pain that she had come to know so well.

But she, and her daughter who had pledged her help, soon came to discover that dying wasn't easy, especially if you're so sick that you can hardly

FIGURE 5–3 Betty Rollin, NBC News correspondent, recounted the story of how she helped her mother, who was suffering from ovarian cancer, end her life. (Reprinted by permission of AP/Wide World Photos)

swallow and if you're not prone to violence. Ida Rollin wanted to die quickly and painlessly, with her family nearby. *Last Wish* (1985) tells the story of a desperate search for a doctor who would write the prescription by which she, with the support of a loving family, could gently end a life that no longer held or promised any meaning for her.

Like the story of Lester Zygmanik, Ida Rollin's story became a highly successful book and eventually a made-for-television movie starring Patty Duke and Jean Stapleton in the roles of Betty Rollin and her mother respectively.

Death at the AMA

A short essay in the January 8, 1988, issue of the *Journal of the American Medical Association* told the story of a fatigued young gynecology resident being awakened in the middle of the night to attend a restless patient. The name of the author was "withheld by request" but when s/he arrived at the unknown patient's room, having only briefly reviewed her chart, s/he discovered "a 20-year-old girl named Debbie [who] was dying of ovarian cancer." She was vomiting relentlessly and her emaciation made her look "much older than 20." She weighed eighty pounds and was suffering from "severe air hunger." A second woman, middle-aged, was with her holding her hand. The author described the scene in the following way:

> Both looked up as I entered. The room seemed filled with the patient's desperate effort to survive. Her eyes were hollow, and she had suprasternal and intercostal retractions with her rapid inspirations. She had not eaten or slept in two days. She had not responded to chemotherapy and was being given supportive care only. It was a gallows scene, a cruel mockery of her youth and unfulfilled potential. Her only words to me were, "Let's get this over with."

With this, the harried young resident retreated to the nurses station to decide on a course of action. "I could not give her health, but I could give her rest" was the conclusion. The nurse was asked to draw 20 mg of morphine sulfate into a syringe and the resident told Debbie and her companion that she would be given something that would "let her rest." The morphine was injected and "within seconds" her breathing slowed and her eyes closed. A few minutes later her breathing slowed even more, then became irregular, and then it stopped. Debbie's unnamed companion "seemed relieved." The author concluded the story with three short words. "It's over, Debbie."

The essay triggered a flood of letters to *JAMA* and raised the issue of the physician's role in euthanasia (actually, to be correct, direct, active, voluntary (?) euthanasia) to a fever pitch. While most of the mail condemned the act, some readers expressed skepticism as to whether such a small dose of morphine could produce such a dramatic result. The editor of *JAMA*, Dr. George Lundberg, was quoted as saying that he and his staff believed—but had not confirmed—that the essay was based on an actual event. Lundberg said that his own staff was divided over whether or not to publish the piece, but two medical peer-review panels urged him to do so. He later defended his decision on the basis of the contribution that it had made to fostering debate on the topic. Along with a collection of representative letters and several essays written in response to the original one, the April 8 issue of *JAMA* carried his summation:

> It [euthanasia] may become one of the predominant medical and ethical debates for the rest of this century. While our early mail was heavily in opposition, our recent letters have run strongly in favor of the act described by the physician and of THE JOURNAL'S courage in publishing about euthanasia. If physicians' letters are any indication, mainstream physician involvement in active euthanasia is unlikely in the near future in this country.   (Lundberg, 1988, p. 2143)

Lundberg went on to acknowledge, however, that both the results of recent polls as well as the letters *The Journal* received were indicative of a different sentiment among members of the general public. He concluded his essay with the following:

> By publishing "It's Over, Debbie," THE JOURNAL demonstrated its belief that the ethics of euthanasia must be debated anew, and it reaffirms the appropriateness of our decision by publishing some of that debate in this issue. During our discussions, we must comprehend the vital social and public policy issues that are involved. Despite the technological revolution, we physicians must continue to honor a tradition that has persevered for thousands of years: the necessity to preserve the best possible life for the longest possible time. When one backs away in any sense from the utter sanctity of maintaining human life, the slope becomes very slippery indeed.   (Ibid.)

The decision by *JAMA*'s editor to publish the story of Debbie's death had created some unexpected problems in the form of a subpoena by a Cook County (Chicago) grand jury which sought to discover the doctor's identity. The subpoena, which had been sought by the state attorney's office, was dismissed by the Circuit Court.

Lundberg's essay was accompanied by a group of letters *The Journal* had received in response to the original essay. Nearly all of them were critical of the act and *The Journal*, the latter because it had failed to clearly dissociate itself from or clearly condemn the behavior. Lundberg decided against this, he stated, in order to foster a spirited debate on the topic. Derek Humphry, of the National Hemlock Society, a group that endorses voluntary, direct, active euthanasia, also wrote a letter strongly criticizing what had allegedly happened and pointing out that this was not what Hemlock was interested in promoting because it was not clearly "voluntary" and the act itself was surreptitious. Hemlock, as we shall discuss later, recognizes the need for certain procedural safeguards if voluntary, direct, active euthanasia for the terminally ill is to be decriminalized.

Some of the critics seemed to resort to rhetorical devices of questionable validity, at least from an empirical standpoint. One suggested that:

> Over is the ethic of the caring physician. Instead, we see emerging the ethic of the killing physician. Over is the ethic of the helping profession. Instead, we see emerging the ethic of the killing profession. If any one physician kills, the mission of our entire profession is endangered. Our civilization had an experience with systematic and institutionalized medical killing earlier in the century [seemingly in reference to Nazi Germany]; many of us naively thought this experience was permanently behind us. Apparently, the killing of patients by physicians is no longer inconceivable to the medical public or American society. It's not over, Debbie, it's only just beginning—again. (Singer, 1988, p. 2096)

Another letter writer recounted the 1920 publication of Karl Binding and Alfred Hoche's, *Permitting the Destruction of Unworthy Life*, which linked the holocaust with the German euthanasia movement. Of course, whether or not the Nazi experience, with its emphasis on racial cleansing and the building of a master race through involuntary killing, is even relevant to the debate over voluntary euthanasia, is also part of the debate itself. It would seem to be difficult to make the argument that mass extermination could ever be described as a "good death."

This same writer also challenged the "relief of suffering" as a valid goal of Debbie's doctor. Rather than being devoid of meaning, suffering, he suggested, can "lead to a more complete knowledge of the self."

> In my practice, many patients seem to have acquired spiritual and psychological benefits from suffering. With skill and knowledge and with reflection on the beauty of life we will be better able to care for the severely ill and suffering of the world. (Lamb, 1988, p. 2097)

Among the supportive letters was one from a well-known medical ethicist who wrote:

> It makes no sense to hide our heads in the sand when many different forms of active euthanasia are currently being practiced in the United States. Discussing these may help bring about a social consensus that would support traditional physician reluctance to engage in active euthanasia.
>
> Problems do exist, however, in prolonging life beyond any reasonable and comfortable limit. These problems must be thoroughly discussed by our health professional societies as well as by our citizens. (Thomasma, 1988, p. 2098)

While the letters from most of the physicians were critical, as Lundberg pointed out in his accompanying essay, "the public" response to *The Journal* differed. One writer described the situation of her father, age eighty-five, who

has been in a nursing home for more than a year. He is incontinent, has lost his memory and ability to comprehend and reason, and is hospitalized periodically for pneumonia, urinary tract infection, dehydration, and so on.

He has now lost his ability to swallow, and since Christmas he has been fed through a tube inserted in his nose. Because he tried to remove the tube, his hands are tied at all times to the bed rails. He is not comatose but he does not recognize his family and he has no understanding of why he is being forced to lie in bed under these circumstances. I believe that if I were asked to make a list of ways in which to torture people, this would have to be placed somewhere near the top.

I am fully aware that a physician's duty is to treat and heal, but when healing is clearly not possible, should not mercy killing be allowed?   (Wilson, 1988, p. 2097)

Another young woman wrote:

I am a 23-year-old legal secretary and I watched my mother die of lung cancer. It was a horrible death and not one that I would like to endure myself. Cancer patients who are terminally ill endure much pain and suffering. I feel very strongly that if such a patient wants to end her life by being injected with morphine or any other drug that will end her pain, then she should have the right. No one should have the right to make someone suffer.   (Davis, 1988, p. 2097)

Yet another woman wrote:

The author of the essay is a brave, caring, and progressive member of his profession. His actions were those of one who values an individual's right of choice—Debbie's choice, my choice, the choices of many who refuse to suffer when hope of recovery is nil.

Physicians are so concerned with saving life that they are overlooking quality of life when the end is imminent. They are willing to withhold treatment at the request of a patient but will ignore a request for a peaceful, painless end. Outdated medical ethics and laws deny humans the final dignity of the "humane" end we afford our pets.

It galls me that all the nay sayers of the medical community who have written to *JAMA* won't look past their protective veil of medical ethics to address an issue that is so overwhelmingly embraced by laymen. Active voluntary euthanasia certainly would be preferred by all those who feel that self-deliverance is better than prolonged pain and suffering. . . .

To all those physicians who would deny me a lethal injection, on request, as I lie dying, I say, " Whose life is it, anyway?"   (Moran, 1988, p. 2098)

The Journal also published two "Commentaries" along with Lundberg's essay. In the first of these, four distinguished physicians admonished that "Doctors Must Not Kill" (Gaylin, Kass, Pellegrino, & Siegler, 1988, pp.

2139–2140). Two of their premises were simple. First, the physician who killed Debbie had committed a felony: premeditated murder. Second, the act was unprofessional and unethical. S/he didn't know the patient, s/he didn't study her chart, s/he didn't converse with her family, and s/he didn't consult with *her* (Debbie's attending) physician. All of this seems to be unassailably true. Their third premise, however, that "Doctors Must Not Kill," is a conclusion, trumpeted with great authority but without benefit of empirical data. They do refer to "tradition" and a 1986 "statement" of the Judicial Council of the AMA which affirmed the principle that a "physician should not intentionally cause death" and they expressed their dismay that this tradition has been and is being challenged, but one searches in vain for any "evidence" that this will produce the ills they seem to fear. One of those fears is that we might become like the Netherlands where, according to them "the barriers to physician killing are gone" and which has resulted in "many well-documented cases" of "uninvited killing by doctors."

The Gaylin et al. essay was followed by a rebuttal of sorts. Vaux argued that the debate about the circumstances of Debbie's death was symptomatic of the "deeper question" that troubles us all. "As I lie dying, will I be offered humane care, will I be done in too soon by some expediency, or will I be subjected to terminal torture?" (Vaux, 1988, pp. 2140–2141).

He reminded readers that "euthanasia" should not be interpreted as referring to "Nazi-like elimination of the sick, old, or unproductive" nor, because it seemingly lacked the element of informed consent by the patient, did "It's Over, Debbie" constitute euthanasia. We would remind our readers at this point that, as discussed in Chapter 2, informed consent is based on a decision by a competent patient who has been apprised of the potential risks and benefits of the proposed "treatment" along with any alternatives that might be available.

Vaux expressed a concern that progress in medicine has brought with it a blurring of the qualities that medically distinguished the living from the dying.

> With our life-prolonging techniques and medications, we have transformed death; we have taken it out of the acute, natural, and noninterventional mode and made it more into a chronic, contrived, and manipulated phenomenon. Deaths as inevitable as Debbie's have been protracted by a range of interventions, including chemotherapy, analgesia, the administration of intravenous fluids and nutrients, and hospitalization itself. Logically and emotionally, we cannot intervene at one phase and then be inactive at another, more painful phase. We cannot modify nature and then plead that nature must be allowed to run its unhindered course. (Ibid., p. 2141)

The debate Lundberg was seeking had become a reality. Yet another series of letters to *JAMA* were published some four months later. The vast majority of these letters, unlike the original collection, were supportive of the anonymous author of "It's Over, Debbie," and critical of the position taken by Gaylin and his associates. One of them in particular, written by another prominent medical ethicist, commented that if this kind of reasoning and "rhetorical overkill" is representative of the training of clinical ethicists, then the entire discipline may well be in trouble! (Brody, 1988, p. 789).

Meanwhile, as the debate over Debbie's death continued in *JAMA*, the issue was also being played out in the political forum in California.

The Humane and Dignified Death Act: Proposition 161

The Humane and Dignified Death Act was drafted by two California lawyers, Robert L. Risley and Michael H. White. Risley's involvement in the right-to-die movement stems from his wife's protracted and painful death from cancer in 1984. The model law they wrote would have amended the California Constitution by adding an "inalienable right of privacy [which would include] the right of the terminally ill to voluntary, humane, and dignified doctor as-sisted aid in dying" (1988). Under the terms of the Act, a terminally ill patient could request a physician to provide "aid in dying," defined as "any medical procedure that will terminate the life of the qualified patient swiftly, painlessly, and humanely." The proposal would also have provided for the appointment of an agent, selected by the patient while competent and specifically authorized to request "aid in dying," who would be able to act on the patient's behalf should he or she become unable to do so. Only "terminally ill" patients would qualify. A terminal condition was defined as "an incurable condition which, re-gardless of application of life-sustaining procedures" would be likely to result in death within six months and where such treatments "only serve to postpone the moment of death of the patient." Diagnosis and certification in writing must be provided by two physicians, one of whom was the attending physi-cian, who had personally examined the patient.

The request would require the same formalities as a more typical advance directive. It would have to be signed in the presence of two witnesses, neither of whom was related to the patient by blood or marriage or who would inherit anything under the terms of a will or operation of law. Also excluded as wit-nesses were the attending physician and any employees of the attending physi-cian or of the health care facility where the patient had been admitted. There were also special safeguards that would have specifically applied to patients in nursing homes.

A directive would be effective for seven years unless revoked earlier. Physicians and health care facilities acting in good faith pursuant to the direc-tive would be protected against civil and criminal liability. There would be, however, no penalty for failing to comply with the terms of the directive unless there was "willful failure to transfer" the patient to a physician who would comply.

While suicide is not a crime anywhere in the United States, the proposal would not have altered that part of California law that identified aiding, advising, or encouraging another to commit suicide as a felony. The proposal simply stated that death resulting from a request for aid in dying does not constitute suicide.

Due to the controversial nature of the proposal, the proponents were unable to find any member of the California legislature who was willing to sponsor it. Convinced that there was considerable support among the public, they decided to try to get the proposal on a statewide ballot by the initiative route. California, like many other states, has a provision for bypassing the legislature and putting issues directly before the voters if a petition signed by a certain percentage of the registered voters is filed with state officials.

Although the referendum initiative ultimately failed to obtain the number of signatures needed to qualify for the ballot, the campaign demonstrated a strong and growing nucleus of popular support which the sponsors sensed that they could count on in the future. In 1992, on the heels of the narrow defeat of a similar proposal by the voters of Washington State, an event that will be discussed later in this chapter, the issue had qualified. When the voters went to the polls on November 3, the initiative, identified as Proposition 161, failed to pass by the same fifty-four to forty-six majority that occurred in Washington. The fact that the proposal failed by only 5 percent of the vote is significant in that it had been opposed by the National Right to Life Committee, the California Pro-Life Council, the California Medical Association, the California Nurses Association, the California Hospice Association, and the Catholic Church. In addition to this formidable source of organized opposition, "every newspaper in the state which editorialized on the subject opposed it" (Andrusko, 1992).

The Kevorkian Controversy

The public debate over euthanasia reached new heights on June 4, 1990, when the national media announced that Dr. Jack Kevorkian (see Figure 5–4), a sixty-four-year-old retired pathologist, had assisted in the "suicide" of Janet Adkins. Adkins, who was fifty-four at the time, had been diagnosed as having Alzheimer's disease. Kevorkian had gained some notoriety through his advocacy for the more humane execution of prisoners. He argued that they should be given the opportunity to choose death by lethal injection coupled with donation of their organs; not only would the killing be less barbaric, he maintained, but it would also help ease a severe shortage of organs for transplant. It was this that seemed to lead to his interest in euthanasia and the development of a "suicide machine," which he labeled a "mercitron" (Kevorkian, 1991) (see Figure 5–5).

As *Time* (Gibbs, 1990) commented shortly thereafter, this was a case

FIGURE 5–4   Dr. Jack Kevorkian. (Reprinted by permission of AP/Wide World Photos)

where neither the physician nor the patient worked very well as a symbol for the euthanasia debate. Janet Adkins, a Portland (Oregon) school teacher was still in the early stages of Alzheimer's and not yet very sick. She was an active and talented woman who, a week before her death, beat her thirty-two-year-old son in a tennis match. It was "more her dread than her disease that drove her to seek Kevorkian's help" (Ibid., p. 69). Even before her illness, she had been a member of the Hemlock Society. She came to Michigan, where Kevorkian lived, because she thought, probably correctly, that she would be unable to get a physician in Oregon to assist her in her suicide. In Michigan, the law was somewhat murky concerning assisted suicide and Dr. Kevorkian, who had consulted with her only by telephone, seemed willing to test it. Convinced that her disease was progressing and that the time she had left to act was limited, she flew to Detroit with her husband, an investment broker. He hoped that she would change her mind and they even purchased a round-trip plane ticket for her . . . just in case.

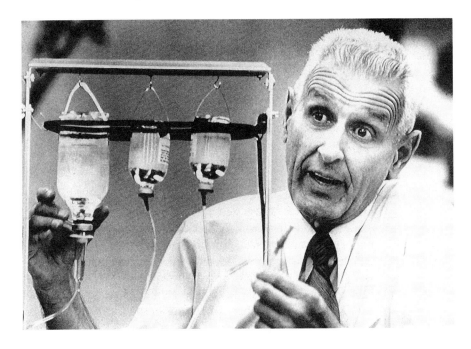

FIGURE 5–5   The "mercitron," a device assembled by Dr. Jack Kevorkian to allow him to "assist" in the suicide of those seeking his help. After his medical license was revoked by the State of Michigan and he could no longer acquire the necessary drugs, he began using carbon monoxide delivered via a mask. (Reprinted by permission of AP/Wide World Photos)

Meanwhile, Dr. Kevorkian was searching for a place where the death could take place. He tried, unsuccessfully, funeral homes, hotels, and vacant office buildings. As a last resort, he turned to his 1968 Volkswagen camper. The setting would be in a public campground.

Dr. Kevorkian, who had been described as "flamboyant" by some, made no efforts to conceal his willingness to challenge the law. On January 24, 1990, nearly six months before Janet Adkin's death, he sent the following letter to the Michigan Department of Licensing and Regulation:

> My purpose is to inform the Department that I have begun a unique medical practice: to assist the rational suicide of patients who are suffering from eminently [sic] terminal illness, severely crippling or painful disease or deformity or trauma, and who, on their own, have decided that the quality of life for them has degenerated to intolerable levels. Candidates for the service must be alert and mentally competent, and their underlying condition must be physical (not psychiatric). The service entails more than one consultation with the patient, their close family members, and their personal physicians. The latter

supply me with case summaries, including their assessment of prognosis. The suicide is accomplished in a painless, fast, and dignified way by means of a device I invented last year. At the time and place of his or her choosing the patient activates the device by touching a switch which cuts off a slow intravenous drip of saline solution and starts infusion of thiopental sodium solution. A minute later the device will infuse a solution of potassium chloride to stop the heart. The procedure will be monitored with a running electrocardiograph to document clinical death. In every instance the local medical examiner will have been given prior notice. (*The People of the State of Michigan* v. *Jack Kevorkian*, 1991, p. 110)

With her husband at her side, Dr. Kevorkian hooked Mrs. Adkins to the machine. The death was described as quick and painless.

As soon as he was convinced that she was dead, Dr. Kevorkian called the police. He was not charged immediately, although a judge did issue a temporary restraining order barring him from assisting with other suicides. Criticism was sharp and quick in coming. A sympathetic piece by Dr. Marcia Angell, executive editor of *The New England Journal of Medicine*, published in *The New York Times*, was a notable exception. After reflecting on what Janet Adkins had awaiting her, Angell asked:

Was it better than what Dr. Kevorkian offered? Maybe. But the answer is not simple and it is probably not the same for everyone in her position. The notion that there is a "correct" ethical answer to this question should give us a pause.

The prospect for Janet Adkins was bleak. Moreover, modern medical care permits longer and longer survival under these circumstances, and patients are often subjected to the full panoply of aggressive treatment simply because it is available. What is someone like Janet Adkins, who valued her independence, to do?

Aware of this predicament, many people have focused criticism not on Mrs. Adkins but on Dr. Kevorkian, for helping her. This is a puzzling position. If suicide under these circumstances is not wrong, then why is it wrong to help? (Angell, 1990)

Dr. Kevorkian, who was dubbed "Dr. Death" or "Jack, the Dripper" by the media, was subsequently charged with murder which, in Michigan, carries a mandatory penalty of life imprisonment without parole. The Oakland County prosecutor was quoted as saying that failure to charge Dr. Kevorkian would turn Oakland County into a suicide mecca for the nation. He was arraigned and freed on bail while awaiting trial. The murder charges were dismissed in December 1990, but another court, on February 5, 1991, made the injunction against the use of his "machine" permanent.

One could, of course, quibble over whether or not Dr. Kevorkian followed the procedures he so carefully set up for himself. Was Mrs. Adkins, for example, suffering from an "imminently terminal illness, severely crippling or painful disease or deformity or trauma?" (*People of the State of Michigan* v. *Jack Kevorkian*, 1991, p. 110). Was her underlying condition truly "physical (not psychiatric)?" (Ibid.). And was there sufficient consultation? To do so, however, one runs the risk of crashing into the trees while searching for the forest. The threshold question is "Was Dr. Kevorkian's act legal?" not was it wise, ethical, or moral. About the latter there is room for disagreement. Concerning the former, we have a right to an answer and, at least in Michigan at that time, the answer is yes.

Although there had been a case in 1919 (*People* v. *Roberts*) in which a husband, Frank Roberts, had been sentenced to life in prison in solitary confinement for helping his wife, who was suffering from multiple sclerosis, commit suicide by giving her Paris green [arsenic] to drink, in 1983 the Michigan Court of Appeals (*People* v. *Campbell*) stated that the Roberts ruling was no longer the law. Unlike Janet Adkins, it had been argued that Katie Roberts was too weak to have actively participated in ending her life. The judge called Roberts' deed "an inhuman and dastardly act" and said that it didn't matter whether his wife wanted to commit suicide. (There was testimony that Katie Roberts had tried to commit suicide the previous year by drinking carbolic acid, a powerful disinfectant.) The Governor of Michigan commuted the life sentence to ten years and Roberts was released after serving slightly more than four.

The 1983 case which, in effect, overruled the *Roberts* decision involved a somewhat more tawdry set of circumstances. Steve Campbell was a young man with "a drinking problem, a drug problem, and an attitude" (McGraw, 1992). He was a high school dropout with a history of arrests. Suspecting that his friend, Kevin Basnaw, was having an affair with his wife, Campbell badgered him, while depressed and drunken, into shooting himself with a gun that Campbell had provided. Although the District Court ordered Campbell to stand trial for murder, on March 21, 1983, a three-judge panel of the State Appeals Court ordered the charges dropped. The Michigan Supreme Court declined to hear the case. It was the decision in *Campbell* that was the basis for the judge's dismissal of the charges against Dr. Kevorkian.

Less than three months after Janet Adkins died, on August 19, Virginia Harper, a sixty-nine-year-old Californian, traveled to Michigan with her seventy-three-year-old husband, Bertram, and committed suicide in a Detroit motel room by swallowing sleeping pills. After she was asleep her husband placed a plastic bag over her head. Mrs. Harper had been diagnosed as having liver cancer. They were accompanied to Michigan by their forty-year-old daughter. On May 10, 1991, Mr. Harper was acquitted on charges of second-degree murder. The jury deliberated less than two hours.

On October 23, 1991, Dr. Kevorkian was again back in the news. This time it was in connection with the deaths of two women, Sherry Miller, age forty-three, and Marjorie Wantz, age fifty-eight. Ms. Miller had multiple sclerosis and Ms. Wantz suffered from a painful and incurable pelvic disease. The former died from inhalation of carbon monoxide using a mask; the latter from a lethal injection via a machine similar to the one used with Janet Adkins. The setting was a cabin in a campground some forty miles from Detroit.

Mrs. Miller had testified in support of Dr. Kevorkian before the court that permanently enjoined the use of his machine. On July 21, 1992, an Oakland County Circuit Court judge again dismissed charges against Dr. Kevorkian reiterating that Michigan has no law against assisted suicide. Moreover, he added, the prosecutors had failed to show that it was Dr. Kevorkian who actually tripped the devices that the two women used to die.

The governor, John Engler, was quoted as urging the legislature to act before the state becomes known as "the suicide state." A bill that would make assisted suicide a felony had been passed by the Senate, but not yet considered by the House. Just shortly before the dismissal of charges occurred, on May 3, 1992, the 300 members of the Delegate Assembly of the Michigan State Medical Society voted to rescind an earlier, January 15, vote of the organization's board which would have endorsed legislation making it a felony for a physician to help a patient commit suicide. While the Society remains on record against it, it says it no longer should be a crime. Prior to that, in November, 1991, Dr. Kevorkian's license to practice medicine was revoked by the State Board of Michigan. They found him to be "a threat to the public health, safety, and welfare requiring emergency action." Since he had retired as a practicing clinical pathologist years earlier, and the act for which he was being reprimanded seemed to members of the State board to lie "outside" the practice of medicine, one can only wonder what the loss of his license might be expected to result in. It certainly didn't deter him from assisting in the deaths of Sherry Miller and Marjorie Wantz.

Dr. Kevorkian was back in the news again on May 15, 1992. This time he had "counseled" fifty-two-year-old Susan Williams, afflicted with multiple sclerosis that had left her incapacitated and blind. He was with her at her home as she self-administered carbon monoxide but, according to his attorney, he did not "assist" in the death. Mrs. Williams' body was found in a bedroom with a mask covering her face and nose. Mrs. Williams' sisters and her twenty-nine-year-old son were also with her at the time of her death; her eighty-one-year-old husband was aware of her decision but not in attendance.

According to newspaper accounts of the case, Mrs. Williams left a letter:

> I don't want to live . . . any longer and feel I have the right to end my life. . . .
> The quality of my life is just existing, not living. . . .
>
> Doctor Kevorkian has counseled me not to do this until I am absolutely sure this is what I want. . . . I pray Dr. Kevorkian will be exonerated of any wrongdoing in this case. I am so thankful he was able to help me.

No charges had been filed at the time. Dr. Kevorkian, according to his attorney, threatened to go on a hunger strike if imprisoned (*The [Toledo] Blade*, May 16, 1992).

On September 29, 1992, Dr. Kevorkian "assisted" in the death of fifty-two-year-old Lois Hawes. Ms. Hawes had been diagnosed with lung cancer which had metastasized to her brain. She had already outlived by several months the time when her death had been expected to occur when her diagnosis had been confirmed. According to press reports, two of her sons, two sisters, and a niece were also present at the suicide, which occurred at the home of one of Kevorkian's supporters.

The suicide came some ten days after the Michigan State Medical Society had rejected Kevorkian's request for help in handling his "patients" and his vow that he would continue his work regardless. According to press reports, Kevorkian studied Ms. Hawes' medical records and a report by an oncologist and also met with a psychiatrist who assured him that she was mentally competent before he aided her in taking her own life. The death sparked a flurry of activity in the Michigan legislature where there were several bills under discussion (*The [Toledo] Blade*, September 28, 1992).

On November 23, 1992, Dr. Kevorkian was present when Catherine Andreyev, age forty-five, a woman from Pennsylvania with breast cancer, died after inhaling carbon monoxide at an Oakland County (Michigan) house. Less than a month later, on December 15, two women who had previously testified in support of Kevorkian at a news conference to protest the proposed legislation ended their lives with his assistance. Marguerite Tate, age seventy, who had amyotropic lateral sclerosis (ALS)—Lou Gehrig's disease—and Marcella Lawrence, age sixty-seven, who suffered from emphysema, heart disease, and severe arthritis, died at Tate's Auburn Hills (Michigan) home after inhaling carbon monoxide. Just hours after the death of the two women, Michigan Governor John Engler signed legislation creating a Michigan commission on death and dying and, pending its recommendation, instituting a ban on assisted suicide. Figure 5–6 traces the sequence of events that began with the death of Janet Adkins.

The commission was to be comprised of a wide variety of people representing a broad spectrum of opinion on the topic of assisted suicide. Members were to include, but not be limited to, nominees from groups such as the American Association for Retired Persons, the American Civil Liberties Union, the Michigan Hemlock Society, Hospice, the Michigan Hospital Association, the Michigan Nurses Association, the Michigan Psychiatric Society and Psychological Association, the State Medical and Bar Associations, and Michigan Right to Life. The commission was charged with producing a report and recommendations within fifteen months that would address:

1. Current data concerning suicide within the state.
2. The proper aims of legislation affecting voluntary self-termination.

The Kevorkian Chronicles

June 4, 1990 — Janet Adkins, age 54, Alzheimer's disease

June 8, 1990 — Kevorkian *temporarily barred* from using machine to assist suicide.

December 13,1990 — *Murder charges* in the death of Janet Adkins dismissed.

February 5, 1991 — *Permanent injunction* against using machine to assist suicide.

October 23, 1991 — Sherry Miller, age 43, multiple sclerosis
Marjorie Wantz, age 58, incurable "pelvic disease"

November 20, 1991 — Michigan Board of Medicine *suspends license.*

February 28, 1992 — *Ordered to stand trial* on murder charges of Sherry Miller and Marjorie Wantz.

May 15, 1992 — Susan Williams, age 52, multiple sclerosis.

July 21, 1992 — *Murder charges* of Miller and Wantz *dismissed.*

September 29, 1992 — Lois Hawes, age 52, lung and brain cancer

November 23, 1992 — Catherine Andreyev (Moon Township, PA), age 45, breast cancer

December 15, 1992 — Marguerite Tate, age 70, ALS

Marcella Lawrence, age 67, emphysema, heart disease, and arthritis

Governor signs into law a *temporary ban* on assisting in suicide

January 20, 1993 — Jack Elmer Miller, age 53, bone cancer

February 4, 1993 — Stanley Ball, age 82, pancreatic cancer and blindness
Mary Biernat, (Indiana resident), age 73, breat cancer

February 8, 1993 — Elaine Goldbaum, age 47, multiple sclerosis

February 15, 1993 — Hugh Gale, age 70, emphysema and congestive heart disease (invalid)

February 18, 1993 — Jonathon Grenz, (Costa Mesa, CA), age 44, cancer of mouth and throat
Martha Ruwart, (Cardiff-by-the-Sea, CA), age 41, duodenal and ovarian cancer

FIGURE 5–6   A chronology of the physician-assisted suicide controversy in Michigan.

The Kevorkian Chronicles (Continued)

February 25, 1993	Legislature approves *bill banning assisted suicide* immediately.
April 27, 1993	California judge *suspends Kevorkian's medical license.*
May 16, 1993	Ron Mansur, age 54, lung and bone cancer
May 20, 1993	*Law declared unconstitutional* by Judge Cynthia D. Stephens of Wayne County Circuit Court.
August 4, 1993	Thomas Hyde, age 30, ALS
August 17, 1993	Prosecutors decide to charge Kevorkian in connection with Hyde suicide.
September 9, 1993	Donald O'Keefe, age 73, bone cancer
October 22, 1993	Merian Frederick, age 72, ALS
November 22, 1993	Ali Khalili (M.D.), age 61, multiple myeloma (bone cancer)
December 13, 1993	*Law declared unconstitutional* by Judge Richard C. Kaufman of Wayne County Circuit Court.
January 27, 1994	*Law declared unconstitutional* by Judge Jessica Cooper of Oakland County Circuit Court.
May 3, 1994	Wayne County jury finds Kevorkian innocent of violating the law against assisting a suicide in the death of Thomas Hyde.
May 4, 1994	U.S. District Court Judge Barbara Rothstein ruled that Washington state law banning doctor-assisted suicide was *unconstitutional.*
May 10, 1994	Michigan Court of Appeals finds assisted suicide law invalid on technical grounds but orders Kevorkian to stand trial on murder charges steming from the deaths of Marjorie Wantz and Sherry Miller.
June 6, 1994	Michigan Supreme Court agrees to hear appeals on the status of the assisted suicide law. Arguments are scheduled for October 4, 1994.

FIGURE 5-6 *(Continued)*

3. The most efficient method of preventing voluntary self-termination.

4. Appropriate guidelines and safeguards regarding voluntary self-termination.

5. Any other factors the commission considers necessary in developing recommendations for legislation.

All meetings of the commission were to be open to the public.

Effective April 1, 1993, and continuing until six months after the commission makes its recommendation to the legislature, the law also makes assistance of suicide a felony punishable by no more than four years imprisonment or by a fine of no more than $2,000, or both. Assisting suicide is defined as providing the physical *means* by which another attempts or commits suicide or participation in a physical *act* by which another attempts or commits suicide. Shortly after its passage, the Michigan branch of the American Civil Liberties Union announced its intention to challenge the constitutionality of the new law.

Undeterred by the new legislation, Dr. Kevorkian was back in the news again on January 20, 1993, when he assisted in the suicide of Jack Elmer Miller, a fifty-three-year-old man with bone cancer. This was followed by another double suicide on February 4—eighty-two-year-old Stanley Ball, who suffered from pancreatic cancer and blindness, and Mary Biernat, a seventy-three-year-old Indiana resident with breast cancer. There would be four additional suicides before the new law became effective. Elaine Goldbaum, a forty-seven-year-old victim of multiple sclerosis, died on February 8. Hugh Gale, a seventy-year-old with emphysema and congestive heart disease ended his life on February 15, and, on February 18, there was yet another double suicide involving two California residents, forty-four-year-old Jonathon Grenz, who suffered from cancer of the mouth and throat, and forty-one-year-old Martha Ruwart, who had been diagnosed as having duodenal and ovarian cancer.

On May 16, 1993, approximately a month and a half after the law became effective, Dr. Kevorkian assisted with the suicide of a fifty-four-year-old sufferer from lung and bone cancer, Ron Mansur. Because a decision in the suit brought by the ACLU was pending, prosecutors decided not to bring charges against him. Four days later, on May 20, Judge Cynthia Stephens of the Wayne County Circuit Court, basing her decision primarily on the technicality that it violated a section of the Michigan Constitution that forbids legislation that addresses more than one subject—it had both created a commission and criminalized assisted suicide—but also writing that there is a constitutionally protected right to commit suicide, issued an injunction against enforcement of the law. That ruling was blocked on June 22 by a two to one decision of the Court of Appeals pending a decision on the constitutionality of the issue (*The [Toledo] Blade*, June 23, 1993).

Between August 4 and November 22, 1993, Dr. Kevorkian assisted with four additional suicides: Thomas Hyde, a thirty-year-old man with amyotrophic lateral sclerosis (ALS); Donald O'Keefe, seventy-three, who had cancer of the bone; Merian Frederick, a seventy-two-year-old woman with ALS; and Ali Khalili, a sixty-one-year-old physician with bone cancer. Kevorkian was charged with violating the law against assisted suicide in the O'Keefe case and, on December 13, 1993, Circuit Court Judge Richard Kaufman, who like Judge Stephens also sits in Wayne County, issued an opinion striking the law as it applied to Dr. Kevorkian. Unlike Judge Stephens, Kaufman did not find the law unconstitutional on the technicality of having more than one purpose. He did, however, strongly assert that the law violated a person's constitutionally protected right to commit rational suicide.

Kevorkian had also been arrested in neighboring Oakland County for his role in the Frederick suicide and began a hunger strike to protest what he regarded as the immorality of the $50,000 bond that had been set as a condition of his release. The Oakland County prosecutor was quoted as saying he did not regard the decisions of the Wayne County courts as binding on the courts in Oakland County. Circuit Court Judge Jessica Cooper, of Oakland County, subsequently reduced the amount to $100 on the condition that Kevorkian wear an electronic monitoring device so that his whereabouts could be known at all times. After hearing arguments on the case, on January 27, 1994, Judge Cooper, like Judges Stephens and Kaufman, ruled that the law was unconstitutional. While the decision was pending before Judge Cooper, Kevorkian promised that he would curtail his activities in assisted suicide and undertake a campaign to gather enough signatures from registered voters to place a proposal for a constitutional amendment legalizing the practice on the Michigan ballot.

On May 10, 1994, a Wayne County jury found Kevorkian innocent of violating the law on assisted suicide in the death of Thomas Hyde. Since Kevorkian had admitted that he had assisted in Mr. Hyde's death, including an interview on national television, this was simply a case of jury nullification. The jurors refused to find that Kevorkian had done anything wrong.

A week later, on May 10, the Michigan Court of Appeals ruled that the law was invalid on technical grounds—refusing to reach the broader constitutional issues addressed by the trial courts—but they ordered that Kevorkian stand trial on the murder charges stemming from the deaths of Marjorie Wantz and Sherry Miller. On June 6, the Michigan Supreme Court agreed to hear appeals on the status of the assisted suicide law. Arguments were scheduled for October 4, 1994.

Unless either the voters or the legislators of the State of Michigan respond by legalizing certain forms of assisted suicide, it is likely that the court decisions will ultimately be appealed to the U.S. Supreme Court. Also, perhaps working its way toward the U.S. Supreme Court is a Federal District Court decision of May 3, 1994, which held that the State of Washington's law that criminalized physician-assisted suicide is unconstitutional (*Compassion in Dying v. Washington*).

Diane: A Case of Death and Dignity

Early in the spring of 1991 another physician, this one quite willing to identify himself by name, told of how he had participated in the death of one of his patients. Like the story of Debbie's death, this one was also told in the pages of a prestigious medical journal, this time *The New England Journal of Medicine* rather than *JAMA*. Dr. Timothy Quill (see Figure 5–7), an internist from Rochester, New York, told how he had prescribed barbiturates for "Diane," a forty-five-year-old patient with acute myelomonocytic leukemia, in sufficient quantity to allow her to take her own life.

Dr. Quill, unlike Debbie's anonymous physician, had enjoyed a long-term physician-patient relationship with Diane. He had seen her through a number of struggles with her health, her family, and her profession. Now, when she felt like she was "really living fully for the first time," it was his unenviable task to tell her that the fatigue she had been experiencing was a symptom of leukemia. He explained to her that long-term cures are possible approximately 25 percent of the time. The treatments, chemotherapy and perhaps bone marrow transplantation, were linked with a number of distinctly unpleasant side effects. No treatment would result in certain death in days, weeks, or at most a few months.

From the beginning, Diane was insistent about refusing treatment. She just wanted to go home and be with her family. The dilemma had been discussed fully with her family and, although they were disappointed with her decision, they sadly accepted it. Dr. Quill, too, accepted it. He realized how difficult treatment could be, relating in his story how "the last four patients with acute leukemia at our hospital had died very painful deaths in the hospital during various stages of treatment," although he did not share this fact with Diane (Quill, 1991, p. 693).

Reading his account of what happened, one gets a true sense of his struggle. Although he had helped arrange for hospice care, it soon became clear that this is not what Diane wanted. She wanted to maintain control of herself and her own dignity during the time remaining and, when this was no longer possible, she wanted to take her life in the least painful way. Realizing that this was more than he could offer or promise but also recognizing that her request made sense, he referred her to the Hemlock Society for "information that might be helpful to her" (Ibid.). Later, when she approached him with a request for barbiturates, Dr. Quill wrote the prescription.

Several months passed. During this time Diane spent her time with her husband and son and her closest friends. At Quill's request, she even spoke to

FIGURE 5–7 Dr. Timothy Quill, who published the story of how he assisted one of his patients in ending her own life in *The New England Journal of Medicine.* (Reprinted by permission of AP/Wide World Photos)

residents at the hospital about "the importance of informed decision making, the right to refuse treatment, and the extraordinary personal effects of illness and interaction with the medical system" (Ibid.). During the last weeks of her life, there was a period of "relative calm and well being," and fantasies of a miracle began to surface, but those hopes soon passed. It was clear to everyone that the end was approaching.

She began saying goodbye to family and friends, including Dr. Quill. He describes the final meeting as follows:

> It was clear that she knew what she was doing, that she was sad and frightened to be leaving, but that she would be even more terrified to stay and suffer. In our tearful good-bye, she promised a reunion in the future at her favorite spot on the edge of Lake Geneva, with dragons swimming in the sunset. (Ibid.)

Her husband called two days later to announce that Diane was dead. Dr. Quill called the medical examiner and reported the death as acute leukemia.

While true, this was not the complete story. Realizing that the mention of suicide would likely result in an ambulance crew, a coroner's investigation and, perhaps, an autopsy, and even the possibility of criminal prosecution and/or professional review, Quill said acute leukemia

> to protect us all, to protect Diane from an invasion into her past and her body, and to continue to shield society from the knowledge of the degree of suffering that people often undergo in the process of dying. Suffering can be lessened to some extent, but in no way eliminated or made benign, by the careful intervention of a competent, caring physician, given current social constraints.   (Ibid.)

The experience obviously affected him deeply. Although he did not technically assist in her suicide—the barbiturates had been prescribed for complaints of insomnia which were rather transparently feigned—Dr. Quill realized that he had helped make it possible, successful, and relatively painless. His essay ended with a reflection.

> I wonder how many families and physicians secretly help patients over the edge into death in the face of such severe suffering. I wonder how many severely ill or dying patients secretly take their lives, dying alone in despair. I wonder whether the image of Diane's final aloneness will persist in the minds of her family, or if they will remember more the intense, meaningful months they had together before she died. I wonder whether Diane struggled in that last hour, and whether the Hemlock Society's way of death by suicide is the most benign. I wonder why Diane, who gave so much to so many of us, had to be alone for the last hour of her life. I wonder whether I will see Diane again, on the shore of Lake Geneva, with dragons swimming on the horizon. (Ibid., p. 694)

Although the differences between Debbie's death and Diane's should be clear, the response to Quill's story was only slightly less dramatic. The District Attorney pledged to conduct an investigation and submitted the case to a Rochester grand jury, which found that no criminal conduct had taken place. He was subsequently charged with, and cleared of, misconduct charges by a panel of the State Medical Board. The Board ruled that his actions were "legal and ethically appropriate" (*The [Toledo] Blade,* 1991). A representative of the National Hospice Association wrote to *The Journal* to state that it "rejected the practice of voluntary euthanasia in the care of the terminally ill" (Levy, 1991, p. 658). One of his peers, commenting on Diane's one-in-four chance of survival, said, "Any physician should be reluctant to let a patient like this forego such an opportunity for life, without applying all his or her powers of persuasion and personally invoking the love of family and friends and the expertise and support of a psychiatrist, the patient's nurses, a clergyperson or patient advocate, a social worker, and maybe a patient or two who risked the uncertainty of treatment in similar circumstances" (Ross, 1991, p. 658).

Another physician questioned whether Quill himself might not have been depressed and perhaps able to benefit from psychiatric intervention (Marzuk, 1991, p. 659). Others voiced an argument, which we will examine more closely later, that perhaps "[t]his society is too likely to accept the death of sufferers rather than the development of effective systems of care and support" (Lynn and Teno, Ibid.). Still another viewed the happenings as the beginning of an inevitable slide down the "slippery slope" (O'Connor, Ibid.). Some said they were "more concerned about the deliberate misrepresentation of the cause of death" (Nolte and Zumwalt, 1991, p. 660). One physician stated that Dr. Quill had a duty to stop Diane from taking her own life; "it is the role of a physician to prevent suicide attempts whenever there is a possibility that they may occur" (Cardo, 1991, p. 658).

On the positive side, Quill was described as "a conscientious physician providing excellent medical care" (Freer, 1991, p. 658), but it was clear that few of his colleagues seemed willing to enter the debate on his side, at least in print.

While Dr. Quill seems to have been the first physician to describe a personal experience in helping a patient to die by prescribing the necessary drugs, just two years earlier *The Journal* carried a widely publicized "Special Article" written by twelve distinguished physicians in which they seemed to strongly endorse actions such as his. In a reprise of an earlier paper (Wanzer et al., 1984) that had discussed the various kinds of appropriate care for the hopelessly ill, but included nothing about the topic of assisted suicide, Wanzer and his colleagues opined that:

> Some physicians, believing it to be the last act in a continuum of care provided for the hopelessly ill patient, do assist patients who request it, either by prescribing sleeping pills with knowledge of their intended use or by discussing the required doses and methods of administration with the patient. [Quill had done both.] The frequency with which such actions are undertaken is unknown, but they are certainly not rare.   (1989, p. 848)

The group summarized its feelings about the ethics of such behavior by stating that all but two of the twelve believed that it "was not immoral for a physician to assist in the rational suicide of a terminally ill person" (Ibid.).

They concluded their position paper with a discussion of the Dutch experience with voluntary, direct, active euthanasia and noted that, presumably, the "majority of physicians" in the United States opposed it. Unlike their attitudes about physician-assisted suicide, however, they failed to inform readers whether that was true within their own small, but influential, group. Since the 1989 paper was subtitled "A Second Look," perhaps we will soon be treated to "A Third Look" to provide us with an answer to that question.

Final Exit

The euthanasia debate received another boost during the summer of 1991 with the publication of a book that quickly climbed to the top of the best-seller lists. *Final Exit* (1991), subtitled *The Practicalities of Self-Deliverance and Assisted Suicide for the Dying*, was written by Derek Humphry, founder and president of the National Hemlock Society, with a foreword by Betty Rollin. Although this was Humphry's second book on this topic, the first—*Let Me Die Before I Wake* (1981)—was published independently by Hemlock. According to Humphry, no mainstream publisher would touch it. Regardless, and despite widespread criticism and condemnation, it sold more than 130,000 copies (Humphry, 1991, p. 19).

Like its predecessor, *Final Exit* was designed as an informational source for people who wish to end lives which, to them, have become medically unbearable. Although Humphry acknowledges that some people who may be suffering from mental or emotional imbalance, but who are not terminally ill, will use the information in the book to commit suicide, he maintains that they would have found a way to take their lives regardless of the availability of his book.

Although he properly warns readers that there are laws against assisting another in committing suicide, Humphry is simply wrong, as the discussion of the Kevorkian cases should illustrate, when he states that "it is against the law everywhere to assist a suicide—no matter what the reason" (Ibid., p. 30). Although the absence of such a law in Michigan is best known, only approximately half of the states have laws making such behavior criminal (see Figure 5–8).

After cautioning readers about the perils of self-deliverance by such means as electrocution, hanging, drowning, shooting (the most commonly used, successful method among men), carbon monoxide from exhaust fumes, and various nonprescription drugs, Humphry provides the reader with an extensive list of prescription medications and the dosage units that would be lethal. He also suggests that if you don't have the help of a physician, it is best to use a loose fitting plastic bag secured tightly around the neck. Commenting on whether the plastic bag should be clear or opaque, Humphry says, "Loving the world as I do, I'll opt for a clear one if I have to" (Ibid., p. 98).

Initiative 119

Although the issue of physician aid-in-dying failed to qualify for the statewide ballot in California in 1988, the situation was different in the State of Washington. After an intense and bitter campaign, the votes were counted on

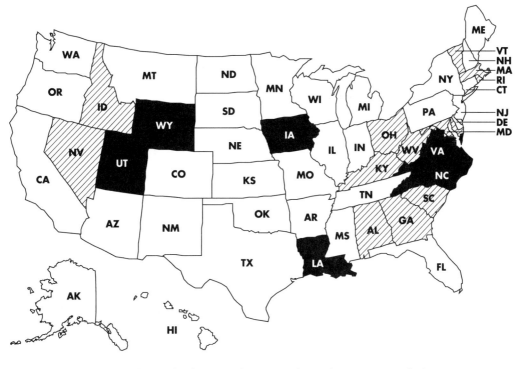

States with statutes that explicitly criminalize assisted suicide: (32 states: Alaska, Arizona, Arkansas, California, Colorado, Connecticut, Delaware, Florida, Hawaii, Illinois, Indiana, Kansas, Maine, Michigan, Minnesota, Mississippi, Missouri, Montana, Nebraska, New Hampshire, New Jersey, New Mexico, New York, North Dakota, Oklahoma, Oregon, Pennsylvania, South Dakota, Tennessee, Texas, and Wisconsin).

Jurisdictions that criminalize assisted suicide through the common law (the District of Columbia and 12 states: Alabama, Georgia, Idaho, Kentucky, Maryland, Massachusetts, Nevada, Ohio, Rhode Island, South Carolina, Vermont, and West Virginia).

States in which the law is unclear concerning the legality of assisted suicide (6 states: Iowa[1], Louisiana[2], North Carolina[3], Utah[3], Virginia[1], and Wyoming.[3]

[1] Case law exists which may or may not be applicable to assisted suicide.

[2] State constitution stipulates that "no law shall subject any person to euthanasia."

[3] State has abolished the common law of crimes and therefore does not explicitly prohibit assisted suicide.

FIGURE 5–8   U.S. map showing various laws regarding assisted suicide. [Reprinted by permission of Choice In Dying (formerly Concern for Dying/Society for the Right to Die), 200 Varick Street, New York, NY 10014–4810; (212)366–5540]

November 5, 1991, and the proposition failed by a narrow margin. If it had passed it would have made Washington the only jurisdiction in the world with legalized voluntary, direct, active euthanasia. Although the Netherlands is often cited as an example of a country with "legalized euthanasia," we will show later in this chapter that such a statement is somewhat misleading.

Out of a total of slightly more than 922,000 votes cast, 54 percent voted to defeat the proposal and 46 percent voted for it. The issue had been decided by slightly less than 5 percent of the voters! The Washington State Medical Association acknowledged that it was "very slow to respond" and commented that, "if approved, [the] vote would have authorized a right to die before patients have a right to health care" (Breo, 1991, p. 304). Even within the membership of the Society, some 16 percent of the physicians opposed actively campaigning against the proposal. Spending on Initiative 119 set a record for the state. Hemlock was credited with raising most of the $1.4 million spent to support the ballot; the Catholic Church was identified as the source of most of the $700,000 spent to oppose it (Ibid., p. 2899).

The Pros and Cons

For many people, euthanasia is an emotional issue, to be decided on the basis of feelings and beliefs, rather than an intellectual one, to be decided on the reasonableness of the arguments put forth. This seems to be especially so among those who have had a personal experience with a loved one dying under extremely stressful circumstances. Regardless of this, it is interesting to examine the arguments, for and against, that have been submitted. For some, this is purely and simply unthinkable because of their religious beliefs. Derek Humphry recognized this in the beginning of his book, *Final Exit*, when he wrote: "If you consider God the master of your fate, then read no further. Seek the best pain management available and arrange hospice care" (Humphry, 1991, p. 21).

It is certainly true that many, but not all, of the world's religions would oppose the varieties of euthanasia that we have been discussing. While it is beyond the scope of this book to review or summarize the teachings of the various religious traditions concerning voluntary, direct, active euthanasia, the interested reader is referred to *Active Euthanasia, Religion, and the Public Debate* (1991).

Not all of the arguments against euthanasia, however, are religiously motivated. While the social and political dimensions of the debate seem to have increased appreciably, the topic itself has been debated for many years. One of the classic expositions of the nonreligious case against euthanasia was written more than thirty-five years ago.

Kamisar (1958) suggests that the major arguments against legalizing voluntary, direct, active euthanasia fall into either of two categories: (1) that it is likely there would be a high incidence of mistake and/or abuse, and (2) that what is voluntary today could very easily become involuntary tomorrow. Concerning the first of these, he includes both cases of mistaken diagnosis (medical error) and irrational choices made by those whose judgment may be clouded by stress or pain.

Mistake and/or Abuse

Kamisar argues that the legalization of euthanasia might lead to the death of patients who mistakenly believe that they are terminally ill. To buttress his argument, he cites several noteworthy cases of medical misdiagnosis, most of them dealing with patients who had been diagnosed as having cancer. As a precautionary safeguard, he quotes approvingly the suggestion that there might be a waiting period, perhaps as along as ten years, before a request for euthanasia might be granted! This, of course, would also tend to greatly reduce the perceived need for euthanasia as well, although it is not clear that this was Kamisar's intention. All of his examples of misdiagnosis were based on cases from the late 1950s and earlier. While it could be argued that while diagnosis is still part of the *art* of medicine and errors *do* occur, the kind of errors that Kamisar cited are far less likely to happen with the technology available to today's diagnostician.

Related to, but distinct from, his discussion of diagnostic error is the question of prognosis. What does it mean, for example, when we say that someone is incurable? While there may be no cure immediately at hand, is it not possible that such a cure may be found tomorrow? Next week? Next month? Next year? If the patient's wish for euthanasia were to be granted, only to learn too late that life could have been saved, it would be a tragedy. Although it is quite true that we do not know *today* what medical miracles will exist *tomorrow,* there is, likewise, no guarantee that such discoveries will happen or, if they do, that they will be available to or desired by any particular patient. In Diane's case, for example, her decision to refuse the conventional treatment was based on her assessment of the chance that it would work and the effect that it would have on the *quality* of her life. Moreover, the likelihood of any miracle cure rescuing a patient from a disease previously thought to be incurable is highly dependent upon the stage to which the disease has progressed. It is unlikely that many, if any, would wish to end their life when first diagnosed; the desire to die quickly and painlessly is typically reserved for much later, at a time when suffering is perceived to have become intolerable. By then they are quite likely to be well beyond any help that a "breakthrough" might offer.

Killing one who is not really desirous of death could fall into the category of either mistake or abuse. If euthanasia were to be limited to those suffering from intolerable pain who had freely chosen to end their lives, then, says Kamisar, we find ourselves in the paradoxical position of granting the wish "only if the patient is both sane and crazed by pain" (1958, citing Frohman, 1956, p. 1222). Or, he asks, how can we be sure that the decision is not influenced by the drugs given to relieve the very pain that prompts the request? How do we know that judgment has not been distorted by depression? How are we to know that the patient has not been coerced, perhaps even by a member of the family, into a decision for death? Or, how are we to know that the physician is not also responding irrationally? Remember that one of Dr. Quill's critics suggested that perhaps he, as well as Diane, could have benefited from psychiatric consultation.

These, of course, are all important points worthy of careful consideration. They are not, however, compelling arguments. Procedural safeguards must be a part of any proposal for legalization of voluntary, direct, active euthanasia, and it is through such protocols that the truly voluntary nature of the request would be assured (Benrubi, 1992).

Dr. Timothy Quill, who contributed so much to the debate over physician-assisted suicide through the report of his experience with Diane in *The New England Journal of Medicine,* has addressed the topic of safeguards. He, along with colleagues Drs. Christine K. Cassel and Diane E. Meier, suggests that it is the responsibility of the patient's primary physician to ensure that the following conditions are satisfied before assisting in a suicidal act:

1. The patient must have a condition that is incurable and associated with severe, unrelenting suffering. Moreover, the patient must understand the condition, the prognosis, and the types of comfort care that are available as alternatives.

2. The physician must ensure that the patient's suffering and the request for assistance are not the result of inadequate comfort care.

3. The patient must clearly and repeatedly, of his or her own free will and initiative, request to die rather than continue suffering. They add, however, that although a too ready acceptance of a patient's request could be perceived as encouragement, it is important not to force the patient to beg for assistance.

4. The physician must be sure that the patient's judgment is not distorted.

5. Physician-assisted suicide should be carried out only in the context of a meaningful doctor-patient relationship. This has been one of the most frequent criticisms of Dr. Kevorkian's actions, suggesting that he, trained as a pathologist, may lack an important dimension that Drs. Quill, Cassel, and Meier, clinicians all, might bring to this process.

6. Consultation with another experienced physician is required to ensure

that the patient's request is voluntary and rational, the diagnosis and prognosis accurate, and the exploration of comfort-oriented alternatives thorough.

7. Clear documentation to support each condition is required. (Quill, Cassel, and Meier, 1992)

Voluntary vs. Involuntary Euthanasia

Kamisar feels that, while voluntary euthanasia is a proposition that is quite vulnerable to attack in its own right, it should also be rejected because it is likely to lead to an even more dangerous practice—involuntary euthanasia. He even maintains that the proponents of voluntary euthanasia are using the issue to create public support that will open the door for the practice of the killing of the old, the ill, and the handicapped who have become burdensome to society. It is this kind of slippery slope argument, the English equivalent of the Arabic philosophers' "camel's nose" paradigm, that seems to be most frequently raised in opposition. According to this argument, we should avoid doing something that may be ethically and/or morally appropriate in its own right if it is likely to lead to that which is ethically and/or morally inappropriate. We must be careful when stepping onto these "slippery slopes" since we can quickly and easily loose our footing and wind up at the bottom of an abyss.

There is, of course, some reason to take this seriously. For instance, it is true that many of the most compelling cases set forth in justification of mercy killing have not been carried out with consent. That was certainly true of most of the cases involving physicians cited earlier in this chapter—Drs. Sander, Montemarano, Kraai, and Hassman. Moreover, it was also true in most of the cases involving mercy killings by family members—Harry Johnson, Louis Greenfield, Louis Repouille, and John Noxon. Whether or not it would be possible to "hold the line" (Jennings, 1991) against quickly ending the lives of permanently unconscious patients for whom we now merely stop treatment, with the consent of their families or surrogate, is difficult to predict. Certainly it could be argued that it was no less merciful to end such lives by a lethal injection than to wait for death resulting from the complications of starvation and/or dehydration as we do now. But it is equally important to recognize that those two issues—voluntary versus nonvoluntary—can be unjoined and considered separately.

This same argument—that we can't be sure where the decision to allow something not presently accepted will lead us—could be, and was, raised against passive euthanasia. Although *Quinlan* was the first case to establish a legal basis for withdrawing LSMT from an incompetent patient *at the request of her family and where there was evidence that this is what she would have chosen for herself,* we have not established a practice of withholding LSMT *without* the consent of the family.

Testifying about this issue before the President's Commission, Dr. Willard Gaylin, President of The Hastings Center, stated:

> It seems to me that in [the slippery slope argument] is a bogeyman that is brought out in every discussion—again it's part of the hard-case problem. . . .
>
> It then occurred to me that there was not a single problem that I was concerned about that didn't exist on a spectrum, and that any time you draw a line on any spectrum some damn fool can get up and point to two things proximal to that line and say "You mean, Dr. So-and-so, you think there's a difference between X and Y." And, of course, there isn't a difference between X and Y, because when you're on a spectrum, wherever you draw the line, you're going to find two proximal points that are almost identical. . . . You . . . [run the risk of going] all thorough your life never drawing a line. (President's Commission, 1983, p. 29)

It should be noted that the President's Commission did *not* endorse voluntary, direct, active euthanasia nor has any other medical, legal, or governmental body in the United States.

More recently, in the pages of *The New England Journal of Medicine*, Singer and Siegler (1990) voiced some of the same arguments put forth by Kamisar. They raise the concern that legalized euthanasia might open the door for *crypthanasia*—secretly practiced involuntary euthanasia which, they allege, is already happening in the Netherlands. Legalizing the practice, they add, is also likely to result in pressures placed on chronically ill or dying patients, perhaps subtly, for them to end their lives to spare their families financial or emotional strain. The right to die quickly could become an obligation to do so. Third, they suggest that "surrogate" euthanasia might evolve in the same way that we now recognize, under some circumstances, the use of a substituted judgment or best interest standard of decision making. They also warn the reader that this could lead to "discriminatory" euthanasia whereby disenfranchised or highly vulnerable groups such as the disabled, the poor, and the elderly, to name a few, might be coerced into ending their lives.

The legalization of euthanasia, they claim, is also likely to have far-reaching and undesirable effects on what they call the "real issues in the care of dying patients" (Ibid., p. 1883). Easing the process of dying will diminish our efforts to cure chronic disease and to develop better methods of pain control. This concern has also been expressed by an official of the National Hospice Association which seems to see euthanasia as antithetical to their goal of comforting the dying (Miller, 1991).

Hospice, a concept that is focused on controlling the pain the dying person may be experiencing, and which will be discussed more fully in Chapter 8, strongly opposes voluntary, direct, active euthanasia. While supporting passive euthanasia (allowing death to occur by withholding or withdrawing LSMT) and indirect, active euthanasia (providing pain control medication which may, as an unintended result, shorten life), they have opposed efforts to legalize "euthanasia." A survey of the membership of the Academy of Hospice Physicians (an international physician organization devoted to hospice care), produced the following ranking of primary reasons for opposing euthanasia:

1. Divert attention away from efforts to provide optimal palliation and more appropriate and compassionate care.
2. Too high a risk of degenerating into abuse, such as involuntary euthanasia or murder.
3. Morally wrong for anyone to ever actively cause a death.
4. Incompatible with medical ethics and would subvert the role of the physician. (Ibid., p. 130)

While it is undisputed that hospice care has provided immeasurable support and comfort to untolled patients and their families, there are concerns of the dying that a total reliance on hospice seemingly fails to address. First, there is an acknowledgment, even by the strongest supporters of hospice, that there are some circumstances where pain cannot be well controlled. While these cases may be few, they cannot be dismissed. Second, relief from physical pain, while it is certainly *one* of the major concerns of the dying, is not the only form of distress that may produce a decision to seek a quick and painless death. There is also, at least for some, a fear of total dependency, loss of dignity, and a concern that their prolonged dying will cause unnecessary suffering for their loved ones. While hospice also recognizes and tries to address these issues, it is often much more difficult to measure success.

Singer and Seigler also express a concern that "euthanasia subverts the social role of the physician as healer" and that accepting it would lead to a loss of "public confidence and trust in medicine as a healing profession" (Singer and Siegler, 1990, p. 1883). To them, "euthanasia strikes at the heart of what it means to be a physician" (Ibid.). They—like Dr. Gaylin and his colleagues, who, in response to the story of Debbie's death, admonished that "doctors must not kill" (Gaylin, 1988)—see an unresolvable conflict between the role of healer and killer. While this may be so for some, this is an assumption rather than a verifiable conclusion; this conflict seems to be handled rather nicely by other healers, such as veterinarians, who have traditionally accepted killing as part of their role. They seem to be able to perform both functions without jeopardizing the trust of those who bring their animals to them for care. That they might get their role of healer and killer confused, even momentarily, does not seem to be a serious concern.

The basis for the medical prohibition against euthanasia is often traced, as it is by Singer and Siegler, to the Hippocratic Oath. While there is debate among medical historians concerning the origins of the oath and many medical schools have abandoned the practice of having graduates recite it, that discussion will be left to others. We would caution the reader at this point that it is necessary to understand the temporal context of the Hippocratic Oath, both in reference to the time when it was written and to any contemporary application. While the oath does carry a pledge that "I will give no deadly medicine to anyone if asked, nor suggest any such counsel," it also forbids charging for teaching the art of medicine to the children of physicians and the surgical removal of kidney or gall stones.

Since the topic of euthanasia and the Netherlands has already been mentioned at several points in this chapter, now would seem to be the appropriate point to examine the situation more closely, for it is there that we might gather some empirical data to help answer some of the questions that have been raised.

Euthanasia and the Netherlands

The Netherlands is often cited as a model of voluntary, direct, active euthanasia in action. Technically speaking, it should be acknowledged that euthanasia is not legal in the Netherlands. The laws on the books clearly prohibit both voluntary, direct, active euthanasia and assisted suicide. These laws, enacted in 1886, state that:

> He who robs another of life at his express and serious wish is punished with a prison sentence of at most twelve years or a fine of the fifth category (Article 293 of the Netherlands Penal Code). A fine of the "fifth category" can reach a maximum of 100,000 guilders, approximately $50,000 at the 1990 exchange rate.
>
> He who deliberately incites another to suicide, assists him therein or provides him with the means is punished, if the suicide follows, with a prison sentence of at most three years or a fine of the fourth category (Article 294 of the Netherlands Penal Code). The fine of the "fourth category" can be a maximum of 25,000 guilders, approximately $12,500 at the 1990 exchange rate. (Gomez, 1991a, pp. 19, 147)

It is, however, tolerated, or rather not prosecuted, if it is performed according to a particular set of circumstances. The practice can be traced back to 1973 when two important events took place. One was the first prosecution of a Dutch physician for participation in active euthanasia. The second was a statement by the Royal Dutch Society for the Promotion of Medicine (KNMG) that said, "[L]egally euthanasia should remain a crime, but that if a physician, after having considered all the aspects of the case, shortens the life of a patient who is incurably ill and in the process of dying, the court will have to judge whether there was a conflict of duties which could justify the act of the physician" (Gevers, 1987, p. 158).

The case involved a physician who had injected her mother, a seventy-eight-year-old nursing home patient who was confined to a wheelchair, incontinent, and suffering from the aftermath of a cerebrovascular accident (stroke). The head nurse at the home testified that the woman had repeatedly expressed a desire to die. She was also described as unwilling to cooperate with rehabilitative efforts and lacking the will to live. She was injected with morphine and died within several minutes. The court in Leeuwarden convicted the physician but ordered the sentence of one week in jail suspended. If there were no other punishable acts committed within the year, the sentence would be completely suspended (de Wachter, 1989; Gomez, 1991a).

Eight years later, in 1981, another lower court, this time in Rotterdam, convicted a layperson of assisting in a suicide. In emphasizing the fact that the defendant was not a physician, the court set out a series of criteria that must be met if an act of euthanasia were to be excused:

1. There must be unbearable suffering on the part of the patient.
2. The desire to die must emanate from a conscious person.
3. The request for euthanasia must be voluntary.
4. The patient must have been given alternatives and must have had time to consider them.
5. There must be no other reasonable solutions to the patient's problem.
6. The death must not inflict unnecessary suffering on others.
7. More than one person must be involved in the decision.
8. Only a physician may actually euthanize the patient.
9. Great care must be exercised in making this decision. (Gomez, Ibid., p. 32)

Although the decision of the court created great public debate, most comments on the decision—both lay and professional—were favorable (Ibid., p. 33).

In 1982, the district court in Alkmaar acquitted a physician who had ended the life of a ninety-five-year-old woman who was frail and in deteriorating health, but without a specified illness. She had repeatedly requested that her life be ended. The Alkmaar court held that the patient had a right to self-determination and that the request was well documented. It concluded that there had been no "material illegality." The prosecutor, feeling that the court had failed to carefully apply the guidelines of the Rotterdam court, appealed the decision to the Court of Appeals in Amsterdam.

The Amsterdam court retried the case in 1983 and, while finding the physician guilty, it assigned no punishment. The physician, in turn, appealed the case to the Supreme Court of the Netherlands. The appeal was supported by the Netherlands Society for Voluntary Euthanasia [Nederlands Vereniging voor Vrijwillige Euthanasie (NVVE)] (Gomez, 1991a, p. 6). The Supreme Court overturned the decision of the appeals court, indicating that the lower court had failed to consider whether the physician had been placed in an "intolerable position" because of a "conflict of duties." It referred the case to the Court of Appeals at The Hague and instructed the court to consider "[w]hether the euthanasia practiced by the defendant would, from an objective medical perspective, be regarded as an action justified in a situation of necessity (beyond one's control)" (Ibid., pp. 36–37).

The court at The Hague, in turn, asked the Dutch Medical Society (KNMG) to give an opinion as to whether there might be such circumstances, "situations of necessity," in which the patient or the physician, or both, would be under such strain that euthanasia would be justified. The KNMG answered in the affirmative and the court, in turn, dismissed the charges against the physician.

Under the current regulations, the Dutch physician who has euthanized a patient must identify the cause of death as euthanasia on the death certificate. Either the physician or the coroner must report to the police that euthanasia has taken place. The police are to report to the district attorney who decides whether or not to prosecute. Prosecutions take place in a district court composed of three judges. If convicted, the defendant can appeal to the Court of Appeals (three judges) and finally to the Supreme Court (five judges) (de Wachter, 1989, p. 3317).

Although the current practice seems to enjoy considerable support among the Dutch, both from the medical profession and the population at large, it is opposed by a vocal minority, including a group of approximately 1,000 of the 30,000+ Dutch physicians. Given the fact that voluntary, direct, active euthanasia is being increasingly debated in this country and that both the proponents and opponents tend to use "evidence" from the Dutch experience rather casually, Battin (1990) has proposed seven caveats that should be considered in such debates:

1. *It must be remembered that there are no hard data about the practice of euthanasia in Holland.* In spite of the requirement that all cases be reported to the Ministry of Justice, it is estimated that only a small fraction are. The reasons for this failure to report will be discussed below.

2. *Exaggerations are frequent.* Rather than being commonplace, euthanasia is rather rare. Of the estimated 120,000 deaths that occur each year in Holland, out of a population of 14.5 million, it is estimated that 6,000 result from euthanasia. This would be approximately 5 percent of all deaths. Ninety-five percent or more of deaths in Holland do *not* occur from euthanasia.

3. *Terminological issues operate to confuse the issue.* In Holland, the term *euthanasia* is used typically to describe what in the United States would be called voluntary, direct, active euthanasia; the modifiers are considered redundant. Dutch critics of the practice, who often speak and publish in the

United States, seem to be guilty of lumping together cases of nonvoluntary, passive euthanasia and voluntary, direct, active euthanasia and thereby greatly inflating the figures on euthanasia. Because of this failure to differentiate between causing death—that is, active euthanasia and allowing death to occur, or passive euthanasia—Battin suggests that much of the opposition in Holland to the former is really opposition to the latter (Battin, 1990, p. 74). This represents a considerable difference between us and the Dutch. While we seem to have become much more comfortable with passive euthanasia where the patient is unable to express an opinion, a position reflected in the line of cases starting with *Quinlan* and continuing through *Cruzan*, the Dutch seem to view this as much more problematic than direct, active euthanasia based on the contemporaneously expressed wishes of the patient.

4. *Legal claims are misleading, either way.* As has been previously discussed, it is clearly erroneous to state unequivocally that euthanasia is legal in Holland. But, on the other hand, it is equally clear that it is seldom punished when carried out in conformity with the guidelines established by the courts. It is this delicate legal status that probably accounts for a tendency toward underreporting.

5. *The institutional circumstances of euthanasia in Holland are easily misunderstood.* Unlike in the United States, in Holland most primary care is provided in the patient's home, or in an office in the physician's home, by the *huisarts* or home physicians. Because the physician typically lives in the neighborhood and makes house calls, there tends to be a much closer relationship between patient and physician. This is a situation that often existed here several generations ago and has since been replaced by the impersonality of the health care system. It also accounts for a greater feeling of trust between providers and consumers.

6. *The economic circumstances of euthanasia in Holland are also easily misunderstood.* Holland, unlike the United States, has a national health care system that provides care for all including hospitalization, nursing home and home care, and the services of a wide array of health care providers. The fears about legalizing the practice in the United States that some have raised, that patients might be pressured into choosing euthanasia because of financial concerns, are not serious problems for the Dutch.

7. *Differences in social circumstances often go unnoticed.* While it is obvious that there are wide disparities in the economic wellbeing of Americans, the Dutch exhibit much greater societal homogeneity. There is also less racial prejudice and virtually no homelessness. Like us, however, the Dutch are a democratic, sophisticated, industrialized, and modern society with a high respect for the freedom and dignity of the individual. That they are concerned with ethics is obvious from the existence of four well-staffed centers for the study of

bioethics (in Amsterdam, Leiden, Utrecht, and Maastrict) in a country with one-twentieth the population of the United States. (Gomez, 1991a, p. 159)

Battin cautions that, as the debate intensifies here, it will be well for us to look more carefully at practices in Holland, but to detach ourselves from the biases we bring to the issue and to look with comparatively objective eyes.

Among the latest information to appear on the status of euthanasia in the Netherlands is the results of a nationwide study on "euthanasia and other medical decisions concerning the end of life (MDEL)" conducted at the request of the Dutch government (van der Maas et al., 1991). Actually three studies were conducted. The first involved detailed interviews with 405 physicians, the second a questionnaire survey of the physicians of 7,000 deceased persons, and the third a prospective study of "about 2,250" deaths among patients who were being cared for by the participants of the first study. In the last of these three, the physicians reported on every death in their practice during the six months following the interview. The report of this commission, known as the Remmelink Commission, after the attorney-general of the Dutch Supreme Court who chaired it, stated that euthanasia—defined as termination of life at the patient's request—occurred in less than 3 percent of all deaths. The actual figures ranged from 1.7 percent in the first study to 2.6 percent in the third. Much more common was a shortening of the patient's life by high doses of opiates intended to relieve pain (indirect, active euthanasia) and death resulting from decisions to abate treatment (passive euthanasia). Each accounted for approximately 17.5 percent of all deaths that occurred in the studies. Assisted suicide, with the patient administering a lethal drug provided or prescribed by the physician, was estimated to occur in .3 percent of all cases. The researchers conclude that the euthanasia debate should be placed into "the much broader context of MDEL [which in itself] is an inevitable consequence of the development of medicine" (Ibid., p. 13).

Euthanasia in Germany

While Holland gives us some, albeit limited, data on the practice of voluntary, direct, active euthanasia, Battin (1991) has suggested that Germany provides a model of a rather different kind of voluntary euthanasia. Unlike the Dutch, who seem to have great trust in their physicians, the Germans, partially because of the painful history of Nazism, appear to believe that doctors should have no role in directly causing death. Active euthanasia is vigorously and widely opposed in Germany and there is accordingly, a disapproval of the Dutch experiment. But, although killing on request is prohibited, assisting another in their suicide is not a violation of the law. Battin describes this as follows:

> Taking advantage of this situation, there has developed a private organization, the *Deutsches Gesellschaft fur Humanes Sterben* (DGHS) or German Society for Humane Dying, which provides support to its very extensive membership in choosing suicide as an alternative to terminal illness. The DGHS provides information about suicide; it assists in gaining access to the means for suicide; and, if requested, then it provides *Begleitung* or "accompaniment" for the person about to commit suicide, sending someone to be with the person who takes a fatal dose, especially if that person is alone or does not have a family supportive of such a choice. The DGHS runs regular ads in the popular magazines, and apparently is familiar to a sizable proportion of the populace. I do not know how frequent are suicides assisted by the DGHS, as distinct from suicides in terminal illness generally, but it seems fair to say that the option of self-produced death is more clearly open in Germany than in Holland or in the United States.   (1991, p. 301)

Battin, who has written convincingly in defense of both voluntary, direct, active euthanasia and assisted suicide, expresses a belief that physician-assisted suicide, carried out in a manner similar to the way Dr. Quill assisted Diane to end her life, is likely to be the model best suited to the United States given the "current state of our own somewhat flawed society" (Ibid., p. 305).

Public Attitudes About Euthanasia

Although the results of statewide balloting in Washington and California are clearly an important indicator of public attitudes about one form—voluntary, direct, active euthanasia for the terminally ill—they are representative only of certain segments of the total population. An interesting summary of national attitudes was reported by Blendon, Szalay, and Knox in the May 20, 1992, issue of *JAMA*.

The data were derived from two sources. The first was a random sample of 1,004 adults throughout the United States. The survey was done by telephone on behalf of the *Boston Globe* and the Harvard School of Public Health. It was conducted in October 1991. The second source of data was an analysis of twenty national opinion surveys conducted by seven polling organizations between 1950 and 1991. Each of these polls were also done by telephone and involved 1,000 to 3,000 randomly sampled adults.

The authors conclude that "public support for legislation that would allow euthanasia and patient self-determination has been growing over time"

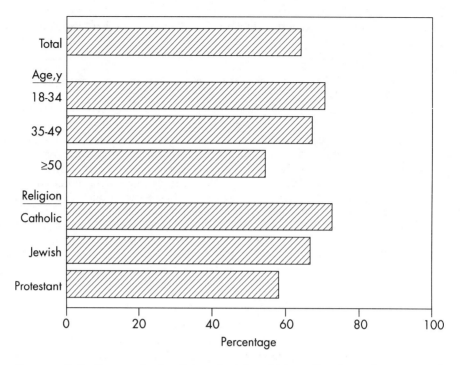

FIGURE 5–9   Support for legalizing physician aid in ending lives of patients with incurable diseases, by age and religion. (Adapted from Bendon et al., 1992, p. 2660)

(Blendon et al., 1992, p. 2659). According to them, support for physicians being allowed to end the lives of patients with incurable diseases if they and their families request it had grown from 34 percent in 1950 to 63 percent in 1991. Unfortunately, they did not differentiate between voluntary, direct, active euthanasia, wherein the physician would actually cause the death to occur, and physician-assisted suicide, where the cause of death would be under the control of the person requesting aid-in-dying.

They also concluded that age, religion, and race are important. As can be seen from Figure 5–9, supportive attitudes seem to be inversely linked to age, with approximately 70 percent of the eighteen- to thirty-four-year-old age group expressing a belief that physicians should be allowed to *administer* lethal drugs if a terminally ill patient requests it; even among "older Americans" (those fifty years of age and older), however, 54 percent are supportive. Physician aid-in-dying is supported by a majority of each of the major faiths in this country, ranging from a high of 72 percent among Catholics to a low of 59 percent among Protestants. Figure 5–10 indicates that white Americans are considerably more likely than blacks to be supportive, and that the differences

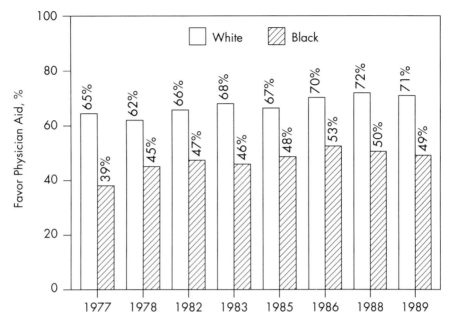

FIGURE 5-10 Support for legalizing physician aid in ending lives of patients with incurable diseases, by race. (Adapted from Bendon et al., 1992, p. 2660)

in the level of support have been relatively constant from 1977 through 1989, the *average* difference being about 20 percent.

The main reason respondents would consider ending their lives was fear that they would be a burden on their family, an answer given by 47 percent, although this answer was more likely to be given by middle-age Americans (57 percent) than either younger (eighteen- through thirty-four-year-olds) or older (fifty years and over) ones (39 percent and 45 percent respectively) (Ibid., 1992, p. 2660). Other reasons given for choosing a speedy and painless death included (1) not wanting to live in pain if seriously ill (20 percent), (2) not wanting to be dependent upon machines (19 percent), and (3) not wishing to continue living if unable to perform most daily activities (12 percent) (Ibid.).

Although respondents were most likely to choose withholding life support and treatment, not including food and water, as a means of intentionally ending their lives (24 percent), 20 percent would consider asking a physician to *administer* lethal drugs or injections and 19 percent would prefer that their physician *prescribe* a lethal drug that they could take by themselves. Only 16 percent would include the withholding of food and water, and fewer still, 11 percent, would ask a family member or close friend to help them end their life. Concerning the withholding of food and water, it should be noted that under the circumstances described in the question, a terminal illness where the patient is awake and in great pain, one would not expect this option to be chosen at all.

Blendon et al. (1992) predict that the effort to change public policy will not only continue but also escalate and that this effort is likely to be successful over time. Even so, they note, if "euthanasia" becomes legally permissible, relatively few Americans would be likely to actually exercise that option.

What, then, does the future seem to hold for the practice of "euthanasia" in this country? While we have no crystal ball to give us the answer, it would appear that several tentative conclusions could be safely drawn. First, given the volatile nature of the debate, it is quite unlikely that we will see anything like a consensus emerging in the near future. Second, unless we are able to do something to restructure the provision of health care in our society, especially the care of sufferers from catastrophic disease such as AIDS, Alzheimer's disease, and various kinds of cancer, the demand for a quick and painless death is likely to continue to increase. And finally, because of both of these, it is likely that the euthanasia debate will be to the first part of the twenty-first century what the abortion debate has been to the last part of the twentieth.

Summary

"Euthanasia" has become one of the most hotly debated topics of the day. Unfortunately, the term is often misused or used in such a way that there is misunderstanding about its meaning. Euthanasia is, quite simply, a good death—a death free of pain or suffering. It is only with the addition of modifiers such as *active* or *passive, direct* or *indirect,* and *voluntary* or *involuntary* (and perhaps *nonvoluntary*) that the full range of meaning takes shape. Passive euthanasia, allowing death to occur by withholding or discontinuing treatment that no longer benefits the patient, has become widely accepted. So, too, has indirect, active euthanasia such as produced by escalating use of pain control drugs realizing that this will likely shorten the patient's life. The intent is to provide relief from pain; the death of the patient is a forseeable but indirect effect of the treatment. It is only those direct acts intended to end the life of the patient, so-called mercy killing, that seem to be so controversial.

Our legal system has demonstrated some ambiguity in dealing with mercy killing. There have been celebrated cases where those who have broken the law have received surprising leniency and, in some cases, no punishment at all. Physicians, at least until Dr. Jack Kevorkian, have been quite unlikely to be successfully prosecuted for assisting in the death of their patients.

The public debate over what has come to be known as assisted suicide has been spurred by the activities of the National Hemlock Society and the stories that have been widely told of those who have assisted in the deaths of others—Betty Rollin's tale of her mother's *Last Wish,* an account in the *Journal of the American Medical Association* by an anonymous resident of his participation in the death of an ovarian cancer patient, and Dr. Timothy Quill's moving story of how he assisted his patient, Diane, in ending her life. Public support for physician assistance in dying can be gauged by the results of statewide balloting in Washington and California where proposals to legalize such were narrowly defeated. No one, however, has done more to push the issue into the public spotlight than a retired Michigan pathologist, Dr. Jack Kevorkian. As of this writing, Dr. Kevorkian had participated in twenty suicides, had been indicted and jailed because he was unable or unwilling to post bail, and had seen three county courts and one appellate court declare the law under which he had been arrested as unconstitutional. It is likely that his case will be appealed to the Michigan Supreme Court and, perhaps, to the U.S. Supreme Court as well.

Neither the proponents nor the opponents of assisted suicide can provide assurances of where, if legalized, it might lead. The Netherlands is often used as an example of what might happen here. Unfortunately, it is used by both the proponents and the opponents to justify their arguments. The Netherlands, however, is quite different from the United States in several important aspects and the practice there is much less frequently assisted suicide than it is physician-administered, aid-in-dying. Comparisons between the United States and the Netherlands, and

Germany, both of which are discussed in the text, need to progress with great care.

Regardless of where we as a society move on this question, it has become increasingly clear that this is an issue that won't go away.

Study Questions

1. How would you define the word *euthanasia*?

2. How does the use of modifiers such as *direct, indirect, active, passive, voluntary, involuntary,* and *nonvoluntary* change that definition?

3. In what ways have the courts been ambiguous in deciding cases of mercy killing?

4. What is the Hemlock Society and what are its goals?

5. What are the differences between Debbie's death, as described by an anonymous resident in *The Journal of the American Medical Association,* and Diane's death, as described by Dr. Quill in the *New England Journal of Medicine*, that would seemingly generate so much condemnation in the former and so much approval in the latter?

6. Although Dr. Kevorkian seems to have a significant following, he has been criticized in ways that Dr. Quill has not. What are those criticisms and upon what differences in the two situations are they based?

7. What are some of the pros and cons in the argument over euthanasia?

8. How is euthanasia handled in the Netherlands? In Germany?

References

Active Euthanasia, Religion, and the Public Debate. (1991). Chicago: The Park Ridge Center.

Andrusko, D. (1992). Assisted suicide measure defeated in California. *National Right to Life News,* 19 (16):4.

Angell, M. (1988). Euthanasia. *NEJM,* 319:1348–1350.

___. 1990. Don't criticize Dr. Death . . . *The New York Times,* June 14, p. A14.

Anonymous. (1988). It's over, Debbie. *JAMA,* 259(2):272.

Battin, M. P. (1990). Seven caveats concerning the discussion of euthanasia in Holland. *Perspectives in Biology and Medicine,* 34(1): 73–77.

___. 1991. Euthanasia: The way we do it, the way they do it. *Journal of Pain and Symptom Management,* 67(5): 298–305.

Benrubi, G. I. (1992). Euthanasia—the need for procedural safeguards, *NEJM,* 326(3):197–198.

Binding, K., and A. Hoche. (1920). *Permitting the Destruction of Unworthy Life.* Leipzig,

Germany: Verlag von Felix Meiner. Translated by Wright, W., P. G. Derr, and R. Salomon. (1992). *Issues in Law and Medicine,* 8(2):231–265.

Blendon, R. J., U. S. Szalay, and R. A. Knox. (1992). Should physicians aid their patients in dying: The public perspective. *JAMA,* 267(19): 2658–2662.

Breo, D. L. (1991). MD-aided suicide voted down; both sides say debate to continue. *JAMA,* 266(20):2895–2900.

Brody, H. (1988). Letter. *JAMA,* 260(6):789.

Cardo, L. J. (1991). Letter. *NEJM,* 325:658.

Choice in Dying News. (1992). 1:2. New York: Author.

Compassion in Dying v. *Washington.* 1994 U.S. Dist. Lexis * 5831.

Davies, J. (1988). Raping and making love are different concepts: So are killing and voluntary euthanasia. *J. Med. Ethics,* 14:148–149.

Davis, D. (1988). Letter. *JAMA,* 259(14): 2097.

de Wachter, M. A. M. (1989). Active euthanasia in the Netherlands, *JAMA,* 262(23): 3316–3319.

Freer, J. P. (1991). Letter. *NEJM,* 325(9):658.

Gaylin, W., L. R. Kass, E. D. Pellegrino, and M. Siegler. (1988). Doctors must not kill. *JAMA,* 259(14):2139–2140.

Gevers, J. K. M. (1987). Legal developments concerning active euthanasia on request in the Netherlands. *Bioethics,* 1:156–162.

Gibbs, N. (1990). Dr. Death's suicide machine. *Time,* June 18, pp. 69–70.

Glantz, L. H. (1987/88). Withholding and withdrawing treatment: The role of the criminal law. *Law, Medicine & Health Care,* 15(4):231–241.

Gomez, C. R. (1991a). *Regulating Death: Euthanasia and the Case of the Netherlands.* New York: The Free Press.

___. (1991b). Euthanasia: Consider the Dutch. *Commonweal,* Supplement, 469–472.

Humphry, D. (1981/82). *Let Me Die Before I Wake.* Los Angeles: The Hemlock Society.

___. (1984). *Jean's Way: A Love Story.* Los Angeles: The Hemlock Society.

___ and A. Wickett. (1986). *The Right to Die: Understanding Euthanasia.* New York: Harper & Row.

___. 1991. *Final Exit: The Practicalities of Self-Deliverance and Assisted Suicide for the Dying.* Eugene, Oregon: The Hemlock Society.

Jennings, B. (1991). Active euthanasia and forgoing life-sustaining treatment: Can we hold the line? *Journal of Pain and Symptom Management,* 6(5):312–316.

Kamisar, Y. (1958). Some non-religious views against proposed "mercy killing" legislation. *Minnesota Law Review,* 42(6): 969–1042.

Kevorkian, J. (1991). *Prescription Medicide: The Goodness of Planned Death.* Buffalo, NY: Prometheus.

Kevorkian at side of suicide victim. *The [Toledo] Blade,* May 16, 1992.

Kevorkian stirs renewed calls for ban. *The [Toledo] Blade,* September 28, 1992.

Lamb, M. H. (1988). Letter. *JAMA,* 259(14):2097.

Levy, M. H. (1991). Letter. *NEJM,* 325:658.

Lundberg, G. D. (1988). "It's over, Debbie" and the euthanasia debate. *JAMA,* 259(14):2142–2143.

Lynn, J., and J. Teno. (1991). Letter, *NEJM*, 325(9):659.

Marzuk, P. M. (1991). Letter. *NEJM*, 325:659.

McGraw, B. (1992). Jealous husband who helped rival's death muddied legal waters. *Detroit Free Press*, June 3.

Mercy killing draws probation. (1987). *Medical World News*, January 26, p. 46.

Miller, R. J. (1991). Hospice care as an alternative to euthanasia. *Law, Medicine & Health Care*, 20(1–2): 127–132.

Mitchell, P. (1976). *Act of Love: The Killing of George Zygmanik*. New York: Alfred A. Knopf.

Moran, E. (1988). Letter. *JAMA*, 259(14):2098.

National Hemlock Society, The. (1989). Supporting the option of active voluntary euthanasia for the terminally ill. *Hemlock Quarterly*, 36: July.

Nolte, K. B. and R. E. Zumwalt. (1991). Letter. *NEJM*, 325:660.

O'Connor, N. K. (1991). Letter. *NEJM*. 325(9):659.

People v. *Campbell*, 335 N.W. 2d 27 (Mich. Ct. App. 1983), appeal denied, 342 N.W. 2d 519 (Mich. 1984).

People v. *Roberts*, 178 N. W. 690 (Mich. 1920).

President's Commission for the Study of Ethical Problems in Medicine and Biomedical and Behavioral Research. (1983). *Deciding to Forego Life Sustaining Treatment*. Washington, D.C.: U.S. Government Printing Office.

Quill, T. E. (1991). Death and dignity: A case of individualized decision making. *NEJM*, 324(10):691–694.

___, C. K. Cassel, and D. E. Meier. (1992). Care of the hopelessly ill: Proposed clinical criteria for physician-assisted suicide. *NEJM*, 327(19): 1380–1384.

Rollin, B. (1976). *First, You Cry*. Philadelphia; J. B. Lippincott.

___. (1985). *Last Wish*. New York: Warner.

Ross, M. T. (1991). Letter, *NEJM*, 325(9):658.

Russell, O. R. (1975). *Freedom to Die: Moral and Legal Aspects of Euthanasia*, New York: Human Sciences Press.

Singer, P. A. (1988). Letter. *JAMA*, 259(14):2096.

___. P. A. and M. Seigler. (199.). Euthanasia—a critique. *NEJM*, 322:1881–1883.

State of Michigan, the People of the v. *Jack Kevorkian*. (1991). Circuit Court for the County of Oakland, reprinted in *Issues in Law and Medicine*, 7(1) 107–121.

Suicide doctor cleared of misconduct charges. 1991. *The [Toledo] Blade*, August 17.

Teno, J. and J. Lynn. (1991). Voluntary active euthanasia: The individual case and public policy. *JAGS*, 39:827–830.

Thomasma, D. C. (1988). Letter. *JAMA*, 259(14):2098.

van der Maas, P. J. et al. (1991). Euthanasia and other medical decisions concerning the end of life. *Lancet* (September 14): 669–674.

Vaux, K. L. (1988). Debbie's dying: Mercy killing and the good death. *JAMA*, 259(14):2140–2141.

Suicide-aid ban back in effect. 1993. *The [Toledo] Blade*, June 23.

Wanzer, S. H., et al. (1984). The physician's responsibility toward hopelessly ill patients. *NEJM*, 310(15):955–959.

____. (1989). The physician's responsibility toward hopelessly ill patients: A second look, *NEJM*, 320:844–849.

Wilson, S. D. (1988). Letter. *JAMA*, 259(14):2097.

Wolf, S. M. (1989). Holding the line on euthanasia. *Hastings Center Report*, (January/February): 13–15.

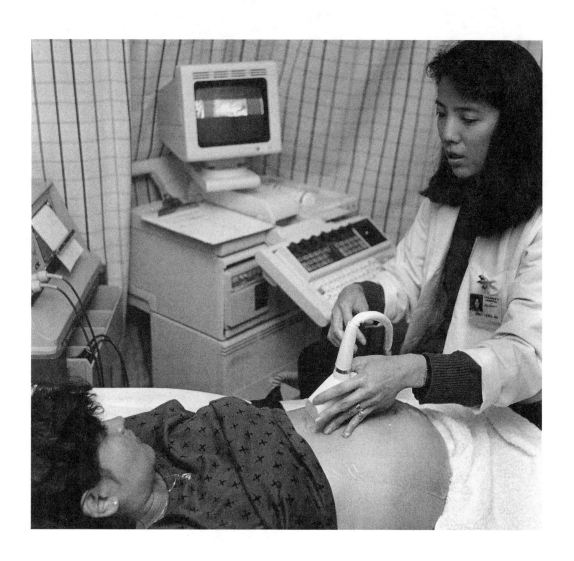

CHAPTER 6

Making Treatment Decisions for Anomalous Newborns

Considering the short life span of many of these children and their frequently very limited ability to perceive or enjoy the benefits of life, we cannot assert with confidence that in every situation there would be a societal consensus that life is preferable to never having been born at all.

Turpin v. *Sortini* (1978), California Court of Appeals

Of all tyrannies a tyranny sincerely exercised for the good of its victims may be the most oppressive. . . . [T]hose who torment us for our own good will torment us without end for they do so with the approval of their own conscience.

C. S. Lewis, *The Humanitarian Theory of Punishment* (1952)

OF ALL THE DECISIONS to be made over whether or not to withhold or withdraw life-sustaining medical treatment, few are more difficult than those involving seriously imperiled neonates. Human parents, as is true of most animals, seem to have an instinctive tendency to love and nurture their offspring. As agonizing as it may often be to make the decision to halt life-sustaining treatment for a terminally ill and/or incompetent adult, even those who have lived a full and rich life, for those who are at the very beginning of life's journey, making such a decision can be truly overwhelming.

Just as the ever-increasing rate of technological development has created changes in the way we die, as described in the earlier chapters, so too has technology greatly altered the type of care provided to seriously ill newborns. Medicine now has the ability to rescue infants who, only a decade or so ago, would have been unable to survive. Unable to cure, the best that could be done was to provide comfort to these fragile infants as they died. Such is no longer the case.

Although the cases that have fueled the controversy about the care provided for anomalous newborns have typically involved infants born with either Down syndrome (Trisomy 21; see Box 6–1) or myelomeningocele (spina bifida), the question of appropriate treatment is likely to be encountered much more frequently in cases of prematurity or low birth weight (LBW). It has been among the latter where improvements in the rates of neonatal survival have been most dramatic. According to the President's Commission (1983), the decline in neonatal mortality since 1970 has been attributable to improved survival rates at specific birth weights, rather than from a change in the proportion of high-risk infants born. Even in 1983, when its report was first published, the Commission was able to state that

> improvement among the smallest infants—those at greatest risk of death and illnesses—has been especially dramatic: for newborns weighing 1000–1500 grams [one pound is equivalent to 454 grams], the mortality rate has dropped from 50% to 20% since 1961; fully half the live-born infants weighing less than 1000 grams [2.2 pounds] now survive, compared with less than 10% just 20 years ago.   (Ibid., p. 197)

Not all premature infants do well. The same can be said of children born with congenital defects, slightly more than 4 percent of the approximately 3.3 million children born in this country each year (Ibid., p. 201). Many of those conditions are by no means rare. Spina bifida, for example, occurs in between 1 and 10 per 1,000 births. Down syndrome is present in 1 of every 600 births, the rates being lower in children born of younger parents and higher in cases of advanced maternal, and perhaps paternal, age. Anencephaly, a condition in which the cerebral cortex is partially or almost entirely absent, occurs in about 1 in 1,000 births. Congenital heart defects are found in approximately 0.7 percent of live births. The incidence of hydrocephaly (fluid in the skull) at birth, not associated with spina bifida, is between 0.3 and 2 per 1,000. Microcephaly, a condition in which the head fails to grow after birth and which often manifests itself in gross retardation, occurs in somewhat less than 1 per 1,000 births. Overall, the frequency of such birth defects that are evident at delivery or soon after is about 15 per 1,000 births (Coburn, 1980, p. 340). Many of these infants will require vigorous medical intervention at birth if they are to survive.

> [But] some infants with low birth weight or severe defects cannot survive for long, despite the most aggressive efforts to save them; others suffer severe im-

BOX 6–1 *Down Syndrome*

Down syndrome [sometimes called Down's syndrome and (especially) in older literature, mongolism] is characterized by the presence of three instead of the normal two of the human chromosomes designated as number 21. Consequently, Down syndrome is also called Trisomy-21. It is characterized by a small flattened skull, flat nose, unusual slanting of the eyes, a protruding, furrowed tongue, a short, thick neck, short broad hands with small fingers that curve inward, short, wide feet with a gap between the first and second toes, short stature, sparse hair, low voice pitch, below average muscle tone, a tendency to hearing impairments and respiratory disorders, and mental retardation. While persons with Down syndrome exhibit a combination of several of these characteristics, it is rare for any one individual to exhibit all of them. Mental development is usually retarded, generally in the moderate to severe range, although it is possible (albeit unusual) for an individual with Down syndrome to have average or even superior intelligence. (U.S. Commission on Civil Rights, 1989, p. 21)

The President's Commission states that although IQs from about 18–92 have been reported, most Down syndrome children have an IQ between 30 and 55; quite a few score less than 30 and only in rare cases does the IQ exceed 70. The higher scores occur in a small percentage of the cases in which all of the person's cells do not carry the chromosomal aberration, a condition known as *mosaicism* (President's Commission, 1983, pp. 202–203).

While the diagnosis of Down syndrome can be made shortly after birth, the intellectual capacity of the child cannot be accurately assessed until much later. It is impossible to accurately predict where on the range between 18 and 92 any individual child will ultimately fall. Some will fall at the higher end of the scale and may even be able to become self-sufficient; others will fall at the lower end of the scale and may never develop even basic life skills such as dressing, feeding, and toileting themselves. Their potential is, quite simply, unknown. Christopher Burke, who plays the role of Corky on the weekly television series "Life Goes On," obviously has a mild form of the disorder and provides an encouraging model of what some people with Down syndrome might accomplish. But, on the other hand, there are some with Down syndrome who require life-long custodial care. While it is clearly incorrect to refer to children with Down syndrome as "blobs," a quotation attributable to Dr. Walter R. Owens, the obstetrician in the *Infant Doe* case, it is also incorrect to place them generically at the other end of the curve. Christopher Burke is not representative of the average person with Down syndrome.

Although traditionally associated with increasing maternal age, some studies suggest that children with Down syndrome receive the extra chromosome from their fathers in up to 25 percent of the cases. Also, because of the increasing use of prenatal diagnosis (amniocentesis) by women thirty-five years of age or older, some 80 percent of the cases (approximately 2,400 of the estimated 3,000 cases a year) are now born to mothers younger than thirty-five years of age.

pairments either as a component of their conditions or as a result of treatments. Thus medicine's increased ability to forestall death in seriously ill newborns has magnified the already difficult task of physicians and parents who must attempt to assess which infants will benefit from various medical interventions, and which will not. Not only does this test the limits of medical certainty in diagnosis and prognosis, it also raises profound ethical issues. (President's Commission, 1983, p. 198)

These issues have been accentuated by a series of events that can be traced back to the mid-1960s and early 1970s. One of these events was the development of transabdominal amniocentesis. Amniocentesis is a process that involves directing a long, hollow needle through the abdominal wall and into the uterus of the pregnant woman. The procedure takes place under local anesthesia and the needle is guided by an ultrasound picture of the uterus. Since the volume of amniotic fluid required for the procedure to be done is inadequate early in pregnancy, the test is usually performed when the woman is no less than fourteen to sixteen weeks pregnant. By studying the exfoliated fetal cells found in the extracted fluid, a genetic assessment of the fetus is possible. While the technique was first used to diagnose Down syndrome *in utero*, the number of genetic disorders that can now be disclosed through this procedure has grown tremendously.

The recognition that it had become possible to detect such genetic defects during pregnancy was one of the factors that led to the attempts to legalize abortion in the early 1960s. Why, the argument was put, if it were possible to detect such genetic defects as Down syndrome and Tay-Sachs disease *in utero*, shouldn't the pregnant woman be given the opportunity to end the pregnancy with a "therapeutic" abortion? These early efforts at reforming the abortion laws met with some success, but they ultimately gave way to efforts to repeal the laws restricting abortion and culminated in the 1973 decision of the U.S. Supreme Court, *Roe* v. *Wade*, which overturned all state laws criminalizing abortion. This had the immediate effect of invigorating a nascent anti-abortion, or pro-life, movement. Although there had been increasing public participation in the abortion debate as the first reforms were implemented, until *Roe* was decided those favoring change—the pro-choice advocates—seemed most vocal.

The Johns Hopkins Baby

Among the developments that set the stage for the controversy over the care of anomalous newborns was an event that occurred at Johns Hopkins Hospital in Baltimore in October 1971. A baby with Down syndrome and an intestinal blockage was born. Down syndrome (formerly called *mongolism* because of the slanted appearance of the eyes) is a genetic defect, characterized by an extra chromosome at the twenty-first location (Trisomy 21). The intestinal blockage, at a point where the stomach emptied into the small intestine, is known as *duodenal atresia*. Unless and until the atresia was surgically repaired the infant could not be given any nourishment by mouth.

The parents decided not to give consent for the corrective surgery and the physicians and hospital administration agreed to honor their wishes. The infant died fifteen days after birth as a result of starvation and dehydration. The physicians and administrators expressed a belief that it would have taken too long to seek the necessary court authorization, an opinion perhaps buttressed by a belief that the court would be unwilling to order surgery on a "mongoloid" baby against the wishes of the parents. Whether their assumption was correct will, of course, never be known.

Written reaction to the death was uniformly critical (Gustafson, 1973). The situation was subsequently recreated on film by the Joseph P. Kennedy, Jr., Foundation. The film, *Who Should Survive?*, was produced to educate the public about the ethical dilemmas confronting modern medicine.

The Rehabilitation Act of 1973

Also during the early 1970s there was a series of investigations into the way in which the mentally handicapped—comprised of both the mentally ill and mentally retarded—were cared for in our society. These investigations revealed the deplorable conditions that existed in many of our state and local institutions. Residents often lived in filthy conditions, were subject to various forms of physical and emotional abuse, and were given care which, at its best, could be described only as custodial. As a result of these investigations, many of the institutions were closed. Congress held hearings into the plight of the "handicapped" and did what it often does when discovering a problem—it threw money at it. Congress passed the Rehabilitation Act of 1973 which, among other provisions, made it a violation of federal law to discriminate against the handicapped in housing, employment, and educational opportunity. The handicapped were to be brought into the mainstream of society by this landmark antidiscrimination legislation but, from the perspective of history, it could be argued that this was an unfulfilled promise.

The Duff and Campbell Paper

It was also in the early 1970s that Drs. Raymond Duff and A. G. M. Campbell published a paper in *The New England Journal of Medicine* describing their experiences with the special-care (neonatal) nursery at Yale-New Haven Hospital. They reported that over a two-year period, of the 299 consecutive deaths that occurred, forty-three (14 percent) were the result of decisions to withhold treatment. Among this group were fifteen infants with multiple anomalies, eight with trisomy, eight with cardiopulmonary disease, seven with meningomyelocele (spina bifida), three with other central-nervous-system disorders, and two with short-bowel syndrome. Parents and physicians together decided in each case that the prognosis for "meaningful" life was extremely poor or hopeless and that treatment should be halted. Duff and Campbell stated that "the awesome finality of these decisions, combined with a potential for error in prognosis, made the choice agonizing for families and health professionals. Nevertheless, the issue has to be faced, for not to decide is an arbitrary and potentially devastating decision of default" (1973, p. 890).

The paper was written, they maintained, because of an increasing concern, both lay and professional, about the quality of life of many of the survivors of neonatal intensive care units. They indicated that "many pediatricians and others are distressed with the long-term results of pressing on and on to save life at all costs and in all circumstances" (Ibid.). As justification for the various decisions to stop treatment, they cited not only the poor quality of life that would exist for those requiring institutionalization but the effect that this would have on their families as well. There was also concern that physicians often pushed too hard, going far beyond the best interest of the child, because of vested interests in their own careers. It was clear that they were trying to entice their professional colleagues to participate in a debate about the appropriate balance between technology and ethics. The technology to rescue more and more severely imperiled babies was improving steadily. The question, as they seemed to see it, was, "Because we have the ability to rescue, does this mean that we also have the obligation to do so?" The answer that they had arrived at was "No."

Duff and Campbell realized the controversial nature of their suggestions, legal as well as ethical.

> What are the legal implications of actions like those described in this paper? Some persons would argue that the law has been broken, and others would contend otherwise. Perhaps more than anything else, the public and professional silence on a major social taboo and some common practices has been broken further. That seems appropriate, for out of the ensuing dialogue perhaps better choices for patients and families can be made. If working out these dilemmas in ways such as those we suggest is in violation of the law, we believe the law should be changed.   (Ibid., p. 894)

In discussing both the Duff-Campbell report and the Johns Hopkins case, Richard A. McCormick, a prominent Catholic theologian and bioethicist, then with the Kennedy Center for Bioethics at Georgetown University and now on the faculty at the University of Notre Dame, acknowledged that they raise the "most agonizing and delicate moral problems" (McCormick, 1974, p. 172). McCormick introduced his essay by recounting the story of Baby Boy Houle, an infant born at Maine Medical Center on February 9, 1974, with "horrible deformities."

His entire left side was malformed; he had no left eye, was practically without a left ear, and had a deformed left hand; some of his vertebrae were not fused. Furthermore, he was afflicted with a trachoesophageal fistula and could not be fed by mouth (see Box 6–2). Air leaked into his stomach instead of going to the lungs (Ibid.). A well-known obstetrician was quoted as saying, "It takes little imagination to think that there were further internal deformities" (Ibid.).

The parents, faced with what they regarded as a bleak prognosis, refused to give consent for the repair of the fistula. Unlike the Johns Hopkins case, several physicians decided to take the case to court. The judge, in approving their petition, stated, "At the moment of live birth there does exist a human being entitled to the fullest protection of the law. The most basic right enjoyed by every human being is the right to life itself" (Ibid.). By this time, the baby's condition had continued to deteriorate and even some of the physicians who had filed the petition were having second thoughts about the surgery. Regardless of this, the surgery was performed and the child died shortly thereafter.

McCormick cautioned against responding to these cases with sloganeering. Such statements as "There is no such thing as a life not worth saving" or "Who is the physician to play God?" do nothing to assist in the discovery of truth. Slogans often "co-opt" this discovery and only thinly disguise a good number of questionable value judgments in the process. "Slogans," says McCormick, "are not tools for analysis and enlightenment; they are weapons for ideological battle" (Ibid., pp. 172–173).

What is needed, he urged, is a "balanced middle path between medical vitalism (that preserves life at any cost) and medical pessimism (that kills when life seems frustrating, burdensome, 'useless')" (Ibid.). Not unlike the recommendations for decision making that will be discussed later in this chapter, McCormick called for a middle course between these twin idolatries of life— attitudes that view death as an unmitigated, absolute evil and life as the absolute good. His middle course would acknowledge

that life is indeed a basic and precious good, but a good to be preserved precisely as the condition of other values. It is these other values and possibilities that found the duty to preserve physical life and also dictate the limits of this duty. In other words, life is a relative good, and the duty to preserve it a limited one. These limits have always been stated in terms of the *means* required to sustain life. But if the implications of this middle position are unpacked a bit, they will allow us, perhaps, to adapt to the type of quality-of-life judg-

---

Box 6–2   Gut Defects: Tracheoesophageal Fistula and Duodenal Atresia

In about 1 of every 3,000 to 4,500 live births, the esophagus is incomplete and the upper part of the esophagus is not connected to the lower part. This condition is called *esophageal atresia*. In about three-fourths of cases of such atresias, the incomplete esophagus (the tube connecting the mouth with the stomach) is linked to the trachea (windpipe). This latter condition is referred to as a *tracheoesophageal fistula* (TE). It occurs in about 1 of 5,000 births.

Atresia of the esophagus prevents food or liquids from getting to the child's stomach. A tracheoesophageal fistula can cause the aspiration of stomach juices if the lower part of the esophagus is joined to the trachea, and aspiration of food and liquids taken by mouth if the upper part of the esophagus is connected to the trachea. These conditions are somewhat more common in babies with Down syndrome than in other children. Each is lethal if untreated, and they are both considered surgical emergencies.   (U.S. Commission on Civil Rights, 1989, p. 21, citations omitted)

In some cases, there is a narrowing or blockage (atresia) at the point where the stomach joins with the small intestine. The uppermost portion of the small intestine is known as the **duodenum** and the condition is therefore called *duodenal atresia*. The blockage prevents food entering the stomach from passing into the duodenum, thereby creating two serious problems. Since absorption of nutrients takes place primarily in the small intestine, a child with duodenal atresia cannot be nourished by mouth. Also, since food entering the stomach from the esophagus will be trapped there, a threat that it will be regurgitated and aspirated into the lungs is created. This could cause either asphyxia or lead to pneumonia and ultimately the death of the child.

---

ment we are now called on to make without tumbling into vitalism or a utilitarian pessimism.   (Ibid., p. 174)

The answer to this dilemma, according to McCormick, lies in adopting a standard based on the *potential for human relationships* for it is there that the meaning, substance, and consummation of life is to be found. Using such a standard would typically mean that an infant with Down syndrome and a tracheoesophageal fistula would be treated, but that an infant with anencephaly (absence of the cerebral cortex) need not be. While these extremes are rather easily identified, there will continue to be situations in the middle—the gray areas—that will require anguishing deliberation and highly individualized decision making.

All of the aforementioned developments—the growth of technology, a growing societal awareness of the plight of the disabled, the intensified public debate over induced abortion, and several widely publicized cases about the appropriate care of imperiled newborns—set the stage, so to speak, for the case that marked the beginning of government intervention into the decision-making process. It began on April 9, Good Friday, 1982, in Bloomington, Indiana.

Infant Doe

A little more than a decade after the birth of the Johns Hopkins baby, a child with similar defects was born at a hospital in Bloomington, Indiana (see Box 6–3). As in the Johns Hopkins case, the parents decided against surgery. They were supported in their decision by their obstetrician-gynecologist, Dr. Walter R. Owens, who pointed out that

> if this surgery were performed and if it were successful and the child survived, that this still would not be a normal child. That it would still be a mongoloid, a Down's syndrome child with all the problems that even the best of them have. That they did have another alternative which was to do nothing. In which case the child [would] probably live only a matter of several days and would die of pneumonia probably. . . . Some of these children . . . are mere blobs.   (U.S. Commission on Civil Rights, 1989, p. 21)

The pediatricians recommended that the child be transferred to a nearby hospital which was equipped to perform the surgery required to repair the fistula. The parents decided that it would be in the best interest of the infant, their other two children, and the family as a whole if the surgery were not performed. At that point, a representative of the hospital asked the Circuit Court to make a ruling. Judge John C. Baker held a hearing at the hospital late in the following evening and ruled that the choice between the course of treatment recommended by Dr. Owen and that of the pediatricians was rightfully that of the parents and that he saw no reason to intervene.

As news of the situation at the hospital began to spread, members of the Right-to-Life movement in southern Indiana became involved. It was reported that a Canadian teacher of the mentally retarded and an Indiana couple with a Down syndrome child of their own had offered to adopt the infant. The local prosecutor filed a motion with the Indiana Supreme Court asking it to intervene and order the surgery but they refused for purely procedural reasons, thus never considering the merits of the petition. On April 15, six days after he had been born, the child, known only as Infant Doe, died of pneumonia while

---

BOX 6–3   *The Medical Facts About Infant Doe*

Nearly a year and a half after the birth of the baby that would come to be known only as Infant Doe, Dr. John E. Pless, a physician at Bloomington Hospital, reported the facts about the case in *The New England Journal of Medicine*. Since the medical records were sealed by the court, this is the best account of the facts that is available.

The mother and father had two healthy children at home. Labor started somewhat early and there was an abnormal volume of "green-tinged" amniotic fluid. The infant was limp and cyanotic at birth with an Apgar score of 2. The one-minute and five-minute Apgar scores were 5 and 7, respectively. A normal score is 10. The initial diagnosis of Down syndrome was based on the appearance of facial characteristics. The presence of a tracheoesophageal fistula was diagnosed after unsuccessfully attempting to place a catheter into the stomach. A chest X-ray revealed a somewhat enlarged heart which—along with poor blood flow to the lower extremities—led to the diagnosis of possible aortic coarctation.

The parents, as is now well known, refused to authorize surgery. The baby was given phenobarbital and morphine as needed to relieve restlessness and pain. The parents visited and held the child frequently until his death six days later.

The TE fistula was confirmed at autopsy as was the diagnosis of Down syndrome. The appearance of other organs was "unremarkable." Dr. Pless concluded his report with the following statements. "This, then, was an infant with obvious Down's syndrome and reparable esophageal atresia and tracheoesophageal fistula, who had signs of fetal distress and did not breathe well after birth. The potential for mental function and social integration of this child, as of all infants with Down's syndrome, is unknown."

(Pless, 1983)

---

attorneys were flying to Washington to ask Justice John Paul Stevens, the justice of the U.S. Supreme Court with jurisdiction for overseeing the 7th Circuit (which includes Indiana), to intercede.

Reaction to Infant Doe's death was swift. The Right-to-Life movement, which had become a well-organized and powerful political force, took the position that this was a predictable outcome for a society which, by allowing the "killing of unborn children" through abortion, had lost respect for human life. Infant Doe's death was a vivid example of where that path had led us.

There was also a strong reaction from the White House. President Reagan, who had taken a strong stand against abortion and had been endorsed by the National Right-to-Life Committee, responded by sending a memorandum to Secretary of Health and Human Services Richard S. Schweiker. The memo

Box 6–4   *A Chronology of the Anomalous Newborn Treatment Dilemma*

Late 1960s and early 1970s	Beginning of widespread development of neonatology and neonatal intensive care units resulting in increased capacity to sustain anomalous neonates.
1971	Johns Hopkins Hospital Down Syndrome Case.
1972	*Wyatt* v. *Stickney*, 344 F. Supp. 373 (M.D. Ala.) One of a series of investigations into the care of the mentally handicapped (mentally ill and retarded) that culminated in Congressional hearings leading to the passage of the Rehabilitation Act of 1973.
1973	*Roe* v. *Wade*, 410 U.S. 113. U.S. Supreme Court decision that struck Texas abortion law prohibiting abortion unless necessary to save the life of the pregnant woman.
	Duff and Campbell's report on treatment decisions in the pediatric intensive care nursery at Yale-New Haven Hospital (*New England Journal of Medicine*, 289:890–894, October 25).
April 9, 1982	"Infant Doe" Case, Bloomington, Indiana.
May 18, 1982	President Ronald Reagan responds to "Infant Doe" through an HHS "Directive to Health Care Providers."
March, 7, 1983	Department of HHS proposes Federal Handicapped Newborn Regulations including development of a "Baby Doe" hotline.
April 14, 1983	Federal Handicapped Newborn Regulations overturned by U.S. District Court due to improper promulgation procedures [*American Academy of Pediatrics* v. *Heckler*, 561 F. Supp. 395 (D.D.C. 1983)].
July 5, 1983	HHS proposes new handicapped infant regulations and solicits public comment (48 *Fed. Reg.* 30, 846).
October 9, 1983	Baby "Jane Doe" born at St. Charles Hospital, Port Jefferson, New York. Parents decide to withhold surgery.
October 20, 1983	Government sues to obtain hospital records claiming authority under the "Infant Doe" regulations. Court rules in favor of the hospital [*United States* v. *Univ. Hosp.*, 575 F. Supp. 607, (E.D.N.Y. 1983), affirmed

Box 6–4 *(Continued)*

	by the Court of Appeals at 729 F.2d 144 (2nd Cir. 1984)].
January 12, 1984	Final rules related to the care of handicapped newborns published by HHS (49 *Fed. Reg.* 1622).
June 11, 1984	HHS regulations struck by Federal court in New York [*American Hospital Association* v. *Heckler*, 585 F. Supp. 541 (S.D.N.Y.)]. The decision was affirmed, without opinion, by the Court of Appeals at 794 F.2d 676 (2nd Cir. 1984).
October 9, 1984	Child Abuse Amendments of 1984, Public Law 98–457, signed into law by President Reagan to become effective October 9, 1985.
June 17, 1985	U.S. Supreme Court agrees to review decision in *American Hospital Association* v. *Heckler*.
January 15, 1986	U.S. Supreme Court hears arguments in *AHA* v. *Heckler*, now captioned as *Bowen* v. *American Hospital Association*. Dr. Otis Bowen, formerly the Governor of Indiana, had succeeded Margaret Heckler as Secretary of HHS.
June 9, 1986	Supreme Court affirms lower court decision in *AHA* v. *Heckler* (*Bowen* v. *American Hospital Association*, 476 U.S. 610).

began: "The recent death of a handicapped newborn child in Indiana . . . raised the question whether federal laws protecting the rights of handicapped citizens are being adequately enforced." The announcement of the memo came several hours after 150 handicapped persons—in wheelchairs, on crutches, or with canes—had staged a protest in Washington. For a chronology of the events which comprise the anomalous newborn treatment dilemma, see Box 6–4.

The Letter from Washington

On May 18, slightly more than a month after the death of Infant Doe, a letter signed by Betty Lou Dotson, Director of the Office for Civil Rights in the Department of Health and Human Services, was mailed to some 6,800 hospitals receiving federal funds, such as Medicare or Medicaid reimbursement. The letter, which has been reproduced in its entirety as Figure 6–1, stated in part that it was a violation of Section 504 of the Rehabilitation Act of 1973 to deny medical care to the handicapped, including people with Down syndrome. The letter also warned that such violations could result in a loss of all federal funds.

In a press release that accompanied copies of the letter furnished to the news media, Secretary Schweiker was quoted as saying:

> In the aftermath of the recent death of a handicapped newborn child in Bloomington, Indiana, there has been a great deal of justified public concern about the protection of newborn infants with birth defects and their right as human beings to receive appropriate medical treatment. President Reagan and I share this concern, and the President has instructed me to make absolutely clear to health care providers in this nation that federal law does not allow medical discrimination against handicapped infants. In providing this notice we are reaffirming the strong commitment of the American people and their laws to the protection of human life.   (*HHS News*, two-page press release, May 18, 1982)

The Infant Doe Regulations

Less than a year later, on March 7, 1983, the Department of Health and Human Services (HHS) published an "Interim Final Rule" designed to address the treatment of handicapped infants. The rule required hospitals receiving federal funds to display poster-size (eleven by fourteen inches) notices in "conspicuous places" in nurseries and in delivery, maternity and pediatric wards. The notices were to state that discriminatory failure to feed and care for handicapped infants was prohibited by federal law, that anyone having knowledge of an infant being denied food or customary medical care should contact the HHS hotline or the state child protective agency, and that the failure to feed and care for infants might violate state law. The posters also included a toll-free telephone number where anonymous callers could report suspected violations. Investigators, either federal or local, would be dispatched to review the medical records to see whether or not the law had been violated.

Health care providers, spearheaded by American Academy of Pediatrics (AAP) (but also including the National Association of Children's Hospitals and Related Institutions and the Children's Hospital National Medical Center) responded by filing suit in the Federal District Court for the District of Columbia against the Department of Health and Human Services, which by then was headed by Margaret Heckler, asking the court to strike the regulations. The AAP argued that the regulations were "arbitrary and capricious," that HHS lacked statutory authority for the regulations, and that the rule impermissibly

Notice to Health Care Providers

SUBJECT: Discriminating Against the Handicapped by Withholding Treatment or Nourishment

There has recently been heightened public concern about the adequacy of medical treatment of newborn infants with birth defects. Reports suggest that operable defects have sometimes not been treated, and instead infants have been allowed to die, because of the existence of a concurrent handicap, such as Down's syndrome.

This notice is intended to remind affected parties of the applicability of section 504 of the Rehabilitation Act of 1973 (29 U.S.C. 794). Section 504 provides that "No otherwise qualified handicapped individual . . . shall, solely by reason of his handicap, be excluded from the participation in, be denied the benefits of, or be subjected to discrimination under any program or activity receiving Federal financial assistance. . . ." Implementing regulations issued by the Department of Health and Human Services make clear that this statutory prohibition applies in the provision of health services (45 C.F.R. 84.52) and that conditions such as Down's syndrome are handicaps within the meaning of section 504 (45 C.F.R. 84.3(j)).

Under section 504 it is unlawful for a recipient of Federal financial assistance to withhold from a handicapped infant nutritional sustenance or medical or surgical treatment required to correct a life-threatening condition, if:

1. the withholding is based on the fact that the infant is handicapped; and
2. the handicap does not render the treatment or nutritional sustenance medically contraindicated.

For example, a recipient may not lawfully decline to treat an operable life-threatening condition in an infant, or refrain from feeding the infant, simply because the infant is believed to be mentally retarded.

We recognize that recipients of Federal financial assistance may not have full control over the treatment of handicapped patients when, for instance, parental consent has been refused. Nevertheless, a recipient may not aid or perpetuate discrimination by significantly assisting the discriminatory actions of another person or organization. 45 C.F.R. 84.4(b) (l) (v). Recipients must accordingly insure that they do not violate section 504 by facilitating discriminatory conduct.

In fulfilling its responsibilities, a Federally assisted health care provider should review its conduct in the following areas to insure that it is not engaging in or facilitating discriminatory practices:

FIGURE 6-1   Notice to Health Care Providers from Betty Lou Dotson, Director, Office for Civil Rights, U.S. Department of Health and Human Services, May 18, 1982.

- Counseling of parents should not discriminate by encouraging parents to make decisions which, if made by the health care provider, would be discriminatory under section 504.

- Health care providers should not aid a decision by the infant's parents or guardian to withhold treatment or nourishment discriminatorily by allowing the infant to remain in the institution.

- Health care providers are responsible for the conduct of physicians with respect to cases administered through their facilities.

The failure of a recipient of Federal financial assistance to comply with the requirements of section 504 subjects that recipient to possible termination of Federal assistance. Moreover, section 504 does not limit the continued enforcement of State laws prohibiting the neglect of children, requiring medical treatment, or imposing similar responsibilities.

Betty Lou Dotson
Director, Office for Civil Rights

FIGURE 6-1 *(Continued)*

intruded into confidential relationships protected by the Constitution. On April 14, Judge Gerhard Gesell invalidated the rule on the grounds that the HHS had violated the Administrative Procedures Act, a procedural rule that regulatory agencies are obligated to follow. HHS had failed to allow a thirty-day period for public commentary prior to implementation of the proposed regulations (*American Academy of Pediatrics* v. *Heckler*, 561 F. Supp. 395 (D.D.C. 1983)).

HHS responded by preparing a revised version of the rule and publishing it in the *Federal Register*, as required under the Administrative Procedures Act, on July 5. To demonstrate that it was responding to several of Judge Gesell's criticisms in striking the previous version of the rule, the revised version included the following:

1. A review of a number of cases in which the Department alleged that treatment had been wrongly denied to handicapped infants.

2. A discussion of several surveys which indicated that denial of treatment to handicapped infants was accepted by the majority of pediatricians. (These studies, and others, will be discussed later in this chapter.)

3. A statement that hospitals could limit placement of notices to nurses' stations, rather than in wards open to the public, to minimize the likelihood of malicious or otherwise unwarranted reporting.

4. A reduction in the size of the notice from 11 by 14 to 8.5 by 11 inches.

5. The addition of a new provision requiring that child protective services agencies receiving federal funds develop protocols for handling reports of violations and reporting promptly to the HHS Office for Civil Rights.

After the new regulations had been proposed, but before they were finalized, a child who would become the focus of attention in yet another test of government intervention was born in Port Jefferson, New York.

Baby Jane Doe

The child was born on October 11, 1983. She had several serious disorders: *meningomyelocele,* a form of spina bifida in which part of the spinal cord protrudes, covered by a thin membrane, forming a sac; *hydrocephaly,* or fluid in the skull; and *microcephaly,* an abnormally small skull. Her parents were told that unless she had surgery to correct the spina bifida and hydrocephaly, her life expectancy ranged from a few weeks to two years. With surgery, she might survive twenty years, but would be severely retarded, epileptic, paralyzed, bedridden, and subject to constant urinary tract and bladder infections.

Because of the seriousness of her condition, she was transferred to State University Hospital at Stony Brook, also in New York, where the surgery could be performed. However, after consulting with neurologists, nurses, social workers and religious counselors, the parents decided against the surgery, opting instead for antibiotic treatment to help prevent infection. Their decision was challenged by a Right-to-Life lawyer, Lawrence Washburn, Jr., who, acting on an anonymous tip, filed suit claiming that the parents were attempting to cause the death of their handicapped child. At a hearing held nine days after her birth, the court ordered that the surgery to close the infant's back be performed. Because there was a challenge by the parents' lawyer to Washburn's standing to sue, the judge, who had been elected to the bench as a nominee of the Right-to-Life party, appointed a county attorney, William E. Weber, as guardian *ad litem* to protect the interests of the child.

Within twenty-four hours, an appellate court had reversed the court-ordered treatment decision, a ruling that would be upheld by the New York

Court of Appeals (the highest court in the state) approximately a week later. About a week after the Court of Appeals had ruled in favor of Baby Jane Doe's parents, the Justice Department brought suit in Federal District Court against University Hospital, claiming that it had a right to review the baby's medical records under the provisions of the Infant Doe regulations that had been proposed but not yet finalized. The court found for the hospital, holding that the records already available established that there had been no discrimination. The government appealed the decision to the Second Circuit Court of Appeals where they also lost. Following the Second Circuit's decision in the University Hospital case, the American Hospital Association amended its complaint in its suit against the Department of Health and Human Services (*AHA* v. *Heckler*) and the American Medical Association filed a separate suit to challenge the Infant Doe Rule. The suit was also joined by the Hospital Association of New York State, the American College of Obstetricians and Gynecologists, the Association of American Medical Colleges, the American Academy of Family Physicians, and individual physicians. These two suits were consolidated and were decided by the U.S. Supreme Court on June 9, 1986. By that time, Secretary Heckler had left the Department and had been replaced by Dr. Otis Bowen, the former governor of the State of Indiana. The case was captioned as *Bowen* v. *American Hospital Association* (476 U.S. 610).

The Court upheld the decisions of the lower courts overturning the Infant Doe Regulations. It was a five to three decision with Justice Rehnquist not participating. As is typical, no reason was offered for his recusal. Justice Stevens announced the judgment of the Court and delivered an opinion in which he was joined by Justices Marshall, Blackmun, and Powell. Chief Justice Burger's concurrence added the crucial fifth vote. Justices White, Brennan, and O'Connor dissented.

The majority offered three reasons for their refusal to uphold the regulations:

1. They concluded that the Department of Health and Human Services had attempted to use §504 of the Act in a way that was never contemplated by Congress when it passed the legislation. There was no evidence that it was ever intended to dictate the kind of medical treatment decisions that the Department was trying to require.

2. They further concluded that there was no evidence in the record that the recipients of federal funds (the hospitals) were guilty of discrimination against the handicapped. It was the parents, the Court argued, who were making the decisions about appropriate treatment and the Department could not penalize them for decisions (discriminatory or otherwise) made by the parents. This would be quite different, they

suggested, if the parents were seeking treatment for their handicapped newborns and the hospitals had refused to provide it.

3. Finally, there was a question of jurisdiction. The majority stated that the Department had no authority to order State agencies to serve as its representatives.

> While the Secretary can require state agencies to document their *own* compliance with 504, nothing in that provision authorizes him to commandeer state agencies to enforce compliance by *other* recipients of federal funds (in this instance, hospitals). State child protective services agencies are not field offices of the HHS bureaucracy, and they may not be conscripted against their will as the foot soldiers in a federal crusade. (*Bowen v. American Hospital Association*, 1986, p. 642)

It seemed that the legacy of Baby Jane Doe would be to bring an end to federal intervention into infant care decisions. While this dispute was being played out in the courts, however, Congress passed the Child Abuse Amendments of 1984. They were signed into law by President Reagan on October 9 and were scheduled to become effective one year later.

The Child Abuse Amendments of 1984

The Child Abuse Prevention and Treatment Act (Public Law 93–247) was signed into law in 1974. It established the National Center on Child Abuse and Neglect in the Department of Health and Human Services. The National Center carries out the following responsibilities:

1. Makes grants to States to implement State child abuse and neglect prevention and treatment programs.
2. Funds public or nonprofit private organizations to carry out research, demonstration, and service improvement programs and projects designed to prevent, identify and treat child abuse and neglect.
3. Collects, analyzes, and disseminates information, e.g., compiles and disseminates training materials, prepares an annual summary of recent and on-going research on child abuse and neglect, and maintains an information clearinghouse.
4. Assists States and communities in implementing child abuse and neglect programs.
5. Coordinates Federal programs and activities, in part through the Advisory Board on Child Abuse and Neglect.   (Child Abuse and Neglect Prevention and Treatment Program, 1985, p. 14878)

The Act has been extended and amended several times since its passage. All fifty states, the District of Columbia, and all U.S. territories (including, but not limited to, Puerto Rico, Guam, and the Virgin Islands) are eligible to apply for grants. The most recent amendment of the Act was triggered by the controversy over the death of Infant Doe.

The Child Abuse Amendments created a revised definition of "medical neglect" that would include withholding medical care, including food and water, from handicapped newborns. In formulating the requirements of the legislation, considerable reliance was placed upon an agreement that was hammered out in negotiations involving various medical groups and groups representing the disabled. The agreement, Principles of Treatment for Disabled Infants, provided the following:

> When medical care is clearly beneficial, it should always be provided. When appropriate care is not available, arrangements should be made to transfer the infant to an appropriate medical facility. Consideration[s] such as anticipated or actual limited potential of an individual and present or future lack of available community resources are irrelevant and must not determine the decisions concerning medical care. The individual's medical condition should be the sole focus of the decision. These are very strict standards.
>
> . . . In cases where it is uncertain whether medical treatment will be beneficial, a person's disability must not be the basis for a decision to withhold treatment. At all times during the process when decisions are being made about the benefit or futility of medical treatment, the person should be cared for in the medically most appropriate ways. When doubt exists at any time about whether to treat, a presumption always should be in favor of treatment. (Joint Policy Statement: Principles of Treatment of Disabled Infants, 1984, p. 550)

The "compromise" was opposed by the American Medical Association (*U.S. Commission on Civil Rights,* 1989, p. 81).

In order for a state to be eligible for funding under the law, it must have policies in place that would assure a method of responding to reports of medical neglect. The supplemental information accompanying the new law offered a short statement on the appropriate standard of care:

> [F]irst, all such disabled infants must under all circumstances receive appropriate nutrition, hydration and medication. Second, all such disabled infants must be given medically indicated treatment. Third, there are three exceptions to the requirement that all disabled infants must receive treatment, or, stated in other terms, three circumstances in which treatment is not considered "medically indicated." (Child Abuse and Neglect Prevention and Treatment Program, 49 Fed. Reg. 48160 (1984) as codified at 45 C.F.R., pt. 1340, proposed December 10, 1984)

The law itself defined the "exceptions" as follows:

The term "withholding of medically indicated treatment" means the failure to respond to the infant's life-threatening conditions by providing treatment (including appropriate nutrition, hydration, and medication) which, in the treating physician's or physicians' reasonable medical judgment, will be most likely to be effective in ameliorating or correcting all such conditions, except that the term does not include the failure to provide treatment (other than appropriate nutrition, hydration, or medication to an infant) when, in the treating physician's or physicians' reasonable medical judgment, (A) the infant is chronically and irreversibly comatose; (B) the provision of such treatment would (i) merely prolong dying, (ii) not be effective in ameliorating or correcting all of the infant's life-threatening conditions, or (iii) otherwise be futile in terms of the survival of the infant; or (C) the provision of such treatment would be virtually futile in terms of the survival of the infant and the treatment itself under such circumstances would be inhumane.   (98 Stat. 1752 §121)

Infant Care Review Committees

Perhaps in an attempt to soften what some might have seen as stridency, the regulations designed for implementation of the new amendments to the Child Abuse Prevention and Treatment Act included a recommendation for in-house review committees rather than direct reliance on governmental oversight. The Department of Health and Human Services, the same agency of the executive branch that had written the ill-fated Baby Doe regulations, prepared both the Final Rule on the Child Abuse Amendments and model guidelines for the establishment of Infant Care Review Committees. HHS stressed that the development of such committees (ICRCs) was merely recommended and not required by any federal laws. The Child Abuse Amendments did, however, require that states develop a plan (procedures) whereby Child Protective Services agencies assume the responsibility for responding to reports of withholding treatment from handicapped newborns. (See Box 6–5 for a parental perspective on "overtreatment" of impaired newborns.)

HHS claimed that the decision to recommend the development of hospital-based review committees had been influenced by the recommendations of the President's Commission (1983). The Commission had concluded that

hospitals that care for seriously ill newborns should have explicit policies on decision-making procedures in cases involving life-sustaining treatment for these infants. . . . Such policies should provide for internal review whenever parents and the attending physicians decide that life-sustaining therapy should be foregone. . . .

Such a review could serve several functions and the review mechanism

B o x 6–5 *On the Death of a Baby*

We were told repeatedly that "someone must be the child's advocate." But how is it possible to be sure in a case like Andrew's [born at 800 grams and fifteen-and-a-half weeks premature] just what that means? Who can determine whether or at what point the child's true advocate is the person proclaiming his right to life or the person proclaiming his right to death? We felt that we as the child's parents were more likely to have feelings of concern for his suffering than the necessarily detached medical staff busy with scores of other cases and "interesting" projects.

However, the "someone" who became our child's self-appointed advocate was the attending physician of the NICU. It was argued that we were not the baby's advocates but merely the parents' advocates. By that logic, why are [the physicians] not recognized as the *doctors'* advocates? For it is useless to pretend that there was ever such a thing as an objective advocate of Andrew's rights. Is any neonatologist, who has, in addition to his ethical commitments as a human being, a professional interest in a baby's problems, a pride in his expertise and in the statistics of success in his unit, and concerns about protecting his reputation in the eyes of his associates, really the right person to be trusted as the baby's sole advocate?

Of course, we were self-interested too. As Andrew's parents, we had a heightened sense of his suffering. Also, we feared the prospect of having to care for the rest of our lives for a pathetically handicapped, retarded child. If this is considered less than noble, what then is the appropriate label for the willingness to apply the latest experimental technology to salvage such a high-risk child and then to hand him over to the life-long care of someone else?

(Stinson and Stinson, 1979, pp. 68–69)

may vary accordingly. First, it can verify that the best information available is being used. Second, it can confirm the propriety of a decision that providers and parents have reached or confirm that the range of discretion accorded the parents is appropriate. Third, it can resolve disputes among those involved in a decision, if necessary, by siding with one party or another in a dispute. Finally, it can refer cases to public agencies (child protective services, probate courts, or prosecuting attorneys) when appropriate. (President's Commission, 1983, p. 227)

HHS further recommended that membership on such committees be comprised of "at least" the following core members:

1. A practicing physician [e.g., a pediatrician, a neonatologist, or a pediatric surgeon].

2. A practicing nurse.
3. A hospital administrator.
4. A social worker.
5. A representative of a disability group.
6. A lay community member.
7. A member of the facility's organized medical staff, who shall serve as chairperson. (*Federal Register*, 1985, pp. 14893–94)

The HHS recommendation presents an interesting contrast, in both the responsibilities of such an in-house review committee as well as its composition, with a comparable recommendation made by the American Academy of Pediatrics (AAP). Whereas the HHS proposal called for Infant Care Review Committees, the AAP referred to such committees as Infant Bioethical Review Committees, realizing the *ethical* nature of at least some of the decisions that they would be asked to review. The HHS designation seemed to disregard, or at least minimize, such a role and to focus (almost) entirely on whether treatment would save the baby's life. This difference is also reflected in the recommended composition of the committee. The AAP recommendation, in addition to the members specified by HHS, called for the inclusion of an ethicist or member of the clergy. While a clergy person was suggested as perhaps a "supplemental" member or advisor by HHS, any role that might be played by an ethicist was noticeably absent from their guidelines. Moreover, although HHS cited the report of the President's Commission as recommending the use of review committees to facilitate sound decision making in cases involving what they referred to as "seriously ill newborns," there is a profound difference in the way that the President's Commission and HHS viewed the process as unfolding. The President's Commission started from the position that parents are the appropriate decision makers and that their decisions are appropriately based on the "best interests" of their infants. Such a standard, best interests, clearly takes into consideration the quality of the child's life, not merely whether it is possible that the life can be saved. The Commission discussed the best interests of the infant in the following way:

> In most circumstances, people agree on whether a proposed course of therapy is in a patient's best interests. Even with seriously ill newborns, quite often there is no issue—either a particular therapy plainly offers net benefits or no effective therapy is available. Sometimes, however, the right outcome will be unclear because the child's "best interests" are difficult to assess.
>
> The Commission believes that decision-making will be improved if an attempt is made to decide which of three situations applies in a particular case—(1) a treatment is available that would clearly benefit the infant, (2) all treatment is expected to be futile, or (3) the probable benefits to an infant from different choices are uncertain. These three situations need to be consid-

ered separately, since they demand differing responses. (President's Commission, 1983, p. 217)

Whether or not a given therapy will provide a "net benefit" to the infant should be based on a weighing of the benefits and burdens of treatment from the infant's own perspective, not on the potentially negative effects on others such as parents, siblings, or society. This, the Commission notes, is a very strict standard that would clearly compel treatment to correct a gut defect in a baby with Down syndrome. Moreover, there are clearly cases in which treatment would be futile. There is no treatment that can benefit an infant born without a cerebrum (anencephaly) or with certain severe cardiac defects. The greatest difficulty concerns those cases where it is unclear whether or not treatment would confer a net benefit. It is with these latter situations that the process of information gathering and dissemination facilitated by an ethics committee can be most useful to both parents and providers. This will reduce the likelihood of two problems the President's Commission was concerned with: (1) that the parents might receive outdated or incomplete information that would limit their capacity to make sound decisions and (2) that decision might be made without careful reevaluation (Ibid., pp. 223–224). Table 6–1 illustrates how the framework proposed by the President's Commission might operate.

Of course, there will always be some uncertainty in deciding whether or not treatment constitutes a net benefit for an infant born with serious anomalies. The Hastings Center Project on Imperiled Newborns (Nolan, 1987) iden-

TABLE 6–1 *Treatment Options for Seriously Ill Newborns—Physician's Assessment in Relation to Parent's Preference*

Physician's Assessment of Treatment Options*	*Parents Prefer to Accept Treatment***	*Parents Prefer to Forego Treatment***
Clearly beneficial	Provide treatment	Provide treatment during review process
Ambiguous or uncertain	Provide treatment	Forego treatment
Futile	Provide treatment unless provider declines to do so	Forego treatment

Source: President's Commission, 1983, p. 218.
*The assessment of the value to the infant of the treatments available will initially be by the attending physician. Both when this assessment is unclear and when the joint decision between parents and physican is to forego treatment, this assessment would be reviewed by intra-institutional mechanisms and possibly thereafter by court.
**The choice made by the infant's parents or other duly authorized surrogate who has adequate decisionmaking capacity and has been adequately informed, based on their assessment of the infant's best interests.

tified three approaches to the uncertainty of decision making in such cases. The first of these was called the *statistical approach*. According to this strategy, premature infants would be denied aggressive treatment if they fell below a cutoff based on age and size. This, they stated, is characteristic of a Swedish approach where infants below 750 grams (approximately 1.5 pounds) are rarely given artificial ventilation.

A contrasting approach would be to begin treatment with every infant where there is even the slightest chance of viability, and to continue active treatment until it becomes certain that the baby will either die or be so severely impaired that the parents could legitimately opt for termination of treatment. This was called the *wait-until-near-certainty approach* and it was suggested that an increasing number of American physicians and institutions employ this strategy.

An intermediate approach, said to be characteristic of British neonatal practice, would be to begin treatment for every infant, but to allow the option of termination before it is absolutely certain that the infant will either die or be so devastatingly disabled that he or she will be unable to relate to others or to the environment. This was termed an *individualized approach*. Physicians would periodically reassess an infant's prognosis, taking into account such factors as severe intraventricular hemorrhages (brain bleed) or other indicators of probable neurological impairment, and would allow termination of treatment if there were a high chance (although not certainty) of severe disability.

Each of these approaches has disadvantages. Under the statistical approach, it is possible that some babies will die who could have survived with minimal, if any, impairment, although physicians and parents will never know which ones.

The wait-until-near-certainty approach is likely to minimize the probability of death where the baby is capable of surviving without devastating impairment. The price of this approach, however, is that some babies will be kept alive who might have experienced an early death as the lesser of two evils. Under the individualized approach, neither of the undesirable outcomes under the other two approaches is minimized. The result will be that some babies will die who otherwise might have lived and that some babies will live who might otherwise have died. Whether either group will be better off for it is likely to be a subject of disagreement. Prognostic uncertainty forces a consideration of which sort of these two mistakes is least tolerable.

Although the wait-until-near-certainty approach might seem perfectly appropriate in the face of *complete* uncertainty—that is, when decision makers have no knowledge at all of the probabilities of the various outcomes occurring—it is not particularly well suited to moral situations in which there are data on which to base predictions. Under the Child Abuse Amendments, each of these strategies would be prohibited.

The decision about whether or how aggressively to treat anomalous newborns has become tremendously complicated by developments in medical technology over the past quarter of a century, by the public debate over sanctity of life versus quality of life ethics, and by the intrusion of government into the medical decision-making process. Decisions that were once regarded as personal and private and were quietly made by parents and physicians (low profile) are now subjected to ever-increasing scrutiny (high visibility). While it is obvious that some of these decisions may not have been in the best interests of some anomalous infants, the frequency of such occurrences is a matter of speculation.

When the HHS published its final version of the Infant Doe rules in the *Federal Register* on January 12, 1984, it included a listing of forty-nine cases that had been reviewed since it first assumed an investigatory role following the birth of the Bloomington infant. However, as stressed by the majority opinion of the Supreme Court in *Bowen*, "by the Secretary's own admission *none* of the 49 cases had 'resulted in a finding of discriminatory withholding of medical care'" (*Bowen* v. *American Hospital Association*, 1985, p. 634). Both the Johns Hopkins and the Infant Doe cases would be examples of discriminatory withholding of treatment but, since these two cases were separated by nearly eleven years, they could hardly serve as the basis for an argument that such forms of discrimination are common occurrences or that the problem had reached such epidemic proportions that government intervention had become necessary.

It is, however, becoming increasingly clear that there has been a shift in attitudes among physicians who care for anomalous newborns regarding the desirability of aggressive treatment. In 1975, when California pediatricians were asked how they would treat an infant like the Johns Hopkins baby, assuming that the parents would agree and that they would have legal immunity, 61 percent said that they would not perform the surgery and that they would provide only that care necessary to keep the baby comfortable until it died. Just 17 percent responded that they would do "everything humanly possible" to save the baby's life (*Treating the Defective Newborn*, 1976, p. 2). In a national study reported in 1977, 85 percent of pediatric surgeons and 65 percent of pediatricians, asked whether they would agree with a parental decision not to treat a baby with Down syndrome and congenital heart disease, answered affirmatively (Shaw, Randolph, and Maynard, 1977). Another study reported that same year, but confined to Massachusetts pediatricians, found that 51 percent would not recommend surgery for a Down syndrome infant with intestinal blockage (Todres et al., 1977). This latter survey was partially replicated in the late 1980s and revealed a rather sharp change in attitude. When asked whether they would acquiesce to the wishes of parents of a Down syndrome baby with duodenal atresia to withhold surgery, 73 percent said that they would recommend surgery and 68 percent said they would seek a court order if the parents refused operative consent. (See Box 6–6 for an example of *parental* emphasis on overtreatment.)

Box 6–6   *The Best Interests of the Child?*

Baby L, a two-year-old girl, was born prematurely (thirty-six weeks, 4.4 pounds) to a thirty-three-year-old woman who had given birth three times previously. There were complications during the pregnancy and at birth the amniotic fluid was thick with meconium. Apgar scores were 1 at one minute, 4 at five minutes, and 5 at ten minutes, all indicative of severe distress. The infant was resuscitated, stabilized, and weaned from mechanical ventilation. She demonstrated responsiveness only to painful stimuli.

There were repeated surgeries—a gastrostomy at one month, stomach surgery at four months, and a tracheostomy at seven months. There were episodes of aspiration and uncontrolled seizures. She was discharged after fourteen months with twenty-four-hour nursing care, but was readmitted within two weeks for recurrent pneumonia. She was repeatedly hospitalized over the next nine months with recurrent pneumonia and four cardiopulmonary arrests. The physicians agreed, unanimously, that continued emergency treatment was not in the best interest of the child, but the mother demanded that everything be done to assure her survival.

The mother petitioned the court to force the physicians to agree to provide emergency treatment if necessary. The dispute was resolved when a pediatric neurologist from another institution agreed to arrange a transfer. Two years later, at the age of four, Baby L remained blind, deaf, and quadriplegic and was fed through the gastrostomy. She averaged a seizure a day and required intensive home nursing care sixteen hours a day. Her mental status was that of a three-month-old infant.

(Paris, Crone, and Reardon, 1990)

Just slightly more than half of the pediatricians (51 percent) expressed a change in attitude concerning treatment of anomalous newborns. Seventy percent of those whose attitudes reportedly shifted stated that it was specific patient care experiences that had most changed their views. Legal pressures and "uncertain and evolving legislation" were cited by 24 percent and 18 percent of the group respectively (Todres et al., 1988).

To the extent that these earlier attitudes on the part of pediatricians may have contributed to a climate supportive of undertreatment and unwarranted deaths of anomalous newborns, some would argue that the pendulum of parental discretion in making treatment decisions had swung too far in the direction of autonomy. The solution proposed by the Reagan administration, however, seemed to have pushed the pendulum too far in the other direction. The United States Commission on Civil Rights, the membership of which consisted entirely of political appointees of the same administration that created the Infant Doe regulations, issued a report urging their reimplementation claiming that the Child Abuse Amendments are not sufficient to prevent medical discrimination against anomalous neonates. Since the Amendments apply, they argue, only to states that accept federal funding for child abuse prevention and treatment programs (and not all do) and they delegate investigation and enforcement to local child protective services agencies, the Commission fears that the law will not be vigorously enforced. The report, which was prepared following a four-year study at a cost of one-half million dollars, has met with substantial criticism, including a dissent from its chairman, who stated that "the interests of handicapped newborns have been sacrificed to a political mission" (U.S. Commission on Civil Rights, 1989, p. 155).

Shapiro (1990) has argued that the report is distorted by the Commission's (1) flawed data-acquisition process, (2) inaccurate and misguided assumptions about medical care of infants with disabilities, (3) inaccurate and misguided assumptions about applicable law, and (4) naive and complete failure to consider the implications for the care of infants with disabilities if its recommendations were to be aggressively followed. For example, she notes that the report fails to even minimally address the dilemmas concerning medical treatment on the frontiers of neonatology—very low birthweight, premature infants—where aggressive treatment all too often does more harm than good.

Tucker has criticized the report, not for rejecting the quality-of-life analysis but for refusing to acknowledge "that death is *sometimes* preferable to life for some severely disabled children."

> Thus, while the commission's conclusion that quality of life analyses are inherently discriminatory is founded on logical analysis and is theoretically and factually sound, the apparent conclusion that there is never a situation in which a disabled infant's quality of life would be intolerable is extreme and unreasonable. (Tucker, 1990, p. 274)

Shapiro and Tucker agree that "the discriminatory treatment discussed at length in the report is largely a thing of the past and that the problem today is overtreatment, rather than undertreatment, of infants with disabilities." Shapiro cites a survey of Kopelman, Irons, and Kopelman (1988) in which 56 percent of the responding members of the Prenatal Pediatrics Section of the American Academy of Pediatrics believed that "infants with an extremely poor prognosis for survival were being overtreated" (1988, p. 677). She describes the problem as follows:

> This overtreatment tendency is not difficult to understand. Physicians whose careers are dedicated to the saving of human lives, and who often must spend many hours in attempting to save a child, tend to regard parents who wish to stop treatment as quitters, as individuals disloyal to the therapeutic enterprise. Moreover, technology has a force and momentum of its own, often described

as the "technological imperative." Health care providers tend to apply a technology in medicine if it is available even if there is no evidence that the application will benefit those who are treated. It is very difficult for physicians to do nothing for a patient, even when doing something harms the patient more than it helps. In addition, the ever increasing risk of malpractice litigation strongly biases physicians in favor of overtreating severely ill newborns. (Ibid., p. 294)

Tucker reminds readers that "reasonable minds can, and do, differ with respect to the question of whether mandatory treatment of *all* seriously ill newborns should be required by law" (1990, p. 284). Both she and Shapiro, whose remarks were originally prepared as invited papers at a conference sponsored by a group of pro-life organizations, concluded that the Commission Report was biased and one-sided and that government should not intrude into the decision-making process concerning anomalous newborns.

It is hard to predict future developments in this area. Contrary to the Commission on Civil Rights' recommendation that the Department of Health and Human Services resurrect the Infant Doe regulations to force the courts, including the Supreme Court, to reconsider their legitimacy, it is highly unlikely that this would happen under the Clinton administration. For the first time in twelve years, there is a president who is committed to personal choice on the matter of abortion, and with a more liberal position on this and other "social issues" government intervention in this area is not likely. That the regulations would have been promoted by a "conservative" administration to begin with is, to some commentators, a bit peculiar.

> Positions in the debate about neonatal [decision-making] are anomalous in ways that bespeak our puzzlement. One might expect, for instance, that conservatives, believing in the family's autonomy and the parent's authority, would want parents to make this decision as freely as they make other medical decisions. Yet many conservatives would use federal power (which they distrust) in the form of anti-discrimination statutes (which they dislike) through conditions on federal aid (which they detest) to intrude into areas of classic state government authority (which they revere). One might expect, for instance, that liberals, believing in the rights of the individual against the state, the autonomy (state-backed, if necessary) of children from their parents, and the rights of groups (like the handicapped) traditionally discriminated against, would favor affirmative action to protect those rights. Yet many liberals would leave these decisions to parents (with, perhaps, the aid of a committee of doctors).   (Schneider, 1988, p. 152, citations omitted)

Of course, all of this discussion about birth anomalies will have a beneficial effect on society if it causes prospective parents to take a careful look at their responsibilities for producing healthy children. The only thing that can be done to prevent the *conception* of children who are likely to be afflicted with a genetic defect is avoiding pregnancy where there is a genetic predisposition in either would-be parent. For those not opposed to abortion, monitoring during pregnancy with either amniocentesis (which is only effective after fourteen weeks of gestation) or the newer technique of chronic villi biopsy (which is effective after eight weeks of pregnancy) are often used where there is a likelihood of genetic defect. Developmental defects, neural tube defects such as spina bifida, can be diagnosed during pregnancy by monitoring alphafetoprotein (AFP) levels in the pregnant woman's blood. Aside from these screening techniques, couples should be mindful of the adverse effects of certain diseases and drugs on the development of the conceptus. Fetal alcohol syndrome, a disorder characterized by developmental defects and mental retardation, is the most frequent birth defect seen today. Other drugs, both therapeutic and recreational, can have serious effects on embryonic and fetal development.

And, finally, there is the need for women to obtain prenatal care from the earliest stages of pregnancy. Many developmental problems, especially prematurity, can be reduced or eliminated by good obstetrical care. The U.S. Department of Health and Human Services has recognized the importance of good prenatal care in setting the National Health Promotion and Disease Prevention Objectives for the year 2000. In its decennial report, *Healthy People 2000* (1992), the problem was described as follows:

> The most prominent risk factor for infant death, low birth weight (less than 2,500 grams), occurred among nearly 7 percent of all births in 1987 and was associated with more than half of all infant deaths. Black babies have twice the risk of having low birth weight. Low birth weight is linked to a variety of nonfatal disorders, including neurodevelopmental conditions, learning and behavior problems, and lower respiratory tract infections. In 1985, approximately 11,000 low-birth-weight infants were born with moderate to severe disabilities. From 1970 to 1981 low birth weight declined about 1.3 percent per year, but has since been stagnant. A number of risk factors have been identified for low birth weight, including: younger and older maternal age, high parity, poor reproductive history (especially history of low birth weight), low socioeconomic status, low level of education, late entry into prenatal care, low pregnancy weight gain, smoking, and other substance abuse. Smoking is estimated to be associated with from 20 to 30 percent of all low-birth-weight births in this country. Illicit drug use as a contributor to low birth weight has increased in some urban areas.
>
> An expectant mother with no prenatal care is three times more likely to have a low-birth-weight baby. Despite the importance of early prenatal care in protecting against low birth weight and infant deaths, nearly one of every four pregnant women in the United States receives no care in the first trimester of pregnancy. A disproportionate share of these mothers has low income, less than a high school education, or is very young. Between 1970 and 1980 there

was a significant trend toward increasing early entry into prenatal care, but that trend has since plateaued. Contributing to this problem is the fact that an estimated 14 million women of reproductive age have no insurance to cover maternity care.   (Ibid., p. 70)

Parenthood is high among the most important responsibilities that one can undertake. We owe it to our children to do all that we can to see that they are born healthy, and, as we will discuss in the next chapter, wanted.

Summary

Making decisions about the appropriate use of LSMT for severely anomalous newborns is one of the most difficult tasks confronting parents and health care providers. As agonizing as it may be to make the decision to halt LSMT for a terminally ill and/or incompetent adult, even those who have lived a full and rich life, for those who are at the very beginning of life's journey, making such a decision can be truly overwhelming.

These decisions were once low-profile, private matters between parents and physicians. Now, because of a variety of circumstances discussed in the text, they have become high visibility and, for that reason, they may often be influenced by considerations other than the best interests of the infant. The argument can be made that these infants have become pawns in the ever-intensifying conflict between proponents of a sanctity-of-life ethic and those who would base treatment upon the quality of life that might be anticipated. The controversy has been fueled by the abortion and euthanasia debates and by advances in neonatal medicine which have resulted in the ability to rescue, if not always fully restore, more and more critically imperiled babies.

Who should make these agonizing decisions? Parents? Physicians? Judges? Or government? This chapter examines each of these alternatives and concludes that the decisions are best made by those who are closest to the infants and who are likely to be affected by the decisions most dramatically—parents and physicians working together. Ethics committees can often provide assistance in this process. Since the debate has shown few indications of diminishing, it is likely that these decisions will continue to be highly scrutinized, perhaps subjecting grieving parents to the additional stress of pursuing the best interests of their anomalous newborn in an adversarial setting.

Study Questions

1. What is meant by the term *anomalous newborn*? Are there other terms that might better describe the problem?

2. Why is it so difficult to predict at birth the degree of mental retardation that might later be exhibited by an infant diagnosed as having Down syndrome (Trisomy 21)?

3. In 1973, Drs. Duff and Campbell published a paper in *The New England Journal of Medicine* revealing that 14 percent of the deaths at the Yale-New Haven neonatal care nursery resulted from decisions to stop life-sustaining treatment. What reasons did they give for making such a revelation?

4. Fr. Richard McCormick, a highly regarded bioethicist, has argued for a "middle path between medical vitalism . . . and medical pessimism." What standard does McCormick advocate as a basis for making decisions about appropriate medical treatment?

5. Upon what legal basis did the Reagan administration rest the right for governmental intrusion into treatment decisions for handicapped newborns? What reasons did the U.S. Supreme Court, in *Bowen* v. *American Hospital Association*, give for invalidating the Infant Doe regulations?

6. What were the major requirements of the Infant Doe regulations?

7. What was the significance of the Infant Doe case? The Baby Jane Doe case? In terms of their effect on public policy concerning the treatment of anomalous newborns, how would you differentiate between these two cases?

8. What are the differences between the requirements of the Infant Doe regulations and those of the Child Abuse Amendments of 1984?

9. Low birth weight is the most prominent risk factor in infant death and a significant factor in disability as well. What are some of the steps that pregnant women can take to reduce the risk of low birth weight?

References

American Academy of Pediatrics v. *Heckler,* 561 F. Supp. 345 (D.D.C. 1983).

Bowen v. *American Hospital Association,* 476 U.S. 610 (1986).

Child Abuse Amendments of 1984 (Pub. L. 98–457) [codified as amended at 42 U.S.C.A. §§5101–5104 (West. Suppl. 1985).]

Child Abuse and Neglect Prevention and Treatment Program/Final Rule. (1985). *Federal Register,* 50(72): 14878–14901.

Coburn, R. C. (1980). Morality and the defective newborn. *Journal of Medicine and Philosophy,* 5(4):340–357.

Dotson, B. L. (1982). Notice to Health Care Providers (letter).

Duff, R. S., and A. G. M. Campbell. (1973). Moral and ethical dilemmas in the special care nursery. *NEJM,* 289:890–894.

Federal Register, April 15, 1985, 45 CFR 1340, DHHS Part IV; Child Abuse and Neglect Prevention and Treatment Program: Final Rule.

Federal Register, April 15, 1985, 45 CFR Part 1340, DHHS Part VI; Model Guidelines for Health Care Providers to Establish Infant Care Review Committees: Notice.

Gustafson, J. M. (1973). Mongolism, parental desires, and the right to life. *Perspectives in Biology and Medicine,* 16(2): 529–557.

Joint Policy Statement. (1984). Principles of Treatment of Disabled Infants. *Pediatrics,* 73:559.

Kohl, M. (Ed.). (1978). *Infanticide and the Value of Life.* Buffalo: Prometheus Books.

Kopelman, L. M., T. G. Irons, and A. E. Kopelman. (1988). Neonatalogists judge the "Baby Doe" regulations. *NEJM,* 318:677–683.

Lewis, C. S. (1952). The humanitarian theory of justice. *Res Judicatae,* 6:224, 228.

McCormick, R. (1974). To save or let die: The dilemma of modern medicine. *JAMA,* 229(2): 172–176.

Nolan, K. (1987). Imperiled newborns: The Hastings Center Project. *Hastings Center Report* (December): 5–32.

Paris, J. J., R. K. Crone, and F. Reardon. (1990). Physicians' refusal of requested treatment: The case of Baby L. *NEJM*, April 5, reprint.

Pless, J. E. (1983). The story of Baby Doe (letter). *NEJM* (September 15): 664.

President's Commission for the Study of Ethical Problems in Medicine and Biomedical and Behavioral Research. (1983). *Deciding to Forego Life-Sustaining Treatment*. Washington, DC: U.S. Government Printing Office.

Roe v. *Wade,* 410 U.S. 173 (1973).

Schneider, C. E. (1988). Rights discourse and neonatal euthanasia. *California Law Review.* 76(1):151–176.

Shapiro, R. S. (1990). Medical discrimination against children with disabilities: A report on the U.S. Commission on Civil Rights. *Issues in Law and Medicine*, 6(3):285–296.

Shaw, A., J. G. Randolph, and B. Maynard. (1977). Ethical issues in pediatric surgery: A national survey of pediatricians and pediatric surgeons, *Pediatrics,* 60:588–599.

Stinson, R. and P. Stinson. (1979). On the death of a baby. *Atlantic Monthly*, (July):64–72.

Todres, I. D., J. Guillemin, M. A. Grodin, and D. Batten. (1988). Life-saving therapy for newborns: A questionnaire survey in the state of Massachusetts. *Pediatrics,* 81(5):643–649.

Todres, I. D., D. Drand, M. C. Howell, et al. (1977). Pediatrician's attitudes affecting decision-making in defective newborns. *Pediatrics,* 60:197–201.

Treating the defective newborn: A survey of physician's attitudes. (1976). *Hastings Center Report* (February):2.

Tucker, B. P. (1990). The U.S. Civil Rights Commission Report, "Medical Discrimination Against Children with Disabilities": A brief commentary. *Issues in Law & Medicine,* 6(3):269–284.

Turpin v. *Sortini*, 182 Cal. Rptr. 337, 346 (1982).

U.S. Commission on Civil Rights. (1989). *Medical Discrimination Against Children with Disabilities*. Washington, D.C.: U.S. Government Printing Office.

U.S. Department of Health and Human Services. (1992). *Healthy People 2000: Summary Report*. Boston: Jones and Bartlett.

CHAPTER 7

Abortion

One's philosophy, one's experiences, one's exposure to the raw edges of human existence, one's religious training, one's attitudes toward life and family and their values, and the moral standards one establishes and seeks to observe, are all likely to influence and to color one's thinking and conclusions about abortion.

Mr. Justice Harry A. Blackmun, *Roe* v. *Wade*, January 22, 1973

We cannot diminish the value of one category of human life—the unborn—without diminishing the value of all human life.

President Ronald W. Reagan, *Abortion and the Conscience of the Nation*, 1984

W<small>HY THE TOPIC OF ABORTION</small> in a book on death and dying, you may be asking yourself. Especially if you happen to be one of the many who consider themselves pro-choice on the abortion question, you may even be somewhat suspicious of our motives. We have chosen to include the topic for two reasons, both of which, to us, seem substantial. First, regardless of one's position on the issue, it would seem reasonable to conclude that a death always occurs with abortion. We do not feel that it forces one to relinquish a pro-choice position to acknowledge that abortion is the intentional termination of nascent human life. How one responds to and/or copes with that fact is certainly worthy of our concern. Second, as should have become apparent to the reader by this point in the book, the abortion controversy seems to be inextricably intertwined with most of the other controversial questions about life and death. The pro-life or anti-abortion lobby was the prime mover in the passage of the Infant Doe regulations through coalition building with advocacy organizations for the handicapped. Moreover, that same powerful pro-life lobby vigorously lobbied to delay the passage of advance directive legislation in some states. Even the judiciary has become caught up in the intensity of the abortion debate. You might recall, for example, Justice Nolan's dissent in the *Brophy* case. In authorizing the removal of Paul Brophy's feeding tube, the Massachusetts Supreme Judicial Court had, in Justice Nolan's view, "now succeeded in imposing their anti-life viewpoint at both ends of life's spectrum" (*Brophy* v. *New England Sinai Hospital, Inc.,* 1986, p. 640).

We recognize that the debate about abortion is intense and often acrimonious. We write this chapter not in an attempt to persuade the reader of the correctness of one particular view over another but, rather, to encourage the reader to examine the debate from several different and perhaps new perspectives. The controversy has become deeply imbedded in our lives, socially, politically, and religiously, and if we are ever going to temper its divisiveness it will only be through an understanding of what the arguments are all about. We do not expect that what we have to say about abortion will be accepted, much less embraced, by all, but we have made a careful effort to be as fair and objective as possible to our approach to the topic. We begin, as we have with most of the other delicate issues we have looked at so far, with a brief historical introduction.

A Brief History of Abortion

Abortion is rooted in antiquity. Although we will be looking at a more recent history, suffice it to say that abortion, along with infanticide, is one of the oldest methods of population control. There are a number of excellent books that discuss abortion in the ancient world and the interested reader is referred to one or more of them (Lader, 1966; Noonan, 1970; Petchesky, 1984; Tribe, 1990). We have chosen to limit our history to the confines of the American experience, beginning with the colonial period and concluding in the present. By doing so we hope to show how attitudes toward abortion have been shaped by a variety of factors, not the least of which has been our enhanced understanding of medicine and the technology explosion that has accompanied it.

The Colonial Period

For nearly two hundred years after the first Pilgrims landed at Plymouth Rock, there were no laws proscribing abortion. The system of laws that developed in this country was based on British common law, and historians tell us that abortion, at least when performed early in pregnancy, did not become a crime in Great Britain until the passage of Lord Ellenborough's Act in 1903. This is not to suggest that abortion was freely accepted. There were religious or ecclesiastical admonitions that can be traced back to the beginning of the Christian era and that undoubtedly formed much of the basis for criminal sanctions against abortion when done late in pregnancy. The dividing point between early (noncriminal) and later abortion was *quickening*, the perception of fetal movement within the womb. Neither in England nor in the colonies was there any attempt to define the precise time of quickening, although there is general agreement today that it probably occurs around the fourteenth week of gestation. Although postquickening abortion carried criminal penalties, there is some disagreement among writers concerning how severe they were and how vigorously they might have been enforced (Lader, 1966; Callahan, 1970; Noonan, 1970, 1979; Tribe, 1990).

The First American Laws

The first abortion laws in the United States were not passed until early in the nineteenth century. Connecticut, in 1821, was the first state to legislate against abortion by passing a law making abortion illegal after quickening. This codified the common law tradition and, by implication, would lead us to believe that early, prequickening abortions continued without legal restraint. The first of the states to make abortion, or attempted abortion, a criminal offense at any stage of pregnancy was New York. The New York law, passed in 1828, served as a model for many of the early anti-abortion statutes. While it barred abortion regardless of quickening, it treated early (prequickening) abortion as a misdemeanor and late (after quickening) abortion as second-degree manslaughter. It also provided an exception for therapeutic abortion if necessary to preserve the life of the pregnant woman. Connecticut did not revise its abortion law to include early abortion until 1860 (Lader, 1966, p. 86), nearly forty years after late abortions had been criminalized. Other states soon followed New York's lead, and by the turn of the century there were laws prohibiting abortion, regardless of the stage of pregnancy, throughout the United States.

There are several proposed reasons for the rapid passage of restrictive laws. Some historians have suggested that the laws were part of a Victorian ethic that prohibited all forms of illicit, that is, nonmarital, sexual intercourse. Sex was seen as acceptable only if it were procreative. Since the availability of abortion provided an escape from unwanted child-bearing, one of the penalties for transgression was weakened if not eliminated. Support for this theory can also be found in the parallel crusade to make contraception illegal. In 1832, Charles Knowlton, a Massachusetts physician, was jailed for publishing a book that detailed four methods of contraception. Although it was conceded that he had broken no laws, he had "offended morality" (Lader, 1966, p. 90). Later, in New York, Anthony Comstock founded the New York Society for the Suppression of Vice and succeeded in getting the legislature to pass "obscenity" laws that would be used to prosecute all forms of "deviant" sexual behavior and possession of books and printed materials about sexuality. These laws would later be used to prosecute Margaret Sanger, founder of Planned Parenthood, when she tried to open birth control clinics in New York.

Comstock was influential in persuading Congress to pass federal anti-obscenity legislation intended to suppress traffic in pornography, which was defined in such a way that it included information about birth control and abortion. He was appointed a special agent of the Post Office and, during the 1870s, used his authority to drive abortionists out of business. The laws he inspired are still referred to today as the Comstock Laws and the term is usually understood to describe efforts to enforce a narrow, rather prudish view of morality on the public at large.

Until forced underground by state laws, and the federal Comstock Laws, abortion was a rather visible part of the American scene in the middle part of the nineteenth century. Abortions were often performed by midwives and other "medical" practitioners, and such services were typically advertised in newspapers. A wide variety of pills and tonics, as well as folk remedies, also were widely promoted as abortifacients. Many of these substances were taken orally and often caused death by poisoning. Another factor contributing to the passage of anti-abortion laws in that era was the intent to end the distribution of toxic substances that often killed pregnant women.

Public health concerns about abortion also included the risk of infection and bleeding. When most of the criminal laws were enacted, abortion was no doubt a hazardous procedure. Antiseptic techniques and blood transfusions were unknown. The former would develop from the work of Lister and Pasteur. Their discoveries were first announced in the late 1860s, but were not generally accepted and widely employed until near the turn of the century. Developing an infection, which was not unlikely, or hemorrhaging could easily result in death. Childbirth-related morbidity and mortality, while not insignificant, were undoubtedly far lower than the incidence of serious illness and death resulting from abortion. One author has estimated that it was probably not until well into the twentieth century that this relationship changed (Means, 1968). Today, it is widely accepted that abortion-related morbidity and mortality are significantly lower than that associated with pregnancy and childbirth.

Demographic concerns contributed to shifting opinions about abortion. Birth rates, especially among the middle and upper classes, had fallen throughout the early part of the nineteenth century and there was a concern that the lower classes, including the immigrants (ethnic and religious minorities which included the Irish, Poles, and Italians, most of whom were Catholic), were reproducing much faster than the "native" population and that they would, in time, no longer be in the minority. While the anti-abortion movement today is often associated with the Catholic Church (more specifically, the hierarchy of the Church), it appears that many of the early laws were passed by Protestants, not Catholics, and that they were intended to ensure that they, the Protestants, remained in the majority.

To some degree, perhaps a lesser one, the early anti-abortion laws were a reaction to attempts by early feminists to change the role of women, to offer an identity aside from the traditional one of wife and mother. That struggle, and the debate about it, is still going on in our society, although the intensity of the controversy would seem to be less today than it was then.

A final issue to be factored into the picture is the role played by the newly organized American Medical Association in moving the anti-abortion agenda. The founding of the AMA in 1847 is seen as a turning point for medicine in this country. Prior to that time, there were no standards for the practice of medicine and there were all sorts of practitioners of the "healing arts." Unlike the educated and exclusively male members of the aristocracy who formed the new breed of "regular" physicians, medicine had been practiced by an assortment of naturopaths, homeopaths, herbalists, and, of course, the midwives—most of them women. The new practitioners sought to gain control over the practice of medicine by driving out the "irregulars." They distinguished themselves from the other practitioners by their opposition to abortion and they helped to mobilize public opinion against it as one way of establishing their sole authenticity.

While none of these various influences, acting alone, probably would have produced the rapid change in the abortion laws that followed, the combined influence was considerable. By the turn of the century, abortion had become illegal.

The American Law Institute Model Abortion Law

It would be nearly a century before the pendulum began to swing in the other direction. In 1962, the American Law Institute (ALI), a prestigious group of lawyers, law professors, and judges who meet regularly to review existing laws and make recommendations for change, proposed a modification of the abortion laws. As part of a broader review of the criminal code, the ALI recommended a model law that would remove most abortions from the criminal code and incorporate them into the medical practice acts of the various states. The proposal would have legalized abortion under any of three circumstances:

1. To preserve the physical or mental health of the pregnant woman.
2. If the fetus (or embryo) were likely to be afflicted with a grave defect.

3. If the pregnancy had resulted from felonious intercourse, that is, rape or incest.

The model law would have required certification by two physicians that the conditions had been met and the abortion would have to be performed in a hospital. While the Institute's report attracted considerable attention, it would be several years before any of the states enacted laws based upon it. A number of factors undoubtedly influenced what seemed to be a rapid shift in public opinion concerning abortion. One of these was the tragic experience of a woman from Phoenix, Arizona. Her name was Sherri Finkbine.

The Shift in Public Attitudes

It was in the summer of 1962 when Sherri Finkbine decided that she wanted to end her two-month-old pregnancy. Mrs. Finkbine, who was thirty years old and the mother of four, had just discovered that the drug she had been taking to alleviate her chest pains, caused by what her physician thought was "nervous tension," was thalidomide. Her prescription had run out, and she had been taking the pills her husband had brought home from a European trip. Her concern started when she began reading reports of fetal deformities linked to thalidomide in Europe where, unlike the United States, the drug had been marketed as a tranquilizer. Thousands of thalidomide babies were born with flipperlike appendages for arms and legs, a condition called *phocomelia*. Many were severely crippled and others had severe facial deformities. The numbers ran into the thousands.

The Finkbines were told that there was a fifty-fifty chance that their baby would be afflicted and they decided not to take that chance. Her physician told her that she would have to apply to a review board at a local hospital for permission to abort. The petition was subsequently approved.

Less than a week before she was scheduled to have the abortion Mrs. Finkbine told a friend, a newspaper editor, of her plight and he asked for permission to publish her story as a warning to other women. Her name would be withheld. She agreed. She failed to anticipate the reaction that followed publication. The County Attorney told a reporter for the paper that he would have to prosecute if a complaint was filed. The hospital board decided to postpone the procedure and Mrs. Finkbine was finally forced to fly to Sweden, where abortion was legal, to end her pregnancy. Her ordeal was carried by the news media throughout the country and undoubtedly prompted many people to examine their attitude toward abortion. Many people were highly critical of her decision, including her employer who fired her as hostess of a children's television show, but many rallied to her support as well. Sherri Finkbine had become a symbol, a reminder for many that abortion, which was typically discussed in hushed tones as a sordid act of wayward women, had touched the life of someone just like them.

A year or so after the Finkbine incident, the United States was hit with the last of a series of rubella epidemics. Rubella, also known as German or three-day measles, is a relatively benign disease of childhood which, once contracted, produces a lifelong immunity. Although the effects on children are seldom serious, if contracted by a woman in the early stages of pregnancy, it can produce devastating effects on the embryo or fetus. The problem has been all but eliminated through wide-scale childhood vaccination programs. The rubella epidemic of 1964–1965, however, left some 20,000 fetal deaths and 20,000 congenital malformations in its wake. It also served as a vivid reinforcement of the ALI recommendation that abortion be offered as an option where there is risk of grave fetal defect.

It was also during this time that scientists were developing the technology that would allow for the monitoring of pregnancy by amniocentesis. This is accomplished by extracting a small volume of amniotic fluid—the liquid that surrounds the fetus *in utero*—from the amniotic sac through a long, hollow needle inserted through the abdomen. Exfoliated fetal cells can be recovered from the fluid and examined under the microscope for evidence of genetic defect. Amniocentesis can detect the presence of a wide variety of serious, some lethal, conditions. Typically, the procedure is performed around the fourteenth week of pregnancy, the earliest that there is a sufficient volume of fluid available, and soon thereafter, the cell cultures will provide the information sought. In the early 1980s another technique for gathering fetal cells—chorionic villi biopsy (CVB)—was developed. CVB makes it possible to do the genetic testing weeks earlier than possible using amniocentesis.

There also seemed to be an awareness building during the early 1960s that, in spite of the anti-abortion laws on the books, large numbers of women were ending their pregnancies illegally, often at great peril to their health and/or life. Since there were no accurate statistics kept that would allow quantification of an illegal act, the number of abortions can only be estimated. The estimates were often based on such things as deaths attributable to abortion and various forms of abortion-related morbidity, primarily infection and hemorrhage. The estimates ranged from 200,000 to 1.2 million abortions performed yearly. Although the degree to which the anti-abortion laws discouraged or prevented women from terminating unwanted pregnancies is a matter of speculation, it is quite clear that the laws had created a two-tiered system of abortion services for American women. Those women with the financial ability to do so often chose to leave the country to have an abortion in various parts of the world where it was legal. Common destinations were places such as Cuba (before the Communist takeover), Japan, or Sweden. Their other option was to pay often exorbitant sums to have an abortion performed, illegally, by a physician willing to risk arrest. Poorer women, however, if they wanted to end an unwanted pregnancy, were often faced with a choice between self-induced abortion and having the abortion done under considerably less safe circumstances than their more affluent sisters. The evidence of botched abortions could be found in hospitals from coast to coast.

The Abortion Law Reform Movement

It was against such a backdrop that the public mood began to shift. Although it took several years from the time that the ALI first recommended a change in state laws, gradually that change began to take place. The first state to change its law criminalizing all induced abortions was Mississippi. Mississippi, seldom thought of as being in the forefront of social reform, changed its abortion law to allow for the termination of pregnancies that had resulted from rape. Since the change seemed to be motivated more by racism, that is, out of a concern that white women may have been unwillingly impregnated by black men, than by any concern about the reality of the problem of unwanted pregnancy as experienced by women, the change in the Mississippi law is usually treated as a footnote in the history of abortion reform. The first state to adopt all of the recommendations of the ALI was Colorado in 1967. North Carolina and California followed its lead. While one of the goals sought by reform of the abortion laws was the elimination, or at least reduction, in the incidence of illegal abortion, it soon became clear that this wasn't happening. Hindsight always has twenty-twenty vision and, from the perspective of history, it is now rather obvious why those early reforms failed to significantly reduce illegal abortion. The primary reason is that most women contemplating abortion, then as now, are not motivated by concerns about their ability to carry a pregnancy to term or about the well-being of the conceptus. Nor, for that matter, will but a small percentage of them have been impregnated through rape or incest. Most pregnant women then, as now, who wanted to end their pregnancies through abortion were motivated by an unwillingness to continue the pregnancy for a variety of reasons that were quite personal to them. They were, quite simply, undesirous of carrying *this particular* pregnancy to term. Consequently, the change in the laws recommended by the ALI only accounted for a tiny percentage of the women who sought abortions. The number of illegal abortions in states passing ALI-type laws was largely undiminished.

It was during this same period that many of the major organizations of physicians, lawyers, and public health workers began issuing position statements favoring greater access to legal abortion. In 1967, the AMA Committee on Human Reproduction urged the adoption of an ALI-like model which included a requirement that two physicians approve the request to abort and that the procedure be performed in a hospital accredited by the Joint Commission on Accreditation of Hospitals (the JCAH is now the JCAHCO, the Joint Commission on Accreditation of Healthcare Organizations). The resolution was adopted by the AMA's House of Delegates. In 1970, the House of Delegates modified this position to state that "abortion is a medical procedure that should be performed by a licensed physician in an accredited hospital only after consultation with two other physicians and in conformity with state law, and that no party to the procedure should be required to violate personally held moral principles" (*Roe* v. *Wade,* p. 143, 1973, citing to Proceedings of the AMA House of Delegates 221, June 1970).

In October 1970, the American Public Health Association, the oldest and largest organization of public health professionals, adopted Standards for Abortion Services. The standards included the following:

A. Rapid and simple abortion referral must be readily available through state and local public health departments, medical societies, or other non-profit organizations.

B. An important function of counseling should be to simplify and expedite the provision of abortion services; it should not delay the obtaining of these services.

C. Psychiatric consultation should not be mandatory. As in the case of other specialized medical services, psychiatric consultation should be sought for definite indications and not on a routine basis.

D. A wide range of individuals from appropriately trained, sympathetic volunteers to highly skilled physicians may qualify as abortion counselors.

E. Contraception and/or sterilization should be discussed with each abortion patient.   (As cited in *Roe* v. *Wade*, 1973, pp. 144–145)

In 1972, the American Bar Association put its stamp of approval on a Uniform Abortion Act that had been drafted by the Conference of Commissioners on Uniform State Laws. Unlike the ALI proposal, the ABA model would have allowed for abortion up until the twentieth week of pregnancy for *any* reason, but would allow abortion beyond that time only if pregnancy would constitute a risk to the life or health of the pregnant woman, or the fetus was afflicted with a "grave physical or mental defect," or if the pregnancy had resulted from incest or rape, including illicit intercourse with a girl under the age of sixteen (as cited in *Roe* v. *Wade*, 1973, pp. 146–147).

By then, the abortion law reform movement, seeing the results of the earlier ALI laws passed by several states, had shifted its emphasis to repeal. The movement, which had began gathering political steam, argued that abortion should be removed from state criminal codes and treated exclusively within the medical practice acts. Their arguments were aided by several state and federal court decisions, beginning in the late 1960s, which had invalidated state abortion laws either on the basis of "unconstitutional vagueness" or as violation of women's "privacy" guarantees under state and/or federal constitutions.

The Repeal of Abortion Laws

The first of the states to repeal their abortion laws was, quite surprisingly, Hawaii. It did so in 1970, and was soon followed by Alaska. They were the last two states to join the union and the only two noncontiguous ones. As the merits of abortion repeal were being debated in the various state legislatures, there were frequently raised concerns about the problem that might occur for the first state to liberalize its law. It was feared, quite appropriately as history would testify, that the state would become an "abortion mecca," drawing women who hoped to end their pregnancies from far beyond their borders. Residency clauses were an attempt to prevent that from happening. Hawaii would provide in-hospital abortions before viability only for those women who had resided there for ninety days or more. Alaska also established a residency requirement, but only thirty days. The effect of both would be to exclude non-residents who wanted to travel there for an abortion. New York, however, was different.

The abortion debate had been a recurrent part of the legislative agenda in New York, as it was in many other states, throughout the end of the 1960s. It had become increasingly acrimonious and devisive. When the legislature was called into session in 1970, abortion opponents, hoping to head off what seemed to be getting closer and closer to passage, decided to introduce an abortion bill so radical that even the supporters of change would be unable to vote for it. The bill called for abortion to be legally available through twenty-four weeks of pregnancy with no hospital or residency requirements. Women would be able to come to New York through the first six months of pregnancy and have an abortion done as an out-patient, which would be considerably less expensive than abortions performed in hospitals. Surprisingly, the bill passed. It would become effective ninety days from its April passage. In July, pregnant women, many of whom had obviously been "saving" their abortions until the new law took effect, descended upon New York. It seems that New York had, indeed, become what other states had feared. It is truly amazing, and a tribute to the health care system, that the state managed to accommodate this demand and did so with a record of safety that was quite good. Although the safety of late abortions is less than with abortion done early in pregnancy, the New York experience demonstrated that even then pregnancy termination could be done with less risk to the pregnant woman than continuation of the pregnancy through birth.

The State of Washington, also in 1970, would be the last to repeal its abortion law. Unlike Hawaii, Alaska, and New York, however, Washington did so by statewide referendum rather than through the legislature. The question was put directly to the voters.

By 1973, the landscape of abortion law in the United States looked something like a patchwork quilt. ALI-type laws had been enacted in thirteen states (Arkansas, California, Colorado, Delaware, Florida, Georgia, Kansas, Maryland,

New Mexico, North Carolina, Oregon, South Carolina, and Virginia). Courts, either state or federal, had invalidated laws in at least nine states (California, Connecticut, Florida, Georgia, Kansas, New Jersey, North Dakota, Texas, and Wisconsin) and the District of Columbia. In addition to this, at least nineteen state medical societies had voted to recommend that the anti-abortion laws of their state be reformed or repealed. Several cases were working their way through the federal judiciary. The one to arrive at the Supreme Court first was the case of an 1854 Texas law that had been declared unconstitutional by a three-judge Federal District Court for the northern district of Texas in 1970.

Roe v. *Wade*

The Texas law, which had made it a crime to perform an abortion unless necessary to preserve the life of the pregnant woman, had been challenged by a single woman, Jane Roe, who sought to have an abortion. Roe, a pseudonym used to protect the identity of the plaintiff, argued that the Texas law violated her constitutional rights, including her right of privacy. Other courts, including the U.S. Supreme Court, had previously ruled that the U.S. Constitution contains a right of privacy which includes freedom from state interference in a variety of personal decisions involving family, marriage, and procreation. The Supreme Court had previously struck down state laws that had prevented parents from sending their children to private schools (*Pierce* v. *Society of Sisters*, 1925), prohibiting foreign language instruction in elementary school (*Meyer* v. *Nebraska*, 1923), prohibiting interracial marriage (*Loving* v. *Virginia*, 1967), calling for sterilization of habitual criminals (*Skinner* v. *Oklahoma*, 1942), and restricting the use of contraceptives, both marital (*Griswold* v. *Connecticut*, 1965) and among single persons (*Eisenstadt* v. *Baird*, 1972). Several federal and state courts, including the California Supreme Court (*People* v. *Belous*, 1969), had begun applying the privacy doctrine to abortion restrictions and finding them invalid.

Roe v. *Wade* (Henry Wade was the District Attorney for the city and county of Dallas who was responsible for enforcing the law) was first heard by the Supreme Court during the 1971/72 term. Without announcing its reason for doing so, the Court adjourned in 1972 without handing down a decision on the Texas law. Instead, they ordered the case held over for reargument during the following term. The parties were back again in the fall of 1972 and on January 22, 1973, the Court, by a seven to two decision, ruled that the Texas law unconstitutionally infringed upon Jane Roe's right to privacy. The majority held that the right of privacy, while not enumerated or specifically mentioned in the Constitution, is founded in the Fourteenth Amendment's concept of personal liberty. It further held that, especially during the early stages of pregnancy, the privacy right was *fundamental*.

Fundamental rights, as identified by the Court, are those that are most highly valued, and any attempt by the state to regulate against them will be viewed with a high degree of suspicion; they will be given "strict scrutiny." Fundamental rights include such things as freedom of speech, religion, association and, of course, privacy. In applying strict scrutiny, the court typically overturns state laws restricting any such rights unless the state can demonstrate a compelling interest in the restriction and show that the law has been drawn in the narrowest possible manner to accomplish the goal. In practice, what this typically means is that once a right has been identified as fundamental, it is unlikely that the government will be able to sustain the heavy burden imposed by strict scrutiny and the law will be declared unconstitutional. Other less important rights, however, may be infringed on by a government showing that there was merely a "rational relationship" between the restriction in question and the result sought and that the law in question is one way, not necessarily the best or least restrictive, to accomplish the goal. In practice, this typically means that such laws are invariably upheld. Now, perhaps, you can understand the significance of the majority's holding in *Cruzan*, that Nancy Cruzan had a *liberty interest* in having her feeding/hydration tube withdrawn; the dissenters argued that such a right was *fundamental*.

Justice Blackmun wrote the opinion for the majority. Blackmun, who prior to appointment to the bench had worked as counsel for the Mayo Clinic, wrote that the right of the pregnant woman was not unqualified; it had to be balanced against important state interests such as protecting the public health or preserving human life. To accommodate these differing interests, that of the pregnant woman and those of the state, Blackmun and his colleagues devised a trimester framework. Pregnancy was divided into three segments, or trimesters, and the rights of the pregnant woman would be balanced against those of the state with the rights of the state increasing, and those of the woman diminishing, as the pregnancy moved closer to term.

1. During the first trimester (approximately twelve to thirteen weeks), the abortion decision was to be left to the "medical judgment of the pregnant woman's attending physician." The reason for this, said the Court, was that during this period abortion mortality is less than that in normal childbirth.

2. During the second trimester, defined as extending from the end of the first trimester until viability, the state could "regulate" the abortion procedure in ways designed to protect the health of the woman. Viability was defined as occurring no sooner than twenty-four weeks and no later than twenty-eight weeks of pregnancy. This was based on evidence submitted at trial and included in the briefs of the parties. Rather than designating a specific time, the court stated that since viability is likely to differ from one pregnancy to another, it should be determined by the medical judgment of the physician.

3. During the stage subsequent to viability, the state could, if it so desired, proscribe (prohibit) abortion entirely except for those situations where it would be necessary to protect the life or health of the pregnant woman.

It is from this statement, that there must always be an exception for abortions deemed necessary to preserve the life or health of the pregnant woman, that the critics of *Roe* have argued that the Court "legalized abortion throughout pregnancy." While it is true that *Roe* did establish that a narrow category of abortions, those judged necessary to preserve the life or health of the pregnant woman, can *never* be prohibited by the state, regardless of the stage of pregnancy, that is no different from the nineteenth-century laws that prohibited all abortions except those necessary to save the life or health of the pregnant woman. In reality, what has happened since *Roe* was decided is not a trend toward later and later abortion but, for a variety of reasons including availability, safety, and expense, one that has been steadily going in the other direction. Women have shown no interest in availing themselves of an opportunity, if indeed there is one, of terminating their pregnancies throughout the entire nine months!

The state of Texas had argued that it had a compelling interest in protecting the life of the unborn from the time of conception. The Court held that that interest did not become compelling until viability, the time when the fetus had the ability to survive independently outside the womb. The state had argued that the conceptus was a person from the moment of conception and, as such, should be protected under the Fourteenth Amendment which guarantees that "no *person* shall be deprived of life, liberty, or property without due process of law." In rejecting that argument, the Court said that the state had "conceded . . . that no case could be cited that holds that a fetus is a person within the meaning of the Fourteenth Amendment" (*Roe* v. *Wade*, 1973, p. 157). *Person,* as it is used in the Constitution, has application only postnatally; it does not include the unborn. At this point, the Court offered the following:

> We need not resolve the difficult question of when life begins. When those trained in the respective disciplines of medicine, philosophy, and theology are unable to arrive at any consensus, the judiciary, at this point in the development of man's knowledge, is not in a position to speculate as to the answer. (Ibid., 1973, p. 159)

While we can understand the Court's frustration in being confronted with this metaphysical question about the origins of life, we would suggest that Blackmun's observation about the beginning of life was unrelated to the question the Court was asked to answer. The question was not, "Is the conceptus—embryo or fetus—alive?" We doubt that there would now be, nor would there have been in 1973, serious scientific disagreement that the answer to that question is yes. While there may perhaps be some philosophical and theological, and perhaps even judicial, disagreement about that, the question is essentially a scientific one. The question that the Court was being asked to decide, however, was not whether the conceptus was alive, but whether it was a "person" and therefore protected under the Fourteenth Amendment. To that question the Court answered no; there was no evidence that embryos or fetuses had ever been considered persons, "in the whole sense of the word," under the Constitution. Whether or not we should treat nascent life, nascent *human* life, as though it were a person is an *ethical* question and one not likely to yield to scientific analysis.

The reaction to the decision in *Roe* was swift. Immediately, pro-life legislators introduced bills in both houses of Congress that would amend the Constitution to extend "personhood" to embryos and fetuses. Amending the Constitution, however, is not an easy process. It has only been done twenty-six times in more than 200 years. The first ten—the Bill of Rights—were approved together in 1791; the last—lowering the voting age to eighteen—was added in 1971. A proposed amendment must first pass both houses of Congress by a two-thirds majority and then be ratified by three-quarters of the states. The proposed Equal Rights Amendment, which would have prohibited discrimination on the basis of sex, was passed by Congress but failed to be ratified within the seven-year period allocated. Although first introduced in the wake of *Roe* and reintroduced regularly ever since, a bill to extend personhood to the "unborn"—the so-called Human Life or Paramount Human Life Amendment—has yet to receive enough votes to pass either house. Another way of amending the Constitution is by a Constitutional Convention. A convention, which has been called only once in American politics, would be assembled at the request of three-quarters of the states. Many constitutional scholars are deeply concerned about the vagueness of the rules that guide a convention and fear that many of our freedoms might be jeopardized by such a process.

The other line of attack on *Roe* was to pass restrictive regulations either at the state or federal level. The state regulations included such things as requirements for spousal consent or notification, that all abortions be performed in hospitals, that there be mandatory waiting periods before an abortion could be performed, and that certain kinds of information be provided to women prior to an abortion. Some states and the federal government passed laws restricting the use of government funds, that is, Medicaid, for abortions. The funding restrictions were upheld by the U.S. Supreme Court; most of the other restrictions were struck down.

Pro-life advocates realized that if they wished to see restrictive laws passed, they would have to work to elect pro-life legislators at both the state and federal level. When Ronald Reagan announced his candidacy for President of the United States in 1979, the pro-life movement responded enthusiastically. Reagan, who had forcefully and repeatedly stated his opposition to "abortion on demand," promised, if elected, to work for the passage of a constitutional amendment to protect unborn children. Running against President Jimmy Carter, Reagan was elected by a huge margin. The Republican platform called for outlawing of abortion and President Reagan set about doing just that by urging Congress to pass a pro-life amendment and by promising to appoint to the federal bench, including the Supreme Court, only those judges who shared his restrictive view of the constitution. It appeared that *Roe*, and its interpretation of constitutionally protected privacy rights, was unlikely to survive.

By 1989 the Reagan court was poised and ready, at the urging of the administration, to overturn *Roe*. The opportunity was in the form of a challenge to a Missouri law that had been declared unconstitutional by two lower federal courts on its way to the Supreme Court. The case was *Webster* v. *Reproductive Health Services* (1989).

Webster v. *Reproductive Health Services*

William A. Webster was the attorney general of Missouri, whose job it was to enforce the laws of the state, and Reproductive Health Services was an abortion clinic that had filed suit hoping to have the restrictions of a 1986 Missouri law declared unconstitutional. Among other provisions of the law were:

1. A preamble declaring that "the life of each human being begins at conception" and "unborn children have protectable interests in life, health, and well-being."
2. A provision that no "public facilities" be used for performing abortions, even if the abortion would be paid for entirely with private funds.
3. A requirement that prior to performing an abortion at a gestational age "reasonably believed" to be 20 weeks or more, where there would be a "possibility" of viability, the physician would be required to perform "tests" to establish gestational age, weight, and lung maturity of the "unborn child."

The plaintiffs argued that the preamble violated *Roe's dicta* that the state may not establish one theory as to when life begins, that the ban on public facilities would—since mid-trimester and later abortions were typically done in hospitals (public facilities)—be the same as banning those abortions, and that the "testing" requirement conflicted with *Roe's* trimester framework. *Roe* said that viability began no sooner than twenty-four weeks and no later than twenty-eight and that the determination of viability was to be judged by the physician. Missouri, they claimed, was intruding during the second trimester in a way that would increase the cost of the abortion, by requiring the use of ultrasonography to gauge the age and weight of the fetus and amniocentesis to assess fetal lung maturity, although neither of those tests were designed to protect the life or health of the pregnant woman. There was no test, they argued, that could be done to determine fetal lung maturity as early as the twentieth week of pregnancy.

It looked certain that *Roe* would fall. There were only three members of the *Roe* majority left on the Court: Justice Blackmun, who wrote the opinion, and Justices Brennan, the only Catholic member of the *Roe* Court, and Marshall, the only African-American. Justice Stevens, who had been appointed by President Gerald Ford in 1975, a moderate who usually voted pro-choice, seemed to be a fourth vote. Justice O'Connor, a Reagan appointee (1981) and the only woman to sit on the high court, had voted with the majority in striking down several other restrictive state laws (*City of Akron* v. *Center for Reproductive Health*, 1983; *Thornburgh* v. *American College of Obstetricians and Gynecologists*, 1986), but she was thought to be leaning toward overturning *Roe*.

Justices Rehnquist and White had been the original dissenters in *Roe*; Rehnquist was now Chief Justice, having been appointed by President Reagan when Chief Justice Burger resigned from the Court in 1986 to head the Commission on the Bicentennial. Reagan filled the slot created by Burger's departure with Antonin Scalia, the first Italian-American to sit on the Court. When Justice Powell resigned in 1987, he was replaced by Anthony Kennedy. Kennedy was actually the president's third choice; the first had been Robert Bork, who asked that his name be withdrawn after it became clear that he would not be recommended by the Senate Judiciary Committee or confirmed by the Senate. Bork was openly hostile both to *Roe* and to the concept of privacy upon which it was based. Bork's replacement was Douglas Ginsberg, who withdrew his name after it had been disclosed that he had smoked marijuana with some students at Harvard Law School during the 1960s. Kennedy was next in line and he was quickly confirmed. It was thought that Rehnquist, White, O'Connor, Kennedy, and Scalia would cast the votes necessary to uphold *Webster* and scuttle *Roe*. They didn't.

The majority, voting along predictable five-to-four lines, upheld the preamble, indicating that it was "simply the expression of a value judgment" that did not limit the right to abortion. Unless and until the state attempted to apply the definition in a restrictive manner, it was free to merely define life in any way it wished. The same majority upheld the ban on performing abortions in public facilities even though, as Justice Blackmun pointed out in dissent:

> The Missouri statute prohibits the performance of abortions in institutions that in all pertinent respects are private, yet are located on property owned, leased, or controlled by the government. Thus, under the statute, no abortion may be performed at Truman Medical Center in Kansas City—where, in 1985, 97 percent of all Missouri hospital abortions at 16 weeks or later were

performed—even though the Center is a private hospital, staffed primarily by private doctors, and administered by a private corporation: the Center is located on ground leased from a political subdivision of the State. (1989 U.S. LEXIS 3290 at *82)

The "testing" requirement was upheld by a three-one–one-four vote known as a *plurality decision*. The five justices voting to uphold the provision agreed in the result but could not agree on the reason. The Chief Justice, joined by Justices White and Kennedy, agreed that the testing provision conflicted with *Roe's* trimester framework and voted to overturn that part, but *only* that part, of *Roe*.

Justice Scalia, in his first opportunity to rule on the constitutionality of a state restriction, seemed eager to demonstrate his desire to overturn *Roe*. He agreed that there was a conflict between Missouri's testing requirement and *Roe's* trimester approach and he would have upheld the former by overruling the latter. Disagreeing with the position espoused by Rehnquist, White, and Kennedy—that the conflict created by the Missouri law called only for a rejection of the trimester portion of *Roe*—and with O'Connor's attempt to harmonize what "merely appeared" to be a conflict—an argument to be discussed below—Scalia demonstrated his impatience with the piecemeal dismantling of *Roe*.

The real question, then, is whether there are valid reasons to go beyond the most stingy possible holding today. Ordinarily, speaking no more broadly than is absolutely required avoids throwing settled law into confusion; doing so today preserves a chaos that is evident to anyone who can read and count. Alone sufficient to justify a broad holding is the fact that our retaining control, through *Roe*, of what I believe to be, and many of our citizens recognize to be, a political issue, continuously distorts the public perception of the role of this Court. We can now look forward to at least another Term [sic] with carts full of mail from the public, and streets full of demonstrators, urging us—their unelected and life-tenured judges who have been awarded those extraordinary, undemocratic characteristics precisely in order that we might follow the law despite the popular will—to follow the popular will. . . .

Given the Court's newly contracted abstemiousness, what will it take, one must wonder, to permit us to reach the fundamental question? The result of our vote today is that we will not reconsider that prior opinion [*Roe*], even if most of the Justices think it is wrong, unless we have before us a statute that in fact contradicts it—and even then (under our newly discovered "no-broader-than-necessary" requirement) only minor problematical aspects of *Roe* will be reconsidered, unless one expects State legislatures to adopt provisions whose compliance with *Roe* cannot even be argued with a straight face. It thus appears that the mansion of constitutionalized abortion-law, constructed overnight in *Roe v. Wade*, must be disassembled door-jamb by door-jamb, and never entirely brought down, no matter how wrong it may be. (Ibid. at *78)

Justice O'Connor voted to uphold the Missouri law because, unlike any of the others, she saw no conflict with *Roe*. Surely, she reasoned, Missouri did not mean to require physicians to perform tests—referring to the testing for fetal lung maturity at twenty weeks or more—if there were no tests that would accomplish that result. Therefore, the statute could be harmonized with *Roe* by reading it only to require such tests when the physician had reason to believe that the fetus was viable. O'Connor expressed her dissatisfaction with what she felt was the arbitrariness of *Roe's* trimester framework, a position she had expressed in previous abortion cases before the Court (*City of Akron v. Akron Center for Reproductive Health*, 1983; *Thornburgh v. American College of Obstetricians and Gynecologists*, 1986). She felt that there was no reason to deny the state a compelling interest in protecting nascent life throughout the pregnancy rather than limiting it to the period subsequent to viability. The appropriate standard in testing the constitutionality of state restrictions was not whether the state's interest was compelling, but whether the restrictions placed an "undue burden" on the woman's right to have an abortion. Although this clearly demonstrated her willingness to overrule *Roe's* trimester framework, since she saw no conflict between *Webster* and *Roe*, that would have to be deferred until a more appropriate time.

Justice Blackmun wrote a strong dissent, which was joined by Justices Brennan and Marshall. Although acknowledging that the Court continued to uphold the "quintessentially intimate, personal, and life-directing decision" of a woman to terminate a pregnancy, the plurality, the dissenters wrote, "implicitly invites every state legislature to enact more and more restrictive abortion regulations in order to provoke more and more test cases, in the hope that somewhere down the line the Court will return the law of procreative freedom to the severe limitations that generally prevailed in this country before January 22, 1973." The opinion, he claimed, was filled with "winks, and nods, and knowing glances to those who would do away with *Roe*" (Ibid. at *81).

The significance of *Webster* was not so much in what it did—narrowly upholding state restrictions on late abortions—but, rather, what it seemed to promise. The Court seemed to be sending a message that, given an appropriate case, and *perhaps* one more vote, it was ready to overrule *Roe*. Justice Blackmun described the situation: "For today, at least, the law of abortion stands undisturbed. For today, the women of this Nation still retain the liberty to control their destinies. But the signs are evident and very ominous, and a chill wind blows" (Ibid. at *111).

The Minor's Rights Cases

In 1990, still waiting for an appropriate case that would allow it to directly confront the central issue in *Roe*—the right of privacy that protected abortion—the Court decided two minor's rights cases. The decisions were handed down on the same day as the decision in *Cruzan*, June 26. In *Hodgson* v. *Minnesota* a five-to-four majority upheld a two-parent notification law. The opinion was written by Chief Justice Rehnquist and joined by Justices Kennedy, White, Scalia, and O'Connor. The law provided a judicial "by-pass" whereby a pregnant minor seeking an abortion had a choice between having her parents notified or convincing a judge that she was either (1) mature enough to make the decision herself or (2) that having the abortion was in her best interest. All but Justice O'Connor wrote that they would have upheld the law even *without* the "by-pass" provision. The other case, *Akron Center for Reproductive Health* v. *Ohio*, was a one-parent notification law, also with a judicial "by-pass," and Justice Stevens joined the *Hodgson* majority resulting in a six-to-three vote.

Although it had become rather routine for the administration to urge the Court to use every abortion case on its docket, regardless of the issue presented, to overturn *Roe*, a Pennsylvania case—*Casey* v. *Planned Parenthood of Southeastern Pennyslvania*—was thought, by many, to provide the first real opportunity to do so. In 1988, President Bush had been elected, running on the same pro-life platform that had been so successful for his predecessor. Bush, who had professed a pro-choice stance before being chosen as Mr. Reagan's running mate, now, like Reagan, took the position that abortion should be illegal, except where necessary to preserve life of the woman or if the pregnancy had resulted from rape or incest. On these latter two conditions, rape and incest, he held a more liberal position than either President Reagan or the Republican Platform Committee. Mr. Bush continued the practice of appointing pro-life judges to the Court. His first opportunity came with the resignation of Justice William Brennen. Perhaps reflecting upon President Reagan's difficulty with the Bork appointment, Bush choose a relatively unknown District Court judge from New Hampshire, David Souter. Souter, who unlike Bork seemed to have said or written little—there was no "paper trail"—had little difficulty with the confirmation process. In 1991, with the resignation of Justice Thurgood Marshall, Mr. Bush nominated Clarence Thomas to replace him. The rest, as they say, is history.

The Senate Judiciary Committee confirmation hearings and the subsequent vote by the full Senate were reflective not only of the fear that Thomas was too conservative, especially on the issue of abortion, but by the fact that he had been accused of sexual harassment by Anita Hill, a former subordinate at the Office of Economic Opportunity who is now a law professor at the University of Oklahoma. He was confirmed by a deeply divided Senate. During the confirmation hearings, when asked about his views on *Roe* v. *Wade*, Thomas professed that he "had no opinion" and that he "never even discussed the case." This was viewed, by some, as rather difficult to accept, given the fact that the decision has been one of the most controversial ones in the history of the Court.

Planned Parenthood of Southeastern Pennsylvania v. Casey

The new Bush-Reagan Court, including Justice Thomas, had its first chance to vote on abortion in the case of a challenge to a restrictive Pennsylvania law. The Pennsylvania legislature passed an "Abortion Control Act" that required, among other provisions:

1. A twenty-four hour waiting period before an abortion could be performed.
2. That the woman contemplating abortion be informed of the availability of information about embryonic and fetal development as prepared by the State.
3. That a married woman seeking an abortion must sign a statement that she has notified her husband.

The District Court held all of the provisions unconstitutional. The Court of Appeals struck only the husband notification provision; the waiting period and information requirements were upheld. The Bush administration urged the Supreme Court to use the case as an opportunity to overturn *Roe*. Although they upheld the ruling of the Court of Appeals, approving the informed consent and waiting period and striking the husband notification provisions, the plurality opinion, which was written by Justices O'Connor, Kennedy and Souter, seemed to seriously undermine the law under *Roe*. Whereas *Roe* recognized the right to privacy, which included the right to terminate an unwanted pregnancy, as a fundamental right under which the state could not prevent a woman from choosing abortion prior to viability, under *Casey* the right was characterized as a liberty interest. Moreover, rather than using viability as the time at which the state's interests in the life of the fetus became compelling, the Court now held that the state had a "profound interest in potential life" *throughout the pregnancy* and that the appropriate test would be whether or not the proposed restrictions placed an "undue burden" on the right to abortion. A divided Court joined with various portions of the O'Connor, Kennedy, Souter opinion. Justice Stevens, who joined the Court after *Roe* had been decided and dissented in *Webster*, agreed with the shift to the undue burden standard but would have struck both the waiting period and the informed consent provisions. The latter, he stated, were designed to persuade a woman not to have an abortion rather than to aid her in making a decision. Justice Blackmun expressed concern that the new undue burden standard would be much more difficult to administer than *Roe's* trimester framework. He would also have upheld the fundamental right/strict scrutiny standard and thereby invalidated the Pennsylvania law. Justice Scalia, as he had in *Webster*, argued that *Roe* should be overruled. Chief Justice Rehnquist and Justice White, the two dissenters in *Roe*, although refusing to join with Justice Scalia in his desire to use *Webster* to overrule *Roe*, now agreed with him that the Pennsylvania law provided an opportunity to do so. Justice Thomas provided the fourth vote on the Court to overrule *Roe*. The anti-*Roe* justices were critical of the new undue burden standard, which they characterized as "created largely out of whole cloth," having no basis in constitutional law, and being difficult to apply. Although the right to abortion survived *Casey*, it did so in a greatly weakened condition. Justice Blackmun had become the sole defender of *Roe* left on the Court, although Justice Stevens seemed to align himself with most, other than the trimester framework, of what *Roe* stood for. Justices O'Connor, Kennedy, and Souter had assumed the role of moderates who had crafted a standard that returned more power to the states to place restrictions on the right to abortion as long as they did not constitute an undue burden, whatever that might mean in practice. Although they upheld the twenty-four-hour waiting period against the claim that it was unconstitutional on its face—as written—they did indicate that it might be found to constitute an undue burden as applied to individual cases. Most importantly, however, it was clear that the Court was only one vote away from overruling *Roe*. Justice Blackmun summed it up in the following way:

> Three years ago, in *Webster v. Reproductive Health Services*, four Members of this Court appeared poised to "cast into darkness the hopes and visions of every woman in this country" who had come to believe that the Constitution guaranteed her the right to reproductive choice. All that remained between the promise of *Roe* and the darkness of the plurality was a single, flickering flame. Decisions since *Webster* gave little reason to hope that this flame would cast much light. But now, just when so many expected the darkness to fall, the flame has grown bright.
>
> I do not underestimate the significance of today's joint opinion. Yet I remain steadfast in my belief that the right to reproductive choice is entitled to the full protection afforded by this Court before *Webster*. And I fear for the darkness as four Justices anxiously await the single vote necessary to extinguish the light.   (1992 U.S. LEXIS 4751 at *136–137, citations omitted)

Justice Blackmun concluded his dissent by commenting on the vastly different view of the world held by the Chief Justice and Justices White, Scalia, and Thomas compared to those who would uphold reproductive choice. They were, in his words, "worlds apart."

> And yet, in another sense, the distance between the two approaches is short—the distance is but a single vote.
>
> I am 83 years old. I cannot remain on this Court forever, and when I do step down, the confirmation process for my successor well may focus on the issue before us today. That, I regret, may be exactly where the choice between the two worlds will be made.   (Ibid. at *169)

The Presidential Election of 1992

Abortion was very much in the forefront of the 1992 presidential campaign. Arkansas Governor Bill Clinton, the Democratic candidate, ran on a platform that vowed to uphold choice and to stem the appointment of anti-*Roe* judges to the Supreme Court. The incumbent president, George Bush, continued to state his opposition to abortion, except where necessary to preserve the life of the pregnant woman or when the pregnancy had resulted from rape or incest. These latter two exceptions were broader than the abortion platform assembled by the Republican National Committee, for whom only the life of the "mother" [pregnant woman] was an acceptable exception. Independent candidate Ross Perot had taken the position that it was not the proper role of government to intrude into the abortion decision, a position presumably like that of the Democrats.

Although abortion was only one of many issues in the campaign, it was an important one for those who had strong feelings about the issue. The National Right to Life Committee ran large notices in several issues of the *National Right to Life News* comparing the abortion positions of the candidates and urging readers to post the information in their churches (see Figure 7–1). On the local levels, opponents of abortion placed ads in newspapers in the days prior to the election admonishing that a vote for Clinton would be anti-Christian. Regardless of this, Governor Clinton won the election with 43 percent of the popular vote (see Box 7–1). Ross Perot captured 19 percent and the incumbent president, George Bush, received 38 percent (*Time*, November 16, 1992, p. 19). During the same election, voters in both Maryland and Arizona approved state proposals that would assure women residents of the right to abortion even if the Supreme Court were to eventually overrule *Roe*.

It is expected that the Clinton victory will begin to reverse the tide of pro-life regulations that had been instituted by the Reagan/Bush White House. For example, in January 1992, President Clinton, by executive order, lifted the ban on abortions performed in military hospitals, both here and abroad. He also revoked the ban on abortion counseling in federally funded (Title X) birth control clinics. There are some 4,000 Title X-funded clinics serving approximately 3.7 million women a year. Most of these clinics, some of which are operated by Planned Parenthood affiliates and others by state and local health departments, offer pregnancy testing and, depending upon the results of the tests, counseling to women concerning their options—prenatal care, adoption services, and abortion. Although most Title X recipients do not provide abortions, restrictions initiated at the direction of former President Reagan would require a forfeiture of federal funding unless they agreed not to discuss abortion with clients. Labeled the "Gag Rule" by the media, the regulations were challenged in the federal courts and upheld by a predictably divided Supreme Court (five to four) on May 23, 1991 (*Rust v. Sullivan*, 59 *Law Week* 4451). Perhaps re-

Where Do The Candidates Stand?

"Faith, family — these are the values that sustain the greatest nation on Earth. And to these values we must add the infinitely precious value of life itself. Let me be clear: I support the right to life."

GEORGE BUSH

GEORGE BUSH

Roe vs. Wade

GEORGE BUSH has steadfastly called for the reversal of Roe v. Wade. As he told a rally of pro-lifers in Washington, D.C., "The Supreme Court's decision in Roe v. Wade was wrong and should be overturned." Bush Appointee Attorney General William Barr said the Justice Department would continue to urge the Court to reverse Roe in future cases.

Appointment of Judges

GEORGE BUSH has sought to appoint judicial conservatives, such as Clarence Thomas, to the courts. Thomas joined three other justices in dissenting from the Court's Casey decision upholding Roe. During the Bush/Reagan years, the pro-abortion majority on the Court has shrunk from 7-2 to 5-4.

Abortion as Birth Control

GEORGE BUSH has banned promotion of abortion as a method of birth control in federally funded clinics.

Unlimited Abortion

GEORGE BUSH has vowed he will veto the "Freedom of Choice Act" (FOCA). FOCA goes well beyond even Roe versus Wade and forbids any significant limits on abortion. The President pledged, "it will not become law as long as I am President of the United States."

Abortion Without Parental Consent

GEORGE BUSH will fight proposals to allow minor girls to obtain abortion without parental consent. The President said, "This idea is crazy."

Government Funding of Abortion

GEORGE BUSH has strongly defended the Hyde Amendment which prohibits the use of federal dollars to pay for abortions, except to save the mother's life.

This insert is provided for information and education purposes only and is not an endorsement of any candidate for elective office. Provided by the National Right to Life Comm., Inc.

Where Do The Candidates Stand?

"I have never wavered in my support of Roe v. Wade... In Arkansas I have fought against mandatory waiting periods and parental and spousal consent laws."

BILL CLINTON

BILL CLINTON

Roe vs. Wade

BILL CLINTON says he has "always been pro-choice" and has "never wavered" in his "support of Roe v. Wade." "I have believed in the rule of Roe v. Wade for 20 years since I used to teach it in law school." (Roe v. Wade allows abortion for any reason, even as a method of birth control, even in the late stages of pregnancy.)

Appointment of Judges

BILL CLINTON says that support for Roe v. Wade would be a "litmus test" for his nominees to the Supreme Court. Referring to the one-vote margin by which the Court recently upheld Roe v. Wade, Clinton said, "As president, I won't make you worry about the 'one justice away' on the Supreme Court."

Abortion as Birth Control

BILL CLINTON has said he would issue an Executive Order repealing this pro-life policy on his first day in office.

Unlimited Abortion

BILL CLINTON has made support for FOCA a key part of his campaign. "I would support a federal Freedom of Choice Act to protect a woman's right to choose."

Abortion Without Parental Consent

BILL CLINTON boasts that he has "fought against" parental consent laws in Arkansas, and says, "I'm opposed to parental consent, by the way, and I oppose a bill that would do that.

Government Funding of Abortion

BILL CLINTON would repeal the Hyde Amendment. Moreover, abortion on demand would be paid for under his national health program.

ROSS PEROT

ROSS PEROT has said he would sign the same radical legislation Clinton supports which would guarantee abortion for any reason . . . even as a method of birth control or for sex selection. He supports tax funding of abortion.

Figure 7–1 Abortion positions of the candidates—1992. (Reprinted by permission of the National Right to Life Committee, Inc., Washington, D.C.)

sponding to criticism that the administration was attempting to stifle free speech or intrude into the physician-patient relationship, President Bush issued a "clarification" that the regulations, which had been promulgated by the Department of Health and Human Services, the same agency that had prepared the Infant Doe regulations, were not intended to apply to any conversations between physicians and their patients, but only to counseling performed by nonphysician employees. Since physicians actually do little of the counseling at Title X agencies, most of it being done by either nurses or other trained counselors, the clarification seemed, to many, to be a distinction without a difference. Since the president's clarification arguably constituted a revision of the regulations, the revised regulations were again challenged in federal court and held unconstitutional on the very same day that Mr. Bush was being voted out

---

Box 7–1   *Abortion and the Presidential Election of 1992*

Although the issue of abortion was raised by all of the candidates in the 1992 presidential election, it was only one of many issues that seemed to be important to some voters. Other issues were jobs and the economy, health care, the budget deficit and the growing dimensions of the national debt, environmental protection, and taxes. According to *Time* magazine, the percentage of voters for each of the candidates who thought the issue of abortion was important was Clinton, 38; Bush, 54; and Perot, 8. By way of comparison, the issue voters identified most frequently as important to their choice of a candidate was the environment for Governor Clinton (74%), foreign policy for President Bush (87%), and the budget deficit for Mr. Perot (37%).

(*Time,* November 16, 1992, p. 48)

---

of office. Twice Congress had voted to reverse the HHS policy but each time it failed to muster the necessary two-thirds majority needed to override a presidential veto. The Bush administration did not appeal the ruling.

Yet another likelihood under a Clinton presidency is the passage of federal legislation that would restrict the rights of individual states to pass laws criminalizing abortion. Several states have already passed such laws or are in the process of doing so. Following the *Webster* decision, Louisiana passed a law banning all abortions except for those necessary to preserve the life of the pregnant woman or to terminate a pregnancy resulting from rape or incest. Anyone performing an illegal abortion would be imprisoned at hard labor for not less than one nor more than ten years and fined not less than ten thousand nor more than one hundred thousand dollars (Buell, 1991). The law was declared unconstitutional by both the Federal District Court and the Court of Appeals and, on March 8, 1993, the U.S. Supreme Court declined review of those decisions. Guam, a territory, passed an even more draconian law. The only exception would be for an abortion that two physicians certify as necessary to save the life of the pregnant woman or prevent *grave impairment* of her health. Illegal abortion would be a felony. The 130,000 residents of Guam are overwhelmingly Catholic and Archbishop Anthony Apuron threatened to excommunicate any member of the twenty-one-member legislature who voted against the law (Ibid.). On November 30, 1992, the U.S. Supreme Court, by a vote of six to three, refused to hear an appeal from the Ninth U.S. Circuit Court of Appeals in San Francisco which, like the Federal District Court, had declared the Guam law unconstitutional. Chief Justice Rehnquist and Justices White and Scalia dissented. If President Clinton upholds his campaign pledge to appoint only federal judges, including Supreme Court justices, who support abortion rights, any further attempts to overturn *Roe* should fail. In the spring of 1994, Justice Blackmon, perhaps sensing that *Roe* was now secure, announced his resignation from the court.

The Freedom of Choice Act (FOCA) would insure that the right to abortion was not restricted by the various state legislatures. The original House and Senate bills (see Figure 7–2) have been amended to include provisions that would guarantee a state's right to require parental consent or notification (presumably with an alternative for judicial bypass), protect unwilling persons from being forced to participate in the performance of abortions to which they are conscientiously opposed, and reaffirm that states have no obligation (unless required to do so by their own constitutions) to pay for abortions (Koslov, 1992).

Freedom of Choice Act

SECTION 1. SHORT TITLE.
This Act may be cited as the "Freedom of Choice Act of 1991."

SECTION 2. RIGHT TO CHOOSE.

(a)   In General. Except as provided in subsection (b), a State may not restrict the right of a woman to choose to terminate pregnancy

  (1)   before fetal viability; or

  (2)   at any time, if such termination is necessary to protect the life or health of the woman.

(b)   Medically Necessary Requirements. A State may impose requirements medically necessary to protect the life or health of women referred to in subsection (a).

SECTION 3. DEFINITION OF "STATE."
As used in this Act, the term "State" included the District of Columbia, the Commonwealth of Puerto Rico, and each other territory or possession of the United States.

Figure 7–2   One of several bills introduced to create federal law to protect the freedom to choose abortion recognized by the Supreme Court in *Roe* v. *Wade*.

Abortion and Public Health

Although abortion is often seen only as a political issue because of the way that it has influenced and been influenced by the political process, it is equally, if not more so, important to consider abortion—both legal and illegal—as a public health issue. Illegal abortion continues to be the leading cause of maternal mortality (deaths due to the consequences of pregnancy and childbearing) in those countries where there is no legal abortion or where the grounds for legal abortion are confined to the need to preserve the life of the pregnant woman. It was primarily a realization that illegal abortion was the cause of so much maternal morbidity (illness) and mortality that medical and public health organizations such as the American Medical Association, the American College of Obstetricians and Gynecologists, and the American Public Health Association helped lead the fight to liberalize abortion laws in the United States in the 1960s. By contrast, legal abortion has proven to be exceptionally safe, safer than both illegal abortion and carrying a pregnancy to term.

The Safety of Abortion

Maternal mortality in the United States currently stands at approximately 6.6 deaths per 100,000 live births. This, however, is a composite figure that includes all women. Deaths resulting from the complications of pregnancy and childbirth among black women, who are less likely to receive good prenatal care, stand at 14.2 per 100,000 live births. Although the risk to her life is certainly not insignificant, for a woman who desires to carry a pregnancy to term, it is one she freely assumes. A woman unwillingly pregnant, however, might well view this increased risk—aside from whatever else might motivate her—as unacceptable. Abortion-related mortality, by comparison, has fallen from 4.1 per 100,000 in 1973—the year that *Roe* was decided—to 0.7 in 1983 (Centers for Disease Control, 1987).

Even that figure, however, is misleading, because it does not consider the timing of the abortion. The earlier in the pregnancy that the abortion is performed, the safer it is. More than half of all abortions are performed at eight weeks of pregnancy or less. The mortality rate for abortions performed at or before eight weeks of pregnancy is 0.2 per 100,000 (Gold, 1990). This would make abortion at this time thirty-three times safer than childbirth for all women and seventy-one times safer than childbirth for black women. Although the risk rises as gestational age increases, and abortions performed at eleven to twelve weeks of pregnancy are three times more dangerous for the woman than those performed at eight weeks or less, even then the risk of death is only 0.6 per 100,000 procedures.

The Morality of Abortion

Although those who oppose abortion often profess to be concerned about the well-being of the woman seeking to terminate her pregnancy, it is our belief that this is somewhat disingenuous. At the core of the debate is a profound disagreement about the absolute sanctity of human life. A sanctity of life ethic asks only if what is to be aborted is human life and, if the answer to that question is yes, then the value of that human life takes precedence over *any* competing claims that the pregnant woman might have. A "pure" sanctity of life ethic might even be interpreted in such a way as to prohibit abortions even where the woman's life is put at serious risk by the continuation of the pregnancy but, for most who oppose abortion, this would constitute a legitimate exception. Because all human life is sacred, opponents would argue, society has an obligation to protect it, especially the lives of the weakest and most vulnerable. Opponents of abortion would argue that human life begins at conception and that the "unborn child"—a term they use to describe the conceptus throughout pregnancy—is a "person" entitled to protection of the law. Abortion, to many who oppose it, is murder.

For those who support the right of a pregnant woman to decide whether she will have an abortion, the right to life of the conceptus must be weighed against the right of the woman to decide whether she will become a mother. To them, the conceptus—at least during the early stages of development—is a form of human life, nascent human life, quite different from the baby or child that it has the potential to become. They might even point out that fertilized ova (zygotes) are spontaneously aborted (miscarried) in nearly half of all pregnancies (Little, 1988), most at a time when the woman doesn't even realize that she was pregnant. Few would consider those early pregnancy losses the same as the death of a baby. Even with later miscarriages (spontaneous abortions) typically up until the twentieth week of pregnancy, there is neither a registration of birth nor death. Only if the newborn survives the birth process, however momentarily, is there a registration of neonatal birth and death.

As for the argument that abortion is murder, this is an assertion without basis in fact. While one can argue that it should be *treated as though it were* murder, one searches in vain for any evidence that this has ever been such in the history of Anglo-American law. Abortion, even during those periods in our history when it was criminalized, was always distinguished from any form of homicide. The abortionist was prosecuted for the crime of abortion, not homicide, and the penalties, if convicted, were considerably less harsh. And, even if it were to be regarded by some as murder, the penalties proposed are typically directed only at the person performing the abortion, not the pregnant woman. Why is it, if this were murder, that the primary accomplice to the act—the one who brought the "victim" to the scene of the crime—is not punished? When President Bush was asked this question during the 1988 campaign against

Governor Michael Dukakis—"How will you punish the women who have illegal abortions?"—after first saying that he "hadn't thought about it" he replied, the next day through his press secretary, that the women wouldn't be punished because they were victims.

The Supreme Court seemed to be addressing this when they stated in *Roe* that "the unborn have never been considered persons, in the whole sense of the word, under the Constitution." Moreover, the mere fact that so many organizations, both professional and religious, have endorsed the right to choose should at least cause us to critically question the assertion that abortion is murder. Groups such as the American Medical Association, the American Bar Association, the American Public Health Association, and the Religious Coalition for Abortion Rights, an ecumenical group of churches representing many of the major faiths, would be unlikely, simply put, to endorse murder (see Box 7–2).

The AMA Report on Abortion

Although their objection to abortion is a moral one, opponents often use distorted statements about the safety of abortion in an attempt to give greater legitimacy to their objective—making abortion illegal. Because of conflicting claims about the safety of abortion, the American Medical Association, at its 1991 Annual Meeting, asked their Council on Scientific Affairs,

> in order to educate and improve the understanding of the American public, [to] perform an objective study of available data on the morality and morbidity associated with illegally induced abortions prior to the US Supreme Court's *Roe* v. *Wade* decision and compare it with the mortality and morbidity incurred by abortions performed today [and] that the results of this study be published in a manner accessible to legislators and the public by the 1992 Annual Meeting.   (Council on Scientific Affairs, 1992, p. 3232)

The report, published in the December 9, 1992, issue of *JAMA*, concluded that there had been a steady and dramatic decline in the mortality of legal abortion from 1973 (when *Roe* was decided) through 1985 (the most recent year for which data were available). As can be seen from Table 7–1, the mortality rate (deaths per 100,000 procedures) fell from 3.3 in 1973 to 0.4 in 1985. The improved safety resulted both from the increasing experience of physicians performing abortions and the earlier stages of pregnancy during which the abortions were performed.

The number of American women ending their pregnancies through induced abortion has remained relatively stable from 1980 through 1985. A sizable proportion of the increase from 1975 through 1979 is a reflection of the growing numbers of young women entering their reproductive years combined

Box 7–2 *Religious Coalition for Abortion Rights*

The Religious Coalition for Abortion Rights (RCAR) is comprised of thirty-five national Protestant, Jewish, and other denominations and faith groups. They are a nonpartisan organization committed to the preservation of religious liberty as it relates to the issue of reproductive freedom. Although its members hold varying viewpoints as to when abortion is morally justified, it is that plurality of belief that supports their conviction that the abortion decision must remain with the individual, to be made on the basis of conscience and personal religious principles, and free from government interference. Members of RCAR include the following:

American Ethical Union

National Service Conference
American Ethical Union

American Humanist Association

American Jewish Committee

American Jewish Congress

B'nai B'rith Women

Division of Homeland Ministries
Christian Church (Disciples of Christ)

Woman's Caucus
Church of the Brethren

Women in Mission and Ministry
The Episcopal Church

Episcopal Urban Caucus

Episcopal Women's Caucus

Federation of Reconstructionist
Congregations and Havurot

Lutheran Women's Caucus

Northern Province
The Moravian Church in America

NA'AMAT USA

National Council of Jewish Women

National Federation of Temple
Sisterhoods

North American Federation of Temple
Youth

Committee of Women of Color
Presbyterian Church (U.S.A.)

Social Justice and Peacemaking
Ministry Unit
Presbyterian Church (U.S.A.)

Women's Ministry Unit
Presbyterian Church (U.S.A.)

Union of American Hebrew
Congregations

Unitarian Universalist Association

Unitarian Universalist Women's
Federation

Board for Homeland Ministries
United Church of Christ

Coordinating Center for Women
United Church of Christ

Office for Church in Society
United Church of Christ

Board of Church and Society
United Methodist Church

Women's Division
Board of Global Ministries
United Methodist Church

United Synagogue of America

Women's American ORT

Women's League for Conservative
Judaism

Women's Rabbinic Network

YMCA National Board

Table 7–1   *Number of Abortions and Abortion-Related Deaths, United States,*
from 1973 through 1985

Year	No. of Legal Abortions	No. of Deaths from Legal Abortion	No. of Spontaneous, Other, and Unknown Abortion Deaths	No. of Deaths from Legal Abortion per 100,000 Procedures
1973	744,610	25	13	3.3
1974	898,570	26	22	2.9
1975	1,034,170	29	15	2.8
1976	1,179,300	11	14	0.9
1977	1,316,700	17	16	1.3
1978	1,409,600	9	10	0.6
1979	1,497,670	18	9	1.2
1980	1,553,890	9	7	0.6
1981	1,577,340	7	3	0.4
1982	1,573,920	11	6	0.7
1983	1,575,000	10	7	0.6
1984	1,577,180	11	7	0.7
1985	1,588,550	6	7	0.4

Source: Adapted from Council on Scientific Affairs, 1992.

with increasing rates of sexual activity, and pregnancy, at earlier ages. Currently, approximately three of every ten pregnancies are terminated by induced abortion. An estimated 21 percent of American women of childbearing age have had one or more abortions (Henshaw, 1987; Tietze, Forrest, and Henshaw, 1988). Although the extent of illegal abortion was unknown prior to 1973, estimates range from 200,000 to 1,200,00 per year (Tietze and Henshaw, 1986). It was estimated that 5,000 to 23,000 illegal abortions continued to take place each year for several years after *Roe* was decided but they seem to be minimal today (Binkin, Gold, and Cates, 1982). Illegal abortion continues to be a major cause of death among women in Latin America (see Box 7–3). A disturbing number of the deaths reported in recent years resulted from attempts at self-induced abortion, most of them among minority women (Ibid.).

Abortion and Subsequent Childbearing

Opponents of abortion sometimes attempt to frighten women away from abortion by claiming that their ability to become pregnant and/or carry a healthy pregnancy to term at a later date will be impaired by abortion. While it is unclear whether multiple abortions might produce such results—the data being

Box 7–3 *Illegal Abortion and Women's Health in Latin America*

According to a recent study by the Alan Guttmacher Institute, the research arm of the Planned Parenthood Federation of America, clandestine abortion has become one of the leading methods of birth control in Latin America. While illegal in every Latin American country except Cuba, abortion takes the lives of thousands of women every year. Contraceptive methods such as birth control pills or intra-uterine devices are not widely used, mostly because family planning education is not easily available.

In Mexico it is estimated that between 1 and 2 million abortions are performed every year and cause the deaths of 25,000 to 30,000 women. In Brazil, with 150 million people, between 1.4 and 2.4 million abortions are performed each year—a rate that exceeds that of the United States where abortion is legal. Some 400,000 women are admitted each year to hospitals from complications and about half of them die.

(Reprinted by permission of the Associated Press)

insufficient to either prove or disprove such—it is clear that early termination of pregnancy is not a risk to subsequent childbearing.

> The CDC [Centers for Disease Control, an arm of the U. S. Public Health Service] concluded that vacuum aspiration, which accounts for 90% of pregnancy terminations in the United States today, does not pose a measurable risk to a woman's future childbearing capacity. They also concluded that a single induced termination of pregnancy by vacuum aspiration does not increase the risk of subsequent infertility or ectopic pregnancy. Women who experienced a single induced abortion are also at no greater risk of future miscarriage, stillbirth, infant mortality, or congenital anomalies, low-birth-weight infants, or major complications during pregnancy or delivery. (Council on Scientific Affairs, 1992, citations omitted)

The Psychological Effects of Abortion

Although representatives of the Right-to Life movement dispute the claims about the safety of abortion, it should be obvious to most that the data indicating the safety of abortion are overwhelmingly convincing. Perhaps mindful of this, opponents have shifted their focus from the physical effects of abortion, aside from those physical effects on the "unborn child," to the psychological sequelae. Women Exploited By Abortion (WEBA) is a pro-life group ostensibly comprised of women who had abortions, regretted their decision to do so , and who now oppose the availability of abortion. They characterize women having abortions as victims who have been manipulated into ending their pregnancies by societal pressures to abort and a withholding of information about the "true nature of abortion" by providers. They often testify in support of legislative proposals to impose waiting periods on women seeking abortions. They claim that abortion has far-reaching and often unpredictable effects on the psyche of women, effects that can be similar to post-combat psychiatric reactions seen in soldiers. They have even formed groups to provide post-abortion counseling to women experiencing such stress-linked reactions. A leaflet distributed by one anti-abortion group describes the alleged problem as follows:

> Most often a woman will feel the consequences of her decision within days of her abortion. If they don't appear immediately, they will appear as she gets older. Emotional scars include unexplained depression, a loss of the ability to get close to others, repressed emotions, a hardening of the spirit, thwarted maternal instincts (which may lead to child abuse or neglect later in life), and intense feelings of guilt and thoughts of suicide. Don't be fooled—every abortion leaves emotional scars.   (Pro-Life Action Ministries, n.d.)

On July 30, 1987, President Ronald Reagan directed his surgeon general, Dr. C. Everett Koop, to prepare a comprehensive report on the psychological impact of abortion on women, presumably to assist the Reagan administration in its efforts to further restrict the availability of abortion. Koop, who was strongly committed to the pro-life cause in his own right, conducted hearings and directed his staff to search the literature on the mental health impact of abortion. Some eighteen months later, in January 1989, Koop sent a letter to President Reagan stating that "in spite of a diligent review . . . , the scientific studies do not provide conclusive data on the health effects of abortion on women" (Koop, 1989, p. 32).

The following month (February 1989), the American Psychological Association convened a panel of experts to conduct their own review of the scientific literature. Their findings were published in preliminary form in April 1990 in *Science*, the journal of the American Association for the Advancement of Science, and later in *American Psychologist* (1992), the journal of the American Psychological Association. They summarized their report as follows:

> The best available studies on psychological responses following legal, nonrestrictive [excluding ALI-type laws] abortion in the United States suggest that severe negative reactions are infrequent. Some individual women may experience severe distress or psychopathology following abortion, but it is not clear whether these are causally linked to the abortion. As former Surgeon General C. Everett Koop (1989) testified before Congress regarding his review of research on psychological effects of abortion, emotional responses may be overwhelming to a given individual, but the problem of the development of significant psychological problems related to abortion is "minuscule from a public health perspective." Studies that have included comparison groups of women who carry to term suggest that the choice made by women regarding their pregnancy is the one that is most likely to be best for them. Women at higher

risk for relatively more negative responses include those who are terminating pregnancies that are wanted and meaningful, who perceive a lack of support from their partner or parents for the abortion, who are more conflicted and less sure of their decision and coping abilities beforehand, who blame themselves for the pregnancy, and who delay until the second trimester.

For the vast majority of women, an abortion will be followed by a mixture of emotions, with a predominance of positive feelings. This holds immediately after abortion and for some time afterward. We do not know about very-long-term effects. However, the positive picture shown up to eight years after abortion makes it unlikely that more negative responses will emerge later.

The best studies available on psychological responses to unwanted pregnancy terminated by abortion in the United States suggest that severe negative reactions are rare, and they parallel those following other normal stresses. The time of greatest distress is likely to be before the abortion. [There is] persuasive evidence that abortion is usually psychologically benign.   (Adler et al., 1992, citations omitted)

A recent paper published in *JAMA*, based on a similar search of the scientific literature, reported that the incidence of psychiatric illness is considerably lower following abortion than following childbirth and that there is "no evidence" of an abortion trauma syndrome (Stotland, 1992).

Existing Threats to the Safety of Abortion

In spite of compelling data demonstrating the safety of abortion, factors currently existing in our society increase the risk to women seeking to end their pregnancies. Mandatory waiting periods, such as those upheld by the Supreme Court in the *Casey* decision, often result in delay in obtaining the abortion. While a delay of one or two days might produce *only* additional mental anguish, expense, and inconvenience, often the waiting periods (depending upon individual clinic practices) delay the abortion for a week or more, thereby subjecting the woman to higher risks when the procedure is done.

Mandatory parental consent or notification laws, such as those upheld by the Supreme Court in *Hodgson v. Minnesota* and *Akron v. Ohio*, also tend to delay the abortion and increase adolescent health risks. Although such laws tend to have wide public support, even among some of those who support unrestricted abortion rights for adult women, there is no convincing evidence that the benefits outweigh the risks. Although opponents of abortion sometimes argue by analogy that "a child can't even get her ears pierced without parental consent, why should she be able to have an abortion without it?," the analogy is an imperfect one. After all, if she doesn't get her ears pierced now because her parents won't consent, she can always choose to do so when she comes of age and her life will be imperceptibly changed by the postponement.

Moreover, when is the last time you ever heard of someone dying from a "back alley" ear piercing?

Among other threats to the safety and/or availability of abortion is the drop in the number of obstetrics and gynecology residency programs offering training in first trimester abortion. In 1985, half of residencies included abortion training as an option; only 23 percent made it a routine part of training (Council on Scientific Affairs, 1992). There is also a problem with access to abortion services for many women. Although 84 percent of the members of the American College of Obstetricians and Gynecologists agreed that elective abortion should be performed under some circumstances, only 34 percent of them actually provided them. Often, they cite unwillingness to experience harassment, both personally and sometimes of their family, by anti-abortion zealots. As of 1988, 83 percent of the counties in the United States lacked an abortion provider, despite the fact that 31 percent of all women aged fourteen to forty-four lived in these counties (Ibid.).

RU 486: The French Abortion Pill

Technology, which has had a major impact on changing the way in which we die throughout this century, has also had an impact on the abortion controversy. Although the basic research began much earlier, the controversy over medical, as opposed to surgical, abortion began on September 23, 1988, when the French government approved the marketing of an abortion pill—RU 486. Although the drug's scientific name is mifepristone and its brand name is Mifegyne, it is best known as RU 486, the name first assigned to it during its developmental stages at Roussel-Uclaf, a French pharmaceutical company (Klitsch, 1989). On October 26, little more than a month after gaining official marketing approval by the ministry of health, officials at Roussel announced the cancellation of their plans to distribute RU 486 because of the "intense pressure" they had been receiving from anti-abortion groups both in France and in the United States. The threats included not only violence, but the boycotting of Roussel-Uclaf products, along with those of their German parent company, Hoechst AG. Two days later, however, French Health Minister Claude Evin ordered Roussel to resume distribution of RU 486 stating that "from the moment governmental approval for the drug was granted, RU 486 became the moral property of women, not just the property of the drug company" (Ibid., p. 1).

The French government was able to apply this kind of pressure on Roussel because it owned 36 percent of the company's stock and also because of French law which states that the government may revoke a company's patent and award the license to another producer if it refuses to make a licensed drug available (Ibid., 1989). Roussel complied with the health minister's order, and

RU 486 has been used in more than 100,000 abortions since then (Rosenfield, 1992).

RU 486 is designed to be used within two to three weeks of a missed menstrual period. Beyond that point, its effectiveness declines since the high levels of progesterone produced by the developing placenta are thought to overwhelm the antiprogesterone effects of RU 486. The drug is taken orally in a 600-mg dose. Used alone, it is 60 to 85 percent effective in inducing menstruation and terminating early pregnancies; when followed by a prostaglandin administered within thirty-six to forty-eight hours, the effectiveness rate is 95 to 100 percent. Prostaglandin (PG) is a naturally occurring hormone that can induce uterine contractions and can be administered either orally, by injection, or by vaginal suppository. The bleeding that occurs as a result of RU 486/PG use is like that of a heavy menstrual period or an early surgical abortion.

RU 486 is thought to work by blocking or inhibiting progesterone receptor sites in the uterine lining. Progesterone, which is first produced by the corpus luteum formed by the cells lining the follicle which had held the ovum, prevents uterine contractions. RU 486, sometimes referred to as an *antiprogesterone,* has a greater affinity for the progesterone receptor sites than does progesterone itself. Deprived of the influence of progesterone in this way, the uterus begins to contract and menstruation occurs, taking with it the fertilized egg that had implanted in the uterine wall.

As currently used in France, the procedure for obtaining a RU 486/PG abortion involves four office visits:

1. A first visit for diagnosis of pregnancy and deciding to terminate the pregnancy;
2. After one week of reflection (required by law in France) a second visit to receive the RU 486 in pill form;
3. A third visit, made 48 hours later, to receive the prostaglandin; and finally,
4. A fourth visit to verify the completeness of the process. (Baulieu, 1992, p. 154)

Since RU 486 has been shown in clinical studies to cross the placenta, women seeking to abort by this method in France are required to agree to a surgical abortion in the event that RU 486/PG fails. There is no evidence thus far of the effects on the fetus should the woman choose to continue the pregnancy at that point.

Under the sponsorship of the World Health Organization (WHO), RU 486 has been clinically tested in several countries, including Sweden, The Netherlands, Hungary, Great Britain, Italy, India, Chile, Hong Kong, and Singapore. It has also been tested in the United States (Banwell and Paxman, 1992). Dr. Etienne-Emile Baulieu, the French scientist who is recognized as the discoverer of RU 486, has been honored in this country with the Lasker Award, described as "America's most prestigious medical honor." The irony of this is that while he traveled to New York to accept the award, the drug for which he was being honored was not then and is not now available for use here. The reason for this is twofold. First, the Reagan and Bush administrations imposed, through the Food and Drug Administration, an Import Alert, first issued in 1988 and again in 1989, banning the importation of RU 486 for personal use. The Import Alert, however, is more of a symbolic barrier than a real one because it merely bars importation unless there is an IND (Investigational New Drug) permit or a NDA (New Drug Application). The former can be obtained by investigators seeking to conduct clinical trials; the latter by a pharmaceutical company wishing to distribute the drug after submitting evidence proving it to be both safe and effective.

Clinical trials have already been conducted here, but Roussel stopped making RU 486 available because of the tense political climate in the United States. To date, no pharmaceutical companies have expressed interest in applying for a NDA. Leaders in the pro-life movement have threatened a consumer boycott against any company that steps forward to market the drug. Given the fact that most, if not all, of the U.S. pharmaceutical corporations are part of multiproduct conglomerates that market everything from toothpaste to bunion pads, a boycott, if effective, could have a crippling effect on the corporate balance sheet. Pro-choice advocates have threatened a counter-boycott against companies refusing to market the drug and the claims of the opposing forces may have resulted in a status quo standoff. One way of skirting the threat of a proposed boycott would be to import the drug under a specially formed single-product corporation where there would be no susceptibility to a broad boycott. One writer has suggested the name Feminist Pharmaceuticals (Buc, 1992).

Early in 1991, the New Hampshire legislature passed a resolution officially welcoming the testing of RU 486 in its state. This was characterized as a gesture to encourage Roussel to overcome its timidity about exporting the drug to the United States. In July 1992, a pregnant woman, Leona Benten, was detained by customs officials in New York for attempting to bring RU 486 into the country for personal use. Ms. Benten, an unmarried social worker from California, had alerted officials that she would be challenging the import ban so that she and a New York-based pro-choice organization could test the constitutionality of the ban in court.

The case was heard before a Federal District Court Judge who ruled that the FDA had acted illegally because it had not made a public announcement or sought public comment before implementing the ban. This is the same argument that was used to strike the first of the Infant Doe regulations which were discussed in Chapter 6. The FDA was ordered to immediately release the impounded dosage to Ms. Benten. Within hours, however, Department of Justice lawyers had convinced the Second U.S. Court of Appeals in Manhattan to block that ruling. A petition was filed with Supreme Court Justice Clarence

Thomas, who has jurisdiction over emergency appeals from New York, Connecticut, and Vermont, and within a matter of days the full Court had rejected the petition by a seven-to-two vote.

RU 486 is thought to have promise for a variety of uses beyond that of early induction of abortion. It has been shown to prevent ovulation when taken on the days immediately preceding regular ovulation. It has also been tested as a "once-a-month" menses inducer. Women taking the pill at the end of their cycle would begin menstruating without knowing whether a fertilized egg was present in the discharge, perhaps thereby diffusing the issue of abortion for both the individual and society. Baulieu (1989) has referred to RU 486 as a *contragestive*—a combination of contraceptive and antigestational agent— to counter the argument that it is an abortifacient.

RU 486 also has potential use as a means of promoting the expulsion of a fetus that has died *in utero* or as a means of softening the cervix before inducing labor or prior to performing a surgical abortion. It may also be useful in increasing uterine contractions in delayed or prolonged labor. Other reports have suggested usefulness in the treatment of breast cancer, glaucoma, and Cushing's syndrome (Klitsch, 1989). Opponents of abortion are fearful that if the drug is made widely available for these uses it will inevitably wind up being used for pregnancy termination as well.

Of course, one of the major concerns about RU 486, from the pro-life perspective, is that it will dramatically change the nature of the abortion controversy. First, medical abortion could be done as an office, as opposed to a clinic, procedure. If there were no abortion clinics to picket, it would be much more difficult to mount a meaningful protest. Since physicians could offer medical abortion as a routine office procedure, there would be no way of knowing which patients were there to end a pregnancy and which were simply being treated for vaginitis or some other routine gynecological problem.

RU 486/PG would also undoubtedly change the imagery of the abortion debate. The visual impact of fully formed fetuses, whether presented as dismembered remains of dilatation and evacuation (D&E) procedures or intra-amniotic saline, would not reflect the reality of the very early abortions triggered by RU 486/PG. Of course, those images are not accurate representations of the early abortions done by vacuum aspiration either, but "medical" abortion appears to be less dramatic than instrumental abortion.

There are also concerns that RU 486 will make abortion too easy, that it will trivialize it and lead to an increase in the number of women having abortions. "Why bother with contraception," the argument goes, "when you can end a pregnancy quickly and easily at the end of a cycle?" Evidence from the French experience with RU 486 doesn't support this. According to some sources, the French abortion rate has remained the same since RU 486 was introduced and the demand for contraception has increased (James, 1992).

On May 17, 1994, Rousell-Uclaf announced that it would give U.S. patent rights for RU 486 to The Population Council, a nonprofit organization. It was rumored that both Rousell-Uclaf and its parent corporation, the German pharmaceutical firm of Hoechst, hoped to thereby escape from the controversy—accompanied by threats of a product boycott—had they agreed to market RU 486 in the United States. The Population Council was expected to begin large-scale clinical trials of RU 486 during the fall. Depending upon the results of those trials, it is possible that the drug will be approved for distribution by sometime in 1996. (RU-486 is significant, both sides agree, 1994).

Fetal Tissue Transplantation

The controversy over human fetal tissue and biomedical research dates back to 1974, when Congress created the National Commission for the Protection of Human Subjects of Biomedical and Behavioral Research and made the formulation of regulations on fetal research the first item on the agenda (Annas and Sherman, 1989). Although the recommendations of the Commission called for an ethics panel to review funding requests, the administration refused to appoint such a panel and, consequently, until quite recently, no federally funded research on either fetuses or *in vitro* fertilization has been done in this country (Ibid., p. 1079).

The controversy over utilization of tissue obtained from aborted fetal tissue was fueled in 1987 by reports by foreign researchers, first from Mexico and then from Sweden, of attempts to treat patients with Parkinson's disease by transplantation of cells obtained from fetal brain tissue. Parkinson's disease results from a deterioration of neurons in a section of the midbrain called the substantia nigra. The fibers from these cells secrete the chemical dopamine in the forebrain regions that help regulate movement. In the absence of normal dopamine secretion there are a variety of impairments including rigidity, difficulty in initiating movements, and tremor. It is estimated that there are currently half a million to a million people, including one in fifty over age sixty, suffering from the disease (Field, 1991). The cause is unknown and there is presently no cure.

Currently available drugs, although sometimes helpful in controlling the symptoms of the disease, have serious side effects. The Mexican researchers expressed optimism with the results of their efforts (Madrazo et al., 1988), but the Swedes were less so (Lindvall et al., 1988). Researchers have since been able to utilize fetal tissue for implantation in patients with diabetes mellitus (pancreatic cells), apalstic anemia, and leukemia, and fetal tissue may be potentially useful in the treatment of Alzheimer's disease, Huntington's disease, spinal cord injury, and neuroendocrine deficiencies (Consultants of the Advisory Committee to the Director of the National Institutes of Health, 1988).

In October 1987, the National Institutes of Health (NIH) submitted a request to the Assistant Secretary for Health, Robert Windom, for approval to fund the transplantation of fetal tissue into the brain of a patient with Parkinson's disease. Shortly thereafter, in March 1988, Assistant Secretary Windom called for the establishment of a special NIH advisory panel to study the ethical, medical, and legal questions of fetal tissue transplants and to make recommendations to the government. Two months later, ostensibly pending the outcome of the advisory panel deliberations, a moratorium was announced on the use of fetuses from elective abortions in federally funded research.

The Human Tissue Fetal Transplant Research Panel was comprised of twenty-one members. They submitted their report on December 5, 1988 (Consultants of the Advisory Committee to the Director of the National Institutes of Health, 1988); it was unanimously accepted by the twenty-six-member advisory committee to the NIH director approximately a week later. However, on September 2, nearly two weeks before the Panel held its first meeting, the White House prepared an executive order that would bar government scientists from using fetal tissue obtained from induced abortion.

The major issue was the source of the fetal tissue. Tissue obtained from spontaneous abortions (miscarriages) is generally considered unsatisfactory for transplantation because of the high rate of fetal pathology.

> It is now well established that about half of such fetuses aborted in the first trimester and 20 percent of those aborted in the second trimester are chromosomally abnormal. Moreover, a variety of microorganisms have been associated with spontaneous abortions, including cytomegalovirus, herpes simplex types 1 and 2, rubella, toxoplasma, and Ureaplasma urealyticum. It would be indefensible to transplant abnormal or infected fetal tissue that could increase both the risk of a transplant failure and that of infection in the recipient. Tissue from spontaneously aborted fetuses should not be used for transplantation into a human subject.   (Annas and Sherman, 1989, p. 1081, citations omitted)

Moreover, in spontaneous abortions there is an inevitable delay between the death of the fetus and expulsion from the uterus and that unknown interval of anoxia would further diminish the usefulness of the fragile neural cells.

The age of the fetal tissue is also important. Best results are obtained if the fetal tissue is sufficiently differentiated but not yet to the point where the cells have begun to produce the molecules that would be likely to trigger a rejection response in the recipient. The argument in favor of fetal tissue transplantation is a simple one. Abortion is legal and, as many would argue, moral. There are approximately 1.5 million abortions performed each year in the United States, approximately half of them during the first eight weeks of pregnancy—dated from the first day of the last menstrual period (LMP)—which would make the tissue potentially suitable for transplantation (Center for Disease Control, 1991). Women will continue to have abortions regardless of whether the fetal tissue is disposed of with biological waste or if it is, with their consent, used for transplantation. The ban on federal funding for research on fetal tissue transplantation only slows the process of evaluating the usefulness of the procedure and may be denying better health to those whose lives might be dramatically improved by a transplant. To argue that this would legitimize abortion is no more logical than to argue that organ transplants legitimize drunk driving, riding motorcycles without helmets, suicide, or homicide just because donors are often obtained from the ranks of these victims.

Opponents of abortion argue that because abortion is morally wrong it would also be wrong to use tissue thereby obtained regardless of the use to which it might be put. They also claim that proper consent cannot be given because the fetus is unable to do so and the pregnant woman forfeits her moral authority to make such a donation once she decides to have the abortion. Furthermore, they contend that fetal tissue transplantation will increase the number of abortions. This would be likely to occur because:

1. It might cause abortion to become more favorably regarded by the general public, especially sick people who might benefit from the technology and their families, and this would make it more difficult to abolish legal abortion.

2. For some women who are ambivalent about terminating their pregnancies, it might tip the scales toward abortion.

These arguments were rejected by the Panel which concluded, with but two dissenting votes, that it is acceptable public policy to support transplant research using fetal tissue. The Panel issued a series of recommendations designed to help insulate the decision to abort from the utilization of fetal tissue thereby obtained. They recommended that:

1. The decision to terminate a pregnancy and the abortion procedure itself should be kept independent from the retrieval and use of fetal tissue.

2. Payments and other forms of remuneration and compensation associated with the procurement of fetal tissue should be prohibited, except payment for reasonable expenses occasioned by the actual retrieval, storage, preparation, and transportation of the tissues.

3. The decision and consent to abort must precede discussion of the possible use of the fetal tissue and any request for such consent as might be required for that use.

4. The pregnant woman should be prohibited from designating the transplant-recipient of the fetal tissue.

5. Anonymity between donor and recipient should be maintained, so that the donor does not know who will receive the tissue, and the identity of the donor is concealed from the recipient and transplant team.

6. The timing and method of abortion should not be influenced by the potential uses of fetal tissue for transplantation or medical research. (Strong, 1991)

On April 20, 1989, *The New England Journal of Medicine* carried a report by the Stanford University Medical Center Committee on Ethics in which forty-four of the forty-six voting members (there were two abstentions) supported research on aborted fetal tissue. They recommended that:

Human fetal tissue should generally be treated with the respect given cadavers, and its use should be governed by the same legal rules.

Women who undergo induced abortions should not be allowed to benefit directly from the subsequent medical use of the fetal tissue, through payment for it, through reimbursement of expenses connected with the abortion, or in any other manner. The National Organ Transplantation Act should be amended to cover human fetal tissue—whether used for transplantation or any other medical purpose—and to exclude abortion-related expenses from its definition of permissible reimbursement.

Because of the possibility that a conflict of interest might affect their advice to patients about abortion, medical personnel who perform induced abortions should not be allowed any direct benefit from the subsequent use of the fetal tissue.

The proper medical use of fetal tissue from spontaneous abortions and from abortions induced because of risk to the mother's life is ethically unobjectionable.

The use of tissue from fetuses aborted for the specific purpose of donating that tissue seems ethically impermissible. The Uniform Anatomical Gift Act should be amended to bar the donation to specific persons of human fetal tissue from induced abortions.

Subject to these conditions, human fetal tissue can be used ethically for medical research and treatment.   (Greely et al., 1989, p. 1096)

In spite of the recommendations of the government's own advisory panel, in November 1989 the new Assistant Secretary for Health, James Mason, announced that the 1988 moratorium on fetal tissue transplantation would be continued indefinitely. Although there were several attempts by Congress, during the Bush administration, to authorize funding for fetal tissue research, they were repeatedly vetoed by the president and attempts to override the vetoes fell short of the necessary votes.

The future of federally funded fetal tissue research will certainly be on the agenda of the Clinton administration. Shortly after he was elected, representatives of more than forty medical research and health advocacy groups signed a letter to President-elect Clinton asking him to end the moratorium by executive order soon after his inauguration (*The [Toledo] Blade,* November 21, 1992). Moreover, the November 26, 1992, issue of *The New England Journal of Medicine*, widely regarded as one of the most prestigious medical journals in the world, carried three papers indicative of successful treatment of Parkinson's disease with transplanted fetal tissue and an editorial calling for a lifting of the federal funding ban. Drs. Jerome Kassirer and Marcia Angel, editor-in-chief and executive editor respectively, stated that "it appears that there are indeed important benefits to be gained by continuing this work."

On January 22, 1993, two days after taking the oath of office as the forty-third president of the United States, Bill Clinton, by executive order, signaled the reversal of the anti-abortion policies of his predecessors, Ronald Reagan and George Bush. As he had promised during his campaign for the presidency, he lifted the ban on fetal tissue transplantation research, ordered a lifting of the so-called "gag rule" that restricted abortion counseling in federally funded birth control programs, eliminated the restrictions that had banned abortions at U.S. military hospitals overseas, if they are paid for privately, and began the process that could result in the importation of RU 486 for personal use, if the Food and Drug Administration determines that there is no justification for the prohibition. He also reversed a 1984 executive order of the Reagan administration, known as the "Mexico City policy," that prevented the United States from providing aid to foreign organizations that perform or promote abortion as part of their population control efforts. These actions, hardly by coincidence, took place on the twentieth anniversary of the U.S. Supreme Court's decision in *Roe v. Wade* (*The [Toledo] Blade,* January 23, 1993).

The Future of Abortion

While trying to predict the future is always risky business, as both weather forecasters and economists can attest, there are some trends concerning abortion that allow us to offer some rather cautious predictions about where abortion is likely to be as we move into the twenty-first century. Of course, the results of the presidential election of 1992 have somewhat bolstered our confidence in such an enterprise. It is likely that the Clinton administration will reverse the anti-abortion policies of the previous twelve years and restore some balance to a federal judiciary, including the Supreme Court, which had tilted strongly against abortion rights. It is also likely that RU 486 or some other abortifacient drug will be made available to American women and that, as we discussed earlier, will likely alter the nature of the abortion debate as well as abortion practices.

The trend toward legalized abortion is worldwide, especially in democratic countries, and it is hard to imagine the United States—the world's leading democracy—moving against that trend. With few exceptions such as Ireland, which will be discussed below, the only countries that restrict the exercise of choice are those inordinately influenced by the Church or by repressive governments or both. The experience in Communist Romania provides an example of what can happen when reproduction becomes an instrument of government.

The Romanian Experience

The October 1992 issue of the *American Journal of Public Health* carried a report by European scientists who analyzed abortion in Romania before, during, and after the reign of President Nicolae Ceaucescu, who installed a repressive government in 1966. The Ceaucescu regime introduced extreme pronatalist policies which included a ban on both contraception and abortion.

> Mandatory pelvic examinations at places of employment were imposed on women of reproductive age. Informers for the security police were stationed in maternity hospitals. Doctors could be prosecuted for performing unauthorized abortions, and nurses were to make unannounced supervisory visits to new mothers to determine whether they were taking proper care of their infants.   (Stephenson et al., 1992, p. 1328)

Prior to 1966, Romanian women—like their neighbors in other Eastern European countries—had access to safe abortion through the country's health care system. The harsh pronatalist policies resulted in the highest maternal mortality rate in Europe and in thousands of unwanted children in institutions. Although the policies were intended to increase the reproduction rate and the population of Romania, they failed to achieve that goal. Although there was a brief rise, the birth rate actually fell and continued to do so as Romanian women switched from legal to illegal abortion.

> Before the 1966 law went into effect, the Romanian maternal mortality rate was similar to those of other Eastern European countries [10 to 15 per 100,000 live births]. Afterward, abortion-related maternal mortality increased to a level 10 times that of any other European country. For the decade 1980 to 1989, the average Romanian maternal mortality rate was 150 maternal deaths per 100,000 live births. Many women obtained abortion illegally, and every year approximately 500 otherwise-healthy women of childbearing age died from postabortion hemorrhage, sepsis, abdominal trauma, and poisoning.   (Ibid., p. 1329, citations omitted)

Those women with unwanted pregnancies who were forced to carry their pregnancies to term often institutionalized their children. Although the number of children in state-run orphanages and other institutions before the overthrow of the government in the December 1989 revolution is unknown, shortly after the revolution approximately 150,000 to 200,000 children were in such institutions.

The newly installed democratic government of Romania was quick to rescind the 1966 law. The maternal morality rate fell by 50 percent in the first year under the new policy. Moreover, new admissions to children's institutions have decreased despite continuation of severe economic conditions.

Reflecting on the twenty-three-year experiment with criminalization of abortion—not unlike the American experience with alcohol prohibition—Stephenson and her colleagues concluded that it had

> resulted in over 10,000 deaths of women from unsafe abortion. The pronatalist policy as a whole resulted in the untoward institutionalization of thousands of children and in an elevated rate of infant deaths. In effect, it also turned otherwise-law-abiding women and their partners into criminals; women learned to fear the government and its representatives. Doctors and other health care providers were victims as well because they were forced to carry out the policies of the state. Working today to improve and strengthen women's health services, Romanian doctors report that many women remain fearful of contact with the health care system.   (Ibid., pp. 1329–1330)

Abortion in Ireland

Yet another example of the problems created by highly restrictive abortion laws can be found in the Republic of Ireland. Although the United Kingdom liberalized its abortion laws in 1967, in politically divided Ireland only women from Northern Ireland, which is controlled by Britain, have access to abortion, although they must travel to England to exercise that right. In the south, The Republic of Ireland, there is a ban on abortion. The Irish abortion law is the most restrictive one in all of Europe.

Early in February 1992, Ireland's attorney general sought and obtained an injunction to prevent a fourteen-year-old girl from traveling to London for an abortion or, more accurately, to punish her for having an abortion in England upon her return to Ireland. The young woman claimed, through her parents, that she had been impregnated after being raped by the father of one of her friends. She had gone to London with her parents to have an abortion and, like the approximately 5,000 Irish women who quietly do so each year, it would have been uneventful had it not been for a conversation between her father and police officials in Ireland. Her father questioned officials as to whether it would be necessary to preserve fetal cell samples for proof of identity in the prosecution of the alleged rapist. It was at that point that the attorney general was notified.

Later that same month, the Irish Supreme Court overturned the injunction. The Court held that the girl should be permitted to have the abortion because she had threatened suicide and under the Irish Constitution there is a provision for an "equal right to life of the mother."

In November, the issue of abortion was put to the Irish voters in the form of three questions. First, should it be legal to distribute information about abortion? Second, should it be legal for Irish women to travel to other countries to have an abortion? And third, should it be legal for Irish physicians to perform abortions to save women's lives?

The referendum was opposed by both sides in the abortion debate. Pro-life forces objected because it was seen as too lenient. Pro-choice advocates argued that it was too restrictive. There was speculation that all three issues would pass after the Catholic Bishop's Conference announced that voters could vote yes or no in good conscience. However, shortly before the vote, several of the bishops, including the Archbishop of Dublin, broke with the hierarchy and urged a no vote. They were joined by Mother Theresa of Calcutta, who was educated in Ireland. By approximately three-to-two majorities, the Irish voters removed a ban on the distribution of information about abortion and made it legal for women to travel to other countries to obtain abortions. Both of these had been advocated by "European leaders" who sought to convince Irish officials that the country should comply with European Community standards of free travel and access to information. By a two-to-one majority, however, they rejected a proposal that would have allowed Irish physicians to perform abortions to save women's lives (Francome, 1992).

Looking for the Middle Ground

The difficulty with abortion is that there seems to be no acceptable middle ground when it comes to unwanted pregnancy. Although it has been twenty years since the Supreme Court decision in *Roe* v. *Wade*, the controversy continues to rage. One thing that both sides should, but don't seem to be able to, agree on is the need to do a much better job in preventing unwanted pregnancy. Even here there is a controversy; a debate within a debate as it were. Pro-life advocates tend to argue that the only acceptable way of preventing pregnancy is through promoting abstinence for the unmarried. Although it is questionable whether such a policy would work among the unmarried, it fails to take into consideration the incidence of unwanted pregnancy within marriage, even when couples have been attempting to prevent conception. Pro-choice proponents are also concerned about reducing unwanted pregnancy but they would do so through better and more readily available contraceptives and better sex education. Neither of these approaches is widely supported in the pro-life movement.

Abortion has been with us since the beginning of recorded history. It has been debated in America for more than 150 years, intensely so for the last 25 of those. Perhaps the time has finally come when we will just have to learn to live in acceptance of our disagreement. That, after all, is what living in a pluralistic society is supposed to be about. And, finally, perhaps we can all work together toward creating a society in which abortion will be seen as less necessary, rather than less accessible.

Summary

Abortion is yet another of those topics that seem to be locked in interminable turmoil. Although references to the practice may be found in writings dating back thousands of years, the American abortion debate can be traced to the events of the nineteenth century which led to the passage of the first state laws making abortion a criminal offense. The intensity of the debate picked up considerably with the state-by-state legalization of abortion that began in the mid-1960s and was sparked even futher by the U.S. Supreme Court's decision in *Roe* v. *Wade* in 1973.

While the nineteenth-century drive to criminalize abortion was led by many in the mainstream of American medicine, today—for a variety of reasons described in the text—the medical profession is one of the strongest proponents of legalization. There seems to be a growing realization that modern medicine has succeeded in making induced abortion, performed early in pregnancy, safer than the alternative of carrying pregnancy to term. Although the Rehnquist court, during the presidencies of Ronald Reagan and George Bush, seemed willing to support a variety of restrictions on abortion such as restrictions on federal and state funding and parental notification and/or consent laws, they have stopped short (but just barely) of overturning *Roe*. The *Webster* and *Casey* cases were the high-water marks for the antiabortion voices on the Court. With the resignation of one of the original *Roe* dissenters and one of its strongest critics, Justice Byron White, President Clinton had the opportunity to appoint Justice Ruth Bader Ginsburg, thought to be a strong supporter of *Roe*, to the Court. Under the Court as it is presently constituted, any challenge to overturn *Roe* would seem destined to fail.

In 1992 Bill Clinton became the first pro-choice president in more than a decade. Shortly after his inauguration, he issued executive orders lifting the moratorium on federally funded research on transplantation of fetal tissue, the import ban on the abortifacient drug RU 486, and the restrictions on abortion counseling in federally funded birth control projects. The Clinton administration has also supported passage of legislation that would make the right to abortion federal law (Freedom of Choice Act) and making blockage of the entrance to abortion clinics a federal offense. The latter, known as the Freedom of Access to Clinic Entrances Act (FACE), was passed by Congress late in 1993. It was signed into law by the president on May 26, 1994 (*The [Toledo] Blade,* May 27, 1994).

Since abortion has been widely available in the United States for more than twenty years, there are considerable data supporting its safety when performed under qualified medical supervision. There are also examples from parts of the world where abortion is still illegal, or has been until very recently, of the health consequences to women of illegal abortion. Because of deeply held convictions about the morality of induced abortion, like the parallel controversies over removing life support (especially feeding tubes) from the permanently unconscious, physician assistance in dying, and withholding treatment from severely anomalous newborns, the abortion debate is likely to be with us for some time to come.

Study Questions

1. What was the distinction that was usually made between legal and illegal abortion in the laws regulating abortion that were passed during the early part of the nineteenth century in America?

2. What were some of the reasons underlying the criminalization of abortion that took place during the middle of the nineteenth century and eventually resulted in abortion becoming illegal, unless necessary to save the life of the pregnant woman, throughout the United States?

3. What were the provisions of the Model Abortion Law proposed by the American Law Institute in 1962?

4. What were some of the factors underlying the shift in public opinion about abortion that took place during the middle of the twentieth century which resulted in the legalization of abortion?

5. How did the U.S. Supreme Court, in *Roe* v. *Wade,* attempt to strike a balance between the right of a pregnant woman to have an abortion and the right of the state to protect the life of the conceptus?

6. What restrictions on abortion performed on a minor have the Supreme Court been willing to uphold that it has not been willing to uphold as applied to non-minors?

7. What is meant by the term *judicial bypass* and how does it work?

8. In the *Casey* decision, the U.S. Supreme Court abandoned the trimester framework that had been enunciated in *Roe.* How did the trimester framework work and what is the new "guideline" under *Casey*?

9. How safe is early induced abortion compared to childbirth?

10. What arguments can be made that induced abortion is immoral? That it is moral?

11. What conclusions about the safety of induced abortion were reached by the Council on Scientific Affairs of the American Medical Association in its 1992 report?

12. What is the evidence for and against the existence of adverse psychological effects, the so-called abortion trauma syndrome, resulting from induced abortion?

13. What is RU 486 and how does it work?

14. Why has the issue of transplantation of fetal tissue become so vigorously debated? What effect is this likely to have on the number of women choosing to end their pregnancies with induced abortion?

References

Adler, N. E., H. P. David, B. N. Major, S. H. Roth, N. F. Russo, and G. E. Wyatt. (1990). Psychological responses after abortion. *Science,* 248:41–44.

___ and H. P. David, B. N. Major, S. H. Roth, N. F. Fusso, and G. E. Wyatt. (1992). Psychological factors in abortion: A review. *American Psychologist,* 47(10):1194–1204.

Akron Center for Reproductive Health v. *Ohio,* 497 U.S. 502 (1990).

Annas, G. J., and S. Elias. (1989). The politics of transplantation of human fetal tissue. *NEJM,* 320:1079–1082.

Banwell, S. S., and J. M. Paxman. (1992) The search for meaning: RU 486 and the law of abortion. *American Journal of Public Health,* 82(10):1399–1406.

Baulieu, E. (1989). Contragestion and other clinical applications of RU 486, an antiproges-terone at the receptor. *Science,* 245:1351–1357.

___. (1992). Updating RU 486 development. *Law, Medicine & Health Care,* 20(3):154–156.

Botched, Illegal Abortions Take Toll in Latin America. (1992). *The [Toledo] Blade,* November 23 at 1.

Brophy v. *New England Sinai Hospital, Inc.,* 398 Mass. 417, 497 NE 2d 626 (1986).

Buc, N. L. (1992). RU 486, the FDA and Free Enterprise. *Law, Medicine & Health Care,* 20(3):224–225.

Buell, S. W. (1991). Criminal abortion revisited. *New York University Law Review,* 66(6):1774–1831.

Callahan, D. (1970). *Abortion: Law, Choice & Morality.* New York: Macmillan.

Centers for Disease Control. (1987). *Morbidity and Mortality Weekly Report.* CDC *Surveillance Summaries,* 36:1SS.

___. (1991). *Abortion Surveillance, United States, 1988.* CDC Surveillance Summaries. Atlanta: Author.

City of Akron v. *Akron Center for Reproductive Health,* 462 U.S. 416 (1983).

Clinton lifts abortion bans. (1993). *The [Toledo] Blade,* January 23.

Consultants of the Advisory Committee to the Director of the National Institutes of Health. (1988). *Report of the Human Fetal Tissue Transplantation Research Panel.* Bethesda, MD: National Institutes of Health.

Council on Scientific Affairs. (1992). Induced termination of pregnancy before and after *Roe* v. *Wade*: Trends in the mortality and morbidity of women. *JAMA,* 268(22):3231–3239.

Eisenstadt v. *Baird,* 405 U.S. 438 (1972).

Election '92 (1992). *Time,* November 16.

Field, R. (1991). Dr. Parkinson's cruel disease. *American Health,* 10(7):54–58.

Francome, C. (1992). Irish women who seek abortions in England. *Family Planning Perspectives,* 24(6):265–268.

Greely, H. T., T. Hamm, R. Johnson et al. (1989). Special report: The ethical use of human fetal tissue in medicine. *NEJM,* 320:1093–1096.

Griswold v. *Connecticut,* 381 U.S. 479 (1965).

Henshaw, S. K. (1987). Characteristics of U.S. women having abortions, 1982–1983. In Stanley K. Henshaw and J. Van Vort (Eds.), *Abortion Services in the United States, Each State and Metropolitan Area, 1984–1985.* New York: Alan Guttmacher Institute.

Hodgson v. *Minnesota,* 497 U.S. 417 (1990).

James, B. (1993). The pill of choice. *Lear's* (January): 57–59+.

Klitsch, M. (1989). *RU 486: The Science and the Politics.* New York: Alan Guttmacher Institute.

Koop, C. E. (1989). A measured response: Koop on abortion. *Family Planning Perspectives,* 21(1):31–32.

Koslov, T. I. (1992). Abortion on the Supreme Court agenda: *Planned Parenthood* vs. *Casey* and its possible consequences. *Law, Medicine & Health Care,* 20(3):243–248.

Lader, L. (1966). *Abortion.* Boston: Beacon Press.

Lindvall, O., S. Rehncrona, B. Gustavii, et al. (1988). Fetal dopamine-rich mesencephalic grafts in Parkinson's disease. *Lancet,* 2:1483–1484.

Little, A. B. (1988). There's many a slip 'twixt implantation and the crib. *NEJM,* 319(4): 241–242.

Loving v. *Virginia,* 388 U.S. 1 (1967).

Madrazo, I., V. Leon, C. Torres, et al. (1988). Transplantation of fetal substantia nigra and adrenal medula to the caudate nucleus in two patients with Parkinson's disease. *NEJM,* 318:51.

Means, C. C. (1968). The law of New York concerning abortion and the status of the fetus, 1664–1968: A case of cessation of constitutionality. *New York Law Forum,* 14(3):411–515.

Medical groups urge Clinton to end ban. (1992). *The [Toledo] Blade,* November 21.

Meyer v. *Nebraska,* 262 U.S. 390 (1923).

Mohr, J. C. (1978). *Abortion in America: The Origins and Evolution of National Policy.* New York: Oxford University Press.

New law shields abortion access. *The [Toledo] Blade,* May 27, 1994.

Noonan, J. T., Jr. (Ed.). (1970). *The Morality of Abortion: Legal and Historical Perspectives.* Cambridge, MA: Harvard University Press.

___. (1979). *A Private Choice: Abortion in America in the Seventies.* New York: The Free Press.

People v. *Belous,* 71 Cal. 2d 954, 458 P. 2d 194 (1969).

Petchesky, R. P. (1984). *Abortion and Woman's Choice.* Boston: Northeastern University Press.

Pierce v. *Society of Sisters,* 268 U.S. 510 (1925).

Pro-Life Action Ministries. (n.d.). *What They Won't Tell You at the Abortion Clinic.* St. Paul, MN (leaflet).

Reagan, R. W. (1984). *Abortion and the Conscience of the Nation.* Nashville: Thomas Nelson Publishers.

Roe v. *Wade,* 410 U.S. 173 (1973).

Rosenfield, A. (1992). RU 486. *AJPH,* 82(10):1325–1326.

Rust v. *Sullivan,* 59 Law Week 4451 (1991).

RU 486 significant, both sides agree. (1994). *The [Toledo] Blade,* May 4.

Skinner v. *Oklahoma,* 316 U.S. 535 (1942).

Stephenson, P., M. Wagner, M. Barer, and F. Serbanescu. (1992). Community: The public health consequences of restricted induced abortion—Lessons from Romania. *American Journal of Public Health,* 82(10): 1328–1331.

Stotland, N. L. (1992). The myth of the abortion trauma syndrome. *JAMA,* 268(15): 2078–2079.

Strong, C. (1991). Fetal tissue transplantation: Can it be morally insulated from abortion? *Journal of Medical Ethics,* 17:70–76.

Thornburgh v. *American College of Obstetricians and Gynecologists,* 476 U.S. 747 (1986).

Tietze, C., and S. K. Henshaw. (1986). *Induced Abortion: A World Review 1986.* Washington, D. C.: The Alan Guttmacher Institute.

___ J. D. Forrest, and S. K. Henshaw. (1988). United States of America. In P. Sachdev (Ed.), *International Handbook on Abortion* (pp. 474–483). Westport, CT: Greenwood.

Tribe, L. H. (1990). *Abortion: The Clash of Absolutes.* New York: W. W. Norton.

Webster v. *Reproductive Health Services,* 492 U.S. 490 (1989), 1989 LEXIS 3290.

CHAPTER 8

The Dying Patient

For my own personal ease I should have died years ago, but though these years have been spent in excruciating pain, I am pleased that I have lived them.

Benjamin Franklin

To Elisabeth Kubler-Ross whose research took the pennies off the eyes of the living so they could see the dying.

Robert Kavanaugh, *Facing Death*

A hospital would insist on a strict diet for a dying diabetic patient. We serve chocolate cake.

Madeline Duffield, Director of Nursing, St. Christopher's Hospice, London

The Individual Experience of Dying

What is it like to receive a terminal diagnosis, to experience the effects of an often progressive, disabling terminal disease, to eventually undergo the dying process? For those of us in the midst of living, answering such questions is based on suppositions about how we would feel and react *if* we were going to die. In grappling with such questions, the actuality of our own ultimate death seems itself to become conjecture or, at least, a difficult concept to grasp. Intellectually, we all know that we are going to die someday; however, some-day seems far in the future. What is it like to be informed that you are going to die soon, to be thrown into the midst of dying while in the midst of living?

For many, learning about the individual experience of dying will become more than a hypothetical, academic exercise. Unless death is sudden and unexpected, as may occur with an accident, homicide, or massive heart attack, it will become a reality. Given the chronic conditions related to most adult mortality, it is uncommon for death to occur completely unanticipated. It has been speculated that anywhere between 100,000 and 1.2 million people in the United States annually become aware of and are forced to cope with their own impending death. It is further speculated that almost half of these persons live with such knowledge for at least three months (Schulz and Schlarb, 1988).

Dying individuals must cope with numerous sources of stress. They deal with various physical, psychological, and social stressors that accompany terminal illness. These might include an array of burdensome physical symptoms and possible progressive disability, psychological distress, an alteration of social roles, and possible draining of the family's financial resources. Additionally, if they are aware of the terminal nature of their condition, they must deal with the psychological stress of anticipating their own dying.

How long must these stressors be endured? What is their magnitude? What kind of care do the dying require? How many know that they are dying? How do they cope? These are among the many questions concerning the circumstances surrounding dying about which we need to learn more.

The last twenty-five years have marked a revolution in the study of death and dying. In spite of the dramatic increase in published research on the topic, serious knowledge gaps remain regarding the experiences of dying patients. In reviewing the past two decades of research, Schulz and Schlarb (1988) found it

> remarkable that there exists so little generalizable factual information about dying persons and their experiences before death, especially in light of the relatively large literature focused on the relatives of the dying patient. For some reason, the dying person has been left out. The data that do exist are . . . flawed, limited in scope, or based on small and non-representative samples. (p. 301)

Dying experiences may vary depending on the individual—his or her cultural background, religion, age, education, socioeconomic status—and the nature of the terminal condition. For example, the experience of dying with multiple sclerosis may be different from that of dying with colon cancer or AIDS. By studying terminal conditions in association with the kinds of questions included in Box 8–1, we may learn more about the range of possible problems encountered by dying patients and appropriate interventions in an attempt to ease their physical and emotional burdens as much as possible.

Much of the research on the experience of dying to date has centered on the psychosocial perspective. Indeed, it has focused almost exclusively on the emotional responses of dying patients. However, little is known about the

Box **8–1**   *Learning More About the Circumstances Surrounding Death*

Learning more about the following in association with various terminal conditions may help us to better understand and assist dying persons. With regard to the dying and specific terminal conditions:

- What is the length of illness prior to death?
- What is the extent of patient disability?
- How much pain is encountered?
- What is the magnitude of psychological distress encountered?
- What coping strategies are employed?
- What is the amount and kind of care needed?
- What is the amount and kind of care received?
- How many patients are aware they are dying?

Source: Adapted from R. Schulz, and J. Schlarb. (1988). Two decades of research on dying: What do we know about the patient? *Omega*, 18:299–317.

kinds of factors determining their responses or the environments in which they die.

Existing research has also centered on younger to middle-aged persons whose normal life expectancy has been cut short, often by cancer. Their situation is not necessarily representative of the majority of deaths in the United States. Most people in this country die during old age. Many of them have endured a long period of progressive physical decline and have suffered various social losses. Death may have different connotations for such individuals. However, given society's negative stereotyped view of the elderly, we must caution against a hastily constructed, age-based reaction to death. The topic needs further study. We have much to learn about the older adult's fears and attitudes toward death, the stress that facing death produces in the later years, and coping strategies that are employed among this group. As Benjamin Franklin (who died in his eighties after a prolonged period of physical discomfort) reminded us, he was glad that death had not come sooner. In our youth-oriented society, we may dismiss death-related concerns for older adults because we think they should be ready to die!

This chapter focuses on selected research on adult dying patients beginning with that of Elisabeth Kubler-Ross whose stage theory of dying has had a profound impact. The contributions of her work, along with criticisms of it, will be examined. Because of the important influences of their developmental level and maturational experiences, material on dying children is presented elsewhere.

The Stages of Dying

The best known conceptualization of the dying process was presented by Elisabeth Kubler-Ross (1969) in her landmark book *On Death and Dying*. Based on interviews with over 200 terminally ill patients, she asserted that five stages or emotional reactions mark the psychological response to dying. They are denial, anger, bargaining, depression, and acceptance.

The first stage, denial, is a common initial reaction to a terminal diagnosis. "No, not me. It can't be true" may be seen as a healthy coping mechanism to buffer the shock of such news. The denial stage is almost always short. However, a long and expensive ritual was used by the following patient in order to support her denial.

> She was convinced that the x-rays were "mixed up." She asked for reassurance that her pathology report could not possibly be back so soon and that another patient's report must be marked with her name. When none of this could be confirmed, she quickly asked to leave the hospital, looking for another physician in the vain hope "to get a better explanation for my troubles. . . ." She asked for examination and re-examination, partially knowing that the original diagnosis was correct, but also seeking further evaluations in the hope that the first conclusion was indeed in error.   (Kubler-Ross, 1969, p. 38)

When denial can no longer be maintained, it is often replaced by feelings of anger, rage, envy, and resentment. "Why me?" becomes the next question. Anger may be displaced and projected on anyone and everyone with whom the patient comes in contact. Although the anger of a terminally ill person should be expected, this stage is perhaps the most difficult for medical staff and family members.

The third stage, bargaining, is an attempt on the patient's part to postpone the inevitable. As indicated by Kubler-Ross, the terminal patient uses the same maneuvers as a child and asks to be "rewarded for good behavior." Bargaining may occur between the patient and health care workers, family, or friends. Most bargains are secretly made with God. They almost always include wishes for the removal of pain and discomfort and for life extension. Kubler-Ross offers the case of a woman who was upset at the prospect of being unable to attend her son's wedding because of her encumbering symptoms. With great effort on her part, she learned self-hypnosis and was able to remain comfortable for several hours at a time.

> She had made all sorts of promises, if she could only live long enough to at-
> tend this marriage. The day preceding the wedding she left the hospital as an
> elegant lady. Nobody would have believed her real condition. She was "the
> happiest person in the whole world" and looked radiant.   (Kubler-Ross, 1969,
> p. 83)

This same woman returned to the hospital and remarked, "Now don't forget, I have another son."

The fourth stage, depression, is characterized by overwhelming feelings of loss. Under such circumstances, it is not a sign of a "psychiatric disorder," but a normal, common, and understandable reaction. Two types of depression are characteristic of this stage. The first, reactive depression, results from the various losses that may accompany serious illness and dying. For example, patients may mourn the loss of an amputated limb or their hair to radiation therapy. Loss of vigor, social role, independence, and ability to engage in former activities are among the numerous other forfeitures that may induce great sadness. Preparatory depression, on the other hand, is a grieving over one's own impending death.

With time, Kubler-Ross believes, the patient may reach the stage of acceptance. It should not be mistaken for happiness or capitulation. It is a stage almost void of feelings. According to Kubler-Ross (1969, pp. 112–113), this is often a time when the dying individual will "contemplate his coming end with a certain degree of quiet expectation." It is as if the struggle is ended and the individual has arrived at "the final rest before the long journey."

These emotional reactions may also be present in the loved ones of the dying. They, too, may experience denial, anger, bargaining, depression, and acceptance while coming to terms with the devastating news. That the timing of these reactions among the various parties may not coincide is another sensitive point. For instance, a dying woman may have come to accept her fate while her husband denies the seriousness of her illness.

Advocates and Critics of Kubler-Ross

Although not empirically tested, Kubler-Ross's stage theory of dying has been openly embraced by many over the years. General readers, high school and college students, doctors and nurses, clergy, family and friends of dying persons, and terminally ill patients themselves are among those who have recited the stages from denial to acceptance. Many have uncritically accepted and freely applied them.

Several years ago, when the stages had become so much a part of the popular vocabulary of death, Kalish (1976) contended that they were in danger of becoming self-fulfilling prophecies. He observed that some health caretakers encouraged, even manipulated, their dying patients through Kubler-Ross's stages. In turn, some patients occasionally became concerned if they were not progressing adequately.

Another author noted:

> It has not been uncommon, in my experience, to hear nurses and doctors, for instance, complain that "this patient will be dying soon and he simply hasn't accepted what is happening to him. Why does he seem to be stuck in denial?" The implication of their complaint is, of course, that one should move "through" denial to some other mode of coping.   (Rainey, 1988, p. 140)

Such stories underscore how often others have interpreted the stages to be sequentially ordered or have affixed a value to them, which was not Kubler-Ross's intent. She cautioned that people do not march through them like robots in the order given. They may bounce back and forth in their emotional reactions or remain in one stage. She did not imply that they were to be rushed through them in any particular order as some have attempted to do. She also indicated that for some it may be inappropriate to die in a stage of acceptance. If one had lived life facing adversity head-on with anger and struggle, then to die with dignity might be to die in a stage of anger.

Although the stage-based model still lingers on for some, many in teaching and clinical practice have moved away from this approach (Corr, 1992, 1993). They fear that it risks stereotyping coping behavior and serves as an obstacle to individualization. The totality of a person's life can be ignored in strict adherence to the stages of dying. The effects of age, gender, religion, ethnic background, and life experience have not been systematically studied as they apply to Kubler-Ross's stage theory.

As Kastenbaum (1991, p. 102) indicated, "We take the entire course of our lives with us into the final months and weeks." He is among many who have written on the inadequacies of the Kubler-Ross model (Corr, 1992; Pattison, 1978; Schulz and Aderman, 1974; Shneidman, 1973, 1980; Weisman, 1972). Weisman (1992) credits him with having put the model "to rest" (see Box 8–2). However, in his evaluation of the Kubler-Ross sequence, Kastenbaum reminds us that some of the practical problems associated with it are attributed to its "hasty and uncritical application by others" (Kastenbaum, 1991, p. 103).

Despite its limitations, Kubler-Ross's work has been of tremendous value in sensitizing us to the needs and rights of the dying (see Box 8–3). It has provided a foundation for studying coping strategies of terminally ill persons. While the notion of stages has been rejected, her observation that people facing death undergo a variety of emotional responses that ebb and flow has not.

Box 8–2   *Shortcomings of the Applications of the Kubler-Ross Stage Theory*

1. *The existence of stages has not been established.* There is nothing to demonstrate that "stages" exist, are five in number, or are those designated. Dying people exhibit "response sets" or moods, but these are not stages or sequenced. Neither are they are limited to the five identified in the model.

2. *There is no evidence that people pass from Stage 1 through Stage 5.* Despite a lack of data, the theory won acceptance. Perhaps its premature approval reflected our social and emotional need to fill the void surrounding information on coping with dying.

3. *The methodology employed in its establishment is narrow and limited.* The psychiatric interview was conducted and analyzed by one person. Furthermore, what patients do and say in the presence of an interviewing psychiatrist is a small and select sample of their behavior.

4. *What was described has become prescribed.* The concept of emotional sets presented in a stage framework has led to its misuse. In standardizing an approach to dealing with the dying person, some caregivers have failed to distinguish between what can happen and what should happen.

5. *The totality of the person is ignored.* An assumed universality of the stages may reduce the dying person to a specimen moving along a predetermined path.

6. *The influence of environmental dynamics on the patient's behavior is neglected.* Patient denial may sometimes reflect the cure orientation of medicine rather than the patient's personality or universality of Stage 1. The process of dying may be strongly influenced by the behavior and attitudes of those in one's social setting.

Source: Adapted from R. Kastenbaum, (1991). *Death, Society, and Human Experience.* New York: Merrill, pp. 101–103.

Many others have lent their clinical experience and research expertise to this perception.

Dying persons are often denied the opportunity to ventilate these emotions, perhaps because they fear burdening others or because the medical or home environment does not encourage or tolerate such open expression. Kubler-Ross implored us to allow the dying to express their emotions. Likewise, she cautioned that we not label or punish them for doing so. For example, those whose words or behaviors seem to deny the diagnosis should not be presumed weak. As we have seen, denial is often a short-lasting initial reaction to buffer the shock of the fatal diagnosis. As we will see later in this chap-

Box 8–3   The Stage-Based Model: Continuing to Learn from Kubler-Ross's Work

C. A. Corr recognizes the tremendous contributions Elisabeth Kubler-Ross has made to better understanding coping mechanisms of dying patients and their families. Although Herman Feifel's (1959) work in the area precedes hers by a decade, she is the recognized pioneer in leading the effort to investigate coping with dying. Corr cautions that despite the impact of her work, it does not represent the first or last word in discussions of the topic. He emphasizes that we cannot allow the learning process to stop with the publication in 1969 of her classic book *On Death and Dying.*

> Although we all benefited from the work of Kubler-Ross, we cannot simply lean upon her work for the rest of time. Instead, we must continually strive to find additional good and further riches within ourselves. In particular, we must look within ourselves to go beyond the inadequacies of the stage-based model for coping with dying that Kubler-Ross set forth so many years ago.   (Corr, 1993, p. 81)

Corr believes that we can continue to learn from the efforts of Elisabeth Kubler-Ross. He further believes that the stage-based model set forth in *On Death and Dying* should not be the focus of our contemporary efforts in this area. He summarizes three central reasons not to focus on the stage-based model as well as three important lessons to learn from Kubler-Ross' work as follows:

Three Reasons Why the Stage-Based Model Should Not Be the Central Legacy of Kubler-Ross' Work:

1. We should not think that there are only five ways to cope with death and dying.
2. We should not think of the five reactions cited by Kubler-Ross as being interlinked stages. These reactions are coping strategies not interlinked elements in a linear standard of measure.
3. These five reactions are not obligatory nor should they be "prescribed" by those helping the dying.

Three Lessons We Should Learn from Kubler-Ross' Work:

1. People who are coping with their dying are *still alive* and may have unfinished needs to address.
2. Those caring for dying persons should actively listen to them in identifying their needs.
3. Dying persons can teach us to know ourselves better.

Source: Adapted from C. Corr, (1993). Coping with dying: lessons that we should learn and should not learn from the work of Elisabeth Kubler-Ross. *Death Studies,* 17:69–83.

FIGURE 8–1 Dr. Elisabeth Kubler-Ross. (Reprinted by permission of AP/Wide World Photos)

ter, it is also an effective coping strategy over the long term for some. Additionally, denial may be reinforced by the curative orientation of medicine. How is the dying cancer patient who is receiving aggressive chemotherapy from a physician and hoping for a possible cure to act? He or she may deny the possibility that the treatment won't work. To do otherwise might make the treatment unbearable. It might also label him or her a bad patient.

Nor should we label those who are openly depressed as weak. To be depressed about dying is normal. We shouldn't expect someone to put on a perpetually "happy face" for us. The dying need a hand to hold, a shoulder to cry on, a friend to talk to. We shouldn't expect them to carry their fears and sadness alone, to keep such feelings constantly bottled up inside.

Likewise, retaliation against those exhibiting anger and frustration isn't appropriate. These feelings should be allowed open expression. Our job isn't to force dying persons to conform to our opinion of how they should react but to be supportive of and responsive to their needs.

At the time that Kubler-Ross's first book was published, death was a taboo subject in U.S. society. Through her dedicated work, she fostered its open discussion. She went on to publish several other books, engage in extensive speaking tours, and conduct regular workshops on the topic. During the 1970s, the name Kubler-Ross became synonymous with caring concern for the terminally ill. In recognizing her unique manner of leading the popular death-awareness movement, one sociologist writes:

> If she was not the one to hold the proverbial candle to the cultural darkness surrounding death, someone else undoubtedly would have done so, for the silence had become deafening. In attending her talks around the country during the 1970s, this author had flashes of being at some old-time revival. The house was always packed and the audience always enthusiastic. (Kearl, 1989, p. 490)

Someone else may have led the movement. However, it is hard to imagine anyone else having done so more sensitively, powerfully, or persuasively. We owe much to this dedicated and compassionate physician. The tribute paid her by Kavanaugh (1972) in the dedication of his book *Facing Death* eloquently depicts the role she has played in the death-awareness movement: "To Elisabeth Kubler-Ross whose research took the pennies off the eyes of the living so they could see the dying."

Alternative Coping Models

It has been proposed that any alternative model to understanding coping with dying should strive to do four things. First, it should provide a basis for understanding individual aspects of coping. It should not imply that there is one right way to cope with dying. Second, it should encourage empowerment for those dying. That is, it should foster their authority in decision making regarding their care. Third, it should stress the shared aspects of coping, thereby drawing people together. Loved ones are not merely passive observers of a dying patient; they are coping with the situation as well. Finally, the model should provide guidance for those who seek to assist dying persons be they doctors, nurses, clergy, or friends and loved ones (Corr, 1992; Weisman, 1992).

Awareness of and Communication About Dying

In the last thirty years, there has been a significant change in the willingness of physicians to inform patients that they are dying (Fitts and Ravdin, 1953; Greenwald and Nevitt, 1982; Klenow and Youngs, 1987; Oken, 1961; Seale, 1991; Veatch and Tai, 1980). In 1961, 88 percent of U.S. physicians surveyed preferred not to tell cancer patients of their diagnosis if the prognosis was grave (Oken, 1961). Almost twenty years later, when the study was repeated by Novack et al. (1979), a marked change was found. Results indicated that 98 percent of responding physicians preferred to tell patients of their diagnosis.

Whether or not patients are informed of their prognosis, they continue to interact with their caregivers. In their classic study of interactions between hospital staff and terminally ill patients, Glaser and Strauss (1965) identified four awareness contexts: closed awareness, suspicion, mutual pretense, and open awareness.

Closed Awareness

Closed awareness occurs when staff know of the impending death but the patient does not. Any talk of death is avoided. This backdrop does not deal with patients as persons but rather as clients to be managed according to an established routine. It does not give them an opportunity to openly express their emotions, put their affairs in order, attend to any unfinished business, or maintain personal control of their living and dying. At one time, this institutional interplay was not uncommon. Today, it is no longer a common method of patient management. As indicated earlier, the present emphasis is on informing patients of their prognosis.

Suspicion

Suspicion involves a modification of closed awareness, wherein patients suspect that the truth about their dying is being withheld. Although uninformed about the life-threatening nature of their illness, patients may pick up on the verbal or behavioral clues of others. Likewise, their physical symptoms may tell them that something is seriously wrong. This situation generally does not continue for long, but evolves into the awareness contexts of mutual pretense or open awareness.

Mutual Pretense

Mutual pretense exists when patients and staff know that death awaits but pretend otherwise. Pretense may be initiated by either party and ends when one of the actors cannot, or will not, sustain it. A change to open awareness may be sudden or gradual, if it occurs at all. However, either party may revert to the pretense context. Thus, there may be fluctuation between pretense and open awareness. Mutual pretense can provide some privacy and dignity for the patient and minimize tensions for the staff. If others initiate the pretense, however, the dying may be cut off from meaningful interaction, feeling forced to keep up the pretense.

Open Awareness

Open awareness occurs when both patients and staff openly acknowledge the terminal prognosis. It allows for meaningful interaction and mutual support. It also facilitates attending to unfinished business and frees the staff from rigid talk and restrained behavior. Open awareness and communication are more customary today than they once were. Many adults want complete disclosure regarding their illness and prognosis. They also want to fully participate in decisions affecting their physical care and personal lives.

In the ideal sense, open awareness appears to be the preferred interactive scheme. However, it may not be for everyone. It can be very stressful. Some people deal best with menacing situations via denial or avoidance. Such as a coping strategy may not be unfavorable as long as it does not endanger anyone. It is possible to accept a terminal diagnosis and receive supportive care, yet avoid talking about it to others and even to display a future orientation. Denial is not uniformly dysfunctional. It may be a way to maintain privacy and to avoid the stress and fatigue of routinely dealing with impending death.

Rainey (1988) notes that denial is neither invariably helpful or harmful. In reference to clinical case conferences concerning dying patients, he remarks:

> Perhaps most troubling has been the tendency to view "openness" and "acceptance" in very positive terms, while assuming that "denial" is invariably pathologic and counterproductive. This has led to unnecessary and often unfortunate confrontations with patients, tactless disclosure, and battering of sorely needed psychological defenses.   (p. 142)

Awareness contexts and their associated interactive schemes were first studied and described in an institutional setting. They are not, however, confined to patients and their formal caregivers. They involve family and friends as well. It should also be noted that patients may operate under one awareness context with one person and under another with someone else. Open awareness may be a comfortable interactive scheme with one person while mutual pretense works best with another.

Dying Trajectories

The research team of Glaser and Strauss was the first to study and clarify the distinctive characteristics of dying in an institutional setting. They observed the social phenomenon of dying in six hospitals in the San Francisco area. The majority of their findings are published in two books: *Awareness of Dying* (1965) and *Time for Dying* (1968). The awareness contexts just outlined are detailed in the former book; dying trajectories are dealt with in the latter.

According to Glaser and Strauss (1968), staff members working with the ill must answer two questions for themselves about every patient: Will the patient die? And if so, when? These questions are important because the staff generates expectations about a patient's death and takes its treatment and other attitudinal cues from the answers that are developed. They expect the patient to linger, to die quickly, or to die at a pace somewhere between the two.

Perceptions about the course that dying will take are referred to as *dying trajectories*. The nature of staff interaction with the patient is closely related to the specific expectations they have formed about the patient's dying. This is true regardless of the accuracy of their expectation. Likewise, patients' perceptions about the course their own dying will take are greatly affected by staff expectations.

Two important cues that contribute to the perception of the dying trajectory are the patient's physical condition and the time-based references to dying made by medical staff members. Physical symptoms are easiest to read and help establish some degree of certainty about the outcome. Time-based cues have numerous reference points. A doctor's expectations about disease progression ("It's going fast," "He's lingering"), the length of the hospital stay, and even the work schedule (can the patient continue to be bathed, fed?) contribute to expectations about how much longer patients will live.

Among the frequent kinds of dying trajectories are the (1) lingering trajectory, (2) quick trajectory leading to expected death, and (3) sudden trajectory leading to unexpected death. The various kinds are typically associated with given types of hospital units and generally yield different patterns of staff activity.

The Lingering Trajectory

When medical staff perceive patients as being in a lingering death trajectory, patients may suffer a loss in perceived social worth and relinquish control over their care. Staff members may feel they have done everything possible to care for a patient and may view a downhill course as inevitable. The death of a patient on a lingering trajectory may seem appropriate to the staff who rationalize that the patient's life is now of limited value. Intense emotional reactions on the part of family at the death may serve to confuse those who have made assumptions about the patient's present limited social worth.

Family and staff may experience stress when the lingering patient does not die "on schedule." As Shneidman (1980) articulates, the good patient dies on time

in accordance with the dying trajectory mapped by the staff. To die too early, unexpectedly, is an embarrassment to hospital staff; but what is more surprising (and of psycho-social interest) is that to linger too long, beyond the pro-

jected trajectory, can be an even greater embarrassment to the hospital staff—
and a great strain on the next of kin who may have premourned and set their
mind's clock for a specific death date, which if not met, becomes painfully
overdue.   (p. 205)

The Expected Quick Trajectory

In contrast to the lingering trajectory, the expected quick trajectory typically
involves acute life-or-death crises. Expected quick trajectories are usually associated with high-risk procedures, dangerous acute events, or surgery. The
usual proximity of family under such circumstances places additional demands
on the staff. They must work intently, under time constraints, while dealing
with family concerns. A given hospital or medical unit's resources, as well as
the perceived social worth of the patient, may influence the type of care delivered.

The Unexpected Quick Trajectory

The unexpected quick trajectory involves an unanticipated crisis that may challenge the professional caregiver's defenses regarding anxiety and death.
Especially stressful to the staff may be the death that they worked earnestly to
prevent. Glaser and Strauss refer to the "poor physician" (who worked hard to
save the patient), not the one who died, as the frequent recipient of staff sympathy. The death that occurs from an unexpected complication or from a condition other than the one being "managed" may be emotionally problematic for
the staff.

In general, noncritical care or nonemergency hospital units may not "expect" critical events to occur, although intellectually they know that they
might. When unexpected-death situations suddenly arise, the staff face special
challenges, challenges to their curative skills and to their continued emotional
composure.

The Occupational Stress of Caring for the Dying

The now classic and often cited studies by Glaser and Strauss of U.S. hospitals
and dying patients documented the impersonal routine of institutional care
and the staff practice of emotional suppression. They also captured some of the
intensity and urgency with which staff mobilize their skills to cure disease and
save lives.

The differing dying trajectories bring with them various sources of occupational stress for medical workers. Running through all of these scenarios of
dying is the failure to cure, to heal, to restore. Physicians, trained as they are in
curative medicine, frequently view the dying patient, consciously or uncon-
sciously, as their failure (Rinaldi and Kearl, 1990). Benoliel (1974) noted that

patient death symbolizes to physicians their powerlessness in the face of death. Sudden, unexpected death may deliver this message with a jolt. Lingering death, perhaps, serves as a protracted reminder. With lingering death, there may be subtle abandonment by the physician characterized by physical withdrawal from direct patient care (in the hospital, house staff assume care), fewer visits, and withholding of expressed warmth and spontaneity (Latimer, 1991).

Hospice Care

While Glaser and Strauss were studying awareness contexts and dying trajectories in the institutional care of dying patients in the United States, Cicely Saunders was working with another approach to caring for dying patients in another part of the world. The celebrated physician, nurse, and social worker was frustrated by the curative emphasis of medicine and the marginalization of the dying. In a biography of her, that frustration was expressed as follows:

> Medicine was about cure, if they couldn't cure doctors felt they had failed; it was about having answers, they had no answers for the dying. Doctors did not consider it their job to ease the process of dying beyond prescribing pain-killing drugs; as far as possible they avoided dying patients, embarrassed by what they saw as failure.   (du Boulay, 1984)

Saunders sought to provide an alternative means of caring for dying patients when she opened St. Christopher's Hospice in London in 1967. The emphasis of this facility was not on heroic life-sustaining measures or regular checks of blood pressure, pulse, and temperature. It did not speak of death in hushed tones (if at all) or marginalize the dying patient. At St. Christopher's, the dying patient was the central concern. Open awareness and communication about serious illness and dying was the norm. The hospice philosophy can be applied in a number of settings. It is a concept of care for the terminally ill that combines various elements while attempting to maintain patient autonomy.

Hospice Philosophy of Care

Hospice care attempts to keep dying persons as comfortable as possible. Thus, its major focus is palliative rather than curative care. Control of pain and other distressing symptoms (nausea, vomiting, shortness of breath, anorexia, constipation, weakness, confusion, and so on) is viewed as a treatment goal in its own right. If a patient's preoccupation with suffering is of such intensity that everything else in life is excluded, then self-control, independence, human dignity, and interpersonal relations are sacrificed.

Also, each patient is seen as a part of a family whose total well-being is affected by the terminal illness of one of its members. Thus, hospice views the family as the unit of care. Caring does not stop when the patient dies but continues for the family during bereavement with the availability of bereavement counselors.

An interdisciplinary team involving physician, nursing, social work, counseling, and volunteer services provides hospice care. It is typical for staff to regularly come together to review their experiences. They may ventilate their stresses and lend support to one another. Hospice is not only concerned with the needs of patients and their families but with those of the staff caring for them as well.

Historical Development of the Modern Hospice Movement

The term *hospice* is derived from Medieval Europe where it indicated a resting place on a long and arduous journey. It has been borrowed in reference to the contemporary task of providing humanistic care to the terminally ill and their families. The roots of today's hospice programs can be traced to the 1800s when Irish Sisters of Charity opened and operated a home for the dying in Dublin. In the early 1900s, they opened a similar facility in London and named it St. Joseph's Hospice. It was in that facility during the 1950s that Cicely Saunders began her work with the dying. There she developed the basic ideas and principles that guide most present-day hospice programs. In 1967, she opened St. Christopher's, the first modern hospice. It has become a model for hospice programs around the world.

Located in Sydenham on London's outskirts, St. Christopher's became a training center for care of the dying. Professionals from all over the world have come to St. Christopher's to study, learn, and work with terminally ill patients. Many of these persons have returned home encouraged to develop similar programs.

The first hospice program in the United States began in 1974 as Hospice, Inc., now known as Connecticut Hospice. Located in New Haven, it began as a coordinated home care program for the dying, utilizing the Visiting Nurses Association, under the medical direction of Sylvia Lack. Dr. Lack had served as the Medical Officer at St. Christopher's and St. Joseph's between 1971 and 1973 before coming to the United States.

There are three major types of hospice programs today. In the United States, the emphasis has been on home-care programs. The goal is to allow terminally ill patients to remain at home in the presence of their families, if possible. The second type of hospice program involves free-standing facilities. These are structures like St. Christopher's that house full-service hospice programs. Only a few of these exist in the United States. Connecticut Hospice now includes a free-standing facility that has been in operation since 1979. The first such institution in the United States was Hillhaven Hospice in Tucson. Now under the shelter of St. Mary's Hospital, it is called St. Mary's Hospice. Hospital-based care is a third type of hospice model, likewise restricted by today's funding mechanisms. In this model, some beds within a hospital are designated for hospice-care patients.

The first U.S. hospice programs were philanthropically financed. Grants, charitable donations, and volunteer workers along with partial payments from some patients kept them afloat. However, as time went on, there was concern about their continued financial viability. Hospice began directing its efforts toward insurance coverage for hospice care. Blue Cross/Blue Shield and various commercial insurance carriers began offering insurance coverage for such services. In 1982, the Tax Equity and Fiscal Responsibility Act (TEFRA) was passed amending the Medicare legislation to include hospice benefits (see Box 8–4). With the enactment of the Medicare benefit, standards were set for certifying hospice care and licensing procedures initiated by the individual states.

Barriers to Hospice Care

In the United States, hospice has evolved from a fringe alternative led by dedicated, idealistic professionals and volunteers to an accepted system of terminal care. Much of this change has been precipitated by the legislation allowing terminally ill patients to receive Medicare-reimbursable services from certified hospice programs. In 1983, when Medicare began offering a hospice benefit, hospices in the United States numbered 516. By 1989, the number had grown to over 1,700 (Rhymes, 1990).

In spite of this growth, hospice continues to serve a minority of terminally ill patients. Likewise, its anticipated use has not materialized. It was projected that by 1985, 40,000 patients would use hospice services. Less than 13,000 actually did (Fraser, Koontz, and Moran, 1986).

There are a number of barriers to hospice care. One of them involves the requirement that patients with a terminal illness have a life expectancy of six months or less. This prognosis must be agreed upon by the patients's physician and the medical director of the hospice program. It can be difficult to determine how much time a patient has left, although to do so is easier during the advanced stages of cancer. Not surprisingly, the overwhelming majority of hospice patients are dying from cancer.

Many others suffering from conditions such as emphysema, amyotrophic lateral sclerosis (ALS or Lou Gehrig's disease), congestive heart failure, or AIDS could benefit from hospice care. However, their prognoses are usually more difficult to evaluate. Because of the difficulty in establishing life expectancy, many patients who could have derived greater benefit on earlier admission to hospice are referred to such programs very late in their illness. Interestingly,

---

BOX 8–4   *Medicare Hospice Benefit*

Medicare (Part A) helps pay for hospice services if all three of these conditions are met:

1. A physician certifies that the patient is terminally ill.
2. The patient elects to receive hospice care instead of standard Medicare benefits for the terminal illness.
3. Care is provided by a hospice program that participates in Medicare.

The patient is responsible for 5 percent of the cost of outpatient drugs or $5 toward each prescription, whichever is less.

Hospice benefits provide respite care which is a short-term stay in an in-patient facility. It provides temporary relief, or respite, to the home caregiver. Each in-patient respite care stay is limited to no more than five days in a row. The patient pays 5 percent of the Medicare-allowed rate for such care. The rate will vary depending on the area of the country.

While receiving hospice care, Medicare continues to pay for all necessary covered services under the standard Medicare benefit program for a condition not related to the terminal illness.

The Medicare hospice benefit does not pay for treatments other than for pain relief and symptom management of a terminal illness.

Source: Adapted from U.S. Department of Health and Human Services. (1993). *The Medicare 1993 Handbook.* Washington, DC: Health Care Financing Administration.

---

the most frequent reason referred patients are not admitted to hospice programs is death before a care program can be established (MacDonald, 1989).

Also, the survival time of a person with a terminal illness can depend on the aggressiveness with which episodic crises are treated. For example, those with AIDS, emphysema, and cancer often die as a result of infection. Whether aggressive treatment of such a complication will provide more quality time for the terminal patient is a point to consider at times. In general, hospice patients are not supposed to receive aggressive, heroic, or life-sustaining measures. How these are defined and whether or not they are ever appropriate for hospice patients is sometimes subject to debate.

Today, there is a concern that treatment procedures in U.S. hospices sometimes may be guided more by economic pressures than by genuine hospice philosophy. Indeed, in the period following the passage of the Medicare Hospice Benefit, management issues began to dominate. Consequently, many hospice directors were uncertain about pursuing Medicare coverage. By 1984, less than 10 percent of eligible programs had sought certification. By the end of the 1980s, only half of the qualified programs had done so (General Accounting Office, 1989).

The strict limitation on in-patient care is one reason why some hospice programs have not sought Medicare certification. Under the legislation, more than 80 percent of a hospice program's patient-care days must be for home care. Thus, less than 20 percent of patient-care days may be spent for in-patient services. This particular requirement was invoked as a Medicare cost-saving device. Many hospices are afraid of the serious financial consequences facing them should their patients need more in-patient services.

Additionally, under the legislation, hospices face a cap on total reimbursement for each hospice patient. This factor is complicated by the responsibility for patient care that is assumed by hospice programs. Once they accept a patient, they are responsible for continued care, both in-patient and home-care services, until the patient's death, regardless of the costs or limitations on Medicare reimbursement.

Medicare cost-containment mechanisms can affect who does and does not receive hospice services. Partially because of limitations on in-patient care and Medicare reimbursement ceilings, it is common for certified programs to require patients to have a twenty-four-hour caregiver in the home. More functionally disabled patients or those without strong family support or financial resources with which to hire caregivers may have limited access to hospice care. One study of hospice referrals found that absence of a caregiver accounted for only 4 percent of patients denied admission (MacDonald, 1989). However, as Rhymes (1990) points out, this may be due to selective referrals. That is, those who get referred to hospices are more likely to have a caregiver in their home or the financial means to hire one.

This criticism is not to suggest that weakened, dying persons do not need in-home caregivers. Even if they are functional when entering a program, they face the likelihood of physical decline, disability, and required assistance. Neither does the criticism suggest that insurance programs provide full-time in-home caregivers. The criticism falls on the system which seems to have encouraged the development of home-care programs at the expense of other in-patient care models. Home care is not possible for everyone. In fact, it may not be appropriate for some patients and their families. As Torrens (1985) charged, "It should not be left to the vague powers of political pressure groups or Medicare reimbursement to shape the proportionate distribution between hospital-based and home care programs" (Torrens, 1985, p. 80).

Is Hospice Successful?

Stories abound about the care delivered by hospice programs; well-controlled, scientific studies do not. Measuring the costs and quality of, and satisfaction with, hospice is a difficult task. Not all hospice programs or their patient populations are the same. Institutional and home-care patients may have differing needs and be at different stages of the disease process, which makes comparisons of the two difficult.

The National Hospice Study, funded and directed by the Health Care Finance Administration, was designed to examine various outcomes for a matched group of hospice and nonhospice terminal patients and their families. It found that home-care costs were less than those of hospital-based programs which tended to match the costs of conventional hospital care. Families expressed greater satisfaction with death occurring at home, but also experienced higher levels of stress. The patients' quality of life (measured via specific indicators) did not significantly differ with the care setting, but pain and symptom management tended to be better in hospital-based hospice programs. Patients receiving hospice care underwent less diagnostic testing and received less aggressive therapy (Greer et al., 1984; Mor, Greer, and Kastenbaum, 1988).

Another widely cited and well-respected report studied terminal patients receiving care in conventional medical and surgical service units of a Veteran's Administration Hospital in Los Angeles. These patients were compared with those receiving care in a hospice unit of the same facility. Greater patient and family satisfaction was recorded for those receiving care in the hospice unit. No significant differences were found between these two settings regarding pain and symptom control or measures of activities of daily living. Hospice care was not associated with a reduced number of in-patient days (Kane et al., 1984).

Perhaps a better measure of hospice's "success" is the general influence it has had on the care of the dying regardless of the setting. Kane et al. speculate that the hospice movement may have sensitized medical practitioners in general, not just those in hospice programs, to better serve the dying. This factor may help to explain their lack of significant differences on various important outcome measures.

A similar conclusion was drawn in a British study comparing care of the dying in St. Christopher's Hospice and selected London hospitals. Comparisons were made during 1967–1969 and again during 1977–1979 on a number of patient outcomes including pain relief. Patients at St. Christopher's demonstrated less pain than did hospital patients in the earlier period, but the two groups were comparable by 1977–1979 (Parkes and Parkes, 1984).

Some evidence from both American and British sources indicates an influence of hospice on hospital care. It suggests that in recent years hospital care may have become more like that of hospice. It

> does not enable an assessment of how widespread this development might be in either country, but it does suggest that a general picture of poor treatment and a "closed awareness context" in hospitals may now be less appropriate. In part, this may be due to the educative effect of the hospice movement, particularly in the area of pain control.   (Seale, 1989, p. 553)

Hospice has influenced continued research on pain relief and its application to the patient-care setting. However, inadequate pain management continues to be a concern. In the mid-1980s, the World Health Organization identified cancer pain as a major world health problem (Stjernsward, 1985). Reasons for unsatisfactory pain control include inadequate professional training and misplaced concerns about narcotic addiction (Atchison, Guercio, and Monaco, 1986; Camp, 1988; Choiniere et al., 1990; Cohen, 1980; Harrison, 1991; Lander, 1990; Marks and Sachar, 1973; Mather and Mackie, 1983; Streltzer and Wade, 1981). The Wisconsin Cancer Pain Initiative exemplifies programs that are working to reform medical and nursing school curricula and educate professionals and the public about pain control (Dahl, Joranson, and Weissmann, 1989).

Appropriate Death

Several years ago, Weisman (1972) introduced the concept of appropriate death. It refers to the kind of death appropriate for each dying person—the type of death we would select for ourselves given the choice. It might be a death that strikes suddenly when we are in the middle of doing what we enjoy most—playing a round of golf on a beautiful, sunny day or living it up on the dance floor. We've all heard remarks such as, "He went out doing what made him happy," or "What a way to go!"

Some, however, might prefer to die in their bed surrounded by loved ones and fully aware of their immediate destiny. Thus, an appropriate death varies according to individual differences; it is likewise influenced by the social and cultural environment.

Near-Death Experiences

What Is an NDE?

What is it like to die? Is there another state of existence beyond this earthly realm? These are questions that have fascinated us surely since the beginning of human consciousness. But, still we have no definitive answers. What we do or don't believe remains a matter of faith or opinion. Some people have experienced brushes with death, having suffered traumatic injury, cardiac arrest, near drowning, or attempted suicide. Some have been in physically and/or psychologically stressful circumstances and thought they might be dying, such as mountain climbers who slipped from a ledge, falling a considerable distance only to land in snow. Many of these people have reported strikingly similar stories of what have come to be called near-death experiences or NDEs. They transcend any account of the mere physical circumstances precipitating a crisis. Rather, they refer to a unique psychological state experienced by those in the midst of what are often near-fatal events.

Do NDEs tell us anything about a life hereafter? Some people think so. They believe they stand testimony to our survival after death. Others think not and have offered alternative explanations. Still, the question remains for many who have examined NDEs and confess uncertainty about their meaning.

The recent discourse on NDEs stems from the pioneering work of Elisabeth Kubler-Ross and Raymond Moody which focused public attention on them during the 1970s. In his 1975 book *Life After Life*, Moody presents numerous case histories of NDEs. They emanate from three separate categories of individual experiences. The first involves experiences of persons who were successfully resuscitated after having been judged or pronounced dead by a physician. The second involves those of persons, who during the course of some traumatic event such as an accident or episode of illness, seemingly came very close to death. The final category includes experiences of people who, as they died, related them to others. These are often termed death-bed visions (Osis, 1961; Osis and Haraldsson, 1977).

Moody noted that there are widely divergent circumstances surrounding the near-death episodes and varying types of persons undergoing them. Yet, the accounts include uncanny similarities. What follows is a listing of the various components of an NDE. It should be pointed out that no one NDE includes all of the elements listed—no two NDEs are exactly alike. None of the components is universally experienced, but each of them is reported in numerous, separate accounts. The order in which they are presented is not rigidly fixed. However, extreme variation in sequencing is unusual. People undergoing an NDE may:

- *Hear themselves pronounced dead.*
- *Experience unusual auditory sensations.* These are interpreted in various ways: some report an irritating buzzing or ringing; others note pleasant, musical sounds.
- *Feel themselves moving through a dark tunnel or space.* This element is sometimes referred to as *transcendence*. It commonly involves a sense of their consciousness passing into a new dimension. It has been varyingly described as a cave, a well, a sewer, or a valley. One man called it the "valley of the shadow of death."
- *Separate from their body.* Known as *autoscopy,* this often involves a floating sensation, a lifting out of the body eventually to drift above it. The

physical body may, thus, be viewed from a detached position of height. Details of what is observed and heard may be recounted later. Some people report an initial desire to get back into their own body. A peaceful, "floating," detachment, yet keen awareness, sets in. With separation, there is an absence of pain.

- *See spirits of others.* These spirits may be those of deceased loved ones including relatives and friends. Sometimes religious figures are mentioned.

- *Encounter a being of light.* A bright light may be seen at the end of a tunnel. Though dim at first, the light eventually takes on an unearthly brilliance. This aspect of the NDE has the most profound effect. It is interpreted as a "being," a "presence." It typically takes on a religious connotation. Jewish persons may identify it as an angel, Christians as Christ, those without a religious background as a powerful presence. The light usually reflects peace and love. It directs people to review and evaluate their lives. It does so in a telepathic and nonaccusatory manner.

- *Sense a border between two dimensions of existence.* A turning point may be sensed whereby people either must "decide" to or are directed to return to their earthly existences or remain in this "other-worldly" plane. Since none of those who have remained dead have ever reported their experiences, we have NDE accounts only of those who returned!

The return is generally not remembered. People eventually "wake up" in their old physical bodies profoundly affected by their experience. They often indicate having been so overwhelmed by feelings of peace and love that they resisted turning away from "the border" they encountered. Finding the proper words to express what happened is difficult. They fear others may laugh at their stories, thus discrediting an experience that has changed them forever. They no longer fear death, but want to live life to the fullest.

Accounts of surreal experiences with elements of what are now termed NDEs can be traced to ancient works such as Plato's *Republic* and religious writings. They are a part of folklore and mythology. One is reminded of the River Styx from classical mythology over which the souls of the dead had to cross when hearing of the decisive border encountered in NDEs. Thus, though systematically organized and presented, Moody's contemporary individual accounts do not represent a remarkably new or different aspect of human experience. History points out they have been universally a part of it (Holck, 1978; Zaleski, 1987).

Since Moody's work, these experiences have been more openly addressed and methodically studied. They are now featured in various scientific journals and detailed in several books recounting research into the area.

Interpretations of NDEs

Theoretical explanations of NDEs generally fall into three broad categories: the metaphysical/transcendental, the psychological, and the physiological. The three categories are not necessarily mutually exclusive.

Metaphysical Explanations. Metaphysical explanations hold that NDEs lend support to the belief that humans survive physical death to enter a world of spiritual existence. Thus, those who have NDEs catch a glimpse of the next life. Although religious and philosophical writings might be expected to stand alone in support of this belief, some intriguing contributions from medicine and psychology have served to bolster it.

Seven years after the publication of Moody's *Life After Life,* Michal Sabom, a practicing cardiologist and faculty member at Emory University School of Medicine, produced another book, *Recollections of Death: A Medical Investigation.* It was the culmination of five years' work including 116 patient interviews.

Moody's book was not a hard-hitting scientific work, nor had he pretended it to be. Sabom was skeptical of its far-out accounts of spiritual flight and critical of its scientific weaknesses. Along with a psychiatric social worker, he began interviewing patients who had been critically ill (Sabom and Kreutziger, 1977).

Rather than limiting his subjects to those who had had an NDE, Sabom, unlike Moody, interviewed a random sample of people who had undergone near-fatal medical events. Three-fourths of them had suffered cardiac arrest. Forty percent of his random sample reported experiencing an NDE. Neither demographic differences nor the cause of the near-death event influenced its probability.

One-third of Sabom's sample experienced autoscopy. Twenty-six of this group had general impressions of what happened to them while they floated above their physical bodies. Curiously, six of the autoscopic sample had sharp, detailed memories of what they had viewed. As their bodies lay unconscious below, they were able to see the particulars of their own cardiopulmonary resuscitation. Later, they were able to describe it vividly. Some reported the color of an oxygen mask, the readings on a meter, the number of electric shocks applied, the number of doctors standing around them, and their topics of conversation including one about golf!

An especially interesting feature of Sabom's work is the attempt to corroborate what patients claimed they saw during an autoscopic event with what actually happened. The latter was determined, where possible, by retrieving information from medical records and personnel. Agreement was established in several instances. CPR techniques known only to the medical staff were among the events recalled by previously unconscious patients and those suffering cardiopulmonary arrest.

Sabom, who began his research as a skeptic, sought to explain how those lying motionless with cardiac arrest and their eyes closed could present such accurate accounts. There are various reports of patients who are able to recount things they heard during periods of unconsciousness. However, the autoscopic memories are striking because visual details are provided as well. It was speculated that, perhaps, his modern-day patients were sophisticated about hospital procedures and resuscitative techniques. Television brings such details into the homes of many who have never actually witnessed them. Perhaps, patients having NDEs complete with autoscopy had not "recalled" the medical details of their own cases but had accurately fantasized CPR techniques because of information provided them through television, magazines, or books. Curiously, Sabom questioned a sample of longtime cardiac patients who had not had NDEs about the details of resuscitation and they were unable to supply the necessary information.

Sabom deemed the NDE to be an authentic experience. Like the majority of Americans surveyed (Klenow and Youngs, 1989), he personally believes in life after death. He does not, however, believe that his research proves any such existence. Alternative psychological or physical explanations may one day account for the NDE. Sabom (1982) suggests that life-threatening crises can precipitate a splitting apart of the mind and body as evidenced in the near-death episodes. How that split occurs and how long it can last remain elusive.

Kenneth Ring, a psychologist, also studied NDEs and believes they do provide evidence of a life hereafter. Much of his work supports the findings of Sabom (Ring, 1980, 1984). He estimates that one in three persons surviving a brush with death reports an NDE (Ring, 1989). He is noted for having developed a scale to evaluate the depth or intensity of an NDE (see Table 8–1).

Many persons who survive a brush with death have no recollection of an NDE as illustrated in Ring's estimates. Likewise, elements of near-death episodes are sometimes experienced by those who are not near death or even in a crisis situation (Gabbard, Twenlow, and Jones, 1981; Walker, 1989). Auditory sensations, features of transcendence, and out-of-the body experiences are among the elements noted in some accounts (Monroe, 1971). For some, these factors detract from a survival explanation for NDEs.

Psychological Explanations. NDEs have also been interpreted as a psychological response to the perceived threat of dying, making them analogous to other stress-induced psychological phenomena (Appleby, 1989; Noyes and Kletti, 1976; Roberts and Owen, 1988). Along these lines, Noyes (1979) identifies depersonalization and hyperalertness as key dimensions of NDEs. Aspects of depersonalization include sensing the self as strange or different, the body apart from the self, peculiar sounds, a strange new world, and an altered passage of time. Hyperalertness characteristics include vivid thoughts as well as sharp vision and hearing. It is believed that these dimensions are related to a neural mechanism that helps us to respond to dangerous situations by blunting

---

Table 8–1   *Ring's Stages of a Near-Death Experience*

Stage 1.	Euphoria	An overwhelming feeling of peace and joy. No pain is felt.
Stage 2.	Out-of-body state	Auditory sensation; autoscopy. May encounter other beings.
Stage 3.	Enters darkness or tunnel	Auditory sensation; transcendence. Other beings present.
Stage 4.	Unearthly world of light	A brilliant light is encountered; a "presence" is felt in the light. No awareness of time and space.
Stage 5.	Enters the light and makes a decision	The presence telepathically asks for a life review. Beings encountered are friendly. A barrier is reached where a decision must be made whether to stay in the unearthly realm or to return to life on earth.

Source: Adapted from K. Ring. (1980). *Life at Death: A Scientific Investigation of the Near-Death Experience.* New York: Coward, McCann, and Georghegan.

---

potentially disorganizing emotions. Hence, people can remain calm and are better able to cope during a crisis.

From a psychological perspective, the NDE may be a defense against the threat of death (Blackmore, 1993). The depersonalized state characteristic of it mimics death.

> In it a person experiences himself as empty, lifeless, and unfamiliar. In a sense he creates psychologically the very situation that environmental circumstances threaten to impose. In so doing, he escapes death, for what has already happened cannot happen again; he cannot die, because he is already dead. (Noyes, 1979, p. 79)

Physiological Explanations. Physiological explanations for NDEs also exist. The mystical dimension associated with NDEs includes memories, feelings of joy, seeing colors or "visions," and experiencing strange bodily sensations. Noyes believes these are possibly explained by the altered tissue states and metabolic imbalances induced by terminal illness or traumatic events.

NDEs have been compared with LSD-induced hallucinations (Grof and Halifax, 1977; Siegel, 1980) and to the effects of therapeutically inhaled carbon dioxide and nitrous oxide (Meduna, 1950; Yacorzynski et al., 1950). Still another explanation holds that they are a remembered birth experience (Siegel, 1980). Further physiological explanations have included the activation of endorphins (brain opiates) during stressful periods. These brain chemicals may be responsible for the sense of calm and peace. A reduced oxygen supply to the brain and the buildup of toxic metabolic byproducts might also explain altered sensations.

In their study, Owens, Cook, and Stevenson (1990) offered some support for each of the theoretical interpretive models. Their patient population included a fairly equal number of subjects who would have died without medical intervention as well as those who believed they were near death during an illness or injury (although they actually were not). All reported NDEs. From a metaphysical/transcendental perspective, the researchers cited the unexplained enhancement of cognitive functioning among those who were actually near death. They noted:

> The hypothesis that the brain is necessary for mental functioning would lead us to expect that, as brain function becomes disturbed, and perhaps in some cases diminishes, a matching impairment of cognitive function would occur. (Owens, Cook, and Stevenson, 1990, p. 1177)

Those not near death had experiences resembling those of people who truly were, lending support to the psychological factors that may be able to induce NDEs. Included here are autoscopy, positive feelings, and panoramic life review. Those whose lives were truly imperiled had some experiences significantly more often than did those whose lives were not. They were more likely to report an enhanced perception of light and enhanced cognitive powers which suggests that physical differences may influence the experience.

Surviving an NDE

Whether or not people who have an NDE enter another dimension of existence, we do know that some of them resume life profoundly affected by their experience. It is estimated that approximately 13 million U.S. adults have had an NDE. Today, due to technological advances, many survive medical crises that once meant certain death, potentially expanding the numbers of individuals undergoing an NDE.

While attending to the physical support of patients, caregivers often neglect the emotional experience of surviving critical illness or injury. Increasingly, the health care literature is calling upon caregivers to be sensitive to and nonjudgmental of any NDE accounts that patients might divulge (Corcoran, 1988; Morse and Perry, 1992; Papowitz, 1986; Oakes, 1981; Orne, 1986; Walker, 1989).

Not all NDEs are peaceful experiences (Rawlings, 1993). Although estimated to represent only 1 percent of NDEs, there are reports of frightening ones. A few individuals have encountered scary figures and forms rather than deceased relatives and religious images. Some of those who were attempting suicide have related feelings of extreme uneasiness, of having made the "wrong choice."

Whatever the emotional tone, it is not uncommon for patients to keep

NDEs to themselves for fear they will be thought of as crazy. Some are confused and harbor unresolved concerns about their NDE. It took one man ten years to talk about his experience again after a physician told him he was o.k. now and to forget about it. He had not forgotten it. For years he had tried to make sense of it. One middle-aged woman was relieved to finally discuss her experience with someone who was familiar with NDEs. As a child, she had almost drowned and had undergone the mysterious phenomenon (Papowitz, 1986).

Children report near-death experiences similar to those described by adults (Herzog and Herrin, 1985; Morse, Conner, and Tyler, 1985; Morse and Perry, 1990, 1992; Serdahely, 1989–1990). That they do should alert parents and health professionals to the critically ill child's emotional state during and after recovery. Children are especially vulnerable to the emotional impact of such events as illustrated in selected pediatric cases.

One seven-year-old boy with kidney failure was admitted to an intensive care unit where he suffered two episodes of cardiac arrest, the second requiring defibrillation. He eventually asked his doctor why he had been held down and beaten when he was "being good." He had apparently witnessed the medical procedure and was confused by it. He could not understand what he had done to deserve the rough treatment which included "hitting me on the chest and sticking needles into me" (Herzog and Herrin, 1985, p. 1074).

These authors also present the case of a three-and-one-half-year-old girl who, on the basis of behavioral clues and verbal statements, was determined to have experienced an NDE at six months of age. She had been critically ill with symptoms of severe circulatory failure. Three years later, when her mother was talking about her grandmother's impending death, the child asked, "Will grandma have to go through the tunnel . . . to get to God?" (Herzog and Herrin, 1985, p. 1074).

A particularly interesting NDE was reported to have occurred at birth! It was recalled through a series of recurring dreams by a twenty-three-year-old woman. Born with the umbilical cord wrapped around her neck, she had suffered cardiopulmonary arrest and had been resuscitated. Her experience would be classified as Stage 4 according to Ring's scheme. She recalled traveling through a tunnel toward a light, but did not enter the light. Her experience was described as frightening and uncomfortable. She said that she fought not to die and to be returned to her body. This young woman believes that the NDE made her a stronger person, and one who takes nothing for granted (Serdahely and Walker, 1990). Such an attitude is commonly reported among those who have experienced the event.

Thus, the intriguing and unexplained NDE has been reported among people of all ages. Human experience and fascination with the event are bound to continue. Although individual belief and opinion will be offered in explanation of the phenomenon, uncertainty regarding its meaning will continue as well.

Summary

Over the last twenty-five years, the research on dying patients has focused mainly on their emotional responses to dying. The research was pioneered by Elisabeth Kubler-Ross, who asserted that several emotional reactions characterize the response to dying. These so-called stages of dying (denial, anger, bargaining, depression, and acceptance) have been openly embraced and systematically criticized. Despite any limitations, her work has been of tremendous value in sensitizing us to the needs and rights of the dying. The needs of dying patients and effective coping strategies remain an important area of study.

The last few decades have been marked by an increased willingness of physicians to inform their patients of a terminal diagnosis. Glaser and Strauss identified four interactive schemes regarding knowledge of the terminal diagnosis called awareness contexts; they are closed awareness, suspicion, mutual pretense, and open awareness. This same research team, the first to clarify the distinctive characteristics of dying in an institutional setting, charges that the nature of staff interactions with patients is closely related to expectations formed about the timing of an individual's dying. They may expect a patient to linger, die quickly, or die at a pace somewhere between the two. Such perceptions about the course that a given death will take are called dying trajectories.

In contrast to the marginalization of the dying in a curative, institutional setting, the hospice philosophy of care focuses on the physical and emotional comfort of dying patients and their families. The first modern hospice, St. Christopher's, was opened in London by Cicely Saunders in 1967. It has since become a model for hospice programs around the world. Hospice programs are of three major types: home-based, free-standing, and hospital-based programs.

The first U.S. hospice opened in Connecticut in 1974. Hospice programs here are largely home based and have gradually moved from being operated with grants and charitable donations, as well as partial payments from some patients, to being supported by insurance coverage. In 1982, Medicare legislation was amended to include hospice care. Standards were thus set for certification and licensure of hospice programs.

The concept of appropriate death, introduced by Weisman, refers to the kind of death appropriate for a given individual—the kind of death we would select for ourselves given the choice. It might be sudden or lingering; it might be experienced alone or surrounded by others. It may have any other characteristics we wish.

However death comes, a universal question has been, "What happens to us after we die?" Is there life after death or is death the end of our existence—period? Although the answer to that question is a matter of faith or opinion, the near-death experience (NDE) indicates for some that we continue in another dimension after our worldly demise. NDEs are reported by approximately one-third of those persons who come very close to dying. Their existence has been demonstrated, but their meaning has not. In addition to the survival or metaphysical explanation, it is theorized that NDEs may be a psychological response to the perceived threat of death or a physiological reaction to the process of physical decline.

Study Questions

1. Outline the Kubler-Ross stage theory of dying. What has been the reaction to it? Identify shortcomings of the model as it has been applied.

2. Discuss awareness contexts and communication about dying.

3. What is a dying trajectory and what is its importance? Differentiate the lingering, expected quick and unexpected quick trajectories.

4. Identify Cicely Saunders, St. Joseph's Hospice, St. Christopher's Hospice, Connecticut Hospice, and Sylvia Lack.

5. What are some of the various characteristics of hospice care? Note the three major types of hospice programs.

6. Discuss some of the barriers to hospice care.

7. Is hospice successful? Explain.

8. What is a near-death experience? What kind of experiences have been reported in NDEs?

9. Present an overview of the major theoretical explanations of NDEs.

References

Appleby, L. (1989). Near death experience: Analogous to other stress induced psychological phenomena. *British Journal of Medicine*, 298:976–977.

Atchison, N., P. Guercio, and C. Monaco. (1986). Pain in the pediatric burn patient: Nursing assessment and perception. *Issues in Comprehensive Pediatric Nursing*, 9:399–409.

Benoliel, J. (1974). Anticipatory grief in physicians and nurses. In B. Schoenberg et al. (Eds.), *Anticipatory Grief*. New York: McGraw-Hill.

Blackmore, S. (1993). *Dying to Live: Science and the Near-Death Experience*. London: Grafton.

Camp, L. (1988). A comparison of nurse's recorded assessments of pain with perceptions of pain as described by cancer patients. *Cancer Nursing*, 11:237–243.

Choiniere, M., et al. (1990). Comparison between patient's and nurse's assessments of pain and medication efficacy in severe burn injuries. *Pain*, 40:143–152.

Cohen, F. (1980). Postsurgical pain relief: Patient's status and nurse's medication choices. *Pain*, 9:265–274.

Corcoran, D. (1988). Helping patients who've had near-death experiences. *Nursing*, 88:34–39.

Corr, C. (1992). A task-based approach to coping with dying. *Omega*, 24:81–94.

Corr, C. (1993). Coping with dying: Lessons that we should and should not learn from the work of Elisabeth Kubler-Ross. *Death Studies*, 17:69–83.

Dahl, J., D. Joranson, and D. Weissman. (1989). The Wisconsin cancer pain initiative: A progress report. *American Journal of Hospice Care,* 6:39–43.

du Boulay, S. (1984). *Cicely Saunders: Founder of the Modern Hospice Movement.* London: Hodder and Stoughton.

Feifel, H. (Ed.). (1959). *The Meaning of Death.* New York: McGraw-Hill.

Fitts, W., and I. Ravdin. (1953). What Philadelphia physicians tell patients with cancer. *JAMA,* 153:901–904.

Fraser, I., T. Koontz, and W. Moran. (1986). Medicare reimbursement for hospice care: An approach for analyzing cost consequences. *Inquiry,* 23:141–153.

Gabbard, G., S. Twenlow, and F. Jones. (1981). Do "near death experiences" occur only near death? *Journal of Nervous and Mental Disease,* 169:374–377.

General Accounting Office. (1989). *Medicare Program Provisions and Payments Discourage Hospice Participation.* Report HRD-89–111. Washington, D.C.: Author.

Glaser, B., and A. Strauss. (1965). *Awareness of Dying.* Chicago: Aldine.

Glaser, B., and A. Strauss. (1968). *Time for Dying.* Chicago: Aldine.

Greenwald, H., and M. Nevitt. (1982). Physician attitudes toward communication with cancer patients. *Social Science and Medicine,* 16:591–594.

Greer, D., et al. (1984). *Final Report of the National Hospice Study.* Providence, RI: Brown University.

Grof, S., and J. Halifax. (1977). *The Human Encounter With Death.* New York: Dutton.

Harrison, A. (1991). Assessing patient's pain: Identifying reasons for error. *Journal of Advanced Nursing,* 16:1018–1025.

Herzog, D., and J. Herrin. (1985). Near-death experiences in the very young. *Critical Care Medicine,* 13:1074–1075.

Holck, F. (1978). Life revisited (parallels in death experiences). *Omega,* 9:1–12.

Kane, R., et al. (1984). A randomized controlled trial of hospice care. *Lancet,* 1:890–894.

Kastenbaum, R. (1991). *Death, Society, and Human Experience.* New York: Merrill.

Kalish, R. (1976). Death and dying in a social context. In R. Binstock and E. Shanas (Eds.), *Handbook of Aging and the Social Sciences.* New York: Van Nostrand Reinhold Co.

Kavanaugh, R. (1972). *Facing Death.* New York: Penguin Books.

Kearl, M. (1989). *Endings: A Sociology of Death and Dying.* New York: Oxford University Press.

Klenow, D., and G. Youngs, Jr. (1987). Changes in doctor/patient communication of a terminal prognosis: A selective review and critique. *Death Studies,* 11:263–277.

Kubler-Ross, E. (1969). *On Death and Dying.* New York: Macmillan.

Lander, J. (1990). Clinical judgements in pain management. *Pain,* 42:15–22.

Latimer, E. (1991). Caring for seriously ill and dying patients: The philosophy and ethics. *Canadian Medical Association Journal,* 144:859–864.

MacDonald, D. (1989). Non-admission: The other side of the hospice story. *American Journal of Hospice Care,* 6:17–19, 40–42.

Marks, R., and E. Sachar. (1973). Undertreatment of medical inpatients with narcotic analgesics. *Annals of Internal Medicine,* 78:173–181.

Mather, L., and J. Mackie. (1983). The incidence of postoperative pain in children. *Pain,* 15:271–282.

Meduna, L. (1950). *Carbon Dioxide Therapy: A Neurophysiological Treatment of Nervous Disorders*. Springfield, IL: Charles C Thomas.

Monroe, R. (1971). *Journeys Out of the Body*. New York: Doubleday.

Moody, R. (1975). *Life After Life*. Atlanta: Mockingbird Books.

Mor, V., D. Greer, and R. Kastenbaum. (1988). *The Hospice Experiment*. Baltimore: Johns Hopkins University Press.

Morse, M., and P. Perry. (1990). *Closer to the Light*. New York: Ivy Books.

Morse, M., and P. Perry. (1992). *Transformed by the Light*. New York: Villard Books.

Morse, M., D. Connor, and D. Tyler. (1985). Near-death experiences in a pediatric population. *American Journal of Diseases in Children*, 139:595–599.

Noyes, R. (1979). Near-death experiences: Their interpretation. In R. Kastenbaum (Ed.), *Between Life and Death* (pp. 73–88). New York: Springer Publishing Co.

Noyes, R., and R. Kletti. (1976). Depersonalization in the face of life-threatening danger: An interpretation. *Omega*, 7:103–114.

Novack, D., R. Plumer, R. Smith, H. Ochitill, G. Morrow, and J. Bennett. (1979). Changes in physician's attitudes toward telling the cancer patient. *JAMA*, 241:897–900.

Oakes, A. (1981). Near-death events and critical care nursing. *Topics in Clinical Nursing*, 3:61–78.

Oken, D. (1961). What to tell cancer patients. *JAMA*, 175:1120–1128.

Orne, R. (1986). Nurse's views of NDEs. *American Journal of Nursing*, 8:419–420.

Osis, K. (1961). *Deathbed Observations by Physicians and Nurses*. New York: Parapsychology Foundation.

Osis, K., and E. Haraldsson. (1977). *At the Hour of Death*. New York: Avon Books.

Owens, J., E. Cook and I. Stevenson. (1990). Features of "near death experience" in relation to whether or not patients were near death. *Lancet*, 336:1175–1177.

Papowitz, L. (1986). Life, death, life. *American Journal of Nursing*, 8:417–418.

Parkes, C., and J. Parkes. (1984). "Hospice" versus "hospital" care—Reevaluation after ten years as seen by surviving spouses. *Postgraduate Medical Journal*, 60:120–124.

Pattison, E. (1978). The living-dying process. In. C. Garfield (Ed.)., *Psychosocial Care of the Dying Patient* (pp. 133–168). New York: McGraw-Hill.

Rainey, L. (1988). The experience of dying. In H. Wass, F. Berardo, and R. Neimeyer (Eds), *Dying: Facing the Facts*. Washington: Hemisphere Publishing Corporation.

Rawlings, M. (1993). *To Hell and Back*. Nashville, TN: Thomas Nelson.

Rhymes, J. (1990). Hospice care in America. *JAMA*, 264:369–372.

Rinaldi, A., and M. Kearl. (1990). The hospice farewell: Ideological perspectives of its professional practitioners. *Omega*, 21:283–300.

Ring, K. (1980). *Life At Death*. New York: Coward, McCann and Geoghegan.

Ring, K. (1984). *Heading Toward Omega*. New York: William Morrow.

Ring, K. (1989). Near-death experiences. In R. Kastenbaum and B. Kastenbaum (Eds.), *Encyclopedia of Death* (pp. 193–196). Phoenix: Oryx Press.

Roberts, G., and J. Owen. (1988). The near-death experience. *British Journal of Psychiatry*, 153:607–617.

Sabom, M. (1982). *Recollections of Death: A Medical Investigation*. New York: Simon and Schuster.

Sabom, M., and S. Kreutziger. (1977). The experience of near death. *Death Education,* 2:195–204.

Schulz, R., and D. Aderman. (1974). Clinical research and the stages of dying. *Omega,* 5:137–144.

Schulz, R., and J. Schlarb. (1988). Two decades of research on dying: What do we know about the patient? *Omega,* 18:299–317.

Seale, C. (1989). What happens in hospices: A review of research evidence. *Social Science and Medicine,* 28:551–559.

Serdahely, W. (1989–1990). A pediatric near-death experience: Tunnel variants. *Omega,* 20:55–62.

Serdahely, W., and B. Walker. (1990). A near-death experience at birth. *Death Studies,* 14:177–183.

Shneidman, E. (1980). *Voices of Death.* New York: Harper & Row.

Shneidman, E. (1973). *Deaths of Man.* Baltimore: Penguin Books.

Siegel, R. (1980). The psychology of life after death. *American Psychologist,* 35:911–931.

Stjernsward, J. (1985). Cancer pain relief: An important global public health issue. In H. Fields, R. Dubner, and F. Cervero (Eds.), *Advances in Pain Research and Therapy* (vol. 9, pp. 555–558). New York: Raven.

Streltzer, J., and T. Wade. (1981). The influence of cultural group on the undertreatment of postoperative pain. *Psychosomatic Medicine,* 43:397–403.

Torrens, P. (1985). Hospice care: What have we learned? *Annual Review of Public Health,* 6:65–83.

Veatch, R., and E. Tai. (1980). Talking about death: Patterns of lay and professional change. *The Annals of the American Academy of Political and Social Science,* 447:29–45.

Walker, F. (1989). A nowhere near-death experience: Heavenly choirs interrupt myelography. *JAMA,* 261:3245–3246.

Weisman, A. (1972). *On Dying and Denying.* New York: Behavioral Publications.

Weisman, A. (1992). Commentary on Corr's "A task-based approach to coping with dying." *Omega,* 2:95–96.

Yacorzynski, G., A. Atkinson, J. Cohen, et al. (1950). *Investigation of Carbon Dioxide Therapy.* Springfield, IL: Charles C Thomas.

Zaleski, C. (1987). *Otherworld Journeys: Accounts of Near-Death Experiences in Medieval and Modern Times.* New York: Oxford University Press.

CHAPTER 9

Bereavement, Grief, and Mourning

Give sorrow words, the grief that does not speak knits the o'erwrought heart and bids it break.

William Shakespeare, *Macbeth,* Act IV, Scene iii

Hearing this, Wilbur threw himself down in an agony of pain and sorrow. Great sobs racked his body. He heaved and grunted with desolation. "Charlotte," he moaned. "Charlotte! My true friend!"

Wilbur on hearing of Charlotte's impending death.

E. B. White, *Charlotte's Web*

EACH YEAR IN the United States countless numbers of people suffer the death of a loved one. Those left behind include spouses, children, parents, siblings, various other relatives, and close personal friends. Not only do these persons endure the actual death of the loved one, but they continue their own existence with the loss imposed by that death. Death robs them of a husband, mother, son, sister, or best friend. In so doing, it catapults them into the ranks of the bereaved.

Bereavement is defined as the state of having sustained a loss. It is most typically used in reference to the loss that death inflicts. However, it also applies to various other significant losses. For instance, we may lose our job,

343

home, marriage, functional ability, or a limb to amputation. With the so-called midlife crisis, we witness the loss of our youth and with it our perception of seemingly endless years stretching out before us. We know our time and our life are limited. These various bereaved states may be associated with feelings of grief.

Grief is the emotional reaction to loss. It is a complex, multidimensional response with physical, psychological, and sociocultural components. Physically, it is triggered by the stress of loss and is generally characterized by distinct symptoms. Psychologically, it is a highly personal experience influenced by one's individual psychological dynamics. Finally, grief is played out within a sociocultural setting that defines the significance of lost relationships and belongings and dictates appropriate behavior.

This chapter is concerned with bereavement imposed by death, the related grief experience, and its expression. Selected states of bereavement are examined.

Bereavement and Grief

When others are bereaved, we generally expect them to be grief-stricken. However, such is not always the case. It is possible to experience a loss and, thus, by definition to be bereaved, without experiencing intense emotion. For example, the death of a biologically close relative such as a parent might not elicit a strong reaction. Time, geographic distance, or a lack of affection may not have allowed a close relationship. Thus, the loss is not deemed significant and is not deeply felt.

When a loss is significant, grief can be overwhelming. Powerful sensations coupled with feelings of deep despair tend to sweep over us in wavelike effect. The physical sensations include tightness in the throat, an empty feeling in the abdomen, shortness of breath, sighing, muscular weakness, fatigue, loss of appetite, and sleep disturbances. These sensations can last from twenty minutes to an hour at a time. They tend to come and go.

Psychologically, pain, sorrow, and loneliness are the source of greatest distress. Additionally, the bereaved may feel anger, guilt, fear, anxiety, a lack of emotional warmth with others, a desire to be left alone, and a preoccupation with the image of the deceased. Grief makes its victims feel scattered, confused, in a fog, and removed from what is going on around them. Maintaining an organized pattern of behavior may be difficult, and some sensations may be felt more strongly than others. Depending on the attachment to the deceased, the ebb and flow of powerful feelings can disrupt the normal pattern of life. Some persons relate that these reactions make them feel like they are going crazy.

Grief can be very painful, so painful that some seek to avoid it by burying themselves in their work. They keep busy, too busy to grieve. Others might escape with tranquilizers, sleeping pills, or alcohol. However, avoidance of grief merely postpones dealing with our feelings. Grief needs to be experienced, to be worked through, to be resolved. It is a means of coming to terms with death, of learning to live without the deceased, of regaining the energy to become involved in our own life again. Making these adjustments begins with acknowledging the loss and the pain.

Factors Influencing Grief

Grief experiences are not all alike. Grief is a highly individual affair. Numerous factors influence the intensity of grief and how easily it is brought to resolution. Some factors can enhance our capacity to accept a given death and come to terms with it. Others can make the task more difficult or can seriously undermine it.

Who Died?

Perhaps the most obvious factor influencing the intensity of the grief experience is the identity of the person who died. Losing someone that we love deeply is one of the most shattering experiences in our life. Such closeness extends beyond romantic love. It involves a father and son, a mother and daughter, two sisters, or an uncle and loving nephew. Strong attachments between two people can provide a sense of gratification, security, stability, and self-esteem, all of which may be shaken when the relationship is severed by death. The loss of such an intense relationship may seem to threaten our own existence, to cause us to question our own reason for going on with life.

Likewise, the identity of the person who died may directly affect our own identity or purpose in life by ending fulfilling roles we once performed. If our life revolved around being a parent, spouse, grandparent, or caregiver, then the death of the significant other can be especially devastating. In such an event, we lose not only our loved one but a large part of who we are as well. Death also voids those roles that had been occupied by the deceased. The greater the number and importance of those roles (source of happiness and love, trusted confidant, lover, best friend, breadwinner, and so on), the more disruptive the death will be.

A relationship that was characterized by a high level of dependency between the deceased and the bereaved can make grief quite difficult. Feelings of abandonment and desertion may accompany the death, intensifying a sense of anger. This reaction is most evident when the bereaved is the distinctly dependent partner. The theme of dependency and fear of abandonment stem back to childhood, but may be aroused when highly dependent adult relationships are threatened by separation. Heightened anger and helplessness can complicate grief for the dependent bereaved adult (Parkes and Weiss, 1983; Raphael, 1977; Raphael and Nunn, 1988).

The Acceptability of a Given Death

A particular death's acceptability can be a major influence on the grief experience. An acceptable death is generally one that is timely. Age is often a measure of death's acceptability; for instance, if one's ninety-year-old parent dies, there may be deep sorrow but usually not prolonged, debilitating grief. Death is seen as appropriate with advanced age. Conversely, the death of a child or young adult is not generally considered acceptable; it is seen as unfair and highly inappropriate. Such a death may be expected to produce intense, prolonged grief. Fulton (1970) distinguishes the grief typically associated with acceptable and unacceptable death as "low grief" and "high grief," respectively.

However, the concept of acceptable, appropriate, or low-grief death is based on generalities and societal determinations. Grief is, as previously noted, a highly individual experience. A so-called low-grief death can result in an intense experience depending on the relationship between the two parties involved.

Stephenson (1985) underscores that the appropriateness of death must be considered from the griever's perspective:

> While the rest of the family may see the death of an elderly member as appropriate . . . the surviving spouse may feel a great deal of rage because he or she might always have expected to die first. The death of the spouse will then be seen as unfair and inappropriate. Only by understanding the meaning of death to the griever can we come to understand the meaning of the grief. (Stephenson, 1985, p. 126)

The Availability of Social Support

However demonstrative or private we might be in our personal expression of grief, it is helpful to have society's permission to grieve. The compassionate acknowledgment of our pain helps to validate the sense of loss and to justify the strong emotions it evokes. Such justification facilitates emotional expression and the resolution of grief.

The absence of a supportive social environment undermines the grieving process by failing to validate the importance of a loss and denying the bereaved an opportunity to openly ventilate their feelings. Such is the case with disenfranchised grief (Doka, 1989). This occurs when the importance of the loss goes unrecognized, as might happen for those who miscarry, are mentally retarded, or are close friends rather than relatives of the deceased. We will briefly examine these examples.

For many individuals, miscarriage is a significant form of loss that provokes a postdeath grief reaction. Survivors of miscarriage used to be viewed as illegitimate mourners. Today, their right to grieve is becoming acknowledged. The amount of grief provoked is determined by the meaning the pregnancy held for the couple. However, its expression is often thwarted in this socially unacknowledged form of parental bereavement. There is no live birth, no baby, nothing to hold. One woman referred to her miscarriage as the "passing of a dream." Survivors of miscarriage should be provided the chance to express their feelings. Too often, the grief is negated with statements such as, "You can have another baby" or "You'll get over this quickly" (Lietar, 1986). Miscarriage can be an intense emotional experience. Maternal grief after miscarriage can be the same as it is for a stillborn or neonatal death (Peppers and Knapp, 1980a).

It is uncertain how those with mental retardation conceptualize death. It appears that, except for the profoundly retarded, their responses to it are very much like those of their non-mentally-retarded peers. They are recognized as being at risk of suffering additional emotional and behavioral problems because of the failure of others to acknowledge their need to grieve (Kloeppel and Hollins, 1989; Oswin, 1989). The mentally retarded are often discouraged from displays of grief, perhaps in fear that these will be too intense or disruptive (Carder, 1987; Lipe-Goodson and Goebel, 1983). Likewise, they are often excluded from wakes, funerals, and memorial services and their symptoms of grief are masked with medications (Moise, 1985). Research into intervention schemes to appropriately assist them through the grief process is needed (Wadsworth and Harper, 1991).

The grief of close friends of deceased persons is largely ignored (Sklar, 1991–1992; Sklar and Hartley, 1990). Referred to as *survivor-friends*, they are considered a hidden population of grievers with virtually no channels for publicly expressing their feelings beyond eulogizing their deceased friend at a funeral or memorial service. As with other disenfranchised grievers, they lack a formal role that allows them to grieve as deeply as they feel.

Disenfranchised grief also exists for those whose relationship with the deceased is not socially approved as with extramarital lovers or homosexual couples. When one of the partners in such a relationship dies, the bereaved individual is usually not formally recognized by the greater community. It provides little opportunity for the significance of the loss to be validated or for grief to be publicly acknowledged. When society does not assign significance to a high-grief death, grieving is made more difficult for the bereaved.

Mode of Death

Anticipatory Grief vs. Sudden Death. The mode or manner in which death occurs can influence the grief process. One aspect of the mode of death is time-related, that is, whether the death was anticipated, bringing an end to a period of illness, or whether it was sudden and unexpected. Sudden, unexpected death produces the most severe reactions.

With knowledge of an impending death, the grieving process can begin before the death occurs—a process called *anticipatory grief.* Anticipatory grief helps prepare the loved one for the death, making grief less intense when death actually happens (Ball, 1977; Glick, Weiss, and Parkes, 1974; Parkes and Weiss, 1983). It provides a chance to draw close, to resolve conflicts, and to say goodbye. Anticipatory grief does not, however, eliminate death's overall impact or the desolation and loneliness that loss can bring.

Furthermore, anticipating the loss of a loved one may take its toll. When there is an extended period of time between the shock of a terminal diagnosis or a potentially life-threatening injury and the eventual death, many conflicting emotions can be experienced along the way. Depending on the disease, there may be good days, bad days, periods of remission, and periods of decline. The ups and downs can bring hope and denial, sorrow and despair, anger and impatience—imposing a virtual emotional roller coaster. Needless to say, this kind of experience can be physically exhausting and emotionally draining. Loved ones may find themselves wondering, "When will this nightmare be over? When will this finally end?" They may then feel guilty for having had such thoughts. Anticipatory grief has been referred to as a "state of emotional limbo," where one cannot resolve a loss that has not yet occurred and cannot escape the fact that it will (Stephenson, 1985).

Sudden, unexpected deaths cause more intense reactions, result in more difficult adjustment, and carry a greater risk of physical and mental disability during bereavement. Evidence regarding the health effects on the bereaved is inconsistent (Stroebe and Stroebe, 1987); however, that sudden death can precipitate debilitating shock and prolonged grief among survivors is accepted.

Sudden accidents are the number-one killer of persons aged forty-four years and under in the United States. Nearly one-third of these traumatic deaths are due to automobile accidents. In a study of persons whose spouse or child died in a motor vehicle crash, it was found that resultant psychological stress continued for years—much longer than had been previously assumed (Lehman and Wortman, 1984–1985).

The answer to the proverbial question, "How long should grief last?" had often been, "Six months to a year." This time frame springs from the pioneer work of Lindemann (1944), a psychiatrist who followed survivors of the well-known catastrophic 1942 fire at Boston's Coconut Grove nightclub. The fire left 491 people dead. Lindemann's work proved to be extremely influential in providing a framework for understanding the symptoms of grief and distinguishing its various forms. Over the years, many aspects of his findings have been retained and others modified, including the notion that grief is normally limited to six months.

For example, Lehman and Wortman (1984–1985) found that the suddenly and unexpectedly bereaved spouses and parents in their study of fatal vehicular crashes were still actively dealing with their loss four to seven years after the death. Subjects reported marked depression and failure to resolve their grief. Their work clearly indicates that under such circumstances, long-term grief is a common response and not a sign of individual coping failure.

Natural, Accidental, Suicide, Homicide. Central to the mode of death is the form that death takes—natural causes, accidental, suicide, or homicide. The time-related features previously discussed are relevant to this aspect of death and the grief experience. However, the mode of death can influence survivor grief in various other ways. Shneidman (1973) refers to those bereaved by suicide as *survivor-victims*. They are, he said,

> invaded by an unhealthy complex of disturbing emotion: shame, guilt, hatred, perplexity. They are obsessed with thoughts about the death, seeking reasons, casting blame, and often punishing themselves. (Shneidman, 1973, p. 34)

Those who lose a loved one to murder face great emotional turmoil. Resolving the loss may be made more difficult by prolonged attempts to solve the crime, drawn out court proceedings and appeals, and media attention. When the body is not recovered (whether or not murder was involved), recovery from grief is more difficult (Simpson, 1979).

Other Factors

Various other factors can influence the grief response. Unfinished business between the deceased and bereaved is one of them. Actions left undone, words left unspoken, or conflicts left unresolved can be a source of great regret and heartache. Extreme ambivalence (feelings of love and hate) in a relationship can also make grief harder to resolve. Such contradictory feelings tend to continue after the death, causing exaggerated guilt and confusion.

Previous encounters with loss may give some indication of individual coping style. They may also provide the bereaved with valuable, if painful, coping experience that prepares them to deal more effectively with present and future losses. On the other hand, too many losses accumulating too soon can compromise one's coping ability and lead to an emotional state referred to as *bereavement overload*.

The personality of the bereaved will play a role in coping. For the dependent personality, grief is likely to be more devastating. It is also reported that those who approach life with a greater degree of determination or purpose tend to cope more effectively with bereavement (Pfost, Stevens, and Wessels, 1989). However, these bits of information should not be used to label people as weak or strong on the basis of the apparent intensity of their response to a loved one's death. Intense feelings for another and intense grief are certainly not a sign of weakness. Feelings of grief are powerful, painful; they can be overwhelming. By coping, we do not mean hiding our feelings or not experiencing devastating pain. We mean carrying on with our life—living up to our responsibilities—finding the strength to carry on in spite of the pain.

It should be obvious to the reader by now that grief is a complex phenomenon. It is influenced by the interplay of numerous factors, some of which have been presented in the foregoing material.

The Grieving Process

In order to resolve grief, one must move away from the shock of a terminal diagnosis or pronouncement of death, through a period of emotional unrest, to, finally, learning to live without the deceased. These steps form a rough sequence that are often termed *stages of grief*. They comprise what is also known as the *grief process*.

Cataloguing the grief experience in such a way does not mean to imply that it consists of a set number of emotional reactions that unfold in a rigid order. The emotional states overlap and intertwine. Experiencing them while moving toward resolution has been compared to engaging in a series of dance steps as opposed to taking a cross-country walk (DeSpelder and Strickland, 1992). Emotionally, we are all over the place.

Perhaps one day we will refrain from calling them stages of grief. As Ericsson (1993, p. 88) warns in her book that so powerfully and eloquently chronicles her own grief experience, "The stages of grief are a hoax. There aren't stages. Only waves of feelings two and three at a time." The stage models of grief attempt to capture the essence of these waves of feelings. They characterize the experience while respecting that individuals pass through it in their own unique way. Some have identified three stages of grief (Averill, 1968; Gorer, 1965), while others have outlined as many as seven (Kavanaugh, 1972). These differences are accounted for by consolidating some reactions and expanding on others.

Stephenson (1985) presents three phases of grief. They include reaction, disorganization and reorganization, and reorientation and recovery.

Phase I: Reaction

The reaction phase begins with shock at the news of the death. It is followed by numbness. People often report feeling as if they are in a daze. They go about the tasks of informing others and making funeral arrangements, functioning on an intellectual level but in an emotional stupor.

Initial emotional numbness in response to extremely threatening situations (physical or emotional) may be part of a life-preserving adaptive mechanism. Rather than emotionally succumbing to a threat, in our numbness we are able to concentrate on life-saving tasks such as running away from an enemy or escaping a burning building. The body's stress response does not distinguish between physically or emotionally based threats. Thus, the blow of another's death results in emotional numbness.

Another early aspect of the reaction phase is bewilderment in which an attempt is made to give meaning to the death. When the death is unexpected or inappropriate, it is harder to make sense of it.

Once the reality of the loss begins to sink in, there is a strong desire to recover the deceased, to bring him or her back. Crying out for the loved one is very common.

Anger is a characteristic reaction. The bereaved may be angry at the deceased for having left, angry at God for having "allowed this to happen," or angry at others who attempt to pull them of out grief or to reinforce the reality of the death. Remarks such as, "You must accept the fact that he is dead" may be met with overt or covert hostility.

Guilt, rational and irrational, is a major dynamic of grief—guilt for any promises not kept, for any business left undone, or for any unkind word uttered. The bereaved may feel guilt for the anger.

Phase II: Disorganization and Reorganization

Recognizing that our loss will not be recovered, deep despair sets in accompanied by varying degrees of sadness, loneliness, and yearning. Activities do not have the meaning they once did. Energy is lacking, motivation is gone, and it is difficult to remain focused. It is usually very hard to initiate and maintain an organized pattern of behavior. When bereaved, we feel scattered, as if we are losing our mind.

A new life has to be built. Vitality and a sense of purpose must be regained. But, before a new life can begin, the old one must be disassembled. Our life is not the same and never will be. We must learn to live without the deceased. Rebuilding is frightening and painful as it springs from a sense of uncertainty and helplessness. Desolation and distress may be swelling inside.

There is often a preoccupation with the deceased, an obsessive review of the past, and a lack of emotional closeness with others. To stop grieving is to desert the deceased and to give up all we have left of him or her. Our grief seems to be all that remains, the only thing we can hold onto. Relinquishing it can produce sorrow, loneliness, and more guilt. Hence, there is resistance to end grief.

Phase III: Reorientation and Recovery

In the final phase of grief, it becomes possible to think of the deceased without disabling pain and overwhelming sadness. Our life is enriched by memories of the dead rather than burdened by them. The deceased gradually takes on a new identity outside of our immediate environment. He or she is now in heaven, the next life, at rest, or simply dead, and, thus, is a part of our past. We, the grieving, are left to adapt to life in this world. As Aries (1981) states, when bereaved we eventually become accustomed to the absence of the deceased. We transfer our obstinate fixation on the once-living person to an internalization of the deceased loved one. Grief is resolved when it is possible to reinvest in life and to pursue new goals, interests, and relationships.

The resolution of grief does not mean that we no longer miss our loved one or that the pain of our loss is ever entirely gone. Losing a truly significant loved one is not something we ever get over. The emptiness is always there. We just learn to live with it. We learn to cope. One mother whose daughter died suddenly and accidentally sought for years to heal her broken heart. She read books, joined support groups, and attended numerous conferences on grief. After many years and all of these efforts, she realized that her heart would always be broken. She realized that that was o.k. There was nothing wrong with her psychologically. She was living her life with her "brokenness" in place. The intensity of grief lessened with time but her sense of loss did not.

In contrast to this three-stage model of grief, Kavanaugh's (1972) scheme identifies seven stages. They are (1) shock and disbelief, (2) disorganization and confusion, (3) volatile emotions, (4) guilt, (5) loss and loneliness, (6) relief, and (7) reestablishment. The reader will recognize these emotional states, though enumerated differently, from the foregoing discussion.

Reflections on Kavanaugh's Seven Stages of Grief

In trying to capture the many emotions that accompany the grieving process, Kavanaugh outlines seven stages of grief. The first is shock. When a loved one dies, the reality of the death is hard to grasp even if it has been anticipated. In shock and disbelief, we may question, "Why?" But, it is not answers we seek at this time. Our question is more a statement of our bewilderment than real. Answers are not appropriate. There are no answers, at least none that will be heard.

Disorganization and confusion mark the second stage of grief. We feel out of touch with our surroundings. We need to be allowed to cry and talk without any demand to be "reasonable." The physical presence of and contact with a trusted friend or loved one is important. It symbolizes that warmth remains in our lives—the warmth of a world that is now out of focus.

The third stage of grief is characterized by volatile emotions—explosive feelings such as helplessness, hurt, frustration, and anger. There is often conflict between an open display of such intense feelings and pressure to be in control of ourselves. We usually hold in a lot because we don't want others to think us weak or unreasonable. And, in our culture, people who grieve with open intensity may be labeled in just that fashion. Physicians may tranquilize us and friends offer explanations or admonish us to be strong. These suppressed feelings can eat away at us; their ventilation depends on individual style and personality. For some, they are acknowledged through sober thoughtfulness or talk. For others, the rage may only find release in ranting and raving or pounding the wall. Blame may be angrily cast at God or the medical profession. Thus, in general, professionals may not be the best at providing consolation at this time. The clergy may feel compelled to defend God's divine plan and the doctor or nurse the quality of medical care. Those consoling mourners need to know that the intense feelings are neither good nor bad—they just are. They need not be justified or explained away. With permissive listening, they will, in time, run their course.

Guilt is the fourth stage of grief. When a loved one dies, we relive our life with that person. In so doing, we often have many regrets; we may dwell on the "if onlys": "If only I had expressed my love more often"; "If only I had visited more"; "If only I hadn't been so grumpy or impatient." One woman chastised herself for months after her father's death for not being stricter with him about his diet and exercise program. She also feared she had added to the stress that possibly triggered his heart attack. Another anguished over not getting her husband to the doctor sooner: "I should have seen this coming".

In time, lesser forms of guilt dwindle. Talking about them in a nonjudgmental atmosphere helps them dissipate. In doing so, we may be eventually reassured that there is little to feel guilty about. At the time, we did the best we could. However, serious, rational, long-standing guilt is much more difficult to deal with. The alcoholic husband who buries his wife having never lived up to his promise to quit drinking will find no easy answers to assuage his guilt. The daughter who truly neglected her elderly mother will get no second chance to make things right. Guilt-ridden mourners must find their own way to make amends. Because of their experience, they may become (if only even on a minute scale) the person they wish they had been. As Kavanaugh (1972, p. 116) states, they may become "a walking memorial to a truth only finally learned in death."

The fifth stage of grief may be the most painful. It is the sense of loss and loneliness that death brings. The one who has died and everything he or she was to us will not be replaced. Only we in our own hearts know and feel the depth of that loss. We grieve alone even in the comfort of family and caring friends. And, we may feel painfully alone. The magnitude of our loss becomes more obvious with time, long after others assume that we should be getting on with our life and over our grief. When we lose someone we deeply love, we become more aware of our needs and dependencies with each passing day. The many:

> threads that bind two human beings together in a relationship, all the interneeds and interdependencies, seem taken for granted until death severs them. The tiny things like odors and . . . toenails, scars and facial wrinkles, the lines of a smile and ways of touching, all become as difficult to forget as bigger treasures like mutual acceptance.   (Kavanaugh, 1972, p. 119)

The sixth stage of grief, relief, is very unsettling. It can cause us to feel more guilt and shame. It is the sense of relief that comes with the death of a loved one. It seems contradictory that we should feel any relief at losing someone we love so dearly. And, indeed, it is. The larger part of us cries out in sorrow and loneliness. Yet, another part of us feels that a weight has been lifted. That weight might be the painful task of watching a loved one suffer and die or seeing major medical expenses accumulate. But, lifted also are the demands that a relationship imposes even if those demands are mingled with rich rewards. With the end of a relationship:

> We are, it is true, freer. If we have lost our spouse, we've also lost the parts of him that could not negotiate an amicable solution to a problem, the dependence, and the prison of that dependence. This exists at the same time and in the same space as the moments of regret.   (Ericsson, 1993, p. 38)

We need to recognize the normality of such feelings. Our feeling relief is not a criticism of our loved one. It is not a betrayal of him or her. It is not a callous indictment of us. It is a normal reaction. A middle-aged woman who was suffering intense grief after her mother's death thought one day, "I would not bring her back even if I could." How strange she felt to be having such thoughts in the midst of her anguished sobbing. "This is so painful," she thought, "that I could not bear to go through it again." She felt relief that the anticipated event she had feared for so many years had happened—her mother could not die again.

Gradually, we reach the final stage of grief, reestablishment. We begin to live our life with a renewed spirit. It cannot come too soon for us without guilt staring us in the face. As we work through our feelings, our grief in all its intensity, reestablishment comes in its own time.

These stages of grief are distinct emotional states not separate, successive feelings that surface in a given order. Some may be fleeting, some may last a very long time. Some may be mild, others intense, and some skipped altogether. They can coexist and intermingle. The process of grief is framed, however, by shock (our initial reaction) and reestablishment.

Various Grieving Responses: What Is Normal?

The physical symptoms of grief and its various emotional states do not represent an all or nothing phenomenon. A few, many, or all of the elements may be experienced. Their expression is tempered by the many previously presented variables. Some elements may be felt more strongly than others depending on the degree of attachment to or dependence on the deceased, the appropriateness of the death, or the manner in which it occurred.

The way in which the grieving process is displayed varies with the bereaved. Feelings are not necessarily obvious to others. On the outside we seem o.k., but on the inside we may be falling apart. In the midst of grief, it is not uncommon to be troubled by a sense of personal inadequacy. We may feel weak, deficient, incapable of coping or, at best, less capable than others. It is important to understand that intense feelings, including a sense of disorganization and despair, are not uncommon in the wake of significant loss.

In moving through the grief process, Worden (1982) recognizes that we face four major tasks:

1. Accepting the reality of death. Even if a death is anticipated or viewed as appropriate, its reality is difficult to grasp emotionally.
2. Experiencing the pain.
3. Adjusting to a changed environment.
4. Withdrawing emotional energy from the deceased so that it can be reinvested in other people and other things.

There is no right way to grieve. Although societal expectations about the expression of grief exist, so too do individual differences. Because of the growing awareness of individual and cross-cultural differences in grief's manifestation, there is caution in delineating "normal" and "abnormal" or pathological grief. Anthropological fieldwork tells us that what we might consider pathological may be common or expected in other cultures (Rosenblatt, Walsh, and Jackson, 1976).

The grieving process includes various responses to death. Our identification of the grieving process earlier in the chapter captures what are viewed as common responses to significant death. However, we are only beginning to grasp the full range of what might be considered normal grieving (Zisook and

Schuchter, 1986). Wortman and Silver (1989) propose that our views on "normal" grief to date have overridden our acceptance of alternative views of adjusting to loss. We have assumed that coping with irretrievable loss means inevitable depression, extreme distress (the absence of which spells repressed grief), and working through the feelings to an eventual recovery within a designated period of time.

Failure to follow this pattern has been equated with pathology. We may evaluate others as recovering *too* soon or taking *too* long, as being *too* distressed or not distressed *enough*. Those who experience a death may harshly judge themselves and their reactions. Unrealistic assumptions and rigid expectations about "normal" grief can be a source of further distress for the bereaved.

Wortman and Silver (1989) charge that many of our assumptions fail to be supported by the research literature. There are no validated guideposts for evaluating normal or abnormal grief. They offer three common patterns of adapting to loss. First, there are those who follow the expected pattern. Over time they move from a phase of intense distress to one of recovery. Second, there are those who do not show intense distress. Their absence of serious grief poses no problem. Finally, there are others who continue to experience a high degree of distress over a much longer period of time.

Kalish (1985) speaks in terms of healthy and unhealthy grief. The designation rests on the extent to which they lead to the long-term well-being and effective functioning of the bereaved. In short, healthy grief should enable the bereaved to accomplish the four major tasks of grief outlined by Worden (1982).

In spite of the allowance for variable grief reactions, some people do have difficulty in accomplishing these tasks and resolving their grief. Conflicted grief may result when the relationship between the bereaved and deceased was filled with strife or ambivalent feelings (see Box 9–1). In a study of spousal bereavement, poor grief recoveries were found when marriages were characterized by ambivalence rather than wholly loving or nonloving feelings. Those whose marriages were filled with conflict exhibited many more problems when interviewed twenty-four to forty-eight months after bereavement than those whose marriages were not (Parkes and Weiss, 1983). Chronic grief exists when the emotional reaction to the death continues to dominate one's life. It is more likely to occur when the bereaved was excessively dependent upon the deceased.

When a recent death or other current loss, even if deemed a low-grief response, triggers an extremely powerful grief reaction, an expression of previously unresolved grief may be suspected. This reaction is known as *recapitulation*. However, current thinking cautions us against being too judgmental or absolute in evaluating another's grief experience. It is quite possible that a new loss might result in acute and time-appropriate grief. Such an expression does

---

Box 9–1   *Some Grief Reactions Discussed in Text*

Anniversary Reaction—powerful grief response (feelings, illness, behavior) triggered by the anniversary of a significant event, especially the anniversary of a death.

Anticipatory Grief—begins in advance of death as with a terminal illness or injury. It can emotionally prepare loved ones for the anticipated death.

Chronic Grief—occurs when the grief reaction dominates one's life for an extended period of time.

Conflicted Grief—a difficult grief reaction occurring when the relationship with the deceased was characterized by conflict and/or ambivalence.

Disenfranchised Grief—occurs when the importance of a loss goes unrecognized by others. The bereaved are denied an opportunity to openly express grief.

Recapitulation—when a recent death or other loss triggers feelings from a previous loss or losses resulting in a powerful grief reaction.

---

not necessarily represent a regression on the part of the bereaved or a delayed response to a previous high-grief death (Brabant, 1989–1990).

For example, a college student begins to suffer intense symptoms of grief including sleeplessness and a loss of appetite. Her mother had died when she was a child, yet she is now beginning to experience grief and spend time at her grave. Rather than viewing her behavior as regressive, we might consider that she is experiencing a "new loss" to her mature self. She is suffering the loss of the mother of the soon-to-be college graduate, the mother of the future bride, the mother with whom a young woman would share her fears, hopes, and dreams at this important stage of her life.

The anniversary reaction involves a similar situation regarding a resurfacing of grief. It refers to a significant alteration in feelings or behavior usually on the death anniversary. The literature is unclear on its meaning. Some view it as a reaction to be expected on occasion (Manning, 1985). Others view it as an expression of repressed or unresolved grief (Brown and Stoudemire, 1983).

Waves of sadness may be present when dates of shared occasions such as holidays, birthdays, and wedding anniversaries approach. An anniversary reaction, however, is a more intense experience. The term is also sometimes used to indicate the anxiety that may occur when individuals attain the age at which a significant person died, usually a parent. They may harbor the notion that they too might die at that age.

Mourning

Mourning in Cross-Cultural Perspective

The expression and resolution of grief are dictated not only by individual psychodynamics and the circumstances surrounding a death, but by the social environment as well. The social setting is the backdrop against which grief is acted out. It influences the way we view and respond to a loss. For example, in a society with a strong extended family system, the death of a more distant relative might be keenly felt. In a society such as our own, dominated by the nuclear family, such deaths are generally not important losses unless we have a special attachment to a given individual.

In addition to influencing our conception of what constitutes a significant loss, the social setting can facilitate or impede the grieving process. In traditional societies, the expression of grief is expected and often encouraged. It is facilitated by custom and ritual, which vary considerably. For example, in some cultures the bereaved are secluded for a period of time during which they are expected to grieve. The process is not rushed.

Likewise, the public display of emotions may be encouraged with weeping and wailing. The old Irish custom of keening (*caoine* in Gaelic) allowed for the open expression of grief. A wailing lament was performed for the dead, usually by an older woman known for her skill. Seemingly, the blatant display of crying permitted those present to engage in their own emotional release (Metress, 1990). It touched their sense of sorrow and loss and provided social approval of its expression.

In some cultures, widows might be expected to dress in black for a year and refrain from any social frivolity. Those familiar with *Gone with the Wind* are reminded of the breech of social custom as the widowed Scarlett O'Hara, clad in black gown and bonnet, danced across the floor with Rhett Butler. Onlookers were aghast and disapproving of her irreverent behavior. Widows were expected to be "in grief," a condition socially demarcated by appropriate apparel and actions.

Mourning is the culturally patterned process by which grief is managed or resolved. The preceding are examples of particular mourning customs of various societies, the latter being characteristic of an earlier time in American history. Those cited all speak to a formal recognition of bereavement and an altered state of functioning.

Although we still might not expect the newly widowed to take too eagerly to the dance floor, in modern America we don't think it healthy for the bereaved to be too sad for too long. Impatience with grief is a characteristic of American society where we seek to resolve the grief process as quickly as possible. Beyond the funeral period, people are expected to cope, to be in control, and not to burden others with open emotional displays. To do otherwise puts them at risk of being labeled emotionally weak and too quick to give into their feelings. In our society, grief is something to be mastered rather than experienced (Stephenson, 1985).

Intellectually, we might recognize the significance of a given loss, but culturally we tend to feel uncomfortable with open displays of feelings, our own or someone else's. Even in conversations between close friends, an expression of sorrowful feelings is likely to be preceded by or ended with apologies, "I shouldn't burden you with my problems." "I'm sorry for going on about this."

In some respects, we give the bereaved double and contradictory messages. After a significant death, we expect them to be grief-stricken. However, society, in restricting its expression, seems to value and require "cheerfulness" (Wright, 1983). Demands to contain grief may perpetuate the notion that prolonged displays are abnormal or pathological (Tait and Silver, 1989; Wortman and Silver, 1989).

The French historian Philippe Aries, who wrote the landmark history on changing attitudes toward death in Western civilization (1981), remarked, regarding grief, that what was once required by individual conscience or social obligation is now forbidden. It is no longer appropriate to show or feel grief (Aries, 1974). It is the strong mourners that we admire. Even though we may be falling apart inside, the social climate encourages the denial of grief and the illusion that we are "over it."

> This may be one of the reasons why some bereaved people have fears of going crazy. All of the anxiety and confusion, all the depths of feeling, seem to be on the inside. The rest of the world continues to move along in its usual way. With little social recognition or tolerance for grieving, the individual can be made to feel as though his or her responses were abnormal or pathological. (Kastenbaum, 1991, p. 269)

In contrast to our containment of grief stand many other cultures and their open demonstration of the various emotions that can accompany it. The Kaingang of southeastern Brazil are a hunting people residing in a harsh mountainous environment. Hunters sometimes die in the hazardous pursuit of food. When they do, their loss is keenly felt by the group. The loss of good hunters can bring hardship to all who are dependent on their skills. Feelings of anger and desertion that accompany bereavement are not denied by the Kaingang. Collectively they represent an important cultural theme in their death ritual and expression of grief.

The desertion theme is reinforced by their belief that some spirits linger in their midst, tempting the living to give up their hard life and join them in the next world. Thus, death stands testimony to desertion. Those left behind to continue in the deceased's absence are betrayed and angry. The body of the deceased is placed on a funeral pyre and strong cries of "deserter" are chanted by the mourners. Feelings of desertion extend beyond the funeral period as the remainder of the group continues to avoid the area where death took place. They will not put themselves in a position of being tempted to abandon the others for an easier existence in the spirit world (Henry, 1964).

Such raw exhibition of emotion may seem "primitive" and bizarre to many in our society. As Kalish (1985) warns, the customs of other societies

> need to be understood in terms of the entire societal milieu, not taken out of context as we tend to do. After all, think how strange our relative lack of ritualized mourning behavior would seem to persons from other cultures. It probably appears that we do not respect our dead relatives, since once the funeral is over, little or nothing is expected from the survivors.   (Kalish, 1985, p. 212)

Studying mourning behavior in cross-cultural perspective should not be an exercise in judging others using our own cultural experience as a standard. It should be a means of gaining respect for the universality of human feelings and the broad range of their possible expression. It can give us insight into our own culture and behaviors as well as those of others.

The containment of feelings has become characteristic of Western, industrialized society in general, with some exceptions.

> Many European cultures, such as those of the Greeks and Italians, have quite clear expectations of open and strong emotional release; whereas Anglo-Saxon society may view public display of feelings as unseemly, praising the person who shows strong emotional control.   (Raphael, 1983, p. 38)

Most of us are socialized from childhood to "keep a stiff upper lip," to "be strong," and not to cry. A consequence of our concern with being in control is that we may have become as intolerant of emotions in others as we are of them in ourselves (Scheff, 1975).

The lack of mourning ritual extends to our personal interaction with the bereaved. "I don't know what to say" is, perhaps, the most common reaction to an anticipated encounter with them. Gorer (1965), whose classic work on contemporary grief and mourning represents the first complete analysis of their twentieth-century rejection, offers a personal experience as a bereaved mourner. A few times after the death of his brother, he refused invitations to cocktail parties, explaining that he was in mourning. Those who invited him reacted with "shocked embarrassment." He got the impression that had the invitation clashed with some esoteric, self-indulgent escapade, his decline would have been understood. Instead, the people, whose invitations he refused, "educated and sophisticated as they were, mumbled and hurried away. They clearly no longer had any guidance from ritual as to the way to treat a self-confessed mourner, and I suspect they were frightened lest I give way to my grief, and involve them in a distasteful upsurge of emotion" (Gorer, 1965, p. 111).

Factors Contributing to Our Lack of Mourning Ritual

Numerous historical factors contribute to our present state regarding the general lack of mourning ritual. The industrialization and bureaucratization of society, along with the movement away from a more traditional, community-based life style, are among them. Prior to the nineteenth century, mourning was more of a community as opposed to an individual affair. People living in smaller, close-knit groups divided their affections among an extended assemblage of family and friends. When a death occurred, it was a notable event for the group, all of whom tended to be affected by the loss. "Mourning expressed the anguish of a community" (Aries, 1981, p. 582). Even though a death brought great individual sadness and grief for one particularly close to the deceased, there was less of a tendency for it to devastate one's whole emotional life. A network of close, intimate relationships remained, and individual grief was validated by the mourning of the group.

Our affections and obvious dependencies are now concentrated on an increasingly smaller number of persons. The large group is fragmented and impersonal. The death of one has less impact on the community. Beyond the funeral service, individuals or families often stand alone in their grief. The family has become the primary support network. However, due to geographic mobility, close contact with family members may be limited. Alternative support systems may not be available. Those living in urban/suburban areas are less likely to be as integrated into their communities as was true many years ago (Stroebe, Stroebe, and Hansson, 1988).

Various Bereaved States

Death of a Spouse

One of the most potentially disrupting and studied forms of bereavement is the death of a spouse. In a major study of spousal loss in those under forty-five years of age, anticipatory grief did not remove the impact of death. Although the widowed often voiced relief that their spouse's suffering had ended, they felt desolated and pained when the death actually occurred (Glick, Weiss, and Parkes, 1974). The anticipation of death, however, had the potential to keep the grief response within certain limits. Sudden death brought the tendency for intense anguish.

The many months following the funeral appeared to be the most difficult. As family and friends got on with their lives, the bereaved were pretty much on their own to deal with the practical problems of adjustment to daily life as well as the emotional burden of the death. Widows felt an urge to openly express their feelings but also an overriding desire not to burden others. Although no formal signs of mourning were apparent, most did withdraw from their regular social life.

Although outward signs of grief were generally absent, internal responses remained. The circumstances surrounding the death were replayed in their minds, over and over—a phenomenon referred to as *obsessional review*. It is believed that such preoccupation with the death is helpful in adjusting to the reality of the loss. After the first year, obsession with the loss for the widows tended to give way to "the present" and a reconstruction of their life. Yet, the sense of attachment to the deceased remained.

Widowers were inclined to be less tolerant of their desire to focus on the past. For them, obsessional review generally lasted only for a few weeks. They were also less likely to openly express their feelings. They appeared to socially adjust to the death more quickly, returning to their previous activities. However, their emotional recovery seemed slower.

This investigation, known as the Harvard Bereavement Study, includes a follow-up report on the progress of the surviving spouses two to four years later. It was found that those who made a good recovery within one year of the loss were doing the best several years later. Unresolved grief included three major types: unexpected grief, conflicted grief, and chronic grief. This finding underscores the effect of the nature of the relationship and the mode of death on the risk for intense or prolonged grief (Parkes and Weiss, 1983).

Lopata (1973, 1979, 1980), a specialist in the study of widowhood, emphasizes that spousal bereavement is largely a problem of women, especially older women. Males are more likely to die before their spouse or to remarry if widowed. She characterizes widows as follows: "They are women in a male dominated society. They are old in a society that venerates youth. Many are grieving and lonely in a country that would deny and ignore such unhappy emotions. They are without mates in a social network of couples" (Lopata, 1973, p. 87). They also are at greater risk of serious financial difficulty than are other women their own age or widowers. She points out that younger widows with children must also provide for their care while dealing with their own grief. Also, regardless of gender, the bereaved spouse must assume new roles formerly held by the deceased whether they be banking and bill-paying responsibilities or cooking and household chores.

While spousal bereavement is a significant life event, evidence is beginning to demonstrate the resiliency of those who have already suffered a loss (Caserta and Lund, 1992). That resiliency may account for the apparent minimal long-term effects of bereavement on physical health among the elderly (Ferraro, 1985; Murrell, Himmelfarb, and Phifer, 1988).

In a summary of research on the health consequences of bereavement, a decline in health is noted during the first year of bereavement followed by a return to levels similar to nonbereaved persons after this time (Stroebe, Stroebe, and Hansson, 1988). Findings also demonstrate that "mortality rates among widows exceed those among married persons; they are also higher for widowers than widows, and persons widowed at younger ages are at somewhat greater excess risk . . . relative to older persons" (Stroebe, Stroebe, and Hansson, 1988, p. 5).

The Bereaved Elderly

Although the elderly may be more experienced at coping with loss, it is necessary to remain sensitive to their individual differences and changing circumstances as well as the general benefit they derive from a loving support system. In our society, older adults are not always provided an outlet for the expression of grief. It has been asserted that, because of their age, the elderly may be expected to "grin and bear" their losses rather than openly grieve (Goodstein, 1984). Loss is expected in old age. When held by family, friends, and health professionals, such an attitude may compel older people to act strong, fearing that doing otherwise might label them as weak.

Various types of losses accumulate with age, underscoring the possibility of intense grief reactions after the loss of a spouse, relative, friend, home, employment, financial security, or pet. The cumulative losses, experienced in sometimes rapid succession, can lead to bereavement overload. Attachments to remaining persons and objects may take on increasing value. Hence, a low-grief loss may generate an intense grief reaction.

Symptoms of grief in the elderly may be attributed to or mistaken for another condition in what is referred to as a *devious pattern of grief* (Goodstein, 1984). As grief itself remains ignored, episodic exacerbation of the symptoms may result. Unresolved grief is one of the most frequently misdiagnosed conditions in the elderly. Those who verbalize continued physical and emotional pain may be dismissed as hypochondriacs.

Death of a Parent

Parental death during adulthood is the most common cause of bereavement in the United States. In spite of this fact, relatively little information exists on its effect. It has been referred to as possibly one of the most critical occasions in adult development, representing an important personal and symbolic life event for middle-aged adults (Douglas, 1990–91).

For most of us, the death of a parent represents the loss of the most unique relationship we will ever have. We lose a person who knew us since our birth and who loved us unconditionally (see Box 9–2). In interviews with those

B o x   9–2   Dear Mom . . . *Memories of a beautiful smile, a quick step, a love of life . . . and more.*

Dear Mom,

It's been a long time since we've had a chance to talk and laugh. It's hard to believe that three years have passed and I've managed to get by without you. There have been so many times when I've wished I could pick up the phone and ask you a question or get on a plane and fly home to see you. But, that was really unnecessary because you taught me how to find my own answers, and because your spirit is always with me.

It's been a hard lesson. There were tears when I thought of what I lost, and there were smiles when I remembered what I had. With each passing year, the smiles—and your memory—grow stronger. Slowly, the image of your death and your sickness are fading, and the real you, the woman with the beautiful smile and the quick step and love of life, is coming back.

As I get older and contemplate the possibility of motherhood, I find myself turning to your life again and again. I wonder if I can ever be even half the mother you were. I wonder if it's possible to have a child who could love me as much as I love you. I find it hard to imagine.

I think about my childhood and remember . . . Things changed when I got older. . . . It's not that you stopped being my mother. It's just that you started being my friend. . . .

College added a new twist. I would come home . . . and tell you all that I had learned. We discussed everything. . . . But, in the midst of our friendship, our happiness, came sickness and death, something we couldn't share, a place we couldn't go together. So we kissed and said our goodbyes, parting as mother and daughter, friends and confidantes.

I grieved at first, then I was angry and resentful, resentful toward God for taking you, resentful toward you for leaving us. That anger has been replaced by sadness and acceptance. It is an empty feeling, knowing that you can never come to visit me, that I can never give back to you all the wonderful things you gave to me.

I have learned to live with that. I have learned to pass by the Mother section in the cardstore without wanting to cry. I have learned to quietly celebrate our life together while other mothers and daughters exchange gifts, send flowers and share stories.

But beneath my composure is one final hurdle waiting to trip me up at the appropriate time. I try to prepare myself for the day when I finally have children of my own, a time I know would have brought us closer together than ever before. But, you will not be here to share first-time mother stories from my childhood. You will not be able to calm my fears with the memories that you, and only you, had locked away in your heart.

Box 9–2 *(Continued)*

Remembrance. The author of the letter gazes lovingly at a wedding photo of her mother hours before she herself walked down the aisle in her mother's bridal gown. (Reprinted by permission of *Catholic New York*/Mary DeTurris)

I know it will be a time for tears. Tears because you will never see my children, and because they will never know what a wonderful grandmother they could have had. I will tell them, but words and pictures can never do you justice.

How will they be able to believe that you could be such a wonderful mother and at the same time such a good friend? My only hope is that somewhere deep inside me is your secret recipe for motherhood. Then I will not have to tell them. I will be able to show them.

With love, friendship and respect,
Your daughter,
Mary

Source: Excerpted from M. DeTurris. (1991). Dear Mom. *Catholic New York*, May 9, p. 13. Reprinted by permission of *Catholic New York*/Mary DeTurris.

who've lost a parent, responses point to the uniqueness of the bond between parent and child (Donnelly, 1987). Those interviewed commented on the irreplaceable loss, the loss of one who provided complete acceptance with allowances for faults and mistakes, and the loss of enduring love. One woman acknowledged that although her husband loved her deeply, she knew that when her parent died no one would ever love her that way again.

The death of a mother is often the most difficult, perhaps, because of the nurturing role she played. It sometimes may be due to the fact that fathers usually die first. Thus, with the mother's death, the adult child is left without any parents. Recapitulation may play a role here; that is, with the death of the mother, there may be a resurgence of grief over the father's death.

It is not uncommon for low grief to be associated with parental death during adulthood. Adult children are absorbed in their own lives with jobs, families, and activities. They may have relocated to another part of the country and see their parents(s) only occasionally. Some detachment from parents thus occurs. Strong ties are now forged with a spouse and children whose deaths are more commonly disruptive than is that of an elderly parent's (Owen, Fulton, and Markusen, 1982–1983). The latter death requires fewer life adjustments for the bereaved adult child.

Wide individual differences do exist in the reaction to an elderly parent's death. The severing of this unique relationship can cause intense, prolonged grief. However, there may be personal and social pressure to deny the significance of the loss. Because the death of an older person is typically viewed as timely and appropriate, intense or prolonged grief is not expected. When it occurs, it may be borne silently and painfully. How many times have we heard someone say, "But, he lived a long life." Although that fact may be comforting, it can also imply that we shouldn't be so grief-stricken.

Although the death of an elderly parent may end a long and full life or terminate painful illness and disability, it still may be frought with intense sorrow. To lose someone we loved dearly, who remained a central figure in our life, is painful whatever his or her age. Someone once said that when we lose a child we lose our future and when we lose a parent we lose our past. This point is well presented in a novel by Helen Hooven Santmyer (1982). She depicts the grief of one of her characters, Christina, after the death of her father: "She could not grieve over his death—not after having heard the struggle for his every breath so many weary years." But, she did grieve: "She grieved that the past, when her father was in his prime, was over and done with, except in her memory" (Santmyer, 1982, p. 729).

The death of a parent is an important symbolic life event. It strips away any illusions of immortality for the middle-aged adult. "He had lost his youth. And with both parents dead, nobody now stood between himself and the grave" (Jaques, 1965, p. 510). Such a loss can be a stimulus for emotional growth. Acceptance of our own mortality can result in greater strength and maturity (Douglas, 1990–1991). The death of a parent has been compared to a "developmental push," forcing us to no longer think of ourselves as children but to assume a more mature stance (Osterweis, Solomon, and Green, 1984).

Death of a Child

The death of a child is recognized as one of the most painful grief experiences. The grief is intense and long-lasting and is followed by many years of sorrow. Although on the surface grief may appear resolved, a dull ache may persist that, on occasion, surfaces with intense sadness, anxiety, and tears. This phenomenon is referred to as *shadow grief* (Peppers and Knapp, 1980b; Knapp, 1986).

The loss of a child at any age is devastating whether a newborn, young child, teenager, or adult child. Age, however, may define certain aspects or issues of parental grief. For example, the loss of a young child may be accompanied by the irrational guilt of having failed as the parent-protector. The death of an adolescent child may be complicated by the typically confrontational parent-adolescent relationship. Exaggerated guilt over unresolved conflicts may place a heavy burden on grieving parents. For those who lose an adult child, there is the severing of a long-term relationship and possibly the secondary stress of losing a caregiver in one's old age.

Rando (1986) summarizes various special considerations that involve the loss of a child. The natural cycle is turned upside down. Parents are supposed to die first, whether their deceased child is two or forty. Also, the death is likely to be sudden and unexpected, often stemming from an accident. Of course, even when this is not the case, the death is still untimely and inappropriate in the life of the parents. Anger and guilt tend to be intensified with the death of a child, with guilt being the most pervasive parental response. Obsessional review occurs in an effort to provide order and gain control over what appears to be an unmanageable event. However, with other children to look after, time for necessary "grief work," including obsessional review, may be diminished.

Parents often lose a significant part of their identity when they lose a child. Their status as a parent, the various roles they play, and their sense of self-esteem are altered even if they have other children. Society provides no formal recognition for their changed status (see Box 9–3).

A child who loses his parents is an *orphan.* A spouse whose mate dies is a *widow* or *widower.* But there is no word to denote a parent whose child has died. There are no social guidelines on how to answer the question that

Box 9–3   *Do You Have Any Children?*

Elaine and Joel had been invited to a wedding. They were now seated at a reception table with family and friends and with a woman who brought her "uninvited baby." The bride later apologized for their having been seated at the table with him. He was eating peas now from a red plastic dish his mother had pulled out of the diaper bag.

She and Elaine had engaged in small talk about the wedding, the bride, and the weather. Eventually, Elaine commented that her baby looked about 6 months old. "Spoken like someone who knows," she said. Then came the question that Elaine was not expecting. "Do you have any children?"

Elaine struggled with the answer. What was she to say? Maybe she should say nothing at all. The answer was too involved. It would only make the woman feel uncomfortable and she hadn't meant any harm.

Elaine's own pregnancy had been quite difficult. For the last four months she had been confined to bed to prevent a premature delivery. She and her husband took every necessary precaution. He left her food in a cooler by the couch before leaving for work. In fact, he gathered everything she might possibly need before he got back home. After all, she was only supposed to get up to go to the bathroom.

The whole family had cooperated. Her mother-in-law visited, cooked a month of meals, and froze them. Then her own mother came and cooked Christmas dinner. They anticipated the next Christmas, when there would be a 9-month-old baby crawling about the tree. The next few months dragged on as the bed rest continued with a few exceptions here and there.

After almost 8 months of pregnancy Elaine was allowed to get up. A baby born at this point of gestation would be strong enough to survive. She cooked, took the dog for a walk, and prepared the nursery. She had been anxious to do that for months. Then after 8 months of pregnancy, Peter was born. He was beautiful with lots of black hair and familiar family features.

Within a short time he began having problems. Breathing difficulties they said. But he was fully developed and not underweight. Everything would be fine. But, everything wasn't fine. His condition worsened, became critical. He had to be transferred to a medical facility where a special breathing machine was available. Peter didn't survive the trip. He died less than 2 days after his birth.

They determined that he had contracted a bacterial infection during delivery. It generally was not dangerous, but Peter didn't live because of it. No one really understood why.

There was a funeral two days later. Elaine spoke at it. "Peter, you didn't live very long, but I got to know you, in a way, during the past months. In your short life you gave me something: you gave me a chance to feel things I had never felt before. And I appreciate that."

She and Joel took a one-month trip to Mexico to get away and be together. They returned and went back to work. It was awkward. People often didn't know what to

Box 9–3 *(Continued)*

say. Sometimes they said the wrong things. Even worse, some said nothing, acting as if nothing at all had happened.

So, here they were at the wedding reception. Elaine still pondering the question. To answer "No" would be painful. It would be like betraying Peter's existence—denying how much he was wanted, loved, and missed. She had to say something.

"No," she said, "I don't have any children."

Source: Adapted from E. Kramer, (1989). A baby named Peter. *Toledo Magazine,* Sept. 3–9, pp. 6–8, 10, 12, 17–19.

plagues bereaved parents, "How many children do you have?"   (Rando, 1986, p. 41)

The criteria typically used to diagnose unresolved grief (intense, disabling, or prolonged) are common to parental bereavement. Likewise, a series of acute grief reactions may appear at what would have been significant turning points in the child's life—the first day of school, first communion, bar/bat mitzvah, high school graduation, college entry, and a lifetime of birthdays. Bereaved parents must "grow up" with the loss.

A marriage is also significantly stressed with the death of a child. Both parents are bereaved, often making each other's most valuable supportive resource (his or her spouse) unavailable. Parents are struggling with their own grief and that of their spouses as well. Most families survive the stress but a small percentage of such marriages ends in divorce.

Sudden Infant Death Syndrome (SIDS) is particularly difficult for bereaved parents (DeFrain, 1991). SIDS is the unexpected death of a previously healthy infant between two weeks and one year of age, unexplained even after a complete autopsy examination. It usually occurs during the first six months of life. The etiology of SIDS is unclear, although several risk factors have been identified. Its suddenness, untimely nature, and the uncertainty surrounding its cause complicate the grief reaction. Anger and tremendous guilt are characteristic of SIDS grief.

AIDS-Related Bereavement

The reader is referred to the work of Bergeron and Handley (1992), who in reviewing the literature on AIDS-related bereavement and grief reactions, constructed a very useful bibliography on the topic. The authors of the bibliography are cofounders of AFTER AIDS Bereavement Services, Inc., an organization that starts and networks self-help AIDS bereavement support groups nationally and internationally.

These authors found a relatively small number of articles on AIDS-related bereavement given the magnitude of AIDS. Most of the available information deals with the loss of gay men to the disease. Box 9–4 provides a listing of factors impacting the grief experience of male lovers of those who died due to AIDS.

Some of the same factors listed in Box 9–4 influence AIDS bereaved family members in general. Additionally, family members may suffer ambivalence because of the conflicts associated with a gay life style in our society and their own possible disapproval of the life style of their deceased loved one.

Family members of deceased IV-drug users face many of the same complicating factors. Children from such families may lose both parents and suffer the dissolution of their home. Those whose loved ones die from AIDS in association with treatment for hemophilia may experience much anger. The anger may be directed at God for allowing them to have had a disease that at one time carried such treatment-associated risks.

Death of a Pet

The death of a pet can represent a significant loss and precipitate a strong grief reaction. Yet, bereaved pet owners may be hesitant to admit the depth of their feelings. While cemeteries and condolence cards for lost pets now exist, open expression of grief for a dead animal is often trivialized. Mourning for pets is still not taken seriously in our society and represents a type of disenfranchised grief.

Weisman (1990–1991) established a bereavement counseling program at a humane society and confirmed the special relationship between humans and their pets. He concluded that while companion animals do sometimes substitute for family and children, grief over their death is no "simple displacement or sublimation of frustrated parental or marital desires" (Weisman, 1990–1991, p. 244). Few of the grief-stricken pet owners he studied were socially isolated, even those who were retired. Many had busy lives, many contacts, and outside activities. Yet, they characterized their relationship with their animals as significant. Grief surrounding their death was real.

Consenting to animal euthanasia is especially difficult and often triggers guilt feelings, despite the animal's illness or extreme age and infirmity. Some owners stay with their animal, offering a gentle touch or loving goodbye as it is euthanized by the veterinarian. Guilt may also be triggered when a pet dies in an accident.

B o x 9–4 *Factors Impacting the Grief Experience of Male Lovers of Those Who Died with AIDS*

- Obsessing about becoming HIV-positive or suffering with AIDS themselves.
- Absence of the recognition given to a spouse in conjugal bereavement (disenfranchised grief).
- The lack of a support system.
- Condemnation of the disease and those who contract it. ("It was their own fault; They got what they deserved.")
- Conflict regarding property settlements and having a say in funeral arrangements.
- Internalized homophobia.
- Inappropriateness of death due to the young age at which AIDS-related death usually occurs.
- Multiple losses leading to bereavement overload if one's friends have died with AIDS as well.
- Caregiver fatigue from the emotional and physical burden of caring for one with AIDS.

Source: Adapted from J. Bergeron and P. Handley. (1992). Bibliography on AIDS-related bereavement and grief. *Death Studies,* 16:247–267.

Helping Those Who Are Grieving

When a friend or relative loses a loved one, we want to comfort them. Often, however, we don't know what to do or say. In actuality, there is nothing we can do to make the pain disappear. However, there are a number of useful principles that may allow us to provide them some comfort and assist them through the grieving process. Some of these principles are found in Box 9–5.

Of paramount importance is that we are patient with those who are grieving. We need to give them time and permission to grieve in their own way. We should allow silence or tears, the expression of anger, guilt, despair, and loneliness, and talk about the deceased. But, don't force these things. Provide an environment tolerant of them. Too often, in the weeks and months and years beyond the funeral period, we assume they are over it. We assume that if we

---

Box 9–5   *Helping Those Who Are Grieving*

The following principles may be useful in assisting those who are grieving:

1. *Don't rush someone through grief.* The grieving period is variable. It may take weeks, months, or years. Impatience with grief is a prevailing characteristic of our society. We need to give our friends and loved ones time to grieve.

2. *Don't trivialize someone's grief.* We might do this by our actions or words. We may act as if they should be getting on with their life, as if nothing happened. We may say hurtful things unknowingly such as, "Be strong" or "She lived a long life" or "This was meant to be." We might also discount certain losses such as that of a beloved pet.

3. *Make your support available especially beyond the funeral period.* The bereaved are often "on their own" after the funeral. They need our support and concern after this period long after the funeral is over.

4. *Allow the deceased to be important during the grieving process.* We can do this by encouraging memories of the deceased.

5. *Give permission to grieve.* We can do this by talking about our own reaction to the death. By engaging in open talk about the deceased and our feelings, we can give the bereaved permission to do the same.

6. *Help the bereaved deal with any guilt or anger.* These are common components of grief and may be rational or irrational. Talking about them can be helpful.

7. *Realize the importance of obsessive review.* The bereaved may be preoccupied with memories of the deceased and how death took place. Provide an environment that allows them to talk about the death.

8. *Remember that grief is highly individual.* Don't expect the bereaved to follow an established set of rules. Allow for individual differences.

9. *Help the bereaved to get on with living, to form new relationships.* Be there for them, but don't rush them into a premature "resolution" of grief.

---

bring it up we will be opening up an old wound, causing them to feel bad. How silly to think they could forget if we just didn't mention it.

One widow told of how her wedding anniversary came and went without anyone mentioning it. She felt betrayed. She spent it alone with her memories bottled up inside of her. How she would have loved to have shared some of those memories. There were so many stories to tell.

A couple who had lost their infant daughter several months before looked forward to dinner out with their friends. It would be so good to be able to finally talk about it. But the other couple never mentioned it the entire evening. The bereaved parents went home feeling frustrated, sorrowful, and alone.

Sometimes when the bereaved talk freely (interpreted by some as too much and for too long) about the deceased loved one, others act as if something is wrong with them. They are "stuck" in grief, not moving on with their lives, being morbid, not getting over it. Three years ago a young woman's best friend died. She had been a major figure in her life. They had shared many special times, intimate feelings, and secrets and had done many crazy things together. She notices that even lively tales of their escapades are received with discomfort or reserve. She refuses to silently harbor her memories. She now precedes a story with, "A good friend of mine who moved away" or "A friend I went to school with." Told in this manner, the stories are openly embraced or laughed at.

As a bereaved mother said fourteen years after her teenage daughter's death, "No one ever talked to me about her. I wanted to talk about her, about her life, I still do." Others told her to get on with her own life, to heal. In spite of their attitude, she realized that getting on with her life did not mean forgetting her daughter or pretending she didn't exist (Engram, 1989).

Grief is a complex reaction to loss influenced by a multitude of factors. Exposure to varied grief responses, hopefully, enhances our understanding of personal reactions to loss and our interactions with those who are bereaved.

Summary

Bereavement is defined as the state of having sustained a loss. Grief is the emotional reaction to loss. It is a complex response with physical, psychological, and sociocultural components. Grief is extremely variable. Numerous factors influence its intensity and the ease with which it is resolved. The factors include the identity of the person who died, the acceptability of a given death, the availability of social support, and the mode of death (including whether it was anticipated or sudden and whether it was from natural or unnatural causes).

In order to resolve grief, we go through a process that carries us from the initial shock of death to learning to live without the deceased. The grief process is often catalogued into stages or phases. Doing so does not imply that a set number of emotional reactions unfold in a rigid order. The stage models of grief attempt to identify major emotional experiences while respecting individual variation. Stephenson's three-stage and Kastenbaum's seven-stage models are reviewed.

While continuing to recognize the usefulness of cataloguing the grief experience, we are moving away from viewing grief as normal or abnormal on the basis of its conforming to or deviating from our expectations. It is recognized, though, that some may have greater difficulty in working through grief and that certain factors can complicate or cause a resurgence of grief. Chronic grief, conflicted grief, anniversary reactions, anticipatory grief, disenfranchised grief, and recapitulation are examined.

The social setting is the backdrop against which grief is played out. It can influence our conception of what constitutes a significant loss as well as dictate how our grief is expressed. In our modern, industrialized society, we tend to be impatient with grief—our own, as well as that of others.

The chapter examines various bereaved states including spousal, elderly, child, parental, and AIDS-related bereavement regarding the grief experience and social factors impacting its expression. The bereavement related to the death of a pet is also explored.

In conclusion, practical guidelines for helping those who are grieving are outlined. We often want to be supportive but don't know how. It is extremely important to provide an environment via our words and actions that permits the expression of emotions and conversation about the deceased.

Study Questions

1. Differentiate bereavement and grief. What kinds of symptoms are associated with grief?
2. Present an overview of the many factors that influence the intensity of the grief reaction and the ease with which grief is resolved.
3. Identify low-grief death, high-grief death, disenfranchised grief, and anticipatory grief.

4. Briefly outline the three phases of grief. Compare them with Kavanaugh's seven stages.

5. According to Worden, what are four major tasks of grief?

6. Explain the statement, "There is no right way to grieve."

7. Identify conflicted grief, chronic grief, recapitulation, and anniversary reaction.

8. What is mourning? Discuss its importance in the management and resolution of grief.

9. Discuss the various bereaved states presented in the chapter.

10. What are some important guidelines to help those who are grieving?

References

Aries, P. (1974). The reversal of death. *American Quarterly,* 26:536–560.

Aries, P. (1981). *The Hour of Our Death.* New York: Alfred A. Knopf.

Averill, J. (1968). Grief: Its nature and significance. *Psychological Bulletin,* 70:721–748.

Ball, J. (1977). Widow's grief: The impact of age and mode of death. *Omega,* 7:303–333.

Bergeron, J., and P. Handley. (1992). Bibliography on AIDS-related bereavement and grief. *Death Studies,* 16:247–267.

Brabant, S. (1989–1990). Old pain or new pain: A social psychological approach to recurrent grief. *Omega,* 20:273–279.

Brown, J., and G. Stoudemire. (1983). Normal and pathological grief. *JAMA,* 250:378–382.

Carder, M. (1987). Journey into understanding mentally retarded people's experiences around death. *Journal of Pastoral Care,* 4:18–31.

Casterta, M., and D. Lund. (1992). Bereavement stress and coping among older adults: Expectations versus the actual experience. *Omega,* 25:33–45.

DeFrain, J. (1991). Learning about grief from normal families: SIDS, stillbirth, and miscarriage. *Journal of Marital and Family Therapy,* 17:215–232.

DeSpelder, L., and A. Strickland. (1992). *The Last Dance.* Mountain View, CA: Mayfield.

DeTurris, M. (1991). "Dear Mom." *Catholic New York,* May 9, p. 13.

Doka, K. (1989). *Disenfranchised Grief.* Lexington, MA: Lexington Press.

Donnelly, K. (1987). *Recovering from the Loss of a Parent.* New York: Dodd, Mead.

Douglas, J. (1990–1991). Patterns of change following parent death in midlife adults. *Omega,* 22:123–137.

Engram, S. (1989). There is no cure for grief, only ways to live with it. *Detroit Free Press,* May 17, p. 14.

Ericsson, S. (1993). *Companion Through the Darkness.* New York: HarperCollins.

Ferraro, K. (1985). The effect of widowhood on the health status of older persons. *International Journal of Aging and Human Development,* 21:9–25.

Fulton, R. (1970). Death, grief, and social recuperation. *Omega,* 1:27.

Glick, I., R. Weiss, and M. Parkes. (1974). *The First Year of Bereavement.* New York: Wiley.

Goodstein, R. (1984). Grief reactions and the elderly. *Carrier Letter,* 99:1–5.

Gorer, G. (1965). *Death, Grief and Mourning.* Garden City, NY: Doubleday.

Henry, J. (1964). *Jungle People: A Kaingang Tribe of the Highlands of Brazil*. New York: Vintage Books.

Jaques, E. (1965). Death and the mid-life crisis. *International Journal of Psychoanalysis*, 46:502–514.

Kalish, R. (1985). *Death, Grief, and Caring Relationships*. Monterey, CA: Brooks/Cole.

Kastenbaum, R. (1991). *Death, Society, and Human Experience*. New York: Merrill.

Kavanaugh, R. (1972). *Facing Death*. New York: Penguin Books.

Kloeppel, D., and S. Hollins. (1989). Double handicap: Mental retardation and death in the family. *Death Studies*, 13:31–38.

Knapp, R. (1986). *Beyond Endurance*. New York: Schocken Books.

Lehman, D., and C. Wortman. (1984–1985). The impact of sudden loss. *The Institute for Social Research Newsletter*, 3, 7.

Lietar, E. (1986). Miscarriage. In T. Rando (Ed.), *Parental Loss of a Child* (pp. 121–127). Champaign, IL.: Research Press Company.

Lindemann, E. (1944). The symptomatology and management of acute grief. *American Journal of Psychiatry*, 101:141–148.

Lipe-Goodson, P., and B. Goebel. (1983). Perception of age and death in mentally retarded adults. *Mental Retardation*, 21:68–75.

Lopata, H. (1973). Living through widowhood. *Psychology Today*, February, 87–92.

Lopata, H. (1979). *Women as Widows: Support Systems*. New York: Elsevier.

Lopata, H. (1980). The widowed family member. In N. Datan and N. Lohmann (Eds.), *Transitions in Aging*. New York: Academic Press.

Manning, D. (1985). *Comforting Those Who Grieve*. New York: Harper & Row.

Metress, E. (1990). The American wake of Ireland: Symbolic death ritual. *Omega*, 21:147–153.

Moise, L. (1985). In sickness and death. *Mental Retardation*, 16:397–398.

Murrell, S., S. Himmelfarb, and J. Phifer. (1988). Effects of bereavement/loss and pre-event status on subsequent health in older adults. *International Journal of Aging and Human Development*, 27:87–107.

Osterweis, M., F. Solomon, and M. Green. (1984). *Bereavement: Reaction, Consequences, and Care*. Washington, DC: National Academy Press.

Oswin, M. (1989). Bereavement and mentally handicapped people. In T. Philpot (Ed.), *Last Things: Social Work with the Dying and Bereaved* (pp. 92–105). Wellington, Surrey, Great Britain: Community Care.

Owen, G., R. Fulton, and E. Markusen. (1982–1983). Death at a distance: A study of family survivors. *Omega*, 13:191–225.

Parkes, C., and R. Weiss. (1983). *Recovery from Bereavement*. New York: Basic Books.

Peppers, L., and R. Knapp. (1980a). Maternal reactions to involuntary fetal/infant death. *Psychiatry*, 43:155–159.

Peppers, L., and R. Knapp. (1980b). *Motherhood and Mourning: Perinatal Death*. New York: Praeger Special Studies.

Pfost, K., M. Stevens, and A. Wessels. (1989). Relationship of purpose in life to grief experiences in response to the death of a significant other. *Death Studies*, 13:371–378.

Rando, T. (1986). Unique issues and impact of the death of a child. In T. Rando (Ed.), *Parental Loss of a Child* (pp. 5–43). Champaign, IL: Research Press Company.

Raphael, B. (1983). *The Anatomy of Bereavement*. New York: Basic Books.

Raphael, B. (1977). Preventive intervention with the recently bereaved. *Archives of General Psychiatry,* 34:1450–1454.

Raphael, B., and K. Nunn. (1988). *Counseling the bereaved.* Unpublished paper.

Rosenblatt, P., R. Walsh, and D. Jackson. (1976). *Grief and Mourning in Cross-Cultural Expansion*. New Haven, CT: Human Relations Area Files.

Santmyer, H. (1982). *. . . And Ladies of the Club*. New York: Berkley Books.

Scheff, T. (1975). Labeling, emotion, and individual change. In T. Scheff (Ed.), *Labeling Madness*. Englewood Cliffs, NJ: Prentice Hall.

Shneidman, E. (1973). *Deaths of Man*. New York: Quadrangle/New York Times.

Simpson, M. (1979). *The Facts of Death*. Englewood Cliffs, NJ: Prentice Hall.

Sklar, F. (1991–1992). Grief as a family affair: Property rights, grief rights, and the exclusion of close friends as survivors. *Omega,* 24:109–121.

Sklar, F., and S. Hartley. (1990). Close friends as survivors: Bereavement patterns in a hidden population. *Omega,* 21:103–112.

Stephenson, J. (1985). *Death, Grief, and Mourning*. New York: The Free Press.

Stroebe, W., and M. Stroebe. (1987). *Bereavement and Health*. New York: Cambridge University Press.

Stroebe, M., Stroebe, W., and R. Hansson. (1988). Bereavement research: An historical introduction. *Journal of Social Issues,* 44:1–18.

Tait, R., and R. Silver. (1989). Coming to terms with major negative life events. In J. Uleman and J. Bargh (Eds.), *Unintended Thought: The Limits of Awareness, Intention, and Control* (pp. 351–383). New York: Guilford Press.

Wadsworth, J., and D. Harper. (1991). Grief and bereavement in mental retardation: A need for a new understanding. *Death Studies,* 15:281–292.

Weisman, A. (1990–1991). Bereavement and companion animals. *Omega,* 22:241–248.

Worden, J. (1982). *Grief Counseling and Grief Therapy: A Handbook for the Mental Health Practitioner*. New York: Springer.

Wortman, C., and R. Silver. (1989). The myths of coping with loss. *Journal of Consulting and Clinical Psychology,* 57:349–357.

Wright, B. (1983). *Physical Disability—A Psychological Approach*. New York: Harper & Row.

Zisook, S., and S. Shuchter. (1986). The first four years of widowhood. *Psychiatric Annals,* 15:288.

CHAPTER 10

Children and Death

Ring around the rosie,
A pocket full of posie,
Ashes, ashes,
All fall down.

Fourteenth-century children's rhyme

THE RARITY OF DEATH among children today makes it an especially shocking and tragic event when it occurs. Their lives having just begun, children are not supposed to die. Their doing so contradicts our expectations. That a child should precede a parent in death seems unnatural, out of step with the normal order of things. However, such was not always the case. Our presumption that children will live, that their dying is inappropriate, is an outgrowth of modern society with its reduced infant and child mortality.

Our ancestors knew all too well about the death of children. In colonial New England, Puritan parents often saw one-fourth to one-third of their offspring die before they were ten years old (Stannard, 1977). As recently as the

379

beginning of the twentieth century, children accounted for 53 percent of the total number of U.S. deaths even though they represented only one-third of the population (Kearl, 1989).

Today, the picture has changed drastically. Those under the age of fifteen account for only 4 to 5 percent of all deaths. Immunizations and antibiotics used against an array of infectious diseases that once struck in murderous epidemics have played an important role in this change. Better living conditions including improved sanitation and nutrition and various improvements in medical care have also been important.

At this writing, the leading causes of death in early childhood are injuries, congenital anomalies, cancer, cardiovascular disease, and homicide (Vanderpool and Richmond, 1990). It is projected that by the time this chapter is read, AIDS, a growing problem among children, will be counted among the top five causes of childhood death (Novello, Wise, Willoughby, and Pizzo, 1989). The leading causes of mortality for adolescents are injuries, homicide, and suicide.

Not only has the frequency and pattern of childhood death changed during the twentieth century, but a child's experience with death has changed as well. Children in the past were regularly confronted with death—if not their own, then that of a sibling or young friend and, possibly, even that of a parent. Most deaths and wakes occurred in the home. Thus, children witnessed serious illness and death first hand. They frequently assisted in the care of the sick and were present at the deathbed, wake, and funeral.

That children were so openly exposed to death at one time is evident in a very old childhood game that has survived to this day. Although its derivation is frequently not realized, the popular "Ring-around-the-rosie" can be traced to the plague of fourteenth-century Europe. This Black Death, as it came to be known, killed one-fourth of England's population alone during the 1300s and continued to push through England and Europe in somewhat frequent intervals for almost three centuries.

"Ring around the rosie, a pocket full of posy, ashes, ashes, all fall down." What do these seemingly inane words mean as recited by today's children? Many a parent might be surprised to find out that this children's rhyme tells of the sickness and death that pervaded the Middle Ages. The "rosie ring" refers to the swollen and inflamed lymph nodes symptomatic of the bacterial infection. "A pocket full of posy" was an amulet worn on the body in the hope that its magical powers would protect one from the illness. "Ashes, ashes" is believed to be a vulgarization of the sneezing sound "achoo" that accompanied the respiratory involvement of the most deadly form of plague. "All fall down," of course, speaks of the death that was literally all around—the death that children witnessed.

Today, most children are not exposed to death. Indeed, it has become rare in their lives. With increased life expectancy, the vast majority of persons who die are over sixty-five years old. Most deaths take place in institutions—hospitals or nursing homes—without children present. And, among some families there is uncertainty about the appropriateness of a child's attendance at a funeral. Ironically, although children are exposed to violence and death through television and movies, actual death has become "unnatural" in their lives.

Where death is concerned, children have come to be viewed as islands of innocence. Seeking to protect them, some adults have attempted to shield children from the truth about serious illness and death, to hide their own grief, and to discourage or avoid its expression in the child. Years of study have demonstrated that open, honest communication about death with children is best. Children think about death and have questions regarding it. When confronted with loss, they know sorrow and grief. Both children and adults should be allowed to channel their questions and emotions.

The purpose of this chapter is to explore death in the lives of today's children. Among the topics included are children's understanding of death, terminally ill children, bereaved children and their grieving, talking with children about death, and suicidal behavior in preadolescent children.

Children's Understanding of Death

Children's understanding of death is shaped by the complex interplay of their level of cognitive development and specific experiences with death. In general, we see that a ten-year-old has a more mature understanding of death than a five-year-old. The precise reason for this is not fully known. Is the more mature understanding a reflection of one's age-related developmental abilities? Or, is it the outgrowth of having amassed more life experiences in ten years of living? While the precise role of each may not be discerned, what we do know is that both developmental level and experience can play an important part in a child's understanding of death.

Developmental and Experiential Approaches

Children undergo a developmental progression from immature to mature thinking about death. Age is sometimes used as a rough indicator of that progression. However, research demonstrates that we cannot use age alone to generalize about how children perceive death. A child's own level of maturation and individual experiences with death are important influences. Children can possess a more sophisticated death awareness at a younger age than early researchers thought possible.

Among the earliest and most significant research conducted on children's perceptions of death is that of Hungarian psychologist Maria Nagy. Studying nearly 400 healthy children in post-World War II Hungary, she maintained that children's ideas about death developed in three age-related stages (Nagy, 1948). Her widely cited work has become a standard against which subsequent research on the topic is often measured. It has also become the subject of criticism for not taking into account various experiential and environmental factors. Nevertheless, with refinement her work remains useful. At this point, let us examine the age-graded developmental model offered by Nagy.

Stage One of Nagy's model involves children from three to five years of age and has also been referred to as the preschool stage. Nagy found that children in this age group consider death as a continuation of life, but in an altered or diminished form. For example, four-year-olds might think that some form of life continues in the grave. They may wonder "how grandpa is going to eat and change his clothes in that box (casket)."

Young children do not understand the finality of death; death, equated with sleep and departure, is viewed as temporary. This fact does not, however, negate the sense of pain and anxiety children may experience with separation/death. Separation at any age (even if believed to be temporary) can be very painful. Nagy noted that the separation theme of death was very significant for this age group.

Stage Two involves the middle childhood years from ages five to nine. Nagy observed that during this stage children come to realize that death is final. Those who have died do not maintain a less active existence nor do they return. Although the permanency of death is realized, it is not viewed as inevitable or as something that must happen to the child. Death may be eluded.

Nagy also noted that the majority of children she studied personified death at this time. Death is "somebody" who takes people away and carries them off. The identification of death as a skeleton was often observed and exemplified in a sampling of excerpts from her reports: "Death is a skeleton . . . so strong it can overturn a ship." "Death is a dead person . . . only bones." "Death is like a skeleton." Death descriptions included a variety of mysterious figures that could be powerful and frightening. Death is "dangerous," it lurks around and can "carry you off," especially at night.

At Stage Three, beginning around age nine or ten, children recognize that not only is death forever (a carryover from Stage Two), but it is universal and inevitable. It happens to everyone, including "me," and it cannot be eluded. "Death is something that no one can escape," related one child who was a month away from being ten years old. Children also begin to attribute death to natural phenomena at this stage (see Table 10–1).

As previously noted, Nagy's work remains useful in helping us to appreciate what children may be thinking or feeling about death. It demonstrates that they are curious about the phenomenon, as did the earlier work of Anthony (1940). Anthony found that children think about and actively try to understand death even though their young lives may be void of any deep personal experience with it.

TABLE 10–1   *Nagy's Age-Graded Developmental Model of Children's Conceptualization of Death*

Stage 1 Ages 3–5 Years	Stage 2 Ages 5–9 Years	Stage 3 Age 9 or 10
1. Death is viewed as a diminished form of life.	1. Finality of death is realized.	1. Death is viewed as universal. a. It happens to everyone, including "me."
2. There is a strong separation anxiety theme. a. Death is equated with sleep and departure.	2. There is belief that death may be eluded.	2. Death is inevitable.
3. Death is viewed as temporary.	3. Death is personified.	3. Death is attributed to natural phenomena.

More recent work maintains that Nagy's adherence to chronological age as an indicator of thoughts about death was too strict (Graham-Poole et al., 1989; Jenkins and Cavanaugh, 1985–1986; Kane, 1979; Koocher, 1973). While such chronological age groupings may serve as an approximate guide, individual development is a more accurate gauge. Although younger children tend to manifest a lower developmental level and older children a higher, more adult level of thinking, individual variation does occur. Some younger children may show a more mature level of thinking. Likewise, some older children may not be as advanced in their death-related thoughts as are others their age (Koocher, 1973). Thus, developmental progression in death-related thoughts is more specifically related to individual cognitive maturation than to chronological age alone.

Since Nagy's work, children's personification of death has not been reported as commonly (Gartley and Bernasconi, 1967; Kane, 1979; Kastenbaum, 1991; Koocher, 1973; McIntire, Angle and Struempler, 1972). It has been suggested that the reason for this may be rooted in the tremendous technical changes that have occurred since Nagy's time. Children may have become socialized to replace personification with more scientific-sounding responses. For example, Kastenbaum relates how one seven-year-old recently equated death with a computer being down and "you can't get it started again." Citing the work of Lonetto (1980), he notes that when enticed to draw death as a person, children still seem to find the task engrossing. Perhaps, our present-day scientific images and language upstage the child's use of "emotionally rich and evocative personification" (Kastenbaum, 1991).

The age-graded developmental model did not take into account social, cultural, religious, and experiential influences on a child's thoughts about death. Numerous studies have suggested that these factors can play a significant role in individual and group differences in such thinking (Anthony and Bhana, 1988–1989; Bluebond-Langner, 1974, 1975, 1977, 1989; McIntire, Angle, and Struempler, 1972; Wenestam and Wass, 1987; Zweig, 1983). One is reminded that Nagy's work involved Hungarian children at the conclusion of World War II. Its universal application to children of all cultures and life experiences has been questioned.

As a result of her work with terminally ill children, anthropologist Bluebond-Langner (1974, 1975, 1977, 1978, 1989) challenged the assumptions of the age-graded, developmental model. She learned that the children she studied, the majority of whom were between ages three and nine (but who ranged from eighteen months to fourteen years), came to know that they were dying. Additionally, they understood the finality of their impending death.

The preceding scenario was in direct conflict with contemporary thinking about childhood conceptions of death. Although Nagy studied healthy children, her results were extrapolated to dying children as well. It was maintained that even if young children could discern the prognosis, they would fail to see it as final.

Bluebond-Langner linked children's ideas about death to their personal experiences. She formulated an experiential model that follows dying children as they acquire knowledge regarding their illnesses: at first, they see themselves as seriously ill and, finally, they understand that they are dying. Her model is presented in the following section on terminally ill children.

Terminally Ill Children

Diagnosis and Communication Patterns

The diagnosis of a fatal disease in a child is a shattering experience. Parents face their own overwhelming emotions at the same time that they must provide care and support to their ill and dying child. Some may want to shield their child from the truth which they feel is too frightening and painful. In the case of a young child, they might feel that the diagnosis wouldn't be understood anyway. Research indicates that a terminally ill child usually knows that his or her illness is serious and, eventually, that it is fatal (Bluebond-Langner, 1978; Spinetta, 1978; Spinetta and Maloney, 1975; Spinetta, Rigler and Karon, 1974; Vernick and Karon, 1965; Waechter, 1971, 1984). Even if not told directly, the child senses the magnitude of the problem by the way he or she feels, the various treatment regimens, hospital stays, and encounters with other sick children, some of whom die. The child sees the sadness in the eyes that look away and the artificiality in the forced smiles of parents who are trying to be brave—careful not to let anything slip, be it the wrong words or powerful emotions.

Honesty and sensitivity are important in dealing with seriously ill children. If parents are truthful and supportive, children generally will ask no more than they are capable of handling emotionally. It takes some time for children to fully realize the gravity of their illness. Thus, their questions and concerns will vary with time and the phase of their disease. At first, they may seek information about their disease and try to understand their pain and discomfort. They may have questions and concerns about their absence from school, home, family, and friends; the hospital/clinic routines; their treatments; and another child's illness or whereabouts after his or her death. As time goes on, they may want to know about their own dying.

Questions should not be avoided or dismissed. If they are, the child may be left with a sense of dread that something is so awful that his or her parents cannot even talk about it. Left alone to deal with questions, the child may formulate his or her own answers based on confusion and misinformation.

Secrets and lies can make all parties anxious. They can break down the child's sense of trust. He or she may wonder, "What else is being concealed? What else have I been lied to about?" Parents also risk someone else telling their child the truth if it has been withheld; that someone could even be a fellow pediatric patient.

Working in the hospital with terminally ill children, Bluebond-Langner (1978) was surprised at their willingness to talk with her and their ability to discuss their disease, treatment, and prognosis. She found that hospitalized children talk with each other about their illnesses and concerns. However, they may refrain from doing so with their parents or other adults if they perceive that it makes them uncomfortable. Bluebond-Langner (1977) found that

> while children want to express their awareness, they do not want to do so at the risk of being left alone. They know that direct expression of awareness could cost them the companionship of those they want near them, their parents. So to assure their continued presence, they practice mutual pretense. (p. 65)

Numerous studies through the years have revealed that children who have open communication about their illness with their family and who understand their illness/treatment demonstrate lower stress levels and improved coping ability (Bluebond-Langner, 1978; Spinetta, 1978; Vernick and Karon, 1965; Waechter, 1971, 1984). Denial and closed communication about the illness can cause problems for the dying child who must work out feelings alone. However, forced openness regarding the illness can be destructive for some families. Some parents are unable to function under the stress of open communication. Some of them will demonstrate maladaptive behavior, becoming remote and withdrawn:

> The goal in working with such families must be to help the family members become aware of the false sense of equilibrium that may come from an excessive denial of the problem, and the harm such denial can cause the sick child. If a temporary use of denial, especially at the beginning, proves to be helpful in allowing the family to pull together adaptive resources, then such short-lived denial can be useful in the overall adaptive effort.   (Spinetta, 1978, p. 48)

In any given family, open or closed communication does not have to be an "all or none" matter. In other words, the child may practice mutual pretense and closed communication with a family member who is most comfortable in that situation while being open with another (Bluebond-Langner, 1978).

During the terminal phase of their disease, some children will psychologically distance themselves from their parents. In some cases, their withdrawal may be an outgrowth of the depression that many dying patients, including children, experience. It is also possible that with this behavior, children may be attempting to pull away and shield their parents from the crushing grief that comes from the loss of a close loved one (Wass and Stillion, 1988).

Awareness of Their Dying

The most detailed information on the terminally ill child's awareness of death is provided by the work of Bluebond-Langner (1974, 1975, 1977, 1978, 1989). She discovered that such children understand death at a younger age than do their healthy peers. Their understanding is born of their daily experiences with illness, experiences that are very different from those of their well counterparts. Thus, she found that children's knowledge of death is not based solely on age or cognitive development per se, but on the experience of being ill and in the company of other children who are likewise ill and some of whom die.

She noted that leukemic children come to realize that they are dying through a prolonged process. That process involves encounters with illness that are paralleled by changes in their self-perception. That perception evolves from the notion of being seriously and acutely ill, to chronically ill, to fatally ill. The five stages in the process of acquiring knowledge about the disease are represented in Figure 10–1. Figure 10–2 illustrates the concomitant changes in self perception.

For the child to pass through the stages of information acquisition and changes in self-perception, significant experiences must occur. For example,

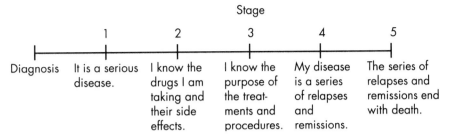

Figure 10–1 Stages in the acquisition of information.

Stage 1 is achieved by observing the reactions of parents and others. Stage 2 is not arrived at until the child has experienced several clinic visits, conversations with other sick children, and a remission. Only when the child undergoes the first relapse will progression to Stage 3 occur. After experiencing several more relapses and remissions, the child moves to Stage 4. When he or she learns that the disease has caused the death of a peer, the child passes to Stage 5 (Bluebond-Langner, 1989).

Children learn about their illness and its consequences from their experiences, by assimilating information from other children, and by observing the behavior of health care workers and family members. They progress through the stages in spite of attempts to shield them from the truth and, according to Bluebond-Langner's observations, without age or intellectual ability impacting the speed or completeness with which they do so. She explains:

> There are 3 and 4-year-olds of average intelligence who know more about their prognosis than very intelligent 9-year-olds. The reason for this is that the 9-year-olds may still be in their first remission, have had fewer clinic visits, and hence less experience. They are only aware of the fact that they have a very serious illness.   (Bluebond-Langner, 1977, p. 54)

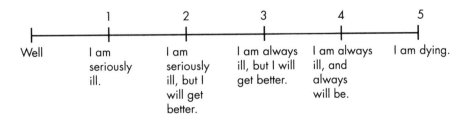

Figure 10–2 Changes in self-perception.

Bluebond-Langner's research has provided insight into the knowledge that some children (namely dying children) have of death. It has also produced renewed questioning of how a child conceives of death. We see from her work that personal experience with one's own dying may allow for a more mature understanding of death at an earlier age than "normal development" might indicate. Generalizing more than that from her work at this time is uncertain.

Care of the Dying Child

Hospital care can be very disruptive for a child. Such is the case even for one who has had a long battle with disease and who because of multiple hospitalizations, has become rather sophisticated about hospital routines. Each admission may bring with it new and unfamiliar experiences and faces. It also carries with it the threat of physical distress from a possible exacerbation of symptoms or from treatment measures. Likewise, the child is separated from normal surroundings and family members and is unable to engage in his or her usual activities.

Pain management of the child is an important issue. Although recent years have seen advances in this area, pediatric pain control lags behind that of adults. There is widespread concern about the undertreatment of children's pain (Duffy et al., 1991) as evidenced in a 1988 Consensus Conference on the Management of Pain in Childhood Cancer.

Several factors compound the problem, among them the scarcity of studies on the severity, prevalence, and management of childhood pain. Additionally, small children may lack the verbal skills to communicate their pain level. An innovative technique developed at the University of Colorado Nursing School in Denver is called an "Oucher." Pediatric patients aged three to twelve are asked to look at a series of pictures of other children's faces displaying various expressions. They are then asked to pick out the picture that best shows how they feel in order to get them to more accurately describe their own pain. Some children may endure pain, however, because of their fear of needles. They don't want a "pain shot." The physician's misplaced fear of addiction has also influenced treatment. On the positive side, pediatric pain management research is increasing (Langreth, 1991).

The concept of hospice care has been extended to children as well as adults. The home care emphasized by hospice programs in the United States can provide a child with familiar surroundings and the company of loved ones. Likewise, it can give parents a sense of control over the care of their child. The decision to provide home care rather than hospital care in the terminal phase of the disease must take into account each family's situation and resources. While hospice can be a blessing for many families, it may place undue strain on others.

The most important factor in providing hospital (rather than hospice) care for a child who eventually dies of cancer is the belief by the physician and family that the cancer may be cured. Choosing hospice is a recognition that death is imminent. Major advances over the last twenty-five years in the treatment of certain childhood malignancies have greatly improved the prospects for survival.

It should be noted that different age groups may bring to the forefront varying behavioral and emotional responses to serious personal illnesses. For small children between ages two and five, separation anxiety is a major issue. The fear of separation/abandonment may be manifested in demanding, negative behavior or panic when a parent leaves the room. Children need reassurance that they will not be abandoned.

For school-age children between ages six and twelve there may be some carryover of the fears and behavior of younger children. Additionally, there may be mutilation anxiety in relation to disfiguring treatments and surgery (Wass and Stillion, 1988). Children in this age group usually work hard to understand their disease, even master it, and to take care of themselves. They may also show sensitive concern for others—wishing to spare their parents any unnecessary stress.

Serious illness and impending death at the adolescent stage may be especially turbulent. Normally, adolescents are setting future goals. In the face of terminal illness, such goals will not be realized; hence, they may feel bitter, angry, and cheated.

Special conflicts must be faced at this normally tumultuous period of life. Just when teenagers are beginning to feel grown up and independent, the limitations and dependency imposed by illness can be very frustrating. Interaction with peers and the related emphasis on physical appearance and "fitting in" give way to separation from friends and classmates and concern over the side effects of medical treatment. Young persons may be forced to deal with severe acne or the swollen moon face secondary to antibiotic or steroid therapy. They may suffer from weight loss, weight gain, hair loss, or amputation of a limb. On the other hand, normal body changes that accompany sexual maturation at this time may be scorned instead of welcomed. They may be reminders of the adulthood that will never be fulfilled.

Bereaved Children and Their Grieving

Factors Influencing a Child's Expression of Grief

In an attempt to spare an "innocent" child pain and sorrow, some adults may deliberately withhold information about sickness and death. Specifics may be talked about in hushed tones. Children may be whisked away to the homes of relatives or friends in an effort to shield them from burdensome encounters and activities. However, children are helped, not hindered, by open communication about illness and death. When information is withheld, children are forced to make sense of the situation on their own. They tend to formulate explanations for what is occurring and for the tension they sense in the adults around them. Such fantasizing is far more unsettling and frightening than the reality of the situation, however sad that reality might be.

Likewise, there may be efforts to minimize a display of grief in bereaved children. Expressions of strong emotion may be met with attempts to distract. Saying "Let's wipe our tears," "Let's go out and play," or "Let's not be so sad," although expressed with caring concern, can deny children the opportunity for needed grieving. Rather than trying to suppress emotions, adults should permit bereaved children to share their feelings and their memories.

Many factors influence children's expressions of grief. Among them are their age, level of cognitive development, experience with death, relationship with the deceased, the nature of the death, and existing family dynamics.

Age and associated level of cognitive functioning can, as we have seen, influence children's understanding of death. It can also influence their reaction to death. The young child may view death as a temporary or sleeplike state, one that assumes continued biological functioning. This point is illustrated in the story of a man who experienced the death of his seventy-five-year-old mother. Driving home from the hospital, he contemplated how his five-year-old daughter Jill would react to her grandmother's death. Upon being told that her Granny had had another stroke and died, Jill's eyes filled with tears. She hugged her father and then wandered around the room before settling into the corner, apparently lost in thought. After some time, she looked up and asked her father, "But, Daddy, won't Granny need her socks?"

Rather than dismissing her question or simply saying no, he sought to understand her concern. He asked the reason for her question. She told him that she had been worried since Granny had left for the hospital without those big gray socks. She always wore them at home to keep her feet warm. Now, she was gone and had left her socks behind. "Isn't she going to be cold without them?" she asked. He could see that his young daughter was trying to grasp the meaning of death and that some of her concerns about it were different from his adult ones (Knowles and Reeves, 1983). Some of those differences might be attributed to her immature reasoning ability. Some, however, might be due to her limited experience with death.

Having endured a loss, the young child may eventually abandon the image of death as a sleeplike state. Recognizing that the dead do not awaken (or come back for their socks), death becomes redefined as a permanent condition (Stephenson, 1985). That redefinition can occur at an early age depending upon prior experience with death. The story of Corey, told in more detail in Box 10–1, exemplifies this situation. When Corey was five years old, her new-

Box 10–1 *When Corey's Sister Died*

When five-year-old Corey started kindergarten, she was eagerly awaiting the birth of her baby sister. Described by her parents as a strong, independent child, she had been involved with preparations for the baby, who would be called Elisabeth, from the beginning. Within twenty-four hours of Elisabeth's birth, Corey would take the lead in being involved with her dying. Elisabeth was born with a rare chromosomal abnormality which, like many such disorders, proved to be incompatible with life. Her visible defects included a cleft lip and palate, elongated thumbs, and low-set ears. Additionally, she suffered from congenital cataracts and cardiac and respiratory irregularities. It was not initially certain how long she would live or in what condition.

Corey, who was told that Elisabeth was very sick, wanted to see her sister. She was allowed to do so from a hallway window several feet from Elisabeth's bassinet. She asked if Elisabeth, hooked up to wires and tubes, would die, and was honestly told that it was possible, but uncertain.

By the next day, more information revealed that Elisabeth was going to die. Corey insisted on a closer look at her dying sister. In preparation, she was told that Elisabeth was not made right and that her face would look strange. She and her parents talked about why Elisabeth would die and how they felt about it.

That afternoon Corey and her parents entered Elisabeth's room. Looking at Elisabeth, who was now free of wires and tubes, Corey exclaimed in the language of the day that her sister looked "Ooo, gross!" Corey then asked if she could touch her. She did so, acknowledging the softness of her skin and her curly red hair. Tearfully, she told Elisabeth that she was loved and that they all wished she did not have to die. Her baby sister responded by moving her tiny arms and legs. Corey was delighted, "She loves me! She knows I'm here!" Corey remained with her sister for some time holding her hand and stroking her bare arm and red hair. When it was time to leave, she said, "We love you Elisabeth. We'll never forget you!"

Corey shocked her parents by telling them that she wanted to see Elisabeth die. Not knowing how long it would be before she died and feeling the statement to be morbid, Corey's parents took her home. That night they received a call that Elisabeth died, peacefully, in the care of a nurse.

The next morning Corey insisted on going to the hospital with her parents who had to sign papers and arrange for an autopsy. At the hospital she announced, "I want to see my sister dead." The head nurse advised that she would be able to do so. Corey was again prepared for what Elisabeth would look like. She would be somewhat blotchy and discolored. Corey looked at her dead sister, who was wrapped in a blanket, with a mixture of sadness and fascination. She touched her and said goodbye, reminding Elisabeth that she was loved and would never be forgotten.

Source: Based on S. Scrimshaw and D. March. (1984). "I had a baby sister once but she only lasted one day." *Journal of the American Medical Association,* 251:732–733.

born sister died. Her parents poignantly related a bereaved Corey's reaction to the loss during the days and weeks that followed (Scrimshaw and March, 1984). Regarding her understanding of the permanence of death at such a young age, they related:

> We have always been very straight-forward with Corey. She was 2 years old when our pet cat died. She watched us bury the cat, then asked when she would come out again. When we said she wouldn't, Corey wanted to know why we couldn't take her to the doctor and get her fixed. By the time her great-grandmother died, Corey was almost 4 years old and understood that death was irrevocable.   (Scrimshaw and March, 1984, p. 733)

One year later, upon the death of her baby sister, Corey had already had quite a bit of experience with death. That she understood the permanence of her dead sibling's departure was underscored, perhaps, in her suggestion to her parents regarding the next baby brother or sister, "How about twins? Then if something happens, we'll still have one." Thus, while age may serve as a rough indicator of a child's understanding of or experience with death, it is not an absolute indicator.

Corey's parents recount that she taught them much about a child's ability to deal with sickness and death. Prior to their experience with Elisabeth, they would have been astonished at the notion of a child seeing a deformed, dying sibling. They would have thought that a child should be protected from emotionally painful sights and experiences. Now, they were thankful they had listened to Corey's wishes. Corey had no nightmares about a mysterious baby she had never seen. Elisabeth's defects had been viewed and acknowledged. But, so had her soft skin, lovely red hair, and responsiveness to Corey.

Corey expressed anger at Elisabeth's death, jealousy at the sight of another family's healthy baby, and guilt. She feared that the cold her mother had caught from her during pregnancy had hurt Elisabeth. These feelings were all discussed. Corey was told that Elisabeth's problem had started very early, long before her mother's cold. Thanks to their open family system, Corey did not have to bear the concerns and fears alone.

Corey's parents had been honest with her, included her in family activities, prepared her for potentially traumatic experiences, and provided an environment that allowed for open expression of feelings (Scrimshaw and March, 1984).

Age may influence the nature or pattern of children's responses to death. Due to their limited attention span, younger children may demonstrate shorter periods of grieving. Initially, adults may think the grief has lifted much sooner than it actually has. In time, they may observe that intermittent grieving becomes the pattern of expression. Also, young children may not appear to be disturbed by the death because they are watching television, riding their bikes, or coloring. In reality, they may have withdrawn into their own private world of grieving.

Sleep disturbances, eating disorders, regressive behavior (such as bed wetting), psychosomatic illness, poor school performance, social withdrawal, and depression are among the symptoms parents might observe in bereaved children, depending upon who died and the circumstances surrounding the death. These factors will be discussed later in the chapter.

Bereavement can be especially problematic for the adolescent. Family and developmental matters can present special issues for them. Relationships fraught with conflict are not uncommon for this age group. If a conflictual relationship is interrupted by death, the course of grief may be more difficult (Harris, 1991).

Adolescents undergo an adult grief process. Yet, it has been noted that they are sometimes "forgotten mourners" (Schachter, 1991–1992). When they lose a family member or a best friend, the focus of attention may be on their own or their friend's parents. The grief of surviving adolescents, be they family or peers, needs to be acknowledged.

However, it should be pointed out that adolescents may be motivated to repress their grief. Fitting in, being a part of a group, and conforming are notoriously important for this age group. They may wish to avoid the stigma of loss or the appearance of being weak or childish. Thus, the adolescent may seek to appear unharmed by death (Garber, 1985).

The family exerts a powerful effect on a child's grieving. That children look to their parents for guidance, particularly in uncommon or extraordinary circumstances, is underscored by Stephenson (1985,1986). Recognizing the rarity of a family death in the lives of most children, he notes that when such a loss occurs parents become important role models "as to how to behave, both socially and emotionally" (Stephenson, 1986, p. 330). In trying to better understand the coping strategy of children who have lost a parent, it is useful to observe the family for the example being set in the home. Children typically mirror the coping method of their surviving parent (Moody and Moody, 1991).

Stephenson (1985) contrasts the closed and open family communication systems as they operate in the face of a death. A closed family system is inclined to be rigid, locking people into tightly defined roles and strict thought and behavioral patterns. It provides little room for change. The significance of a death is not openly acknowledged or discussed. Family members, including children, are emotionally isolated. They do not react to the loss with an open show of honest emotion. Such a display would be considered too disruptive to family functioning. These patterns are frequently experienced by children referred for psychiatric counseling (Stephenson, 1986).

The open family system tends to provide a more supportive, nurturing environment. When a death occurs, the impact of a family loss is openly recognized, allowing for an honest display of emotion. "While this might seem to evoke more severe emotional responses among family members than would a refusal to acknowledge the importance of the loss, it is an indication that the family may be acknowledging the severity of the loss" (Stephenson, 1985, p. 185). In such a system, adults express their own thoughts and feelings, thus permitting children to do the same. Parents and children facilitate each others' grieving.

It is acknowledged that children of all ages should be permitted (but not forced) to attend funerals. Having permission to do so lets them feel that they are a part of the natural order of things (Schafer and Lyons, 1986). Be they family members, classmates, or friends of the deceased, they are afforded the opportunity to say goodbye (Cohn, 1987). In a study of adolescent experiences with the death of a peer, attendance at a friend's wake, funeral, or memorial service was identified as helpful in dealing with feelings (Schachter, 1991–1992).

Death of a Parent

Parental death is especially tragic for children. In the United States, approximately 6 percent of children under age eighteen lose one or both parents (Palombo, 1981). In addition to the sorrow and loneliness emanating from the death of a parent as a source of security, attention, and love, feelings of abandonment may be present. Indeed, children may feel doubly abandoned. Surviving parents who are managing their own grief may have less energy to devote to their children. Thus, children may psychologically lose their remaining parent, temporarily, to grief.

Anger and guilt are also part of parental loss. Some guilt may be related to the conflict that is so frequently a part of parent-child relations and to the magical thinking of children. On the one hand, the child may have been angry at the deceased parent on numerous occasions, even wished the parent dead in order to have his or her own way. Now, with the parent dead, there may be some sense of responsibility. "Did my parent die because I wished him or her dead?" Aside from this possibility, the child may feel guilty for not having been the perfect child. Questions such as "Why did I talk back?"; "Why didn't I clean my room?"; or "Why didn't I take out the garbage?" may weigh heavily on their minds.

Some studies show behavioral differences between children who have experienced parental death as compared with children who have not (Berlinsky and Biller, 1982). A greater incidence of emotional disturbances and maladjustment are among the difficulties cited. Children may react with uncooperative behavior, aggression, or hostility. Some may withdraw (Wass, 1984). Early loss has been linked to children's increased susceptibility to depression, school problems, and delinquency (Cheifetz, Stavrakakis, and Lester, 1989; Elizur and Kauffman, 1982; Kaffman and Elizur, 1983; Kliman, 1968; Raphael, 1983; Rutter, 1966).

It should not be extrapolated from such work that all children suffering the death of a parent are headed for major difficulties or psychiatric disturbances. It is a mistake to consider all cases of parental loss as being alike (Palombo, 1981). Although the death of a parent is a very traumatic event carrying the potential for serious problems, children are quite resilient (Wass and Stillion, 1988). With proper emotional support, they may overcome their loss without serious or prolonged difficulty (Furman, 1974; Stephenson, 1986). More studies are needed on children who do well after the death of a parent. Much of the available information on behavior and parental death is derived from cases that have been referred for therapy (Sekaer and Katz, 1986).

The long-term effects of childhood bereavement have also been a concern. Although the research findings are contradictory, it has been suggested that such children are more vulnerable to physical and emotional problems during their adult lives. A recent study on the effects of negative childhood experiences on adult psychiatric status examined parental death before the age of ten. Results suggest that parental death does not interact with recent events to increase the likelihood of psychiatric problems (Landerman, George, and Blazer, 1991).

Death of a Sibling

The death of a brother or sister is another type of traumatic loss for the child. As with other forms of bereavement, the surviving child may display various behavioral disorders. Having experienced the death of a young person (as opposed to a grandparent, for instance), children may feel vulnerable and fear for their own health.

Closed communication within families can contribute to the onset of emotional/behavioral problems. Many problems might be averted or ameliorated by giving children factual information at the diagnosis and throughout the course of treatment of their dying sibling (Koocher and O'Malley, 1981). An understanding of the illness and an open environment where they are free to ask questions is important. On the one hand, this setting allows them the opportunity to relate their own fears and to ask about their own good health, if that is a worry. It also helps to allay the mystery and fantasizing about "what is wrong." Additionally, it allows them to feel that they are being included in this significant family affair.

Well siblings come to learn about dying and death through their observations of and interactions with the dying child (Bluebond-Langner, 1989). In a study of well siblings of cystic fibrosis patients, age was not a significant factor in how they viewed the disease, but it did influence the sophistication with which they communicated their views (Bluebond-Langner, 1991).

As serious disease progresses and enters the terminal phase, siblings face an array of potential problems. One is that parents do not have the time for them that they used to. Children commonly associate the attention they receive with how much they are loved. Now, parents are preoccupied with their dying child and may be physically and emotionally drained. Although being as sensitive and attentive as possible to the needs of their well children, the demands on their time are often tremendous. They may not be able to go to all of the ball games and school plays. They may not have the time to take long walks or to watch bike rides as they once did. Likewise, dying children may cling to their parent(s), seemingly excluding the well sibling from the relationship they once shared. Consequently, well children might feel jealous, resentful, and neglected.

Well children may feel unimportant. They may feel left out, shifted from place to place, and deceived if not kept abreast of events. In short, they may feel like nonpersons (Grollman, 1967).

As the home life becomes disrupted, frustrations may mount. Friends may not come over as much as they used to or they can't spend the night anymore. The well children may feel bewildered about what the future holds for them and their family.

> The well siblings of terminally ill children live in houses of chronic sorrow. The signs of sorrow, illness, and death are everywhere, whether or not they are spoken of. The signs are written on parent's faces: "My mother always looks tired now," and "Even my Dad's crying a lot." (Bluebond-Langner, 1989, p. 9)

Children's grief reactions are influenced by a number of factors, including their relationship to the deceased sibling and the manner in which the child died (Stephenson, 1986). Sibling relationships are typically characterized by some degree of conflict, whether it be jealousy, rivalry, or, even hostility.

> In losing a sibling the child loses a playmate, a companion, someone who is a buffer against the parents, someone who may love and comfort him, someone with whom he identifies and whom he admires. In short he loses someone dearly loved as well as perhaps envied and rivalrously hated. (Raphael, 1983, p. 114)

The relationship can be influenced by birth order. Younger brothers or sisters may feel the pressure of replacing the deceased—"filling their shoes"—while older siblings may feel guilty for ever having felt burdened by the younger child (Rogers, 1967; Rosen, 1986; Rosen and Cohen, 1981). It is common for older children to wish that their younger siblings would "go away," "leave me alone," or "quit tagging along." Those normal thoughts may create a burden of guilt after the younger child dies.

Sibling relationships have been described as lying somewhere between two extremes. At one end, a vigorously negative or distant relationship may exist; at the other extreme, the relationship may be very intimate and mutually interdependent. An intense grief reaction is more likely to occur when the sibling association is characterized by either extreme (Rosen, 1986).

Accidental death may carry with it unanswered questions and some element of cause or blame. When death is by suicide, the surviving children may feel rejected by their sibling and also must endure the subsequent emotional unrest in the household (Stephenson, 1986).

Guilt after sibling death may emanate from various factors. As previously noted, normal sibling rivalry may cause regret/guilt for past feelings and behavior. Surviving children also may feel guilty for their sense of relief that "it's not me who got sick and died!" There also may be survival guilt, a notion that they are less deserving and should have died instead. Magical thinking may be held responsible for the loss: "I wished him dead and it happened!" These are just some of the various sources of guilt that surviving children might experience.

Some children may be reluctant to express their grief for fear of further upsetting their parents (Fulton, Gottesman, and Owen, 1982; Wass and Stillion, 1988). A twelve-year-old boy who lost his sister reported that his mother cried a lot and his father just didn't talk about it. He stayed in his room so that he would not bother either parent.

Talking with Children about Death

Dealing with death in a child's life can be awkward for an adult. Questions must be answered and feelings confronted. That the subject is difficult and often minimally discussed or avoided has been documented in numerous reports (Furman, 1974; McNeil, 1984; Stillion and Wass, 1979; Wass, 1986; Wass and Stillion, 1988). What follows are some principles that might be useful in talking to children about death.

The loss of a pet is the earliest, possibly only, death-related experience for most American children. This loss, rather than being minimized, can be used to teach children about death and the feelings it provokes (Box 10–2). It can be an occasion for children to openly ask questions and to discuss any concerns or beliefs they have about death. It also can be a time for them to learn that it is O.K. to be sad and O.K. to cry. Holding a funeral ceremony and burying the pet allows them to commemorate the pet and to say good-bye.

When death occurs, children should be given concrete information in a simple, direct, and honest manner. Euphemistic and metaphorical explanations should be avoided. Some examples include assertions that "God took him to heaven"; "The angels carried him away"; "God wanted her because she was

BOX 10–2   R.I.P. Amanda, 1983–1994

Last month we lost a member of the family. Amanda passed away. She was our golden retriever, a month shy of 11 years old—or almost 77 in dog years.

The world can be divided into two types of people: animal lovers and others. The latter never will understand the grieving, the profound sense of loss, the huge void when a longtime pet dies.

For our three children this was the most immediate experience of dying they have known. Yet Amanda's final days served as a family catharsis. For all the sadness and tears, it was a great bonding experience; my wife and I discovered that our kids have strengths that we never fully appreciated.

Amanda was a looming presence in all our lives. She was a gift to Jeffrey, now 12 years old, on his second birthday. The two of them literally grew up together. She was at the door when his younger brother and then younger sister arrived home for the first time. Amanda was too sweet to ever moonlight as a watchdog, yet the children always thought her a comforting protector; she encouraged that ruse.

She was in the center of every festive occasion. At Christmas she reveled in her presents—often with more appreciation than the kids showed—although they always were the same sort of bones and rubber toys. She loved birthdays not merely because she always got some of the cake, though that was special. She just adored happy times.

Then there was Amanda the mother. Over 14 months she had two litters, 15 puppies. Both pregnancies were unplanned, but fortunately they were the result of a steady relationship with a boy of her own faith—a neighbor golden of Republican extraction named Winston. Our two boys, especially Jeffrey, saw her bring lives into this world and witnessed the marvelous nurturing instincts of a mother.

Most of all she was a constant companion and friend. On those days when my wife and I came home from work tired, frustrated or even angry, Amanda always was there with her tail wagging, a smile on her face, overjoyed that her family was together. When the children fought or were punished, Amanda always was there to console them. She taught us far more than we realized, both about perspective and family. She gave us a rare commodity: unconditional love.

Over the final days, she also taught us a lot about how to die with grace, and how to deal with it. Days before she died, my brother, the world's most compassionate veterinarian, sent two books for the younger kids: "The Tenth Good Thing About Barney" by Judith Viorst, and "When a Pet Dies" by Fred Rogers of "Mr. Rogers' Neighborhood" fame. Anyone going through this trauma will find these books invaluable.

But it was her real master, Jeffrey, himself still months away from being a teenager, who had to struggle most valiantly with the realities of an imminent loss. Her kidneys had failed and she went downhill quickly. The only humane course was to put her to sleep, but Jeffrey wanted to bring her home for one last night. It could have been maudlin; it wasn't.

Box 10–2 (*Continued*)

Jeffrey spent the night with Amanda. They had hours of precious time alone. As sick as she was, our golden retriever never lost her congenital sweetness or genial smile; she never complained. Initially resistant to putting her to sleep, Jeffrey that evening called my brother—who lives near Philadelphia—and after a long discussion said simply, "I think she's ready to go."

The next morning right before I took her to the veterinarian, he again told her how important she had been to him. Jeffrey's forte never has been sharing with siblings, but he then urged his younger brother and sister to tell her goodbye, too. Five-year-old Lauren had a final girl-to-girl with her. Then as we were about to drive away, Benjamin, age seven, kissed her on the head and softly said, "Bye-bye, Amanda, I'll see you in heaven."

Source: "R.I.P. Amanda, 1983–1994," by Albert R. Hunt. *The Wall Street Journal,* June 2, 1994, p. A12. Reprinted with permission of The Wall Street Journal © 1994 Dow Jones & Company, Inc. All rights reserved.

so good"; or "Daddy went away." Such explanations can cause confusion and fear. Children may wonder why God takes people away, if other good people (including "me") will be taken away as well, or why my daddy left me if he really loved me. The claim that "Grandma is sleeping" (besides being false) may cause children to be fearful of sleep. Speculating about sleep and death can make for some very frightening fantasies.

The anxiety of separation and the fear of desertion may bother children whether or not these feelings are directly expressed. It may be important to indicate that the loved one did not want to die and leave them behind. Children should be reassured that they are still loved and will not be abandoned.

An open environment where children are free to ask questions should be provided. Such a setting allows them to question when the need arises. One big tell-all does not close the book on the death. Queries, concerns, and feelings are part of the ongoing process of dealing with loss.

Children should also be allowed to express feelings. They may suffer the same feelings as adults but show them differently. This factor is important to bear in mind as illustrated in cases of mothers who were disturbed that their children appeared to respond inappropriately to sibling death. Various mothers related their children reacted to the news with, "Good, now I can have all his toys."

Later it came to be realized that this was the sibling's way of expressing anger with the deceased for leaving them (a feeling shared by the parents), of holding on to a part of the deceased (a desire of the parents as well), and also of expressing all the long-suppressed hurt at being neglected by the parent (a guilt felt by the parents).   (Bluebond-Langner, 1977, p. 63)

Suicide in Preadolescent Children

That children would engage in suicidal behavior is shocking and unthinkable. That they do is a tragic reality. Approximately 12,000 children aged five to fourteen are admitted to the hospital annually as a result of suicidal activity. However, the actual incidence of attempted as well as completed suicide for this age group is particularly difficult to evaluate. While it is widely recognized that the incidence of suicide in the United States is underreported for all age groups, the Division of Vital Statistics does not report the deaths of children under ten as suicide (Pfeffer, 1985). Thus, the less than 1 percent incidence of childhood suicide reported by the U.S. Bureau of the Census (1988) may be misleading.

Fasko and Fasko (1990) indicate that it is wrong to presume that children are too young to consider suicide: "Regardless of whether they perceive death as permanent or temporary, children do make attempts to achieve death, and one must not discount overt or covert suicide threats simply on the basis of age" (Fasko and Fasko, 1990, p. 14).

A number of reasons for suicidal behavior in children have been offered, including attempted self-punishment, escape, reunion with a loved one, and amendment of an intolerable situation (Rosenthal and Rosenthal, 1984). Although further research is needed, abusive situations, depression in the child or parent, a family history of suicide, and family instability to the extent that it is perceived by the child as stressful are among the factors that increase the risk of suicidal behavior in children (Fasko and Fasko, 1990; Weiner, 1982).

Summary

The death of children is especially tragic and shocking. Its occurrence seems out of step with the natural order of things. Such was not always the case. Our ancestors knew all too well about the death of children. In earlier days it was a regular, though still tragic, event. As recently as the beginning of the twentieth century, children accounted for 53 percent of all U.S. deaths. Today, thanks to immunizations, antibiotics, and improved living conditions, including improved sanitation and nutrition, those under age fifteen account for four to five percent of all U.S. deaths.

Children's experiences with death have changed as well. In the past, they regularly confronted death. Most deaths and wakes occurred in the home. Today, death—with the exception of that portrayed on television or in movies—is a rare event in their lives. Most deaths occur in hospitals or nursing homes without children present. Today, some parents are concerned about the appropriateness of children attending viewings and funerals. Honest communication with children about death is healthy and encouraged, as is giving them the opportunity to participate in the activities surrounding death.

Children's understanding of death is shaped by the complex interplay of their level of cognitive development and their experience with death. Nagy advocated an age-based developmental model, maintaining that children's ideas about death developed in three age-related stages. Her work has been a standard for studying childhood conceptualizations of death. With refinement, it remains useful. More recent work indicates that strict adherence to chronological age as an indicator of children's ideas about death is inappropriate. Chronological age may serve an approximate guide, but individual development is a more accurate gauge. The age-graded model does not take into account social, cultural, religious, and experiential influences on a child's thoughts about death. Each can play a significant role. Bluebond-Langner formulated an experiential model by which dying children acquire knowledge about their illness; she described the transformation they undergo as they see themselves as seriously ill and, finally, dying.

Special concerns exist for dying children. These include the disruption imposed by hospitalization, pain management, hospice care, and the various responses to serious illness and dying manifested by differing age groups.

Bereaved children need the opportunity to express their emotions, to talk about death, and to ask questions. Age, level of cognitive development, experience with death, relationship with the deceased, the nature of the death, and family dynamics all influence a child's grief experience. Parental death is especially difficult. In addition to the many emotions of grief, children may experience strong feelings of abandonment. This factor is complicated by the fact that they may also lose their surviving parent, temporarily, to grief. The conflict so common to the parent-child relationship and children's magical thinking may complicate their grief. They feel guilty for not being the perfect child and maybe for having previously wished their parent dead when they didn't get their own way. Behavioral differences between children who are and are not suffering parental loss as well as the long-term effects of such bereavement are areas of ongoing study. With proper emotional support, such children typically overcome their loss without serious or prolonged problems.

The death of a sibling represents another traumatic loss for a child. Open communication with well children about their sibling's terminal diagnosis and dying is important. Well siblings face an array of potential problems including a lack of parental time and attention, disruption of home life, and a perception of being left out. Their grief is influenced by their relationship with the dead sibling, the manner by which death occurred, guilt, and magical thinking.

Talking with children about death is awkward for many adults. The death of a pet can be used to teach children about death and grief. Their questions and feelings should be allowed expression. They should be given honest answers and concrete information. Euphemisms such as, "The angels carried him away" should be avoided.

Approximately 12,000 children between five and fourteen years of age are annually admitted to U.S. hospitals as a result of suicidal activity. The true incidence of attempted and completed suicide for this age group is especially difficult to evaluate. Numerous reasons for suicidal behavior in children have been offered.

Study Questions

1. How has the frequency and pattern of childhood death changed during the twentieth century?

2. Discuss the age-graded developmental model regarding a child's understanding of death. In so doing, present Nagy's stages and an overview of the significance and criticism of her work.

3. How important to terminally ill children is open communication about their illness? Explain your answer.

4. Note the importance of Bluebond-Langner's work regarding terminally ill children's awareness of their dying.

5. Note several factors that compound the problem of pediatric pain control.

6. How does a child's age influence behavioral and emotional responses to serious personal illness?

7. What types of factors influence children's expression of grief? Explain.

8. Identify some special concerns regarding the death of a parent and the death of a sibling for bereaved children.

9. Present some principles that might be useful in talking to children about death.

10. Discuss the frequency of, and identify various reasons for, suicidal behavior in children.

References

Anthony, S. (1940). *The Child's Discovery of Death.* New York: Harcourt Brace and World.

Anthony, Z., and K. Bhana. (1988–1989). An exploratory study of Muslim girls' understanding of death. *Omega,* 19:215–228.

Berlinsky, I., and E. Biller. (1982). *Parental Death and Psychological Development.* Lexington, MA: Lexington Books.

Bluebond-Langner, M. (1974). I know, do you?: Awareness and communication in terminally ill children. In B. Schoenberg et al. (Eds.), *Anticipatory Grief.* New York: Columbia.

Bluebond-Langner, M. (1975). *Awareness and Communication in Terminally Ill Children: Pattern, Process, and Pretense.* Doctoral dissertation, University of Illinois.

Bluebond-Langner, M. (1977). Meanings of death to children. In H. Feifel (Ed.), *New Meanings of Death* (pp. 48–66). New York: McGraw-Hill.

Bluebond-Langner, M. (1978). *The Private Worlds of Dying Children.* Princeton, NJ: Princeton University Press.

Bluebond-Langner, M. (1989). Worlds of dying children and their well siblings. *Death Studies,* 13:1–16.

Bluebond-Langner, M. (1991). Living with cystic fibrosis: The well sibling's perspective. *Medical Anthropology Quarterly,* 5:133–152.

Cheifetz, P., G. Stavrakakis, and E. Lester. (1989). Studies of the affective state in bereaved children. *Canadian Journal of Psychiatry,* 34:688–692.

Cohn, J. (1987). The grieving student. *Instructor:* 76–78.

Duffy, C., P. Pollack, M. Levy, E. Budd, L. Caulfield, S. Spielberg, and G. Koren. (1991). Home-based palliative care for children: A feasibility study. In D. Papdatou and C. Papadatos (Eds.), *Children and Death* (pp. 209–216). New York: Hemisphere.

Elizur, E., and M. Kaufman. (1982). Children's bereavement reactions following the death of the father: II. *Journal American Academy of Child Psychiatry,* 21:474–480.

Fasko, S., and D. Fasko, Jr. (1991). Suicidal behavior in children. *Psychology, A Journal of Human Behavior,* 27:10–16.

Fulton, R., D. Gottesman, and G. Owen. (1982). Loss, social change, and the prospect of mourning. *Death Education,* 6:137–153.

Furman, E. (1974). *A Child's Parent Dies: Studies in Childhood Bereavement:* New Haven: Yale University Press.

Garber, B. (1985). Mourning in adolescence: Normal and pathological. *Adolescent Psychiatry,* 12:371–387.

Gartley, W., and M. Bernasconi. (1967). The concept of death in children. *Journal of Genetic Psychology,* 110:71.

Graham-Pole, J., H. Wass, S. Eyberg, L. Chu, and S. Olejnik. (1989). Communicating with dying children and their siblings: A retrospective analysis. *Death Studies,* 13:465–483.

Grollman, E. (1967). *Explaining Death to Children.* Boston: Beacon Press.

Harris, E. (1991). Adolescent bereavement following the death of a parent: An exploratory study. *Child Psychiatry and Human Development,* 21:267–281.

Jenkins, R., and C. Cavanaugh. (1985–1986). Examining the relationship between the development of the concept of death and overall cognitive development. *Omega,* 16:193–200.

Kaffman, M., and E. Elizur. (1983). Bereavement responses of Kibbutz and non-Kibbutz children following the death of the father. *Journal of Child Psychology and Psychiatry,* 24:435–441.

Kane, B. (1979). Children's concepts of death. *Journal of Genetic Psychology,* 134:141–153.

Kastenbaum, R. (1991). *Death, Society, and Human Experience.* New York: Merrill.

Kearl, M. (1989). *Endings: A Sociology of Death and Dying.* New York: Oxford University Press.

Kliman, G. (1968). Death in the family. In G. Kliman (Ed.), *Psychological Emergencies of Childhood*. New York: Grune and Stratton.

Knowles, D., and N. Reeves. (1983). *But Won't Granny Need Her Socks?* Dubuque, IA: Kendall/Hunt.

Koocher, G. (1973). Childhood, death, and cognitive development. *Developmental Psychology*, 9:369–375.

Koocher, G., and J. O'Malley. (1981). *The Damocles Syndrome*. New York: McGraw-Hill.

Landerman, R., L. George, and D. Blazer. (1991). Adult vulnerability for psychiatric disorders: Interactive effects of negative childhood experiences and recent stress. *Journal of Nervous and Mental Disease*, 179:656–663.

Langreth, R. (1991). Pediatric pain: Helping children cope with medical pokes and probes. *Science News*, 139:74–75.

Lonetto, R. (1980). *Children's Conception of Death*. New York: Springer.

McIntire, M., C. Angle, and L. Struempler. (1972). The concept of death in midwestern children and youth. *American Journal of Diseases of Children*, 123:527.

McNeil, J. (1984). Death education in the home: Parents talk with their children. In H. Wass and C. Corr (Eds.), *Childhood and Death* (pp. 293–313). Washington, D.C.: Hemisphere.

Moody, R., and C. Moody. (1991). A family perspective: Helping children acknowledge and express grief following the death of a parent. *Death Studies*, 15:587–602.

Nagy, M. (1948). The child's view of death. *Journal of Genetic Psychology*, 73:3–27.

Novello, A., P. Wise, A. Willoughby, and A. Pizzo. (1989). The final report of the U.S. DHHS Secretary's Work Group on Pediatric HIV infection and disease: Content and implications. *Pediatrics*, 84:547–555.

Palombo, J. (1981). Parent loss and childhood bereavement: Some theoretical considerations. *Clinical Social Work Journal*, 9:3–33.

Pfeffer, C. (1985). Suicidal fantasies in normal children. *Journal of Nervous and Mental Disease*, 173:78–84.

Raphael, B. (1983). *The Anatomy of Bereavement*. New York: Basic Books.

Rogers, R. (1967). Children's reaction to sibling death. In E. Dunlap and M. Weisman (Eds.), *Psychosomatic Medicine: Proceedings of the First International Congress of the Academy of Psychosomatic Medicine*. Amsterdam, NY: Excerpta Medica Foundation.

Rosen, H. (1986). *Unspoken Grief*. Lexington, MA: D. C. Heath.

Rosen, H., and H. Cohen. (1981). Children's reaction to sibling loss. *Clinical Social Work Journal*, 9:211–219.

Rosenthal, P., and S. Rosenthal. (1984). Suicidal behavior by preschool children. *American Journal of Psychiatry*, 141:520–525.

Rutter, M. (1966). *Children of Sick Parents*. Oxford: Oxford University Press.

Schachter, S. (1991–1992). Adolescent experiences with the death of a peer. *Omega*, 24:1–11.

Schafer, D., and C. Lyons. (1986). *How Do We Tell the Children*. New York: Newmarket Press.

Scrimshaw, S., and D. March. (1984). "I had a baby sister but she only lasted one day." *JAMA*, 251:732–733.

Sekaer, C., and S. Katz. (1986). On the concept of mourning in childhood. *The Psychoanalytic Study of the Child*, 41:287–314.

Spinetta, J. (1978). Communication patterns in families dealing with life-threatening illness. In O. Sahler (Ed.), *The Child and Death* (pp. 43–46). St. Louis: Mosby.

Spinetta, J., and L. Maloney. (1975). Death anxiety in the outpatient leukemic child. *Pediatrics,* 56:1034–1037.

Spinetta, J., D. Rigler, and M. Karon. (1974). Personal space as a dying child's measure of isolation. *Journal of Consulting and Clinical Psychology,* 42:751–756.

Stannard, E. (1977). *The Puritan Way of Death: A Study in Religion, Culture, and Social Change.* New York: Oxford University Press.

Stephenson, J. (1985). *Death, Grief, and Mourning.* New York: The Free Press.

Stephenson, J. (1986). Grief of siblings. In T. Rando (Ed.), *Parental Loss of a Child* (pp. 321–337). Champaign, IL: Research Press.

Stillion, J., and H. Wass. (1979). Children and death. In H. Wass (Ed.), *Dying: Facing the Facts* (pp. 208–235). Washington, D.C.: Hemisphere.

U.S. Bureau of Census. (1988). *Statistical Abstract of the United States* (108th ed.). Washington, DC: U.S. Government Printing Office.

Vanderpool, N., and J. Richmond. (1990). Child health in the United States: Prospects for the 1990s. In L. Breslow, J. Fielding, and L. Lave (Eds.), *Annual Review of Public Health: II* (pp. 185–205). Palo Alto: Annual Reviews Inc.

Vernick, J., and M. Karon. (1965). Who's afraid of death in the leukemia ward? *American Journal of Diseases of Children,* 109:393–397.

Waechter, E. (1971). Children's awareness of fatal illness. *American Journal of Nursing,* 71:1168–1172.

Waechter, E. (1984). Dying children: Patterns of coping. In H. Wass and C. Corr (Eds.), *Childhood and Death* (pp. 51–60). Washington, DC: Hemisphere.

Wass, H. (1984). Parents, teachers, and professionals as helpers. In H. Wass and C. Corr (Eds.), *Helping Children Cope with Death: Guidelines and Resources* (pp. 90–103). Washington, DC: Hemisphere.

Wass, H. (1986). Death education for children in the home and at school. In R. Turnbull (Ed.), *Terminal Care* (pp. 215–228). Washington, D.C.: Hemisphere.

Wass, H., and J. Stillion. (1988). Death in the lives of children and adolescents. In H. Wass, F. Berardo, and R. Neimeyer (Eds.), *Dying: Facing the Facts* (pp. 200–228). Washington, DC: Hemisphere.

Weiner, I. (1982). *Child and Adolescent Psychopathology.* New York: John Wiley & Sons.

Wenestam, C., and H. Wass. (1987). Swedish and U.S. children's thinking about death: A qualitative study and cross-cultural comparison. *Death Studies,* 11:99–122.

Zweig, A. (1983). Children's attitudes toward death. In J. Schowlater et al. (Eds.), *The Child and Death* (pp. 36–48). New York: Columbia University Press.

CHAPTER 11

Suicide

And he was rich—yes, richer than a king,
And admirably schooled in every grace,
In fine, we thought he was everything
To make us wish that we were in his place.

So on we worked, and waited for the light,
And went without the meat, and cursed the bread;
And Richard Cory, one calm summer night,
Went home and put a bullet through his head.

Edward Arlington Robinson, "Richard Cory"

Suicide is an exasperating act as often as it is pitiable. . . . It appears
to cast a subversive judgement upon the social polity as a whole,
that which was supposed to work in life—religion, family,
friendship, commerce and industry—did not; and furthermore, it
"frightens the horses in the street" as Virginia Woolf once
defined . . . (before she killed herself).

E. Hoagland

The Underreporting of Suicide

Last year in the United States approximately 31,000 cases of suicide were reported. A cross-section of U.S. society is represented in these numbers. People
of both genders and all ages, socioeconomic levels, racial, religious, and occupational groups are claimed by this phenomenon that is consistently one of the
ten leading causes of death in the United States.

Suicide statistics are of limited accuracy, however, in portraying the true
numbers of persons who take their own lives. Real figures may be two to three
times those reported (Blumenthal, 1988). Medical examiners surveyed corrob-

orate that reported cases probably reflect less than one-half of the actual numbers (Jobes, Berman, and Josselson, 1986).

Several factors are responsible for the underreporting of suicide. While death certificates register the mode or manner in which death occurs (natural, accidental, suicide, or homicide), there are no uniform criteria to define or identify a suicide. A working group representing coroners, medical examiners, statisticians, and public health agencies has developed and submitted operational criteria that may assist coroners and medical examiners in a determination of suicide (Rosenberg et al., 1988). The findings of this interdisciplinary group were given prominence in the Centers for Disease Control's weekly publication and are contained in Box 11–1.

Another factor contributing to the underreporting of suicide is the stigma associated with such a death. In the face of family or community pressure, decision makers may be disinclined to label a death a suicide. And, the absence of uniformly applied criteria makes it easier for them to do so. Many "accidental" drownings, "accidental" gunshot wounds, and "accidental" poisonings may, indeed, be suicides. Finally, cases may be underreported because of inadequate information on which to make a determination of suicide as a cause of death.

The Psychological Autopsy

A research tool known as the psychological autopsy has, over the past several years, contributed to our knowledge of suicide. Introduced in the 1960s by the National Institute of Mental Health, its intent is to fill in knowledge gaps about suicide. It involves a retrospective review and reconstruction of the events immediately preceding the real or suspected suicidal death. Through interviews with one or more persons who had contact with the decedent during the weeks or months prior to death, an attempt is made to comprehend his or her clinical, psychological, and social background. The psychological autopsy is instrumental in obtaining much of the information cited in Box 11–1. Referred to as "the psychological correlate of the medical autopsy" (Younger et al., 1990), the psychological autopsy can allow one to better establish if a given death was, indeed, a suicide. As the noted suicidologist Edwin Shneidman pointed out some years ago:

> The most serious fault in the certification of equivocal death is the lack of any attempt to establish the *intention* of the decedent in regard to his own demise. The decedent's intention—not his stomach or lung contents or his brain pathology—is what operationally distinguishes suicide from the other three

Box 11–1   *Operational Criteria for Determining Suicide*

Death established as:

Self-Inflicted: There is evidence that death was self-inflicted. This may be determined by pathologic evidence (autopsy), toxicologic, investigatory, and psychologic evidence and by statements of the decedent or witnesses.

Intentional: There is evidence (explicit and/or implicit) that, at the time of injury, the decedent intended to kill himself/herself or wished to die and that the decedent understood the probable consequences of his/her actions.

This evidence may include:

- Explicit verbal or nonverbal expression of intent to kill self.
- Implicit or indirect evidence of intent to die, such as preparations for death inappropriate or unexpected in the context of the decedent's life.
- Expression of farewell or the desire to die or an acknowledgement of impending death.
- Expression of hopelessness.
- Expression of great emotional or physical pain or distress, or effort to procure or learn about means of death or to rehearse fatal behavior.
- Precautions to avoid rescue.
- Evidence that decedent recognized high potential lethality of means of death.
- Previous suicide attempt.
- Previous suicide threat.
- Stressful events or significant losses (actual or threatened).
- Serious depression or mental disorder.

Source: From L. Davidson et al. (1989). Operational criteria for determining suicide. *Morbidity and Mortality Weekly Report,* 37:773–774, 779–780.

modes [natural, accident or homicide]. And the decedent's intention cannot be found in the test tube or under the microscope. . . .

Often, however, it can be discovered by conscientious interviewing of people who knew various aspects of his life style and specific behavior immediately prior to his death. A total autopsy ought to include the services of the behavioral scientist—psychologist, psychiatrist, sociologist, social worker. We call this procedure the "psychological autopsy."   (Shneidman, 1976, p. 248)

In addition to providing insight into the manner by which a given individual death occurs, the psychological autopsy has an important long-term, community function. Its application to large numbers of individual suicides may generate information to aid in characterizing susceptible persons and in designing appropriate intervention strategies.

Characteristics that are associated with an increased probability of a given phenomenon are known as *risk factors*. Our knowledge of risk factors for suicide is incomplete. Even when death certificates identify it as the mode of death, they contain little information to associate the self-destructive act with any particular characteristics. For example, they do not indicate factors such as the decedent's history of employment, socioeconomic status, drug or alcohol use, family structure, mental illness, or family history of suicide.

The psychological autopsy was developed as part of a suicide prevention plan, the goal of which is to identify risk factors amenable to detection and treatment. Characterizing the most vulnerable in our population would assist in improving the design, implementation, and evaluation of prevention strategies (Saltzman, Levenson, and Smith, 1988).

Suicide Statistics: An Overview

Suicide rates are calculated for the nation as a whole as well as for various population groups. The rates are based on the number of suicides per 100,000 persons in a given population designation. For example, a national suicide rate of 12 means that within a given year, approximately 12 people for every 100,000 in the U.S. population will take their own lives.

Although underestimating actual numbers, suicide statistics allow us to monitor long-term trends and to note differing rates among age groups and between the sexes. While the overall suicide rate in the United States has remained about the same for many years, there have been two significant age-related trends. The suicide rate has soared for young people between fifteen to twenty-four years of age and declined slightly for the elderly, although elderly rates have increased recently (McIntosh, 1989; Meehan, Saltzman, and Sattin, 1991; National Center for Health Statistics, 1987). The highest suicide rate continues to be seen among the nation's older adults.

At every age, white males are at an increased risk of suicide. They account for approximately 70 percent of all such deaths. The rate of completed suicides for males is three to four times that of females except among the elderly for whom the male-female ratio increases even further (McIntosh, 1985; National Center for Health Statistics, 1987; Rosenberg et al., 1987). Women *attempt* suicide three times as often as men but they tend to use potentially less lethal means such as drug overdosing or wrist slashing. The lethality of means refers to the probability that one will die from a particular method such as gunshot, hanging, jumping, or drug/alcohol ingestion. The use of firearms, the highly lethal and leading means of suicide for males, is growing for females.

The suicide rate for whites is twice that of African-Americans. However, sharp growth in the rate among young African-American men has been noted. Among religious groups in this country, Protestants have the highest suicide rate (Blumenthal, 1988).

Suicide Attempts

A suicide attempt is an act of intentional self-harm, the outcome of which could be but is not fatal. The ratio of attempted to completed suicides is eight to one (Davidson, 1986). However, this figure is an approximation at best. Attempted suicide is not a reportable condition. Furthermore, we have no system for accurately defining it or evaluating the frequency with which it occurs (Meehan et al., 1992).

Those who engage in suicidal behavior, "attempters" and "completers," are frequently viewed as two separate yet overlapping groups. Those who attempt suicide tend to act unsuccessfully and repeatedly. They also tend to be younger and female. Their behavior, sometimes termed *parasuicide,* may be a dramatic cry for help and one more step in an ongoing path of self-destruction. Suicide attempts should always be taken seriously. Ten percent or more of attempters will eventually succeed in taking their own lives (Blumenthal, 1988).

Those who complete suicide tend to be older and male. They also tend to use more lethal methods. Their first attempt at self-destruction is usually successful. However, it is possible that someone who fully intended to commit suicide may fail to do so. Likewise, an attempt that was intended to fail may succeed.

Selected At-Risk Populations

Youth Suicide

Reported cases of suicide in children between the ages of five and fourteen exist, but are rare. Suicidal behavior, however, is not rare, as is demonstrated by the 12,000 children hospitalized annually for deliberate self-destructive acts (U.S. Department of Health and Human Services, 1986; Fasko and Fasko, 1991). Reported suicides for the nation's youth, designated as those between fifteen and twenty-four years of age, are alarmingly high. In 1977, for the first time, the suicide rate for this age group surpassed that for the nation as a whole (Saltzman, Levenson, and Smith, 1988).

During the first half of the twentieth century, the youth suicide rate was stable and one-half the national rate. Things began to change in the mid-1950s when the youth suicide rate began to rise markedly. By 1980, it had almost tripled. In 1984, suicide became the second leading cause of death for this age group (Rosenberg et al., 1987). By the end of the 1980s, the youth suicide rate stood at 12.9—a major increase over its 1950 measure of 4.5.

Data indicate that among those fifteen to twenty-four years of age, white males have the greatest risk of suicide (Centers for Disease Control, 1988). In fact, the increase in youth suicide is due primarily to the rising male rate. The percentage increase in youth suicide rates for one fourteen-year study period (1970–1984) illustrates this point. During this time, the male rate increased 53.0 percent while the female rate rose 4.8 percent.

The Centers for Disease Control has identified youth suicide as a priority concern. The group is studying suicide patterns in an attempt to determine risk factors that can designate subpopulations of teens (ages fifteen to nineteen) and young adults (ages twenty to twenty-four) at greatest risk (Rosenberg et al., 1987). A family history of suicide, feelings of hopelessness, and mental illness have been correlated with an increased risk of suicide (Beck et al., 1985; Kosky, 1983; Motto, Heilbron, and Juster, 1985; Sudak, Ford, and Rushforth, 1984). Other factors cited and under further study include drug and alcohol abuse and emotional stress. Some of the more frequently noted risk factors for youth suicide, as well as selected suicide prevention strategies, are noted in Boxes 11–2 and 11–3, respectively.

Exposure to suicide—either directly through the loss of a friend or associate or indirectly through a news report or film—has also been considered a possible risk factor for youth suicide. Apparent "outbreaks" of suicide or suicide attempts by young people in a given community within a relatively short period of time are referred to as *serial, copycat,* or *cluster suicides.* Currently a novel feature of suicide among young people, these clustered events suggest the possibility that suicide may have a socially "contagious" effect (Davidson and Gould, 1988; Robbins and Conroy, 1983).

Cluster suicides tend to mimic the suicide method as is indicated in the following two cases. The first involves an apparent suicide pact that took place in New Jersey. The second concerns a series of suicides that followed a television documentary broadcast in West Germany.

Case 1. In March 1987, four teenagers committed suicide by locking themselves inside a thirteen-car garage and sitting in a car with a running engine. Two were males aged eighteen and nineteen and two were females aged sixteen and seventeen. The two young males died of a synergism of carbon

---

B o x 11–2 *Some Risk Factors Associated with Youth Suicide*

- Male more likely than female
- White more likely than black
- Previous suicide attempt
- Depression and affective disorder
- Substance abuse
- Exposure to suicide
- A family history of suicide
- The presence of firearms in the home

---

monoxide poisoning, cocaine and alcohol; the two young women of a synergism of carbon monoxide and cocaine.

Within days of these deaths, the community responded with various efforts to prevent other suicides. School officials provided counselors for students thought to be at high risk, such as those with a history of suicide attempts or those who were close friends of the victims. A local suicide hotline and a walk-in center were started. The garage where the deaths occurred was locked and placed under periodic police surveillance.

In spite of these measures, six days later a seventeen-year-old male and a twenty-year-old female attempted suicide in the same garage by the same method. A policeman found them unconscious after noticing that the garage door lock was broken. The door was removed (Centers for Disease Control, 1988).

Case 2. Klerman (1987), from the Department of Psychiatry, Cornell University Medical Center, reported on a television documentary concerning youth suicide that aired in West Germany. It featured an explicit portrayal of a young man who died when he threw himself before a moving train. Surrounded by controversy, the documentary was replayed one year later. A significant increase in suicide by railroad trauma in the weeks following both television showings was documented by the Mannheim Mental Health Institute.

Cases such as these generate concern over the possible influence of exposure to suicide, the public health responsibilities of the media, and the development of appropriate community intervention strategies when a youth suicide

B o x 11–3   *Youth Suicide Prevention Approaches*

- Working with youth to identify feelings and coping mechanisms.
- Early identification and treatment referral of youth at high risk of suicide.
- School-based screening programs.
- Crisis centers and telephone hotlines.
- Training of health care professionals in the treatment of conditions that can lead to suicide.

occurs. It appears that serial suicide accounts for no more than 1 to 5 percent of all youth suicides (Gould, Wallenstein, and Kleinman, 1987). In spite of this fact, when youth suicide or suicide clustering occurs, community efforts at further prevention are considered appropriate (O'Carroll, Mercy, and Steward, 1988).

The degree to which exposure to another's suicide enhances the danger of imitating that act is being debated. In a study of two Texas clusters, research revealed that exposure did not increase the probability of suicide in those not already at risk. The researchers cautioned that young people who are at risk of suicide may be deeply affected by exposure to another's self-destructive act. Those who did kill themselves were more likely to demonstrate risk factors prior to the clustering. These included a previous suicide attempt, losing a close friend or relative to violent death, or a recent breakup with a boy or girl-friend.

It is feared that sensational coverage and romanticizing of suicide might foster an affinity with the victim for a suicide-prone individual. Such a person might be left with an impression of suicide as a powerful act eliciting attention from family, friends, and peers, even if posthumously. Consequently, some recommend against repetitive media coverage and large memorial gatherings at schools (Davidson et al., 1989).

The population model proposes that the youth suicide rate fluctuates according to the number of persons in that age group and their proportion to the remainder of the population. Thus, in 1955, when there were 21 million people between the ages of fifteen and twenty-four, representing 13 percent of the total U.S. population, the youth suicide rate was low. In 1977, when the rate had climbed to an all-time high of 13.3, there were 41 million youth, comprising 18 percent of the population (Hollinger, Offer, and Ostrov, 1987; Simmons, 1987).

It is theorized that as their numbers increase, so does competition for available resources such as academic honors, spots on athletic teams, admission to college/university programs, and jobs. Heightened competition may thus lead to increased stress (Blumenthal, 1984, 1988; Hollinger, Offer, and Ostrov, 1987) and increased risk of suicide. Young people in this country have experienced a rise in other behaviors indicative of social stress such as drug/alcohol abuse, eating disorders, and crime and delinquency (Blumenthal, 1988). Interestingly, a relatively high youth suicide rate occurred at the start of the twentieth century when young persons comprised a greater percentage of the entire population (Hendin, 1986; Hollinger, Offer, and Ostrov, 1987).

The youth suicide rate plateaued in 1980 as the last of the baby boom generation moved into adulthood and the number of adolescents fell. On the basis of census data, the number of adolescents will continue to decline into the mid-1990s and then increase again. If the population model is correct, the youth suicide rate should be expected to follow the same pattern.

Hollinger, one of the developers of the population model, feels that the suicide rate in older people also is influenced by population numbers and relative proportions. However, he maintains that their suicide rate is inversely related to their numbers. Large numbers of older persons might work for them rather than against them. Greater numbers may mean greater political pressure for improved economic and health care services and less reason for despair (Simmons, 1987).

The population model should not be confused with the cohort model which follows suicide rates in a specific birth group or cohort over time. The latter model hypothesizes that a shared, time-related experience such as the year or decade of birth is associated with illness rates, and, in this case, suicide rates throughout life. The cohort model is concerned, for example, with following a specific generation/group such as the baby boomers throughout time. The population model does not follow a cohort; rather, it continues to focus on a specific age group.

Suicide by the Elderly

Suicide rates increase with age for both genders. For women, they peak in midlife, typically around the age of fifty. Why suicide peaks for middle-aged women is not fully understood. Perhaps, the number of social and physical life changes that occur at this time, including the risk of widowhood, influence the situation. With the peaking of female suicide, the closest rate differential between the sexes occurs; nevertheless, the rates for middle-aged men are over twice those for women (McIntosh, 1991).

Although the greatest *number* of suicides occur among white, middle-aged men, the highest *rate* occurs among the elderly. The latter situation is related to the size of the respective populations. Because there are more middle-aged men, even a lower rate among them translates into more deaths.

The elderly, defined as those persons sixty-five years and older, represent over 12.5 percent of the population and account for about 25 percent of reported suicides. The rate is highest for white males, especially those in their eighties. Once again, during old age, we see that white men commit suicide at a greater rate than females in general or African-American men whose suicide rate peaks between ages twenty-five to thirty-four.

It is speculated that the sharp age-related loss of status that older white men in our society undergo might serve to explain their higher suicide rates. In contrast, racism and sexism have not afforded African-American men and most women the power and influence enjoyed by white males earlier in life. Thus, these groups do not suffer the same drastic loss of status with age (Butler, Lewis, and Sunderland, 1991).

The elderly are more likely to successfully complete the self-destructive act and, hence, have the smallest ratio of attempted to completed suicide. Perhaps, this is because suicide is less likely to be a call for help among this age group. Also, firearms are the most common method by which older people take their own lives (Casey, 1991).

Suicide may be more underreported for the elderly than for any other age group. Older persons are more likely to be taking medications for multiple chronic conditions and are, chronologically, nearer to death. They can stop taking life-sustaining drugs or deliberately overdose on prescribed medications without generating any suspicion (Glass and Reed, 1993). Also, some fatal accidents in this group may go unquestioned and actually be disguised suicides (Blazer, Bachar, and Manton, 1986).

Among the conclusions cited in a study concerning the overall decline in medical autopsy rates with age was that

> clinicians, family members and medical examiners may be prone to attribute certain deaths incorrectly to "natural causes." It is not unlikely that a number of elderly persons found dead have not died from the ubiquitous labels of "cerebrovascular disease" or "arteriosclerotic heart disease" but perhaps from drug overdose—accidental or self-induced—or even homicide. One wonders if the low autopsy rate among the elderly . . . is masking such cases. (Ahronheim, Bernholc, and Black, 1983, p. 1185)

Depression is a precipitating factor in suicide. It varies from the transient state of feeling sad, blue, or down to the severe depression manifested by psychotic withdrawal. While depression is the most common mood/emotional disorder found in older adults, the present generation of older people is extraordinarily free of major depressive disorders. Major depression is more common in today's younger cohorts (Blazer, 1989; Blazer, Hughes, and George, 1987; Butler, Lewis, and Sunderland, 1991; Meyers et al., 1984).

Nevertheless, it has been estimated that depression may be related to 50 to 75 percent of late-life suicides (Katz et al., 1988). Depression-related deaths among the elderly have been termed the most preventable because they result from giving up rather than from a major depressive illness (Butler, Lewis, and Sunderland, 1991). Depression may follow various physical, psychological, financial, and social losses associated with the process of aging. These losses can accumulate to create despair.

That "old age" alone is a rational or sound reason for taking one's life is sometimes offered. Frequently, this notion is tied to concerns about disease and infirmity. The older man facing a long and costly illness, the older woman disabled by a degenerative disease, or the Alzheimer's patient undergoing a progressive loss of intellectual abilities are cases in point. Indeed, U.S. opinion polls underscore that many believe health problems are an acceptable reason for suicide (Sawyer and Sobal, 1987). While they are probably more importantly implicated in suicide by the elderly, their primary role is being questioned by some (Brown et al., 1986).

Unfounded assumptions presently obscure the exact nature of suicide among the elderly (Richardson, Lowenstein, and Weissberg, 1989; Younger et al., 1990). Ageism can

> tempt us to misunderstand the case as an example of "rational suicide" or a psychologically sound person's "right to die." Although we do not preclude the possibility of "rational suicide," we suspect that there is a strong cultural bias to overlook the forces and motives implicated in cases of suicide by elderly people. (Younger et al., 1990, p. 1174)

The psychological autopsy could allow us to better understand forces contributing to suicide in older adults (Alexopoulos, 1991; Osgood and McIntosh, 1986). Findings indicate that informants are available to assist with a psychological autopsy in the majority of elderly suicides (Younger et al., 1990). However, this remarkably useful tool has not been rigorously applied to suicide by the elderly. Perhaps this fact is also related to a negative view of aging. Impressions about the futility and hopelessness of growing old may preclude an investigation and the discovery of potentially manageable risk factors. Caution must be exercised against hastily viewing suicide in the older adult as a legitimate solution to the incurable state of "being old."

Likewise, there is concern that what might appear as a rational suicide in the face of infirmity may on occasion be a self-sacrificing act. As Richmond (1988) maintains, although he is opposed to suicide, he respects a person's genuine choice to take his or her life. His concern is that taking one's life to avoid being a burden to others does not represent genuine choice.

The suicide rate for future generations of elderly persons is open to speculation. The cohort model maintains that suicide rates are directly related to the relative size of a birth cohort in comparison with other groups in the population (Ahlberg and Shapiro, 1984; Murphy and Wetzel, 1980). For example, the baby boom generation experienced a high youth suicide rate. If the cohort model is accepted, we would expect the high rate to follow them as they enter the ranks of the elderly. They would continue to suffer the stress of a large population in competition for limited resources.

For the baby boom generation, the pressures of old age may be compounded by certain demographic and economic issues. The decreased numbers and percentages of young people in the future work force may threaten to compromise social support systems. Likewise, the reduced family size of this cohort will provide a smaller social network (Blazer et al., 1986). The population model previously discussed recognizes the stresses imposed upon a large birth cohort. However, it does not presuppose that a large cohort will experience high suicide rates throughout time.

Risk Factors and Possible Warning Signs

Various risk factors for suicide are the subject of much study. Some important sociodemographic factors have already been presented in the foregoing discussion of youth and elderly suicide. Other associated elements may include being separated, divorced, or recently bereaved or having experienced a sudden change in social/economic status. The latter factor may bring to mind the classic image of the financial tycoon who jumped to his death during the stock market crash of the Great Depression of the 1930s.

A previous suicide attempt is a very powerful predictor of suicide (Blumenthal, 1988; Linehan, 1986). Ten to twenty percent of attempters will go on to successfully end their own lives. Additionally, three-fourths of those who commit suicide provide some indication of their intent either by a previous attempt or by talking about killing themselves (Kastenbaum, 1991). Thus, those who talk about suicide should not be dismissed. Threats should be taken seriously.

Physical illness, social isolation, family history of suicide, and a psychiatric diagnosis have also been identified as risk factors. An abundant amount of research supports the statement that suicide risk is increased with virtually every major psychiatric diagnosis (Blumenthal, 1988).

Warning signs of suicide might include giving away personal items, appearing withdrawn, exhibiting a change in personality, or talking about suicide. Depression is another possible warning sign. However, it is sometimes the case that one who has apparently recovered from a period of "feeling down" is at risk of suicide. Deciding to commit the act, which is viewed as an escape from one's troubles, may be the reason for an unexpected or unexplained improvement in mood.

Grief Reactions and Suicide Bereavement

Those family members or close friends who survive the loss of a relative and/or loved one to suicide are often referred to as *suicide survivors*. The state of loss they are experiencing is termed *suicide bereavement*. Several years ago, Shneidman (1973) proposed that suicide bereavement was, perhaps, the greatest public health problem of suicide. Afterall, bereaved survivors, estimated to be in the millions, far outnumber those who complete the act. Despite the fact that so many are left to endure the aftermath of such a death, there has been a paucity of research on the nature of grief reactions and their resolution among suicide survivors. Although the topic needs further study, some recent investigations provide meaningful insight.

In their study of suicide bereavement among spouses, Barrett and Scott (1990) concluded that suicide survivors experience more grief reactions than those who survive the loss of loved ones to other forms of death. The suicide survivor deals with the common grief reactions that are a part of losing a family member. These responses include physical symptoms, hopelessness, anger, guilt and possible self-destructive behavior. Additionally, they face reactions that result from a death other than by natural causes—one viewed as preventable and shameful. They also must face the trauma of sudden death that typically intensifies the grief experience. Finally, they suffer the additional stress of dealing with death due to suicide, which includes feelings of rejection, embarrassment, and confusion.

Although the grief experience may be more intense for the suicide survivor, Barrett and Scott conclude that recovery is not singularly determined by the mode of death or the grief reactions it occasions. Furthermore, recovery of suicide survivors seems similar to that of other bereaved individuals two to four years after their loss.

Possible differences in grief reactions between various relatives surviving suicide are uncertain and warrant further research. For example, are there differences in the grief experiences for a parent, child, spouse, or sibling? Potential differences are presently subject to much conjecture. McIntosh and Wrobleski (1988) engaged in an exploratory study of assumed differences in the grief experiences of those variously related to the deceased. They concluded that, with some exceptions, suicide survivors have similar grief experiences.

Explaining Suicide: Sociopsychological Models

Although it has been the subject of study for many years, no one really understands why some people commit suicide. Various theories attempting to shed light on this complex human behavior have generally fallen into one of two theoretical models. The sociological model seeks an explanation for suicide within the social environment. It is based on the classic work of French sociologist Emile Durkheim which culminated in *Le Suicide,* first published in 1897. This work was translated into English in 1951 and represents the theoretical foundation upon which sociological research on suicide is based.

The psychological model of suicide seeks to understand the self-destructive act on the basis of mental and emotional processes taking place within the individual. The earliest psychological explanations for suicide were developed by Viennese psychologist Sigmund Freud (1917/1955; 1923/1955).

Today, a more integrated approach seeks explanations for suicide in both the social and psychological context. Such an approach will be presented after a brief overview of the two major theoretical models.

Sociological Models of Suicide

Durkheim noted that suicide rates varied on the basis of social groupings. Indeed, rates do vary from country to country and within countries on the basis of age, gender, marital status, religion, and so on. He maintained that such variation resulted from society's influence and control over the individual. Under this premise, the strength or weakness of the bond between individuals and the social groups to which they belong is a determining factor for suicide.

Durkheim formulated four categories of suicide: egoistic, altruistic, anomic, and fatalistic. They are associated with social dynamics and are reflected in the degree of integration and regulation that individuals encounter in society. At this point, we will define and compare these various categories of suicide.

Egoistic Suicide. Egoistic suicide is associated with a lack of social integration, where weak bonds exist between the individual and society. Persons with few deep social ties are left to their own coping devices. Durkheim found, and recent research tends to corroborate, that marital status and family ties influence the risk of suicide (Stack, 1982). Social ties and the risk of suicide are inversely related, said Durkheim, not only to the degree of integration with domestic society but with religious and political society as well. According to this maxim, the more we feel a part of something, be it family, a religious group, or the political climate of society, the less likely we are to take our own life.

Altruistic Suicide. Whereas egoistic suicide results from too little social integration, altruistic suicide occurs as a result of an exaggerated concern for or identification with society. In societies that maintain very strong holds on their members, persons may be willing to kill themselves for the sake of the group and/or the beliefs and principles it espouses. For instance:

> In 1986, during a large protest, a young Korean student publicly set himself on fire and then leaped from a building. A meaningless death? From the stu-

dent's viewpoint, it was a means of showing the Korean government the
strength and depths of his beliefs and of those who supported him. Buddhist
monks were making similar statements when they burnt themselves to death
in the streets of Viet Nam to protest the escalation of the War there.
(LaGreca, 1988, p. 242)

This type of self-directed martyrdom tends to be uncommon in Western societies. However, soldiers who willingly perish in heroic and self-sacrificing acts
could be termed victims of altruistic suicide.

A society's expectations and customs may dictate altruistic forms of suicide. Harakiri, or ritual disembowelment, was practiced in medieval Japanese
society among dishonored warriors. In India, the now illegal practice of suttee
involved women throwing themselves on their husbands' funeral pyres. This
act was influenced by the power of Hindu scripture and the belief that it guaranteed widows continuing residence with their husbands in the next life.
Japanese Kamikaze pilots of World War II were charged with the suicidal mission of crashing their airplanes into enemy ships, an act involving the greatest
personal sacrifice for one's group. All of these are examples of behavior
strongly influenced by group expectations and individual integration with society.

Anomic Suicide. Anomic suicide may occur when an individual's relationship to society is disrupted, leaving him or her with a sense of normlessness.
Many circumstances can produce this situation, including divorce, the death of
a significant person such as a spouse, and the loss of a job. Persons undergoing
such critical disruption to their lives feel anxious, lonely, and isolated. They
may feel abandoned. Their world seems loosely regulated and chaotic which
leaves them more vulnerable to suicide. Economic change, hardship, and unemployment are related to an increased risk of suicide (Marshall and Hodge,
1981; Platt, 1984).

Societies undergoing rapid social change are likewise characterized by a
sense of normlessness. Traditional customs and rules no longer provide the behavioral guidelines they once did. Inhabitants of such societies no longer have
the same sense of belonging. Signs of behavioral stress, including suicide, surface.

Fatalistic Suicide. Durkheim's fourth category, fatalistic suicide, suggests
that an oppressive, controlling society may stimulate suicide by blocking individual goals and opportunities. Fatalistic suicide is the polar opposite of
anomic suicide as measured by extremes of social regulation.

Durkheim's work did not focus on individual intention or the psy-
chopathological dimensions of suicide. It does not shed light on why one person in a given situation takes his or her life and someone else does not. Still,
his work is respected for demonstrating the significance of social factors in sui-

cide. It continues to be examined for its appropriateness in understanding suicide. That examination often involves criticism or refinement of his work
(Gibbs and Martin, 1964; Kamerman, 1988; Martin, 1968; Stafford and Gibbs,
1985). Read the following material and think about how you would categorize
the Jonestown deaths. Do you believe the deaths were suicide? If your answer is
yes, into which of Durkheim's classifications would you place them and why?

Jonestown Commune, The People's Temple Cult, 1978

How would you classify the "suicides" that occurred at the Jonestown com-
mune of the People's Temple cult in Guyana? They have been questionably referred to as a modern example of altruistic suicide. The media described them
as the largest mass suicide in history.

In the jungles of the northeast corner of South America, the Reverend Jim
Jones led over 900 members of his cult community to their deaths. Anyone
who saw film footage or still photographs of that 1978 event will not forget the
overwhelming scenes of bodies that lay strewn around the grounds of
Jonestown. From paper cups, cult members had swallowed Kool-Aid laced with
cyanide and tranquilizers. Thus, the members of a unique community died.
Their leader also died from a gunshot, presumably fired by his own hand.

This bizarre example of group behavior and social control promoted
Kastenbaum (1991) to call for a reexamination of Durkheim's neglected concept of sociocide. Sociocide occurs when the "spirit" of a group, termed its collective representation, becomes sullen, morose, and self-destructive. Persons
who are well integrated into the group are especially vulnerable to the dysfunctional community mood. The group is held together by self-destructive forces
that can eventually rip it apart.

Was the final act of the more than 900 Americans comprising the People's
Temple Cult the end result of their collective representation? Perhaps. Fear and
hardship had enabled Jones to recruit his followers, many of whom were black
and/or older women and men. Their Social Security benefits, small bank accounts, and real estate holdings had been signed over to the People's Temple.
Some had even been persuaded by Jones to adopt children who were former
wards of the state of California and eligible for certain social benefits. The benefits were in turn given to the People's Temple. The cult grew and as it did relatives became increasingly suspicious and fearful.

Jones, concerned about defectors, surrounded himself with armed body
guards and degraded and punished those suspected as disloyal. To avoid de-
fection, he moved his group from San Francisco to the isolation of Guyana.
Eventually, Congressman Leo Ryan and a delegation of concerned family members traveled to Guyana to investigate the situation. Ryan, along with several of
his congressional aides, TV reporters, and some would-be defectors, were
killed there, triggering the mass death that followed shortly thereafter.

From an audiotape and accounts of the few survivors, it is known that not all of the dead voluntarily committed suicide. Some had the drink forced down their throats. Also, residents had lived in Guyana under extremely stressful conditions without access to their passports or money. Approximately one-third of the community consisted of children under sixteen years of age, a group for whom the notion of voluntary suicide under such circumstances is inappropriate.

Harris (1981), an anthropologist, questions if the larger implications of the Jonestown affair have been misunderstood. The media's emphasis on the apparent "mass suicide" distracted us from examining the factors that helped Jones recruit so many who became dependent on him. In speaking of the People's Temple cult, Harris (1981) offers:

> Like tens of millions of other ordinary people, Jones' followers felt weak, neglected, isolated. They were under intense pressure from the rising costs of housing and medical care and the high incidence of street crimes. And as blacks, many of them had experienced the stings of racism and had grown weary of being treated as inferior citizens. Bizarre as their solution to these problems may seem, would it not be a mistake to ignore the similarity between them and the many million of other Americans who also now feel defenseless and isolated?   (p. 156)

Eighteen months before Jim Jones and his followers died, he had talked at an antisuicide rally held at San Francisco's Golden Gate Bridge—the leading location for suicide in the world. Concerned Bay Area residents had formed an ad hoc committee out of their interest in promoting a suicide deterrent for the bridge.

At the rally, Jones spoke of suicide victims as casualties of society. He lamented that basic values, decency, and human kindness were becoming less evident. Helpless and despondent, those for whom society provided nowhere else to go brought their burdens to the Golden Gate, said Jones. The bridge stood testimony to human invention and technological genius. For Jones, it also symbolized social failure (Seiden, 1979).

Psychological Models of Suicide

Sociological study has devoted attention to the fact that various groups of people are at an increased risk of suicide. That risk fluctuates across cultures and over time, presumably as social circumstances vary. Today, in U.S. society groups at greatest risk of suicide include the elderly, young people between the ages of fifteen and twenty-four years, white males, and Native Americans.

The psychological study of suicide is concerned with better understanding what factors contribute to the individual act (Hendin, 1991). In other words, what makes an individual, whatever the social group membership, take his or her life while others in that same group do not? While we may never know the definitive answer to that question, we can isolate psychological factors that increase the likelihood of one's doing so. As previously noted, various such risk factors have been identified, including a sense of hopelessness, social isolation, and a psychiatric diagnosis.

Freud hypothesized that people take their own lives for "intrapsychic" reasons—that is, because of psychological factors within the individual. He viewed suicide in the context of unconscious hostility, a theory that has been expanded by others (Menninger, 1985). Over the years, various and multifaceted psychological theories of suicide have been delineated.

The suicidal act is viewed as an attempt to force change. Life is unbearable and suicide will eliminate the problem. Suicide attempts that are unsuccessful at bringing change may be repeated. DeSpelder and Strickland (1992) summarize valuable insights derived from the psychological model of suicide:

1. The acute suicidal crisis is time limited. It is of brief duration, generally lasting hours or days. It may recur, however.

2. The suicidal individual tends to be ambivalent about killing him or herself. Fantasies of rescue usually accompany suicidal plans.

3. Most suicidal events involve the victim and a significant other in some way.

Psychiatric models of suicide assume that the majority of persons who take their own lives are mentally ill or suffer from a serious emotional disorder. Severe depression is the dominant explanation of suicide. Other related disorders include psychoses, extreme neuroses, and personality disorders, including drug dependency and alcoholism.

An Integrated Approach

At the outset of this discussion it was stated that both social and psychological factors must be incorporated into a consideration of suicide. As Shneidman contends, "understanding suicide—like understanding any other complicated human act such as drug or alcohol misuse or antisocial behavior—involves insights drawn from many fields that touch on man's entire psychological and social life" (Shneidman, 1976, p. 5).

Blumenthal and Kupfer (1986) presented a theoretical overlap model for understanding suicidal behavior (see Box 11–4). It posits that five domains of risk factors operate across the life cycle for all age groups. These five domains include psychiatric diagnosis, personality disorders and traits, psychosocial and environmental factors, genetic and familial variables, and biochemical factors. The existence of contributing factors from each of these domains is assumed to increase the risk of suicide. The model attempts to explain why only some individuals with a given psychiatric disorder go on to attempt or com-

---

B o x 11–4   *The Overlap Model*

The five domains comprising the overlap risk factor model are:

1. The *psychiatric diagnosis* is important. The risk for suicide is increased with al-most every major psychiatric disorder.

2. *Personality traits* such as aggression, impulsivity, and hopelessness are impor-tant in relation to suicide and may cross diagnostic groupings. Personality dis-orders, such as borderline personality disorder and antisocial personality dis-orders, are highly correlated with suicidal behavior.

3. *Psychosocial factors, life events, and chronic medical illness* are risk factors. Increased negative life events, decreased social supports, a chronic medical ill-ness, and exposure to suicide are contributory. Also, many who take their own lives have had a recent humiliating life experience.

4. *Genetic and familial factors* that predispose to suicide are identified.

5. *Biological factors* under study include neurochemical and biochemical vari-ables that may identify a vulnerability state for suicide. A deficiency of the neurotransmitter serotonin appears to be associated with aggressive, violent, suicidal behavior across psychiatric diagnostic groupings.

Source: Adapted from S. Blumenthal, (1988). A guide to risk factors, assessment, and treatment of suicidal patients. *Medical Clinics of North America,* 72:937–971; and S. Blumenthal and D. Kupfer. (1986). Generalizable treatment strategies for suicidal behavior. *Annals of the New York Academy of Science,* 487:327–340.

---

plete suicide (and why a great many others do not). Those who do commit sui-cide may have greater overlap of risk factors. The overlap model provides a comprehensive framework for studying suicidal behavior by incorporating the contributions of numerous explanatory models.

Suicide Intervention

Crisis Intervention Centers

Since the 1960s, we have seen the establishment of suicide crisis centers and telephone hotlines. Such centers have typically provided twenty-four-hour telephone availability of persons (usually volunteers) trained in suicide intervention. The major goal of such centers is to reduce the chance of suicide during an acute emotional crisis. Over the years, the mission of these centers has expanded to include assistance to callers with other emotional or psychological crises. Most of them are now called crisis intervention centers.

During the course of the telephone call, the volunteer attempts to assess the lethality of the caller. For example, is the anonymous caller holding a gun or is he or she considering buying one tomorrow? The latter situation is still taken seriously, but it allows the volunteer/counselor more time. Callers are encouraged to ventilate their feelings in a nonjudgmental atmosphere. Possible solutions other than suicide are discussed. Callers may be assisted in receiving additional help beyond this short-term resource.

Individual Assistance

What can you do if you suspect that someone you know is suicidal? First of all, it is important to realize that you cannot take responsibility for the actions of another. You can be available as a good listener or friend. But, in the end, the ultimate responsibility does not lie with you. Second, there are no magic words or techniques that are guaranteed to prevent the act. There are, however, some useful guidelines to follow:

1. Take suicidal threats seriously. It is a myth that someone who talks about suicide won't really do it. Three out of four people who kill themselves provide some sort of previous indication either by a prior attempt or through something they have said. Someone who threatens to take his or her own life is considered at risk of doing so.

2. Don't be judgmental. One of the most productive things you can do is provide an open listening environment. By making value judgments, you may create frustration and guilt and cut off any further confiding of self-destructive inclinations. "Why would you want to do that with all you have to live for?" or "That's morally wrong!" may make the person feel he or she has to justify his or her pain in someone else's eyes or that the person can't justify his or her pain (even though it is very real)!

3. Don't belittle those who threaten suicide. "You couldn't do that" or "You're all talk" may challenge them to prove otherwise.

4. Listen to them. Brushing off their concerns or resisting conversation may be interpreted as further rejection. They may feel unworthy of attention. Just listening to another can be an important gesture of caring concern. It may also be quite productive in allowing them to alleviate stress by talking about their feelings and problems.

5. Help them to see alternatives to suicide. Most persons contemplating

suicide are ambivalent about it. They aren't certain if they want to live or die. "Is there anything else that you can do to deal with your present situation?" "Have you ever felt like this before? What did you do then?" are the kinds of questions that may help them to focus on other things in their life.

6. If they have been drinking or using drugs, consider them to be at increased risk of taking their life. Substance abuse intensifies feelings and can reduce self-destructive inhibitions.

7. Don't be fooled by an apparent improvement in mood. Often when people are feeling very down or depressed they do not have the energy to kill themselves. However, they may decide to do so during this time. As they move out of the depressed state, they feel a sense of relief about their decision. A sense of control over their situation and the knowledge that a release from their problems is imminent may serve to lift their spirits. All the while they may be gathering the strength with which to commit the act.

8. Familiarize yourself with available resources in your community. You may be of help in providing information about resources such as crisis intervention centers or counseling services.

Summary

Several factors are responsible for the underreporting of suicide. One is that there are no uniform criteria for identifying a suicide; another is the stigma associated with the act. In the face of community pressure, authorities may be disinclined to label a death as such. Also, there may be inadequate information with which to determine the actual mode of death. The psychological autopsy can help in establishing if a death was due to suicide. It involves a retrospective analysis of the events leading up to the death. Through interviews with those who had contact with the deceased an attempt is made to better understand his or her physical, psychological, and emotional states in order to determine if the death was a self-destructive act. Besides providing insight into the manner in which an individual death occurred, the psychological autopsy can also help us to identify characteristics that increase the risk of suicide. The information generated can help in the design of suicide-prevention strategies.

While suicide statistics underestimate the true frequency of the act, they do allow us to monitor long-term trends and to note differing rates based on characteristics such as gender and age. At every age, white males are at an increased risk of suicide, accounting for 70 percent of all such deaths. Women attempt suicide three times as often but they tend to use less lethal means. The lethality of means refers to the probability that a given method will result in death. Firearm use, the most highly lethal and leading means for men, is growing for females.

A suicide attempt is an intentional act of self-harm that could be, but is not, fatal. Those who engage in suicide attempts (attempters) and those who successfully complete the act (completers) are often viewed as separate yet overlapping groups. Suicide attempts must be taken seriously as some attempters will eventually succeed in taking their life.

Among the at-risk populations for suicide in the United States are the young (those between ages fifteen and twenty-four) and the elderly (those over age sixty-five). White males are at greatest risk in both of these groups. Cluster suicides, unique to the young, involve so-called "outbreaks" of suicide or suicide attempts in a given locale within a short period of time. They tend to mimic the suicide method. The degree to which exposure to suicide increases the risk of imitating the act is being debated. Some research demonstrates that it is those at risk prior to clustering who are most likely to kill themselves. The population and cohort models attempt to explain why certain groups are at greater risk of suicide. The reason for the high suicide rate among the elderly is the subject of study. Whether or not future generations of older adults will continue to exhibit a high rate is uncertain.

Besides gender and age, various other risk factors for suicide are identified. Warning signs of suicide are also considered.

Bereavement due to suicide may be the greatest public health problem associated with the act. For every individual act, there are countless numbers of persons left to carry on in the wake of such death. The grief associated with suicide is intense and compounded by various factors. However, research indicates that grief recovery is not solely determined by the manner of death.

Various theories have been generated in an attempt to explain why some people take their own lives. They generally fall into one of two models. The sociological model seeks to explain suicide via the social environment. That model is based on the classic work of Durkheim, who formulated four categories of suicide: egoistic, altruistic, anomic, and fatalistic. The psychological model seeks to understand suicide on the basis of an individual's mental and emotional processes. The earliest such explanations were developed by Freud. The integrated approach maintains that both social and psychological factors operate to explain suicide.

Since the 1960s, there has been an increase in the number of suicide crisis centers and telephone hotlines. The major goal of such centers is to reduce the chance of suicide during an acute emotional crisis. Over time, these centers have expanded to provide assistance to callers with other emotional or psychological crises. On an individual basis, there are some guidelines that we can follow if we suspect someone we know is suicidal. However, there is no guaranteed means of preventing suicide. In the end, the ultimate responsibility does not lie with us.

Study Questions

1. Why is suicide underreported?
2. What is a psychological autopsy and what functions does it serve?
3. How are suicide rates calculated? What do the suicide statistics tell us about who is at greatest risk of suicide?
4. Distinguish suicide attempters from completers.
5. Present an overview of youth suicide. Identify cluster suicides and the population model.
6. Present an overview of suicide among the elderly.
7. Characterize the grief reaction for those who are bereaved due to suicide.
8. How does the sociological model seek to explain suicide? Discuss the four categories of suicide introduced by Durkheim.
9. How does the psychological model seek to explain suicide? What is the overlap model?
10. Explain the purpose of crisis intervention centers.
11. Note some useful guidelines to follow in providing individual assistance to someone who may be thinking about suicide.

References

Ahlberg, D., and M. Shapiro. (1984). Socioeconomic ramifications of changing cohort size: An analysis of U.S. post-war suicide rates by age and sex. *Demography,* 21:97.

Ahronheim, J., A. Bernholc, and W. Black. (1983). Age trends in autopsy rates. *Journal of the American Medical Association,* 250:1182–1186.

Alexopoulos, G. (1991). Psychological autopsy of an elderly suicide. *International Journal of Geriatric Psychiatry,* 6:45–50.

Barrett, T., and T. Scott. (1990). Suicide bereavement and recovery patterns compared with nonsuicide bereavement patterns. *Suicide and Life-Threatening Behavior,* 20:1–15.

Beck, A., R. Steer, M. Kovacs and G. Garrison. (1985). Hopelessness and eventual suicide: A 10-year prospective study of patients hospitalized with suicidal ideation. *American Journal of Psychiatry,* 142:559–563.

Blazer, D. (1989). Depression in the elderly. *NEJM,* 320:164–166.

Blazer, D., J. Bachar, and K. Manton. (1986). Suicide in late life: Review and commentary. *Journal of the American Geriatrics Society,* 34:19–25.

Blazer, D., D. Hughes, and L. George. (1987). The epidemiology of depression in an elderly community population. *Gerontologist,* 27:281–287.

Blumenthal, S. (1984). *An Overview of Suicide Risk Factor Research.* Paper presented at the Annual meeting of the American Psychiatric Association, Los Angeles.

Blumenthal, S. (1988). Suicide: A guide to risk factors, assessment and treatment of suicidal patients. *Medical Clinics of North America,* 72:4:937–971.

Blumenthal, S., and D. Kupfer. (1986). Generalizable treatment strategies for suicidal behavior. *Annals of the New York Academy of Science,* 487:327–340.

Brown, J., et al. (1986). Is it normal for terminally ill patients to desire death? *American Journal of Psychiatry,* 143:208.

Butler, R., M. Lewis, and T. Sunderland. (1991). *Aging and Mental Health.* New York: Merrill.

Casey, D. (1991). Suicide in the elderly: A two-year study of data from death certificates. *Southern Medical Journal,* 84:1185–1187.

Centers for Disease Control. (1988). Cluster of suicides and suicide attempts—New Jersey. *Morbidity and Mortality Weekly Report,* 37:213–216.

Davidson, L. (1986). Study of suicide attempts during a cluster of suicides. Paper presented at the Epidemic Intelligence Service Conference, April 14, Atlanta.

Davidson, L., et al. (1989). An epidemiologic study of risk factors in two teenage suicide clusters. *JAMA,* 262:2687–2692.

Davidson, L., and M. Gould. (1988). Contagion as a risk factor for youth suicide. In U.S. Department of Health and Human Services, *Report of the Secretary's Task Force on Youth Suicide.* Vol. 2: *Risk Factors for Youth Suicide.* Washington, DC: U.S. Government Printing Office.

DeSpelder, L., and A. Strickland. (1992). *The Last Dance.* Palo Alto: Mayfield.

Durkheim, E. (1897/1951). *Suicide.* New York: The Free Press.

Fasko, S., and D. Fasko. (1991). Suicidal behavior in children. *Psychology, A Journal of Human Behavior,* 27:11–16.

Freud, S. (1923/1955). Beyond the pleasure principle. In J. Strachey (Ed.), *The Standard Edition of the Complete Works of Sigmund Freud.* London: Hogarth.

Freud, S. (1917/1955). Mourning and meloncholea. In J. Strachey (Ed.), *The Standard Edition of the Complete Works of Sigmund Freud* (pp. 247–252). London: Hogarth.

Gibbs, J., and W. Martin. (1964). *Status Integration and Suicide: A Sociological Study.* Eugene: University of Oregon Press.

Glass, J., and S. Reed. (1993). To live or die: A look at elderly suicide. *Educational Gerontology,* 19:767–778.

Gould, M., S. Wallenstein, and M. Kleinman. (1987). *A Study of Time-Space Clustering of Suicide: Final Report.* Atlanta, GA: Centers for Disease Control.

Harris, M. (1981). *Why Nothing Works: The Anthropology of Daily Life.* New York: Simon and Schuster.

Hendin, H. (1986). Suicide: A review of new directions in research. *Hospital and Community Psychiatry,* 37:148–154.

Hendin, H. (1991). Psychodynamics of suicide, with particular reference to the young. *American Journal of Psychiatry,* 148:1150–1158.

Hollinger, P., D. Offer, and E. Ostrov. (1987). Suicide and homicide in the United States: An epidemiologic study of violent death, population changes, and the potential for prediction. *American Journal of Psychology,* 144:215–219.

Jobes, D., A. Berman, and A. Josselson. (1986). The impact of psychological autopsies on medical examiners' determination of manner of death. *Journal of Forensic Social Science,* 31:177–189.

Kamerman, J. (1988). *Death in the Midst of Life.* Englewood Cliffs, NJ: Prentice Hall.

Kastenbaum, R. (1991). *Death, Society and the Human Experience.* New York: Merrill.

Katz, I., S. Curlik, P. Nemetz, et al. (1988). Functional psychiatric disorders in the elderly. In L. Lazarus (Ed.), *Essentials of Geriatric Psychiatry.* New York: Springer.

Klerman, G. (1987). Clinical epidemiology of suicide. *Journal of Clinical Psychiatry,* 48:12 (suppl.):33–38.

Kosky, R. (1983). Childhood suicidal behavior. *Journal of Child Psychology and Psychiatry,* 24:457–468.

LaGreca, A. (1988). Suicide: Prevalence theories and prevention. In H. Wass, F. Berardo, and R. Neimeyer (eds.), *Dying: Facing the facts* (pp. 229–255). Washington DC: Hemisphere.

Linehan, M. (1986). Suicidal people: One population or two? *Annals of the New York Academy of Science,* 487:16–33.

Marshall, J., and R. Hodge. (1981). Durkheim and Pierce on suicide and economic change. *Social Science Research,* 10:101–114.

Martin, W. (1968). Theories of variation in the suicide rate. In J. Gibbs (Ed.), *Suicide* (pp. 74–96). New York: Harper & Row.

McIntosh, J. (1985). Suicide among the elderly: Levels and trends. *American Journal of Orthopsychiatry,* 55:288–293.

McIntosh, J. (1989). Official U.S. elderly suicide data bases: Levels, availability, omissions. *Omega,* 19:337–350.

McIntosh, J. (1991). Middle-aged suicide: A literature review and epidemiological study. *Death Studies,* 15:21–37.

McIntosh, J., and A. Wrobleski. (1988). Grief reactions among suicide survivors: An exploratory comparison of relationships. *Death Studies,* 12:21–39.

Meehan, P., J. Lamb, L. Saltzman, and P. O'Carroll. (1992). Attempted suicide among young adults: Progress toward a meaningful estimation of prevalence. *American Journal of Psychiatry,* 149:41–44.

Meehan, P., L. Saltzman, and R. Sattin. (1991). Suicides among older United States residents: Epidemiologic characteristics and trends. *American Journal of Public Health,* 81:1198–1200.

Menninger, K. (1985). *Man Against Himself.* New York: Harcourt, Brace and World.

Meyers, J., M. Weissman, G. Tischler, et al. (1984). Six-month prevalence of psychiatric disorders in three communities: 1980–1982. *Archives of General Psychiatry,* 41:959.

Murphy, J., and R. Wetzel. (1980). Suicide risks by birth cohort in the United States, 1949–1974. *Archives of General Psychiatry,* 37:519.

National Center for Health Statistics. (1987). *Monthly Vital Statistics Report,* 36:1–48.

O'Carroll, P., J. Mercy, and J. Steward. (1988). CDC recommendations for a community plan for the prevention and containment of suicide clusters. *Morbidity and Mortality Weekly Report: Supplement,* 37/S-6:1–12.

Osgood, N., and J. McIntosh. (1986). *Suicide in the Elderly: An Annotated Bibliography and Review.* New York: Greenwood Press.

Platt, S. (1984). Unemployment and suicidal behavior: A review of the literature. *Social Science and Medicine,* 19:93–115.

Richardson, R., S. Lowenstein, and M. Weissberg. (1989). Coping with the suicidal elderly: A physician's guide. *Geriatrics,* 44:43–51.

Richmond, J. (1988). The case against rational suicide. *Suicide and Life-Threatening Behavior,* 18:285–289.

Robbins, D., and R. Conroy. (1983). A cluster of adolescent suicide attempts: Is suicide contagious? *Journal of Adolescent Health Care,* 3:253–255.

Rosenberg, M., et al. (1988). Operational criteria for the determination of suicide. *Journal of Forensic Science,* 33:1445–1456.

Rosenberg, M., et al. (1987). The emergence of youth suicide: An epidemiologic analysis and public health perspective. *Annual Review of Public Health,* 8:417–440.

Saltzman, L., A. Levenson, and J. Smith. (1988). Suicides among persons 15–24 years of age, 1970–1984. *Morbidity and Mortality Weekly Report,* 37:SS-1:61–68.

Sawyer, D., and J. Sobal. (1987). Public attitudes toward suicide: Demographic and ideological correlates. *Public Opinion Quarterly,* 5:92.

Seiden, R. (1979). Rev. Jones on Suicide. *Suicide and Life Threatening Behavior,* 9:116–119.

Shneidman, E. (1973). *Death of Man.* New York: Quadrangle Books.

Shneidman, E. (1976). The death certificate. In E. Shneidman (Ed.), *Death: Current Perspectives* (pp. 241–251). Palo Alto: Mayfield.

Shneidman, E. (1976). Current overview of suicide. In E. Shneidman (Ed.), *Suicidology: Contemporary Developments.* New York: Grune and Stratton.

Simmons, K. (1987). Adolescent suicide: Second leading death cause. *JAMA,* 257:3329–3330.

Stack, S. (1982). Suicide: A decade review of the sociological literature. *Deviant Behavior: An Interdisciplinary Journal,* 4:41–66.

Stafford, M., and J. Gibbs. (1985). A major problem with the theory of status integration and suicide. *Social Forces,* 63:643–660.

Stillion, J., H. White, P. Edwards, and E. McDowell. (1989). Ageism and sexism in suicide attitudes. *Death Studies,* 13:247–261.

Sudak, H., A. Ford, and N. Rushforth (Eds). (1984). *Suicide in the Young.* Boston: John Wright-PSG, Inc.

U.S. Department of Health and Human Services. (1986). *Suicide.* HHS Publication No. (ADM) 86–1489. Washington, DC: U.S. Government Printing Office.

Willis, R. (1987). Suicide risk in elderly persons: Diagnosis and management. *Mt. Sinai Journal Medicine,* 54:14–17.

Younger, S., D. Clark, R. Oehmig-Lindroth, and R. Stein. (1990). Availability of knowledge-able informants for a psychological autopsy study of suicides committed by elderly people. *Journal American Geriatrics Society,* 38:1169–1175.

CHAPTER 12

Medical Science and Post-Death Activities

The boast of heraldry, the pomp of power,
And all that beauty, all that wealth e'er gave,
Awaits alike the inevitable hour,
The paths of glory lead but to the grave.

Thomas Gray, "Elegy Written from a Country Churchyard"

UNIVERSALLY, the major ritual observance surrounding death is the funeral. In modern societies such as our own, certain other procedures may be followed after death. These involve various medically related activities including the filing of the death certificate; the investigation of violent, suspicious, or unexpected deaths; the post-mortem examination of the body, and the donation of organs and tissues for the purpose of transplantation as well as the donation of the body for anatomical study. This chapter examines various post-death activities.

The Death Certificate

Death is officially registered via a death certificate. This document constitutes legal proof of death and is mandated in all U.S. jurisdictions. It influences various activities including the distribution of life insurance benefits and property. It also provides public functions: by registering the cause of death, it serves as a public health record monitoring our nation's experience with fatal diseases. The manner or mode of death (natural, accident, suicide, homicide, or undetermined) is also noted on the death certificate, as illustrated in Figure 12–1.

Investigating Death: Medical Examiners and Coroners

In the United States, medical examiners and coroners are responsible for investigating violent, suspicious, or unexpected deaths and deaths that are unattended by a physician. State laws specify the types of death that are investigated, the official(s) responsible for investigations, and the qualifications of the official(s). Depending on the jurisdiction, approximately 20 percent of all deaths fall under the authority of the medical examiner or coroner (Centers for Disease Control, 1989). However, it does not follow that all cases under their jurisdiction result in an investigation. For instance, a medical examiner may choose not to investigate the case of an eighty-year-old man with a history of congestive heart failure who dies in his home unattended by a physician.

The medical examiner is a licensed physician with training in pathology, generally forensic pathology. In the latter, medical knowledge is applied to questions of law, including determining and certifying the cause of death. Medical examiners are appointed by various governmental administrators or boards, depending upon the locale.

Coroners are elected. There are usually no specific statutory requirements for their training. However, in some locales coroners are required to be physicians. There are three basic types of death investigation systems in the United States (see Box 12–1 and Figure 12–2).

These officials have the authority to investigate suspected suicides and homicides; accidental deaths; workplace deaths; deaths that occur in jail; deaths resulting from alleged negligence, drug intoxication, or poisoning; deaths that occur at home without an attending physician present, and various others. For the public good, there may be interest in determining how a death occurred and, through gaining such knowledge, in establishing preventive strategies where possible. For example, unsafe industrial work sites or consumer products (including children's toys) may come to our attention through the investigations of medical examiners and coroners.

Box 12–1   *Death Investigation Systems*

The three basic types of death investigation systems are:

1. *Medical Examiner.* Nineteen states and the District of Columbia have a state chief ME who is responsible for investigating deaths for the entire state. The chief ME is usually appointed and must be a licensed physician with training in pathology. Deputy or county MEs, who are supervised by the chief ME, are appointed by either the chief ME or a county board of supervisors or commissioners. In Mississippi, county MEs are elected.

   Three states have county or district MEs but no state chief ME. Florida has 24 district MEs appointed by the governor. Arizona and Michigan have county MEs appointed by each county's board of supervisors.

2. *Coroner.* Twelve states have county or district coroners who are responsible for investigating deaths within each county. The coroner is elected, and there are usually no specific statutory requirements for training.

3. *Mixed Medical Examiner and Coroner.* Thirteen states have county or district death investigation systems, some of which are directed by MEs and some by coroners. In these states, no one person has supervisory responsibility for the state. However, three states—Arkansas, Kentucky, and Montana—have an appointed state chief ME and elected county coroners.

Source: From Centers for Disease Control (1989). Death investigation—United States, 1987. *Morbidity and Mortality Weekly Report,* 38:1.

Autopsies

The autopsy is a post-mortem examination. The term is derived from the Greek and means "seeing for oneself." It reflects the physician's practice of examining the body after death in order to determine or confirm the cause of death and to gain a better understanding of disease processes and their effects on body tissues and functioning.

Since the 1940s and 1950s, there has been a dramatic decline in the autopsy rate in many Western nations including the United States, where the autopsy rate fell from 50 percent in 1950 to its present rate of approximately 12 to 15 percent (Centers for Disease Control, 1988; Geller, 1983; McPhee and Bottles, 1985; Roberts, 1978).

Should we be concerned about the decline? Some would say no. The amount of time, effort, and money required for autopsies isn't worth it. After

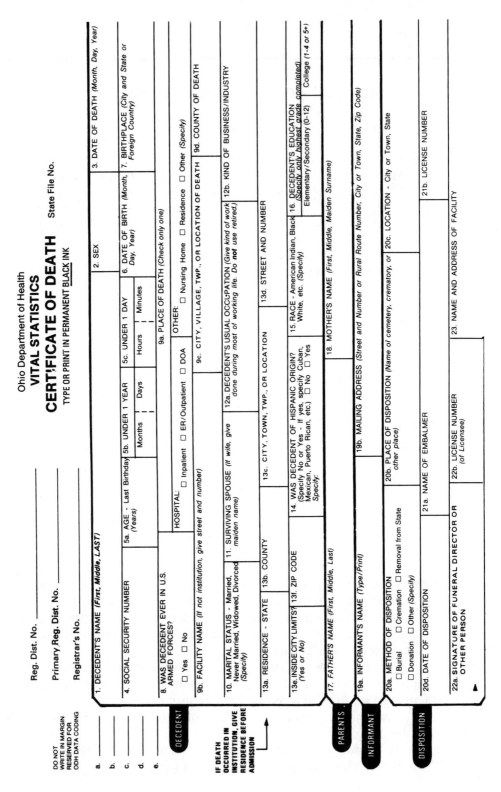

Figure 12–1 Certificate of Death.

438

REGISTRAR

24. REGISTRAR'S SIGNATURE ▲

25. DATE FILED *(Month, Day, Year)*

26a. SIGNATURE OF PERSON ISSUING PERMIT ▲

26b. DIST. No.

27. DATE PERMIT ISSUED

f.
g.
h.
i.

CERTIFIER

28a. CERTIFIER *(Check one)*

☐ CERTIFYING PHYSICIAN
To the best of my knowledge, death occurred at the time, date, and place, and due to the cause(s) and manner as stated.

☐ CORONER
On the basis of examination and/or investigation, in my opinion, death occurred at the time, date, and place, and due to the cause(s) and manner as stated

28b. TIME OF DEATH   M

28c. DATE PRONOUNCED DEAD *(Month, Day, Year)*

28d. WAS CASE REFERRED TO CORONER?
☐ Yes ☐ No

28e. SIGNATURE AND TITLE OF CERTIFIER ▲

28f. LICENSE NUMBER

28g. DATE SIGNED *(Month, Day, Year)*

29. NAME AND ADDRESS OF PERSON WHO COMPLETED CAUSE OF DEATH   *(Type/Print)*

j.
k.
l.
m.

CAUSE OF DEATH

30. PART I. Enter the diseases, injuries, or complications that caused the death. Do not enter the mode of dying, such as cardiac or respiratory arrest, shock, or heart failure. List only one cause on each line. TYPE OR PRINT IN PERMANENT BLACK INK

Approximate Interval Between Onset and Death

IMMEDIATE CAUSE (Final disease or condition resulting in death)

a. _____
DUE TO (OR AS A CONSEQUENCE OF):

Sequentially list conditions, if any, leading to immediate cause. Enter **UNDERLYING CAUSE** (Disease or injury that initiated events resulting in death) **LAST**

b. _____
DUE TO (OR AS A CONSEQUENCE OF):

c. _____
DUE TO (OR AS A CONSEQUENCE OF):

d. _____

PART II. *Other significant conditions* contributing to death but not resulting in the underlying cause given in Part I.

n.
o.
p.
q.
r.
s.
t.
u.

31a. WAS AN AUTOPSY PERFORMED?
☐ Yes ☐ No

31b. WERE AUTOPSY FINDINGS AVAILABLE PRIOR TO COMPLETION OF CAUSE OF DEATH?
☐ Yes ☐ No

32. MANNER OF DEATH
☐ Natural   ☐ Pending Investigation
☐ Accident
☐ Suicide   ☐ Could not be Determined
☐ Homicide

33a. DATE OF INJURY *(Month, Day, Year)*

33b. TIME OF INJURY   M

33c. INJURY AT WORK?
☐ Yes ☐ No

33d. DESCRIBE HOW INJURY OCCURRED

33e. PLACE OF INJURY - At home, farm, street, factory, office building, etc. *(Specify)*

33f. LOCATION *(Street and Number or Rural Route Number, City or Town, State)*

SEE INSTRUCTIONS ON OTHER SIDE

HEA 2717
5152.06 Rev. 3/91

Figure 12–1   *Continued*

439

INFORMATION CONCERNING THE BURIAL OF DECEASED MEMBERS AND FORMER MEMBERS OF THE ARMED FORCES OF THE UNITED STATES

FUNERAL DIRECTORS ARE REQUIRED BY LAW TO FURNISH THE FOLLOWING ADDITIONAL INFORMATION FOR DECEASED MEMBERS OR FORMER MEMBERS OF THE ARMED FORCES.

Name of deceased _____ Date of death _____

State of birth _____ Date of birth _____

Branch of service _____ Date of entry into service _____

Type of separation or discharge from service _____ Date _____

Name of cemetery _____ Date of burial _____

Location of cemetery

County _____ City _____

Township _____ Village _____

Name or number of section in cemetery _____

Number of lot _____ Number of grave _____

Information relative to a deceased veteran may be secured from the Veteran's Discharge Papers.

INSTRUCTIONS - CAUSE OF DEATH

The cause of death means the disease, abnormality, injury, or poisoning that caused the death, **not** the mode of dying, such as cardiac or respiratory arrest, shock, or heart failure.

In **Part I**, the **immediate** cause of death is reported on line (a). Antecedent conditions, if any, which gave rise to the cause are reported on lines (b), (c), and (d). The **underlying** cause should be reported on the last line used in Part I. No entry is necessary on lines (b), (c), and (d) if the immediate cause of death on line (a) describes completely the train of events. **ONLY ONE CAUSE SHOULD BE ENTERED ON A LINE.** Additional lines may be added if necessary. Provide the best estimate of the interval between the onset of each condition and death. Do not leave the interval blank; if unknown, so specify.

In **Part II**, enter other important diseases or conditions that may have contributed to death but did not result in the underlying cause of death given in Part I.

Figure 12-1 *Continued*

30. PART I. Enter the diseases, injuries, or complications that caused the death. Do not enter the mode of dying, such as cardiac or respiratory arrest, shock, or heart failure. List only one cause on each line.

		Approximate Interval Between Onset and Death
IMMEDIATE CAUSE (Final disease or condition resulting in death) →	a Rupture of myocardium	Mins.
	DUE TO (OR AS A CONSEQUENCE OF):	
Sequentially list conditions, if any, leading to immediate cause. Enter **UNDERLYING CAUSE** (Disease or injury that initiated events resulting in death) **LAST**	b Acute myocardial infarction	6 days
	DUE TO (OR AS A CONSEQUENCE OF):	
	c Chronic ischemic heart disease	5 years
	DUE TO (OR AS A CONSEQUENCE OF):	
	d	

PART II. Other significant conditions contributing to death but not resulting in the underlying cause given in Part I

Diabetes, Chronic obstructive pulmonary disease, smoking

31a. WAS AN AUTOPSY PERFORMED? ☒ Yes ☐ No

31b. WERE AUTOPSY FINDINGS AVAILABLE PRIOR TO COMPLETION OF CAUSE OF DEATH? ☒ Yes ☐ No

32. MANNER OF DEATH
☒ Natural ☐ Pending Investigation
☐ Accident
☐ Suicide ☐ Could not be Determined
☐ Homicide

33a. DATE OF INJURY (Month, Day, Year)	33b. TIME OF INJURY	33c. INJURY AT WORK?	33d. DESCRIBE HOW INJURY OCCURRED
	M	☐ Yes ☐ No	

33e. PLACE OF INJURY—At home, farm, street, factory, office building, etc. (Specify)

33f. LOCATION (Street and Number or Rural Route Number, City or Town, State)

CAUSE OF DEATH

---

30. PART I. Enter the diseases, injuries, or complications that caused the death. Do not enter the mode of dying, such as cardiac or respiratory arrest, shock, or heart failure. List only one cause on each line.

		Approximate Interval Between Onset and Death
IMMEDIATE CAUSE (Final disease or condition resulting in death) →	a Cerebral laceration	10 mins.
	DUE TO (OR AS A CONSEQUENCE OF):	
Sequentially list conditions, if any, leading to immediate cause. Enter **UNDERLYING CAUSE** (Disease or injury that initiated events resulting in death) **LAST**	b Open skull fracture	10 mins.
	DUE TO (OR AS A CONSEQUENCE OF):	
	c Automobile accident	10 mins.
	DUE TO (OR AS A CONSEQUENCE OF):	
	d	

PART II. Other significant conditions contributing to death but not resulting in the underlying cause given in Part I

31a. WAS AN AUTOPSY PERFORMED? ☐ Yes ☐ No

31b. WERE AUTOPSY FINDINGS AVAILABLE PRIOR TO COMPLETION OF CAUSE OF DEATH? ☐ Yes ☐ No

32. MANNER OF DEATH
☐ Natural ☐ Pending Investigation
☒ Accident
☐ Suicide ☐ Could not be Determined
☐ Homicide

33a. DATE OF INJURY (Month, Day, Year)	33b. TIME OF INJURY	33c. INJURY AT WORK?	33d. DESCRIBE HOW INJURY OCCURRED
11/15/85	1 p. M	☐ Yes ☒ No	2-car collision—driver

33e. PLACE OF INJURY—At home, farm, street, factory, office building, etc. (Specify) Street

33f. LOCATION (Street and Number or Rural Route Number, City or Town, State) Route 4, Raleigh, Ohio

CAUSE OF DEATH

Figure 12–1 *Continued*

441

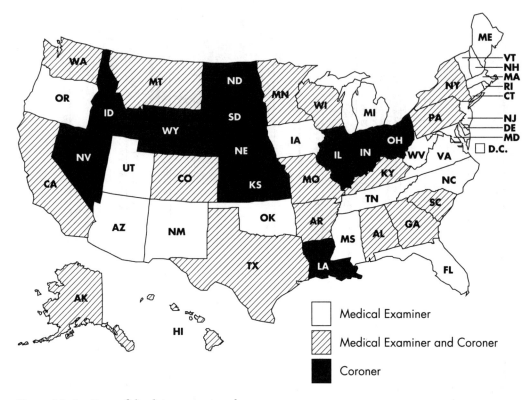

Figure 12–2 Type of death investigation, by state.

all, modern diagnostic techniques seem to tell us all we need to know about a patient's condition and the eventual cause of death. And, what good is there in determining with certainty the cause of a death that has already occurred?

However, there is great concern that the decline carries many negative consequences. The medical literature is filled with reports that demonstrate the continued relevance of the autopsy to quality medical care and to the overall health of the nation. Because of this evidence, various strategies for increasing the autopsy rate are being considered. At this point, let us examine several possible benefits of the autopsy as well as several reasons for its decline. Having done that, we will present some of the proposals that have been suggested for improving the autopsy rate.

Benefits of the Autopsy

The purpose of an autopsy is not merely to determine the cause of death (Souder and Trojanowski, 1992). One of its many benefits is to serve as a teaching and research tool. At one time, a 90 percent autopsy rate was not uncommon for teaching hospitals where such a rate was a mark of a high-quality facility (MacEachern, 1952). Indeed, it was among the criteria medical students used to evaluate prospective hospitals for their internships (Hill and Anderson, 1991). Student doctors, attending and house physicians, and pathologists attended the autopsy and discussions concerning its results. Why? Because autopsies demonstrate much about various disease processes, their interrelationships with one another and degenerative changes, as well as the variation in normal tissues and anatomical structures. Such information can add much to our knowledge of disease and its proper treatment and management. Much of our current knowledge about health and disease was derived from autopsies.

As teaching and research tools, autopsies can be used to assess individual responses to therapy and to evaluate the outcome of various surgical, medical, and drug treatments. Unfortunately, the rate at which they are performed does not make use of their potential to add to our collective knowledge—knowledge that can lead to the improved medical care of others.

Autopsies also can allow a clinical diagnosis to be confirmed, refined, or corrected (Mosquera and Goldman, 1993). The autopsy has been referred to as the ultimate medical consultation (Bowman and Williams, 1984) and the final peer review (Butler, 1991). Serving in such a capacity, it can provide knowledge that contributes to improved diagnostic techniques, better patient management, and, in some cases, increased survival for others (Nemetz, Ludwig, and Kurland, 1987; Pounder et al., 1983; Saladino, 1984). Byard and Bourne (1990) underscore the importance of autopsy in pediatric cases where the symptoms of disease are often subtle or nonspecific, especially in early infancy, making diagnosis more difficult and subject to error. In one study of 172 consecutive perinatal deaths, autopsy represented the sole means of establishing the diagnosis in 26 percent of the cases (Meier et al., 1986). Autopsy findings have the potential to add to improved diagnosis by correlating ante-mortem symptoms with changes and diagnoses established at autopsy.

Among the elderly, who reflect the lowest autopsy rate of between 1 and 3 percent, errors in clinical diagnosis are not uncommon (Ahronheim, Bernholc, and Clark, 1983; Campion et al., 1986; Hill and Anderson, 1991). In one review, nearly 20 percent of deaths attributed to heart disease were found at autopsy to be caused by tuberculosis or cancer. Almost 10 percent attributed to stroke were found to be due to other causes (Britton, 1974).

Errors in diagnosis as to the cause of death have led to concerns about the accuracy of our death certificate data and, ultimately, that of our national mortality statistics. Upon physician completion of death certificates, they are entered into local, state, and national files. Those statistics are used to establish research, treatment, and disease prevention priorities. Inaccurate statistics can lead to inadequate or inappropriate health care resource allocations and other inappropriate health care decisions. Evidence indicates that death certificate data are very unreliable (Glasser, 1981; Gloth and Burton, 1990; Hill and Anderson, 1988; Percy, Stanek, and Gloeckler, 1981). The director of the National Center for Health Statistics referred to the cause of death on death certificates as "far from perfect" (Altman, 1988).

Many reasons have been given for the inaccuracy. The completion of the death certificate is not usually viewed as an important job by physicians (Kircher and Anderson, 1987). The certificate is generally filled out hurriedly and perfunctorily. Its proper completion and the importance of such is not emphasized in medical school or residency training programs. The common practice of listing cardiopulmonary arrest as the cause of death provides no useful information. However, even if great care is taken in completing the death certificate, without an autopsy there is a 10 to 25 percent error rate in the recorded cause of death (Hill and Anderson, 1988).

Besides influencing medical education and research, diagnostic capabilities, and the accuracy of vital statistics, autopsies may exert an effect in numerous other areas. They can help to uncover information about "new diseases" such as Legionnaire's disease or AIDS or those about which we have limited knowledge such as Alzheimer's disease. They also can help in the identification of environmental hazards.

Finally, autopsies can have a beneficial effect on the family because they provide important information about inherited disorders and assist in the grieving process. Grief often provokes feelings of guilt. Loved ones may fear they gave inadequate care. Documentation of the seriousness of a condition and its inevitable outcome can be helpful to the bereaved (Byard and Bourne, 1990; Hill and Anderson, 1991; Valdes-Dapena, 1984).

The Decline in Autopsies

There are many reasons for the dramatic decline in the autopsy rate. Increased diagnostic confidence is a major factor; it has reduced physician requests for an autopsy. The notion that it will not reveal anything significant that wasn't already known before death is largely related to the rapid advances in medical technology. CAT scans, MRIs, endoscopies (inspection of a body cavity with a special instrument), and numerous other diagnostic procedures seem to have left the autopsy behind. Yet, these modern diagnostic procedures haven't had a significant effect on the discrepancy rate between what doctors diagnose as the cause of death and what is found at autopsy (Goldman et al., 1983; Hill and Anderson, 1988, 1991; Landefeld et al., 1988).

Fear of malpractice litigation may also contribute to the reduced number of autopsy requests. Additionally, in this era of modern curative medicine, death is often viewed as a failure. In such a climate, physicians often do not request or attend post-mortem exams for their patients (Friederici and Sebastian, 1984).

Obtaining consent for an autopsy can sometimes be difficult. Except for those mandated by medical examiners or coroners, written authorization by the next of kin is required. Families may have varied reasons for refusing permission. They may feel that their loved ones have already "suffered enough," that their bodies already have been subjected to enough poking, prodding, and invasive procedures. Culture may also play a role in attitudes toward autopsy (Perkins, Supik, and Hazuda, 1993). Also, insurance programs including Medicare do not reimburse autopsies and they are expensive. If family members consent to the procedure, it is they who must often foot the bill. Costs of autopsies ordered by a medical examiner or corner are paid by the county or state.

Economics discourages autopsies because of the manner in which pathologists are paid for their services. Hospital pathologists bill for each laboratory or surgical service they provide (a fee-for-service reimbursement scheme). However, as a part of their hospital-based employment contract, they are generally required to accept a fixed reimbursement for performing all of the autopsies that the hospital requests within a designated period of time. There are many demands on their time for laboratory and surgical pathology (analyzing tissue specimens/biopsies). These services appear to be given greater priority and are considerably more lucrative for the pathologist.

The hospital's autopsy-related costs are paid from the general account:

> The hospital director therefore views the autopsy service as equivalent to the laundry or cafeteria: a money loser that must be accepted with modest grace . . . Some pathologists have instituted a charge to the family—often quite high—that is not covered by insurance, and provides an effective deterrent to autopsy performance.   (Hill and Anderson, 1991, p. 71)

Furthermore, there is no longer the pressure that there once was for hospitals to request autopsies. Since 1971, the Joint Commission on Accreditation of Health Care Organizations (JCAHO) has eliminated the 20 percent autopsy rate previously required for hospital accreditation.

Proposals for the Future

Merely increasing the number of autopsies performed will not necessarily yield significant benefits. They need to be well done. Likewise, autopsy data that is not shared or networked may be lost and become "orphan data" (Nelson, 1976). They wind up in a physician's and a hospital's file without yielding any benefits.

Many have identified the need to increase our national autopsy rate as a part of a coordinated program (Ahronheim, Bernholc, and Clark, 1983; Hill and Anderson, 1991; Landefeld et al., 1988; McPhee and Bottles, 1985).

> If all patients who died while being administered a new drug were autopsied, the collected findings might be expected to provide early information about its effectiveness, or early warnings about unanticipated effects. Autopsies on all persons who have worked in environments suspected of harboring toxic hazards should quickly provide some information about the danger of those environments. When a new disease is identified and tentatively characterized, autopsies on all patients whose death is suspected to be due to that disease would quickly fill in many gaps of knowledge.   (Hill and Anderson, 1991, p. 62)

Implied in this statement is the understanding that such data would be studied and compared in a systematic way.

Proposals to bring back the autopsy include altering consent laws. Some have suggested that autopsies become routine unless an individual objected during life, or unless a family member objects. In several Scandinavian countries, hospitals routinely seek permission for autopsy at the time of admission. Any system for increasing the rate must be respectful of individual and/or religious objections to the procedure.

Increased rates are, however, dependent on more than individual or family consent. Various other suggestions for improving the autopsy rate include providing better financial support for the procedure, reinstating autopsy requirements for hospital accreditation, centering teaching around the autopsy, and educating health care professionals, as well as the public, about its importance (McPhee and Bottles, 1985).

Organ and Tissue Donation

As we have seen, the information gleaned from autopsies can increase our knowledge and add to the public good. Organ donation represents another dramatic way in which the body of the deceased can be used to benefit others. At one time, the notion of removing healthy, living tissue from a dead person was in the realm of science fiction. Today, it is a technical reality (see Tables 12–1 and 12–2). Since the 1960s, medical machinery has allowed oxygenated blood flow to perfuse the organs of dead patients, facilitating their removal for transplantation. Improved surgical techniques and antirejection drugs now permit the transplantation of the heart, lungs, liver, pancreas, and kidneys as well as the tissues listed in Box 12–2.

In spite of technical capabilities, many potential organ recipients do not benefit from transplantation because of the shortage of organs. During 1990, as many as 2,200 people died while waiting for a transplant. Many of these were in end-stage cardiac or liver failure with no other options for their survival. Unlike these patients, those in chronic kidney failure may be kept alive for variable periods by dialysis (Kittur et al., 1991).

TABLE 12–1   *Number of Transplants, by Organ, 1985–1990*

	1985	1986	1987	1988	1989	1990
Heart	719	1,368	1,438	1,663	1,700	2,085
Heart-Lung	30	45	49	74	68	50
Kidney	7,695	8,976	9,094	9,004	8,706	9,560
Cadaveric and Living						
Liver	602	924	1,199	1,711	2,164	2,656
Lung	—	—	—	33	119	262
Pancreas	130	140	142	250	419	549
TOTAL	9,176	11,453	11,922	12,735	13,176	15,164

Source: United Network for Organ Sharing.

At the end of 1990, while 21,982 persons were on U.S. waiting lists for various organs, there were 4,248 cadaveric organ donors (Kittur et al. 1991). The number of cadaveric donors is significant because they are the source of most organ donations. The National Cooperative Transplantation Study found that the number of such donors remained relatively unchanged (4,000–4,357) during the four-year period observed. The demand for organs almost doubled during the same period of 1987–1991. The study also found that the annual number of potential donors is between 6,900 and 10,700, lower than the earlier estimates of 25,000 (*Latest Word*, 1992).

TABLE 12–2   *One-Year Survival Rate, by Organ, 1988*

	Patient Survival Rate, %	Organ Graft Survival Rate, %
Heart	83 (+/−1.0)	82 (+/−1.0)
Heart-Lung*	57 (+/−5.7)	57 (+/−5.8)
Kidney (cadaveric donor)	92 (+/−0.4)	81 (+/−0.5)
Kidney (living, related donor)	97 (+/−0.4)	91 (+/−0.8)
Liver	76 (+/−1.1)	69 (+/−1.3)
Lung*	48 (+/−8.7)	48 (+/−9.0)
Pancreas*	89 (+/−2.3)	71 (+/−3.1)

Source: United Network for Organ Sharing.
*The limited number of procedures performed may distort these figures.

Box 12–2   *Tissue Donation*

Vital organs such as heart, liver, kidney, heart-lung, and pancreas, as well as any or all of the following tissues can be donated:

- Bones—Ilia (hip bones), long bones of the legs and arms, knee joints, ribs, mandible (jaw bones—only in cases of cremation or when the body will not be viewed) and bone marrow.
- Skin—Only a thin layer (about the thickness of a peeling sunburn) is removed, and only from areas that do not show during viewing.
- Dura Mater—A protective covering of the brain.
- Fascia Lata—The covering over the thigh muscle.
- Cartilage
- Ligaments
- Tendons
- Veins
- Eyes and corneas

Bone is used in treating cancerous defects of the extremities and face, disabling spinal problems, scoliosis, birth defects, and for reconstructive surgery of major joints.

Bone marrow is used for research for the treatment of leukemia (especially in children) and nuclear accidents.

Skin is used in the treatment of severely burned patients. Soft tissue (dura, fascia, tendons, and ligaments) is used to treat defects caused by tumors and trauma and to repair tendons, ligaments, and in treatment of sports injuries.

Source: From the Northwest Ohio Tissue Bank, St. Vincent Medical Center, Toledo, Ohio.

Encouraged Volunteerism: The Uniform Anatomical Gift Act and Required Request Legislation

The donation of organs in the United States has been based on encouraged volunteerism. People are encouraged to donate their organs/tissues through a written document such as a donor card (see Figure 12–3). Volunteerism is seen to promote the social values of altruism and kindliness without invading individual rights. Volunteerism of organs became an established policy with

UNIFORM DONOR CARD

Name____

In the hope that I may help others, I hereby make this anatomical gift, if medically acceptable, to take effect upon my death. The words and marks below indicate my desires

I give: (a)_____any needed organs or parts

(b)_____only the following organs or parts

____

Specify the organ(s) or part(s)

for the purposes of transplantation, therapy, medical research or education;

(c)_____my body for anatomical study if needed.

Limitations or
special wishes if any:______________________________

Signed by the donor and the following two witnesses in the presence of each other:

Signature of Donor — Date of Birth of Donor

City & State — Date Signed

Witness — Witness

This is a legal document under the Uniform Anatomical Gift Act or similar laws.
For further information consult your organ procurement organization:

Life Connection
of Northwestern Ohio
(419) 893-4891

Figure 12–3 Uniform Donor Card.

the passage of the Uniform Anatomical Gift Act (UAGA) of 1968. By 1971, some form of this legislation had been adopted in all fifty states and the District of Columbia. In recognizing the legal status of the donor card, the UAGA provides a favorable legal environment for the donation of human tissues/organs after death.

The basic provisions of the UAGA are as follows:

1. Persons eighteen years or older may donate all or part of their body after death for transplantation or medical research and education.
2. A donor's valid statement of gift supersedes the rights of others.
3. If a donor has not acted during life, survivors may do so.
4. Physicians who accept anatomical gifts relying on valid documents are immune from legal action.

5. The time of death is to be determined by a physician not involved in a transplant.

6. The donor may revoke the gift or it may be rejected.

In light of the actual number of potential donors, the encouraged volunteerism of the UAGA has failed to provide the needed numbers of organs. Despite massive and expensive educational and publicity campaigns undertaken by groups such the National Kidney Foundation, the message seems not to have been heard. Surveys indicate that the general population is well informed about organ donation and the shortage of donor organs. They also show that the public is not opposed to organ donation. Seventy-five to eighty percent of adults surveyed are in favor of it. Yet, the vast majority of them have not signed donor cards (Gallup Organization, Inc., 1985, 1986, 1987; Kittur et al., 1991).

Whether or not a donor card has been signed, individuals are encouraged to discuss their feelings about organ donation with their families. This action can increase the chance of having their wishes followed should they ever be in a position to serve as an organ donor. Ninety-eight percent of all organ donors originate from intensive care units. The potential donor is there usually as a result of an accident. In dealing with their fatally injured patients, the medical staff confront families in the midst of their sorrow, shock, and disbelief. In spite of the UAGA, it is families who have the final say in organ donation. Often times, families have not been approached regarding organ donation in light of the tragedy they were enduring. As one New York State legislative aide expressed, "We do not have a shortage of donors. . . . We have a shortage of askers" (Cate and Laudicina, 1991).

Over the past several years, states have adopted what is known as required request legislation. Under this legislation, hospitals are required to identify potential organ/tissue donors and to inform families of their option to donate. They have been required to do so as a condition of participation in Medicare/Medicaid. Like the UAGA, such legislation is based on the principle of encouraged volunteerism. In the latter case, it is the volunteerism of families that is encouraged. The term *required request* is misleading as families are not requested to make a donation. Rather, they are required to be informed of donation opportunities. For this reason, the legislative policy is often referred to as *routine inquiry*. The inquiry is generally made by a transplant coordinator who is a member of the nursing staff.

Because the present system of altruism has not increased organ donations, alternative methods of organ procurement have been proposed (Caplan, 1984, 1987; Singer, 1990). The ethical issues related to obtaining organs is an important concern (Rhodes, 1994; Younger and Arnold, 1993). Most controversial among them is the sale of organs (Essig, 1993) which is strictly prohibited in the United States. Other more viable options to the altruistic model include donor/family compensation and a policy of presumed consent.

Sale of Organs, Donor/Family Compensation, and Presumed Consent

The sale of organs from cadavers or living persons is outlawed in the United States via the National Organ Transplant Act of 1984. Organ sales and purchases are federal crimes punishable by imprisonment of up to five years, or fines of up to $50,000, or both.

A few years ago, an international market in buying, selling, and distributing kidneys was reported. Payments to live kidney donors in some countries were among the practices cited. One tissue-typing laboratory in Bombay, India, recorded 648 paid donors during an eight-month period in 1985. Some prisoners in the Philippines were reported to donate kidneys in exchange for earlier paroles. And, in Japan, a loan shark was said to give his debtors the option of repaying him in kidneys (Bermel, 1986). Such practices have been described as "the plundering of peasants' parts for profit" (Keller, 1984, p. 16).

Arguments against the sale of human organs are based on protecting the vulnerable from exploitation. Medical benefits should not be pursued at the physical expense of the socially and economically deprived. Neither, it is maintained, should the poor be "induced by money to offer the material resources of their bodies" or to co-opt "their own health into a saleable commodity in the marketplace of human replacement parts" (Dickens, 1977, p. 165).

Arguments in support of organ sales are based on increasing their supply and on allowing individual freedom through the act of selling. For the interested reader, these arguments are summarized by MacDonald and Valentin (1988). While it is recognized that some persons unwilling to donate organs would sell them (Caplan, 1983), some findings suggest that if organ sales were permitted, many persons who would benevolently give their organs would neither donate nor sell them (Pessemier, Bennaor, and Hanssens, 1977). In any event, the sale of organs would probably diminish the supply of "free organs" (MacDonald and Valentin, 1988).

The libertarian argument in support of legalizing organ sales is based on the belief that, in a free society, individuals ought to be able to do whatever they wish with their bodies as long as they harm no one else. It recognizes no distinction between the lawfulness of allowing persons to sell their labor in hazardous occupations such as coal mining and selling their nonvital body organs. Be it a kidney or the labor of a coal miner that is sold, a shortening of life is expected (Chapman, 1984). It is further argued that rather than exploiting the poor, the sale of nonvital organs could possibly provide them with the singular opportunity to better their lives through the acquisition of large amounts of money (Brams, 1983).

Whatever arguments might be mustered in favor of organ sales, the reader is reminded that they are outlawed in the United States where reports of un-regulated organ-buying in developing countries are viewed as morally repre-hensible.

However, discussion of modest donor/family compensation is beginning in the United States. A public survey of the acceptability of such a compensatory system as an alternative method for increasing organ donations was conducted by a subcommittee of the Ad Hoc Donations Committee established by the United Network for Organ Sharing (UNOS). UNOS, located in Richmond, Virginia, was congressionally established by the National Organ Transplant Act. It is a central office assisting in matching donor organs with potential re-cipients. It follows the status of all donated organs in the United States and maintains a transplant waiting list for all would-be recipients.

Compensations considered in the UNOS survey were: (1) a payment to the donor family to assist in funeral expenses, (2) a cash payment to the donor's estate, (3) a cash payment to a charity chosen by the donor or family, and (4) a low-cost life insurance policy redeemable on organ donation by the deceased policy holder. A nonfinancial compensation was also included. It would confer "preferred status" on the waiting list for those declaring themselves as potential organ donors, or for any of their relatives, if they should ever require an organ transplant (Kittur et al., 1991).

Fifty-two percent of those surveyed indicated it was acceptable to offer such compensation in an attempt to increase organ donations. Only 5 percent feared that this type of financial compensation carried the potential for abuse. Those surveyed rank-ordered the various forms of compensation as follows: (1) preferred status, (2) a $2,000 payment for funeral assistance, (3) payment to a charity, (4) a limited life insurance policy, and (5) a $2,000 payment to the donor's estate.

The final type of organ procurement system we will consider is presumed consent. If such legislation were passed, it would permit the removal of ca-daver organs unless the deceased carried a "nondonor" card, or had placed his or her name in a central computer register indicating opposition to such a practice, or the next of kin raised an objection.

Proponents of presumed consent point to the fact that opinion polls con-sistently demonstrate that the majority of Americans are supportive of organ donation. By providing a mechanism for those who are not to opt out of the program, we may increase the supply of organs without abusing individual rights. Presumed consent is viewed by many as the most effective alternative to our present system of encouraged volunteerism for increasing the organ sup-ply. Due to its potential for doing so, a National Kidney Foundation Conference concluded that the system is worthy of further consideration (Kittur et al., 1991). Presumed consent exists in several countries; Austria, Belgium, Denmark, Finland, France, Norway, and Singapore all have opting-out legislation (Roels et al., 1990; Teo, 1991).

In addition to its potential for increasing the organ supply, advocates of presumed consent point to its other benefits. Routine organ removal under medically appropriate circumstances would create a social climate expectant of organ donation unless an objection was raised. Organ removal would become a ritual part of death. In so doing, it would relieve the emotional burden of the hospital staff in inquiring about organ donation and that of the family in making a decision at such a traumatic time (Caplan, 1983; Thukral and Cummins, 1987). The reader is reminded that the majority of organ donors eminate from sudden, unexpected death—a time when the family is shocked and in turmoil. "When we find ourselves in . . . boundary situations—when our lives have become unravelled—we need ritual, routine, and automatic procedures. These procedures ought to be those that reflect our collective judgement expressed in more normal times" (Muyskens, 1978, p. 96). Presumed consent would also reduce the costs of public education and promotional campaigns that are involved in encouraged volunteerism. These costs now run in the millions of dollars (Caplan, 1983).

Opponents of presumed consent find the routine taking of organs unethical because it interferes with autonomous behavior. Opting out with nondonor cards or the computer registry depends on individuals taking action on their objections to serve as organ donors. If they fail to take action, their wishes may be violated. It has also been argued that taking organs under this system denies individuals and their families the profound experience of benevolent gift giving (Ramsey, 1970). Although the circumstances surrounding the act may be tragic, families may derive comfort from actively making a donation.

A limited form of presumed consent is in effect in the United States under removal statutes or remit of medical examiner laws. Cases under the jurisdiction of a medical examiner allow the removal of corneas when no known objection exists. A 1991 amendment to the UAGA in the State of Texas permits the medical examiner to approve removal of visceral organs and tissue from cadavers if the "next-of-kin are not located after reasonable effort within 4 hours of pronouncement of brain death" (Kittur et al., 1991, p. 1443).

Cadaver Dissection and Medical School

The UAGA and the uniform donor card provide not only for the transfer of human tissues and organs but for the donation of the body for the purpose of medical education and anatomical study. Medical students across the country take gross anatomy during their first year of medical school. The course, which is the foundation of their medical education, also introduces them to what has been called their "first patient"—the cadaver.

Traditionally, the highly charged emotional and psychological experience of human dissection has been treated in a matter-of-fact manner. However, a growing number of medical schools are developing programs to deal with the emotional experience of working with the cadaver (Blackwell et al., 1979; Marks and Bertman, 1980; Schoenberg, 1991; Schotzinger and Best, 1987–1988). These include orientation programs that attempt to psychologically prepare students for the task. And, the task is more stressful than it appears on the surface. Students are often afraid they will become ill or appear too emotional. Many have disturbing dreams about their cadavers. Hiding feelings has been the norm in fear of negative reactions from their classmates and professors (Coombs and St. John, 1979; Knight, 1973; Segal, 1988).

Concerns about violating the body of another person have been expressed. One medical student put it this way: "We were doing something that would be a crime in our society if we weren't medical students, and that kind of violation of someone's body and privacy, that's significant" (Schoenberg, 1991, p. 27). Another student at the Northeastern Ohio Universities College of Medicine commented on the benefits of the orientation program. The chairperson of the anatomy program, said the student, had

> emphasized the fact that it was the wish of the people who donated their bodies to have their bodies used for this educational purpose. That made it a lot easier for me knowing that I wasn't violating that person's wishes. They really wanted their body to be used for that purpose. (Schotzinger and Best, 1987–1988, p. 219)

Memorial services at the conclusion of the class have developed at many medical schools. These are typically organized by students and attended by students, faculty, and donor families. At one school, the ceremony included a short walk to a cemetery near the medical school where the cremated remains of the cadavers are buried. The stone marking their burial plot reads, "They gave in death for those in life." Gratitude is a common theme at the services. As one student expressed, "A lot of people were really grateful for what the cadaver had given us and for what these people gave so that we could learn. The memorial service was our way of giving something back and somehow saying, 'thank you'" (Schotzinger and Best, 1987–1988, p. 221).

In reflecting on the mortality we all face, the poet Thomas Gray remarked that inevitably "the paths of glory lead but to the grave." Today, various after-death activities involving the body such as autopsies, organ donation, and body donation for medical education lead to the greater good. In their deaths, many have contributed to the advancement of knowledge and to procedures that prolong life for others.

Summary

Universally, the major ritual surrounding death is the funeral. In modern societies such as ours, various other post-death activities occur including the filing of a death certificate. Other possible activities are the investigation of violent, suspicious, or unexpected deaths by a coroner or medical examiner, an autopsy, the donation of organs or tissues for transplantation, and the donation of the body for anatomical study. This chapter presents an overview of these various medically oriented, after-death rituals.

All deaths are officially registered via a death certificate. This document serves as legal proof of death and thus influences the distribution of insurance benefits and property. By registering the cause of death it also serves as a public health record of the diseases that cause Americans to die. The mode of death, be it natural, accidental, suicide, or homicide, is also recorded.

In the United States, medical examiners and coroners are responsible for investigating violent, suspicious, or unexpected deaths as well as those unattended by a physician according to the dictates of state law. The medical examiner is appointed; coroners are elected.

The autopsy is a post-mortem examination performed not just by a coroner's or medical examiner's authorization. It is conducted by a pathologist, in general, to determine or confirm the cause of death and to gain a better understanding of disease processes. Since the 1940s, the U.S. autopsy rate has dramatically declined. This situation has been the subject of serious concern because of the many benefits that autopsies can provide. The decrease is related to several factors. Various proposals have been suggested for improving the autopsy rate so that the information generated may benefit others.

Organ donation represents another dramatic way in which the body of the deceased can be used to benefit others. In spite of technical capabilities, many potential organ recipients don't benefit from transplantation because of the shortage of organs. In the United States, organs are donated in the spirit of volunteerism. The U.S. program of encouraged volunteerism was established with the passage of the Uniform Anatomical Gift Act and is likewise reflected in the required request legislation recently adopted by several states. Despite the fact that surveys indicate that the majority of Americans are in favor of organ donation, encouraged volunteerism has not increased the number of organ donations. Therefore, alternative methods of organ procurement have been proposed. Most controversial is the sale of organs, which is prohibited in the United States. Other, more viable options for increasing the organ supply are a donor/family compensation program and a policy of presumed consent.

The body also may be donated for the purpose of medical education. Medical students encounter cadaver dissection during their first year of medical school; medical schools are now developing programs to help them deal with the emotional aspects of working with cadavers. Memorial services at the conclusion of a gross anatomy class are among such programs.

Study Questions

1. What functions are served by the death certificate?

2. Differentiate a medical examiner from a coroner. What are their functions?

3. Present an overview of the status of autopsies today, the benefits they provide, reasons for their decline, and proposals for increasing the number performed.

4. What is encouraged volunteerism as it relates to organ donation? Present an overview of the Uniform Anatomical Gift Act and required request legislation. Have these programs been successful?

5. Is the sale of organs for transplantation allowed in the United States? Explain. What are some of the pros and cons of selling human organs?

6. What is the United Network for Organ Sharing? Note some donor/family compensation options considered in the UNOS survey.

7. Explain presumed consent as a method for organ procurement. Present some arguments for and against this organ-procurement system.

8. How are some of today's medical schools helping their students deal with the emotionally charged experience of human dissection?

References

Ahronheim, J., A. Bernholc, and W. Clark. (1983). Age trends in autopsy rates. *JAMA*, 250:1182–1186.

Altman, L. (1988). Sharp drop in autopsies stirs fears that quality of care may also fall. *The New York Times*, July 21.

Bermel, J. (1986). Organs for sale: From marketplace to jungle. *Hastings Center Report*, 16:3–4.

Blackwell, B., et al. (1979). Humanizing the student-cadaver encounter. *General Hospital Psychiatry*, 4:315–321.

Bowman, H., and M. Williams. (1984). Revitalizing the ultimate medical consultation. *Archives of Pathology and Laboratory Medicine*, 108:437–438.

Brams, M. (1983). Transplantable human organs: Should their sale be authorized by state statutes? *American Journal of Law and Medicine*, 3:183–195.

Britton, M. (1974). Clinical diagnostics: Experience from 383 autopsied cases. *Acta Medica Scandinavia*, 196:211–219.

Butler, R. (1991). Autopsy: The final peer review. *Geriatrics*, 46:11–12.

Byard, R., and A. Bourne. (1990). The autopsy: A dying art? A paediatric perspective. *Journal of Paediatric and Child Health*, 26:119–121.

Campion, E., V. Reder, A. Mulley, and G. Thibault. (1986). Age and the declining rate of autopsy. *Journal of the American Geriatrics Society*, 34:865–868.

Caplan, A. (1983). Organ transplants: The costs of success. *Hastings Center Report*, 13:23–33.

Caplan, A. (1984). Organ procurement: It's not in the cards. *Hastings Center Report,* 14:9–12.

Caplan, A. (1987). Sounding board: Ethical and policy issues in the procurement of cadaver organs for transplantation. *Human Organ Transplantation,* 272:275.

Cate, F., and S. Laudicina. (1991). *Transplantation White Paper.* Richmond, VA: United Network for Organ Sharing.

Centers for Disease Control. (1988). Autopsy frequency—United States, 1980–1985. *Morbidity and Mortality Weekly Report,* 37:191–194.

Centers for Disease Control. (1989). Death investigation—United States, 1987. *Morbidity and Mortality Weekly Report,* 38:1–4.

Chapman, F. (1984). The life-and-death question of an organ market. *Fortune,* 112:108–112.

Coombs, R. and J. St. John. (1979). *Making It in Medical School.* New York: Spectrum Publications.

Dickens, B. (1977). The control of living body materials. *University of Toronto Law Journal,* 27:142–167.

Essig, B. (1993). Legal aspects of the sale of organs. *Mount Sinai Journal of Medicine,* 60:59–64.

Friederici, H., and M. Sebastian. (1984). An argument for the attendance of clinicians at autopsy. *Archives of Pathology and Laboratory Medicine,* 108:522–523.

Gallup Organization, Inc. (1985, 1986, 1987). *The U.S. public's attitude toward organ transplants/donation.*

Geller, S. (1983). Autopsy. *Scientific American,* 248:124–136.

Glasser, J. (1981). The quality and utility of death certificate data. *American Journal of Public Health,* 71:231–233.

Gloth, M., and J. Burton. (1990). Autopsies and death certificates in the chronic care setting. *Journal of the American Geriatrics Society,* 30:151–155.

Goldman, L., R. Sayson, S. Robbins, L. Cohn, M. Bettman, and M. Wisberg. (1983). The value of the autopsy in three medical eras. *NEJM,* 308:1000–1005.

Hill, R., and R. Anderson. (1988). *The Autopsy Medical Practice and Public Policy.* Stoneham, MA: Butterworths.

Hill, R., and R. Anderson. (1991). The autopsy crisis reexamined: The case for a national autopsy policy. *Milbank Quarterly,* 69:51–78.

Keller, B. (1984). Gut issues. *New Republic,* 15–17.

Kircher, T., and R. Anderson. (1987). Cause of death: Proper completion of the death certificate. *JAMA,* 258:349–352.

Kittur, D., D. Hogan, V. Thukral, L. McGraw, and J. Alexander. (1991). Incentives for organ donation? *Lancet,* 338:1441–1443.

Knight, J. (1973). *Medical Student: Doctor in the Making.* New York: Appleton-Century-Crofts.

Landefeld, C., M. Chren, A. Myers, R. Geller, S. Robbins, and L. Goldman. (1988). Diagnostic yield of the autopsy in a university hospital and a community hospital. *NEJM,* 318:1249–1254.

Latest Word. (1992). The gift of life. *Hastings Center Report,* 22:45.

MacDonald, J., and E. Valentin. (1988). The brave new world of organ transplantation: Issues and challenges from a consumer affairs perspective. *Journal of Consumer Affairs,* 22:119–135.

MacEachern, M. (1952). More autopsies: They are vital to medical progress. *Hospitals,* 26:58–146.

Marks, S., and S. Bertman. (1980). Experience with learning about death and dying in the undergraduate anatomy curriculum. *Journal of Medical Education,* 55:48–52.

McPhee, S., and K. Bottles. (1985). Autopsy: Moribund art or vital science? *The American Journal of Medicine,* 78:107–113.

Meier, P., D. Manchester, R. Shikes, W. Clewell, and M. Stewart. (1986). Perinatal autopsy: Its clinical value. *Obstetrics and Gynecology,* 67:349–351.

Mosquera, D. and M. Goldman. (1993). Surgical audit without autopsy: Tales of the unexpected. *Annals of the Royal College of Surgeons of England,* 75:115–117.

Muyskens, J. (1978). An alternative policy for obtaining cadaver organs for transplantation. *Philosophy and Public Affairs,* 8:96.

Nelson, A. (1976). Orphan data and the unclosed loop: A dilemma in PSRO and medical audit. *NEJM,* 295:617–619.

Nemetz, P., J. Ludwig, and L. Kurland. (1987). Addressing the autopsy. *American Journal of Pathology,* 128:362–370.

Percy, C., E. Stanek, and L. Gloeckler. (1981). Accuracy of cancer death certificates and its effect on cancer mortality statistics. *American Journal of Public Health,* 71:242–250.

Perkins, H., J. Supik, and H. Hazuda. (1993). Autopsy decisions: The possibility of conflicting cultural attitudes. *Journal of Clinical Ethics,* 4:145–154.

Pessemier, E., A. Bennaor, and D. Hanssens. (1977). Willingness to supply human body parts: Some empirical results. *Journal of Consumer Research,* 4:131–140.

Pounder, D., M. Horowitz, R. Roland, and D. Reid. (1983). The value of the autopsy in medical audit: A combined clinical and pathological assessment of 100 cases. *Australia/New Zealand Journal of Medicine,* 13:478–482.

Ramsey, P. (1970). *The Patient as Person.* New Haven: Yale University Press.

Rhodes, R. (1994). A review of ethical issues in transplantation. *The Mount Sinai Journal of Medicine,* 61:77–82.

Roberts, W. (1978). The autopsy: Its decline and a suggestion for its revival. *NEJM,* 299:332–338.

Roels, L., Y. Vanrenterghem, M. Waer, M. Christiaenss, J. Gruwez, and P. Michielson. (1990). Three years experience with a "presumed consent" legislation in Belgium: Its impact on multi-organ donation in comparison with other European countries. *Transplant Proceedings,* 22:2078–2079.

Saladino, A. (1984). The efficacy of the autopsy in medical quality assurance. *Clinics in Laboratory Medicine,* 4:165–183.

Schoenberg, N. (1991). Anatomy of compassion. *The [Toledo] Blade* (November 12): 27.

Schotzinger, K., and E. Best. (1987–1988). Closure and the cadaver experience: A memorial service for deeded bodies. *Omega,* 18:217–227.

Segal, D. (1988). A patient so dead: American medical students and their cadavers. *Anthropological Quarterly,* 61:17–25.

Singer, P. (1990). A review of public policies to procure and distribute kidneys for transplantation. *Archives of Internal Medicine,* 150:523–527.

Souder, E. and J. Trojanowski. (1992). Autopsy: Cutting away the myths. *Journal of Neuroscience Nursing,* 24:134–139.

Teo, B. (1991). Organs for transplantation: The Singapore experience. *Hastings Center Report,* 21:10–13.

Thukral, V., and G. Cummins. (1987). The vital organ shortage. In R. Belk (Ed.), *Advances in Non-Profit Marketing* (Vol. 2). Greenwich, CT: JAI Press.

Valdes-Dapena, M. (1984). The postautopsy conference with families. *Archives of Pathology and Laboratory Medicine,* 108:447–450.

Younger, S., and R. Arnold. (1993). Ethical, psychosocial, and public policy implications of procuring organs from non-heart-beating cadaver donors. *JAMA,* 269:2769–2774.

CHAPTER 13

The Ritualization of Death
Funerals and Disposition of the Body

They say such nice things about people at their funerals that it makes me sad to realize that I'm going to miss mine by just a few days.

Garrison Keillor

Funerals: Functions, Historical Change, and Controversy

Through the years, the way in which humans have disposed of their dead has varied according to culture, religion, personal preference, and even geographic area. For example, among some native peoples of the Arctic, surface burial was common. The frozen ground made it impractical to dig a grave and there were no trees with which to produce a crematory fire. Thus, the corpse was often covered with stones to form a rock vault.

Deliberate burial dates back to the Neanderthals. Their remains have been found within the outlines of pits that intrude upon the normal layering of the earth. This evidence indicates that their bodies were placed in deliberately dug graves rather than dragged some distance from their encampments to be devoured by vultures and other scavengers. The latter would have been a much easier task for the survivors, but they were motivated to do more in the face of death.

Archaeologists have uncovered items that survivors ceremonially placed in the Neanderthal graves. At Teshik Tash in Russia, goat horns surrounded the remains of a child. And, at Shanidar Cave in Iraq, pollen analysis indicates that flowers were left in a grave dating back over 70,000 years. Thus, humans have a long history of ritualizing death. That some form of funeral ritual has existed for much of human history and across the many cultural traditions speaks to its importance (see Box 13–1).

Functions of Funerals

Death rituals are viewed as rights of passage (van Gennep, 1909/1960). As such, they provide formal recognition of the transition from one stage in the life cycle to another and the changed status that transition brings. Death ceremonies help to psychologically remove the deceased from this earthly existence to the symbolic world of the dead. Likewise, they publicly mark the changed status of survivors, reuniting them in their new roles with society.

Funerals serve other individual and community functions, some of which will be briefly summarized. For individuals, funerals can increase the reality of death. They may be more important in doing so when death is sudden and unexpected. They also provide a legitimate public occasion for expressing and validating grief. The worth of the deceased is evidenced by the presence of others who have made time to attend the ceremony and by their expressed tributes and condolences. The pain of the bereaved is, thus, justified. Funerals also provide social support for the survivors. Additionally, they give the bereaved something to do. In the initial phase of grief, survivors are shocked and disorganized. Arranging and attending the funeral (as well as attending to other post-death activities such as insurance matters, settling of the estate, and so on) gives some predictability and organization to an otherwise uncontrollable situation. Also, with their focus on death, funerals present a significant opportunity to reflect on our own mortality. Hence, they can reinforce the value of life and make us think about what is really important to us.

For the community, funerals may reaffirm ethnic or religious identity. They also emphasize the cohesiveness of the family or larger group beyond the loss of one of its members (see Figure 13–1). Devastating loss brings a sense of overwhelming loneliness and disruption. The gathering of family, friends, and colleagues reminds us that there are others in our world—that structure, organization, and life do go on. Social order is reaffirmed. As a socializing experience, funerals help children to learn about death and about the comfort, love, and support that humans can provide each other in times of crisis.

B ox 13–1   *Newgrange: Pyramid in the Round*

The construction of passage graves thousands of years ago, during the late Stone Age, stands testimony to the technological sophistication of their builders as well as to the importance they placed on the proper disposal of the dead. These graves are a western European phenomenon found along the Atlantic seaboard from Ireland to Scandinavia to Spain. Older than the Egyptian pyramids, they, along with the temples of Malta, are the first momentous architectural monuments in prehistoric Europe. There are many in Ireland where Newgrange, the most spectacular of these graves, is found.

Like other such graves, Newgrange is a massive stone structure housing a burial chamber that is entered by means of a long hallway or passage from the outside—hence, the name passage grave. The entire complex is covered by a mound of earth and stone (see photo).

Newgrange

The burial chamber, located deep within the recesses of this spectacular "house for the dead," as one of its leading authorities refers to it (Harbison, 1988), holds cremated remains. Some skeletal material indicates that a few of the dead placed there were not cremated. Various artifacts including pottery, beads, and tools as well as massive stone basins are also found there. The latter are believed to have temporarily held cremated bone while burial rites were performed (see photo).

Built approximately 4,500 years ago, Newgrange is a wonder of the ancient world. It stands over 45 feet high, is 280 feet in diameter, and holds over 200,000 tons of precisely placed stones. It is hard to imagine that such an engineering feat was accomplished so many years ago without the help of modern equipment. Imagine trying to build it today equipped with nothing more than Stone Age tools.

Perhaps even more remarkable is the natural illumination of the burial chamber that only occurs once a year at the winter solstice. The builders of Newgrange deliberately placed a small opening above its entry door. Because of the exact positioning

Box 13–1 (Continued)

Stone Basins

of that opening and Newgrange's construction, something very eerie happens. For a few days surrounding the solstice, with the sun on the horizon, a thin ray of light enters that opening and runs the the length of the passageway to light up the burial chamber. It does so for a 17- to 20-minute period. Then, as the sun rises in the sky, the light departs. For the rest of the year, this burial spot deep within the tomb once again lies blanketed in darkness.

Just who was buried at Newgrange and why such effort was put into the building of this "pyramid in the round," as Harbison calls it, we do not know. Their efforts must have been motivated by a deep respect for the dead and a belief in an afterlife. Thousands of years later, we marvel at the knowledge of astronomy and engineering principles that Stone Age people possessed. Over the years, scientific knowledge has accumulated and technology has advanced, but we still have something profoundly in common with those who lived at the time of Newgrange. For us, as for them, the mystery of life and death remains.

Source: Based on P. Harbison, (1988). *Pre-Christian Ireland.* London: Thames and Hudson Ltd.

Funerals also mirror the values and expectations of a society. Culturally patterned responses to death provide an opportunity to examine the nature of life within a given society. Underscoring the importance of studying death rituals for this purpose, Huntington and Metcalf (1979), maintain that

in all societies . . . the issue of death throws into relief the most important cultural values by which people live their lives and evaluate their experiences.

FIGURE **13–1** Cesar Chavez funeral. The Rev. Jesse Jackson walks alongside former California Governor Jerry Brown as Brown helps carry the casket of United Farm Workers leader Cesar Chavez. The importance of ritual to the community and the simplicity of the casket are portrayed in this glimpse of the 3 1/2 mile funeral procession. (Reprinted by permission of AP/Wide World Photos)

> Life becomes transparent against the background of death, and fundamental social and cultural issues are revealed. (p. 2)

In other words, we can learn a lot about life in a given society by examining the nature of its funerals. The funeral practices of a society "are conditioned by the form and complexity of the organizational characteristics of the society itself" (Binford, 1971, p. 23).

Since the mid-1800s, many changes in our society have occurred. They have altered our experience with death as well as our funerals, which have been characterized as "unemotional, commercialized, and often materialistic" (Stephenson, 1985, p. 214). These same words have been used to describe our modern day society.

Historical Change in Funeral Structure

During the early years of our country, families managed the affairs surrounding death. It was a family member or neighbor who prepared the body, washing and dressing it. This job was generally handed down from one generation to another. A local cabinetmaker usually constructed the coffin which was a simple pine container. Washed, dressed, and placed in the coffin, the body was waked or viewed in the home before the funeral ceremony and burial.

The increasing urbanization of the 1800s began to change several aspects of the funeral. People living in cities became dependent on an array of occupational specialists. You no longer baked bread; you bought it. You no longer had a cow to milk, you bought milk from a dairy. And, you no longer prepared the body of a deceased loved one. This task was sometimes performed by furniture dealers who sold coffins or by nurses who offered their services to the public. Eventually, it was assumed by those who began directing the funeral ceremony as well.

Initially, those who "undertook" the responsibility for the funeral did so as a sideline occupation. They were typically the furniture dealers who made coffins or livery men who supplied carriages for transporting corpses. Funeral directing eventually became a full-time occupation, and by 1882 the organization now known as the National Funeral Director's Association (NFDA) was formed.

The establishments where the corpses were prepared and held for viewing became known as funeral parlors or funeral homes. These titles reflect the previous location of these activities, which had been the family parlor or home. The smaller houses of city dwellers generally did not provide the space to allow for the display of the body and large gatherings of family and friends. And, during the late 1800s another service was being introduced by funeral directors that was not easily performed in private homes—embalming.

Prior to embalming, corpses had been kept on ice to allow time for those who had to travel to attend the viewing and funeral. During the mid-nineteenth century, two undertakers introduced a coffin known as a corpse cooler. It had a special compartment for holding ice and was fitted with a spigot for draining water as the ice melted. Interestingly, a number of factors worked to eliminate this contraption and to allow for the eventual widespread practice of embalming.

Physicians, surgeons, and chemists had an interest in preserving bodies to allow for anatomical study and medical education. They were among the first to experiment with preservative chemicals for this purpose. During the Civil War, their knowledge and experience with these chemicals was put to use on a much larger scale. Many undertakers had received government contracts to oversee the care and shipment home of the bodies of the war dead. The preparation of so many bodies was a massive task and the journeys home were long. Although embalming was not officially required, it was desirable as there were reports of airtight coffins splitting open under the pressure of gasses generated by the decomposing corpses. Thus, physicians were hired by undertakers to infuse the bodies with preservative chemicals.

After the war ended, some funeral directors began to use these chemicals in their preparation of bodies for viewing. However, most were content to stay with the ice cooling practice and resisted embalming, as did most of the general public. Among the latter, embalming was seen as a mutilation of the corpse and a violation of religious teachings.

Chemical manufactureres, however, had plans for the continued large-scale use of their products. They had financially gained from the sale of preservative chemicals during the Civil War. After the war, they sought a broader market for their chemicals. One salesman convinced an anatomy instructor to organize an embalming class at a medical college in Cincinnati, Ohio. He did and in 1882 the first training session was held. These efforts eventually led to the Cincinnati School of Embalming. Undertakers attending the embalming demonstrations became convinced of the value of the technique to their occupation. In time, a reluctant public was eventually persuaded as well. The practice of draining body fluids and simultaneously infusing preservative chemicals alleviated the popular fear of being buried alive as discussed in Chapter 1. Once the embalming process was under way, all could be assured that it was a dead body that was placed in the ground!

Thus, by the turn of the twentieth century, some funeral establishments were not only providing parlors for viewing the dead, but rooms for the embalming and general preparation of the body, and even chapels, thereby eliminating the need to travel to a place of worship. The funeral, which had been managed previously by families in their homes, was in the midst of being transformed into a commercial enterprise managed by funeral directors. Those interested in a more detailed account of the evolution of American funeral practices are referred to the work of Habenstein and Lamers (1962) and Farrell (1980) from which much of the foregoing is derived.

Historical Change in the Character and Functional Significance of the Funeral

Change did not end with the structure and management of the American funeral. Other aspects of the funeral changed as well. With increasing urbanization, society became more materialistic and secular and less community oriented. These changes also became reflected in the character and functional significance of the funeral ceremony.

Elaborate funeral goods became a part of the overall materialism of American society. Coffins, hearses, and funeral homes became much more embellished over the years. Coffins evolved from plain pine boxes into caskets made from various materials ranging from less expensive woods (pine, chestnut, red cedar) that are typically cloth covered, to expensive hardwoods (birch, cherry, mahogany, maple, oak), to metals (iron, bronze, copper, steel). A considerable range of fabrics line the insides of these once simple containers.

Transportation of the body has become costly. Hearses as well as limousines for survivors are kept shiny and up to date. The once simple funeral home is now more often than not an imposing structure itself in possession of spacious rooms dressed in expensive wallpaperings, carpeting, and stylish furnishings.

Ironically, as funerals became more embellished, other forces operated to exert an effect on their significance. What used to be an important community event is now most often a private family affair. Today, the death of any one individual may go unnoticed in the anonymity of mass society, save for close family and friends. Some maintain that today's funerals, the origins of which stem from a time when people mourned as a part of a bereaved community, sometimes no longer provide the support they once did. People may blindly follow social customs out of a sense of duty but derive little or no personal satisfaction. It sometimes may be the case that today's funeral as "a ceremony that invites all to mourn a death presents serious difficulties for the person who has come to believe his grief is private and personal" (Fulton, 1976, p. 342).

The present, very private nature of death and bereavement is in keeping with the general lack of mourning behavior presented in Chapter 9. The public expression of grief is squeezed into a three-day period. Beyond the funeral, the bereaved are often left to carry their grief alone. In these times of contained grief, the funeral may appear perfunctory and routine, punctuating an otherwise private experience. Paradoxically, it has been suggested that for some, funeral purchases may be one of the few remaining means of honoring the dead:

> Because people increasingly lack both the ceremonial and social mechanisms that once existed to help them cope with death, monetary expenditures have taken on added importance as a means for allowing the bereaved to express (both to themselves and others) their sentiments for the deceased. For with so few modes of expression remaining to the bereaved, funeral expenditures serve as evidence of their concern for both the dead and the conventional standards of decency in their community of residence. (Pine and Phillips, 1970, p. 416)

In general, U.S. culture has become deritualized (Mandlebaum, 1959). Ceremonies, including the funeral, have been deemphasized (Fulton, 1965; Kamerman, 1988; Stephenson, 1985). Ceremonial displays are characterized by a number of attributes that are no longer held in high regard in contemporary American life. They are often viewed as religious or historically grounded symbols of little importance in a secular, rational, and future-oriented society. They may be seen to offer empty, sentimental gestures in a culture that emphasizes science and reason over emotions.

The demographics of dying seem to be playing a role in diminishing the importance of the funeral. The majority of those dying in the United States are elderly. Their deaths, considered timely and appropriate, often come after a period of physical decline and/or segregation from mainstream life. For many families, anticipatory grief is triggered in witnessing the decline or institution-alization of an elderly loved one. Under such circumstances, funerals marking their death may seem less necessary (Fulton and Fulton, 1971).

In light of these various changes, "we might expect a trend away from elaborate public ritual and toward simplified public rites" (Pratt, 1981, p. 328). Kamerman (1988) sees the growth of memorial societies as an indication of the deritualization of the funeral. Memorial societies, to be discussed later in this chapter, promote a simplified and lower cost disposal of the body, in contrast to the elaborate and increasingly expensive funeral with which so many are familiar.

Modern-day conventional funerals also have served to insulate mourners from the reality of death. Funerals do not stand alone in this regard. That they have come to do so is in keeping with various changes in the United States' death-related experiences. As life expectancy increased with the advance of the twentieth century, individual encounters with death became postponed. Death is not the all-too-frequent visitor among the young that it once was. Likewise, it has become institutionalized. The sick and dying are now most often cared for in hospitals and nursing homes. After death, the body of the deceased is prepared by a funeral director, generally to be viewed and buried from a funeral home. Death is not the familiar event so intimately experienced by our ancestors. It is avoided in numerous ways and is cloaked in mystery. In modern society

> the reality of death runs counter to many values central to the American image. The result is a feeling of dread and an avoidance of death as well as anything that serves to remind us of its existence. The funeral industry has responded to our increasing secularism and death avoidance by providing more services that defend against the stark finality of death. (Stephenson, 1985, p. 208)

For example, over the years the shape of coffins has changed as have the complexions of the deceased they contain. They no longer conform to the outline of their contents—a human body—as do those plain pine boxes we see in Western movies or horror films. They have become rectangular and the preferred term is now *caskets*. Frequently fitted with sealer gaskets, their construction seems to promise to keep out the elements and to preserve the body (Consumer's Union, 1977; Farrell, 1980; Mitford, 1963). Embalming fluid now contains pigments giving the corpse more lifelike color and makeup adds a final finishing touch.

The Occupational Stigma of Funeral Directing

The occupation of funeral directing involves what anthropologists would call culturally unclean or polluting work. In doing what no one else wants to do, funeral directors become stigmatized. Years ago when relatives or neighbors prepared the body for burial, they did so out of necessity. Funeral directors, on the other hand, choose to do it. To most, it seems a strange person that would elect to handle the dead (Pine, 1975); in so doing, they enter what has been called the "forbidden zone" (Lesy, 1987, p. 5).

Funeral directors have identified their handling of the dead and the notion that they profiteer from death and grief as the two most stigmatizing features of their job. Thompson (1991) examined various techniques funeral directors use in an attempt to diminish or cope with the occupational stigma.

Foremost, funeral directors have symbolically redefined their work. In so doing, they negate as much of what they actually do as possible. Language plays a large part in achieving this goal. Table 13–1 provides a list of terms avoided by the funeral industry as well as what are considered more appropriate substitutions. Language can be very stigmatizing. For example, *funeral director* is less harsh than *embalmer, mortician,* or *undertaker,* which are terms carefully avoided by most of those in the funeral business. Some who work solely as embalmers avoid that term, referring to themselves as funeral directors when asked what they do for a living. By further referring to themselves as bereavement counselors or grief therapists, funeral directors emphasize their work with the living rather than the dead.

Another stigma-managing technique is role distancing. This practice involves detaching themselves from what they do and how others perceive them because of their job. Various patterns emerge, the three most common being emotional detachment, humor, and countering the stereotype of the funeral director. Regarding emotional detachment, morticians, when embalming, often report that they concentrate on the mechanical aspects of their work rather than on the "person" they are preparing. As one said:

> When I picked up the body, it was a person. When I get done, . . . it becomes a person again. But in here its just something to be worked on. I treat it like a mechanic treats an automobile engine—with respect, but there's no emotion involved. It's just a job that has to be done.   (Thompson, 1991, p. 414)

Humor is a backroom tactic that varies from impromptu comments to well-told jokes. It is not unlike the humor that has been recorded among medical students when dealing with a corpse (Hafferty, 1988; Knight, 1973). Countering the stereotype of the funeral director may be attempted with the type of clothing worn (for instance, avoiding black suits) or the personality presented, realizing that on the job a certain reserve is demanded.

Characterizing the job of funeral directing as a profession rather than a trade also bolsters the image and reduces the occupational stigma. Licensure and certification, membership in professional organizations, journals such as *Casket* and *Professional Mortician,* and attendance at annual conventions all contribute to a sense of professionalism.

TABLE 13–1   *The Language of Funeral Directing*

Avoided Terms	Appropriate Substitutes
ashes	cremains
burial	interment
cemetery, graveyard	final resting place
coffin	casket
corpse, dead bodies	remains, the deceased, loved one, Mr. Jones
dead, death	passing on, lying in repose, loss, passing away
embalmer, mortician, undertaker	funeral director
emblaming	preservation, restoration
embalming room	preparation room
funeral	service
hearse	funeral coach
mortuary	funeral home
pick up a body	make a call
tombstone	monument

Additionally, the job security and good income of funeral directors help to compensate for their lack of occupational prestige. This factor provides still another means of personally managing or coping with the negative image they carry.

Finally, funeral directors emphasize their service role above all other aspects of their job. Advertisements typically focus on this orientation. In stressing services to the living—arranging and directing the funeral and comforting the bereaved—the dead are deemphasized. Merchandizing is deemphasized as well. Thus, the service component diverts attention from the two most stigmatizing aspects of funeral directing, handling the dead and selling profitable merchandise.

There is a current trend for funeral directors to serve as "preneed counselors" whereby they assist customers in the advance planning of funerals. This trend has been stimulated by the growth of memorial societies and the criticism of funeral directors for the sale of elaborate funeral merchandise. Preneed planning relieves survivors of the burden of decision making and its financial implications at a time when they are grief-stricken. This role may grow in importance in symbolically redefining the work of the funeral director and in reducing the stigma of making money at the expense of those in the midst of grief (Thompson, 1991). A more extensive consideration of preplanning for funerals as well as prepaying for them, is presented later in the chapter.

In spite of the stigma associated with funeral directing and the criticism to which the funeral industry has been subjected, the valuable role played by funeral directors is recognized (Binger et al., 1969; Glick, Weiss, and Parkes, 1974). Likewise, there are many reports of the bereaved finding their interactions with funeral directors to have been helpful and supportive (Anglim, 1976; Carey, 1979; Cook, 1981, 1983; Doka, 1984–1985; Kalish and Goldberg, 1979–1980; Khlief, 1975; Lieberman and Borman, 1982; Winn, 1981).

Controversy

The American funeral industry has been subjected to serious criticism over the last thirty years (Bowman, 1959; Consumer's Union, 1977; Federal Trade Commission, 1978; Harmer, 1963; Mitford, 1963). Much of that criticism has focused on the sale of profitable funeral merchandise to confused and grief-stricken consumers. It is charged that funerals have become overly embellished and unnecessarily expensive. Bowman (1959) asserts that funerals are so costly and elaborate that they have lost their basic dignity and fundamental meaning.

Others, while recognizing that the bereaved can be easily victimized, believe that much of the anger directed at the funeral industry is misplaced. It is agreed that funerals have become materialistic, but so has U.S. society in general. "To accuse the American public of being too involved with material possessions—too wrapped up in worldly pursuits—is a valid criticism" (Stephenson, 1985, pp. 228–229). Blaming the funeral director for our materialism is too one-sided, too simplistic. We are again reminded that the nature of a given society's funerals mirrors the cultural values by which people in that society live their lives.

The United States is a country whose national motto seems to have become "shop 'til you drop." Our traditional holidays have been turned into shopping excursions and the father of our country reduced to the emblem of "the Washington's Birthday Sale" (Kamerman, 1988, p. 79). Even going back to school has become commercialized. Advertisements encouraging children to start the new school year wearing the "right" clothes seem to have superseded those for purchasing needed pencils and paper. Charges of persons "buying" the affection of others abound. So, we have expensive funerals! So, we have mourners saying goodbye to the deceased with the ostentatious display of funerary goods! Some would raise the question, "Why should funerals be any different?" And, "Why should funeral directors be blamed for American materialism?"

In its investigation of the charges against the funeral industry, the Federal Trade Commission (FTC) recognized the right of individuals to arrange funerals of their choice regardless of the expense. However, it concluded that those arranging funerals often did so under severe handicap and that they needed assistance with their task. Too often that assistance came from funeral directors who played two conflicting roles in the transaction. On the one hand, they appeared as disinterested professionals there to serve the bereaved at their time of need. On the other, they were salespersons of goods and services who financially benefited from the sale of high-profit items.

Those to whom funeral directors sell are, as the Federal Trade Commission (1984) pointed out, under severe handicap. They are under a time constraint. The body of the deceased must be removed to the mortuary within hours after death. There is little time to shop around. Likewise, the bereaved are usually under extreme distress. There are few business transactions wherein consumers are in such a disadvantaged position or where their normal bargaining power is so diluted. Finally, most are inexperienced at arranging funerals. Fifty percent have not previously done so. They lack information about what is required and about what options are available.

Furthermore, the FTC concluded that the general marketing strategy for much of the funeral industry made it difficult for consumers to obtain information about funeral goods, service options, and prices. They also charged the industry with attempting to thwart the development of memorial societies and potentially lower cost alternatives to embalming with open-casket viewing and earth burial. For instance, the Chairman of the Board of Pierce Mortuary Colleges, which is owned by Pierce Chemicals, a major producer of embalming fluids (Kearl, 1989), wrote an editorial about cremation in the trade journal *Professional Mortician:* "The connotation isn't always good because in many cases, the human body was still alive when the fire was lighted. Joan of Arc is a good example and it was a means of punishment for many others" (Pierce, 1983, p. 10). Statements such as this appear to attempt to discourage cremation by creating negative images and feelings toward it.

The FTC Funeral Rule

Out of concern for the consumer's disadvantaged position, the FTC developed a Trade Regulation Rule on Funeral Industry Practices, more commonly called the Funeral Rule. It became effective on April 30, 1984 (Federal Trade Commission, 1984). It requires funeral directors to provide detailed and specific information about funeral prices and legal requirements to those who make funeral arrangements. It allows consumers to purchase only the goods and services they select, except for those required by law, and requires funeral establishments to obtain authorization for embalming.

The FTC began a mandatory review of the Funeral Rule in 1988 to determine if it was helping consumers and whether it should be amended or terminated. The report concluded that the rule is providing pro-competitive and informational benefits to consumers. Its retention without substantial modification, but with certain amendments, was advised. The amended rule became effective July 19, 1994.

Telephone Price Disclosure

The original rule required funeral directors to tell those who phoned about the "terms, conditions, or prices" of funeral goods or services that price information was available over the telephone. This provision was designed to increase consumer access to price information and, possibly, to reduce their reluctance to ask about prices.

After reviewing the practice, the FTC decided that it did more harm than good. Some consumers had been offended by the funeral director's automatic and uninvited statement about price information, feeling that it was an indication of a preoccupation with their ability to afford and eventually pay for funeral services. And, funeral providers were resentful about having to make this statement at such a delicate time—that being their initial contact with the consumer. They feared appearing callous and insensitive (Federal Trade Commission, 1994).

The FTC believes that consumers rarely seek price information from funeral providers due to a general reluctance to do so and not because they believe such information cannot be obtained over the phone. Thus, mandating funeral directors to inform their callers that prices are available via the telephone does not appear to give consumers any new information that increases their likelihood of price shopping.

The FTC amended rule now requires funeral establishments to provide price and other readily available information over the telephone to consumers who request it. The FTC believes that this amendment, along with other features of the Funeral Rule, maintains the integrity of its intention to increase consumer awareness of price information and the exercise of choice in selecting funeral goods and services.

Those so inclined can use the telephone to compare prices among funeral establishments. However, consumers should be aware that price disclosures over the phone may be inexact. For example, questions about casket prices will probably receive a general answer indicating a price range. It would be necessary to inquire about a specific make of casket to receive more specific information.

General Price List

It was pointed out earlier that consumers are reluctant to request price information from funeral providers. They do, however, value receiving information about prices and options in funeral goods and services early in the funeral transaction (Federal Trade Commission, 1994). Those who inquire in person about arranging for a funeral must be given a general price list. This list, which consumers can take home and keep, displays the cost of each funeral service and item offered by the facility. Also, the general price list is required to include disclosure statements about specific legal rights and requirements concerning funeral arrangements. These include disclosures regarding embalming, the use of caskets for cremation, outer burial containers (if their prices are on the general price list), and cash advance provisions (which involve items such as obituary notices, flowers, and memorial cards). Information about required purchases must also be included.

Embalming

Funeral providers are required to present consumers with information about embalming to aid them in deciding whether or not they wish to purchase this service. According to the Funeral Rule, the funeral provider *may not* (1) falsely state that embalming is required by law or (2) charge for unauthorized embalming unless it is required by state law. The provider *must* disclose in writing that, except in specific cases, embalming is not required by law.

The disclosure statement regarding embalming that appears on the general price list reads:

> Except in certain special cases, embalming is not required by law. Embalming may be necessary, however, if you select certain funeral arrangements, such as a funeral with viewing. If you do not want embalming, you usually have a right to choose an arrangement which does not require you to pay for it, such as direct cremation or immediate burial.   (Federal Trade Commission, 1983)

Caskets for Cremation

Some consumers select direct cremation, which is cremation without a viewing or other ceremony with the body of the deceased present. It is also referred to as *immediate cremation.* When a direct cremation is selected, the funeral provider must indicate that an inexpensive alternative container is available to hold the deceased. Alternative containers may be constructed of materials such as fiberboard or composition materials.

Containers are destroyed during cremation. Selecting an alternative container rather than a more expensive casket can lower funeral costs. Under the Funeral Rule, funeral directors may not tell consumers that state or local laws require a casket for direct cremation. If the funeral provider arranges for direct cremations, the following disclosure statement must be placed on the general price list.

> If you want to arrange a direct cremation, you can use an alternative container. Alternative containers encase the body and can be made of materials

like fiberboard or composition materials (with or without an outside covering). The containers we provide are (specify containers). (Federal Trade Commission, 1983)

Outer Burial Containers

Outer burial containers (OBCs) range from simple, less expensive grave liners to more elaborate and costly burial vaults. These enclosures are placed in the ground to hold the casket. Many cemeteries require OBCs because they help to prevent graves from sinking.

According to the Funeral Rule, funeral directors must place the following disclosure on the OBC price list or, if the OBC prices are listed on the general price list, in immediate conjunction with those prices:

> In most areas of the country, state or local law does not require that you buy a container to surround the casket in the grave. However, many cemeteries require that you have such a container so that the grave will not sink in. Either a grave liner or burial vault will satisfy these requirements. (Federal Trade Commission, 1983)

If state or local law in the area(s) where the funeral provider operates does not require a container to surround the casket in the grave, then the phrase "in most areas of the country" need not be included in this disclosure.

Cash Advance Provisions

Cash advance items are goods or services that the funeral director pays for on the consumer's behalf. These include flowers, memorial cards, clergy honoraria, obituary notices, and shipping cases. Some funeral directors charge consumers their cost for such items; others add a service fee to their cost. It is deceptive for funeral providers to fail to disclose to consumers that the price charged for cash advance items is not the same as the cost to the funeral provider when such is not the case.

If the funeral provider charges a service fee or receives a rebate, commission, or trade or volume discount on a cash advance item, the following disclosure must be placed in the itemized statement of funeral goods and services selected: "We charge you for our services in obtaining: (specify cash advance items)" (Federal Trade Commission, 1983).

Required Purchases

The consumer does not have to purchase unwanted goods or services unless they are required by state law. According to the Funeral Rule, the funeral provider is required to disclose this fact in writing on the general price list.

Any specific law that requires the purchase of a given item must be disclosed on the Statement of Funeral Goods and Services Selected.

Statement on Funeral Goods and Services Selected

The funeral provider is required to provide the consumer with an itemized statement of the funeral goods and services selected. It is given to consumers after they have made their selections for a funeral or other disposition of human remains. It contains specified information including the total cost of selected goods and services. If the exact cost of cash advance items is unknown at that time, a "good faith estimate" of their cost must be written on the statement. A fee for basic professional services of the funeral director and staff is permitted as a nondeclinable item. As such, it allows funeral providers to recover overhead costs and to secure a profit.

Casket-Handling Fee

A major intent of the Funeral Rule was to make price information more available to consumers. Historically, funeral providers had objected to price advertising. Likewise, they typically charged consumers a "package deal," bundling most prices together rather than itemizing individual goods and services supplied. Consequently, consumers did not benefit from competitive pricing.

Coincidentally, with the rule, a third-party, casket-seller industry emerged. Consumers who purchase lower cost caskets from these sellers are typically charged a casket-handling fee by funeral directors. The practice is defended as a means of recouping overhead costs and allowing for a profit.

Traditionally, operating expenses have been recouped through casket markup. Thus, consumers supplying their own caskets purchased from a third-party pay their proportionate share of operating costs via the casket-handling fee. In 1988, the average handling fee was $500, a sum almost equal to the then average wholesale casket cost of $517, and 60 percent of the average casket markup of $821 (Federal Trade Commission, 1994).

The FTC recognizes the right of funeral providers to recover operating costs and make a profit. It points out that the Funeral Rule permits such by allowing a markup on items selected and by permitting funeral directors to charge a basic professional services fee. The latter is recognized as the one nondeclinable fee that allows recovery of overhead costs. The FTC finds charging separate casket-handling fees an unfair practice that thwarts a competitive funeral market.

The Funeral Rule has been amended to prohibit funeral providers from charging consumers who buy a casket from a third-party a nondeclinable fee in addition to the basic professional services fee. Thus, they may increase the basic services fee, which they have been reluctant to do. When adding this charge to the basic services fee, they must disclose that they are doing so with a statement indicating that the fee is added to the "total cost of your funeral arrangements if you provide the casket" (Federal Trade Commission, 1994).

Preservative and Protective Claims

FTC investigations indicated that funeral goods and services do not indefinitely preserve the dead body. Under the Funeral Rule, funeral providers may not claim that funeral goods or services will indefinitely delay the natural decomposition of the body. The rule also prohibits them from claiming that funeral goods will protect the body of the deceased from gravesite substances such as water or dirt when such is not true.

Memorial Societies

A memorial society is a nonprofit, nonsectarian group whose members desire a simple, dignified alternative to an elaborate and increasingly costly funeral. They accomplish this goal through a contract or informal arrangement with one or more local funeral directors. Memorial society members are entitled to take advantage of various options for a predetermined cost. The lower cost of these services is related to the modest items selected, such as plain cloth-covered caskets, and to the bargaining power of volume group purchasing through the memorial society.

It is typical for members of a memorial society to prearrange with a cooperating funeral director for an immediate cremation or immediate earth burial. The funeral director agrees to arrange all necessary paperwork and pick up the body of the deceased to transport it in a simple container to the crematory or cemetery. Some members choose embalming with viewing in a plain casket before cremation or burial.

Members of a memorial society typically pay a lifetime membership fee to the organization. It is usually around $25.00 per individual. Some societies charge modest annual dues. Of course, the funeral director's charges for contracted services must also be paid at the time of death. Membership is transferrable among all societies in the United States.

Upon joining, members are given a prearrangement form. It is a simple document that allows for detailed individual funeral planning. Members designate which is preferred—burial, cremation, or body donation. They also can outline the kind of service(s) they want, although this degree of detail or planning is not necessary. Advantages of preplanning and setting aside money for a funeral as well as some disadvantages of prepaying for one are outlined in Box 13–2.

A recommended way to set aside money for a funeral is the *Totten Trust*. It is not a means of prepaying for a funeral. It is an individual trust or savings plan designated for a particular purpose—in this case, your funeral. With the Totten Trust, money:

- Equal to the present cost of a funeral is deposited in a certificate of deposit, money market account, or passbook.
- Can be withdrawn from it by the holder at any time.
- Is payable to a trustee of your choice to be used for your funeral.
- Is available immediately after death without the delay of probate proceedings.
- Accumulates interest helping to cover costs increased by inflation.

Insurance-funded plans are another way to set aside money for a funeral. These are life insurance policies or annuity contracts to provide for a death benefit. Funeral directors often sell such insurance and prefer to be the designated beneficiary. Often-called "preneed plans," they are not linked with any specific funeral merchandise or services.

In addition to helping individuals arrange for lower cost alternatives to the conventional funeral, memorial societies also keep members up to date on legal requirements and provide educational materials on funeral practices and problems. Their national office, located in Madison, Wisconsin, serves as a clearinghouse for consumer complaints as they relate to funeral transactions.

The growth of memorial societies is significantly related to a growing minority of persons who are critical of pretentious, materialistic funerals. Since the first memorial society was formed in 1939, the Continental Association of Funeral and Memorial Societies has added many others, scattered throughout the United States, to its ranks.

Immediate Disposition Companies

Immediate disposition companies generally provide for immediate burial or immediate cremation without the services of a funeral home. They hold the body under refrigeration until all necessary papers (such as a death certificate and cremation permit) have been signed and submitted. Disposition usually occurs in two days or less.

Although they sometimes have "society" in their name, they are not to be confused with memorial societies. The latter cooperate with full-service mortuaries to provide a range of funeral options.

Box 13–2   *Funeral Preplanning and Prepaying*

Today, we frequently hear about pre-need planning for funerals. Pre-need is a term used by the funeral industry in reference to making and paying for funeral arrangements before death.

Some Advantages of Preplanning for Your Funeral	*Some Advantages of Prepaying for Your Funeral*
1. If your wishes are followed, your family is released of making funeral choices under the stresses of a severe time constraint as well as grief.	1. It insures that money is available to pay for your funeral.
2. It provides time for comparison shopping at different funeral homes.	2. It can provide peace of mind for you and your family.
3. It stimulates family discussion and decision making.	
4. It provides an opportunity for you to have input as to what you would like, which may be a source of comfort to you before and to your family after your death.	

While there are advantages to preplanning one's funeral as well as setting aside money for it, there are several disadvantages to paying in advance.

Disadvantages to Prepaying for Your Funeral

1. Your family may not know that you have prearranged and prepaid for your funeral.
2. Should you move, your prepaid plan may not be transferrable.
3. The establishment that you gave your money to may not be in business at the time of your death.
4. The money you pay out today may not cover the inflated funeral costs of tomorrow. Less expensive merchandise may be substituted or your family may need to provide additional money.
5. If you pay in installments and do not complete the payments, your refund may be reduced by a sales charge as high as 30 percent.
6. If you pay in installments and die before all payments have been made, your agreement may not be fully honored.
7. You may need funeral payments for other purposes, sometimes emergencies.

Source: Adapted from *Prepaying for Your Funeral: Benefits and Dangers.* Continental Association of Funeral and Memorial Societies, Inc., Madison, Wisconsin.

Disposal of the Body

Earth Burial, Entombment, and Cremation

Most people in the United States are buried in the earth after their death. The cost of burial generally includes several separate items: (1) the burial plot within the cemetery, (2) the outer burial container required by most cemeteries for earth burial, (3) the opening and closing of the grave, and (4) the grave marker or memorial monument. Cemeteries often charge for installing the grave marker or monument. Some, likewise, charge a fee for the perpetual care of the grave. Others include that fee in the cost of the burial plot. The amount marked for perpetual care (in some states 10 percent of the price) is put in a trust fund to provide for continued upkeep of the grave. A lack of cemetery space is a growing problem. With at least two million deaths occurring annually in the United States, grave space is rapidly diminishing.

Entombment in a mausoleum is another disposal option. The casket is placed above ground in a burial crypt or chamber. Individual burial crypts are arranged in rows stacked one above the other in the greater structure known as a *mausoleum*. Most mausoleums are built on cemetery grounds. In these "tall buildings" that house the dead, the bodies are arranged closer together than can be accomplished with earth burial. Their individual appeal and ability to save space is limited. The costs of entombment typically involve the crypt, its opening and closure, the memorial plaque, and perpetual care of the mausoleum.

Cremation involves reducing the body to bone ashes and bone fragments through the use of intense heat. The water content of the body is evaporated and the carbon content is incinerated, leaving inorganic bone ash (Consumer's Union, 1977). The cremation chamber may reach temperatures of 2,000 to 2,500°F, thereby reducing the human body to from five to seven pounds or more of ashes and bone fragments within an hour and a half. Cremation time varies with the size of the body, the type of container used, and the kind of cremation chamber.

Once the cremation chamber cools, the cremated remains are removed for processing. Using an electromagnet, any metal from the container that held the body is removed. Sometimes people wonder what happens to the gold in teeth. During the cremation process, it may vaporize or form BB-size pellets that often fall between the cracks of the fire brick lining the cremation chamber. If keeping the gold is important to the family, it should be removed prior to cremation. However, dentists may refuse such a request and the cost of retrieving it would probably exceed the value of the gold (Santoro and Bilodeau, 1987).

Among the bone ashes after processing are fragments of bone that range in size from tiny to three- to four-inch pieces. Many crematoriums pulverize these fragments into smaller pieces. They are then placed in a simple container usually made of plastic or cardboard and lined with a plastic bag. They may remain in these simple containers or urns of variable cost may be purchased if desired. Actually, the cremated remains may be placed in any kind of container for the family's keeping. Something durable and nonbreakable is wisest. When the noted author John Steinbeck died, his family placed his ashes in a favorite silver box which held them until they were eventually scattered.

There are several options regarding what to do with the cremated remains. They may be buried or placed in a columbarium niche. Columbariums are structures containing many recessed areas, or niches, for housing cremated remains. They are usually located within a cemetery mausoleum. Also, some churches have such niches in their walls or those of their gardens for holding the cremated remains of their members. Since these remains are sterile, posing no health threat, they may be kept by family members or scattered. The scattering of ashes is legal in most jurisdictions. However, if a family chooses to do this, someone should check to be certain that the remains have been pulverized. There have been instances of larger, recognizable bone fragments found and turned into law enforcement officials who, suspecting foul play, began an investigation (Santoro and Bilodeau, 1987).

Most religions allow cremation. The Greek and Jewish Orthodox faiths oppose it, as do some other religions. The Roman Catholic Church, which once had a ban on cremation, now permits it; that ban was lifted with the Vatican II Council in 1964.

Cremation may be an inexpensive option to conventional burial. However, if it is preceded by a viewing in an expensive casket and the full use of a funeral facility, the family is faced with the usual funeral expenses. Rental caskets are a cost-saving option for those who select cremation after a viewing and funeral service. The body is delivered to the crematorium in an alternative container in which it is cremated.

Cremation is one answer to the growing lack of cemetery space. It is more common in some other countries such as England and Japan where land is at a premium and cemetery space greatly limited. The percentage of cremations in the U.S. is steadily increasing.

After-Death Ceremonies

After-death ceremonies include funeral, memorial, and committal services. With a funeral service, the body is present in an open or closed casket. It is thus held soon after death. A funeral service may take place within the funeral home or at one's place of worship. Though it doesn't happen much today, it is also possible to have a funeral service in a private home as was the custom years ago.

With a memorial service, the body is not present. It is frequently held after an immediate cremation, immediate burial, or when the body hasn't been recovered. The service generally occurs a short time after death, although the time and place are both optional. Since the body is not present and there is no worry about its maintenance, a memorial service can be held days or weeks after the death, which allows family and friends who live at a distance to come together at a more convenient time. Timing might revolve around their schedules, the clearing of bad weather, or the arrival of a significant date in the life of the deceased. The memorial service may be religious or secular, simple or elaborate, indoors or outside.

A committal service may be held in place of or in addition to a funeral or memorial service. It is held at the graveside or mausoleum, the crematory chapel, or at the scattering of ashes—those places where the remains are committed to their final rest. In the case of John Steinbeck, whose love for the California coast and fascination with its marine life are reflected in so many of his writings, that final rest and committal service took place on Point Lobos, overlooking the Pacific Ocean. His ashes, after having been placed to rest for a time in the garden—a garden was always a special feature of his home—were brought by his family to the ocean. They were brought to an oceanside cliff that he loved and where he and his sister had played as children. The favorite silver box holding his remains was opened. And, as his biographer describes: "A young priest with red hair and white robe . . . took a handful of dust and let it drift with the wind. ' . . . ashes to ashes, dust to dust . . . ' An otter played in the sea below, and above a gull circled and cried out against the sky" (Benson, 1984, p. 1038). The disposition of his body and the related committal ceremony seem a fitting tribute to his life and the things he held dear.

Thus, we see that the disposal of the body and after-death services can take many forms or combinations thereof. Many continue to prefer a viewing in a mortuary followed by a church funeral and earth burial with a committal service. Others will opt for an immediate earth burial with no committal ceremony to be followed by a memorial service within days or weeks. Another family may elect to have an open-casket viewing in a mortuary followed by a cremation without services of any kind. And, there are still others who will bury the cremated remains after a funeral service and with a committal ceremony. In the larger society, recognizing that religious, ethnic, and personal differences do exist, there are no rigid rules about what must or should be done.

As we have seen, societal changes can alter our perspectives on death and the form and function of rituals marking this important transition. The therapeutic value of after-death ceremonies in their many forms has not received much serious research attention. However, on a positive note, people today probably have greater freedom than ever before to accept or reject funeral services and other after-death ceremonies on the basis of their personal needs and desires.

Recognizing that styles of funerals and after-death services can and do change and that minimal ceremonialization at a given death may not be inappropriate, we are cautioned to reflect on the various functions that are served by gathering to recognize a death and the changed status of the bereaved. An impulse to preclude after-death ceremonies "can have unintended consequences . . . The social meaning and intrinsic value of human life itself, moreover, may be implicitly denied by the failure to acknowledge our mortality" (Fulton, 1988).

Summary

The final disposition of the body is a universal task facing the bereaved. The form it takes and the ceremony surrounding it vary. Funerals provide many individual and community functions. Historically, a number of forces have acted to change our experiences with death and the structure of our funerals. What was once a significant community event managed by families in their homes is now a more private, commercial enterprise managed by funeral directors.

Funeral directors are stigmatized by the job they do. They have identified their handling of the dead and the notion that they profiteer from death and grief as the two most stigmatizing features of their work. They employ various techniques in attempting to diminish and cope with their occupational stigma.

The U.S. funeral industry has been subjected to serious criticism over the last thirty years. Much of the criticism has focused on the sale of profitable and overly elaborate merchandise to confused and grief-stricken consumers. Recognizing the materialism of U.S. society and the rights of individuals to arrange funerals of their choice (regardless of the expense), the Federal Trade Commission charged that the average consumer was at an extreme disadvantage in arranging a funeral. Assistance was needed and provided with the Trade Regulation Rule on Funeral Industry Practices, more commonly called the Funeral Rule.

The Funeral Rule became effective April 30, 1984. Funeral directors are now mandated to provide specific information about funeral prices and legal requirements to those who make funeral arrangements.

Most persons in the United States undergo earth burial after their death. However, a lack of cemetery space is a growing problem. Entombment in a mausoleum is another option. The casket is placed above ground in an individual crypt that is contained in the larger structure, known as a mausoleum. Cremation involves reducing the body to ashes and bone fragments through the use of intense heat.

Various after-death ceremonies include the funeral, memorial, and committal services. With a funeral service, the body is present in either an open or closed casket. With a memorial service, it is not. A committal service may be held in place of or in addition to a funeral or memorial service. Its location may be the burial or entombment site, the crematorium, or where ashes are scattered.

Study Questions

1. Present an overview of the various individual and community functions provided by funerals.
2. Describe the historical change in funeral structure from that managed in the private home by families to the commercial enterprise managed by funeral directors.
3. How have changes in U.S. society influenced the character and functional significance of the funeral?
4. What have funeral directors identified as the two most stigmatizing features of

their work? How do funeral directors attempt to diminish or cope with the stigma of their occupation?

5. What kind of criticism has the U.S. funeral industry been subjected to over the last thirty years? Does the criticism seem justified? Explain.

6. Present an overview of the Funeral Rule.

7. What is a memorial society? What kinds of benefits does it offer its members?

8. Funeral preplanning and prepaying are becoming more common. Note some advantages of preplanning and prepaying for one's funeral. What are some disadvantages of prepayment?

9. What is a Totten Trust? What are preneed plans as they relate to funerals?

10. What are immediate disposition companies?

11. What does the cost of earth burial generally entail?

12. Contrast earth burial, entombment, and cremation.

13. Contrast the various after-death ceremonies.

References

Anglim, M. (1976). Reintegration of the family after the death of a child. In I. Martinson (Ed.), *Home Care for the Dying Child: Professional and Family Perspectives* (pp. 144–167). New York: Appleton-Century-Crofts.

Benson, J. (1984). *The True Adventures of John Steinbeck, Writer*. New York: Penguin Books.

Binford, L. (1971). Mortuary practices: Their study and their potential. *American Antiquity*, 36:6–29.

Binger, C., et al. (1969). Childhood leukemia: Emotional impact on patient and family. *NEJM*, 208:414–418.

Bowman, L. (1959). *The American Funeral*. Washington, DC: Public Affairs Press.

Carey, R. (1979). Weathering Widowhood: Problems and adjustment of the widowed during the first year. *National Reporter*, 2:1–5.

Consumer's Union. (1977). *Funerals: Consumers' Last Rights*. New York: Pantheon.

Cook, J. (1981). Children's funerals and their effect on familiar grief adjustment. *National Reporter*, 4:1–2.

Cook, J. (1983). A death in the family: Parental bereavement in the first year. *Suicide and Life-Threatening Behavior*, 13:42–61.

Doka, K. (1984–1985). Expectation of death, participation in funeral arrangements, and grief adjustment. *Omega*, 15:119–129.

Farrell, J. (1980). *Inventing the American way of Death: 1830–1920*. Philadelphia: Temple University Press.

Federal Trade Commission. (1978). *Funeral Industry Practices: Final Staff Report to the Federal Trade Commission and Proposed Trade Regulation Rule*. Washington, DC: Bureau of Consumer Protection.

Federal Trade Commission. (1983). Trade Regulation Rule; Funeral Industry Practices. *Federal Register*, 48.

Federal Trade Commission. (1984). *Compliance Guidelines: Trade Regulation Rule on Funeral Industry Practices*. Washington, DC: U.S. Government Printing Office.

Federal Trade Commission. (1994). *Funeral Industry Practices Trade Regulation Rule. Final Amended Trade Regulation Rule.* Washington, DC: Bureau of Consumer Protection.

Fulton, R. (Ed.). (1965). *Death and Identity.* New York: Wiley.

Fulton, R. (Ed.). (1976). *Death and Identity.* Bowie, MD: The Charles Press.

Fulton, R. (1988). The funeral in contemporary society. In H. Wass, F. Berardo, and R. Neimeyer (Eds.), *Dying: Facing the Facts* (pp. 257–277). Washington, DC: Hemisphere.

Fulton, R., and J. Fulton. (1971). A psychological aspect of terminal care: Anticipatory grief. *Omega,* 2:91–99.

Glick, I., R. Weiss, and C. Parkes. (1974). *The First Year of Bereavement.* New York: Wiley.

Habenstein, R., and W. Lamers. (1962). *The History of American Funeral Directing.* Milwaukee: Bulfin.

Hafferty, F. (1988). Cadaver stories and the emotional socialization of medical students. *Journal of Health and Social Behavior,* 29:344–356.

Harbison, P. (1988). *Pre-Christian Ireland.* London: Thames and Hudson Ltd.

Harmer, R. (1963). *The High Cost of Dying.* New York: Collier.

Huntington, R., and P. Metcalf. (1979). *Celebrations of Death.* New York: Cambridge University Press.

Kalish, R., and H. Goldberg. (1979–80). Community attitudes toward funeral directors. *Omega,* 10:335–346.

Kamerman, J. (1988). *Death in the Midst of Life.* Englewood Cliffs, NJ: Prentice Hall.

Kearl, M. (1989). *Endings: A Sociology of Death and Dying.* New York: Oxford University Press.

Khlief, B. (1975). The sociology of the mortuary: Attitudes to the funeral, funeral director, and funeral arrangements. In O. Margolis et al. (Eds.), *Grief and the Meaning of the Funeral* (pp. 37–46). New York: MSS Information.

Knight, J. (1973). *Medical Student: Doctor in the Making.* New York: Appleton-Century-Crofts.

Lesy, M. (1987). *The Forbidden Zone.* New York: Farrar, Straus, and Giroux.

Lieberman, M., and L. Borman. (1982). Widows view the helpfulness of the funeral service. *National Reporter,* 5:2–4.

Mandelbaum, D. (1959). Social uses of funeral rites. In H. Fiefel (Ed.), *The Meaning of Death* (pp. 189–217). New York: McGraw-Hill.

Mitford, J. (1963). *The American Way of Death.* New York: Simon and Schuster.

Pierce, W. (1983). Editorial Comment. *Professional Mortician,* 46:10.

Pine, V. (1975). *Caretaker of the Dead: The American Funeral Director.* New York: Irvington.

Pine, V., and D. Phillips. (1970). The cost of dying: A sociological analysis of funeral expenditures. *Social Problems,* 17:405–417.

Pratt, L. (1981). Business temporal norms and bereavement behavior. *American Sociological Review,* 46:317–333.

Santoro, P., and P. Bilodeau. (1987). Cremation with dignity. In L. Carlson (Ed.), *Caring for Your Own Dead* (pp. 24–32). Hinesburg, VT: Upper Access Publishers.

Stephenson, J. (1985). *Death, Grief, and Mourning.* New York: The Free Press.

Thompson, W. (1991). Handling the stigma of handling the dead: Morticians and funeral directors. *Deviant Behavior: An Interdisciplinary Journal,* 12:403–429.

van Gennep, A. (1909/1960). *The Rites of Passage* (translated by M. Vizedon and G. Caffee). Chicago: University of Chicago Press.

Winn, R. (1981). Perceptions of the funeral service and post-bereavement adjustment in widowed individuals. *National Reporter,* 4:1–8.

Epilogue

So live, that when thy summons comes to join
The innumerable caravan, which moves
To that mysterious realm, where each shall take
His chamber in the silent halls of death,
Thou go not, like the quarry-slave at night,
Scourged to his dungeon, but, sustained and soothed
By an unfaltering trust, approach thy grave,
Like one who wraps the drapery of his couch
About him, and lies down to pleasant dreams.

William Cullen Bryan, "Thanatopsis"

To everything thing there is a season
and a time to every purpose under the heaven;
A time to be born, and a time to die.

Ecclesiastes 3:1

Students who enroll in courses on death and dying sometimes express their surprise that, rather than being morbid and depressing, they often find the experience to be life-affirming and uplifting. While the topic is quite serious, and sometimes gravely so (no pun intended), the time spent contemplating our own mortality and the many ways that death and dying are part of the fabric of our daily life also can cause us to look closely at those things that give joy and meaning to our life and, thereby, result in a renewed enthusiasm for life and living. As Sherwin Nuland writes in his best-selling book, *How We Die*, "*Ars moriendi* is *ars vivendi*: The art of dying is the art of living" (1994, p. 268). We hope that the text has inspired such feelings in you.

As we stated in the Preface, when we began planning this text we set out to write a book on medicine for nonphysicians, law for nonlawyers, and public policy for nonpoliticians. Here, too, we hope that we have succeeded in some way in helping you become more comfortable with the often specialized language of these disciplines. We hope that we have given you some tools so that you might not only understand better, but that you might also interact more comfortably with, those who make their living in the policy arena of death and dying. Our goal was to help make death, and the many ways of dying that precede it, less a stranger and thereby help to dispel much of the fear and anxiety that is always intensified by ignorance.

We hope that you now understand the difference between the traditional cardiopulmonary and the more recent brain-referenced bases for diagnosing death. Often those who stand at the bedside of their "brain dead" loved ones struggle to realize that the warm, pulsating and breathing-assisted form lying before them is no longer alive. So, too, we hope that you understand the difference in the decision that undergirds the removal of life support from the "brain dead" from that which withholds or withdraws life-sustaining treatment from the dying or permanently unconscious patient. Although these very different issues are still sometimes conflated by the media, we hope that you will bring a keener and more critical presence to your reading of such "cases" in your daily newspaper or learning about them from your evening newscast.

Because we believe that each of us must be a partner with our physicians and other health care providers, we have sought to empower the reader by helping you to understand your rights as a consumer. With an understanding of these rights, however, comes a correlative responsibility: the responsibility for seeking out the information necessary to inform your decisions and to take responsibility for your actions.

In many ways we are a death-denying society. We often find it difficult to talk about death and dying and, perhaps because of that, even those closest to us may not clearly understand our desires about the kind of medical care that we would consider appropriate when we are no longer able to make decisions for ourselves. We have tried to motivate the reader to plan for this contingency, not only by encouraging discussions about these questions, but by urging the greater use of advance directives. Either living wills or durable powers of attorney for health care, and usually both, are now legally recognized in every state and, by their use, it is possible to spare our loved ones needless agony in trying to make the "right" decision about the use of life-sustaining medical treatment. Although we strongly endorse the use of such advance directives—one of the nicest gifts that you can give to those who love you—we caution the reader to make sure that the directive fully and clearly represents his or her personal desire, regardless of any restrictions such as terminal illness or permanent unconsciousness that might be written into the enabling statute.

We hope that the text has also helped prepare the reader to better participate in the public policy debates that are likely to continue over the topics of direct, active euthanasia, physician-assisted suicide, the medical treatment of anomalous newborns, and the many ramifications of the abortion controversy. Each of these is quite complex, and the way in which they are resolved will be of great importance in shaping the evolution of our society. We have tried to demonstrate that complexity and, particularly, an understanding that the kind of answers that we get will be dependent upon the questions that we ask.

Death, of course, is a universal fact of life. Each of us will one day die and, before doing so, it is likely that our life will be touched by the deaths of others that we love and care deeply about. Understanding something about the psychological and social dimensions of death and dying will undoubtedly help us to cope more effectively with those experiences. By understanding how the experience of dying is influenced by causes, timing, and circumstances, it is likely that we can better comfort the dying and better cope with the imminence of our own death. Although the process of dying has been greatly changed by ever-growing changes in medical technology, the hospice movement has provided an important and welcome alternative for those who would prefer a more personal and "natural" death.

Not until each of us is touched by the death of someone we love will we come to fully understand the meaning of bereavement, grief, and mourning. What we have tried to do in the text is to prepare the reader for those experiences by looking at them as universal, somewhat predictable, and necessary experiences. The intensity of these feelings is likely to be magnified by the death of a child, and children, more than the rest of us, are particularly in need of support and guidance in understanding and coping with the loss of a loved one. While it is our wish that each of you will be touched as little as possible by these "necessary losses," perhaps something that we have written will help ease the pain and speed the healing during those inevitable times when we mourn our losses.

Furthermore, we hope that you will not be touched by the untimely death of a loved one or friend to suicide. The grief resulting from such a loss is confounded by exaggerated feelings of desertion, guilt, and anger. Should someone you know suffer such a loss, we hope that what you have read here will make it easier to be there for them rather than to withdraw from what might otherwise seem an uncomfortable, avoidable encounter.

Death in today's modern world is sometimes followed by various medically oriented activities including the autopsy, organ transplantation, or the donation of the body for medical education. Hopefully, you are now better prepared should you ever have to make a decision regarding them.

Finally, we hope you better understand the many options that exist today regarding funeral/memorializing ceremonies and the final disposition of human remains. How you choose to ceremonially mark the death of a loved one and whether you choose cremation, entombment, or earth burial is less bound, today, by convention than, perhaps, at any other time in human history.

Becoming educated about death and dying can be a truly liberating experience. We often fear most those things that we understand least. The goal that guides our continuing efforts as educators is the elimination of the ignorance in which irrational fear so often grows. We hope that you have learned as much from reading this book as we have in writing it for you.

Reference

Nuland, S. B. (1994). *How We Die*. New York: Knopf.

Subject Index

Author and Publications Index